Handbook of Research on Asian Business

Handbook of Research on Asian Business

Edited by

Henry Wai-chung Yeung

Professor of Economic Geography, National University of Singapore

Edward Elgar
Cheltenham, UK • Northampton, MA, USA

Published by
Edward Elgar Publishing Limited
Glensanda House
Montpellier Parade
Cheltenham
Glos GL50 1UA
UK

Edward Elgar Publishing, Inc.
William Pratt House
9 Dewey Court
Northampton
Massachusetts 01060
USA

A catalogue record for this book
is available from the British Library

Library of Congress Cataloguing in Publication Data
Handbook of research on Asian business / edited by Henry Wai-chung Yeung.
    p. cm. — (Elgar original reference)
Includes bibliographical references and index.
    1. Asia—Commerce. 2. Asia—Economic integration. 3. International trade.
    4. Asia—Foreign economic relations. I. Yeung, Henry Wai-chung. II. Series.

HF3752.3.H36 2006
338.095—dc22

                                                            2006008421

ISBN-13: 978 1 84376 960 6 (cased)
ISBN-10: 1 84376 960 3 (cased)

Printed and bound in Great Britain by MPG Books Ltd, Bodmin, Cornwall

Contents

PART III BUSINESS–STATE RELATIONS

PART IV BUSINESS, DEVELOPMENT AND POLICY ISSUES

Figures

Tables

Notes on contributors

F. Gerard Adams (PhD, University of Michigan, USA) is Visiting Professor in the College of Business Administration at Northeastern University in Boston. He moved there in 2001 after many years in Philadelphia at the University of Pennsylvania. He is married to Heidi Vernon. After receiving his PhD in 1956, he was a business economist in the petroleum industry and served in government at the CEA in Washington and at the OECD in Paris. He spent 36 years at the University of Pennsylvania, where he was professor of economics. In addition to his teaching, he was involved in academic governance, as head of the Faculty Senate, and in business consulting and forecasting. He has taught abroad frequently as a visiting professor at the Sasin Graduate Institute of Business Administration of Chulalongkorn University in Bangkok and the Johns Hopkins Center in Nanjing, China. Adams' research interests have ranged widely. He has worked on a broad range of empirical studies including models of nations, regions, commodity markets, energy, industries, firms and the linkages between these models. His recent research has focused on the economics of development and crisis in East Asia. He is author of numerous articles and a number of books, among them *Industrial Policies for Growth and Competitiveness, Export Instability and Economic Growth, Stabilizing World Commodity Markets, The Business Forecasting Revolution, The Macroeconomic Dimensions of Arms Reduction, Economic Activity, Trade and Industry in the US–Japan–World Economy, East Asian Development: Will the East Asian Growth Miracle Survive?, Public Policies in East Asian Development: Facing New Challenges, E-Business and the New Economy, East Asia, Globalization, and the New Economy*.

Tim G. Andrews (PhD, Brunel University, UK) is Senior Lecturer in International Management at Strathclyde Business School, University of Strathclyde. He has published a series of conceptual and empirical articles examining cross-cultural issues pertaining to the management of Western MNCs in Southeast Asia. Recent articles have appeared in the *Asia Pacific Journal of Management, Journal of International Business* and *Asia Pacific Business Review*. He is the co-author of *Multinationals in Southeast Asia* and co-editor of the *Working in Asia* book series. Current research within the region explores the impact of cultural variance on the intracorporate implementation of electronic communication programmes in Thailand.

Cristina Chaminade (PhD, Autonomous University of Madrid, Spain) is Assistant Professor in Innovation Studies at the Centre for Innovation, Research and Competence in the Learning Economy (CIRCLE), Lund University (Sweden) and Visiting Professor at the HHL Leipzig School of Business (Germany). Her doctoral thesis was awarded Best Thesis in Economics (UAM). Before joining CIRCLE, she worked at the UAM researching on innovation policy for small firms. Between 1997 and 2003, she was the Spanish delegate in the OECD Work Groups on National Systems of Innovation, and on Innovative

Clusters and International Scientific Co-operation (Global Science Forum). She has been Head of the Innovation Unit of the Spanish Entrepreneurial Association of Electronic and Telecommunication Industries (ANIEL). Her research focuses mainly on innovation policy, particularly how to promote innovation and knowledge creation in different industries and firms, with a special interest in developing regions.

Tung-lung Steven Chang (PhD, George Washington University, USA) is Professor of Marketing and International Business at the College of Management, Long Island University, C.W. Post campus. He has taught MBA classes at the headquarters of Northrop Grumman, Olympus, Symbol Technologies and Verizon. Dr Chang has centred his research on the global expansion and marketing strategy of multinational corporations. His research has been published by *Journal of World Business, International Marketing Review, Journal of Global Marketing, Competitiveness Review* and *International Finance Review*, among others. Dr Chang is the recipient of Keller Grants, a United Nations Development Program Grant, and a National Science Foundation grant. He previously served as a member of the New Jersey State Export Finance Company's Advisory Council.

Cindy M.Y. Chung (PhD, University of British Columbia, Canada) is Assistant Professor at the Marketing and International Business Division in the Nanyang Business School at the Nanyang Technological University. She obtained her doctorate in marketing. Her research interest is in the area of consumer behaviour, specifically relating to consumer word-of-mouth, the price–quality relationship, and cross-cultural consumption issues. She teaches consumer behaviour at the undergraduate and graduate levels.

Andrew Delios (PhD, Richard Ivey School of Business, Canada) is Associate Professor and Head of the Department of Business Policy, NUS Business School, the National University of Singapore. He is the author or co-author of more than 50 published journal articles, case studies and book chapters. His articles have appeared in such journals as the *Academy of Management Journal, Administrative Science Quarterly, Strategic Management Journal, Strategic Organization* and *Journal of International Business Studies.* He has authored five books, including *International Business: An Asia–Pacific Perspective* and *Strategy for Success in Asia.* He has written case studies and conducted research on companies involved in Canada, China, India, Italy, Hong Kong, Japan, Singapore and Vietnam. His research looks at foreign investment issues in emerging economies, particularly by Japanese multinationals, and the governance, strategy and performance of China's listed companies.

Christopher M. Dent (PhD, University of Hull, UK) is Senior Lecturer in the East Asian Economy in the Department of East Asian Studies at the University of Leeds, UK. His research interests centre on the international political economy of East Asia and the Asia–Pacific. He is more specifically interested in new trade policy developments in the Asia–Pacific; the foreign economic policies of Singapore, South Korea and Taiwan; East Asian developing countries, multilateralism and globalization; East Asia's economic relations with the European Union; theories of international economic security; and theories of regionalism. Published books include *New Free Trade Agreements in the Asia–Pacific* (2006); *Asia–Pacific Economic and Security Co-operation* (editor, 2003); *The*

Foreign Economic Policies of Singapore, South Korea and Taiwan (2002); *Northeast Asian Regionalism: Learning from the European Experience* (co-editor, 2002); *The European Union and East Asia: An Economic Relationship* (1999); *The European Economy: The Global Context* (1997). Christopher Dent is also author of over 50 academic articles and papers, and is currently writing a book on the recent proliferation of free trade agreement (FTA) projects in the Asia–Pacific.

M. Krishna Erramilli (PhD, University of Arkansas, USA) is Vice-Dean, Office of Executive Education at the Nanyang Business School, Nanyang Technological University, Singapore. He taught in the US for many years before joining NTU, where he also headed the Marketing and International Business Division. He has published in top journals, including *Journal of Marketing* and *Journal of International Business Studies*, in addition to presenting papers at numerous international conferences. His research interests are in international market entry strategy, international business theory and international competitive advantage.

Axèle Giroud (PhD, University of Bradford, UK) is Senior Lecturer in International Business at Bradford University School of Management. She has previously worked in the University of Paris I, Panthéon-Sorbonne. She has conducted several research projects on Asian and multinational firms' activities in the region. She is interested in issues of knowledge transfer, multinational firms' linkages in host economies and multinational strategies in Asia. She has taken part in several international seminars (notably some organized by the United Nations), and has published articles and book chapters, as well as completing several research reports for major organizations, such as the Japanese Bank for International Cooperation, the British Department for International Development and the ASEAN Secretariat. She recently published *Transnationals, Technology and Economic Development* (2003) and *Multinationals and Asia: Organizational and Institutional Relationships* (2005).

Doug Guthrie (PhD, University of California, Berkeley, USA) is Professor of Management and Organization at the Stern School of Business and also holds a joint appointment in the Department of Sociology at New York University. His primary areas of research focus on organizational theory, the impact of corporations on the social sector and the impact of foreign companies in China. He is author of *Dragon in a Three-Piece Suit: The Emergence of Capitalism in China* (1999) and, more recently, *China and Globalization: The Economic, Political and Social Transformation of Chinese Society* (2006).

Gary G. Hamilton (PhD, University of Washington, USA) is Professor of Sociology in the Jackson School of International Studies at the University of Washington. He has published numerous books and articles, including most recently *Emergent Economies, Divergent Paths: Economic Organization and International Trade in South Korea and Taiwan*, with Robert C. Feenstra (2006), *Commerce and Capitalism in Chinese Societies* (2006), *Cosmopolitan Capitalists: Hong Kong and the Chinese Diaspora at the end of the 20th Century,* editor and contributor (1999), *The Economic Organization of East Asian Capitalism,* with Marco Orrù and Nicole Biggart (1997) and *Asian Business Networks*, editor (1996).

Ying Ho is a PhD student in Marketing at The Chinese University of Hong Kong, Shatin, Hong Kong. Her research focuses on cross-cultural marketing, service marketing and consumer behaviour. She has published in *Journal of International Marketing*, *Journal of Database Marketing and Consumer Strategy Management*, and *Cornell HRA Quarterly*. She obtained her BBA at The Chinese University of Hong Kong, and her MSc in International Business at the University of Manchester Institute of Science and Technology, UK.

Kam-hon Lee (PhD, Northwestern University, USA) is Professor of Marketing at The Chinese University of Hong Kong, Shatin, Hong Kong. His research areas include business negotiation, cross-cultural marketing, marketing ethics, social marketing and tourism marketing. He has published in *Journal of Marketing*, *Journal of Management*, *Journal of Business Ethics*, *Journal of International Marketing*, *Cornell HRA Quarterly*, and other refereed journals. He also serves on the editorial boards of various international and regional journals.

Peter Ping Li (PhD, George Washington University, USA) is Professor of Management at California State University, Stanislaus. His primary academic interest lies in the development of holistic, dynamic and dialectical frameworks with regard to the impact of cultural values and dynamic changes on the global strategic management. In particular, his recent research focuses on re-examining the extant theories of international business and strategic management from the cultural and social perspective of China and East Asia, especially the issue of informal networks for business exchanges. Dr Li has published in various academic journals, including *Organization Studies*, *Asia Pacific Journal of Management, Journal of Organizational Change Management*, *Management & Organizational Review*, *Journal of Global Information Management*, *Advances in International Comparative Management*, *International Executive* (currently *Thunderbird International Business Review*) and *Advances in Chinese Industrial Studies*, among others.

John A. Mathews (PhD, Imperial College, London, UK) is Professor of Strategic Management at Macquarie Graduate School of Management, Macquarie University in Sydney. He is the author of *Tiger Technology: The Creation of a Semiconductor Industry in East Asia*, as well as *Dragon Multinational: A New Model of Global Growth*. He is widely published in the academic literature, most recently with a paper in *California Management Review* on strategy and the crystal cycle, and in *Research Policy* on innovative capacity in East Asia. He has worked with UNCTAD, UNIDO and the World Bank. Professor Mathews was a Visiting Scholar at the Rockefeller Foundation Study Center at Bellagio, in Italy, in September 2004.

Pavida Pananond (PhD, University of Reading, UK) is Assistant Professor at the Department of International Business, Logistics and Transport, Thammasat Business School, Thammasat University, Bangkok, Thailand. She has published in *ASEAN Economic Bulletin*, *Asia–Pacific Journal of Management* and *Journal of Asian Business*. Her research interests include post-crisis changes of Thai multinationals, the globalization of Thai management, and the evolution and international expansion of Thai business groups.

Mike W. Peng (PhD, University of Washington, USA) is Provost's Distinguished Professor of Global Strategy at the University of Texas at Dallas. Prior to joining UTD, Dr Peng was an associate professor at the Ohio State University. Professor Peng is widely regarded as one of the most prolific and most influential scholars in global strategy. He has published over 40 journal articles and three books, including, most recently, *Global Strategy* (2006). He has served on the editorial board of the *Academy of Management Journal*, *Academy of Management Review*, *Journal of International Business Studies* and *Strategic Management Journal*. He is currently an editor of the *Asia Pacific Journal of Management*, and has been appointed as its editor-in-chief for 2007–9.

Misha Petrovic (PhD, University of Washington, USA) is Postdoctoral Research Fellow in the Department of Sociology, University of Washington. He received his MA in sociology and political science from CEU, Prague and the University of Lancaster. His doctoral dissertation deals with the making of global markets for consumer goods. He specializes in economic sociology and globalization studies. He co-authored several articles on global retailing and its impact on the global economy, including 'Making global markets: Wal-Mart and its suppliers', in *Wal-Mart: Template for 21st Century Capitalism*, edited by Nelson Lichtenstein (2005).

Nicholas A. Phelps (PhD, University of Newcastle, UK) is Reader in Economic Geography at the School of Geography, University of Southampton. He is author of *Multinationals and European Integration* and co-editor of *The New Competition for Inward Investment*. His research interests are in the geography and economic impacts of multinational companies and foreign direct investment (FDI), the political economy of FDI attraction, and the agglomeration of economic activity.

Piyush Sharma is a Research Associate and final year doctoral candidate in the Marketing and International Business Division of the Nanyang Business School at Nanyang Technological University (NTU), Singapore. Piyush earned his bachelor's degree in Electrical Engineering from University of Delhi and MBA in Marketing from Indian Institute of Management, Bangalore in India. He has over 20 years of professional experience in a wide range of industries and has been involved in teaching, research and executive education at NTU. His research interests include hedonic consumer behaviours, international marketing and services marketing.

Kulwant Singh (PhD, University of Michigan, USA) is Associate Professor of Business Policy, NUS Business School, National University of Singapore. He has published more than 40 papers, chapters and cases on issues related to strategy and competition in rapidly changing environments. His papers have appeared in such journals as the *Academy of Management Journal*, *Strategic Management Journal*, *Organization Science*, *Industrial and Corporate Change* and *Journal of Management*. He has published three books, including, most recently, *Strategy for Success in Asia* (2005).

Bharadhwaj Sivakumaran (PhD, University of Maryland, USA) is Assistant Professor at the Department of Management Studies, Indian Institute of Technology, Chennai, India. His research primarily focuses on variety-seeking behaviour, impulse buying behaviour, cross-cultural buying behaviour, and order of entry effects. He has presented numerous papers in all the leading marketing conferences.

Paz Estrella Tolentino (PhD, University of Reading, UK) is Lecturer in International Business at the School of Management and Organizational Psychology, Birkbeck College, University of London. Among her publications is *Technological Innovation and Third World Multinationals* (1993). The book is based on her PhD dissertation that received the 1989 Academy of International Business Richard N. Farmer Prize for the best PhD thesis on international business.

Eric W.K. Tsang (PhD, University of Cambridge, UK) is Associate Professor of Strategic Management at Wayne State University, USA. His research interests include organizational learning, strategic alliances, research methodology and Chinese management issues. He has published widely in leading management journals, such as *Academy of Management Executive*, *Academy of Management Review*, *Human Relations*, *Journal of Business Venturing*, *Journal of International Business Studies*, *Journal of Management Studies*, *Organization Studies* and *Strategic Management Journal*.

Lai Si Tsui-Auch (PhD, Michigan State University, USA) is Associate Professor at the Nanyang Business School, Nanyang Technological University of Singapore. Her current research focuses on business groups, trust and distrust in organizations and bureaucratic rationality. Her research has been published in such journals as *Organization Studies*, *Journal of Management Studies*, *Management Learning*, *Journal of Asian Business*, *International Sociology*, *International Journal of Urban and Regional Research*, *Development and Change* and *Gazette*. She is currently a member of the Editorial Board of *Organization Studies* and of *The Qualitative Report*.

Jan Vang (PhD, Lund University, Sweden) is Assistant Professor at Copenhagen Institute of Technology, Aalborg University in Copenhagen, Denmark, as well as researcher at CIRCLE at Lund University, Sweden. His research focuses on the globalization of innovation systems, with special attention to Asia and Scandinavia, and to so-called 'creative industries'. He has written and (co)-edited numerous books, special issues and papers.

Heidi Vernon (PhD, Boston University, USA) is Professor of Management and Director of International Alliances at Northeastern University. She has been Senior Professor at Prasetyia Mulya Graduate School of Management in Indonesia. She is a specialist in strategic and cultural aspects of international business. Professor Vernon is the author of three books: *Lowell: The Corporations and the City* (1992), *Strategic Management in the Global Economy* (1997) and *Business & Society; A Managerial Approach* (1998). She is on editorial and review boards of professional journals and is also the author of numerous articles and papers. She has been a consultant to the World Bank, the United Nations Development Program, and the Harvard Institute for International Development. Professor Vernon has presented papers at numerous conferences around the world, and has done research on the role of women in international business, the role of culture in business, and the issues of international management. She has spent many years travelling, consulting, and teaching in Asia.

Junmin Wang is a doctoral candidate in the Department of Sociology at New York University. She is currently working on a dissertation on the transformation of the tobacco industry in China during the economic reforms.

Friedrich Wu (PhD, University of Washington, USA) is Adjunct Associate Professor of International Political Economy at the Nanyang Technological University in Singapore. He was a former Director of Economics at the Singapore Ministry of Trade and Industry, and Vice President/Head of Economic Research at the DBS Bank, the largest banking group in Singapore and in Southeast Asia.

Wei Wei Xu is a PhD student in the Business Policy Department of the NUS Business School, National University of Singapore. She received her Masters degree in economics at Beijing Normal University. Her research interests include international strategic management and corporate governance in emerging countries. Currently, she is looking at how the ownership structure influences the internationalization patterns of multinational firms in China.

Henry Wai-chung Yeung (PhD, University of Manchester, UK) is Professor of Economic Geography at the Department of Geography, National University of Singapore. He was a recipient of the National University of Singapore Outstanding University Researcher Award (1998), the Institute of British Geographers Economic Geography Research Group Best Published Paper Award (1998), the Commonwealth Fellowship (2002) and the Fulbright Foreign Research Award (2003). His research interests cover, broadly, theories and the geography of transnational corporations, Asian firms and their overseas operations and Chinese business networks in the Asia–Pacific region. Professor Yeung has published widely on transnational corporations from developing countries, in particular Hong Kong, Singapore and other Asian newly industrialized economies. He is the author of three monographs: *Transnational Corporations and Business Networks* (1998), *Entrepreneurship and the Internationalisation of Asian Firms* (2002) and *Chinese Capitalism in a Global Era* (2004). He is also the editor or co-editor of another four books: *The Globalisation of Business Firms from Emerging Markets* (1999), *Globalisation and the Asia Pacific* (1999), *Globalization of Chinese Business Firms* (2000) and *Remaking the Global Economy: Economic–Geographical Perspectives* (2003). He has over 70 research papers published in internationally refereed journals and 30 chapters in books. He is editor of *Environment and Planning A*, *Economic Geography*, and *Review of International Political Economy*, Asia–Pacific editor of *Global Networks*, and business manager of *Singapore Journal of Tropical Geography*. He sits on the editorial boards of eight other international journals, including *Asia Pacific Journal of Management*, *European Urban and Regional Studies* and *Journal of Economic Geography*.

Acknowledgments

When my commissioning editor, Francine O'Sullivan, first asked me two years ago if I would be interested in pursuing this project, I thought the timing was perfect for such a volume, and that the job should not be too daunting precisely because of the paucity of the existing literature on Asian business. In retrospect, I have come to the realization that this is indeed a daunting job that requires enormous energy and persistence to bring it to fruition. In this regard, I want to express my gratitude to the following people and institutions for making this *Handbook* a reality – something I can be truly proud of.

My contributors, all leading experts in their respective fields, deserve the highest form of appreciation. All 30 contributors graciously accepted my initial invitation to contribute and wrote their chapters in a timely and professional manner that made my editorial role much less painful. While they kindly endured and responded to my specific comments on their chapters (some were harsh and mean), I am very glad that the revised chapters have mostly taken on board the critical issues raised by a 'ruthless' editor. Meanwhile, several individuals should be acknowledged here: Andrew Aeria, Dieter Ernst, Hafiz Mirza and Dennis Tachiki. Because of a variety of unforeseen circumstances, I am unable to include their contributions in this *Handbook*. However, I would like to thank them for their interest in this project and their continual support.

Moreover, I would like to thank my home institution, the National University of Singapore, for funding a major research project (R-109-000-050-112) of which this *Handbook* represents a tangible outcome. My research assistant, Angela Leung, has done a superb job in supporting my editorial role in this *Handbook* project. I am very grateful for her unfailing support, sometimes even from a distance during her holidays at home in Seattle.

My publisher, Edward Elgar, and commissioning editor, Francine O'Sullivan, have been most patient with the progress of this project. I am very grateful for their continual support of my research work in general and their confidence in this *Handbook* project in particular. The generous financial support from my publisher in securing the relevant copyright permission should also be acknowledged here.

Finally, I must express my greatest gratitude and love for my wife, Weiyu, and daughter, Kay. They have endured this entire project. During the final stage of editing the chapters, our second child, Lucas, was born. Consequently, all three of them had to live with me for weeks when I edited the chapters in my PowerBook right in front of them. For their endless love and great fun, I dedicate this *Handbook* to them.

Henry Wai-chung Yeung
Singapore
January 2006

1.   Unpacking the business of Asian business

Henry Wai-chung Yeung

The rise of Asia as an important region for global business has been widely recognized as one of the most significant economic phenomena in the new millennium. In his February 2005 speech delivered at Lancaster University's Management School, Stephen Green, the Group CEO of HSBC Holdings plc – the global bank that arguably knows Asia best – noted that the rise of Asia 'will fundamentally reshape the world's economic landscape in the decades ahead . . . At HSBC we believe developing markets will provide about half the growth in demand in the world economy over the next 25 to 30 years. And we believe that China and India will be core to that . . . I would go further and say that the economic modernisation of Asia is the most seismic consequence yet of the globalization of human commerce' (Green, 2005: 1, 4). Many business and economic indicators have conclusively shown the superlative upward trajectories of Asian firms and Asian economies: the number of leading Asian firms listed in *Fortune Global 500* is growing rapidly; the GDP per capita of Asian economies is increasing dramatically, and thereby creating huge domestic consumer markets; Asia is attracting a large proportion of the world's foreign direct investment, and becoming a favourite investment destination for global corporations; China and India alone are contributing to a substantial portion of the world's manufactured products and IT services; and the list of achievements by Asian firms and Asian economies goes on and on.

While substantive academic studies of Asian business have been in existence for several decades now, there is relatively little systematic integration of our knowledge and research on Asian business (see also Leung and White, 2004). Most of the existing studies either focus on business and management issues in specific Asian firms (Calingo, 1996; Hamlin, 1998, 2000; Turpin and Shen, 1999) and Asian economies (for example Japan, Indonesia and Hong Kong), or champion an all-embracing Asian-style/way of management (for example Chen, 1995; Lau *et al.*, 2000; Backman and Butler, 2003; Warner, 2003; Tipton, 2005). The former research approach tends to place much emphasis on economy-specific characteristics, at the expense of broader regional and global forces, in shaping business and management issues in a particular economy. In some cases, the analytical focus is highly limited to micro-management issues within Asian firms. On the other hand, the latter approach often caricatures the great diversity of management practices in Asia, and makes sweeping generalizations that call for an exceptional view on how a singular form of Asian business differs from the so-called 'Western' practices in business and management. An unfortunate consequence of either approach is that Asian business becomes rather mystified as either unique to specific Asian economies or similar across all Asian economies. These approaches are clearly unsatisfactory, as Asia is becoming much more articulated into the global economy. We need a more holistic approach that combines micro-level analysis of Asian firms and industries, with macro-contextual analysis of local, national, regional and global influences on Asian business.

   This introductory chapter aims to shed light on our state-of-the-art understandings of Asian business in relation to three important analytical themes: (1) Asian firms and networks; (2) Asian states, institutions and business systems and (3) global commodity/value chains and global production networks. The focus here is neither exclusively on business firms themselves nor on specific national economies. Rather, I aim to introduce this *Handbook*, not by telling what each chapter is about, but by situating individual chapters or groups of chapters within one or more of the above interrelated strands of analytical literature. Before I proceed to unpack each of these strands of literature, I need to contextualize their relevance to this *Handbook*. First, in each of the three analytical themes, there are specific theoretical perspectives that help organize research efforts and advance our knowledge of Asian business. They are developed not only by researchers in business and management schools, but also by academics in a wide range of cognate social science disciplines, such as international economics, political economy, economic sociology, regional studies, development studies and economic geography. The collective body of literature introduced in this chapter is therefore highly interdisciplinary and transcends particular functional areas in Asian business (for example marketing or organizational behaviour).

   Second, the presentation sequence of these three strands of theoretical literature reflects the *analytical scale* of their central claims. More specifically, individual firms, national economies and global processes are the three scales at which these theoretical perspectives and their associated analytical studies are organized. While some of the chapters in this *Handbook* are only implicitly embedded in these theoretical perspectives, other chapters have drawn explicitly upon particular theoretical perspectives to develop their understanding of the nature and organization of Asian business. This chapter thus provides an overall theoretical reference point for understanding the research topics and materials reviewed in subsequent chapters.

   Third, it must be noted that these three strands of theoretical literature represent cutting-edge research on Asian business since the 1980s. My choice of this time line is intentional, as Asian business, with the exception of Japanese business, has emerged as a serious academic research focus only since the 1980s. The past 25 years witness a tremendous surge in academic interests in Asian business. This chapter serves to bring together this diverse body of academic studies, in order to showcase the influential research on Asian business for both retrospective and prospective reasons. With hindsight, these perspectives can help us understand the evolution of Asian business to their current state of the art. However, any research programme should be forward-looking, and thus we should develop prospective insights that help guide future research on Asian business. Some of these research agenda will be examined in the concluding section of this chapter.

ASIAN FIRMS AND NETWORKS

The first significant strand of theoretical literature relates to business firms in Asia, whether they originate from Asian economies or are foreign firms investing in Asia. In general, this strand of literature is concerned with business strategy and organization in Asia (see also chapters in Part I of this volume). While focusing their conceptual lenses on the firm level, these studies have made significant progress towards identifying the causal firm-specific factors that contribute to their business performance in Asia and beyond. In this analytical context, two approaches particularly stand out, amongst a whole range of other lesser and, sometimes, competing perspectives: the resource-based view of the firm and organizational networks theory.

The intellectual antecedents of the *resource-based view* (RBV) of the firm have now been well mapped out (Barney, 1991, 2001; Peng, 2001; see also Chapter 5 in this volume). In this view, the performance of Asian firms or firms in Asia is directly linked to their access to firm-specific resources, such as capital, technology, markets and managerial skills. As reviewed in Chapters 2 and 3, a significant number of studies of Asian business have focused on their resource endowments as the independent variable that explains their business and organizational outcomes. Despite its origin in industrial economics (see Penrose, 1959), to a large extent, the RBV perspective has been adopted by researchers based in business schools and management studies throughout the world to study such empirical issues as knowledge transfer, success of joint ventures, organizational choice, and so on.

While the RBV-inspired work has identified a whole range of firm-specific factors in explaining the performance of Asian business, there is too much analytical privilege offered to *intra-firm* resources, at the expense of *inter-firm relationships*. These latter relationships form the focal point for theoretical perspectives related to organizational networks. This body of literature has made a significant impact on our understanding of firm performance through pioneer work on business and organizational networks in Asia. Unlike the RBV-linked work, this genre of work focuses primarily on how business networks are formed and organized in specific Asian economies. It also differs from the business systems theory to be explained later, because the state and non-state institutions are not as important as theorized in the business networks theory.

There are primarily two aspects to this body of work on business and organizational networks in Asia. The first group of work relates to the role of interpersonal relationships in explaining business performance and organizational outcomes in Asia. The second examines the role of business groups in Asia at the inter-firm level. Both strands of literature owe their conceptual antecedents to several important sociological studies of Asian economies in the late 1980s and the early 1990s (see Hamilton and Biggart, 1988; Hamilton, 1991; Orrù *et al.*, 1997). In particular, these earlier sociological studies have identified the critical importance of interpersonal relationships in the organization of business activities in Asia. For example, in many Asian economies with a substantial economic presence of ethnic Chinese (for example Hong Kong, Taiwan and Singapore), the role of interpersonal relationships or *guanxi* is critical to understanding business activities (see also Chapters 4 and 5 in this volume). As mainland Chinese opens to global business, *guanxi* relationships seem to continue to play a significant role in business ventures and marketing activities in China (see also Chapters 6 and 9–10 in this volume).

Meanwhile, the role of business groups in inter-firm relationships is quite distinctive in Asian business. From the Japanese *keiretsu* (Gerlach, 1992; Richter, 1999a; Kensy, 2001; Beamish *et al.*, 2002; Paprzycki, 2004) to the South Korean *chaebol* (Jwa, 2002; Chang, 2003; Jwa and Lee, 2004) and the Chinese family conglomerate (Wong, 1988; Redding, 1990; Yeung, 1998, 2004; Hamilton, 2005), business groups are significant collective players in Asian business, and they have received a fair share of theoretical and empirical attention (see also Hamilton, 1991; Richter, 1999b; Dacin and Delios, 2005; Chapters 2–3 in this volume). These studies have shown that, despite the advancement of globalization forces, business groups in Asia remain highly resilient to organizational change and transformations (Carney, 2005; see Chapters 15 and 18 in this volume). In particular, business groups in Asia are found to be significant players in their domestic economies, organized around dominant firms and/or families, highly diversified in the scale and scope of their business operations and, in many cases, highly internationalized in their geographic presence. As explained in the next section, the organization of economic activities in Asia is significantly different from Anglo-American capitalism, in which there is a strong separation between the ownership and control of business firms.

Insofar as the above studies are concerned, there is a strong tendency towards focusing on the strategy, organization, management and marketing activities of business firms in Asia in their home economies (see also chapters in Part II of this volume). Few of them have examined a relatively recent phenomenon, the *internationalization of Asian firms*. While the early 1980s witnessed a spate of empirical studies of the emergence of the so-called 'Third World multinationals' associated with such researchers as Wells (1983) and Lall (1983), the next wave of studies came only much later, in the mid-1990s, when these Asian transnational corporations (TNCs) began to make serious inroads into the global marketplace (Yeung, 1999, 2002; Yeung and Olds, 2000; Beausang, 2003; see also Chapters 20–22 in this volume). Until very recently (for example Guillén, 2002; Mathews, 2002; Chen, 2003; Yang, 2005), this substantial body of literature has relatively little crossfertilization with the above studies of business strategy and organization of firms in Asian economies. This is perhaps a reflection of the domination of economics perspectives in a majority of empirical studies of the internationalization of Asian firms (see Yeung, 1999).

To sum up, the past 15 years have seen the rapid emergence of academic studies of the business strategies of Asian firms and the organization of their business networks from a variety of theoretical perspectives. As illustrated in the chapters in Parts I and II of this volume, the Asian firm serves as an important analytical category to unpack the intricate nature of Asian business. While drawing upon both macroeconomic and micro-firm-specific analyses, these studies of Asian business have shed light on both the cross-sectional profiles of Asian firms and their dynamic transformations over time. As we are approaching a better understanding of Asian firms, we begin to realize that Asian business is certainly not just about Asian firms. Equally, if not more, important are the institutional contexts, political economies and business systems in which these firms are embedded. Here, we encounter another whole set of theoretical perspectives that are developed through rigorous social scientific investigations into Asian economies.

ASIAN STATES, INSTITUTIONS AND BUSINESS SYSTEMS

As we move from Asian firms and their corporate strategy and management to broader political–economic considerations, we are compelled to examine the role of Asian states, institutions and business systems in shaping the organization of Asian business. In other words, there is only so much that firm-level studies can tell us about Asian business. This is where the literature on Asian business (rather than just Asian firms) draws upon the critical theoretical insights offered in major social science disciplines, such as comparative political economy, economic sociology, institutional economics, development studies, and so on. As pointed out by Mike Peng in Chapter 3 (see also Peng, 2003; Peng *et al.*, 2005), we simply cannot fully grapple with the intricacies of business strategy and organization in Asia by focusing exclusively on firm-level variables and behaviour. There is no doubt that firms are the key drivers of business activities in Asia and beyond. However, there is now a large body of theoretical literature that points to the deeply embedded relationships between capitalist firms (and, even, non-capitalist firms, as in the case of transitional economies such as China) and the wider societal context (see chapters in Part III of this volume). In this subsection, I focus on three interrelated theoretical perspectives that are developed specifically from the Asian context.

First, since the mid-1980s, a number of influential political economists and political scientists have collectively popularized the *developmental state theory* that fundamentally explains the superior economic performance of selected Asian economies in relation to the strong administrative guidance of their respective developmental states (Vogel, 1979; Johnson, 1982; Amsden, 1991, 2001; Haggard, 1990; Wade, 1990; Woo-Cumings, 1999; Hamilton-Hart, 2002; cf. Boyd and Ngo, 2005). In this theoretical perspective, Asian states are featured strongly in terms of their direct and indirect interventions in the national economies. In direct terms, strong states in Japan and the Asian newly industrialized economies (NIEs) – such as South Korea, Taiwan and Singapore – not only prioritized economic development as the prime goal for their policy interventions, but also engaged in explicit pro-business policies during the various stages of their industrialization programmes and, to a significant extent, the post-industrial era. These state interventions existed in the form of promoting certain leading national firms as 'national champions' through strategic industrial policies and tax and export incentives. In some cases, the state took a direct interest in the establishment, ownership and continual management of business groups in these Asian economies (for example Singapore and Taiwan). Such leading firms as Singapore Airlines and Taiwan Semiconductor Manufacturing Company (TSMC) are good examples of such state-driven initiatives (see also Chapters 15–16 in this volume).

In an indirect way, these Asian states also engaged foreign firms, in the form of inward foreign direct investment (FDI), to kick-start their developmental processes. As shown in Chapters 12–14 and 19 in this volume, these favourable government policies towards foreign investors have made a very significant impact on a variety of indicators of national economic development, ranging from innovative capacity, industrial linkages and industrial upgrading to business opportunities, managerial capabilities and labour skills. For example, Taiwan's formidable position in the global electronics industry today would not be possible without these direct and indirect interventions by the Taiwanese government during the past three decades (see Chapter 16 in this volume). Equally, state intervention and transnational capital must be credited for much of Singapore's well-known achievement in economic development (see Chapters 12 and 15 in this volume). The implications of these state interventions in Asian economies are that business strategy and organization, whether domestic Asian firms or foreign firms in Asia, cannot be solely understood as rational economic decision making in the absence of powerful influences at the broader structural and institutional levels. Despite the great diversity in the specific national institutional contexts, Asian business is as much about business firms as about states and their embedded institutions.

This argument thus brings us to the second, but closely related, theoretical perspective that focuses specifically on *institutions* and *institutional change* in Asian economies. Partly linked to cognate theoretical developments in institutional economics (Hodgson, 1988, 1994; North, 1990), economic sociology (Granovetter and Swedberg, 1992; Smelser and Swedberg, 1994, 2005; Nielsen and Koch, 2004) and organizational analysis (DiMaggio and Powell, 1991; DiMaggio, 2001), this research interest emphasizing the role of institutions in Asian economies has made a fundamental contribution to our understanding of business activities in Asia. Beginning with the work by Hamilton and Biggart (1988) on business networks as the institutional foundation of Asian economies, a whole variety of theoretical and empirical studies of institutions has mushroomed during the past two decades. This diversity in literature has made it rather difficult to identify them separately (see also Chapter 3 in this volume).

Broadly speaking, however, there are at least two strands of studies in this vast literature. One strand works on the state–business nexus, the other on the role of social institutions in Asian business. The political economy dimension of *state–business relationships* has undoubtedly attracted a significant amount of research attention during the past two decades. Partly related to the developmental state literature, this body of work focuses on how state-driven institutional structures have provided favourable opportunities for business firms in Asian economies (see also chapters in Part III of this volume). We now know a great deal about the rise of numerous major business groups in Asian economies in relation to pro-business state-sponsored institutional frameworks (for example banking systems, industrial structures, R&D frameworks, labour markets, and so on), particularly in mainland China (Guthrie, 1999; Keister, 2000; see also Chapters 6 and 22 in this volume), Indonesia (Robison, 1986), Malaysia (Gomez, 1999), Singapore (Low, 1998; see also Chapter 15 in this volume), South Korea (Fields, 1995; Kim, 1997; Lee, 1997), Taiwan (Shieh, 1992; Fields, 1995; see also Chapter 16 in this volume) and Thailand (Hewison, 1990). By unpacking the political economy of these pro-business institutional structures, these studies have incorporated politics and power relations in their analysis of business actors and their relationships with broader institutional power dynamics. As a consequence, we can better understand the dynamics of Asian business, particularly at times of institutional change in an era of accelerated economic globalization (see also Chapters 3 and 18 in this volume).

Another strand of the literature on institutions in Asian business focuses on the role of *social organization* in providing the institutional foundation of Asian business. Here, the emphasis has been placed on how social and cultural institutions in Asia interact with economic incentives to promote business and entrepreneurial activities. Collectively, these studies have shown how variations in social and cultural institutions have made a significant difference to the business strategy and management practices of firms from different Asian economies (see Orrù *et al.*, 1997; Biggart and Guillén, 1999) and the ways in which marketing activities of business firms are influenced (see Chapters 7–8 and 10 in this volume). For example, personal relationships or *guanxi* have been identified as a form of social institution that engenders business transactions among related parties. Unlike the culturalist explanation of this *guanxi* factor in relation to Confucian traditions (for example Redding, 1990; Haley *et al.*, 1998; cf. Chapter 17 in this volume), this institutionalist perspective on *guanxi* sees these complex webs of interpersonal relationships as social institutions, rather than cultural practices, that emerge from peculiar political, economic and social contexts in Asia (see Yang, 1994; Chung and Hamilton, 2001; Guthrie, 2002; Yeung, 2004; Chapter 4 in this volume). As the forms of social organization in these

Asian economies change and become transformed over time, particularly in relation to globalization tendencies, there are important implications for our understanding of the dynamics of Asian business in a global era (see also Yeung, 2000; Chapters 6, 15 and 18 in this volume).

While the developmental state theory and institutional analysis focus respectively on the state and institutional structures, the third theoretical perspective brings them together to form a comprehensive analysis of Asian business at the level of *business systems*. Originally formulated by organizational sociologist Richard Whitley (1992, 1999), this business systems perspective has been developed to explain the management, organization and performance of Asian firms in relation to their home-economy business systems (for example authority systems, institutional structures, labour relations and capital markets). Similar to the developmental state theory and institutional analysis, this perspective affords much more explanatory power to *internal* factors within individual Asian economies. The most significant difference, however, remains that the business systems perspective encompasses a much broader range of explanatory variables than either the developmental state theory or institutional analysis (see also Westney, 1996; Jakobsen and Torp, 2000; Yeung, 2000, 2002; Redding, 2005; Chapter 20 in this volume). This perspective situates firm-specific practices within the broader business systems in which these firms are embedded. The business systems perspective, however, is not without its analytical problems. The most significant one is its excessive focus on the highly imposing structuring effects of nation-specific factors, at the expense of processes that operate beyond the national scale – at the regional and global scales. As explained in the next section, these broader processes are well theorized in analytical perspectives that incorporate these regional and global processes at work.

In summary, Asian business is best understood as a complex outcome of firm-specific decisions and strategies, and their interaction with wider political and social institutions in Asia. When these institutions become sufficiently influential, they form a unique configuration of a business system that can leave long-term impacts on the ways in which business activities and firm practices are conducted in Asia. The three interrelated theoretical perspectives examined in this section are highly relevant for our understanding of both Asian firms and foreign firms in Asia, because they focus on the business environment internal to respective Asian economies. By going beyond individual firm-level analysis, these broader perspectives differ from the strategic management and the business organization approach described in the previous section; they contribute to a more comprehensive understanding of Asian business as an organizational outcome shaped by a variety of actors (for example firms and states) and institutional structures (for example capital and labour markets). These perspectives showcase how firm-level analysis per se is insufficient in grappling with such extra-firm issues as political economic processes, institutional influences and the dynamics of business systems.

GLOBAL COMMODITY/VALUE CHAINS AND GLOBAL PRODUCTION NETWORKS

While the theoretical perspectives and associated empirical studies in the above two sections have shed very useful light on the *modus operandi* of firms in Asia (local or foreign) and the wider business systems in which these firms are embedded, there is one significant element that remains relatively undertheorized in these perspectives: regional and global forces. These forces are critically important insofar as we are concerned with how Asian economies and, therefore, Asian firms are articulated or integrated into the global economy. This articulation requires us to understand not only the internal dynamics of business within Asia, but also, more crucially, the processes through which Asian economies participate in regional and global economic processes and business activities. In other words, while the perspectives outlined in the previous two sections are highly competent in telling us about the why and the how of Asian business in Asia, they are not really able to inform us much about the ways in which Asian business contributes to global business. In this section, I examine two interrelated theoretical perspectives that put *regional and global processes* at the forefront of their analytical foci: the global commodity/value chain (GCC/GVC) perspective and the global production networks (GPN) perspective. Similar to the perspectives introduced in the previous section, these two perspectives originate from social scientific investigation into *transnational processes* that link different economies and countries together in a chain- and network-like configuration of business and economic activities.

In many ways, the *global* commodity/value chain perspective owes its theoretical origin to earlier sociological studies of economic development. Influenced by Immanuel Wallerstein's world-system framework, in which different countries are sorted in a cascading order of core, semi-periphery and periphery economies, the GCC/GVC analysis gained prominence after the mid-1990s, following the innovative work by Gary Gereffi and Miguel Korzeniewicz (Gereffi and Korzeniewicz, 1990, 1994). Together with other researchers in development studies, they have constructed an analytical framework that focuses on the global scale (Schmitz, 2004; Gereffi, 2005; Gereffi *et al.*, 2005). The GCC/GVC analysis, in particular, has been shown to provide enormously important insights into a wide range of economic development issues, such as industrial upgrading, technological and employment change, market expansion, trade patterns, and so on.

In terms of its relevance for Asian business, the GCC/GVC perspective has been applied directly to the study of how Asian supplier firms are integrated into the strategic decisions of global buyers from North America and Western Europe in a wide range of industrial sectors, such as clothing (Gereffi, 1999; Hassler, 2003; see also Chapter 11 in this volume) and electronics (Borrus *et al.*, 2000; McKendrick *et al.*, 2000; Sturgeon, 2003; see also Chapter 16 in this volume). The GCC/GVC perspective therefore enables us to understand much better why industrial firms in export-intensive Asian economies are organized and configured, not just in relation to their firm-specific strategy and resources or their home-economy business systems (see above sections), but, more importantly, in accordance with the strategic need of global buyers. The perspective introduces a very significant *external* or *exogenous* factor influencing the management and organization of Asian business. In both Chapters 11 and 16 in this volume, the contributors have demonstrated clearly how Asian firms and states are responding to global demand, mediated through the relevant GCCs/GVCs, with appropriate industrial policies and business strategies.

The GCC/GVC analysis, however, does suffer from some analytical shortcomings that can be remedied through the global production networks framework (see Dicken *et al.*, 2001; Henderson *et al.*, 2002; Hess and Yeung, 2006). First, while the chain concept in the GCC analysis brings multiple geographical scales, particularly the global scale, to the forefront of its analysis, the geography of GCCs remains weakly developed and under-theorized, no doubt a reflection of the origin of the framework in development studies and economic sociology. The issue of territoriality is highly aggregated in the GCC framework, identifying the spatial units of analysis, such as countries and economies, as either core or periphery. This is where the GPN framework in economic geography makes stronger claims, because it deals with how actors in various GPNs are anchored in different places (for example specific regions within a country) and multiple scales (from the national to the local scale). A more recent refinement of the GPN framework in Coe *et al.* (2004) has made an explicit analytical link between GPNs and (subnational) regional development – a core issue for economic geographers since the 1980s. Similarly, the work by Coe and Hess (2005) and Coe and Lee (2006) shows how large retailers in Europe are directly involved in the development and restructuring of important supplier networks in East Asian economies. Johns' (2006) work also shows how Asian producers of video games are increasingly incorporated into global production networks that span different regions and territories.

Second, the institutional dimensions of the GCC/GVC analysis seem to be hijacked by its privileging of governance structures. The former includes the role of state policies and institutional conditions in shaping development outcomes in different places and regions in Asia (see also chapters in Part III of this volume). The GCC/GVC analysis places much greater emphasis on alternative governance structures that are associated with the peculiar configuration of GCCs/GVCs in different industries and sectors. For example, in the clothing industry, the key driver is argued to be global buyers, who dictate the terms of garment manufacturing. In the automobile industry, lead firms (assemblers) drive the entire GCC/GVC through their assembly plants located in different regions and countries. The GPN perspective, however, argues that global buyers do not necessarily always dictate the governance structures in these networks, because of substantial variations in national institutional contexts (see discussion in the previous section). For example, Dicken and Hassler (2000) allude to the possibility of country-specific business networks in shaping the governance of clothing GPNs in Indonesia. Similarly, Chapter 16 in this volume shows how the Taiwanese government has been actively involved in reconfiguring its position in the global electronics GPN, from mainly playing the OEM (original equipment manufacturing) role to increasingly emphasizing the ODM (original design manufacturing) and, eventually, the OBM (original brand manufacturing) role.

Taken together, the GCC/GVC and the GPN perspectives have collectively gone beyond focusing exclusively on Asian firms and institutions as the primary explanatory variable for Asian business. By introducing global processes as an *external* dimension of Asian business, these perspectives are highly important for understanding the strategy and performance of Asian firms, the development outcomes of individual Asian economies, and the design and adoption of relevant business and economic policies. By focusing on both global firms and their production networks in Asia, and the articulation of these networks into the global marketplace, these theoretical perspectives offer new insights into the interconnections between actors and processes in Asian business and the global economy.

CONCLUSION AND FUTURE RESEARCH AGENDA

The above strands of theoretical literature and the collective contributions to this *Handbook* provide a solid ground for unpacking the nature and organization of Asian business. Despite its enormous variety and complexity spanning a large number of countries and economies in the region, the messy 'business' of Asian business has been made much more accessible and intelligible by these organizing frameworks and theoretical perspectives. In particular, the above collective body of work on Asian business has made a significant difference to social scientific studies of business organizations and economic activities. By challenging the conventional wisdoms in management and organization studies (see also Wright *et al.*, 2005), regional and development studies and international political economy, these Asia-specific studies have not only added new empirical insights to our existing stock of knowledge on global business. More importantly, they have contributed to cutting-edge theoretical advancement in all of these fields, by developing these empirical insights into appropriate conceptual frameworks that find relevance in other contexts outside Asia. As some of the contributors in this volume have argued (for example Chapters 3, 8, 10 and 16), research on Asian business can provide fertile ground for breakthrough theoretical work (see also Yeung and Lin, 2003). This *Handbook* is intended to be a testimony to such an ambitious goal in social scientific research on global business.

While the contributions in this *Handbook* may point to some level of maturity of research on Asian business, nevertheless, our research 'business' is far from over, for at least two reasons. First, as Asia continues to grow relentlessly and to be integrated into the global economy, business activities and economic organization in Asia will likely be transformed over time (see also Chapters 8, 15 and 18 in this volume). We need fresh theoretical and empirical insights into these transformative processes that come to influence the evolution of Asian business and economies. These insights will be highly useful for both academic research and practical policies. Second, academic research in the social sciences, including business and management studies, continues to be dominated by Anglo-American-centric research. This explicit bias in social scientific knowledge is particularly clear in the various studies critically reviewed by some of the contributors to this *Handbook* (for example Chapters 2, 3, 10 and 20; see also Yeung, 2001). Research on Asian business can certainly help to redress this fundamental bias in our research world.

What then are the future research agenda that can fulfil the above two highly important missions? While I will leave topically specific research agenda (for example strategy, marketing, and development and government policies) to the various contributors in this volume, here I will focus on three key elements of this future research agenda. First, we need much more integration of concepts and ideas across different research fields and disciplines. As is evident in my brief survey of the various theoretical perspectives in this chapter and the contributions to this volume, such *integration across fields* remains inadequate and underdeveloped. In the substantive area I know best – ethnic Chinese family firms and business networks in Asia – we continue to find a bifurcation of micro-level research on the strategy, organization and performance of these ethnic firms in their own right, and macro-level research on the societal systems in which these firms and their business networks thrive. Very few studies manage to cross this unfruitful micro–macro divide in our research efforts, let alone integrate them in a meaningful and original manner. This integration across fields is both necessary and challenging for next generation scholarship to emerge from research into Asian business. If conducted successfully, it will help to bridge the disciplinary divide that is so common in the social sciences and business schools throughout the world.

One particularly encouraging analytical direction in this regard is concerned with the *institutionalist perspective*. While I have already reviewed this approach briefly earlier in the chapter (see also Chapter 3 in this volume; Peng, 2003; Peng *et al.*, 2005), institutional research has enormous potential in future studies of Asian business. Unlike the Anglo-American capitalism in which business firms are relatively more separated from their institutional environments (for example state structures and investors), institutional systems in Asia are much more complex and intertwined with individual actors such as owners, investors, firms and states. Consequently, the changing dynamics of Asian economies provides an excellent experimental setting for observing and analysing how institutional change shapes business organization and processes, and vice versa. In other words, Asian business is in itself a uniquely dynamic phenomenon that can potentially lead to new and fresh insights through theoretically grounded empirical research. Future research on Asian business is likely to take into account institutions and institutional contexts in Asia a lot more seriously, whether researchers are dealing with the strategy and performance of firms, the significance and transformations of business networks, or, even, interconnections between Asian business and global production networks. Institutional research will emerge from its 'backburner' status – a description used in Chapter 3 of this volume – to become the forefront analytical framework, organizing a diverse range of empirical research on Asian business.

Second, future research on Asian business must go beyond individual cases of firms and economies to incorporate an explicitly *comparative* lens in research design. Too often we have seen rigorous studies of particular Asian firms in their domestic contexts (for example Japanese firms in Japan, South Korean firms in South Korea, and so on). This relative lack of comparative empirical research can be detrimental to the collective advancement of our knowledge of Asian business and beyond. We need more comparative research into intra-Asian business and extra-Asian business. By comparing the nature and organization of firms from different Asian economies, and between Asian and non-Asian economies, we should be able to develop better theoretical and empirical insights into Asian business. For example, the GCC/GVC and GPN work reviewed earlier has explicitly incorporated the comparative angle. In doing so, these perspectives shed very important light on how firms from different Asian economies are organized and compete in the global economy. Linked to the institutionalist perspective, this comparative analysis of firms and economies from Asia can identify significant similarities and differences across these firms and economies, and, in doing so, allow for causal analysis of the underlying mechanisms and processes that account for these similarities and differences. This is where comparative analysis offers the most important potential for new theoretical insights that cannot be provided for through empirical studies of homogeneous units or samples.

Finally, dynamic Asia in the new millennium clearly requires us to reorient our research tools away from static cross-sectional analysis to more dynamic and longitudinal analysis. The *dynamics of change and transformation* will undoubtedly become the key research focus in the near future, but, as many of the contributors in this volume have shown, we are still far away from arriving at a set of dynamic analytical frameworks that can handle these changes and transformations in Asian business. This research endeavour needs not only collective efforts and commitment by researchers from different disciplinary backgrounds, but also better access to research data and resources. Insofar as longitudinal research is concerned, there is a dearth of historical data about Asian business that are analytically comparable and consistent. The institutional structures and incentive systems of today's academia are also unfavourable towards such time-consuming longitudinal research. The future of research on Asian business is clearly both challenging and exciting. With all of its weaknesses and inadequacies, I hope this *Handbook* will provide a good starting point for tackling these important future research agenda, in a way that will bring research on Asian business into the mainstream understanding of global business and global economic change.

REFERENCES

Amsden, Alice H. (1991), 'Diffusion of development: the late industrializing model and Greater Asia', *American Economic Review*, **81**(2), 282–6.

Amsden, Alice H. (2001), *The Rise of 'The Rest': Challenges to the West From Late-Industrializing Economies*, New York: Oxford University Press.

Backman, Michael and C. Butler (2003), *Big in Asia: 25 Strategies for Business Success*, New York: Palgrave Macmillan.

Barney, Jay B. (1991), 'Firm resources and sustained competitive advantage', *Journal of Management*, **17**, 99–120.

Barney, Jay B. (2001), 'Resource-based theories of competitive advantage: a ten-year retrospective on the resource-based view', *Journal of Management*, **27**(6), 643–50.

Beamish, Paul W., A. Delios and S. Makino (eds) (2002), *Japanese Subsidiaries in the New Global Economy*, Cheltenham, UK and Northampton, MA, USA: Edward Elgar.

Beausang, Francesca (2003), *Third World Multinationals: Engine of Competitiveness or New Form of Dependency?*, New York: Palgrave Macmillan.

Biggart, Nicole W. and M. F. Guillén (1999), 'Developing difference: social organization and the rise of the auto industries of South Korea, Taiwan, Spain, and Argentina', *American Sociological Review*, **64**, 722–47.

Borrus, Michael, D. Ernst and S. Haggard (eds) (2000), *International Production Networks in Asia: Rivalry or Riches*, London: Routledge.

Boyd, Richard and T.-W. Ngo (eds) (2005), *Asian States: Beyond the Developmental Perspective*, London: RoutledgeCurzon.

Calingo, Luis Ma. R. (1996), *Strategic Management in the Asian Context: A Casebook in Business Policy and Strategy*, Chichester: John Wiley & Sons.

Carney, Michael (2005), 'Globalization and the renewal of Asian business networks', *Asia Pacific Journal of Management*, **22**(4), 337–54.

Chang, Sea-jin (2003), *Financial Crisis and Transformation of Korean Business Groups: The Rise and Fall of Chaebols*, Cambridge: Cambridge University Press.

Chen, Min (1995), *Asian Management Systems: Chinese, Japanese and Korean Styles of Business*, London: Routledge.

Chen, Tain-Jy (2003), 'Network resources for internationalization: the case of Taiwan's electronics firms', *Journal of Management Studies*, **40**(5), 1107–30.

Chung, Wai-Keung and G.G. Hamilton (2001), 'Social logic as business logic: guanxi, trustworthiness, and the embeddedness of Chinese business practices', in Richard P. Appelbaum, W.L.F. Felstiner and V. Gessner (eds), *Rules and Networks: The Legal Culture of Global Business Transactions*, Oxford: Hart Publications, pp. 325–46.

Coe, Neil and M. Hess (2005), 'The internationalization of retailing: implications for supply network restructuring in East Asia and Eastern Europe', *Journal of Economic Geography*, **5**(4), 449–73.

Coe, Neil and Yong-Sook Lee (2006), 'The strategic localization of transnational retailers: the case of Samsung-Tesco in South Korea', *Economic Geography*, **82**(1), 61–88.

Coe, Neil, M. Hess, H. Yeung, P. Dicken and J. Henderson (2004), ' "Globalizing" regional development: a global production networks perspective', *Transactions of the Institute of British Geographers*, New Series, **29**(4), 468–484.

Dacin, Tina and A. Delios (eds) (2005), 'Special issue: networks in Asia Pacific business', *Asia Pacific Journal of Management*, **22**(4), 315–463.

Dicken, Peter and M. Hassler (2000), 'Organizing the Indonesian clothing industry in the global economy: the role of business networks', *Environment and Planning A*, **32**(2), 263–80.

Dicken, Peter, P. Kelly, K. Olds and H. Yeung (2001), 'Chains and networks, territories and scales: towards an analytical framework for the global economy', *Global Networks*, **1**(2), 89–112.

DiMaggio, Paul J. (ed.) (2001), *The Twenty-First-Century Firm: Changing Economic Organization in International Perspective*, Princeton, NJ: Princeton University Press.

DiMaggio, Paul J. and W.W. Powell (eds) (1991), *The New Institutionalism in Organizational Analysis*, Chicago: University of Chicago Press.

Fields, Karl J. (1995), *Enterprise and the State in Korea and Taiwan*, Ithaca: Cornell University Press.

Gereffi, Gary (1999), 'International trade and industrial upgrading in the apparel commodity chain', *Journal of International Economics*, **48**(1), 37–70.

Gereffi, Gary (2005), 'The global economy: organization, governance, and development', in Neil J. Smelser and R. Swedberg (eds), *The Handbook of Economic Sociology*, 2nd edn, Princeton, NJ: Princeton University Press, pp. 160–82.

Gereffi, Gary and M. Korzeniewicz (1990), 'Commodity chains and footwear exports in the semi-periphery', in William G. Martin (ed.), *Semipheripheral States in the World Economy*, Westport, CT: Greenwood Press, pp. 45–68.

Gereffi, Gary and M. Korzeniewicz (eds) (1994), *Commodity Chains and Global Capitalism*, Westport, CT: Praeger.

Gereffi, Gary, J. Humphrey and T. Sturgeon (2005), 'The governance of global value chains', *Review of International Political Economy*, **12**(1), 78–104.

Gerlach, Michael L. (1992), *Alliance Capitalism: The Social Organization of Japanese Business*, Berkeley: University of California Press.

Gomez, Edmund Terence (1999), *Chinese Business in Malaysia: Accumulation, Accommodation and Ascendance*, Surrey: Curzon.

Granovetter, Mark and R. Swedberg (eds) (1992), *The Sociology of Economic Life*, Boulder, CO: Westview Press.

Green, Stephen (2005), 'The rise and rise of Asia', The Professor Sir Roland Smith Chief Executive Lecture, Lancaster University Management School, 14 February 2005 (available at http://www.lums.lancs.ac.uk), accessed on 31 October 2005.

Guillén, Mauro F. (2002), 'Structural inertia, imitation, and foreign expansion: South Korean firms and business groups in China, 1987–95', *Academy of Management Journal*, **45**(3), 509–25.

Guthrie, Douglas (1999), *Dragon in a Three-Piece Suit: The Emergence of Capitalism in China*, Princeton, NJ: Princeton University Press.

Guthrie, Douglas (2002), *Social Connections in China: Institutions, Culture, and the Changing Nature of Guanxi*, Cambridge: Cambridge University Press.

Haggard, Stephen (1990), *Pathways from the Periphery: The Politics of Growth in the Newly Industrializing Countries*, Ithaca, NY: Cornell University Press.

Haley, George T., Chin-Tiong Tan and Usha C.V. Haley (1998), *The New Asian Emperors: The Overseas Chinese, Their Strategies and Competitive Advantages*, Oxford: Butterworth-Heinemann.

Hamilton, Gary G. (ed.) (1991), *Business Networks and Economic Development in East and South East Asia*, Hong Kong: Centre of Asian Studies, University of Hong Kong.

Hamilton, Gary G. (2005), *Commerce and Capitalism in Chinese Societies: The Organization of Chinese Economies*, London: RoutledgeCurzon.

Hamilton, Gary G. and Nicole Woolsey Biggart (1988), 'Market, culture, and authority: a comparative analysis of management and organization in the Far East', *American Journal of Sociology (Supplement)*, **94**, S52–94.

Hamilton-Hart, Natasha (2002), *Asian States, Asian Bankers: Central Banking in Southeast Asia*, Ithaca, NY: Cornell University Press.

Hamlin, Michael Alan (1998), *Asia's Best: The Myth and Reality of Asia's Most Successful Companies*, Singapore: Prentice Hall.

Hamlin, Michael Alan (2000), *The New Asian Corporation: Managing for the Future in Post-Crisis Asia*, San Francisco: Jossey-Bass.

Hassler, Marcus (2003), 'The global clothing production system: commodity chains and business networks', *Global Networks*, **3**(4), 513–32.

Henderson, Jeffrey, P. Dicken, M. Hess, N. Coe and H. Yeung (2002), 'Global production networks and the analysis of economic development', *Review of International Political Economy*, **9**(3), 436–64.

Hess, Martin and H. Yeung (2006), 'Whither global production networks in economic geography? Past, present and future', *Environment and Planning A*, **38**(7), 1193–204.

Hewison, Kevin (1990), *Bankers and Bureaucrats: Capital and the Role of the State in Thailand*, New Haven: Yale University Press.

Hodgson, Geoffrey M. (1988), *Economics and Institutions: A Manifesto for a Modern Institutional Economics*, Cambridge: Polity Press.

Hodgson, Geoffrey M. (1994), *Economics and Evolution: Bringing Life Back into Economics*, Cambridge: Polity Press.

Jakobsen, Gurli and Jens Erik Torp (eds) (2000), *Understanding Business Systems in Developing Countries*, London: Sage.

Johns, Jennifer (2006), 'Video games production networks: value capture, power relations and embeddedness', *Journal of Economic Geography*, **6**(2), 151–80.

Johnson, Chalmer (1982), *MITI and the Japanese Economic Miracle*, Stanford: Stanford University Press.

Jwa, Sung-Hee (2002), *The Evolution of Large Corporations in Korea: A New Institutional Economics Perspective of the Chaebol*, Cheltenham, UK and Northampton, MA, USA: Edward Elgar.

Jwa, Sung-Hee and In Kwon Lee (eds) (2004), *Competition and Corporate Governance in Korea: Reforming and Restructuring the Chaebol*, Cheltenham, UK and Northampton, MA, USA: Edward Elgar.

Keister, Lisa A. (2000), *Chinese Business Groups: The Structure and Impact of Interfirm Relations During Economic Development*, Oxford: Oxford University Press.

Kensy, Rainer (2001), *Keiretsu Economy – New Economy? Japan's Multinational Enterprises from a Post-Modern Perspective*, New York: Palgrave.

Kim, Eun Mee (1997), *Big Business, Strong State: Collusion and Conflict in Korean Development*, Albany: SUNY Press.

Lall, Sanjaya (1983), *The New Multinationals: The Spread of Third World Enterprises*, Chichester: Wiley.

Lau, Chung-Ming, Kenneth K.S. Law, David K. Tse and Chi-Sum Wong (eds) (2000), *Asian Management Matters: Regional Relevance and Global Impact*, London: Imperial College Press.

Lee, Yeon-ho (1997), *The State, Society and Big Business in South Korea*, London: Routledge.

Leung, Kwok and S. White (eds) (2004), *Handbook of Asian Management*, Boston: Kluwer Academic.

Low, Linda (1998), *The Political Economy of a City-State: Government-Made Singapore*, Singapore: Oxford University Press.

McKendrick, David G., R.F. Doner and S. Haggard (2000), *From Silicon Valley to Singapore: Location and Competitive Advantage in the Hard Disk Drive Industry*, Stanford: Stanford University Press.

Mathews, John A. (2002), *Dragon Multinational: A New Model for Global Growth*, Oxford: Oxford University Press.

Nielsen, Klaus and C.A. Koch (eds) (2004), *Institutionalism in Economics and Sociology: Variety, Dialogue and Future Challenges*, Cheltenham, UK and Northampton, MA, USA: Edward Elgar.

North, Douglass (1990), *Institutions, Institutional Change, and Economic Performance*, New York: Cambridge University Press.

Orrù, Marco, N.W. Biggart and G.G. Hamilton (1997), *The Economic Organization of East Asian Capitalism*, London: Sage.

Paprzycki, Ralph (2004), *Japanese Interfirm Networks: Adapting to Survive in the Global Electronics Industry*, London: RoutledgeCurzon.

Peng, Mike W. (2001), 'The resource-based view and international business', *Journal of Management*, **27**(6), 803–29.

Peng, Mike W. (2003), 'Institutional transitions and strategic choices', *Academy of Management Review*, **28**(2), 275–96.

Peng, Mike W., Seung-Hyun Lee and Denis Y.L. Wang (2005), 'What determines the scope of the firm over time? A focus on institutional relatedness', *Academy of Management Review*, **30**(3), 622–33.

Penrose, Edith (1959), *The Theory of the Growth of the Firm*, Oxford: Basil Blackwell.

Redding, S. Gordon (1990), *The Spirit of Chinese Capitalism*, Berlin: De Gruyter.

Redding, S. Gordon (2005), 'The thick description and comparison of societal systems of capitalism', *Journal of International Business Studies*, **36**(2),123–55.

Richter, Frank-Jürgen (ed) (1999a), *Business Networks in Asia: Promises, Doubts, and Perspectives*, Westport, CT: Quorum Books.

Richter, Frank-Jürgen (1999b), *Strategic Networks: The Art of Japanese Interfirm Cooperation*, New York: International Business Press.

Robison, Richard (1986), *Indonesia: The Rise of Capital*, Sydney: Allen & Unwin.

Schmitz, Hubert (ed.) (2004), *Local Enterprises in the Global Economy: Issues of Governance and Upgrading*, Cheltenham, UK and Northampton, MA, USA: Edward Elgar.

Shieh, G.S. (1992), *'Boss' Island: The Subcontracting Network and Micro-Entrepreneurship in Taiwan's Development*, New York: Peter Lang.

Smelser, Neil and R. Swedberg (eds) (1994), *The Handbook of Economic Sociology*, Princeton, NJ: Princeton University Press.

Smelser, Neil and R. Swedberg (eds) (2005), *The Handbook of Economic Sociology*, 2nd edn, Princeton, NJ: Princeton University Press.

Sturgeon, Timothy J. (2003), 'What really goes on in Silicon Valley? Spatial clustering and dispersal in modular production networks', *Journal of Economic Geography*, **3**(2), 199–225.

Tipton, Ben (2005), *The Asian Firm*, Cheltenham, UK and Northampton, MA, USA: Edward Elgar.

Turpin, Dominique and Xiaobai Shen (eds) (1999), *Casebook on General Management in Asia Pacific*, Basingstoke, Hampshire: Macmillan Business.

Vogel, Ezra F. (1979), *Japan as Number One: Lessons for America*, Cambridge, MA: Harvard University Press.

Wade, Robert (1990), *Governing the Market: Economic Theory and the Role of Government in East Asian Industrialization*, Princeton, NJ: Princeton University Press.

Warner, Malcolm (ed.) (2003), *Culture and Management in Asia*, London: RoutledgeCurzon.

Wells, Louis T. Jr (1983), *Third World Multinationals: The Rise of Foreign Investment from Developing Countries*, Cambridge, MA: The M.I.T. Press.

Westney, D. Eleanor (1996), 'Special Issue in Asian Business Systems', *Journal of Asian Business*, **12**(1), 1–112.

Whitley, Richard (1992), *Business Systems in East Asia: Firms, Markets and Societies*, London: Sage.

Whitley, Richard (1999), *Divergent Capitalisms: The Social Structuring and Change of Business Systems*, New York: Oxford University Press.

Wong, Siu-lun (1988), *Emigrant Entrepreneurs: Shanghai Industrialists in Hong Kong*, Hong Kong: Oxford University Press.

Woo-Cumings, Meredith (ed.) (1999), *The Developmental State*, Ithaca, NY: Cornell University Press.

Wright, M., I. Filatotchev, R. Hoskisson and M.W. Peng (2005), 'Strategy research in emerging economies: challenging the conventional wisdom', *Journal of Management Studies*, **42**(1), 1–33.

Yang, Dexin (2005), *China's Offshore Investments: A Network Approach*, Cheltenham, UK and Northampton, MA, USA: Edward Elgar.

Yang, Mayfair Mei-Hui (1994), *Gifts, Favors and Banquets: The Art of Social Relationships in China*, Ithaca, NY: Cornell University Press.

Yeung, Henry Wai-chung (1998), *Transnational Corporations and Business Networks: Hong Kong Firms in the ASEAN Region*, London: Routledge.

Yeung, Henry Wai-chung (ed.) (1999), *The Globalisation of Business Firms from Emerging Economies*, two vols, Cheltenham, UK and Northampton, MA, USA: Edward Elgar.

Yeung, Henry Wai-chung (2000), 'The dynamics of Asian business systems in a globalising era', *Review of International Political Economy*, **7**(3), 399–433.

Yeung, Henry Wai-chung (2001), 'Redressing the geographical bias in social science knowledge', *Environment and Planning A*, **33**(1), 2–9.

Yeung, Henry Wai-chung (2002), *Entrepreneurship and the Internationalisation of Asian Firms: An Institutional Perspective*, Cheltenham, UK and Northampton, MA, USA: Edward Elgar.

Yeung, Henry Wai-chung (2004), *Chinese Capitalism in a Global Era: Towards Hybrid Capitalism*, London: Routledge.

Yeung, Henry Wai-chung and George C.S. Lin (2003), 'Theorizing economic geographies of Asia', *Economic Geography*, **79**(2), 107–128.

Yeung, Henry Wai-chung and K. Olds (eds) (2000), *Globalization of Chinese Business Firms*, New York: Macmillan.

PART I

Business Strategy and Organization

2.   Strategy research in Asia
Andrew Delios, Wei Wei Xu and Kulwant Singh

Research on strategy in Asia has made substantial contributions to the development of strategy theory and research (Hoskisson *et al.*, 2000). This chapter focuses on developing and extending recent ideas about new theoretical and empirical insights on strategy that emerge when we consider the Asian context. We do not attempt to provide a comprehensive overview of research on strategy in Asia. Instead, we aim to facilitate the development of the theory of strategy as situated in the context of firms operating in Asia. We adopt a pragmatic approach in which we focus on current and significant research on Asia, with observations drawn from research published in journals in the 1995 to 2004 period.

In developing our ideas in this chapter, we focus on two particular streams of research: product diversification and geographic diversification of multinational corporations (MNCs). In reviewing the literature in these areas, we attempt to be representative, not exhaustive. We identify trends and tabulate our literature review to support our conclusions on the direction of strategy research in Asia.

THE ASIAN CONTEXT

What makes strategy in Asia a different phenomenon that warrants investigation separate from studies situated in other empirical contexts? We discuss five sources of differences below. First, however, we must recognize that Asia is a convenient term for addressing a territorial unit that ranges from Pakistan to Japan's Hokkaido, and Mongolia to New Zealand's Stewart Island. Clearly, there is great diversity and room for segmentation in this vast region (Singh and Delios, 2005). Cognizant of its inherent diversity and broad scope of coverage, we adopt this wide-ranging and non-specific term, 'Asia'.

In adopting this convenient definition, we are implicitly making an important suggestion, that Asian culture, and culture in general, has a limited impact on business strategy (cf. Chapter 17 in this volume). Real cultural differences exist within and across countries in Asia, and between Asia and other regions of the world. These differences can influence human resource management, organization structure and other aspects of business operations (Chen, 2001; Fukuyama, 1995; Hamilton and Biggart, 1988; Luo, 2000; Redding, 1990; Westwood, 1997). Yet culture is just one aspect of a nation's environment that can influence the success of business strategy, and we believe, a relatively unimportant one. Indeed, influences on strategy and firm performance attributed to culture can be explained more effectively by the country's stage of development and related factors, such as socio-political, market and institutional developments (Biggart and Hamilton, 1992; Clegg *et al.*, 1990; Hamilton and Biggart, 1988; North, 1990; World Bank, 2001). Accordingly, we develop our perspective on strategy in Asia using an institutional economics perspective (North, 1990; see also Chapter 3 in this volume).

Emerging and developed economies in Asia are characterized by varying degrees of development in government, business, legal and other types of institutions (Peng, 2000). These differences in national institutional environments are key factors that differentiate strategy in Asia from that elsewhere (Whitley, 1992). For example, institutions in many Asian countries are less developed than in the countries of the European Union or North America (see chapters in Part III of this volume). Underdeveloped financial markets, inadequate financial intermediaries, poor corporate governance and underdeveloped banks characterize most Asian economies. Coupled with poorly developed communications infrastructures and lax corporate reporting requirements, these institutional features restrict information flows and impede market efficiency. Other institutional characteristics include inadequately trained, inflexible and relatively unproductive labour; scarce management talent; unreliable property rights protection; few consumer protection regulations and organizations; inefficient or corrupt governments; inefficient judicial systems, and weak enforcement of laws and contracts (Johnson *et al.*, 2000; Khanna and Palepu, 1997; La Porta *et al.*, 1999; World Bank, 2001).

These institutional weaknesses can distort the efficient functioning of factor and product markets, limit opportunities, and inhibit firms from profitably pursuing opportunities that firms in institutionally developed economies can explore. Institutional environments differ across economies and have an impact on the organization and conduct of business activity. They are therefore important influences on strategy. While obviously a simplification of institutional environments in Asia, this brief description emphasizes the idea that an effective perspective on strategy in Asia begins with a focus on national institutions (Peng, 2006; Singh, 2004). We comment on some of the formal and informal institutional characteristics below.

Governments in Asia

An important feature of the business environment in Asia is the role played by governments and their affiliated agencies and corporations. Governments in Asia adopt a mix of direction, regulation and pursuit of free market orientations (Aoki *et al.*, 1996; Hamilton and Biggart, 1988; Lasserre and Schutte, 1995; Wade, 1990; World Bank, 1993). Asian governments have combined intervention with free market support. Most governments in Asia participate directly in business when this is necessary or profitable; they are doing so with greater frequency and – this is a controversial conclusion – more effectively than governments in many other regions. As a result, Asian governments have been promoters, partners, regulators and actors in business. These governments assist firms in many areas, but also compete against them, or stage conditions under which competition is heightened. This requires firms operating in Asia to engage in more complex relationships with regulators and governments than they would in equally developed countries in other regions.

Governance Systems

A combination of cultural, firm and institutional differences makes corporate governance in Asia different (Khan, 1999). Asian family-based corporate governance systems differ significantly from the equity market or bank-led governance systems that dominate respectively in North America and Western Europe and that exist to lesser degrees in some economies in Asia. The different composition, characteristics and interests of major owners in Asia, and the underlying differences in legal systems and other traditions that support such governance, dictate the need for different frameworks and analyses for studies concerning effective governance systems.

Business Networks

Business networks or business groups exist in most countries, but the prominence of business networks and their influence in Asia makes them more significant components of business systems and economies than in other regions. Typical business networks include *keiretsu* in Japan, *chaebol* in South Korea, ethnic Chinese family business groups across much of Asia, government-linked corporations in Singapore, politically connected conglomerates in Malaysia and Indonesia, and other family businesses in most countries (Hamilton and Biggart, 1988; Lasserre and Schutte, 1995; Richter, 1999). The broad reach and size of these business networks gives them a powerful presence and the ability to undertake investments and acquisitions, to transfer resources, to overcome regulatory and political barriers and to enter markets in many host economies. Any study of strategy in Asia therefore needs to understand the presence, influence and operations of these business networks and groups.

Institutional Diversity

For most of the last three decades of the twentieth century, Asia has enjoyed rapid economic growth and less rapid, but progressive, development in its supporting institutions. As this development is not uniform, social, legal, regulatory, language, governance and business systems differ substantially across and within economies in Asia. These differences are compounded by differing histories, geographies, cultures, economies and colonial experiences within which these supporting institutions are embedded. Economic systems differ significantly in Asia: some economies have relatively large and free markets that offer firms considerable strategic flexibility, while others are restrictive and highly regulated (Weder, 1999). Countries in the region also differ in respects that are unrelated to their stages of economic and political development, varying greatly in sociocultural, political and technological sophistication. These differences have led to greater disparity in physical, human, institutional and public infrastructure in Asia than in other regions. Again, there is a concomitant need for strategy research to incorporate insights into the origins and consequences of these regional disparities in economic, cultural and political institutions.

PRODUCT DIVERSIFICATION IN ASIA

Product diversification and geographic diversification are two central and important themes among the diverse research being undertaken in Asia (Leung and White, 2004). The first issue relates primarily to the issue of firms diversifying across industries, while the second relates primarily to their undertaking multinational operations that will be addressed in the next section. These two phenomena emerged as prominent strategies for firms during the 1970s to 1990s period of rapid development in many Asian economies. As Asian markets continue to grow and mature, firms will continue to face these diversification issues.

Product diversification is a central focus of academic and practitioner interest in strategy (Goold *et al.*, 1994; Palich *et al.*, 2000; Rumelt *et al.*, 1994). We begin our review of strategy in Asia by evaluating the issue of product diversification. The foundation for this review is provided by the studies detailed in Table 2.1 of the Appendix.

Why do Asian Firms Diversify?

Strategy research on diversification asks the following important questions: What should be the scope of a firm? Why do firms diversify? What types of firms diversify? How do firms diversify? What are the outcomes of diversification? Williamson (1975) and Gort (1984) argue that diversification is fundamentally a risk-spreading practice that firms adopt to reduce unpredictable changes in profitability in different industrial sectors. Diversification can be a risk-spreading strategy, but it is typically large, stable and economically healthy organizations that lead diversification efforts. Hence, other reasons might better explain why firms diversify.

In Asia, Guthrie (1997) has shown that changing markets and responsibilities have led to increased diversification in the transitional Chinese economy (see also Chapter 6 in this volume). Poorly performing firms often struggle to survive in a rapidly changing market system that is associated with administrative instability. Firms located at the upper level of China's administrative hierarchy are forced to handle responsibilities that previously belonged to the domain of the state.

Moreover, Li *et al.* (1998) found that two motives drive managers to diversify in the context of China. The first is related to building resources and skills necessary for firm growth. The second represents an attempt to manage the external environment by entering into a new business. Li *et al.* (1998) also noted that both central and local governments in China play an important role in a firm's diversification decisions. For instance, state-owned enterprises are more likely to diversify than non-state-owned firms, because of preferential conditions and resources offered by the government to its firms (Li *et al.*, 1998; Lu *et al.*, 2000). Part of the explanation for this trend, according to Lu *et al.* (2000), is that governmental resources are usually general, such as capital, land property, information, business licences and administrative personnel. These resources do not provide competencies in a particular industry, although they can support diversification to different industries. Lu *et al.* (2000) pointed out that firms with government support are better able than other firms to overcome entry barriers to diversifying.

Examining Taiwanese firms, Hamilton (1997) noted that a unique ownership structure can be an important driver of firm diversification. When a family-owned firm is passed from one generation to the next, ownership, rather than managerial authority, is often shared equally. As a result, an enterprise can be divided into a number of horizontally connected firms that operate either in different industries or in different geographical areas. Diversification is thus a consequence of the sharing of family-held assets. Owners that have a large share of their wealth in a single firm may try to reduce the risk of concentrated wealth by having their firms diversify, thus avoiding diluting their own control by spreading their investments across firms.

Building on research that focuses on the context-specific nature of diversification and the impact of organizational ownership on diversification strategy, Ramaswamy *et al.* (2002) explored how the different objectives and monitoring predispositions of distinct ownership groups can influence diversification strategy. Their study of firms in India shows that diverse ownership groups adopt different postures in monitoring and influencing diversification. Their findings show that holdings of for-profit institutional investors and mutual fund companies are negatively related to firms' unrelated diversification.

Strategy research has evaluated managerial motives as a force for firm diversification (Besanko *et al.*, 2000). Agency theorists note that, instead of pursuing economic efficiency and/or enhancing shareholder wealth, executives are motivated to pursue a diversification strategy in attempts to increase their private benefits (Jensen, 1986; Hoskisson and Hitt, 1990). Using a sample of 145 Singapore firms, Chen and Ho (2000) provided evidence on the level and value of corporate diversification. They found that the level of diversification is negatively related to outside blockholder ownership, but is unrelated to insider owner- ship. They also found a significant loss of value from diversification only for those firms with low managerial ownership, suggesting that value-reducing diversification may stem from agency problems. Outside block ownership does not have a significant impact on the value of diversification. Although outside blockholders may act as a deterrent to the level of diversification, there is no evidence that they can effectively reduce agency problems for those firms with low managerial ownership.

Managing Diversification

The management of diversified firms has been a key issue in strategy research (Chandler, 1962; Steer and Cable, 1978; Williamson, 1975), with the multidivisional (M-form) struc- ture attracting particularly attention. Hill *et al.* (1992) showed that a related diversified firm will be better served by adopting a cooperative organization, while an unrelated diversified firm will be better served by adopting a competitive organization. For busi- nesses in Asia, the organization structure and diversification relationship has not been extensively examined.

Integrating institutional and organizational perspectives, Kim *et al.* (2004) demon- strated the paths of strategy and structure evolution of diversified business groups in South Korea. In the early stage of industrialization in South Korea, when the external market was underdeveloped, diversified business groups emerged as necessary organiza- tional forms to secure access to intermediate products and services. With the advancement of the institutional environment in South Korea, the significance of business groups' generic capabilities as efficient internal markets substituting for inefficient external markets has declined. South Korean firms have had to restructure themselves with competitive M-form structures, or to refocus into related businesses using the cooperative M-form structure to gain an organizational fit with their new environment. This result is consistent with our perspective that improvements in market efficiency in Asian economies will reduce the internal market benefits of diversification.

Using Taiwanese business groups as the sample, Chu (2001) empirically examined and compared the efficacy of two approaches to managing diversification: an economic and structural approach and a cultural approach. The first represents a contingency approach in which strategy–structure fit is a key determinant of a diversified business group's performance. The second is a cultural approach that focuses on the use of strong shared values to minimize opportunistic behaviour. Both approaches can improve firm performance.

Impact on Performance

The relationship between diversification and performance has long been a central issue in strategy research (Datta *et al.*, 1991; Goold *et al.*, 1994; Hoskisson and Hitt, 1990; Montgomery, 1994; Palich *et al.*, 2000). Increasing diversification can have a positive impact on performance due to economies of scope and scale, greater exploitation of internally generated resources, increased market power, risk reduction and learning. At the same time, the costs of diversification, primarily the costs of managerial and organizational complexity, increase with greater diversification, particularly unrelated diversification. This leads to the conclusion that the benefits of diversification will decline if expansion goes beyond an optimal point for a firm.

Despite extensive research, empirical analyses of diversification's effects on performance have yielded mixed results (Palich *et al.*, 2000; Markides and Williamson, 1994). Hitt *et al.* (1997), Datta *et al.* (1991), Geringer *et al.* (1989) and Grant *et al.* (1988) provided some support of a positive relationship, though often only for international (geographic) diversification. Yet a sizeable literature (for example Markides, 1995) has documented that diversified US firms underperform focused competitors. The unreliability of the general diversification–performance relationship makes it a research issue that deserves close attention in Asia. In addition, distinct contextual factors in Asia, including institutional and economic development, different firm ownership structures and government policies, may limit the generalizability of diversification–performance research to Asia. Research on diversification in Asia could help establish boundary conditions for current theories on the diversification–performance relationship.

Khanna and Palepu (1997, 2000) identified five aspects of institutional environments in emerging economies that may influence the impact of diversification on firm performance. Specifically, the lack of well-established product, financial and labour markets, weak laws and regulations, and the inconsistent enforcement of contracts in emerging economies can make it difficult for firms to pursue resource and competency building as focused businesses. Nachum (2004) added that developing economy firms typically lack the firm-specific advantages required to support a focused strategy (Amsden, 1998). Nachum (2004) further contended that government policies in many developing countries reward diversification through low-cost loans, greater access to foreign exchange, and a multitude of rent-creating opportunities (Chudnovsky and Lopez, 2000; Ungson *et al.*, 1997) that are likely to have a favourable impact on performance.

Using these arguments, Nachum (2004) found empirical evidence to support a positive association between product and geographic diversification and firm performance in 22 developing economies, most of which were in Asia. Strong support was also found for the impact of the external environment in which diversification occurs. Firms based in different regions have different diversification preferences, and these choices affect the performance outcomes of diversification.

In a developed country context, Delios and Beamish (1999) demonstrated that geographic scope was positively associated with firm profitability in Japan, even when the competing effect of proprietary assets was considered. Increasing geographic scope is a response to the development and possession of proprietary assets that is reflected at the downstream end through diversification across businesses. Although geographic scope was positively related to performance, product diversification was not. This is consistent with Geringer *et al.*'s (2000) finding that the unique aspects of the Japanese business environment might lead to different strategies, objectives and outcomes as compared to similar firms in the Euro-American context. Japanese firms tend to focus on employment, sales growth or market share instead of profits. Japanese capital markets accept lower returns, and tight relationships between manufacturing firms and affiliated banks reduce financial performance pressures. In essence, lower costs of capital and low performance pressures allow greater diversification, as this strategy supports other objectives.

Claessens *et al.* (2003) examined the vertical relatedness and complementarity of product diversified firms across nine Asian economies. They found that vertical relatedness and complementarity has positive effects on short- and long-term performance of diversified firms, with the effects more pronounced for complementarity than for vertical relatedness. They concluded that firms in less developed economies have more opportunities for short-term profits by exploring complementarity, as the learning hurdle is low in this type of expansion. In the long run, firms in more developed economies, such as Japan, have less severe capital misallocation problems when they pursue complementary diversification. This is because markets in these economies are more effective in monitoring resource allocation.

ASIAN MULTINATIONALS AND STRATEGY

Product diversification has long been a characteristic of firms in Asia. By contrast, geographic diversification or the growth of Asian multinationals is a more recent phenomenon (see also Chapters 20–22 in this volume). Indeed, according to UNCTAD (2004), firms based in Asia are collectively the largest and fastest-growing outward investors in the developing world. With a foreign direct investment (FDI) stock of US$635 billion in 2003, Asia accounted for 75 per cent of the total outward FDI stock of all developing economies. Asia also contributed to 80 per cent of outward FDI flows, or an annual average of US$46 billion in 2000–2003. Hong Kong was the largest source of FDI, followed by China, Malaysia, Singapore, South Korea and Taiwan as other important outward investors.

Research

Empirical research and theory development on geographic diversification and multinational firms has traditionally focused on multinational enterprises (MNEs) based in North America, Japan and Western Europe. Asian MNEs are a recent phenomenon and have attracted limited empirical research attention, despite their growing proliferation and importance (Pananond and Zeithaml, 1998; Luo, 1999; see also Chapter 20 in this volume). Early studies on Asian MNEs tended to contrast their characteristics with those of developed country MNEs (Lall, 1983; Wells, 1983; Tolentino, 1993). As noted earlier, the growth of Asia has resulted in increased intraregional direct investments (Dobson and Chia, 1997). FDI is being undertaken from one regional economy to another, beginning with Japan, followed by South Korea, Taiwan, Hong Kong and Singapore, and then by economies such as Indonesia, Malaysia and Thailand (Toh and Low, 1994; Guisinger, 1991).

As MNEs from Japan have had a long history of competing in international markets and have been extensively studied, we concentrate on MNEs from other parts of Asia. In general, MNEs from developing countries differ from those from developed countries in terms of ownership patterns, size of investment, market entry strategies, sources of funding and the influence of the home country (Lall, 1983; Wells, 1983; Yeung, 1999). Research on MNEs in Asia, as summarized in Table 2.2 in the Appendix, has focused on their characteristics and strategies, their governance and operations, and their perform-ance.

Characteristics and Strategies of Asian MNEs

Much of the research on Asian MNEs has examined their basic characteristics and strat-egies. These studies tend to be descriptive, although some are deductive, hypothesis-testing analytical studies. The general objective of these studies has been to develop a better understanding of Asian MNEs as situated in different economies in Asia. Young *et al.* (1996), for example, illustrated the technology transfer process in Asian MNEs investing in China. In the growth of these MNEs, technology transfer begins with inward transfers through equipment purchases, then moves to joint ventures and extends through the acquisition of R&D firms in developed countries. The internationalization process of these firms, in terms of target country and mode of entry, is determined by the motiv-ations for the investment. Market-seeking investments are made in culturally and geo-graphically proximate countries. Efficiency-seeking investments are directed to developed countries. The internationalization of these firms is also aided by the development of capabilities for technological learning and for managing joint ventures obtained by part-nering with foreign partners in joint ventures in China.

Lee and Beamish (1995) found that, for South Korean investments in developing coun-tries, the need for a local partner's knowledge is a more important driver than government restrictions in stimulating the formation of joint ventures in the host countries. Most South Korean firms took minority ownerships in their joint ventures and were more satisfied with their joint ventures in developing countries than in developed countries. Lee and Beamish (1995) concluded that MNEs' joint venture characteristics differ by stages of development in both the home and the host countries.

Sim and Pandian (2003) examined Taiwanese and Singapore MNEs in the textile and electronics industries in order to understand their motivations, patterns and sources of competitive advantage. They found that the internationalization strategies of Taiwanese and Singapore firms rely on cost-based competencies and other location-based advan-tages. These advantages in turn hinge on an extensive web of ethnic networks, and are aided by government support. Ethnic networks have not been a key part of conventional MNE theory, reinforcing the idea that social and institutional frameworks are a distin-guishing feature that should be included in the analysis of Asian MNEs.

Zin (1999) explored the outward FDI of Malaysian firms to understand their business strategies. International expansion is driven by market-seeking motives as well as resource and regulatory barriers concerns. Unlike most MNEs from developed countries, Malaysian firms have diverse value chain orientations, from stand-alone firms to those implementing complex, integrated production strategies. In the latter cases, firms tend to decentralize the management of their overseas subsidiaries.

Rajan and Pangarkar (2000) evaluated a major theme in MNE research: entry mode strategies. Drawing upon the well-established eclectic framework of Hill *et al.* (1990), they found that three broad categories of variables, relating to control, cost and competence, affect entry modes used for foreign expansion. Singapore MNEs' entry mode choices are strongly influenced by strategic motive and desire to exploit synergies. If firm-specific assets are transferred as part of an FDI, there is a strong tendency to adopt entry modes that offer greater control over subsidiary operations, a result consistent with prior work on American and Japanese MNEs.

Governance and International Operations

As of today, we know relatively little about the corporate governance of Asian MNEs (Hamilton, 1996), although the issue of ownership and governance is now receiving greater attention. As countries differ significantly in the institutional contexts in which corporate governance is embedded (Au *et al.*, 2000; Claessens *et al.*, 2000; Gedajlovic and Shapiro, 1998; Li, 1994; Pederson and Thomsen, 1997; Peng, 2000), a lack of knowledge about corporate governance of MNEs from developing countries is a notable shortcoming.

Based on interviews with Hong Kong MNE executives, Yeung (1997) found that social and business networks are important elements of a firm's internationalization efforts, with political connections creating substantial FDI opportunities. Business connections and personal relationships are fundamental for the establishment of governance structures by which Hong Kong firms manage their Southeast Asian operations. Personal trust and experience are important for the coordination and control of international operations.

Peng *et al.* (2001) researched the patterns of corporate governance of MNEs from Thailand and found that, relative to non-MNEs, Thai MNEs have more densely connected interlocks of board directors, occupy more central locations in the interlocks network and appoint more military directors (see also Chapter 21 in this volume). These military directors may allow firms to tap into unique political resources (Boddewyn and Brewer, 1994).

Performance

MNEs enjoy several sources of advantage over domestic firms (Dunning, 1988; Rugman, 1979). Examples of these advantages include the achievement of economies of scale and scope (Grant *et al.*, 1988; Kogut, 1985), gaining cost benefits through locating operations in less costly regions, and learning from locating subsidiaries in competitive markets (Kogut, 1985). As with product diversification research, most studies of MNE performance have been carried out in developed countries. There is little information on the performance of Asian MNEs.

Among studies of Asian MNEs, Wan (1998) examined the relationship between geographic diversification, product diversification and the performance of Hong Kong MNEs. He found an equal level of product diversification among Hong Kong firms, regardless of the level of geographic diversification. Interestingly, Hong Kong MNEs do not perform better than domestic firms, although geographic diversification has a positive impact on profit stability and sales growth. Domestic firms in Hong Kong tend to have lower costs than Hong Kong MNEs as the latter face the additional cost burden of international coordination. Internationalization increases sales but not profitability.

Similarly, Han (2002) investigated South Korean FDI in China and proposed that three main factors, technology, internationalization experience and ownership patterns, may influence the performance of South Korean firms in China. The labour intensity of technology in a foreign subsidiary and the suitability of manufacturing technology for local conditions are major influences on subsidiary performance.

Extant MNE Theories and the Asian MNE Context

As indicated in Table 2.2 in the Appendix (see also Pangarkar, 2004), a general conclusion from research on international expansion is that Asian MNEs differ substantially in their characteristics, operations and performance from those MNEs based in North America, Western Europe and Japan. This raises a key research question: How applicable are extant theories of MNEs in Asia? Despite numerous attempts to contribute to MNE theory development by drawing on the context of Asia, theoretical knowledge of Asian MNEs remains inadequate (Yeung, 1994, 1999, 2002). Until the mid-1990s, mainstream MNE research regarded developing country MNEs as, paradoxically, either idiosyncratic or too similar to other MNEs to warrant separate study (Giddy and Young, 1982; Mathews, 2002), yet firms and their constituent resources are geographically embedded in specific social, business and institutional infrastructures (Yeung, 1998). This explains why firms are more likely to commence international expansion through a process of moving first to the most familiar or similar countries. This in turn leads to the view that MNEs cannot be studied without a specific investigation of their home and host environments.

A number of recent studies have examined developing country MNEs, in particular those from Asia. Attempts to integrate Asian MNE theory into MNE theory tend to focus on two approaches: first, the application of MNE theory to Asian MNEs and, second, using research on Asian MNEs to enhance extant MNE theory. MNE theory needs to address a variety of challenges from the experience of Asian MNEs. One such issue is how a theory founded on competitive advantages can explain the emergence of latecomer Asian MNEs. MNE theory needs to respond to these challenges, just as strategy theory did to the challenge of strategic alliance and networks in Asia during the 1980s and the 1990s.

Li (2003) attempted to respond to this challenge by drawing on the experiences of Taiwan's Acer Group (see also Mathews, 2002). One conclusion from Li (2003) is that ownership advantages – fundamental to the Ownership, Location, Internalization (OLI) model in explaining MNE success – may not be necessary for success of international operations, a result supported in Makino *et al.*'s study (2002). In direct contrast to OLI theory predictions that ownership advantages lead to overseas investments, Taiwanese firms such as Acer engage in FDI to build ownership advantages.

Shapiro *et al.* (2003) took a related approach to examine ethnic Chinese family firms in Asia. They contended that, though ethnic Chinese family firms are unique products of their cultural heritage (Fukuyama, 1995; Hall and Xu, 1990) and their social contexts (Hamilton and Biggart, 1988; Whitley, 1992), they can be understood with reference to the OLI constructs of Dunning (1993). They suggested that the ownership advantages of ethnic Chinese family firms reside in intangible proprietary assets in the form of human and social capital. These assets include specific managerial capabilities and their personal managerial networks, and are often related to family ties. In line with these ownership advantages, location advantages stem from the ability of an ethnic Chinese family firm to expand to less developed economies in which they have personal relationships and networks, and where formal rules and regulations tend to be dominated by informal codes for negotiating and striking deals. Although these observations may not require a fundamental re-evaluation of MNE theory, they suggest how adaptation may be required for the application of MNE theory in an Asian context.

Pangarkar (2004) further provided a valuable summary of research on Asian multinationals. As with research on product diversification, research on geographic diversification and Asian MNEs can move forward by focusing on the impact of institutional considerations. Pangarkar (2004) suggested that research be guided by (1) identifying whether an Asian MNE is government-linked or not; (2) identifying the Asian MNE's extent of internationalization; (3) identifying its product diversification; (4) looking at the range of value added activities it performs; and (5) examining a firm's ethnic origins and its relational ties.

A typology of Asian MNEs (for example expatriate MNEs, government-linked MNEs, ethnic MNEs, undiversified global MNEs, diversified global MNEs) would aid research in the same way that the classification of MNEs in America and Europe (transnational, multinational, international, ethnocentric, polycentric, and so on) has in research on the strategy, structure and performance of MNEs in general. The main idea, which is consistent with the general thrust of this chapter, is to identify the points at which research on Asian MNEs can be unified. This then creates the starting conditions for linking this research with general research on MNEs and FDI.

RESEARCH IMPLICATIONS AND FUTURE DIRECTIONS

Comparative Studies

Strategy research is dominated by comparative approaches that evaluate similarities and differences across a range of phenomena. A particular focus has been to compare results from Asian and other contexts, usually the US. Another approach is to draw comparisons between economies within Asia. According to Tsang and Kwan's (1999) categorization, these replication studies are 'empirical generalizations' or 'generalizations and extensions'. While we agree with the focus on identifying similarities and differences, several problems exist with this approach.

First, most of the studies fail to provide insights into the causes of differences. Although discussions of behavioural differences are often explicitly or implicitly linked to cultural or cognitive differences among managers, these studies are generally not based on systematic empirical research. Relatedly, similarities are usually not explained even though they may occur among organizations and processes embedded in environments that are significantly different in terms of institutions, stage of development, geographic endowment and other dimensions. Explaining the absence of differences is potentially as useful as explaining their presence.

Second, mechanisms linking orientations, actions and performance have often been ignored in comparative research in Asian contexts. The majority of research themes are subsumed under 'what are the differences in orientations, behaviours and performance?'. How the orientations give rise to choices or the choices to performance is rarely investigated. There are some notable exceptions though. Wiersema and Bird (1993), Xie *et al.* (1998) and Amba-Rao (1994), among other studies, showed how different processes can lead to the same orientations having different actions, or how varied actions can have different performance implications depending on the context.

Third, the US context has served as the primary reference point in comparative research, while comparisons of Asian and non-US contexts are sparse. Most researchers ask the question: 'How do results in the Asian context differ from results in the US?' In many ways, the US is so different that it becomes an invalid reference point for Asia. Developing countries in other regions may be more useful reference points, particularly in studies that seek to control for influences in terms of stages of economic development. Comparisons with US findings and contexts may reflect relevant and interesting questions, but, at the integrative level, they may provide an incomplete picture. Interestingly, we also have few insights into similarities and differences among Asian contexts. This is an important research failure because, for many phenomena, within-group variation in Asia may be greater than across-group variations relative to other regions.

Interaction between Institutions and Organizations

Instead of adapting passively to institutional environments, Oliver (1991) argued that firms can actively shape their institutional environments by developing strategic responses. In essence, both firms and institutions are endogenous to an environment. Thus it would be meaningful to develop studies examining firms' strategic efforts to influence their environments, instead of assuming that they are limited to reactive behaviours (Bluedorn *et al.*, 1994). This approach is especially necessary given the prioritization of economic development among many Asian governments, their focus on nurturing domestic firms, their extensive use of government-linked corporations and their extensive economic intervention (see Chapter 15 in this volume). Dominant explanations for firms internationalizing have not adequately addressed the influence of institutions, such as home-country governments, on the emergence of MNEs. This lack of attention may reflect assumptions that governments have no useful or legitimate roles to play in free trade-based economies. The very different approaches of governments and other institutions in Asia can improve our understanding of product and geographic diversification, amongst other important research issues.

This perspective on institutions extends the ideas of a firm's sustainable competitive advantages (Oliver, 1997) from an institutional to an economics perspective. It concerns the way firms restructure themselves in response to institutional change. This focus also involves the study of multinational firms' investment decisions in emerging economies under different institutional contexts. It can be a promising research strand to examine the role and effects of institutions in reducing the transaction costs of product and market changes. This point emphasizes the need to examine interactions between institutional theory and other theoretical approaches.

CONCLUSION AND FUTURE RESEARCH

Much strategy research in an Asian context is either descriptive (Lu *et al.*, 2000; Carney, 1998; Pananond and Zeithaml, 1998; Zutshi and Gibbons, 1998) or based on survey data (Young *et al.*, 1996; Li *et al.*, 1998; Zin, 1999; Sim and Pandian, 2003; Ahlstrom *et al.*, 2004). Cross-national research based on data, which can be replicated and yield sufficient explanatory power for inferences about cross-national differences, would help move forward Asian strategy research.

If these data can be put into place, Asian countries, as characterized by rapid institutional changes, provide the necessary institutional variance to develop and test theory, particularly ideas related to the speed and nature of institutional change and its influence on firm strategies. Institutional factors also have many dimensions that change at different rates. As noted by Tolbert and Zucker (1996), the process of institutionalization should be of interest in future theoretical and empirical work. The pace of institutional and economic changes in Asia often alter radically cost and resource availability within particular locations, prompting MNEs to relocate their operations across countries in the region. This has led to a phenomenon that is common in Asia, but that has received little attention in MNE theory: country exit strategies. As this issue has only been examined from a geopolitical perspective in MNE research, it will be useful to examine this question in Asian contexts from FDI and MNE perspectives.

This observation suggests that researchers should employ longitudinal designs to capture the process elements of institutional effects and compare experiences in economies at different stages of this process. An additional benefit of conducting such research in Asia is that it is often possible to study many phenomena and trends from their very emergence, minimizing the 'left censoring' problem associated with conducting studies in mature economies. Ultimately such an approach would facilitate the exploitation of the main benefit for which, we believe, strategy research on firms in Asia has the greatest potential: a heightened understanding of the confluence of institutions and strategy. Context becomes an important and rigorous defining element in understanding the antecedents to, and consequences of, business-level and corporate-level strategies. Achieving this objective will simultaneously improve our theoretical understanding of strategy in Asia and improve strategy theory in general.

REFERENCES

Ahlstrom, D., M.N. Young, E.S. Chan and G.D. Bruton (2004), 'Facing constraints to growth? Overseas Chinese entrepreneurs and traditional business practices in East Asia', *Asia Pacific Journal of Management*, **21**, 263–85.

Amba-Rao, S. (1994), 'U.S. HRM principles: cross-country comparisons and two case applications in India', *International Journal of Human Resource Management*, **5**, 755–78.

Amsden, A. (1998), 'South Korea: enterprising groups and entrepreneurial government', in A.D. Chandler Jr, F. Amatori and T. Hikino (eds), *Big Business and the Wealth of Nations*, Cambridge: Cambridge University Press, pp. 336–67.

Aoki, M., H.K. Kim and M. Okuno-Fujiwara (1996), *The Role of Government in East Asian Economic Development*, Oxford: Clarendon.

Au, K., M.W. Peng and D. Wang (2000), 'Interlocking directorates, firm strategies, and performance in Hong Kong: towards a research agenda', *Asia Pacific Journal of Management*, **17**(1), 29–47.

Aw, Bee Yan and G. Batra (1998), 'Firm size and the pattern of diversification', *International Journal of Industrial Organization*, **16**(3), 313–31.

Besanko, D., D. Dranove and M. Shanley (2000), *Economics of Strategy*, 2nd edn, New York: John Wiley.

Biggart, N.W. and G.G. Hamilton (1992), 'On the limits of a firm-based theory to explain business networks: the Western bias of neoclassical economics', in N. Noria and R.G. Eccles (eds), *Networks and Organizations*, Boston: HBS Press, pp. 471–90.

Bluedorn, A.C., R.A. Johnson, D.K. Cartwright and B.R. Barringer (1994), 'The interface and convergence of the strategic management and organizational environment domains', *Journal of Management*, **20**, 201–62.

Boddewyn, J. and T. Brewer (1994), 'International-business political behavior: new theoretical directions', *Academy of Management Review*, **19**, 119–43.

Carney, M. (1998), 'A management capacity constraint? Obstacles to the development of the overseas Chinese family business', *Asia Pacific Journal of Management*, **15**(2), 137–62.

Chandler, A.D. Jr (1962), *Strategy and Structure: Chapters in the History of the Industrial Enterprises*, Cambridge, MA: MIT Press.

Chang, S.J. and J. Hong (2000), 'Economic performance of group-affiliated companies in Korea: intragroup resource sharing and internal business transactions', *Academy of Management Journal*, **43**(3), 429–48.

Chen, M.J. (2001), *Inside Chinese Business: a Guide for Managers Worldwide*, Boston, MA: HBS Press.

Chen, S. and K.W. Ho (2000), 'Corporate diversification, ownership structure, and firm value: the Singapore evidence', *International Review of Financial Analysis*, **9**, 315–26.

Choi, Jeong-Pyo and T. Cowing (2002), 'Diversification, concentration and economic performance: Korean business groups', *Review of Industrial Organization*, **21**, 271–82.

Chu, W. (2001), 'Contingency organizations and shared values: multiple logics in managing diversification', *Asia Pacific Journal of Management*, **18**, 83–99.

Chudnovsky, D. and A. Lopez (2000), 'A third wave of FDI from developing countries: Latin American TNCs in the 1990s', *Transnational Corporations*, **9**(2), 31–74.

Claessens, S., S. Djankov and L. Lang (2000), 'The separation of ownership and control in East Asian corporations', *Journal of Financial Economics*, **58**, 81–112.

Claessens, S., S. Djankov, J. Fan and L. Lang (2003), 'When does corporate diversification matter to productivity and performance? Evidence from East Asia', *Pacific-Basin Finance Journal*, **11**, 365–92.

Clegg, S., W. Higgin and T. Spybey (1990), *Capitalism in Contrasting Cultures*, New York: de Gruyter.

Datta, D.K., N. Rajagopalan and A. Rasheed (1991), 'Diversification and performance: critical review and future directions', *Journal of Management Studies*, **28**, 529–58.

Delios, A. and P. Beamish (1999), 'Geographic scope, product diversification, and corporate performance of Japanese firms', *Strategic Management Journal*, **20**(8), 711–27.

Dobson, W. and S.Y. Chia (eds) (1997), *Multinationals and East Asian Integration*, Singapore: International Development Research Centre, Canada and Institute of Southeast Asian Studies.

Dunning, J. H. (1988), 'The eclectic paradigm of international production: a restatement and some possible extensions', *Journal of International Business Studies*, **19**, 1–31.

Dunning, J.H. (1993), *Multinational Enterprises and the Global Economy*, New York: Addison-Wesley.

Erramilli, M.K., S. Agarwal and S.S. Kim (1997), 'Are firm specific advantages location specific too?', *Journal of International Business Studies*, **28**(4), 735–57.

Feenstra, R., T. Yang and G.G. Hamilton (1999), 'Business groups and product variety in trade: evidence from Southern Korea, Taiwan and Japan', *Journal of International Economics*, **48**, 71–100.

Ferris, S.P., K. Kim and P. Kitsabunnarat (2003), 'The costs (and benefit?) of diversified business groups: the case of Korean chaebols', *Journal of Banking and Finance*, **27**, 275–97.

Fukuyama, F. (1995), *Trust: The Social Virtues and the Creation of Prosperity*, New York: Free Press.

Gedajlovic, E. and D.M. Shapiro (1998), 'Management and ownership effects: evidence from five countries', *Strategic Management Journal*, **19**, 533–53.

Gedajlovic E., D.M. Shapiro and B. Buduru (2003), 'Financial ownership, diversification and firm profitability in Japan', *Journal of Management and Governance*, **7**, 315–35.

Geringer, J.M., P.W. Beamish and R.C. da Costa (1989), 'Diversification strategy and internationalization: implications for MNE performance', *Strategic Management Journal*, **10**(2), 109–19.

Geringer, J.M., S. Tallman and D. Olsen (2000), 'Product and international diversification among Japanese multinational firms', *Strategic Management Journal*, **21**, 51–80.

Giddy, I.H. and S. Young (1982), 'Conventional theory and unconventional multinationals: do new forms of multinational enterprise require new theories?', in A.M. Rugman (ed.), *New Theories of the Multinationals Enterprise*, London: Croom Helm, pp. 55–78.

Goold, M., A. Campbell and M. Alexander (1994), *Corporate-Level Strategy: Creating Value in the Multibusiness Company*, New York: John Wiley.

Gort, M. (1984), *Diversification and Integration in American Industry*, Westport, CT: Greenwood.

Grant, R.M., A.P. Jammine and H. Thomas (1988), 'Diversity, diversification, and profitability among British manufacturing companies, 1972–1984', *Academy of Management Journal*, **31**, 771–801.

Guisinger, S. (1991), 'Foreign direct investment flows in East and Southeast Asia: policy issues', *ASEAN Economic Bulletin*, **8**, 29–46.

Guthrie, D. (1997), 'Between markets and polities: organizational responses to reform in China', *American Journal of Sociology*, **102**, 1258–1304.

Hall, R.H. and W. Xu (1990), 'Run silent, run deep: a note on the ever pervasive influence of cultural differences on organizations in the Far East', *Organization Studies*, **11**, 596–616.

Hamilton, G.G. (1996), *Asian Business Networks*, Berlin: Walter de Gruyter.

Hamilton, G.G. (1997), 'Organization and market processes in Taiwan's capitalist economy', in M. Orrù, N.W. Biggart and G.G. Hamilton (eds), *The Economic Organization of East Asian Capitalism*, Thousand Oaks, CA Sage, pp. 237–93.

Hamilton, G.G. and N.W. Biggart (1988), 'Market, culture and authority: a comparative analysis of management and organization in the far east', *American Journal of Sociology*, **94**, S52–S94.

Han, C.M. (2002), 'Korea's direct investments in China: technology, experience, and ownership factors in performance', *Asia Pacific Journal of Management*, **19**, 109–26.

Hill, C., M.A. Hitt and R.E. Hoskisson (1992), 'Cooperative versus competitive structures in related and unrelated diversified firms', *Organization Science*, **3**, 501–21.

Hill, C., P. Hwang and W.C. Kim (1990), 'An eclectic theory of the choice of international entry mode', *Strategic Management Journal*, **11**, 117–28.

Hitt, M.A., R.E. Hoskisson and H. Kim (1997), 'International diversification: effects on innovation and firm performance in product-diversified firms', *Academy of Management Journal*, **40**, 767–98.

Hoskisson, R. and M.A. Hitt (1990), 'Antecedents and performance outcomes of diversification: a review and critique of theoretical perspectives', *Journal of Management*, **16**, 461–509.

Hoskisson, R.E., L. Eden, C.M. Lau and M. Wright (2000), 'Strategy in emerging economies', *Academy of Management Journal*, **43**(3), 249–67.

Jensen, M.C. (1986), 'Agency costs of free cash flow, corporate finance, and takeovers', *American Economic Review*, **76**, 323–29.

Johnson, S., S. Boone, A. Breach and E. Friedman (2000), 'Corporate governance in the Sian financial crisis', *Journal of Financial Economics*, **3**(4), 305–60.

Khan, H. (1999), 'Corporate governance of family businesses in Asia: what's right and what's wrong', ADBI working paper no. 3, ADB, Tokyo, Japan.

Khanna, T. and K. Palepu (1997), 'Why focused strategies may be wrong for emerging markets', *Harvard Business Review*, **75**(4), 41–51.

Khanna, T. and K. Palepu (2000), 'Is group affiliation profitable in emerging markets? An analysis of diversified Indian business groups', *Journal of Finance*, **55**(2), 867–91.

Khanna, T. and J.V. Rivkin (2001), 'Estimating the performance effects of business groups in emerging markets', *Strategic Management Journal*, **22**, 45–74.

Kim, H., R.E. Hoskisson, L. Tihanyi and J. Hong (2004), 'The evolution and restructuring of diversified business groups in emerging markets: the lessons from chaebols in Korea', *Asia Pacific Journal of Management*, **21**, 25–48.

Kim, W.S. (2003), 'Wealth effects of international investments and agency problems for Korean multinational firms', *Journal of International Financial Management and Accounting*, **14**(3).

Kogut, B. (1985), 'Designing global strategies: profiting from operational flexibility', *Sloan Management Review*, **26**, 27–38.

Kwon, Yung-Chul (2002), 'Korean multinationals' foreign direct investment projects: variability in the micro- and macro-level determinants', *The International Trade Journal*, **16**(2).

La Porta, R., F. Lopez-de-Salines and A. Shleifer (1999), 'Corporate ownership around the world', *Journal of Finance*, **54**(2), 471–517.

Lall, S. (1983), *The Third World Multinationals: The Spread of Third World Enterprises*, Chichester: J. Wiley and Sons.

Lasserre, P. and H. Schutte (1995), *Strategies for Asia Pacific*, London: Macmillan.

Lee, C. and P.W. Beamish (1995), 'The characteristics and performance of Korean joint ventures in LDCS', *Journal of International Business Studies*, Third Quarter, 637–54.

Lee, J. and D. Belvins (1990), 'Profitability and sales growth in industrialized versus newly industrialized countries', *Management International Review*, **30**, 87–100.

Leung, K. and S. White (2004), 'Taking stock and charting a path for Asian management research', in K. Leung and S. White (eds), *Handbook of Asian Management*, London: Kluwer Academic Publishers.

Li, J. (1994), 'Ownership structure and board composition: a multi-country test of agency theory predictions', *Managerial and Decision Economics*, **15**, 359–68.

Li, M. and Y. Wong (2003), 'Diversification and economic performance: an empirical assessment of Chinese firms', *Asia Pacific Journal of Management*, **20**, 243–65.

Li, P. (2003), 'Toward a geocentric theory of multinational evolution: the implications from the Asian MNEs as latecomers', *Asian Pacific Journal of Management*, **20**, 217–42.

Li, S., M. Li and J.J. Tan (1998), 'Understanding diversification in a transition economy: a theoretical exploration', *Journal of Applied Management Studies*, **7**(1), 77–94.

Lim, G.E. and T.Y. Teck (1995), 'Diversification strategies, firm characteristics and performance among Singapore firms', *International Journal of Management*, **12**(2), 223–33.

Lins, K. and H. Servaes (1999), 'International evidence on the value of corporate diversification', *Journal of Finance*, **54**, 2215–39.

Lu, Y., R. Yeh, H. Lan and H. Chow (2000), 'Strategic choice of organizational structure under diversification strategies', in C. Lau, K.K.S. Law, D.K. Tse and C. Wong (eds), *Asia Management Matters*, London: Imperial College Press, pp. 169–203.

Luo, Yadong (1999), 'Dimensions of knowledge: comparing Asian and Western MNEs in China', *Asia Pacific Journal of Management*, **16**, 75–93.

Luo, Yadong (2000), *Guanxi and Business*, River Edge, NJ: World Scientific.

Luo, Yadong (2002), 'Product diversification in international joint ventures: performance implications in an emerging market', *Strategic Management Journal*, **23**, 1–20.

Makino, S., C. Lau and R. Yeh (2002), 'Asset-exploitation versus asset-seeking: implications for location choice of foreign direct investment from newly industrialized economies', *Journal of International Business*, **33**(3), 403–21.

Markides, C.C. (1995), 'Diversification, restructuring and economic performance', *Strategic Management Journal*, **16**(2), 101–18.

Markides, C. and P.J. Williamson (1994), 'Related diversification, core competences and corporate performance', *Strategic Management Journal*, **15**, 149–65.

Mathews, J.A. (2002), *Dragon Multinational*, New York: Oxford University Press.

Montgomery, C. (1994), 'Corporate diversification', *Journal of Economic Perspectives*, **8**, 163–78.

Nachum, L. (2004), 'Geographic and industrial diversification of developing country firms', *Journal of Management Studies*, **41**(2), 273–94.

North, D. (1990), *Institutions, Institutional Change, and Economic Performance*, New York: Cambridge University Press.

Oh, D., C.J. Choi and E. Choi (1998), 'The globalization strategy of Daewoo Motor Company', *Asia Pacific Journal of Management*, **15**(2), 185–204.

Oliver, C. (1991), 'Strategic responses to institutional process', *Academy of Management Review*, **16**, 145–79.

Oliver, C. (1997), 'Sustainable competitive advantage: combining institutional and resource-based views', *Strategic Management Journal*, **18**, 697–713.

Palich, L.E., L.B. Cardinal and C.C. Miller (2000), 'Curvilinearity in the diversification-performance linkage: an examination of over three decades of research', *Strategic Management Journal*, **21**, 155–74.

Pananond, P. and C.P. Zeithaml (1998), 'The international expansion process of MNEs from developing countries: a case study of Thailand's CP Group', *Asia Pacific Journal of Management*, **15**(2), 163–184.

Pangarkar, N. (2004), 'The Asian multinational corporation: evolution, strategy, typology and challenges', in K. Leung and S. White (eds), *Handbook of Asian Management*, London: Kluwer Academic Publishers.

Pederson, T. and S. Thomsen (1997), 'European patterns of corporate ownership', *Journal of International Business Studies*, **28**, 759–78.

Peng, M.W. (2000), *Business Strategies in Transition Economies*, Thousand Oaks, CA: Sage.

Peng, M.W. (2006), *Global Strategy*, Cincinnati: Thomson South-Western.

Peng, M.W., K. Au and D. Wang (2001), 'Interlocking directorates as corporate governance in third world multinationals: theory and evidence from Thailand', *Asia Pacific Journal of Management*, **18**, 161–81.

Rajan, K. and R. Pangarkar (2000), 'Mode of entry choice: an empirical study of Singaporean multinationals', *Asia Pacific Journal of Management*, **17**, 49–66.

Ramaswamy, K. and M. Li (2001), 'Foreign investors, foreign directors and corporate diversification: an empirical examination of large manufacturing companies in India', *Asia Pacific Journal of Management*, **18**, 207–22.

Ramaswamy. K., M. Li and B. Petitt (2004), 'Who drives unrelated diversification? A study of Indian manufacturing firms', *Asia Pacific Journal of Management*, **21**, 403–23.

Ramaswamy, K., M. Li and R. Veliyath (2002), 'Variations in ownership behavior and propensity to diversify: a study of the Indian corporate context', *Strategic Management Journal*, **23**, 345–58.

Redding, S.G. (1990), *The Spirit of Chinese Capitalism*, Berlin: Walter de Gruyter.

Richter, F.J. (1999), *Business Networks in Asia. Promises, Doubts, and Perspectives*, London: Quorum Books.

Rugman, A.M. (1979), *International Diversity and the Multinational Enterprise*, Lexington, MA: Lexington Books.

Rumelt, R.P., D. Schendel and D.J. Teece (1994), *Fundamental Issues in Strategy: A Research Agenda*, Boston, MA: Harvard Business School Press.

Shapiro, D.M., E. Gedajlovic and C. Erdener (2003), 'The Chinese family firm as a multinational enterprise', *The International Journal of Organizational Analysis*, **11**(2), 105–22.

Sim, A.B. and M.Y. Ali (2001), 'Western multinational enterprises: a comparative analysis of Western, Japanese, NIC, and LDC firms', *Asia Pacific Business Review*, **8**, 37–57.

Sim, A.B. and J.R. Pandian (2003), 'Emerging Asian MNEs and their internationalization strategies – case study evidence on Taiwanese and Singaporean firms', *Asia Pacific Journal of Management*, **20**, 27–50.

Singh, K. (2004), 'Towards the development of strategy theory: contributions from Asian research', in K. Leung and S. White (eds), *Handbook of Asian Management*, London: Kluwer Academic Publishers.

Singh, K. and A. Delios (2005), *Strategy for Success in Asia*, Singapore: Wiley.

Steer, P. and J. Cable (1978), 'Internal organization and profit: an empirical analysis of large U.K. companies', *The Journal of Industrial Economics*, **27**, 13–30.

Toh, M.H. and L. Low (1994), 'The state of play of direct foreign investment in Asia', *Journal of Asian Economics*, **5**(1), 65–84.

Tolbert, P.S. and L.G. Zucker (1996), 'The institutionalization of institutional theory', in S.R. Clegg, C. Hardy, and W.R. Nord (eds), *Handbook of Organization Studies*, London: Sage, pp. 175–90.

Tolentino, P.E. (1993), *Technological Innovation and Third World Multinationals*, London: Routledge.

Tsang, E. and K.M. Kwan (1999), 'Replication and theory development in organization science: a critical realist perspective', *Academy of Management Review*, **24**, 759–80.

UNCTAD (2004), *World Investment Report: The Shift Towards Services*, (www.unctad.org).

Ungson, G.R., R.M. Steers and S.H. Park (1997), *Korean Enterprise: The Quest for Globalization*, Boston, MA: Harvard Business School Press.

Wade, R. (1990), *Governing the Market*, Princeton, NJ: Princeton University Press.

Wan, C. (1998), 'International diversification, industrial diversification and firm performance of Hong Kong MNCs', *Asia Pacific Journal Of Management*, **15**, 205–17.

Weder, B. (1999), *Model, Myth or Miracle. Reassessing the Role of Governments in the East Asian Experience*, New York: United Nations University Press.

Wells, L.T. (1983), *Third World Multinationals: The Rise of Foreign Investment from Developing Countries*, Cambridge, MA: MIT Press.

Westwood, R. (1997), 'Harmony and patriarchy: the cultural basis for "Paternalistic Headship" among overseas Chinese', *Organization Studies*, **18**, 445–80.

Whitley, R. (1992), *Business Systems in East Asia. Firms, Markets and Societies*, London: Sage.

Wiersema, M.F. and A. Bird (1993), 'Organizational demography in Japanese firms: group heterogeneity, individual dissimilarity, and top management team turnover', *Academy of Management Journal*, **36**, 996–1025.

Williamson, O.E. (1975), *Markets and Hierarchies*, New York: Free Press.

World Bank (1993), *The East Asian Miracle. Economic Grouth and Public Policy*, New York: Oxford University Press.

World Bank (2001), *Building Institutions for Markets. World Development Report, 2002*, Washington, DC: World Bank.

Xie, J., X.M. Song and A. Stringfellow (1998), 'Interfunctional conflict, conflict resolution styles, and new product success: a four-culture comparison', *Management Science*, **44**, 192–206.

Yeung, H.W.C. (1994), 'Transnational corporations from Asian developing countries: their characteristics and competitive edge', *Journal of Asian Business*, **10**(4), 17–58.

Yeung, H.W.C. (1997), 'Business networks and transnatinal corporations: a study of Hong Kong firms in the ASEAN region', *Economic Geography*, **73**(1), 1–25.

Yeung, H.W.C. (1998), 'Capital, state and space: contesting the borderless world', *Transactions of the Institute of British Geographers*, **23**, 291–309.

Yeung, H.W.C. (1999), 'Introduction: competing in the global economy: the globalization of business firms from emerging economies', in Henry Yeung (ed.), *The Globalization of Business Firms from Emerging Economies*, Cheltenham, UK and Northampton, MA, USA: Edward Elgar.

Yeung, H.W.C. (2002), *Entrepreneurship and the Internationalisation of Asian Firms: An Institutional Perspective*, Cheltenham, UK and Northampton, MA, USA: Edward Elgar.

Young, S., C.H. Huang and M. McDermott (1996), 'Internationalization and competitive catch-up processes: case study evidence on Chinese multinational enterprises', *Management International Review*, **36**(4), 295–314.

Young, M.N., D. Ahlstrom, G.D. Bruton and E.S. Chan (2001), 'The resource dependence, service, and control functions of boards of directors in Hong Kong and Taiwanese firms', *Asia Pacific Journal of Management*, **18**, 223–44.

Zin, R. (1999), 'Malaysian reverse investments: trends and strategies', *Asia Pacific Journal of Management*, **16**, 469–96.

Zutshi, R.K. and P. Gibbons (1998), 'The internationalization process of Singapore government-linked companies: a contextual view', *Asia Pacific Journal of Management*, **15**(2), 219–46.

APPENDIX

Table 2.1 Product diversification: recent literature and findings in Asia (1995–2004)

Author(s)	Location	Sample	Research themes	Research findings
Lim and Teck (1995)	Singapore	41 firms	• Diversification–performance relationship	• Negative moderating effect of size on the diversification–performance relationship
Guthrie (1997)	China	81 industrial firms	• Influences of contextual factors (performance and location of administrative level) on diversification	• Organizations with poor economic health more likely to adopt diversification • Firms at upper levels of administrative hierarchies more likely to adopt diversification
Hamilton (1997)	Taiwan	96 large business groups	• Ownership, organizational structure and diversification	• Family ownership has an influence on firm diversification • Network-like organizational structure
Li et al. (1998)	China	Case study of eight firms	• Purposes and motivation of diversification	• State-owned and non-state owned firms diversify with different motives • Diversification is used as a growth strategy to capture opportunities and deploy skill and resources
Wan (1998)	Hong Kong	81, including 47 multinational corporations	• Impact of international and industrial diversification on performance	• Positive impact on profitability stability and sales growth, but not on profitability • Industrial diversification enhances profitability stability, but reduces profitability
Aw and Batra (1998)	Taiwan	Data drawn from Taiwanese Census of Manufacturers	• Product and geographical market diversification	• Large firms are more diversified while small and medium-sized firms diversify into export markets rather than different product markets

Table 2.1 (continued)

Author(s)	Location	Sample	Research themes	Research findings
Delios and Beamish (1999)	Japan	399 manufacturing firms	• Geographic scope, product diversification and performance relationship	• Geographic scope is positively associated with firm profitability • Performance is not related to the extent of product diversification
Lu et al. (2000)	China	Case study of 15 firms	• Contextual factors and diversification	• Foundation conditions and ownership structures have an impact on a firm's degree of diversification
Geringer et al. (2000)	Japan	108 largest Japanese manufacturing multinationals	• The relationship of performance to product and international diversification	• Product diversity varies between *keiretsu* and non-*keiretsu* firms, but performance is not much different • Performance also varies over time considerably, but strategies are less variable
Chang and Hong (2000)	South Korea	317 groups with a total of 12 019 affiliated companies	• Corporate effects on performance	• At the group level, both related and unrelated diversification achieve higher performance
Khanna and Palepu (2000)	India	1309 firms	• Diversification–structure–performance relationship	• A quadratic relationship between performance and group diversification • Group structure adds value
Chen and Ho (2000)	Singapore	145 firms	• Ownership, diversification and performance	• No correlation between insider ownership and the level of diversification • A weak negative correlation between outside block ownership and the level of diversification • Diversified firms are valued less than single segment firms
Ramaswamy and Li (2001)	India	94 firms	• Ownership and product diversification strategy	• The level of foreign representation on the board of directors is likely to

				• dampen unrelated diversification strategies
Chu (2001)	Taiwan	31 firms	• Diversification strategy and structure (and performance)	• Both approaches can lead to satisfied economic performance and they are supplementary; diversified firms employing simultaneously two management logics will outperform firms with only one logic
Ramaswamy et al. (2002)	India	88 firms	• Ownership and diversification strategy	• Diverse ownership groups adopt different postures in monitoring and/or influencing organizational diversification
Luo (2002)	China	134 international joint ventures (IJVs)	• Product diversification and performance	• The relatedness of an IJV's products with that of its foreign and local parents is positively associated with its performance
Choi and Cowing (2002)	South Korea	25 of the largest *chaebols* over 1985–95	• Relationships involving corporate diversification, concentration and economic performance	• Changes in internal member firm concentration affect *chaebol* profits • A quadratic relationship exists between group profits and the number of member firms
Li and Wong (2003)	China	106 firms	• Investigate the joint effect of both related and unrelated diversification strategies on firm performance in an emerging economy setting	• Both resource building and utilization through concentration and related diversification and institutional environmental management through unrelated diversification are important for firm performance, but they must be considered together
Gedajlovic et al. (2003)	Japan	Two sample sets: 355 firms and 212 firms from 1986–91	• Impact of equity ownership by financial institutions on firm performance in Japan for 1986–91	• While ownership by financial institutions is associated with unprofitable diversification, such ownership is, on balance, positively associated with firm profitability

Table 2.1 (continued)

Author(s)	Location	Sample	Research themes	Research findings
Ferris *et al.* (2003)	South Korea	759 *chaebol* firm-year observations and 1316 non-*chaebol* firm-year observations from 1990 to 1995	• Costs and benefits associated with the operation of a diversified business group	• *Chaebol*-affiliated firms suffer a value loss relative to non-affiliated firms • *Chaebol* firms possess greater debt capacity and consequently enjoy lower tax burdens • The costs associated with *chaebol* membership exceed its benefits
Kim *et al.* (2004)	Japan	295 firms	• Benefits accruing from *keiretsu* affiliation differ across member firms, depending on their power in (or dependence on) the *keiretsu*	• Powerful *keiretsu* member firms are able to place more emphasis on growth in pursuing product and international diversification, whereas less powerful *keiretsu* member firms are subject to strong monitoring and emphasize profitability
Ramaswamy *et al.* (2004)	India	150 manufacturing firms during 1993–4	• Compares the influence of institutional investors and banks with the influence of CEOs and boards on unrelated diversification	• External constituents collectively have more influence on unrelated diversification than CEOs and boards • Institutional investors tend to discourage unrelated diversification, but banks are quite supportive of such moves
Lee and Belvins (1990)	Japan, South Korea and Taiwan, as compared to the US	400 firms (100 in each country)	• Determinant of performance	• Diversification is not important to performance determinants, at least in Japan and Korea samples
Feenstra *et al.* (1999)	South Korea, Taiwan and Japan	50 largest *chaebol* in Korea, 96 largest groups in Taiwan,	• Trade pattern of product diversity, business group structure	• Japanese firms exceed either Taiwanese or South Korean firms in product variety. South Korean firms market particular with high volume production,

Author (year)	Sample	Topic	Findings
	and 16 largest *keiretsu* in Japan		but are more limited in product variety; Taiwan exports more high-priced intermediate inputs, whereas South Korea exports relatively more high-priced final goods
Lins and Servaes (1999)	174 and 227 German, 808 and 778 Japanese, 391 and 341 British firms in Germany, Japan and UK firms in 1992 and 1994	• Diversification and shareholders' wealth	• The effect of diversification on firm value is different; the value of diversification is related to the institutional structure of a country • In Japan, firms with a strong association to an industrial group would be less diversified than independent firms
Khanna and Rivkin (2001)	14 emerging markets; Various data sources	• A comparison of performance among firms affiliated with group and outside of groups	• Differences in profitability vary across institutional contexts • In some countries, business group affiliates earn higher accounting profits than do otherwise comparable unaffiliated firms
Claessens *et al.* (2003)	East Asian economies; 10 000 firm years in nine East Asian economies during 1991–6	• Diversification–productivity	• The learning-by-doing and the misallocation-of-capital effects vary systematically with the types of business combination and the levels of economic development
Nachum (2004)	Over ten Asian economies; 345 firms in 22 developing countries	• Impact of industrial and geographical diversification activities of developing country firms on their performance	• Significant and positive association between industrial and geographic diversification and performance, and considerable variation of these relationships across developing regions and diversification strategies

Note: Table is adapted (with the addition of literature from 2000 to 2004) from Lu *et al.* (2000).

Table 2.2 Geographic diversification (Asian multinationals): recent literature and findings (1995–2004) (Japan excluded)

Author(s)	Context	Sample	Research themes	Main findings
Lee and Beamish (1995)	South Korean firms in LDCs	108 firms	• Characteristics, motivation and performance	• Relative to JV from developed countries, differences are found in terms of stability, venture creation rationale, satisfaction level with performance, and the relationship between control and performance and between ownership and control
Young et al. (1996)	State-owned MNCs from China	5 firms	• Motivations, stage achieved in the internationalization process	• Leapfrogging of stages in the internationalization process • Firm-level and host-country factors predominantly influence mode choice
Yeung (1997)	Hong Kong firms in Southeast Asia	111 firms	• Business networks; mechanisms of Southeast Asian operations	• Hong Kong firms and their Southeast Asian operations are socially and culturally embedded in networks of relationships
Erramilli et al. (1997)	South Korean MNCs	177 subsidiaries (by 132 firms)	• Level of ownership by Korean MNCs in developing versus other countries	• The influence of firm-specific advantage may be contingent upon the characteristics of both home- and host-country locations
Carney (1998)	Ethnic Chinese family businesses	50 firms	• Development of proprietary competencies	• In contrast to prevailing cultural and institutional accounts, extant theory of the family firm and of organizational networks provides an alternative explanation of observed investment strategies and organizational structure
Pananond and Zeithaml (1998)	Charoen Pokphand group (Thailand)	1 firm	• International expansions process (geographic and sectoral participation)	• While existing resources feature prominently, determining the direction and the success of expansion, the accumulation of new expertise becomes even more significant in the long run

Study	Sample		Focus	Findings
Oh et al. (1998)	Daewoo Motor Company (Korea)	1 firm	• Globalization strategy	• Emerging market MNEs can follow non-sequential and non-linear internationalization process
Wan (1998)	Hong Kong MNCs	81 firms	• Industrial diversification, geographic diversification and performance	• Hong Kong MNCs are more internationalized than domestic firms, but they do not perform better
Zutshi and Gibbons (1998)	Government-linked MNCs from Singapore	2 firms	• Internationalization process	• Describes the evolution of two government-linked companies in Singapore and reviews their internationalization strategy
Zin (1999)	Malaysian investment abroad	7 firms	• Motivations, business strategies	• Finding new markets as the main reason for locating overseas • Most MIA takes the form of stand-alone affiliates • Most decentralize decision making regarding the management of these subsidiaries
Rajan and Pangarkar (2000)	Singaporean MNEs	1100 firms	• The choice of foreign mode of entry (as provided by equity stakes)	• Control, cost and competence affect the equity stake in an overseas venture
Peng et al. (2001)	Thailand based MNEs	200 firms	• Do the interlocks network attributes and individual board directors of MNEs differ systematically from those of non-MNEs?	• Compared with non-MNEs, MNEs in Thailand (1) have more densely connected interlocks, (2) occupy more central locations in the interlocks network, and (3) appoint more military directors
Sim and Ali (2001)	IJVs from western, Japan, NIEs and LDC in Bangladesh	58 IJVs	• Characteristics, difference from various contexts	• Reveal difference among the IJVs originating from the four country group, which suggest significant effect of country national origins on IJVs
Young et al. (2001)	Ethnic Chinese firms in	47 firms	• The extent to which the functions of resource dependence, service	• The service and control functions are less pronounced for East Asian boards,

Table 2.2 (continued)

Author(s)	Context	Sample	Research themes	Main findings
	Hong Kong and Taiwan		and control are performed, primarily by outside board members	while the resource dependence function is more pronounced • The governance of the region is being moved closer to international practices by a new generation of leaders
Han (2002)	Korean investors in China	91 firms	• Determinants of performance: technology, internationalization experience, and ownership patterns	• The labour intensity of technology involved in FDI and the appropriateness of manufacturing technology to the local conditions affect the performance • The internationalization experiences also affect the profitability • The level of local ownership has a positive impact on performance
Kwon (2002)	Korea	123 firms	• The relative importance of the determinants of Korean multi-nationals' FDI	• Propose a framework for the analysis of the determinants of FDI that incorporates project variables at the micro level and country variables at the macro level
Makino et al. (2002)	Taiwan	328 firms	• Location choice	• Motivation has a significant impact on the choice of their investment location, yet this impact is moderated by the capabilities • Both asset-exploitation and asset-seeking aspects of investments are predictive of the NIE firms' location choice of investment
Li (2003)	Acer Group from Taiwan	1 firm	• Extant MNE theories to the MNEs from the developing countries as latecomers	• The extant MNE theories need modifications (so as to apply to the MNEs from the developing countries as

Study	Context	Sample	Focus	Findings
				• latecomers) and enhancements (so as to explain better all MNEs)
Li (2003)	Taiwan's Acer group	1 firm	• Evolutionary pattern	• Gaining initial competitive advantages by combining the location-specific advantages of their home countries and the developed countries
Sim and Pandian (2003)	Taiwanese and Singaporean MNEs in the textile and electronics industries	12 firms	• Internationalization characteristics and strategies	• The emerging Taiwanese and Singaporean MNEs, while exhibiting characteristics such as those described in extant theories, also show some differences
Kim (2003)	Korea	30 firms	• The wealth effects of FDI announcements by Korean firms	• Cross-border investments increase shareholder wealth • They do not obtain the firm-specific technological advantages over international competitors
Shapiro et al. (2003)	Ethnic Chinese family firms	N/A	• Examine the strategic behaviour of ethnic Chinese family firms by applying Dunning's eclectic theory	• Like the classic Western MNE, the ethnic Chinese family firm can be understood as a viable mechanism for capitalizing on particular configurations of OLI advantages in international markets
Ahlstrom et al. (2004)	Ethnic Chinese start-up firms in the East Asian economies of Hong Kong, Singapore and Taiwan	41 entrepreneurs	• Characteristics of ethnic Chinese business culture's impact on the success of ethnic Chinese firms	• Traditional business practices are hindering the building of firms that can be taken public and experience the high growth consistent with vibrant entrepreneurial firms

Note: Table is adapted with alteration from Pangarkar (2004).

3. Towards an institution-based view of business strategy in Asia

Mike W. Peng

This chapter focuses on a key research question: why do strategies of firms from different countries and regions differ?[1] This is the very first question among the five most fundamental questions in strategic management raised by Rumelt *et al.* (1994: 564).[2] Since the diversity of firm strategies around the world can arise as the result of many possible forces internal or external to the organization, this question engenders a wide variety of disparate answers from economists (Nelson, 1991) and sociologists (Carroll, 1993). Thus far, strategy researchers have primarily focused on industry conditions (Porter, 1980) and firm resources (Barney, 1991) as drivers of firm differences, leading to competition- and resource-based perspectives respectively.

Drawing from recent research on Asian business organizations, I argue that, in addition to these existing theories, a new, institution-based view has emerged to account for differences in business strategy. A number of scholars have already suggested that, in addition to industry and firm-level conditions, a firm also needs to take into account wider influences from sources such as the state and society when crafting and implementing its strategies (DiMaggio and Powell, 1991; Oliver, 1997; see also Chapters 6 and 15 in this volume). These influences are broadly considered as institutional frameworks (North, 1990; Scott, 1995). When applied to strategy research, this new perspective can consequently be called an *institution-based* view of business strategy (Peng, 2000a, 2002, 2003, 2006; Peng and Heath, 1996).

Since no firm can be immune from institutional frameworks in which it is embedded, there is hardly any dispute that institutions matter. In order to make further theoretical progress, researchers must 'tackle the harder and more interesting issues of how they matter, under what circumstances, to what extent, and in what ways' (Powell, 1996: 297). This chapter therefore has three objectives. First, extending my earlier theoretical work (Peng, 2000a, 2002; Peng and Heath, 1996), this chapter outlines the broad contour of the new, institution-based view of business strategy. Second, I review the recent Asian management literature to assess the progress made in the direction Powell (1996) calls for (see also Chapter 2 in this volume). Given that most existing research takes place in North America and Western Europe, a focus on Asia allows us 'to vary institutional contexts'; otherwise, 'it is difficult if not impossible to discern the effects of institutions on social structures and behaviours if all our cases are embedded in the same or very similar ones' (Scott, 1995: 146). Informed by research on a number of Asian countries, four substantive areas are reviewed: (1) supplier strategies, (2) entrepreneurial strategies, (3) diversification strategies, and (4) growth strategies. While this is not an exhaustive list of research areas, I believe that they represent a broad spectrum of research interests through which the institution-based view of business strategy can be illustrated. Finally, current research is critiqued and future research directions are suggested.

UNDERSTANDING INSTITUTIONS

According to North (1990: 3), institutions are 'the rules of the game in a society or, more formally, are the humanly devised constraints that shape human interaction'. Similarly, Scott (1995: 33) defines institutions as 'cognitive, normative, and regulative structures and activities that provide stability and meaning to social behavior'. An 'institutional framework' is therefore defined by Davis and North (1971: 6) as 'the set of fundamental political, social, and legal ground rules that establishes the basis for production, exchange, and distribution'.

Under the label of 'new institutionalism', there are differences between two versions. The economist's version focuses more on efficiency (North, 1990; Williamson, 1985), whereas the sociologist's version concentrates more on legitimacy (DiMaggio and Powell, 1991; Scott, 1995). Delineating the theoretical boundaries between these perspectives is beyond the scope of the present chapter. In the spirit of previous institutional work in strategy (for example, Oliver, 1997; Peng and Heath, 1996), this chapter takes an *integrative* approach, drawing upon the broad institutional literature to examine how institutions bear upon the strategy problem.

Institutional frameworks interact with organizations by signalling which choices are acceptable and supportable. As a result, institutions help reduce uncertainty for organizations. Institutional frameworks are made up of both formal and informal constraints (North, 1990). *Formal* constraints include political rules, judicial decisions and economic contracts. *Informal* constraints, on the other hand, include socially sanctioned norms of behaviour that are embedded in culture and ideology (Scott, 1995). North (1990) suggests that, in situations where formal constraints fail, informal constraints will come into play to reduce uncertainty and provide constancy to organizations. These insights have important implications for the development of an institution-based view of business strategy (Peng, 2000a, 2003, 2006).

AN INSTITUTION-BASED VIEW OF BUSINESS STRATEGY

Strategies are about choices. An analysis of business strategy thus needs to 'recognize the exercise of choice by organizational decision makers' (Child, 1972: 10). Given the influence of institutional frameworks on firm behaviour, any strategic choice that firms make is inherently affected by the formal and informal constraints of a given institutional framework (North, 1990; Oliver, 1997). Viewed from such a perspective, much of the strategy literature that largely focuses on Western firms does not discuss the specific relationship between strategic choices and institutional frameworks. Indeed, the influence of the 'environment' has long been featured in the literature (Lawrence and Lorsch, 1969). However, what has dominated this research is a 'task environment' view that focuses on economic variables such as market demand and technological change. Until recently, scholars have rarely looked beyond the task environment to explore the interaction among

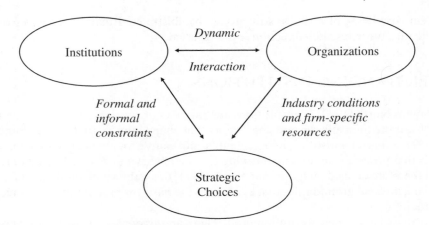

Figure 3.1   Institutions, organizations and strategic choices

institutions, organizations and strategic choices. Instead, a market-based institutional framework has been taken for granted.

Such an omission is unfortunate because it is precisely the institutional frameworks in developed economies that prompt Western firms to choose certain strategies and constrain them from choosing others (Peng and Heath, 1996). Today, we are much more conscious of the importance of the relationships between organizations and institutions. Treating institutions as independent variables, an institution-based view of business strategy focuses on the dynamic interaction between institutions and organizations, and considers strategic choices as the outcome of such an interaction (Figure 3.1). Specifically, strategic choices are not only driven by industry conditions and firm-specific resources that traditional strategy research emphasizes (Barney, 1991; Porter, 1980), but also reflect the formal and informal constraints of a particular institutional framework which decision makers confront (Oliver, 1997; Scott, 1995).

Since the 1990s, more scholars have come to realize that institutions matter (Powell and DiMaggio, 1991; Scott, 1995) and that strategy research cannot just focus on industry conditions and firm resources (Khanna and Palepu, 1997; Peng, 2000a). As argued by Hoskisson *et al.* (2000), institutional theory appears to be a highly insightful approach when probing into organizational strategies in Asia. While taking institutions seriously is only a first step, working out the analytic logic of their influence is the second, and explicating the underlying mechanisms comes next. This chapter can be considered as a part of this broad intellectual movement in search of a better understanding of the relationship among institutions, organizations and strategic choices (Peng, 2002, 2003, 2006). Next, I turn to four substantive areas of recent research in a variety of Asian economies to illustrate how the institution-based view has evolved.

SUPPLIER STRATEGIES

While most strategy research focuses on Western firms, Williamson (1991: 87) argues that it has become virtually 'impossible to discuss the matter of business strategy long without the issue of Japanese economic organization surfacing'. Of particular concern to strategy researchers is the *keiretsu* network – the webs of inter-firm relations that envelop many Japanese firms (Gerlach, 1992) and now increasingly involve other Asian firms (Peng *et al.*, 2001a). Specifically within such a network, independent suppliers seem to be willing to site their factories close to major manufacturers such as Toyota and Honda in the absence of a long-term contract. Such a high degree of asset specificity creates economic value by reducing delivery time and costs and by increasing the efficiency of more just-in-time deliveries (Dyer, 1997). However, according to research in the US (Williamson, 1985), such a high degree of asset specificity is likely to result in high transaction costs. This is because the value of suppliers' location-specific assets will depreciate considerably when they no longer have a contract with manufacturers and/or when suppliers want to deliver to other manufacturers located elsewhere. Consequently, suppliers are predicted to be unwilling to site their factories in a vulnerable location, and manufacturers often need to engage in costly vertical integration. In contrast to such thinking, some Japanese firms seem to have an unlikely combination, namely, high asset specificity and low transaction costs, thus presenting a research puzzle to researchers (Dyer and Nobeoka, 2000). More recently, as *keiretsu* networks are extended throughout Asia, how indigenous Asian firms 'buy in' becomes an interestingly new issue (Peng *et al.*, 2001a).

One way to solve the puzzle is to invoke the difference in national cultures between Japan and Western countries such as the US (Dore, 1987). A high propensity to cooperate is believed to be rooted in the Japanese culture and, consequently, a high degree of inter-firm cooperation is more likely. Beyond this simplistic culturalist perspective, more recent work has increasingly focused on the institutional frameworks in which Japanese firms are embedded (Hill, 1995). Specifically, while Japan has developed a set of formal legal frameworks based on the American model during the postwar decades, they are not used extensively. Instead, Japanese firms tend to place a greater emphasis on informal constraints, such as consensus and trust building, instead of formal contracts. In other words, 'the informal constraints of Japanese society do a *relatively* better job of holding opportunism in check than those of many Western societies', resulting in both a high degree of specialization and low transaction costs (Hill, 1995: 129, original emphasis). The upshot is that major Japanese automobile manufacturers such as Toyota and Honda can avoid costly vertical integration typically found in Western automobile companies, while still benefiting from close cooperation with suppliers (Dyer and Nobeoka, 2000).

Although research on Japanese supplier strategies has demonstrated that inter-firm strategies can be organized differently and still generate competitive advantage (Peng *et al.*, 2001a), this work is a *weak* test of the institutional perspective. This is because the national cultures of Japan and Western countries are so different that it is difficult to partition out the impact of institutional influences independently of national cultural influences. The next section reviews some recent work that takes on such a challenge.

ENTREPRENEURIAL STRATEGIES

A strong test of the institutional perspective needs to demonstrate that institutions matter independently of national cultures (Lau and Ngo, 2001). Such work has only begun recently. Most research in this area starts with a cross-cultural perspective, that is, comparing and contrasting the impact of different national cultures on firm behaviour. For example, the dramatic contrasts between mainland Chinese and American cultures have attracted a number of cross-cultural studies that report significant differences. However, critics argue that many *cross-cultural* studies do not accomplish their objectives; rather, they end up being *cross-national* studies that reflect the impact of environmental factors such as different formal and informal institutional frameworks in various countries (Farh *et al.*, 1997: 441; Kelley and Worthley, 1981: 164). It is therefore difficult to conclude whether the observed differences between subjects in two different countries are due to cross-cultural or to cross-national differences (Lau and Ngo, 2001).

One solution is to introduce a third sample from Hong Kong or Taiwan (McGrath *et al.*, 1992). Subjects in Taiwan and Hong Kong are assumed to share the cultural roots of their counterparts in mainland China, and operate in a different market economy. However, since Taiwan and Hong Kong represent a third national environment, employing these samples, although representing substantial progress, is still unable to allow researchers to isolate the role of national institutions independently of the cultural effect, or vice versa (Mitchell *et al.*, 2000).

Attempting to fill such a gap, Tan and Peng (2002) employ a rigorous and quasi-experimental design to isolate better the role of cultural and national differences. It is widely known that ethnic Chinese are an entrepreneurial people, as evidenced by the wealth they generate throughout Southeast Asia and now increasingly in North America and Western Europe (Fukuyama, 1996; see also Chapter 18 in this volume). However, entrepreneurial activities in mainland China were kept at a minimum during the Maoist period until the late 1970s. Since then, the emergence of entrepreneurship in mainland China seems to indicate that it is the development of market-supporting institutions – both formal and informal – that gives birth to a new wave of entrepreneurship (Peng, 2001a). Similar to Lau and Busenitz (2001), Tan and Peng (2002) test this proposition by focusing on entrepreneurs who have founded new businesses in China. Specifically, we draw on three samples, namely, mainland Chinese, Chinese Americans and Caucasian Americans. These samples represent two distinctive national environments (mainland China versus the US) and two different cultures (Chinese versus American). We measure the differences in entrepreneurs' perception of the environment and their strategic orientations. Two competing hypotheses are generated. First, if the *national* institutional effect predominates, then Chinese American and Caucasian American entrepreneurs will show relatively similar patterns of response compared with those of mainland Chinese entrepreneurs. Conversely, if the *cultural* effect predominates, then mainland Chinese and Chinese American entrepreneurs will show relatively similar patterns of response when compared with those of their Caucasian American counterparts (Tan and Peng, 2002).

The introduction of the Chinese American sample thus 'bridges' the two national samples. On the one hand, these entrepreneurs compete with their Caucasian American counterparts in the same national environment. On the other hand, Chinese American entrepreneurs, despite their immigration experience, have been found to maintain significant cultural similarities to counterparts in their former homeland. For example, while other immigrant groups may try to 'blend in', Chinese Americans often emphasize their cultural uniqueness, as evidenced, for example, in the distinctive decorations of Chinatowns in major American cities (Fukuyama, 1996). Under the joint impact of cultural and environmental influences, the response of Chinese American entrepreneurs therefore cannot be predicted a priori in a single direction, and has to be entertained through two competing hypotheses.

Our empirical results lend strong support for the institutional perspective (Tan and Peng, 2002). Specifically, Chinese American and Caucasian American entrepreneurs tend to share more similarities in terms of their environmental perceptions and strategic orientations when compared with their counterparts in mainland China. Despite a presumed cultural link between mainland Chinese and Chinese American samples, these two groups differ significantly in many dimensions. These results therefore provide some preliminary evidence suggesting that it is institutional frameworks, rather than national cultures, that drive entrepreneurship. Given that the institutional environments between mainland China and the US are radically different, our findings are hardly surprising. More work may need to concentrate on 'partially similar' cases (Lau and Ngo, 2001; Shenkar and von Glinow, 1994), for example by comparing and contrasting firm strategies in different Asian economies to which we now turn.

DIVERSIFICATION STRATEGIES

Since the 1970s, research in North America and Western Europe suggests that, on average, firms with a higher level of diversification are less profitable than firms with a lower level of diversification (Hoskisson and Hitt, 1994; see also Chapter 2 in this volume). What seems to hurt performance the most is a strategy of conglomerate (or unrelated) diversification. Consequently, unrelated conglomerates have largely become a thing of the past in major developed economies since the 1980s and the 1990s. In contrast, highly diversified conglomerates known as 'business groups' have often been found extensively in Asian economies, such as China (Keister, 2000; Peng, 1997), Hong Kong (Au *et al.*, 2000; Wan, 1998), India (Khanna and Palepu, 2000), South Korea (Chang and Hong, 2000) and Taiwan (Chung, 2001; Hamilton and Feenstra, 1995).

Seen through a Euro-American lens, the persistence and emergence of these diversified conglomerates throughout Asia may appear to be puzzling (Granovetter, 1994). A culturalist perspective would suggest that the national cultures of these emerging economies tend to foster these culturally important practices. The validity of this view, however, is questionable in light of significant cultural differences among this diverse group of countries. Another perspective suggests that, as a highly institutionalized organizational form due to historical reasons, these conglomerates persist in these 'backward' countries with few performance benefits. A stronger proposition, often embraced by Western media, consultants and advisors to Asian governments, is that these conglomerates actually destroy value and therefore should be dismantled. Rigorous evidence supporting this proposition, however, is rare. Preliminary findings actually suggest that, in contrast to the conventional wisdom in the West, there seems to be discernible performance *benefits* associated with conglomerates in emerging economies, as Khanna and Palepu (2000) and Khanna and Rivkin (2001) find in India and Indonesia. Other scholars report similar findings in Hong Kong (Wan, 1998), Singapore (Lim and Teck, 1995) and Taiwan (Chung, 2001). These findings thus confront researchers: how to reconcile the striking differences in diversification strategies from developed and emerging economies?

The answer seems to lie in the institutional perspective with a focus on the underlying formal and informal institutional frameworks permeating these economies. While emerging economies in Asia are hardly uniform, their formal institutions tend to fall short, to varying degrees, of providing support for low transaction-cost business operations in three critical areas: (1) a credible legal framework; (2) a stable political structure; and (3) functioning strategic factor markets (Khanna and Palepu, 1997; Peng and Heath, 1996).

Throughout Asia, because of the weaknesses of formal institutions, 'informal constraints rise to play a *larger* role in regulating economic exchanges in these countries during the transition' (Peng and Heath, 1996: 504, added emphasis). The main informal constraints come from three sources. First, *interpersonal* relations among executives serve as a focal point for valuable managerial networking. Although managers all over the world devote a considerable amount of time and energy to cultivating interpersonal ties, managers in Asia, owing to a lack of publicly available, reliable information about market opportunities, perhaps 'rely more heavily on the cultivation of personal relationships to cope with the exigencies of their situation' (Child, 1994: 150). By engaging in reciprocal, preferential and mutually supportive networking, managers in diversified conglomerates who often come from the same family, clan and/or educational background are able to reduce uncertainty in their decision making.

Second, *external* connections linking these executives and key stakeholders, especially government officials, are also a crucial part of these informal institutional constraints (Boddewyn and Brewer, 1994; Oliver, 1997). Given the need to combat environmental uncertainty, it is not surprising that managers maintain a 'disproportionately greater contact' with government officials (Child, 1994: 154). For example, in China, Peng and Luo (2000) find that connections with officials appear to be more important than ties with other managers in terms of their impact on firm performance. In Thailand, Peng *et al.* (2001b: 171) document that 42 of the top 200 listed firms have *active-duty* military officers serving as directors on the board. These officers may provide important 'political resources' (Boddewyn and Brewer, 1994) and 'institutional capital' (Oliver, 1997) for firms in such an unstable environment. Bribes, gifts, cronyism and other corrupt practices may be part of working with the bureaucracy, but that is not the whole story. In many cases, educating officials is more important than exchanging favours (Khanna and Palepu, 1997). Conglomerates can leverage their government contacts and present to officials a united front of the interests of diverse industries and businesses represented by a single group, thus minimizing the risk of overloading the bureaucracy.

Finally, the *reputation* of conglomerates serves as an informal, but strong, signalling device to reduce uncertainty for customers and investors. In consumer markets throughout Asia, independent consumer protection organizations are rare, and government watchdog agencies are often ineffective (Khanna and Palepu, 1997). As a result, consumers are reluctant to trust new brands (see chapters in Part II of this volume). Conversely, since established brands wield tremendous power, conglomerates with a quality reputation can leverage their names to enter new industries, including unrelated ones.

When attracting financial investors, the reputation of conglomerates becomes a valuable, unique and hard-to-imitate competitive advantage (Barney, 1991). It is interesting to note that, in contrast to the US, where Internet business is dominated by start-ups that have raised significant capital, Internet services in Asia are predominately provided by established conglomerates that can raise external financing more easily and provide internal funding. Such an ability to raise capital, as well as to allocate capital internally, compensates for a crucial void in the underdeveloped financial markets. In addition to financial investors, foreign direct investors are also more likely to be attracted to established conglomerates than to unknown independent firms in emerging economies. Again, the reputation and prestige of established business groups reduce search costs for foreign investors. These costs can be tremendous because of the lack of information and the steep learning curve in these countries (Luo and Peng, 1999).

Overall, informal constraints offer some constancy and predictability in the absence of well-developed formal market-supporting institutions. Specifically, diversified conglomerates are able to compensate for the lack of formal institutional constraints by performing basic functions by themselves, such as allocating capital, obtaining market information and enforcing contracts. In contrast, specialized organizations (for example, stock exchanges, market research firms, law firms and the courts), as part of the formal institutions in developed economies, will handle these responsibilities and thus reduce the need to support these costly activities within the firm.

Taken together, research on diversification strategies in Asia not only highlights the explanatory power of the institutional perspective, but also reminds us of the institutional embeddedness of the recent findings of diversification research in developed economies. It is important to note that the negative relationship between conglomerate diversification and performance was actually not found during an earlier era in the West (Matsusaka, 1993). Instead, financial markets' response to unrelated acquisitions was found to be *positive* during the 1960s. These findings thus document 'a dramatic reversal in [US] investor sentiment toward diversification – positive in the 1960s, neutral in the 1970s, and negative in the 1980s' (Matsusaka, 1993: 358). During the 1960s, external capital markets in the US were less developed in terms of firm-specific information disclosure than during later decades. For example, relative to the current period, there was less access by the public to databases, analyst reports and other sources of information that could reduce transaction costs for external investors and firms. As a result, conglomerates in the US at that time were perceived ex ante by external capital markets to have an advantage in their abilities to allocate capital internally, a logic very similar to the favourable reaction of external markets to conglomerates in some Asian economies now. In short, the institutional perspective highlights the historical specificity of a particular relationship between diversification and performance that may not hold true longitudinally and spatially (Peng *et al.*, 2005).

GROWTH STRATEGIES

Before the current economic transition, firms in China were not interested in growth (Tan and Litschert, 1994). A fascinating aspect of the transition process is that firms there are now compelled to grow to be more competitive in the emerging ocean of market competition, thus presenting strategy researchers with a previously non-existent question first raised by Peng and Heath (1996): how do firms in transition economies such as China achieve growth?

Existing research on the growth of the firm suggests that there are typically three strategies for growth, namely, generic expansion, mergers and acquisitions, and/or networks and alliances (Penrose, 1959; Williamson, 1985). Work on firm growth in transition economies highlights the institutional prerequisites that support each of these three growth strategies. Specifically, generic expansion calls for a staff of capable managers. Mergers and acquisitions require functioning strategic factor markets. Developing networks and alliances needs to build trust and mutual understanding. While the institutional frameworks supporting the first two growth strategies are primarily formal ones, those for the last strategy are of an informal nature based on interpersonal relationships (Peng, 2000a).

Empirical work has been initiated in China, first through a qualitative phase building on three longitudinal case studies conducted over a seven-year period (Peng, 1997). This work has recently moved to a quantitative phase (Peng and Luo, 2000). Several interesting findings emerge. First, generic expansion, based on firms' own resources, is typically infeasible initially because of the lack of certain critical resources at most firms (for example technology). In fact, some of these firms may need to 'shrink' by turning around from persistent performance problems (Bruton *et al.*, 2001). Second, handicapped by both a lack of capital and a lack of formal strategic factor markets, most firms cannot hope, at least initially, to acquire necessary resources through mergers and acquisitions. Many so-called mergers have been mandated by the government in an effort to bail out ailing state-owned firms (Peng *et al.*, 1999). Third, an informal, network-based growth strategy is typically favoured by a variety of firms (Peng and Heath, 1996). They usually rely on developing interorganizational networks by tapping into the complementary resources at partner firms in order to jointly pursue growth opportunities (Peng, 1997; White, 2000).

Specifically, state-owned firms like to team up with foreign firms and private firms in order to access financial capital, advanced technology and entrepreneurial energy (Peng, 2000b; Shenkar and Li, 1999). Non-state firms are interested in obtaining some political support from the government by collaborating with state-owned firms (Lau and Busenitz, 2001; Peng, 2001a). Foreign firms tap into the capabilities of domestic partners in order to navigate the uncertain waters of economic transition (Beamish, 1993; Luo and Peng, 1999; Peng, 2000b; Yan and Gray, 1994). Finally, micro, interpersonal ties among managers in multiple firms are translated into macro, interorganizational relations that can lead to better firm performance: in short, a *micro–macro* link (Peng and Luo, 2000). Further, another extension of such a micro–macro link can be found in Lau and Busenitz (2001) who link the micro, entrepreneurial cognition with the macro, entrepreneurial strategies and performance in China.

Given that strategic choices are inherently affected by managers' national cultures (Hofstede, 1991), it is not surprising that Chinese managers who have a widely noted cultural propensity to rely on informal ties resort to personal connections to achieve organizational goals (Chen, 2001; see also Chapter 4 in this volume). However, Boisot and Child (1996), Peng (1997, 2000a), Peng and Heath (1996) and Xin and Pearce (1996) argue that, in addition to cultural influences, institutional imperatives during the transition may further necessitate the extensive reliance on personalized exchange relationships. Such an institutional interpretation is borne out by similar findings from transition economies throughout Central and Eastern Europe (Grabher and Stark, 1997). These countries include the Czech Republic (Spicer *et al.*, 2000), Hungary (Stark, 1996) and Russia (Linz and Krueger, 1998; Puffer, 1994). Note that in these countries there is little influence of ethnic Chinese (or Asian) culture that puts a premium on interpersonal ties. Nevertheless, the emergence of a network-based strategy that 'blurs' existing organizational boundaries and creates 'recombinant property' (Stark, 1996) has been widely reported. It is evident that, despite cultural differences, similar institutional imperatives during the transition must have played an important role in leading to similar growth strategies throughout transitional economies (Peng, 2000a).

While initial research finds that growth strategies in transition economies such as China converge on networks and alliances, it is important to caution that this is a *dominant* strategy, not the *only* strategy (Peng and Heath, 1996: 517). A network-based strategy is not without its problems. The first is the lack of codification of information, routines and capabilities. The second is the lack of a formal governance basis; often, members do not operate as unified groups. Decision making in these networks tends to be case-by-case, with extensive negotiations and bargaining among members. These loosely structured, largely informal networks are based on trust, reputation and mutual understanding that, unfortunately, can be exploited when there are divergent economic interests and/or the enforcement mechanism is weak (Peng, 2000a: 64). As a result, there is a recent move throughout China to establish large and fully incorporated enterprises and business groups with a unified command-and-control structure and subsidiaries, as opposed to loosely connected network members (Keister, 2000). Some of these groups, such as the 'red chips' listed in Hong Kong and New York, have ventured abroad with some success (Au *et al.*, 2000).

These activities increasingly call for a strategy of mergers and acquisitions to achieve growth (Peng *et al.*, 1999). Such a need, in turn, has fuelled the urgency to strengthen formal institutional constraints, namely, to establish an adequate legal framework to allow for such market-based transactions (Zhang and Peng, 2000). In other words, the failure of formal institutional frameworks has led to the reliance on informal constraints that results in a network-based strategy. Furthermore, the problems of such a strategy call for strengthening formal institutions. The dynamic interaction between institutions and organizations in Figure 3.1 thus comes a full circle. Specifically, it evolves precisely in a manner described by North (1990: 5) in that strategic choices made by organizations are influenced by the institutional framework, and 'in turn, they influence how the institutional framework evolves'.

CONTRIBUTIONS, CRITIQUES AND EXTENSIONS

Contributions

While a short chapter such as the present one is certainly unable to do justice to such a vast and expanding literature,[3] it is evident that significant progress has been made in the past decade or so. At least two major contributions emerge. First, through developing and extending an institution-based view of business strategy, research on Asian organizations has addressed head-on the very first fundamental question in strategic management, 'why firm strategies differ', identified by Rumelt *et al.* (1994). Note that this new perspective does not imply a rejection of existing work based on competition- and resource-based views. Elsewhere (Peng, 2001b: 821), I have argued that there is substantial room to integrate the more established resource-based view with the emerging institution-based view of business strategy. It is important to note that these perspectives are not mutually exclusive. The institution-based view supplements and enriches mainstream strategy research by drawing attention to the often overlooked importance of institutions, both formal and informal, that are broader than the traditional notion of national cultural differences (Hoskisson *et al.*, 2000; Peng *et al.*, 2005; Wright *et al.*, 2005).

The recent growth of interest in institutional research is probably a reaction to its 'back-burner' status in the strategy research agenda for a long time. Moreover, not only does existing strategy research focus largely on the West, but so does most institutional work. As a result, the importance of institutions fades into the background and is generally ignored by most strategy researchers. A focus on Asian economies is therefore theoretically important because it allows us to highlight the importance of institutional forces (Scott, 1995: 146). In other words, Asian economies have become 'viable research laboratories' (Shenkar and von Glinow, 1994: 56). Such work, I believe, has provided the *strongest* support for the institution-based view. This is because research in developed economies, where the 'rules of the game' are taken for granted, has had a difficult time separating the institutional effect on firm strategy and performance independently of economic and cultural effects. Research on non-Western economies, on the other hand, has not only clearly demonstrated that institutions matter, but also made significant progress to take on the challenge suggested by Powell (1996: 297) to specify the *nature* of such a link in terms of 'how they matter, under what circumstances, to what extent, and in what ways'.

Second, in addition to advancing strategy research, institution-based research on business strategies in Asian economies also contributes to institutional theory by demonstrating the benefits of integrating with efficiency-oriented research. Some institutional theorists suggest that the 'new institutionalism . . . comprises a *rejection* of rational-actor models' often found in efficiency-based research (DiMaggio and Powell, 1991: 8, added emphasis). While such a perspective may be insightful when studying educational institutions and public bureaucracies, where institutional research initially rose, recent work argues against pitting 'strategic and institutional', 'substantive and symbolic', and 'economic and social' factors against each other (Powell, 1996: 295). When institutional theory moves away from schools and bureaucracies to assert its influence in the arena of efficiency-driven business organizations, a focus on efficiency outcomes becomes necessary (Oliver, 1997; Scott, 1995). Otherwise, the usefulness of institutional theory in explaining performance-driven organizational phenomena such as business strategy is limited.

In our particular case, traditional institutional analysis would suggest that certain strategies (for example supplier relations in Japan, conglomerate diversification in India and South Korea) persist simply because such a practice is widely adopted (or institutionalized) independently of evidence that it 'works'. Such a perspective, however, has difficulty in accommodating the emerging evidence documenting concrete performance benefits associated with these strategies (Khanna and Palepu, 2000; Khanna and Rivkin, 2001). At this conjuncture, an integrative approach incorporating both the institutional perspective and the efficiency perspective would be sensible. The challenge for strategy researchers is to uncover the underlying mechanisms that relate institutions to organizational strategies, and then to link them with firm performance (Peng and Luo, 2000).

Critiques and Extensions

Originating in the 1970s, the new institutionalism in the social sciences was still in its adolescence by the 1980s (Scott, 1995), and its application to strategic management is a more recent development (Oliver, 1997). Note that virtually all key references reviewed in the four substantive sections were published in the 1990s and beyond. As a result, there are a number of important problems that existing research has yet to address. Perhaps foremost is the need for more theoretical development that addresses the question first raised by Coase (1937): 'What is the nature of the firm?' A lot of existing work on 'firm' strategies does not agree on what exactly a firm is. A firm in the West has relatively clear legal boundaries characterized by hierarchical control by top management (Williamson, 1985). A firm, especially the large conglomerate, in many Asian economies tends to have 'blurring' boundaries permeated by personal connections, partial ownerships and board interlocks. Such a loosely defined organization is often called a 'business group' (Granovetter, 1994). The difficulty in defining firm (or group) boundaries has not only led to empirical problems when measuring their size, strategy and performance (Khanna and Rivkin, 2001), but also resulted in a conceptual debate on whether these organizations qualify as 'firms'.

Specifically, Hamilton and Feenstra (1995: 58) argue that the narrowly defined Coasian firm with clear boundaries 'does not have the same empirical and conceptual significance throughout the world but, rather, is a prominent feature . . . only in modern Western societies'. While research on *keiretsu* networks in Japan has forced strategy researchers to examine the validity of our conceptualization of the firm based on the Western model, more recent work finds that similar networks dominate the organizational landscape in many Asian countries. A traditional answer is to suggest that these organizations are 'outliers' operating under a different set of logic, and that the field can afford to ignore them and develop 'grand' theories (mostly focusing on Western economies). However, in light of the growing importance of Asian economies and their increased integration with the rest of the world, such an answer becomes indefensible, if we, as a field, ever endeavour to approach a *global* science of organizations (Peng *et al.*, 2001a). While delineating the essence of this debate is beyond the scope of this chapter, future conceptual progress on what constitutes a 'firm' is clearly needed when carrying out strategy research in both Western and non-Western economies.

Second, most existing research is of a static nature. Scholars propose and test *linear* directions, for example close supplier relations and conglomerate diversification lead to better performance. The *dynamic* aspects of the complex relationships have been rarely explored. For example, supplier relations that are too close may introduce rigidities in product designs, resulting in a loss of much-needed flexibility. It is not known, however, how close the relationship with suppliers is 'too close'. After all, conglomerates in Asian economies confront the same problems that plague those in the West: the more activities a firm engages in, the harder it is for the head office to coordinate, control and invest properly in different member units. Therefore 'how much scope is too much' remains to be explored. It is evident that, beyond a point of inflection, further diversification will only backfire (Chang and Hong, 2000; Lee *et al.*, 2007). In future research, how to identify such a point of inflection in highly dynamic and uncertain institutional environments remains a major research challenge.

Finally, how national cultures, interacting with institutional frameworks, affect strategic choices needs to be explored in more depth. Will strategies in Asian economies converge on Western models? Given that individual managers making strategic decisions are influenced by their own national cultures (Hofstede, 1991), convergence is not likely to be the case, at least in the short run (Chen, 2001). On the other hand, complete divergence is also not feasible in today's increasingly integrated global economy. By implication, what seems more likely is 'crossvergence', in that strategies in non-Western economies will continue to be different from those observed in the West and, yet, beyond some point of inflection discussed above, gradually moving toward more similar (but not the same) strategies, as more market-supporting institutions are developed (Young *et al.*, 2002; see also Chapters 8 and 18 in this volume). Currently, we know very little about how these cultural processes manifest themselves in strategic choices and therefore need to pay attention to these processes in future research.

CONCLUSIONS

This chapter has focused on why firm strategies differ, by exploring the underlying institutional frameworks that drive strategic choices. Since 'frame-breaking experiences only come from examining and comprehending organizations operating in other places and other times' (Scott, 1995: 151), business strategies in Asian organizations have recently attracted significant research attention. Overall, research in this area has increasingly appeared in leading journals, thus starting to disseminate this knowledge and assert its influence in the mainstream literature (Peng, 2001b; Peng *et al.*, 2001c; Wright *et al.*, 2005; see also Chapters 2 and 10 in this volume). To be sure, the studies reviewed in this chapter, mostly published in the 1990s, are just the early wave of research probing into the complex and dynamic relationships among institutions, organizations and strategic choices. They are certainly not the final words on them. Companies' strategic moves and our learning about them are not likely to stop soon. One thing for sure is that the importance of institutional influences on business strategies will be increasingly appreciated in the new millennium, thus necessitating more attention from researchers and practitioners, as well as policy makers not only in Asia, but also around the world (Peng, 2006).

NOTES

1. This chapter is adapted from an article originally published in the *Asia Pacific Journal of Management*, 2002, **19**(2), 251–67. Additional work on this chapter was supported in part by a National Science Foundation CAREER grant (SES 0552089, formerly known as a Young Investigator Award). Work on the original article was supported in part by the Center for International Business Education and Research, Center for East Asian Studies, and Office of International Affairs, The Ohio State University. I thank Henry Yeung, C.M. Lau and the two anonymous *APJM* reviewers for their encouragement and guidance on this chapter, and Yi Jiang and Kenny Oh for research assistance. The views expressed are mine and not necessarily those of the funding agencies.
2. The other four most fundamental questions are (1) How do firms behave? (2) How are strategy outcomes affected by strategy processes? (3) What determines the scope of the firm? (4) What determines the international success and failure of firms? While other questions can be raised, according to Rumelt *et al.* (1994: 570), they 'all relate in one way or another' to these five questions.
3. For a detailed review of management and organizational research on Greater China, see Peng *et al.* (2001c). See also Chapters 2, 6 and 10 in this volume.

REFERENCES

Au, K., M.W. Peng and D. Wang (2000), 'Interlocking directorates, firm strategies, and performance in Hong Kong: towards a research agenda', *Asia Pacific Journal of Management*, **17**(1), 29–47.

Barney, J. (1991), 'Firm resources and sustained competitive advantage', *Journal of Management*, **17**, 99–120.

Beamish, P. (1993), 'The characteristics of joint ventures in the People's Republic of China', *Journal of International Marketing*, **1**(2), 29–48.

Boddewyn, J. and T. Brewer (1994), 'International-business political behavior: new theoretical directions', *Academy of Management Review*, **19**, 119–43.

Boisot, M. and J. Child (1996), 'From fiefs to clans and network capitalism: expanding China's emerging economic order', *Administrative Science Quarterly*, **41**, 600–628.

Bruton, G., D. Ahlstrom and J. Wan (2001), 'Turnaround success of large and midsize Chinese owned firms: evidence from Hong Kong and Thailand', *Journal of World Business*, **36**, 146–65.

Carroll, G. (1993), 'A sociological view on why firms differ', *Strategic Management Journal*, **14**, 237–49.

Chang, S.J. and J. Hong (2000), 'Economic performance of group-affiliated companies in Korea: intragroup resource sharing and internal business transactions', *Academy of Management Journal*, **43**, 429–49.

Chen, M.-J. (2001), *Inside Chinese Business*, Boston: Harvard Business School Press.

Child, J. (1972), 'Organizational structure, environment, and performance: the role of strategic choice', *Sociology*, **6**, 1–22.

Child, J. (1994), *Management in China During the Age of Reform*, Cambridge, UK: Cambridge University Press.

Chung, C. (2001), 'Markets, culture, and institutions: the emergence of large business groups in Taiwan, 1950s–1970s', *Journal of Management Studies*, **38**, 719–45.

Coase, R. (1937), 'The nature of the firm', *Economica*, **4**, 386–405.

Davis, L. and D. North (1971), *Institutional Change and American Economic Growth*, Cambridge, UK: Cambridge University Press.

DiMaggio, P. and W. Powell (1991), 'Introduction', in W. Powell and P. DiMaggio (eds), *The New Institutionalism in Organizational Analysis*, Chicago: University of Chicago Press.

Dore, R. (1987), *Taking Japan Seriously*, Stanford, CA: Stanford University Press.

Dyer, J. (1997), 'Effective interfirm collaboration: how firms minimize transaction costs and maximize transaction value', *Strategic Management Journal*, **18**, 535–56.

Dyer, J. and K. Nobeoka (2000), 'Creating and managing a high-performance knowledge-sharing network: the Toyota case', *Strategic Management Journal*, **21**, 345–67.

Farh, J., C. Earley and B. Cheng (1997), 'Impetus for action: a cultural analysis of justice and organizational citizenship behavior in Chinese society', *Administrative Science Quarterly*, **42**, 421–44.

Fukuyama, F. (1996), *Trust: The Social Virtues and the Creation of Prosperity*, New York: Free Press.

Gerlach, M. (1992), *Alliance Capitalism: The Social Organization of Japanese Business*, Berkeley: University of California Press.

Grabher, G. and D. Stark (eds) (1997), *Restructuring Networks in Post-Socialism*, Oxford: Oxford University Press.

Granovetter, M. (1994), 'Business groups', in N. Smesler and R. Swedberg (eds), *Handbook of Economic Sociology*, Princeton, NJ: Princeton University Press, pp. 453–75.

Hamilton, G. and R. Feenstra (1995), 'Varieties of hierarchies and markets: an introduction', *Industrial and Corporate Change*, **4**, 51–91.

Hill, C. (1995), 'National institutional structures, transaction cost economizing, and competitive advantage: the case of Japan', *Organization Science*, **6**, 119–31.

Hofstede, G. (1991), *Cultures and Organizations*, New York: McGraw-Hill.

Hoskisson, R. and M. Hitt (1994), *Downscoping*, New York: Oxford University Press.

Hoskisson, R., L. Eden, C.M. Lau and M. Wright (2000), 'Strategy in emerging economies', *Academy of Management Journal*, **43**, 249–67.

Keister, L. (2000), *Chinese Business Groups*, New York: Oxford University Press.

Kelley, L. and R. Worthley (1981), 'The role of culture in comparative management: a cross-cultural perspective', *Academy of Management Journal*, **24**, 164–73.

Khanna, T. and K. Palepu (1997), 'Why focused strategies may be wrong for emerging markets', *Harvard Business Review*, July–August, 41–51.

Khanna, T. and K. Palepu (2000), 'Is group affiliation profitable in emerging markets? An analysis of diversified Indian business groups', *Journal of Finance*, **55**, 867–91.

Khanna, T. and J. Rivkin (2001), 'Estimating the performance effects of business groups in emerging markets', *Strategic Management Journal*, **22**, 45–74.

Lau, C.M. and L. Busenitz (2001), 'Growth intentions of entrepreneurs in a transition economy: The People's Republic of China', *Entrepreneurship Theory and Research*, Fall, 5–20.

Lau, C.M. and H. Ngo (2001), 'Organization development and firm performance: a comparison of multinational and local firms', *Journal of International Business Studies*, **32**, 95–114.

Lawrence, P. and J. Lorsch (1969), *Organization and Environment*, Homewood, IL: Irwin.

Lee, K., M.W. Peng and K. Lee (2007), 'From diversification premium to diversification discount during institutional transitions', *Journal of World Business* (in press).

Lim, G. and T. Teck (1995), 'Diversification strategies, firm characteristics, and performance among Singapore firms', *International Journal of Management*, **12**, 223–33.

Linz, S. and G. Krueger (1998), 'Enterprise restructuring in Russia's transition economy: formal and informal mechanisms', *Comparative Economic Studies*, **40**, 5–52.

Luo, Y. and M.W. Peng (1999), 'Learning to compete in a transition economy: experience, environment, and performance', *Journal of International Business Studies*, **30**(2), 269–96.

Matsusaka, J. (1993), 'Takeover motives during the conglomerate merger wave', *RAND Journal of Economics*, **24**, 357–79.

McGrath, R., I. MacMillan, I. Yang and W. Tsai (1992), 'Does culture endure, or is it malleable? Issues for entrepreneurial economic development', *Journal of Business Venturing*, **7**, 441–58.

Mitchell, R., B. Smith, K. Seawright and E. Morse (2000), 'Cross-cultural cognitions and the venture creation decision', *Academy of Management Journal*, **43**, 974–93.

Nelson, R. (1991), 'Why do firms differ and how does it matter?', *Strategic Management Journal*, **12** (winter), 61–74.

North, D. (1990), *Institutions, Institutional Change, and Economic Performance*, Cambridge, MA: Harvard University Press.

Oliver, C. (1997), 'Sustainable competitive advantage: combining institutional and resource-based views', *Strategic Management Journal*, **18**, 679–713.

Peng, M.W. (1997), 'Firm growth in transition economies: three longitudinal cases from China, 1989–96', *Organization Studies*, **18**(3), 385–413.

Peng, M.W. (2000a), *Business Strategies in Transition Economies*, Thousand Oaks, CA: Sage.

Peng, M.W. (2000b), 'Controlling the foreign agent: how governments deal with multinationals in a transition economy', *Management International Review*, **40**(2), 141–65.

Peng, M.W. (2001a), 'How entrepreneurs create wealth in transition economies', *Academy of Management Executive*, **15**(1), 95–108.

Peng, M.W. (2001b), 'The resource-based view and international business', *Journal of Management*, **27**(6), 803–29.

Peng, M.W. (2002), 'Cultures, institutions, and strategic choices: towards an institutional perspective on business strategy', in M. Gannon and K. Newman (eds), *The Blackwell Handbook of Cross-Cultural Management*, Cambridge, UK: Blackwell, pp. 52–66.

Peng, M.W. (2003), 'Institutional transitions and strategic choices', *Academy of Management Review*, **28**(2), 275–96.

Peng, M.W. (2006), *Global Strategy*, Cincinnati: Thomson South-Western.

Peng, M.W. and P. Heath (1996), 'The growth of the firm in planned economies in transition: institutions, organizations, and strategic choice', *Academy of Management Review*, **21**(2), 492–528.

Peng, M.W. and Y. Luo (2000), 'Managerial ties and firm performance in a transition economy: the nature of a micro–macro link', *Academy of Management Journal*, **43**(3), 486–501.

Peng, M.W., S. Lee and J. Tan (2001a), 'The *keiretsu* in Asia: implications for multilevel theories of competitive advantage', *Journal of International Management*, **7**(4), 253–76.

Peng, M.W., K. Au and D. Wang (2001b), 'Interlocking directorates as corporate governance in Third World multinationals: theory and evidence from Thailand', *Asia Pacific Journal of Management*, **18**(2), 161–81.

Peng, M.W., Y. Lu, O. Shenkar and D. Wang (2001c), 'Treasures in the china house: a review of management and organizational research on Greater China', *Journal of Business Research*, **52**(2), 95–110.

Peng, M.W., S. Lee and D. Wang (2005), 'What determines the scope of the firm over time? A focus on institutional relatedness', *Academy of Management Review*, **30**(3), 622–33.

Peng, M.W., Y. Luo and L. Sun (1999), 'Firm growth via mergers and acquisitions in China', in L. Kelley and Y. Luo (eds.), *China 2000: Emerging business issue*, Thousand Oaks, CA: Sage, pp. 73–100.

Penrose, E. (1959), *The Theory of the Growth of the Firm*, New York: Wiley.

Porter, M. (1980), *Competitive Strategy*, New York: Free Press.

Powell, W. (1996), 'Commentary on the nature of institutional embeddedness', *Advances in Strategic Management*, **13**, 293–300.

Powell, W. and P. DiMaggio (eds) (1991), *The New Institutionalism in Organizational Analysis*, Chicago: University of Chicago Press.

Puffer, S. (1994), 'Understanding the bear: a portrait of Russian business leaders', *Academy of Management Executive*, **8**(1), 41–54.

Rumelt, R., D. Schendel and D. Teece (eds) (1994), *Fundamental Issues in Strategy: A Research Agenda*, Boston: Harvard Business School Press.

Scott, W.R. (1995), *Institutions and Organizations*, Thousand Oaks, CA: Sage.

Shenkar, O. and J. Li (1999), 'Knowledge search in international cooperative ventures', *Organization Science*, **10**, 134–43.

Shenkar, O. and M. von Glinow (1994), 'Paradoxes of organizational theory and research: using the case of China to illustrate national contingency', *Management Science*, **40**, 56–71.

Spicer, A., G. McDermott and B. Kogut (2000), 'Entrepreneurship and privatization in Central Europe: the tenuous balance between destruction and creation', *Academy of Management Review*, **25**, 630–49.

Stark, D. (1996), 'Recombinant property in East European capitalism', *American Journal of Sociology*, **101**, 993–1027.

Tan, J. and R. Litschert (1994), 'Environment–strategy relationship and its performance implications: an empirical study of the Chinese electronics industry', *Strategic Management Journal*, **15**, 1–20.

Tan, J. and M.W. Peng (2002), 'Culture, nation, and entrepreneurship: implications for an emerging economy', working paper, Fisher College of Business, The Ohio State University.

Wan, C. (1998), 'International diversification, product diversification, and firm performance of Hong Kong MNCs', *Asia Pacific Journal of Management*, **15**, 205–17.

White, S. (2000), 'Competition, capabilities, and the make, buy, or ally decisions of Chinese state-owned firms', *Academy of Management Journal*, **43**, 324–41.

Williamson, O. (1985), *The Economic Institutions of Capitalism*, New York: Free Press.

Williamson, O. (1991), 'Strategizing, economizing, and economic organization', *Strategic Management Journal*, **12** (winter), 75–94.

Wright, M., I. Filatotchev, R.E. Hoskisson and M.W. Peng (2005), 'Strategy research in emerging economies: challenging the conventional wisdom', *Journal of Management Studies*, **42**(1), 1–33.

Xin, K. and J. Pearce (1996), '*Guanxi:* good connections as substitutes for institutional support', *Academy of Management Journal*, **39**, 1641–58.

Yan, A. and B. Gray (1994), 'Bargaining power, management control, and performance in U.S.–China joint ventures: a comparative case study', *Academy of Management Journal*, **37**, 1478–1517.

Young, M., M.W. Peng, D. Ahlstrom, G. Bruton and Y. Jiang (2002), 'Governing the corporation in emerging economies: a principal–principal agency perspective', working paper, The Chinese University of Hong Kong.

Zhang, B. and M.W. Peng (2000), 'Telecom competition, post-WTO style', *China Business Review*, May–June, 12–21.

4. *Guanxi* as the Chinese norm for personalized social capital: toward an integrated duality framework of informal exchange

Peter Ping Li

The apparent success of China's economic transition and its unique institutional context has attracted growing academic interest in recent years (for example Tsui *et al.*, 2004). The focus of the research is on how to explain the institutional context for China's successful economic transition (Boisot and Child, 1996; Cao *et al.*, 1999; Li, 2005a). The commonly evoked notion for explaining China's institutional context and its reform experience is *guanxi* (loosely translated as 'personal ties'), but there are debates about its nature, content, process, antecedents and consequences (see Gold *et al.*, 2002 for a review). Besides, there is much conceptual confusion regarding the distinction and similarity between *guanxi* and social capital (Gold *et al.*, 2002; Lin, 2001a), while the study of social capital suffers from conceptual confusions regarding the level of analysis, content and process (Adler and Kwon, 2002; Burt, 2001; Lin, 1999, 2001b; Portes, 1998; Woolcock, 1998). A systematic research on *guanxi* could shed new light on not only the reform experience of China, but also the debates over *guanxi* and social capital. Further, both *guanxi* and social capital are informal norms (Adler and Kwon, 2002; Li, 1998), whose roles have been largely neglected, especially its links with formal ones (Li, 2005a; Pejovich, 1999). Hence, the significance of *guanxi* as an informal norm lies in its potentials for the development of more geocentric theories by integrating the distinctions and interactions between formal and informal institutions across countries (Boisot and Child, 1996; Li, 1998; Lovett *et al.*, 1999; see also Chapter 3 in this volume).

This chapter reconciles and synthesizes the different views about *guanxi* in the institutional context of China in contrast to those about social capital in the institutional context of the West. I apply the *duality lens* (that is perceiving each phenomenon as consisting of two distinctive (often opposite) and yet interactive elements) to developing an integrated framework of informal exchange, with exchange event, tie and institution as the three-level component as well as strong, weak and total *guanxi* as the three-form component of a social–economic exchange paradigm. Both kin and non-kin strong *guanxi* ties are pervasive in China and East Asia, whereas group-based non-kin weak social ties are pervasive in the West. With its central function of 'bending the rules', especially under the most challenging conditions of high uncertainty, *guanxi* can be both positive and negative. The most positive effect of strong *guanxi* lies in its unique roles of not only preventing the negative, but also promoting the positive, via trust and relationship citizenship behaviours (RCB) to replace the ineffective formal rules or supplement the effective formal rules. The most negative effect of *guanxi* lies in its unique role of fostering systemic corruption, thereby suppressing or sabotaging the effective formal rules.

The central theme of this chapter is that the formal–informal duality largely delineates the antecedent, content-process and consequence of *guanxi*. Via the lens of formal–informal duality, we can methodically analyse the debates over *guanxi* so as to build an integrated framework of informal exchange. I argue that *guanxi* is unique: (1) *guanxi* is the dominant norm in China and is deeply rooted in the Chinese culture (for example Confucianism); (2) strong *guanxi* is the basic form of *guanxi* for both kin and non-kin ties with the integrated instrumental–sentimental role as *guanxi* capital (that is in contrast to the non-kin ties with instrumental roles as social capital for the basic form of social ties in the West) and (3) *guanxi* can be positive and negative, with the proper version of *guanxi* as more effective than formal rules for postmodern societies. The rest of the chapter is organized into four sections. The first section introduces the lens of informal–formal duality and discusses the nature and features of *guanxi* via this lens. The second section focuses on the antecedents of *guanxi*. The third section focuses on the consequences of *guanxi*. The last section concludes with specific suggestions for future research and specific implications for managerial practice.

THE STRENGTH AND STRUCTURE OF *GUANXI*

The Duality of Formal and Informal Exchanges

An emerging implicit consensus in social science is that *guanxi* and social capital are informal in nature (Bourdieu, 1986; Coleman, 1990; Gold *et al.*, 2002; Li, 1998; Lin, 2001a, 2001b; Lovett *et al.*, 1999; Portes, 1998; Woolcock, 1998; Yang, 1994). To understand the informal nature of *guanxi* and social capital, we need to define explicitly informal exchange, tie and institution so as to clearly distinguish them from formal ones. Despite its central importance, however, there are few explicit definitions of formal or informal elements. Most researchers simply adopt the terms without defining them, including institutional research (for example North, 1990; Pejovich, 1999) and organization research (for example Das and Teng, 2001; Poppo and Zenger, 2002; Williamson, 1993). Further, the critical distinction and interaction between formal and informal elements, which have been the core of the social exchange perspective, have largely been neglected in the study of network structure (for example Coleman, 1990; Burt, 2001), strategic alliance (for example Das and Teng, 2001), social embeddedness (for example Granovetter, 1985) and tie strength (for example Levin and Cross, 2004).

To differentiate systematically the formal from the informal, we must explicitly define formality and informality. We can integrate different notions of formal–informal dimensions in terms of explicit versus implicit codification (Cardinal *et al.*, 2004; Helmke and Levitsky, 2003; Scott, 2003), precise versus open-ended agreement (Jones *et al.*, 1997), imposed versus spontaneous formation (Cardinal *et al.*, 2004; Helmke and Levitsky, 2003; Morand, 1995), external versus internal source (Das and Teng, 2001), tight versus loose enforcement (Morand, 1995), legal versus social power (Jones *et al.*, 1997), objective versus subjective approach (Cardinal *et al.*, 2004) and personal–impersonal process (Cardinal *et al.*, 2004; Morand, 1995; Scott, 2003). We identify five primary dimensions of formality–informality (Li, 2005a): (1) codification, (2) formation, (3) enforcement, (4) power, and (5) person. *Informality* refers to the nature of social ontology (for example exchange events and ties) as implicitly assumed, endogenously formed and flexibly enforced by horizontal peers in a personalized process (people-oriented, subjective, affective, sentimental and particularistic). *Formality*, as explicitly prescribed, is exogenously formed and rigidly enforced by vertical authority in a depersonalized process (task-oriented, objective, cognitive, instrumental and universalistic).

According to the five criteria, social exchange, relational contract, *guanxi*, social capital, friendship, network form, non-verbal communication, tacit knowledge and intuitive cognition tend to be strongly informal; clan control, loose strategic alliance, religion, cultural values, ethical norms and transformational leadership tend to be weakly informal; formal control, economic exchange, law, authority, ownership, hierarchy form, transactional leadership, verbal communication, explicit knowledge and analytic cognition tend to be strongly formal; market price, market form and decentralized decision making tend to be weakly formal. We argue that formal and informal elements can be further classified in terms of specific content and relative strength within their own categories. Specifically, strongly informal elements (for example trust) can be divided into stronger ones (for example affective trust) and weaker ones (for example cognitive trust); weakly informal elements (for example social norms and values) can be divided into stronger ones (for example shared values) and weaker ones (for example imposed norms); strongly formal elements (for example authority and law) can be divided into stronger ones (for example tight enforcement of legal rules and authoritarian control) and weaker ones (for example loose application of legal rules and participative management); and weakly formal elements (for example market price) can be divided as stronger ones (for example regulated pricing) and weaker ones (for example free pricing).

If we consider *institution* as a system to regulate the content and process of exchange (as events or ties) between embedded actors (cf. North, 1990), we can divide institutions into formal rule and informal norm. While institution is a macro-level unit of analysis, exchange event and tie are two lower-level units of analysis. Specifically, exchange event or action is a micro-level unit of analysis, whereas exchange tie or relationship (that is a repeated pattern of exchange events or actions – as an exchange norm – between two actors) is a mid-level unit of analysis as a bridge between exchange event and exchange institution. Consequently, events, ties and institutions are interrelated as exchange-related entities at three different levels. Hereafter, we study *guanxi* as a mid-level mediator between exchange event as practice and exchange institution as regulation. In this sense, *guanxi* has dual roles: the discrete behaviours of *guanxi* as specific events, and the generic routines of *guanxi* as a pervasive norm, thus an informal institution. This is consistent with the perspective of social exchange (Blau, 1964; Cook and Emerson, 1978). In particular, we relate the notion of *guanxi* to the notion of total trust as the anchor (antecedent) and embodiment (consequence) of all exchange ties. This notion differentiates and integrates various types of trust (for example personalized strong trust is related to strong tie, while depersonalized weak trust is related to weak tie) with various types of exchange mode (for example strong trust and strong tie are related to the exchange mode of commitment, whereas weak tie and weak trust are related to the exchange mode of control).

The Duality of Strong and Weak Natures

The defining nature of *guanxi*

Despite its popularity in both practice and research, there is no universally accepted conceptualization of *guanxi*. Previous attempts to define it specifically have been controversial (see Bian, 2001; Chen and Chen, 2004; Gold *et al.*, 2002; Lin, 2001a; Luo, 2000 for reviews). The central issue of the debate lies in the unique nature of *guanxi* in contrast to the notion of social capital. We adopt the duality perspective to distinguish and integrate both converging and diverging views regarding the essential dimensions of *guanxi*, so as to develop three notions of it (that is weak, strong and total *guanxi*). Further, we link the three notions of *guanxi* to the three notions of trust (that is weak, strong and total trust) and social capital (that is weak, strong and total social capital).

The converging consensus lies in two essential characters of *guanxi* (that is institutional and interpersonal), whereas the diverging debate lies in the other two essential characters (that is instrumental or sentimental and positive or negative). First, most scholars view *guanxi* as a cultural norm, thus an informal institution (for example Chen and Chen, 2004; Fei, 1992 [1947]; Jacobs, 1979; King, 1991; Li, 1998; Liang, 1986 [1949]; Luo, 2000; Pye, 1995; Yang, 1994; cf. Guthrie, 1998). In particular, they regard the pervasiveness of *guanxi* in China as evidence of weak formal institutions and the need for *guanxi* as an informal substitute. Second, all scholars consider *guanxi* as interpersonal ties, and most regard *guanxi* as particularistic or personalized, thus primarily at the dyadic level and secondarily at the network (for example kinship- or clan-specific) level (for example Chen and Chen, 2004; Farh *et al.*, 1998; Jacobs, 1979; King, 1991; Kipnis, 1997; Li, 1998; Lovett *et al.*, 1999; Luo, 2000; Yan, 1996; Yang, 1994).

Third, scholars debate over the functional nature and the sources of *guanxi* (Bian, 2001; Lin, 2001a). Some regard *guanxi* capital as largely instrumental, as in the case of non-kin weak ties (for example Gold, 1985; Luo, 2000; Pye, 1995; Xin and Pearce, 1996). Others regard *guanxi* capital as largely sentimental, as in the case of kin strong ties (for example Fei, 1992 [1947]; Liang, 1986 [1949]). Still others regard *guanxi* capital as both instrumental and sentimental, as in the case of non-kin strong ties (for example Chen and Chen, 2004; Chung and Hamilton, 2001; Hwang, 1987; Kipnis, 1997; Li, 1998; Lin, 2001a; Yang, 1994). It is worth noting that *guanxi* as non-kin weak tie with instrumental capital at the network level is similar to social tie and social capital. *Guanxi* as strong tie with instrumental and sentimental capital at the dyadic level is distinct from social tie and social capital (Li, 2005b; cf. Bourdieu, 1986; Coleman, 1990; Lin, 2001b; Portes, 1998; Putnam, 2004). If we focus on the similarity between social tie (social capital) and *guanxi* (*guanxi* capital), we can adopt the notion of weak *guanxi*. If we focus on the distinction between them, we can adopt the notion of strong *guanxi*. If we study both weak and strong *guanxi*, we can adopt the notion of total *guanxi*. In this sense, if we redefine social tie and social capital into three notions (that is weak, strong and total social tie and social capital), we may regard *guanxi* (*guanxi* capital) as the Chinese version of social ties (social capital) rooted in the unique institutional context of China, with the interplays between weak formal institutions and strong informal ones in the history of China.

Fourth, scholars debate over the effect and fate of *guanxi* in modern societies (Gold *et al.*, 2002). Despite their general agreement over the unique role of *guanxi* as an informal norm to 'bend the rules', they differ in their ethical evaluations and judgments of this role. Some regard *guanxi* as largely negative and transitory (for example Gold, 1985; Guthrie, 1998). Others regard it as largely positive and persistent (for example Bian, 2001; Lovett *et al.*, 1999; Yang, 2002). Still others regard it as both positive and negative, contingent upon the specific contexts and different forms of *guanxi* (for example Li, 2005a; Pye, 1995).

Building on the above discussion, we define *total guanxi* as an informal norm of social ties that regulates and facilitates privileged access to personalized exchange at both dyadic and network levels. According to this definition, strong *guanxi* is a strongly informal norm for the privileged access to more personalized exchange (both instrumental and sentimental) largely at the dyadic level, whereas weak *guanxi* is a weakly informal norm for the privileged access to less personalized exchange (primarily instrumental), largely at the network level. To highlight the distinction between *guanxi* (capital) as a unique phenomenon in China and social tie (capital) in the West, we focus on non-kin strong *guanxi* (capital) in contrast to weak social tie (capital). As the strong form of informal exchange, strong *guanxi* is related to other informal elements (for example friendship, sentiment and trust), but distinctive from formal ones (for example legal contract, market price and hierarchy authority) (Li, 1998).

Specifically, the nature of strong *guanxi* can be best delineated by its sentimental, personalized, dyadic, reciprocal, long-term and indeterminate features (Chen and Chen, 2004; Chung and Hamilton, 2001; Fei, 1992 [1947]; Gold *et al.*, 2002; Hwang, 1987; King, 1991; Kipnis, 1997; Li, 1998; Liang, 1986 [1949]; Lin, 2001a; Lovett *et al.*, 1999; Luo, 2000; Yan, 1996; Yang, 1994). First, strong *guanxi* is sentimental with personalized sentiment as a major component, distinctive from weak *guanxi* (weak social capital) based on instrumental consideration (Portes, 1998; cf. Pye, 1995). Second, strong *guanxi* is personalized as the exchange of private favours due to personalized rational, moral and affective trust. It is different from the universalistic tie based on depersonalized trust (Hosmer, 1995) or group-specific weak *guanxi* (or weak social capital) based on clan trust (Coleman, 1990; Putnam, 1993). Third, strong *guanxi* is dyadic with ego–alter ties (that is ego ties) as the primary ties, alter–alter ties (that is alter ties) as the secondary ties, and indirect ties between ego and alters (that is indirect ties) as the least important ties to constitute a focal person's centrifugal network. As a web-shaped network with the strongest ties at the core and the weaker ties at the more peripheral layers (Fei, 1992 [1947]), it is thus distinct from indirect ties at the network level (Burt, 2001).

Fourth, strong *guanxi* is reciprocal to mutual obligations and rights based on shared interests, values and sentiments. Fifth, strong *guanxi* is long-term with mutual commitment to repeated exchanges. Sixth, strong *guanxi* is indeterministic with both uncertain information and flexible expectation about the cost and benefit of repeated exchanges in terms of the time, quantity and quality of reciprocal favours. It is asymmetrical in the sense that each specific exchange is unequal because it is biased for one party at a time (with the recipient owing personal debt, that is *renqing*). So strong *guanxi* can be developed and maintained only with reciprocal favours over a long-term process of repeated exchanges.

These six features of strong *guanxi* resemble the pattern variables for the informal paradigm in contrast to the formal one (Parsons, 1951, 1960). Among these six features, the sentimental, personalized and indeterminate features are the most salient since they differentiate strongly informal ties from either weak informal or formal ties (Chung and Hamilton, 2001; Li, 1998, 2005b). In the rest of this chapter, I use total *guanxi* and *guanxi* as well as non-kin strong *guanxi* and strong *guanxi* interchangeably unless specified otherwise.

The Duality of Content and Structure Components

The levels of *guanxi*
Besides its features at the dyadic level, *guanxi* has other features at higher levels of network and system. By definition, *guanxi* ties reside in an ego network with ego ties as the primary ties, alter ties as the secondary ties, and ego's indirect ties as non-*guanxi* third-party ties. It is thus a multi-level centrifugal web (Fei, 1992 [1947]; Li, 1998; Luo, 2000; cf. Wellman *et al.*, 2002). First, strong ego ties constitute the micro-level strong *guanxi* ties. Second, direct ties, including strong and weak *guanxi* (that is weak ego ties) as well as alter ties, constitute the mid-level total *guanxi* network. Third, all ties (direct and indirect ties) constitute the macro-level overall system. I argue that the concept of 'network' should be reserved for defining direct ties. A generic structure with indirect ties should be referred to as 'systems'. Further, the micro-level *guanxi* tie and mid-level *guanxi* network are the core elements, whereas the macro-level overall system is a non-core one (Wellman *et al.*, 2002; cf. Burt, 2001; Gulati *et al.*, 2000). Our research focus should be on the levels of *guanxi* tie and *guanxi* network. It is worth noting that *guanxi* events flow via *guanxi* ties within *guanxi* network, but non-*guanxi* events flow via non-*guanxi* indirect ties within the non-*guanxi* portion of the overall system. Further, the study of *guanxi* tends to focus on strong *guanxi* at the dyadic level with dyad as the unit of analysis, but the study of social capital tends to focus on weak social capital at the network level with network as the unit of analysis.

In contrast to the traditional top-down multi-level approach (for example Burt, 2001; Coleman, 1990), I propose a bottom-up cross-level approach. This approach includes the analysis of the position and status of direct ties across the levels of tie and network, as well as the analysis of the range and density of both direct and indirect ties across the levels of network and system (Wellman *et al.*, 2002). Differently from the extant structural analysis, we explicitly distinguish ego ties from alter ties. The features of alter ties are thus not directly correlated with those of ego ties, including range, density, centrality, equality, closure and hole (cf. Burt, 2001).

The components of *guanxi*
Closely associated with the nature and level of *guanxi*, there are two major components (Gold *et al.*, 2002; Lin, 2001a), the attribute of *guanxi* at the tie level, and the structure of *guanxi* across the levels of tie and network. The attribute of *guanxi* refers to the inner quality of *guanxi*, as measured by the rational–cognitive, moral–norm and emotional–affective aspects (Chung and Hamilton, 2001; Hwang, 1987; Li, 1998). First, the rational–cognitive aspect lies in the role of shared interests embedded in *guanxi* as the informal means for economic, political and other formal ends. Second, the moral–norm aspect lies in the role of shared values embedded in *guanxi* as both moral means and moral ends in themselves. Third, the emotional–affective aspect lies in the role of shared sentiments embedded in *guanxi* as both affective means and affective ends in themselves. The

fundamental distinction between the rational–cognitive aspect and the other two is that both the moral–norm and emotional–affective aspects render *guanxi* not only the informal means, but also the informal ends in themselves (for example identity, pride, friendship and love; Kipnis, 1997; Li, 1998; Yang, 1994).

In other words, *guanxi* should be both instrumental and sentimental (Chen and Chen, 2004; Chung and Hamilton, 2001; Hwang, 1987; Jacobs, 1979; Kipnis, 1997; Li, 1998; Lin, 2001a). It is this duality feature that distinguishes informal ties from formal ties (Putnam, 1993) and stronger ties from weaker ties (cf. Bian, 1997; Granovetter, 1973, 1983). Finally, it is critical to differentiate the personalized morality of *guanxi* (that is internalized values) from the depersonalized morality of weak social capital at group or community level. Specifically, while personalized morality is the obligation to someone with strong ties (Hwang, 1987; Kipnis, 1997; Yang, 1994), generalized morality is the obligation to all members of large communities (Putnam, 1993) or local circles (Coleman, 1990), with or without direct ties. In sum, the dimensions of shared interests, values and sentiments can measure the attributes of *guanxi* at the dyadic level, similar to personalized trust (Li, 2005b).

The structure of *guanxi*

The structure of *guanxi* refers to the outer quality of ego ties, as measured by the scale–scope aspect and the position–status aspect (Wellman *et al.*, 2002). First, the scale–scope aspect lies in the range of ego ties (that is both the extent or breadth and the diversity or non-equivalence of ego ties). It includes the external ego holes: the absence of ego ties as direct access to the required resources available outside the boundary of *guanxi*, thus the lack of ego diversity or the need for new ego ties beyond the local closure. The density of alter ties (that is the extensity or breadth of direct ties between alters) includes the internal alter holes: the absence of alter ties as direct access to the required resources available inside the boundary of *guanxi*, thus the lack of alter diversity or the need for new alter ties within the local closure. Closure and hole are the key constructs about the boundary of ties at various levels, in order to separate internal direct ties from external indirect ties (Coleman, 1990), as well as the diversity of ties at various levels to gauge the need for new ties (Burt, 2001). Closure and hole must both be redefined as multifaceted variables that supplement or complement each other (Uzzi, 1997).

A narrow and rigid closure would result in a high internal density of alter ties and a tendency toward harmonization and homogeneity, with fewer external alter holes and more external ego holes. A broad and flexible closure would result in a low internal density of direct ties and a tendency toward conflict and diversity. A balance between stable closure and permeable hole is highly desirable (Burt, 2001). Moreover, the position–status aspect lies in the centrality and equality of ego ties (that is the significance and match of ego ties with ego, alter or both as owners of strategic resources or brokers for structural holes, cf. Burt, 2001; Gold *et al.*, 2002). The dining-and-wining *guanxi* clique is an example of the former (Bian, 2001). The personal authority of paternalism in the traditional Chinese patron–client ties and the corruption-based patron–client ties between bureaucrats and entrepreneurs in the present Chinese local corporatism are examples of the latter (Li, 2005a; Pye, 1995). In sum, the dimensions of range, density, centrality and equality measure *guanxi* structure.

THE ANTECEDENTS AND PROCESSES OF *GUANXI* ·

The Duality of *Guanxi* Context

It has been generally accepted that the fundamental precondition of *guanxi* is high uncertainty (see Gold *et al.*, 2002 for a review) that is due either to the historical social instability and the traditional psychological insecurity in China (Li, 1998; Pye, 1995; Redding, 1990), or to the weak formal institutions and the dual-track economic transition in modern China (Li, 2005a; Oi, 1999). Although both the historical and modern roots of China's realistic or perceived high uncertainty are important for *guanxi*, we focus on the uncertainties related to the universal implications of *guanxi* (Li, 1998; Lovett *et al.*, 1999): (1) the negative uncertainty regarding the vulnerability or risk of formal exchanges (for example transaction cost) and hostile market changes (for example the erosion of monopoly position), and (2) the positive uncertainty regarding the privilege or opportunity of informal exchanges (for example transaction value in terms of structural hole and strategic alliance for co-exploitation and co-exploration) and munificent market change (for example the emergence of opportunities for entrepreneurship). Built on personalized trust, *guanxi* has the unique potential to transform high uncertainties into high certainties (Li, 2005b).

The benefit of *guanxi* is reflected in the growing literature about dynamic competition due to accelerating technological advance and global integration (D'Aveni, 1994; Eisenhardt, 1989) as well as the increasing importance of knowledge-based dynamic capabilities (Eisenhardt and Martin, 2000) and strategic alliance (Gulati, 1995; Ilinitch *et al.*, 1996; Miles and Snow, 1994). According to the literature, there are actually two generic types of uncertainty. The first type refers to the exchange-related risk or option at the tie level, while the second type refers to the market-related risk or option at the macro level. It is suggested that informal routines are the most effective for exploration under a highly uncertain environment. In a stable environment, market and technological changes occur not only less frequently, but also more predictably. All firms can rely more on the existing explicit knowledge in a process of exploitation (Helfat, 1997; March, 1991). In a dynamic environment, market and technological changes occur not only more frequently, but also less predictably. Firms must rely more on the emerging implicit knowledge in a process of exploration (Brown and Eisenhardt, 1998; March, 1991). *Guanxi* is appropriate for both exchange-related and market-related uncertainties (Li, 1998; Lovett *et al.*, 1999). In sum, both exchange-related and market-related uncertainties are the primary preconditions for *guanxi*.

The Duality of the *Guanxi* Base

There is a serious debate over the fundamental bases for *guanxi* (see Nathan, 1993, for a review). Some regard *guanxi* as deeply rooted in the Chinese cultural values (for example Fei, 1992 [1947]; Pye, 1995; Redding, 1990; Yang, 1994), while others view *guanxi* as contingent on the context of weak formal institutions in modern China (for example Guthrie, 1998; Oi, 1999; Walder, 1986). Differing from these dichotomous views, we adopt an integrated perspective that *guanxi* is rooted in both cultural heritage and institutional context (Gold *et al.*, 2002; Li, 1998). We believe that cultural heritage, as the most fundamental informal institution, is directly related to not only other informal institutions, but also all formal institutions. The historical interaction between informal and formal institutions is responsible for the historical and present-day pervasiveness of *guanxi* in China (Li, 1998; Yang, 1994). It is logical to hypothesize that the rational–cognitive aspect of *guanxi* is primarily due to weak formal institutions, but the moral–norm and emotional–affective aspects of *guanxi* are primarily due to strong informal institutions. The Chinese have historically played down the rational–legal role of formal institutions, while advocating the moral–emotional role of informal institutions (Yang, 1994). The core of Confucianism is to structure the society as an extended family (Li, 1998). While the idealistic value of treating all the members of society as part of the family has been historically abused by the elite to suppress the development of formal institutions, informal institutions have been adopted by the Chinese people to subvert or counter the abuse of state power. Consequently, the path-dependent emphasis on informal institutions has led to weak formal institutions and further exacerbated the addiction to informal institutions in China (Li, 1998; Yang, 1994). In sum, it is the cultural value and the political choice of both the ruling elite and ordinary people that are jointly responsible for both weak formal institutions and strong informal institutions in China.

Besides the above two determinants, there is a third factor that is most relevant in today's environment of high uncertainty: the inherent imperfection or failure of formal institutions with regard to their inability to function effectively under the condition of high uncertainty (Li, 1998). In contrast, informal institutions thrive not only in the context of weak formal institutions typical of traditional societies, but also in the context of imperfect formal institutions common in postmodern societies (Boisot and Child, 1996; Li, 1998; Lovett *et al.*, 1999; Yang, 2002). A case in point is that China's economic transition seems to be bypassing the typical path of establishing strong formal institutions (for example law) as the precondition for the development of the market via a new path of readjusting informal institutions (Boisot and Child, 1996; Li, 2005a; Oi, 1999). It is still too early to draw definitive conclusions about the long-term success of the gradualist approach (Li, 2005a). It is obvious that the new path is not without its problems, the biggest of which is the systemic corruption in China (Li, 2005a). It seems that the best path would be an integration of formal and informal institutions (Li, 1998, 2005a; Lovett *et al.*, 1999).

As with special personal ties, *guanxi* is typically built up on the bases of prior repeated exchanges and future expected exchanges (Li, 1998). *Guanxi*-building can be viewed as a three-phase process: (1) the pre-*guanxi* phase from no tie to weak tie; (2) the *guanxi* proper phase from weak tie to strong tie, and (3) the post-*guanxi* from strong tie to weak tie (Chen and Chen, 2004; Li, 1998; Yang, 1994). There are two basic sources of initiating *guanxi*-building (Chen and Chen, 2004; Chung and Hamilton, 2001; Farh *et al.*, 1998; Hwang, 1987; Li, 1998): (1) ascribed (for example kinship and relational demographics), and (2) achieved (for example friendship and third-party transfer). We share the view that the immediate family members should be excluded from the *guanxi* network, but relatives and other kinships can be included in the *guanxi*-building process (Chung and Hamilton, 2001; cf. Chow and Ng, 2004). The initiation of personalized obligation and personal affectation at the pre-*guanxi* phase and their further development at the *guanxi* phase are the time-consuming outcomes of repeated informal exchanges. In sum, a 2×2 matrix table can summarize the bases and forms of *guanxi*: (1) strong kin, (2) weak kin, (3) strong non-kin, and (4) weak non-kin.

THE CONSEQUENCES AND ROLES OF *GUANXI*

The Duality of the *Guanxi* Role

There is a growing recognition that the roles of informal institutions should be analysed in relation to those of formal institutions (for example Helmke and Levitsky, 2003; Li, 2005a; Pejovich, 1999). It is clear that both formal and informal institutions are required for a society to function properly because both institutions play different roles with unique strengths and weaknesses. Informal institutions seem more effective for complex exchanges at a local level, while formal institutions seem more effective for simple exchanges at a global level (North, 1990). Further, both formal and informal institutions have their own inherent limitations. The worst imperfection of formal institutions may be bureaucracy, whereas the worst imperfection of informal institution may be cronyism; the worst for both would be systemic corruption (Li, 2005a).

In general, formal and informal institutions exist not only owing to the weak status of their counterparts but also owing to the imperfections of their counterparts (Boisot and Child, 1996; Li, 1998, 2005a; Lovett *et al.*, 1999). It is widely accepted that formal institutions emerge because of the inherent imperfections of informal institutions (for example ineffective for global exchange: North, 1990). Much less recognized is that the pervasiveness of informal institutions in modern societies is also due to the inherent imperfections of formal institutions (Boisot and Child, 1996; Li, 1998; Lovett *et al.*, 1999), rather than the inevitable effect of path-dependent development conditioned by the cultural bias (cf. North, 1990). There is a growing recognition that informal institutions become imperative for postmodern societies, since formal institutions fail to facilitate complex exchanges under high uncertainty because of their imperfect character (Boisot and Child, 1996; Li, 1998; Lovett *et al.*, 1999; Uzzi, 1997). Informal norms in general and *guanxi* in particular play two critical roles based on trust (Li, 2005b): (1) to provide access to privileged resources, and (2) to provide access to privileged exchanges. Both roles are imperative under high uncertainty. In other words, informal institutions are both instrumental and sentimental (formal institutions are only instrumental), so that they are able to play the above roles. As the strongest (that is the most instrumental and sentimental) informal norm, *guanxi* is able to offer the best access to privileged resources unavailable to formal rules, and the best access to privileged exchanges unattainable by formal rules. *Guanxi* not only prevents the negative (that is reducing transaction cost via trust as commitment), but also promotes the positive (that is enhancing transaction value via trust as commitment) as long as the pursued shared interest is not in conflict with the public interest (Heimer, 1992; Li, 1998, 2005a; Lovett *et al.*, 1999; Yang, 2002).

The Duality of the *Guanxi*–Trust Link

Trust as embedded in *guanxi*
We relate the three notions of *guanxi* to the three notions of trust with the former as the anchor (antecedent) and embodiment (consequence) of the latter: (1) weak *guanxi* is related to depersonalized trust; (2) strong *guanxi* is related to personalized trust; and (3) total *guanxi* is related to total trust (Li, 2005b). We argue that we must adopt the notion of trust-as-mode (defined as a behavioural choice as a demonstration of one's trustworthiness), if

we study the direct link between *guanxi* and trust, and the notion of trust-as-attitude (defined as a psychological attitude as a perception of others' trustworthiness) for the study of the indirect link between *guanxi* and trust. This is consistent with the structurationist perspective (Sydow, 1998), as well as the implementation intention perspective (Gollwitzer and Sheeran, 2004). We also argue that personalized sources provide the bases for proactive and promotional trust-as-mode and its derived strong trust-as-attitude, while depersonalized sources provide the bases for reactive and preventive weak trust-as-attitude that derives from control or disposition. In this sense, personalized trust as the mode of commitment results from strong *guanxi* and results in RCB related to one's self-initiated and self-regulated trustworthiness.

This view is consistent with the argument that relational trust building and formal task control are two distinctive yet interactive exchange modes as a duality (Long and Sitkin, 2004). Hence, total trust can be viewed as an interaction between personalized and depersonalized trust-as-attitude as two psychological components of total trust (Molm *et al.*, 2000; Morrow *et al.*, 2004; Rao *et al.*, 2005), as well as a distinction between trust-as-mode and control as two behavioural modes. The former refers to the behavioural component of total trust instead of the latter (Nooteboom, 2002; Saparito *et al.*, 2004; cf. Dirks and Ferrin, 2002; Long and Sitkin, 2004; Mayer and Argyres, 2004; Rao *et al.*, 2005). For instance, the evidence that instrumental trust (based on self-interest) is positively related to relational trust (based on shared interests) shows the supplementary link between depersonalized and personalized trust as two types of attitude. The evidence regarding the mediating effect of relational trust on the link between selfish behaviour and altruist behaviour suggests the conflict between trust-as-mode (relationship commitment) and control as two types of mode (Saparito *et al.*, 2004). Furthermore, the meta-analytic review (Dirks and Ferrin, 2002) shows that cognitive trust – less personalized (weaker) than affective trust – is more related to attitudinal outcomes (for example job satisfaction and organizational commitment). Total trust (with both cognitive and affective components), however, is more related to mode-related behavioural outcomes (for example job performance and organizational citizenship behaviours [OCB]), especially when the target of trust (trust referent) is a direct supervisor as opposed to organizational leadership (with the former tie as much more personalized than the latter tie).

We regard personalized trust as the mode of commitment because it defines and governs informal exchange ties at various levels (Granovetter, 1985; Lewis and Weigert, 1985; Li, 1998, 2005b; Uzzi, 1997; Yamagishi *et al.*, 1998; cf. Adler, 2001; Bradach and Eccles, 1989). In this sense, the primary *raison d'être* for personalized trust to serve as the mode of commitment is that it anchors and embodies informal exchange ties and facilitates the strongly or weakly informal exchanges of interest, value and sentiment at both dyadic and network levels (Gibbons, 2004; Li, 1998; Morrison, 2002; Nooteboom, 2002; cf. Child, 2001; Molm *et al.*, 2000; Rao *et al.*, 2005). This is well reflected by the mediating effect of trust on both positive (for example Konovsky and Pugh, 1994; Levin and Cross, 2004; McAllister, 1995; Pillai *et al.*, 1999; Vangen and Huxham, 2003; Wieselquist *et al.*, 1999) and negative associations (for example Robinson, 1996; Saparito *et al.*, 2004; Simons and Peterson, 2000) between the antecedents and consequences of all informal exchanges (for example strong tie, procedural justice, OCB, knowledge transfer, strategic choice, psychological contract and task conflict). We regard the mediating role of trust-as-mode in the relationship between strong *guanxi* and RCB as essential to the core model of trust building, with trust-as-mode as the embodiment or consequence of strong *guanxi* and the anchor or antecedent of OCB.

Trust-as-mode as the mediator between strong tie and RCB

The mechanisms and processes for trust-as-mode to serve as the mediator between strong *guanxi* and RCB can be delineated by the following features of strong trust (Gibbons, 2004; Granovetter, 1985; Li, 1998, 2005b; Nooteboom, 2002; Saparito *et al.*, 2004; Uzzi, 1997): (1) rational goodwill with reciprocal interests; (2) moral goodwill with reciprocal values; and (3) affective goodwill with reciprocal sentiments. The key to the mediating role lies in the unique feature of duality value and duality effect of strong trust. Trust-as-mode considers exchange ties not only as the means for the extrinsic ends, but also as the intrinsic ends in themselves (for example pride and friendship; Li, 1998; Li and Chang, 2004). It is a sentimental element that distinguishes strong tie from weak tie as the measure of trust strength (cf. Bian, 1997; Granovetter, 1983) and RCB from in-role behaviours (Lawler and Yoon, 1996; McAllister, 1995; Seo *et al.*, 2004).

Owing to relationship-specific reciprocal interests, values and sentiments, strong *guanxi* ties automatically lead to the choice of relationship commitment and thus trust-as-mode. Empirical evidence suggests that strong ties generate more trust, commitment and sentiment than weak ties (for example Molm *et al.*, 2000; Reagans and McEvily, 2003). In this sense, strong trust embodies strong tie for a privileged access to the strongest goodwill of all exchange partners. So strong trust can be regarded as personalized strong social capital at the dyadic and network levels (Bradach and Eccles, 1989; Gibbons, 2004; Gulati, 1995; Granovetter, 1985; Li, 1998, 2005b; Powell, 1990; Uzzi, 1997; cf. Adler, 2001; Barney and Hansen, 1994; McEvily *et al.*, 2003; Ouchi, 1980; Sako, 1998). For instance, recent empirical evidence (Rao *et al.*, 2005) shows that personalized trust is the core of strong tie that explains 25.3 per cent of the common variance between inter-firm trust and exchange tie. This finding contrasts with the 4.2 per cent of the common variance explained by depersonalized trust in terms of facilitative government. There is also evidence that strong trust embedded in friendship tie is effective in developing people-related knowledge (that is know-who), in contrast to task-related knowledge (that is know-how) (for example Gibbons, 2004; Morrison, 2002).

Furthermore, the distinction between instrumental and sentimental elements is related to that between people-oriented and task-oriented behaviours. The former tends to be sentimental as strong commitment, whereas the latter tends to be instrumental as weak commitment (Gibbons, 2004; McAllister, 1995; Settoon and Mossholder, 2002). Finally, Levin and Cross (2004) found that personalized dyadic trust is the embodiment of strong interpersonal ties that tend to mediate the relationship between strong tie and knowledge transfer. Both Gulati (1995) and Uzzi (1997) found that strong tie tends to lead to trust-as-mode as a substitute for control. The tight link between strong tie and trust-as-mode is extraordinarily reflected in situations where negative outcomes cannot affect trust-as-mode and RCB. This is because strong tie can buffer and soften the potentially damaging impact of partners' negative behaviours on one's trust-as-mode and subsequent RCB (for example Robinson, 1996; Saparito *et al.*, 2004; Simons and Peterson, 2000).

Empirical evidence also shows that trust-as-mode has a direct effect on OCB in general and RCB in particular (for example Konovsky and Pugh, 1994; McAllister, 1995; Pillai *et al.*, 1999; Wieselquist *et al.*, 1999). McAllister (1995) found that affective trust is positively related to strong OCB, whereas cognitive trust (as measured by depersonalized reputation and role) is negatively related to strong OCB. This is consistent with the view that sentiment defines the role of trust-as-mode as relationship commitment that induces strong pro-relationship behaviour (for example reciprocal OCB as RCB) to ensure successful cooperation. In this sense, RCB refers to intrinsically committed pro-relationship behaviours to strengthen exchange ties beyond the requirements of formal rules or roles (McAllister, 1995; cf. Organ, 1988). There are two basic types of RCB: strong RCB as people-oriented with strong sentiment from strong commitment, and weak RCB as task-oriented with weak sentiment from weak commitment (McAllister, 1995).

Here, we regard trust-as-mode as the mediator between strong tie and strong RCB. The supporting evidence for this view is strong. For instance, reciprocal tie (as a personalized strong tie) mediates the link between affective commitment (as trust-as-mode) and RCB (Molm *et al.*, 2000). Affective trust mediates the link between high interaction frequency (as a measure of strong tie) and strong RCB (McAllister, 1995). Commitment (as trust-as-mode) mediates the link between interdependency (as a measure of strong tie) and pro-relationship behaviour (as RCB) (Wieselquist *et al.*, 1999). Trust as a macro motive (as trust-as-mode) mediates the link between procedural justice (as a measure of possible strong tie) and OCB (Konovsky and Pugh, 1994). Covenantal relationship (as a version of trust-as-mode) mediates the link between workplace values (as a measure of strong tie) and OCB (Van Dyne *et al.*, 1994). Trust mediates the relationship between transformational leadership (as a measure of strong tie) and OCB (Pillai *et al.*, 1999). In this sense, strong *guanxi* or social tie is the anchor and embodiment of trust, while strong trust is the core of strong *guanxi* capital or strong social capital. In sum, strong *guanxi*, trust-as-mode and RCB constitute the core of the model of an interactive trust-building cycle.

The Duality of *Guanxi* Implications

The special roles of informal institutions in general and *guanxi* in particular bear two key implications. First, as the ultimate roles of institutions are not only problem-solving, but also ideal-achieving, it is critical to have a balance between formal (for global yet simple exchanges) and informal institutions (for local yet complex exchanges). Second, it is critical to have a balance between old informal ties (related to the issue of system closure for the familiarity and stability of old ties) and new informal ties (related to the issue of structural hole for the freshness and flexibility of new ties). For a proper balance between formal and informal institutions, they should be comparable and compatible (Helmke and Levitsky, 2003; Li, 2005a), as suggested by the formal–informal interaction thesis (Pejovich, 1999). First, formal and informal institutions should be comparable to supplement or complement each other. If not comparable, the more powerful one may easily replace or even suppress the less powerful one to the extent that the latter fail to counterbalance the dominance of the former (Li, 2005a).

Second, formal and informal institutions should be compatible to supplement or complement each other (Pejovich, 1999). If not compatible, they may sabotage or undermine each other when they are comparable, or the more powerful one may suppress or subdue the less powerful one (Helmke and Levitsky, 2003; Li, 2005a). Only when formal and informal institutions are both comparable and compatible will they supplement each other with compatible roles and comparable forces (Li, 2005a; Lovett *et al.*, 1999). For instance, formal institutions can delineate explicit limits within which informal institutions are allowed to exploit fully their potentials. For example, *guanxi* should be promoted so long as it does not seek private interest at the expense of public interest measured by economic efficiency and social justice. The empirical evidence about the interplay between formal and informal institutions can be found in the complementary roles of equity and personal tie, as well as the curvilinear correlation between trust and transaction cost (that is trust can reduce transaction cost only up to a point) (Uzzi, 1997).

For the balance between different informal institutions, it is critical to have a proper mix of old and new ties within the closure of network without structural holes (ibid.). First, for the most effective function of *guanxi* in terms of privileged access and complex enforcement, the most desirable ties are both strong and diverse. It is obvious that strong ties are required for the unique functions of informal institutions in general and *guanxi* in particular (Bian, 1997; Gold *et al.*, 2002; Li, 1998). Similarly, diverse ties are imperative for direct access to all the necessary resources, as well as the efficient enforcement of complex exchanges (Ruef, 2002). It is critical to separate the issue of tie strength from that of tie diversity (Burt, 2001; Lin, 1999). Contrary to the predictions of the homophily hypothesis (that is social similarity breeding tie strength: McPherson *et al.*, 2001) and the strength of weak tie argument (Granovetter, 1983; Lin, 1999), strong *guanxi* tends to be more diverse than weak social ties of weak social capital. This is because the former are more *instrumental* (more sentimental as well) than the latter (Bian, 1997; Gold *et al.*, 2002). The homophily hypothesis should be more applicable to the weak ties of social capital than to strong *guanxi* because the former are more sentimental than instrumental.

Besides, strong ties can also readily serve as the bridges or brokers for structural holes (Burt, 2001; Bian, 1997). Rather than being confined to kinship and old friendship, most strong *guanxi* ties derive gradually from new friends developed through third party transfer due to instrumental requirements (Bian, 1997; Li, 2005a; Yang, 1994). If we assume that indirect ties tend to be more diverse, indirect ties can still be strong in the sense that they are both strongly tied to third parties (Bian, 1997). Furthermore, primarily concerned with non-repeated exchanges in the case of job search, the strength of weak tie argument bears limited, if any, relevance for the study of informal institutions in general and *guanxi* in particular. This is because the latter's primary role is to facilitate repeated exchanges. Finally, tie strength as an attributive variable for a privileged access is not directly related to tie diversity as a structural variable for a generic access. Empirical evidence suggests that strong ties are best for the transfer of tacit or informal information and knowledge, while weak ties are best for the transfer of explicit or formal information and knowledge, regardless of diverse or similar nature or source (Hansen, 1999). There is also evidence that strong ties tend to be more effective for the exchange between the embedded actors with diverse (for example hierarchical or unequal) social statuses or resources (Bian, 1997; Granovetter, 1983). Even Granovetter (1983) admits that not all weak ties are diverse – only those serving as the bridges or brokers for the structural holes. In sum, strong ties are not necessarily less diverse than weak ties. So tie strength should be treated separately from tie diversity.

Second, we must conceptualize system closure and structural hole as two complementary variables (Burt, 2001). The two can be directly related to the issue of tie age, namely, old ties or new ties. System closure can be redefined as a measure of the boundary or scope of networks (primarily concerned with the familiarity and stability of old ties inside networks, cf. Coleman, 1990). Structural hole can be redefined as a measure of the diversity or variety of networks (primarily concerned with the freshness and flexibility of new ties outside networks, Burt, 2001). In that sense, the closure of *guanxi* ties is the local boundary of strong ties; that of *guanxi* network is the mid-level boundary of direct ties; and that of *guanxi* system is the global boundary of all ties (for example organization, community, nation and the world). Similarly, the hole of *guanxi* ties is the diversity of strong ties in a local closure; that of *guanxi* network is the diversity of direct ties in a mid-level closure; and that of *guanxi* system is the diversity of all ties in a global closure. Redefined as such, closure and hole become two complementary dimensions of *guanxi* structure directly related to the issue of tie age. For example, the external holes (that is the lack of diversity among the old ties in a network) are calls for new external ties (Burt, 2001). According to the above argument, tie diversity is directly related to tie age and both are more structural than attributive because both are closely linked to such structural variables as closure and hole. Consequently, like tie diversity, tie age is not directly related to tie strength (as an attributive variable of *guanxi*).

Third, both old and new ties are necessary for the effectiveness of informal institutions in general (Burt, 2001) and *guanxi* in particular (Gold *et al.*, 2002). Although not directly related to each other, the issues of tie age and tie strength are still indirectly related. For instance, while not all old ties are strong and similar, the strongest ties will be old by definition and more likely to be less diverse than new ties. Not all weak ties are new and diverse, but the newest ties will be weak by definition and more likely to be more diverse than old ties. In other words, while both old and new ties can be strong or weak, as well as diverse or similar, new ties tend to be weaker and more diverse than old ties, at least initially. In that sense, we should keep a balance between strong and weak ties. Owing to dynamic changes, prior strong ties may turn into weak ties and prior weak ties may turn into strong ties (Li, 2005a; Yang, 1994). In addition, strong and weak ties play different roles with different inherent imperfections (Hansen, 1999; Uzzi, 1997). For instance, a strong tie is best for complex exchanges under high uncertainty, but its development is slow and its impact narrow (not necessarily less diverse). A weak tie is best for simple exchanges under low uncertainty, but its development is fast and its impact broad (not necessarily more diverse) (Lin, 1999). In sum, we need to balance old ties with new ties and strong ties with weak ties.

The Duality of *Guanxi* Fate

Generally, not all types of *guanxi* can be sustainable for the long term. The types of *guanxi* with long-term positive effect will thrive, but those with long-term negative effect will vanish (cf. Guthrie, 1998; Yang, 2002). Specifically, *guanxi* that serve both private and public interest will most likely have long-term positive effects, but those that serve short-term private interest at the expense of public interest will most likely have negative effects (Li, 2005a). Further, the hierarchical or unequal *guanxi* may vanish, while the horizontal or equal *guanxi* may thrive (Bian, 2001; Yang, 2002). It is worth noting that there exist no perfect *guanxi*. Every type of *guanxi* has certain positive aspects at certain times, but the same type of *guanxi* will turn negative in the same or other aspects at other times. Further, the individualism-oriented rational–legal formal paradigm in the West is not inherently superior to the collectivism-oriented moral–affective informal paradigm in the East (Chung and Hamilton, 2001; Hitt *et al.*, 2002; Li, 1998; Lin, 2002; Lovett *et al.*, 1999; Yang, 2002). The dichotomy of modernity and traditionality is problematic because it is inaccurate to equate modernity or traditionality with the cultural values of individualism–collectivism and universalism–particularism (cf. Farh *et al.*, 1998).

Influenced by Weber (1951), those who associate individualism and universalism with modernity tend to discount collectivism and particularism. They often view the absence of Western-type institutions in the East as a sign of poor social development (for example Luhmann, 1979; North, 1990). However, we argue that this is not necessarily the case (Boisot and Child, 1996; Li, 1998; Roniger, 1994). As suggested by Boisot and Child (1996), modernization in Europe (that is a process from fief to bureaucracy and then to Western-style market) is not repeated by China's path of modernization (that is a process from fief to clan and then to Eastern-style market–network capitalism). Roniger (1994) also points out that it is not a sign of economic and social underdevelopment to have a strong patron–client relationship in a society. It is just a special type of social formation closely related to specific types of cultural bias. If modernity is indeed related to individualism–collectivism in a U-shaped relationship (that is simple society related to individualism; complex society related to collectivism; and more complex society related to individualism; see Murdock and Provost, 1973; Triandis *et al.*, 1988), we may hypothesize that extremely complex society (for example our globalizing society) is truly related to collectivism. From this perspective, the informal phenomena of *guanxi*, trust and network form represent the future rather than the past. It is interesting to note that the emerging network form resembles the centrifugal shape of the Chinese *guanxi* web (Li, 1998).

Some scholars argue that depersonalized weak tie is more critical to the modern society as the direct substitute for personalized strong tie in the traditional society (for example Bachmann, 2001; Giddens, 1990; Luhmann, 1979; Pearce, 2001; Yamagishi *et al.*, 1998; Zucker, 1986). Citing the emerging trend toward network form as a unique organizational form, other scholars (for example Gibbons, 2004; Heimer, 1992; Li, 1998; McEvily *et al.*, 2003; Powell, 1990; Uzzi, 1997; cf. Adler, 2001) contend that personalized strong tie will be more imperative in the postmodern society as the direct substitute for weak tie in the modern society. Still others suggest that both strong and weak ties are needed as hybrid forms with particularistic and universalistic elements in both modern and postmodern societies (Adler, 2001; Lane and Bachmann, 1996). We adopt an integrated view that both strong and weak ties with personalized and depersonalized trust will be significant in the postmodern society, with the strong forms as the core and the weak ones as the non-core components of total tie and trust in the postmodern society. We echo the view that the West and the East are converging toward network capitalism (for example Boisot and Child, 1996; Chung and Hamilton, 2001; Dunning, 1995; Hitt *et al.*, 2002; Li, 1998, 2005b; Lovett *et al.*, 1999; Yang, 2002). The West can incorporate the elements of personalized obligation and personal affection into its paradigm (that is a paradigm shift from its overemphasis on weak ties toward the stronger ties), whereas the East can incorporate the elements of generalized obligation and law into its own paradigm (that is a paradigm shift from its overemphasis on strong ties toward the weaker ties).

CONCLUSION

Adopting the duality lens, we have discussed the distinction and interplay between strong *guanxi* (social) and weak *guanxi* (social) ties as total informal ties, as well as the distinction and interplay between *guanxi* (social) tie and *guanxi* (social) capital. In particular, we have integrated *guanxi* tie, trust-as-mode, and RCB into an interactive model of *guanxi* building. We have argued that *guanxi*, as an informal norm, not only prevents the negative, but also promotes the positive, thanks to its privileged access to personalized trust, the core of *guanxi* (social) capital. This privilege is both instrumental and sentimental, thus the most desirable for exchanges under high uncertainty. This privilege is built through an interactive process between strong tie, trust-as-mode, and RCB pattern. We hypothesize that the whole world is converging toward a balanced system with comparable and compatible formal and informal institutions. To contribute to this convergence, we must build alternative theories based on the culture and experience of the East to supplement or even supersede the established theories based on the culture and experience of the West (for example for the work on relational rationality, see Lin, 2002; for the work on Chinese relationalism, see Hwang, 2000; for the work on geocentric framework of network form, see Li, 1998; for the work on indigenous Chinese tie, affection and trust, see Yang, 2001).

This chapter is an attempt in that direction by highlighting the duality epistemology and the duality ontology of total *guanxi* and total trust from the Chinese perspective, as well as the geocentric perspective (Li, 1998, 2005b). Further research is needed to specify the contingencies for the positive effect of *guanxi* (Pye, 1995), especially in the practice of strategic alliance and teamwork for knowledge exploration (Li, 2005b). The essential practical implications of *guanxi* include the need for the design of an alliance network to resemble the shape of a centrifugal web, as well as attention to the management of work-related emotions, trust and 'know-who' (in contrast to know-how).

REFERENCES

Adler, P.S. (2001), 'Market, hierarchy and trust: the knowledge economy and the future of capitalism', *Organization Science*, **12**, 215–34.

Adler, P.S. and S. Kwon (2002), 'Social capital: prospects for a new concept', *Academy of Management Review*, **27**, 17–40.

Bachmann, R. (2001), 'Trust, power and control in trans-organizational relations', *Organization Studies*, **22**, 337–65.

Barney, J.B. and M.H. Hansen (1994), 'Trustworthiness: can it be a source of competitive advantage?', *Strategic Management Journal*, **15** (Special Winter Issue), 175–90.

Bian, Y. (1997), 'Bringing strong ties back in: indirect ties, network bridges, and job searches in China', *American Sociological Review*, **62**, 366–85.

Bian, Y. (2001), '*Guanxi* capital and social eating in Chinese cities: theoretical models and empirical analysis', in N. Lin, K. Cook and R.S. Burt (eds), *Social Capital: Theory and Research*, New York: Aldine de Gruyter, pp. 275–95.

Blau, P. (1964), *Exchange and Power in Social Life*, New York: Wiley.

Boisot, M. and J. Child (1996), 'From fiefs to clans and network capitalism: explaining China's emerging economic order', *Administrative Science Quarterly*, **41**, 600–628.

Bourdieu, P. (1986), 'The form of capital', in J.G. Richardson (ed.), *The Handbook of Theory and Research for the Sociology of Education*, New York: Greenwood, pp. 241–58.

Bradach, J.L. and R.G. Eccles (1989), 'Price, authority, and trust: from ideal types to plural forms', *Annual Review of Sociology*, **15**, 97–118.

Brown, S.L. and K.M. Eisenhardt (1998), *Competing on the Edge: Strategy as Structural Chaos*, Boston, MA: Harvard Business School Press.

Burt, R.S. (2001), 'Structural holes versus network closure as social capital', in N. Lin, K.Cook and R.S. Burt (eds), *Social Capital: Theory and Research*, New York: Aldine de Gruyter, pp. 31–56.

Cao, Y., Y. Qian and B.R. Weingast (1999), 'From federalism, Chinese style, to privatization, Chinese style', *Economics of Transition*, **7**, 103–31.

Cardinal, L.B., S.B. Sitkin and C.P. Long (2004), 'Balancing and rebalancing in the creation and evolution of organizational control', *Organization Science*, **15**, 411–31.

Chen, X.P. and C.C. Chen (2004), 'On the intricacies of the Chinese *guanxi*: a process model of *guanxi* development', *Asian Pacific Journal of Management*, **21**, 305–24.

Child, J. (2001), 'Trust – the fundamental bond in global collaboration', *Organization Dynamics*, **29**, 274–88.

Chow, I.H. and I. Ng (2004), 'The characteristics of Chinese personal ties (*guanxi*): evidence from Hong Kong', *Organization Studies*, **25**, 1075–93.

Chung, W. and G.G. Hamilton (2001), 'Social logic as business logic: *Guanxi*, trustworthiness, and the embeddedness of Chinese business', in R.P. Appelbaum, W.L.F. Felstiner and V. Gessner (eds), *Rules and Networks: the Legal Culture of Global Business Transaction*, Oxford: Hart Publishing, pp. 325–46.

Coleman, J.S. (1990), *Foundations of Social Theory*, Cambridge, MA: Harvard University Press.

Cook, K.S. and R.M. Emerson (1978), 'Power, equity and commitment in exchange networks', *American Sociological Review*, **43**, 721–39.

D'Aveni, R.A. (1994), *Hypercompetition: Managing the Dynamics of Strategic Management*, New York: Free Press.

Das, T.K. and B. Teng (2001), 'Trust, control and risk in strategic alliances', *Organization Studies*, **22**, 251–84.

Dirks, K.T. and D. Ferrin (2002), 'Trust in leadership: meta-analytic findings and implications for research and practice', *Journal of Applied Psychology*, **87**, 611–28.

Dunning, J.H. (1995), 'Reappraising the eclectic paradigm in an age of alliance capitalism', *Journal of International Business Studies*, **26**, 461–91.

Eisenhardt, K.M. (1989), 'Making fast strategic decisions in high-velocity environment', *Academy of Management Journal*, **32**, 543–76.

Eisenhardt, K.M. and J.A. Martin (2000), 'Dynamic capabilities: what are they?', *Strategic Management Journal*, **21**, 1105–21.

Farh, J.L., A.S. Tsui, C. Xin and B.S. Cheng (1998), 'The influence of relational demography and guanxi: the Chinese case', *Organization Science*, **9**, 471–88.

Fei, X. (1992 [1947]), *From the Soil: the Foundation of Chinese society, trans. Gary G. Hamilton and Wang Zheng*, Berkeley, CA: University of California Press.

Gibbons, D.E. (2004), 'Friendship and advice networks in the context of changing professional values', *Administrative Science Quarterly*, **49**, 238–62.

Giddens, A. (1990), *The Consequences of Modernity*, Cambridge: Polity Press.

Gold, T.B. (1985), 'After comradeship: personal relations in China since the Cultural Revolution', *China Quarterly*, **104**, 657–75.

Gold, T., D. Guthrie and D. Wank (eds) (2002), *Social Connections in China: Institutions, Culture, and the Changing Nature of Guanxi*, London: Cambridge University Press.

Gollwitzer, P.M. and P. Sheeran (2004), 'Implementation intentions and goal achievement: a meta-analysis of effects and processes', working paper, New York University.

Granovetter, M. (1973), 'The strength of weak ties', *American Journal of Sociology*, **78**, 1360–80.

Granovetter, M. (1983), 'The strength of weak ties: a network theory revisited', *Sociological Theory*, **1**, 201–33.

Granovetter, M. (1985), 'Economic action and social structure: the problem of embeddedness', *American Journal of Sociology*, **91**, 481–510.

Gulati, R. (1995), 'Does familiarity breed trust? The implications of repeated ties for contractual choice in alliances', *Academy of Management Journal*, **38**, 85–112.

Gulati, R., N. Nohria and A. Zaheer (2000), 'Strategic networks', *Strategic Management Journal*, **21**, 203–15.

Guthrie, D. (1998), 'The declining significance of *guanxi* in China's economic transition', *The China Quarterly*, **154**, 254–82.

Hansen, M.T. (1999), 'The search–transfer problem: the role of weak ties in sharing knowledge across organization subunits', *Administrative Science Quarterly*, **44**, 82–111.

Heimer, C.A. (1992), 'Doing your job and helping your friends: universalistic norms about obligations to particular others in networks', in N. Nohria and R.C. Eccles (eds), *Networks and Organizations*, Boston, MA: Harvard Business School Press, pp. 143–64.

Helfat, C.E. (1997), 'Know-how and asset complementarity and dynamic capability accumulation: the case of RandD', *Strategic Management Journal*, **18**, 339–60.

Helmke, G. and S. Levitsky (2003), 'Informal institutions and comparative politics: a research agenda', paper presented at the Conference of Informal Institutions and Politics in Latin America, University of Notre Dame.

Hitt, M.A., H. Lee and E. Yucel (2002), 'The importance of social capital to the management of multinational enterprises: relational networks among Asian and Western firms', *Asia Pacific Journal of Management*, **19**, 353–72.

Hosmer, L. (1995), 'Trust: the connecting link between organisational theory and philosophical ethics', *Academy of Management Review*, **20**, 379–403.

Hwang, K.K. (1987), 'Face and favour: the Chinese power game', *American Journal of Sociology*, **92**, 944–74.

Hwang, K.K. (2000), 'Chinese relationalism: theoretical construction and methodological considerations', *Journal for the Theory of Social Behavior*, **30**, 155–78.

Ilinitch, A.Y., R.A. D'Aveni and A. Lewin (1996), 'New organisational forms and strategies for managing in hypercompetitive environment', *Organisation Science*, **7**, 211–20.

Jacobs, J.B. (1979), 'A preliminary model of particularistic ties in Chinese political alliances: KanCh'ing and Kuanhsi in a rural Taiwanese township', *The China Quarterly*, **78**, 237–73.

Jones, C., W.S. Hesterly and S.P. Borgatti (1997), 'A general theory of network governance: exchange conditions and social mechanisms', *Academy of Management Review*, **22**, 911–45.

King, A.Y. (1991), 'Kuan-hsi and network building: a sociological interpretation', *Daedalus*, **120**, 109–26.

Kipnis, A.B. (1997), *Producing Guanxi: Sentiment, Self, and Subculture in a North China Village*, Durham, NC: Duke University Press.

Konovsky, M.A. and S.D. Pugh (1994), 'Citizenship behavior and social exchange', *Academy of Management Journal*, **37**, 656–69.

Lane, C. and R. Bachmann (1996), 'The social constitution of trust: supplier relations in Britain and Germany', *Organization Studies*, **17**, 365–95.

Lawler, E.J. and J. Yoon (1996), 'Commitment in exchange relations: test of a theory of relational cohesion', *American Sociological Review*, **61**, 89–108.

Levin, D. and R. Cross (2004), 'The strength of weak ties you can trust: the mediating role of trust in effective knowledge transfer', *Management Science*, **50**, 1477–90.

Lewis, J.D. and A. Weigert (1985), 'Trust as a social reality', *Social Forces*, **63**, 967–85.

Li, P.P. (1998), 'Towards a geocentric framework of organizational form: a holistic, dynamic and paradoxical approach', *Organization Studies*, **19**, 829–61.

Li, P.P. (2005a), 'The puzzle of China's township–village enterprises: the paradox of local corporatism in a dual-track economic transition', *Management and Organization Review*, **1**, 197–224.

Li, P.P. (2005b), 'The duality of trust-as-attitude and trust-as-mode: a relationship-embedded model of interactive trust-building cycle', working paper, California State University, Stanislaus.

Li, P.P. and S.T. Chang (2004), 'A holistic framework of e-business strategy: the case of Haier in China', *Journal of Global Information Management*, **12**(2), 44–62.

Liang, S. (1986 [1949]), *The Essential Meanings of Chinese culture*, Hong Kong: Zheng Zhong Press.

Lin, N. (1999), 'Social networks and status attainment', *Annual Review of Sociology*, **25**, 467–87.

Lin, N. (2001a), '*Guanxi*: a conceptual analysis', in A.Y. So, N. Lin and D. Poston (eds), *The Chinese Triangle of Mainland–Taiwan–Hong Kong*, Westport, CT: Greenwood, pp. 153–66.

Lin, N. (2001b), *Social Capital: A Theory of Social Structure and Action*, New York: Cambridge University Press.

Lin, N. (2002), 'How the East and the West shall meet', *Development and Society*, **31**, 211–44.

Long, C.P. and S.B. Sitkin (2004), 'Trust in balance: how managers integrate trust-building and task control', working paper 2004-10-002, Olin School of Business, Washington University.

Lovett, S., L.C. Simmons and R. Kali (1999), '*Guanxi* versus the market: ethics and efficiency', *Journal of International Business Studies*, **30**, 231–48.

Luhmann, N. (1979), *Trust and Power*, Chichester: Wiley.

Luo, Y. (2000), *Guanxi and Business*, Singapore: World Scientific.

March, J. G. (1991), 'Exploration and exploitation in organisational learning', *Organisation Science*, **2**, 71–87.

Mayer, K. and N.S. Argyres (2004), 'Learning to contract: evidence from the personal computer industry', *Organization Science*, **15**, 394–410.

McAllister, D.J. (1995), 'Affect- and cognition-based trust as foundations for interpersonal cooperation in organizations', *Academy of Management Journal*, **38**, 24–59.

McEvily, B., V. Perrone and A. Zaheer (2003), 'Trust as an organizing principle', *Organization Science*, **14**, 91–103.

McPherson, M., S. Lynn and J.M. Cook (2001), 'Birds of a feature: homophily in social networks', *Annual Review of Sociology*, **27**, 415–44.

Miles, R.E. and C.C. Snow (1994), *Fit, Failure, and the Hall of Fame: How Companies Succeed and Fail*, New York: Free Press.

Molm, L., N. Takahashi and G. Peterson (2000), 'Risk and trust in social exchange: an experimental test of a classical proposition', *American Journal of Sociology*, **105**, 1396–1427.

Morand, D.A. (1995), 'The role of behavioral formality and informality in the enactment of bureaucratic versus organic organizations', *Academy of Management Review*, **20**, 831–72.

Morrison, E.W. (2002), 'Newcomers' relationships: the role of social network ties during socialization', *Academy of Management Journal*, **45**, 1149–60.

Morrow, J.L., M.H. Hansen and A.W. Pearson (2004), 'The cognitive and affective antecedents of general trust within cooperative organizations', *Journal of Managerial Issues*, **16**, 48–64.

Murdock, G.P. and C. Provost (1973), 'Measurement of cultural complexity', *Ethnology*, **12**, 379–92.

Nathan A.J. (1993), 'Is Chinese culture distinctive? A review article', *Journal of Asian Studies*, **52**, 923–36.

Nooteboom, B. (2002), *Trust: Forms, Foundations, Functions, Failures and Figures*, Cheltenham, UK and Northampton, MA, USA: Edward Elgar.

North, D. (1990), *Institutions, Institutional Change and Economic Performance*, New York: Cambridge University Press.

Oi, J.C. (1999), *Rural China takes off: Institutional Foundations of Economic Reform*, Berkeley, CA: University of California Press.

Organ, D.W. (1988), *Organizational Citizenship Behavior: the Good Soldier Syndrome*, Lexington, MA: Lexington Books.

Ouchi, W.G. (1980), 'Markets, bureaucracies and clans', *Administrative Science Quarterly*, **25**, 129–41.

Parsons, T. (1951), *The Social System*, New York: Free Press.

Parsons, T. (1960), 'Pattern variables revisited: a response to Robert Dubin', *American Sociological Review*, **25**, 467–83.

Pearce, J.L. (2001), *Organization and Management in the Embrace of Government*, Mahwah, NJ: Lawrence Erlbaum Associates.

Pejovich, S. (1999), 'The effects of the interaction of formal and informal institutions on social stability and economic development', *Journal of Markets and Morality*, **2**, 164–81.

Pillai, R., C.A. Schriesheim and E.S. Williams (1999), 'Fairness perceptions and trust as mediators for transformational and transactional leadership: a two-sample study', *Journal of Management*, **25**, 897–933.

Poppo, L. and T. Zenger (2002), 'Do formal contracts and relational governance function as substitutes or complements?', *Strategic Management Journal*, **23**, 707–25.

Portes, A. (1998), 'Social capital: its origins and applications in modern sociology', *Annual Review of Sociology*, **22**, 1–24.

Powell, W.W. (1990), 'Neither market nor hierarchy: network forms of organization', in L. Cummings and B.M. Staw (eds), *Research in Organizational Behavior*, Greenwich, CT: JAI, pp. 295–336.

Putnam, R.D. (1993), *Making Democracy Work. Civic Traditions in Modern Italy*, Princeton, NJ: Princeton University Press.

Putnam, R.D. (2004), 'Education, diversity, social cohesion and "social capital"', research paper, OECD Education Ministers Conference on Raising the Quality of Education for All, Dublin, Ireland, March.

Pye, L.W. (1995), 'Factions and the politics of *guanxi*: paradoxes in Chinese administrative and political behavior', *The China Journal*, **34**, 35–53.

Rao, A.N., J.L. Pearce and K. Xin (2005), 'Governments, reciprocal exchange and trust among business associates', *Journal of International Business Studies*, **36**, 104–18.

Reagans, R. and B. McEvily (2003), 'Network structure and knowledge transfer: the effects of cohesion and range', *Administrative Science Quarterly*, **48**, 240–67.

Redding, S.G. (1990), *The Spirit of Chinese Capitalism*, New York: De Gruyter.

Robinson, S.L. (1996), 'Trust and breach of psychological contract', *Administrative Science Quarterly*, **41**, 574–99.

Roniger, L. (1994), 'The comparative study of clientelism and the changing nature of civil society in the contemporary world', in L. Roniger and A. Gunes-Ayata (eds), *Democracy, Clientelism, and Civil Society*, London: Lynne Rienner, pp. 1–18.

Ruef, M. (2002), 'Strong ties, weak ties and islands: structural and cultural predictors of organizational innovation', *Industrial and Corporate Change*, **11**, 427–49.

Sako, M. (1998), 'Does trust improve business performance?', in C. Lane and R. Bachmann (eds), *Trust within and between Organizations: Conceptual Issues and Empirical Applications*, Oxford: Oxford University Press, pp. 88–109.

Saparito, P.A., C.C. Chen and H.J. Sapienza (2004), 'The role of relational trust in bank–small firm relationships', *Academy of Management Journal*, **47**, 400–410.

Scott, W.R. (2003), *Organizations: Rational, Natural and Open systems, 5th edn*, Eaglewood Cliffs, NJ: Prentice-Hall.

Seo, M., L.F. Barrett and J.M. Bartunek (2004), 'The role of affective experience in work motivation', *Academy of Management Review*, **29**, 423–39.

Settoon, R.P. and K.W. Mossholder (2002), 'Relational quality and relationship context as antecedents of person- and task-focused interpersonal citizenship behavior', *Journal of Applied Psychology*, **87**, 255–67.

Simons, T.L. and R.S. Peterson (2000), 'Task conflict and relationship conflict in top management teams: the pivotal role of intra-group trust', *Journal of Applied Psychology*, **85**, 102–11.

Sydow, J. (1998), 'Understanding the constitution of interorganizational trust', in C. Lane and R. Bachmann (eds), *Trust within and between Organizations: Conceptual Issues and Empirical Applications*, Oxford: Oxford University Press, pp. 31–63.

Triandis, H.C., R. Bontempo, M.J. Villareal, M. Asai and N. Lucca (1988), 'Individualism and collectivism: cross-cultural perspectives on self-in-group relationships', *Journal of Personality and Social Psychology*, **54**, 323–38.

Tsui, A.S., C.B. Schoonhoven, M.W. Meyer, C. Lau and G.T. Milkovich (eds) (2004), 'Organization and management in the midst of social transformation: the People's Republic of China', *Organization Science*, **15**, 133–44.

Uzzi, B. (1997), 'Social structure and competition in inter-firm networks: the paradox of embeddedness', *Administrative Science Quarterly*, **42**, 35–67.

Van Dyne, L., J.W. Graham and R.M. Dienesch (1994), 'Organizational citizenship behavior: construct redefinition, measurement, and validation', *Academy of Management Journal*, **37**, 765–802.

Vangen, S. and C. Huxham (2003), 'Nurturing collaborative relations: building trust in interorganizational collaboration', *Journal of Applied Behavioral Science*, **39**, 5–31.

Walder, A.G. (1986), *Communist Neo-traditionalism: Work and Authority in Chinese Industry*, Berkeley, CA: University of California Press.

Weber, M. (1951), *The Religion of China: Confucianism and Taoism*, New York: Free Press.

Wellman, B., W. Chan and W. Dong (2002), 'Networking *guanxi*', in T. Gold, D. Guthrie and D. Wank (eds), *Social Connections in China: Institutions, Culture, and the Changing Nature of Guanxi*: Cambridge: Cambridge University Press, pp. 221–42.

Wieselquist, J., C.E. Rusbult, C.A. Foster and C.R. Agnew (1999), 'Commitment, pro-relationship behavior, and trust in close relationships', *Journal of Personality and Social Psychology*, **77**, 942–66.

Williamson, O.E. (1993), 'Calculativeness, trust and economic organisation', *Journal of Law and Economics*, **36**, 453–86.

Woolcock, M. (1998), 'Social capital and economic development: toward a theoretical synthesis and policy framework', *Theory and Society*, **27**, 151–208.

Xin, K.R. and J.L. Pearce (1996), 'Guanxi: connections as substitutes for formal institutional support', *Academy of Management Journal*, **39**, 1641–58.

Yamagishi, T., K.S. Cook and M. Watabe (1998), 'Uncertainty, trust, and commitment formation in the United States and Japan', *American Journal of Sociology*, **104**, 165–94.

Yan, Y. (1996), *The Flow of Gifts: Reciprocity and Social Networks in a Chinese Village*, Stanford, CA: Stanford University Press.

Yang, C.F. (ed.) (2001), *The Interpersonal Relationship, Affection, and Trust of the Chinese: From an Interactional Perspective*, Taipei: Yuan Liou Publishing (in Chinese).

Yang, M.M. (1994), *Gifts, Favors, and Banquets: the Art of Social Relationships in China*, Ithaca, NY: Cornell University Press.

Yang, M.M. (2002), 'The resilience of *guanxi* and its new deployments: a critique of some new *guanxi* scholarship', *The China Quarterly*, **170**, 459–76.

Zucker, L. (1986), 'Production of trust: institutional sources of economic structure, 1840–1920', in B.M. Staw and L.L. Cummings (eds), *Research in Organizational Behavior*, vol. 8, Greenwich, CT: JAI Press, pp. 53–111.

5. Transferring knowledge to enterprises in China

Eric W.K. Tsang

The rapid economic growth of China has caught the world's attention. China is gradually emerging as a great economic power. The Chinese government has employed inward foreign direct investment (FDI) as a key element of its economic development strategy since the late 1970s, when the country's economic reforms started. During the early stage of the economic reforms, the Chinese government learned from the experience of restructuring thousands of loss-making state enterprises that modern management techniques were sorely needed for the country's continued economic development: 'We must consciously sum up China's historical experience and study the concrete conditions and requirements for the economic growth. In addition, we must draw upon the world's advanced methods of management, including those of capitalist countries, that conform to the laws of socialized production' (Central Committee of the Communist Party of China, 1984). The absorption of technological and management know-how naturally became one of the official objectives of attracting FDI. To date, thousands of foreign firms have provided not only their capital, but also knowledge to this socialist country – an unprecedented phenomenon in human history (see also Chapter 6 in this volume).

On the theoretical front, inspired by Edith Penrose's seminal work, *The Theory of the Growth of the Firm*, a recent development in management research is to analyse and develop a firm's strategy by focusing on its resources, instead of the external environment. This more inward-looking approach is known as the *resource-based view*. By focusing upon knowledge as the most strategically important resource of the firm, some scholars are in the process of developing a knowledge-based theory of the firm (Grant, 1996). From this knowledge-based view, FDI can be interpreted as 'the transfer of an intermediate good, called knowledge, which embodies a firm's advantage, whether it be the knowledge underlying technology, production, marketing or other activities' (Kogut and Zander, 1993: 628). Empirical studies have found that transfer of knowledge within a multi-unit firm is laborious, time-consuming and difficult (Szulanski, 2000). It is reasonable to expect that inter-firm transfer of knowledge across national borders is even more problematic.

This chapter reviews the transfer of knowledge by foreign firms to enterprises in China based on both theoretical and empirical literatures. Knowledge transfer is a process of systematically organized exchange of information and skills between entities. The definition of knowledge here encompasses more than technology, and includes management skills and techniques. This definition is in line with the Chinese government's objective of absorbing both types of knowledge. The transfer process discussed in this chapter consists of knowledge communicated from the foreign firm to its China operation, whether joint venture or wholly owned subsidiary. There are thus three key elements involved: the source organization, the knowledge and the recipient organization. The characteristics of each have important implications for the transfer process. Owing to space limitations, the discussions below will focus on the more important characteristics.

CHARACTERISTICS OF SOURCE ORGANIZATIONS

There are two broad characteristics of the source organization that determine the extent and success of knowledge transfer: knowledge base and deployment of expatriates. The former is a firm-level factor and the latter is an individual-level factor. The two are somewhat related, as the knowledge held by an organization is largely determined by the knowledge of its members.

Knowledge Base

As firms specialize in particular product or service types, firm-specific knowledge generally accumulates over time (Dierickx and Cool, 1989). Not all firms are equally adept at knowledge creation, and thus firms are heterogeneous in the knowledge they possess (Barney, 1991). When firms expand abroad, they tend to transfer their ownership advantages, in the form of firm-specific knowledge, to foreign operations in order to overcome the inherent disadvantages of operating in alien environments (Dunning, 2001). The ability to do so relies heavily on their knowledge bases that are developed in a path-dependent manner.

In an empirical study of 62 firms of various national origins, Wang *et al.* (2004) found that, while all these firms possessed some kind of knowledge useful to their China operations, the actual extent of knowledge contributed was affected by the richness of their knowledge bases. For example, the core competence of a Taiwanese bicycle manufacturer in their sample was in managing labour-intensive production and assembly processes. The knowledge transferred to its China operation consisted of primarily mature and standardized technologies. In contrast, a leading American manufacturer of microprocessors constructed a state-of-the-art assembly and test plant for flash memory chips in China and transferred advanced semiconductor manufacturing technology to the plant. In brief, the ability of a foreign firm to contribute knowledge is constrained by its existing stock of knowledge.

Sometimes, a foreign firm diversifies and forms a joint venture in China that operates in a different industry. In this case, the Chinese partner of the venture often possesses better technical expertise with respect to that industry than its foreign counterpart. The foreign firm may still want to transfer its management skills to the venture with the aim of complementing the Chinese partner's technical expertise. The problem is that traditionally Chinese tend to place more emphasis on technical rather than management expertise. A person without a relevant technical background is regarded as a layman (*waihang* in the Chinese language), no matter how much management experience the person has. In China, having a *waihang* who leads experts in the trade (*neihang*) is not regarded as an acceptable arrangement. In particular, conflicts may arise when the changes suggested by the foreign firm interfere with the technical aspects of the operation. For example, in Tsang's (2001) study of 18 foreign-invested enterprises in China, the foreign partners of a joint venture proposed to change the existing shift schedule of factory workers in order to better utilize the manpower. The Chinese partner opposed this, saying that the change would affect their efficient production procedures that were originally designed by the Chinese engineers. The Chinese did not have much confidence in the proposal mainly because the foreign partners were not in the same industry as the venture.

Deployment of Expatriates

More often than not, expatriates serve as agents of knowledge transfer, and are responsible for transferring headquarters' practices to overseas affiliates. Expatriates are usually expected to teach the locals how things are done at the headquarters. Lyles and Salk's (1996) study of knowledge transfer to Hungarian joint ventures indicates that expatriate managers play a crucial role in the process. Winter (1995) argues that these managers should be familiar with headquarters' practices and warns against recruiting new staff for this purpose. This is especially the case for the most senior person assigned to the overseas operation, because the role played by the leader in creating a conducive learning environment is of primary importance. This person should be able to gain not only the trust, but also the respect, of local staff. Possessing relevant work experience and technical knowledge is essential.

In Tsang's (2003) study, for example, the foreign partner of a joint venture assigned a newly recruited executive to China to assume the position of general manager. The person had worked in several textile factories in China and did not have any experience in the venture's business of manufacturing industrial equipment. He told the joint venture staff on the day of his arrival that he joined the foreign partner just a week earlier and came from the textile industry. He then had a hard time in the joint venture as people simply did not believe that he had the expertise for leading the venture. In contrast, the general manager of another joint venture had worked in the foreign partner for over 20 years, and had been the general manager there in charge of operations before he was assigned to China. His local colleagues showed their respect for his experience and expertise. Because of his wealth of experience, he was able to tackle the problems arising from knowledge transfer very effectively.

Another factor concerns cultural distance. Child and Rodrigues (1996) argue that national cultural differences may foster feelings of distancing and conflict between expatriate and local staff in an international joint venture, and hinder the transfer of knowledge between the two groups of people. Thus shortening the cultural distance between expatriate and local staff would facilitate knowledge transfer, and pre-assignment training might help in this respect. Tung (1986) describes several types of training programme that can better prepare a manager for posting to China. The programmes include language training, factual information about China's history, the economic and political situation, culture assimilators to sensitize trainees to the different kinds of situation that may arise in China, and so on. The aim is to prepare personnel for cross-cultural encounters. In Sergeant and Frenkel's (1998) study of managing people in China, a few of their respondents, who were expatriates, received cross-cultural training. These respondents were of the opinion that the training was useful and they would like to have more. Yet, in Tsang's (1999a) study of 12 Singapore firms that invested in China, only one of them made use of such training.

A related factor is language proficiency. Transferring knowledge to a foreign country requires clear, unambiguous communication between the transferor and the recipient. Speaking the same language is a crucial means of ensuring such communication. In an empirical study of post-acquisition managerial learning in Central Eastern Europe, it was found that both expatriate and local managers mentioned language problems as the greatest barrier to successful learning (Villinger, 1996). Similarly, in their intensive case studies of knowledge transfer by four foreign firms to China, Buckley *et al.* (2004) found that their respondents singled out language differences as the biggest concern for management. The Singapore firms in Tsang's (1999a) study also recognized the importance of having expatriate managers who could speak Chinese.

Since the English proficiency level in China is generally low, foreign firms of non-Chinese origin may consider hiring ethnic Chinese living in Hong Kong, Taiwan and Singapore as expatriate managers. As cautioned above, these people should be first trained at the headquarters so that they become familiar with the practices there before taking up their positions in China. Marcotte and Niosi (2000) describe a successful case of a new organizational culture taking root in a Sino-foreign joint venture. The anchor person was an ethnic Chinese from Hong Kong, who was a director of the Japanese partner and the executive director of the joint venture. He combined his intimate knowledge of Chinese culture with his rich experience of Japanese management in order to build the new culture.

Finally, commitment of human resources by the foreign firm is a crucial factor. Assigning a sufficient number of expatriates to China, especially at the initial stage of operation, seems to be necessary for facilitating learning among Chinese managers. Owing to resource constraints, some foreign firms may try to carry out knowledge transfer by assigning their managers to China on a part-time basis, such as working two weeks a month in China. A key problem of using part-time expatriates is that most of these managers do not have proper titles in China. Consequently, they may not be able to obtain the necessary cooperation from local staff. In an empirical study of Sino-Swedish joint ventures, Sharma and Wallström-Pan (1997: 377) quote one expatriate as saying that 'Experts who sit on the side to help production but are not actually supervisors do not get any respect from the Chinese. . . . No one goes to them for advice, unless they have some kind of position or title.'

Another problem of having part-time expatriates is the difficulty of following through the implementation of practices brought in by the foreign firm. Those firms that used part-time expatriates in Tsang's (2001) study were usually not very successful in transferring their knowledge to China. A further problem is that building personal relationships, or *guanxi*, in China is critical for business success (Tsang, 1998; see also Chapter 4 in this volume). Having good *guanxi* with local staff surely facilitates knowledge transfer, yet cultivating *guanxi* requires serious effort and considerable time. Part-time expatriates are not well positioned to provide this.

CHARACTERISTICS OF KNOWLEDGE

Knowledge may be analysed using many different angles or dimensions. The most common classification of knowledge is probably the distinction between tacit and explicit knowledge originated by Polanyi's (1967: 4) famous saying that 'we know more than we can tell'. This distinction is relevant to knowledge transfer in general. Another characteristic of knowledge, namely the extent of social embeddedness, is particularly pertinent to knowledge transfer in the context of China.

Tacitness

Knowledge generally consists of two components, explicit and tacit. Polanyi (1967) defines tacit knowledge as non-verbalizable, intuitive and unarticulated. Explicit knowledge, on the other hand, is codifiable and can be transmitted in formal, systematic language. Two major determinants of the proportion of tacit knowledge in a technology are its age and complexity. Robinson (1991) identifies the 11 phases of a technology life cycle from discovery to disappearance. A mature technology that reaches a later phase of its life cycle has been widely used and standardized in industry. Much of the previously uncodified information on the technology will have become codified (Teece, 1977). On the other hand, cutting-edge technology is still in a state of flux. There have been very few previous applications. Engineering drawings, working procedures and manuals are being constantly modified. Few concrete details have been codified.

Complexity of a technology refers to 'the number of critical and interacting elements embraced by an entity or activity' (Kogut and Zander, 1993: 633). Regardless of its age, simple technology is normally in the form of explicit knowledge. Complex technology, nevertheless, cannot be codified in full, even if it is mature. Compare the technology of making a bicycle with that of making an airplane. The complexity of the latter implies that it contains a much higher tacit component than the former. As the Chinese government intends to acquire advanced technology that is expected to be relatively new and complicated, the issue of transferring tacit knowledge becomes pertinent.

If knowledge is rather tacit, the learning process in the recipient organization can be complex and difficult (Marcotte and Niosi, 2000) and it has to be transferred through intimate human interactions (Tsang, 1997). In other words, tacitness demands dedicated efforts from both the source and recipient organizations. Employees of the source organization will likely face difficulties in trying to articulate the tacit components of knowledge, because they are not clearly aware of them (see Nonaka, 1994). The difficulties are aggravated if the source and recipient organizations come from countries that are very different in terms of the cultural, economic and political environments. Unfortunately, this is often the case for knowledge transfer to China.

In their study of 28 Canadian firms that invested in China, Marcotte and Niosi (2000) found that tacit knowledge constituted a substantial part of the total knowledge transferred. The tacit nature of knowledge left much room for multiple problems of interpretations on the part of the Chinese. In the extreme case, there were serious misunderstandings and disagreements regarding the strategic orientation in two of the joint ventures. The Canadian firms faced the burden of transcending the cultural and institutional barriers of communication in order to teach their technologies effectively. Those firms that lacked the requisite resources failed to achieve their objective of knowledge transfer.

Li-Hua (2004) conducted an in-depth study of the construction of the Xiaolangdi Hydroelectric Network across the Yellow River in China. The project, which was started in 1994 and completed in 2000, involved a number of foreign firms, mainly from Europe. There was active transfer of construction technologies, project management techniques and other related knowledge to China throughout the life of the project. He found that the local partners were keen to have knowledge transferred by their foreign counterparts, particularly tacit knowledge such as management know-how, problem solving and decision-making techniques. Informal channels, in the form of social occasions and chance meeting at work, served as important means through which tacit knowledge was transferred. In contrast, explicit knowledge was often transferred through formal channels such as training sessions, seminars and meetings. Tacit knowledge represents a challenge for researchers. As indicated by Li-Hua's (2004) study, transfer of tacit knowledge is much harder to track than that of explicit knowledge.

Social Embeddedness

Another classification frequently used in research on technology transfer is the distinction between physical and organizational technologies that are labelled by some researchers as hard and soft technologies, respectively (for example, Morgan, 1991; Von Glinow and Teagarden, 1988). Physical technologies correspond to ordinary people's concept of the term 'technology', which is associated with machinery, engineering, production processes, and other technical matters. The term 'organizational technologies' refers to the knowledge of organizational structures and processes that do not involve physical technologies, or involve them only peripherally (Westney, 1991). More often than not, physical technologies are more tangible and well-defined than organizational technologies. For instance, among advanced manufacturing technologies, numerical control machines are physical and just-in-time production systems are organizational technologies.

The distinction between physical and organizational technologies is particularly useful when investigating knowledge transfer across borders. In a study of international transfer of physical technologies, Teece (1977) found that substantial transfer costs were involved. Westney (1991) argues that transferring organizational technologies across borders is more complex than transferring physical technologies. Since organizational technologies are less codified and more interdependent with their social context than physical technologies, their transfer from one country to another inevitably entails planned or unplanned change and innovation. For example, in analysing the problems associated with implementing 16 emerging physical and organizational technologies in the domestic context, Aggarwal (1995) concludes that technical problems encountered in adopting physical technologies can be overcome through R&D. On the other hand, organizational technologies usually face problems revolving around retraining and attitudinal change of employees, which may take a long time to resolve.

It is reasonable to expect that the behavioural problems related to organizational technologies will be even more serious when these technologies are transferred from one country to another. For instance, when summarizing the training experience of foreign firms in China, Melvin (1996: 22) distinguishes between hard skills and soft skills, which to some extent correspond to physical and organizational technologies, respectively:

Hard-skills training is relatively straightforward; many expatriate trainers are generally impressed with the ability of Chinese trainees to learn new concepts quickly. But soft-skills training, which involves breaking down long-held attitudes, is often more difficult to implement. To keep operations running smoothly, Chinese managers and employees must understand *why* it is important to do something a certain way, not just what to do or how to do it.

A key reason for the difficulty of transferring organizational technologies is that they are often more socially embedded than physical technologies. While organizational technologies are generally less codified and more interdependent with the social context than physical technologies (Westney, 1991), there are great variations among organizational technologies. The contrast between financial management and human resource management (HRM) is a good illustration. In line with the open door policy, China has been transforming its Soviet-based accounting system. International accounting practices are being gradually introduced into the country. Accounting standards and practices are well codified and somewhat independent of the social context. As such, it is expected that they should be readily transferable. In Tsang's (2001) study, for example, the transfer of accounting practices was smooth.

Transferring HRM practices is a completely different story. HRM is one of the most often cited problems faced by foreign investors in Sino-foreign joint ventures (Tsang, 1994). The old HRM system in Chinese state enterprises was very much a socially constructed product firmly embedded in the former socialist production model (Warner, 1993). Tsang (1994) classifies the causes of HRM problems in Sino-foreign joint ventures into those that are of Chinese cultural origin and those that originate from the existing institutional environment. To complicate matters further, the Chinese partner of a joint venture often insists that personnel issues are 'internal' matters and are off limits to foreign scrutiny (Hendryx, 1986). Tsang (2001) found that the person directly in charge of HRM was usually a local Chinese manager. This would make the transfer of HRM practices difficult as the foreign firm was not in direct control of the matter. Wholesale transfer of HRM practices from foreign countries to China is therefore unlikely. More often than not, substantial adjustment to suit the local context is required (Lu and Björkman, 1997). A case in point is the performance-based reward system that is often preferred by foreign firms. Owing to the legacy of egalitarianism practised in state enterprises, Chinese supervisors tend to distribute bonuses to their subordinates evenly, defeating foreign firms' intention of tying bonus to performance (Child, 1994).

CHARACTERISTICS OF RECIPIENT ORGANIZATIONS

The recipient organization is the context in which knowledge transfer takes place. This section discusses two characteristics of the recipient organization that affect the dynamics of knowledge transfer. The first characteristic concerns the ownership type: whether the recipient is a wholly owned subsidiary or joint venture. The second one is about the way that a joint venture is established: whether it is a greenfield investment or an acquisition.

Ownership Type

China has made available a variety of channels, ranging from wholly owned subsidiaries to licensing, for attracting the inflow of foreign capital. Judging by the attention paid by the Chinese government in terms of legislation and promotion efforts, joint ventures appear to be the most preferred channel. This is understandable. In a joint venture set-up, expatriate and local managers work together on a long-term basis and the venture offers an excellent environment for the Chinese to acquire knowledge from the foreign partner. However, many problems experienced by foreign investors in running Sino-foreign joint ventures have gradually surfaced over the years (Shenkar, 1990). To avoid these problems, many foreign firms have started to opt for wholly owned subsidiaries (Vanhonacker, 1997). Today, joint ventures and wholly owned subsidiaries remain two major FDI options in China (see also Chapter 9 in this volume). The two options have different implications for knowledge transfer. Geppert (1996) argues that managerial learning is embedded in a specific social context. The two investment options constitute different social contexts in which learning takes place.

As mentioned above, Child and Rodrigues (1996) discuss the role of social identity, which in turn affects the perceived social distance between the parties involved, in the transfer of knowledge in international joint ventures. If the perceived social distance is high, the transfer is likely to be impeded. Tsang's (2001) study indicates that, compared with wholly owned subsidiaries, the presence of a Chinese partner in a joint venture generally increases the distance between expatriate and local managers. This is reflected in daily communications. In these joint ventures, the terms 'the Chinese side' (*Zhongfang*, in Chinese) and 'the foreign side' (*waifang*) were frequently used by both local and expatriate managers when they described the situations in the ventures. The distinction between the Chinese and the foreign sides was particularly prominent when inter-partner relationships were having problems. Moreover, local managers tended to identify themselves with the Chinese partners, even though they themselves were recruited into the ventures by the foreign partners. It appears that the Chinese partner naturally becomes a reference group for local managers to identify with. In contrast, local managers of wholly owned subsidiaries were more likely to regard themselves as members of the foreign parent companies, particularly if the managers had received overseas training in the parent companies. This sense of belonging would motivate the local managers to learn from their expatriate counterparts, and thus facilitate the process of knowledge transfer.

The need to collaborate with the Chinese partner can become a barrier to knowledge transfer in a joint venture. Training (critical for improving the absorptive capacity of local employees) is a case in point. The level of investment in training in a joint venture depends on consensus between partners. For example, there were one wholly owned subsidiary and three joint ventures in Buckley *et al.*'s (2004) sample. Recruitment and training in the three joint ventures was constrained by the need to bargain with the Chinese partners over human resource issues. Their training programmes were less systematic and intensive than that of the wholly owned subsidiary because the Chinese partners undervalued training. In particular, during difficult times, training was treated lightly or even ignored in the joint ventures. Similarly, in Wang *et al.*'s (2004) study, wholly owned subsidiaries could decide the budget on training at their sole discretion. Foreign partners of joint ventures, however, needed to discuss with their Chinese counterparts, who preferred distributing the profit as dividends rather than spending it on training. As a result, wholly owned subsidiaries provided more comprehensive training programmes than joint ventures.

More than two decades ago, Mansfield and Romeo (1980) found that firms tended to transfer advanced technologies abroad through wholly owned subsidiaries rather than joint ventures or other entry modes. This finding still holds today, for several reasons.

First, all the benefits generated from knowledge transfer to subsidiaries are retained by the parents. This motivates firms to devote more resources to the transfer. Second, with full control over the transfer process and without the need to worry that partners may mis-appropriate their proprietry knowledge, firms feel more secure about transferring the latest technologies to their subsidiaries. This is especially the case for transferring know-ledge to developing countries, such as China, where the record of patent protection is poor. In Wang *et al.*'s (2004) study, for instance, two firms transferred basic and applied R&D technologies and cutting-edge manufacturing technologies only to their sub-sidiaries, while some firms transferred only mature technologies to their joint ventures.

Leakage of knowledge is particularly a concern when the Chinese partner of a joint venture subsequently forms another joint venture with a competitor of the foreign partner. For example, one of the joint ventures studied by Buckley *et al.* (2004) was Beijing Jeep, established by Beijing Automotive Works and American Motor Corporation in 1983. Some managers who received management training in the venture later moved back to Beijing Automotive Works, which subsequently launched a new joint venture with Hyundai in 2002. Similar incidents happened in the other two joint ventures of the study. As a result, the authors found that transfer of knowledge to the three joint ventures was slower and poorer in quantity and quality than to the wholly owned subsidiary.

Finally, knowledge is a critical component of power in the joint venture context. The foreign firm usually begins as the stronger partner thanks to its technological supremacy relative to the Chinese. It may therefore hesitate to teach its Chinese counterpart whole-heartedly. This is because of the worry that, once the Chinese have mastered the know-ledge concerned, the balance of power begins to swing in favour of the Chinese side (see Tsang, 1999b). When the Chinese partner has exhausted the knowledge transfer possibil-ities that can be offered by the foreign partner, it may move out of the partnership, operate either on its own or with others, and use the proprietary knowledge it has acquired from the foreign partner. The longer it takes for the Chinese to reach that stage, the greater the bargaining power and the better the position of the foreign partner. In brief, it is some-times in the best interest of the foreign partner to slow down its pace of transferring knowledge to its joint venture.

Greenfield versus Acquisition Joint Ventures

A joint venture can be established from scratch (greenfield) or by taking over an existing organization (acquisition). Acquisition joint ventures are common in transition economies, such as China and Russia. One of the aims of the Chinese government in attracting foreign investments is to restructure the huge number of inefficient state enter-prises (see also Chapter 6 in this volume). As a result, many Sino-foreign joint ventures have been established by acquiring the existing assets of state enterprises. Under this arrangement, the Chinese partner, a state enterprise, usually contributes its factory and machinery to the venture. The foreign partner injects capital and new machinery into the venture. The Chinese staff, who were originally employed by the state enterprise, con-tinue to work in the venture, though there are normally some layoffs. This acquisition type of joint venture contrasts with a greenfield investment whereby the joint venture is based on a new operation built from scratch and new staff are recruited from the labour market. The two types of joint ventures differ only in terms of how they are established, and are exactly the same in all the other aspects. They are subject to the same Chinese joint venture laws.

An acquisition joint venture is different from an ordinary acquisition, defined as 'purchase of stock in an already existing company in an amount sufficient to confer control' (Kogut and Singh, 1988: 412), in several respects. First, a joint venture is a separate legal entity distinct from its parent companies and enjoys, to a varying extent, operational autonomy. This is often not the case for an acquisition that usually involves a greater degree of integration between the acquirer and the acquired firm in order to achieve operating synergy (Nahavandi and Malekzadeh, 1988). Second, the Chinese partner of a Sino-foreign joint venture can exert substantial influence on the way the venture should be run, even if the partner is a minority shareholder (Schaan, 1988). The Chinese partner's influence is enhanced by the fact that the venture is located in China. Third, resources and capabilities of the foreign partner are normally perceived as more efficient than those of the Chinese partner. This is because the foreign partner usually possesses more advanced technologies and is more experienced in competing in the international market. For acquisitions effected between domestic companies or between companies of developed countries, such a perceived differential of efficiency does not normally exist.

The distinction between greenfield and acquisition joint ventures is important because, in the latter case, the foreign partner normally has to implement a strategy of dismantling or restructuring the existing backward system of a state enterprise, on the one hand, and installing its own, on the other. The former involves organizational 'unlearning', and the latter organizational learning. In other words, compared with greenfield joint ventures, acquisition joint ventures need to go through an additional step of organizational unlearning that refers to the discarding of existing knowledge to make way for new knowledge.

Agócs (1997) argues that change programmes or interventions implemented in organizations are often met with resistance. Individuals have a tendency toward maintaining the status quo (Heath *et al.*, 1993); that is, they want to carry on with existing ways of doing things to which they have been accustomed. Tsang's (2003) study of five acquisition joint ventures found significant resistance to the restructuring processes carried out by the foreign partners. Indicators of resistance posed by local staff included passivity, grievances against change, continuing a practice that has been officially replaced by a new one, hidden sabotage, delay in reaching a key milestone of implementing a technology, and so on.

Resistance to restructuring hinders knowledge transfer. For example, in Tsang's (2001) sample, there were two joint ventures that were in the same line of business, had the same foreign partner and were established at almost the same time in China. The only major difference was that one was a greenfield investment, whereas the other was an acquisition. At the time of the study, the expatriate managers of the acquisition joint venture were still tackling the resistance to some of their technologies posed by their Chinese colleagues. In contrast, the greenfield joint venture had already properly implemented many of the technologies, with some modifications, brought in by the foreign partner.

Among the factors discussed by Tsang (2003) that affect resistance, of particular relevance to knowledge management is the age of the former state enterprise on which an acquisition joint venture is established. Organizational age is an important source of inertia inhibiting change (Ginsberg and Buchholtz, 1990). The strong roots of existing practice in the past 'guide and legitimate established modes, and they represent both repositories of learned experience and the foundations for structures of existing interests' (Child *et al.*, 1987: 108). This is related to the concept of organizational memory that refers to 'stored information from an organization's history that can be brought to bear on present decisions' (Walsh and Ungson, 1991: 61). Knowledge of an organization is stored not only in the non-human component of its organizational memory such as manuals, policies, files, information systems, and so on, but also in the collective memory of its members. Usually, it is the human component of organizational memory that forms the greatest obstacle to change (Nystrom and Starbuck, 1984). A key determinant of inertia is therefore the age of an enterprise when it is converted into a joint venture. The older the enterprise, the more fossilized the collective memory becomes. Operational knowledge of an old enterprise may become part of the members' work habits, and habits are difficult to get rid of.

Until recently, state enterprises in China rarely went bankrupt. Once a state enterprise was established, it used to exist forever, regardless of its performance. For instance, when the former enterprise was converted into one of the joint ventures in Tsang's (2003) sample, it was 37 years old, even older than the foreign partner. As the executive director from the foreign partner exclaimed, 'This is an old factory with old machines and old guards.' The enterprise was a pioneer in China in manufacturing the type of industrial equipment that the joint venture produced. Chinese staff of the venture, who were originally with the enterprise, took pride in this record and in the long history of the enterprise. To a certain extent, they were trapped by past successes. Some changes initiated by the foreign partner caused a lot of eyebrows to be raised. They sometimes could not understand why a certain procedure that had been practised for years had to be abandoned. Their logic was that the procedure must be fine; otherwise it would not have lasted for so long. In other words, the foreign partner had to explain in detail the supremacy of its technologies and know-how.

Another problem concerned the human relations inside the above joint venture. State enterprises used to provide life employment and 'cradle-to-grave' welfare coverage for their employees. A state enterprise is, in a sense, more like a social community than a production unit (Shenkar, 1996). The implication is that, the older the state enterprise, the more complicated the human relations among its employees will be. This was exactly the situation in the venture. There were several cliques deeply entrenched in the organization. The Chinese deputy general manager said, 'Implementing a change that upsets the status quo of these cliques is like moving mountains'. This comment was verified by a failed attempt to install a new organizational structure that would improve internal coordination and communication. Though she appreciated the new structure suggested by the foreign partner, the deputy general manager said, 'You can't put long-time enemies in the same team and hope that they will work together'.

The complicated nature of transforming a state enterprise implies that the effort required on the part of the foreign partner of an acquisition joint venture should not be underestimated. Some expatriate managers in Tsang's (2003) study mentioned that the task was a lot more difficult than they had expected initially. In particular, the experience can be very frustrating when transfer of knowledge encounters unexpected resistance. In sum, the processes of establishing a joint venture on a greenfield site and of transforming a former socialist enterprise into a joint venture are so different that they deserve separate treatment by both practitioners and researchers. Unfortunately, the literature on international joint ventures rarely addresses this important issue.

CONCLUSION

The emerging knowledge-based theory of the firm maintains that knowledge is the most strategically important firm resource (Grant, 1996). The basic argument is that a firm's idiosyncratic know-how and ability to create, acquire, transfer and exploit knowledge are critical to its success (Steensma and Lyles, 2000). Knowledge management has therefore been increasingly recognized as a key managerial function necessary for achieving competitive advantage (Argote and Ingram, 2000).

For firms having FDIs, whether joint ventures or wholly owned subsidiaries, in emerging economies, they have to transfer their technologies and know-how to these operations in order that they can exploit their ownership advantages. This is especially the case for China where many world-class firms have established their footholds. Foreign firms compete more among themselves than against the relatively backward Chinese firms. How effective and efficient knowledge is transferred to their operations in China is a critical success factor. The above discussions clearly show that knowledge transfer is a complex process, yet firms can reduce the chances of making mistakes through a better understanding of the process. A major objective of this chapter is to contribute towards such an understanding.

Successful knowledge transfer also benefits China as a whole. As stated at the beginning of the chapter, acquiring advanced technology and management expertise is a key national objective. China has been highly successful in attracting FDI, but many imperfections remain in terms of effective technology transfer and learning (Buckley *et al.*, 2004). A crucial problem is related to the official preference for joint ventures, based on the rationale that the joint venture offers the Chinese partner an opportunity to learn and absorb both physical and organizational technologies from the foreign partner. However, empirical research has found that, for various reasons, foreign firms tend to transfer better technologies to wholly owned subsidiaries rather than joint ventures. This is an important policy dilemma that has to be addressed by the Chinese government.

Although this chapter has covered most of the important factors affecting the transfer of knowledge by foreign firms to China, it has several limitations. It should be noted that the topic itself is complicated. The above discussions have focused on some of the key issues and excluded others, such as industrial experience of the source organization, levels of learning, learning intent of the recipient organization, and training of local employees.

Another limitation is that the framework of the chapter is organization-based; that is, the organization is the unit of analysis and serves as the context where knowledge is originated or transferred. An emerging approach is to analyse knowledge transfer, using the network as the unit of analysis (Inkpen and Tsang, 2005). In their recent study of transfer of R&D capabilities to China in the automotive industry, Zhao *et al.* (2005) adopt a so-called 'dual network' perspective. They examine how the source networks and recipient networks in which joint venture partners operate influence interorganizational transfer and diffusion of capabilities. This perspective, though more complicated, provides some interesting insights and is especially relevant to studies of knowledge transfer from multinational corporations to large local firms.

Finally, this chapter has covered only the transfer of knowledge from foreign firms to their operations in China. This direction of knowledge flow has been the subject of most of the empirical research in this area. Nevertheless, Tsang (1999c) argues that internationalization itself is a learning process. Firms learn from their overseas collaborative experience even though they may not acquire any specific skills from their venture partners. There is thus a reverse flow of knowledge from their operations abroad to themselves. Tsang (2002) reports an empirical study of the factors affecting knowledge acquisition by Singapore firms in China.

REFERENCES

Aggarwal, S. (1995), 'Emerging hard and soft technologies: current status, issues and implementation problems', *Omega*, **23**(3), 323–39.

Agócs, Carol (1997), 'Institutional resistance to organizational change: denial, inaction and repression', *Journal of Behavioral Economics*, **16**(9), 917–31.

Argote, Linda and Paul Ingram (2000), 'Knowledge transfer: a basis for competitive advantage in firms', *Organizational Behavior and Human Decision Processes*, **82**(1), 150–69.

Barney, Jay (1991), 'Firm resources and sustained competitive advantage', *Journal of Management*, **17**(1), 99–120.

Buckley, Peter J., Jeremy Clegg and Hui Tan (2004), 'Knowledge transfer to China: policy lessons from foreign affiliates', *Transnational Corporations*, **13**(1), 31–72.

Central Committee of the Communist Party of China (1984), *A Decision of the Central Committee of the Communist Party of China on Reform of the Economic Structure*, Beijing: The Communist Party of China.

Child, John (1994), *Management in China During the Age of Reform*, Cambridge, UK: Cambridge University Press.

Child, John and Suzana Rodrigues (1996), 'The role of social identity in the international transfer of knowledge through joint ventures', in Stewart R. Clegg and Gill Palmer (eds), *The Politics of Management Knowledge*, London: Sage, pp. 46–68.

Child, John, Hans-Dieter Ganter and Alfred Kieser (1987), 'Technological innovation and organizational conservatism', in Johannes M. Pennings and Arend Buitendam (eds), *New Technology as Organizational Innovation*, Cambridge, MA: Ballinger, pp. 87–115.

Dierickx, Ingemar and Karel Cool (1989), 'Asset stock accumulation and sustainability of competitive advantage', *Management Science*, **35**(12), 1504–11.

Dunning, John H. (2001), 'The eclectic (OLI) paradigm of international production: past, present and future', *International Journal of the Economics of Business*, **8**(2), 173–90.

Geppert, Mike (1996), 'Paths of managerial learning in the East German context', *Organization Studies*, **17**(2), 249–68.

Ginsberg, Ari and Ann Buchholtz (1990), 'Converting to for-profit status: corporate responsiveness to radical change', *Academy of Management Journal*, **33**(3), 445–77.

Grant, Robert M. (1996), 'Toward a knowledge-based theory of the firm', *Strategic Management Journal*, **17**(Winter Special Issue), 109–22.

Heath, Chip, Marc Knez and Colin Camerer (1993), 'The strategic management of the entitlement process in the employment relationship', *Strategic Management Journal*, **14**(Winter Special Issue), 75–93.

Hendryx, Steven R. (1986), 'Implementation of a technology transfer joint venture in the People's Republic of China: a management perspective', *Columbia Journal of World Business*, **21**(1), 57–66.

Inkpen, Andrew C. and Eric W.K. Tsang (2005), 'Social capital, networks, and knowledge transfer', *Academy of Management Review*, **30**(1), 146–65.

Kogut, Bruce and Harbir Singh (1988), 'The effect of national culture on the choice of entry mode', *Journal of International Business Studies*, **19**(3), 411–32.

Kogut, Bruce and Udo Zander (1993), 'Knowledge of the firm and the evolutionary theory of the multinational corporation', *Journal of International Business Studies*, **24**(4), 625–45.

Li-Hua, Richard (2004), *Technology and Knowledge Transfer to China*, Aldershot: Ashgate.

Lu, Yuan and Ingmar Björkman (1997), 'HRM practices in China-Western joint ventures: MNC standardization versus localization', *International Journal of Human Resource Management*, **8**(5), 615–28.

Lyles, Marjorie A. and Jane E. Salk (1996), 'Knowledge acquisition from foreign parents in international joint ventures: an empirical examination in the Hungarian context', *Journal of International Business Studies*, **27**(5), 877–903.

Mansfield, Edwin and Anthony Romeo (1980), 'Technology transfer to overseas subsidiaries by U.S.-based firms', *Quarterly Journal of Economics*, **95**(4), 737–50.

Marcotte, Claude and Jorge Niosi (2000), 'Technology transfer to China: the issues of knowledge and learning', *Journal of Technology Transfer*, **25**, 43–57.

Melvin, Sheila (1996), 'Training the troops', *China Business Review*, March–April, 22–8.

Morgan, Bruce (1991), 'Transferring soft technology', in Richard D. Robinson (ed.), *The International Communication of Technology: A Book of Readings*, New York: Taylor & Francis, pp. 149–66.

Nahavandi, Afsaneh and Ali R. Malekzadeh (1988), 'Acculturation in mergers and acquisitions', *Academy of Management Review*, **13**(1), 79–90.

Nonaka, Ikujiro (1994), 'A dynamic theory of organizational knowledge creation', *Organization Science*, **5**(1), 14–37.

Nystrom, Paul C. and William H. Starbuck (1984), 'To avoid organizational crises, unlearn', *Organizational Dynamics*, Spring, 53–65.

Penrose, Edith T. (1959), *The Theory of the Growth of the Firm*, Oxford, UK: Blackwell.

Polanyi, Michael (1967), *The Tacit Dimension*, London: Routledge & Kegan Paul.

Robinson, Richard D. (1991), 'Toward creating an international technology transfer paradigm', in Richard D. Robinson (ed.), *The International Communication of Technology: A Book of Readings*, New York: Taylor & Francis, pp. 9–23.

Schaan, Jean-Louis (1988), 'How to control a joint venture even as a minority partner', *Journal of General Management*, **14**(1), 4–16.

Sergeant, Andrew and Stephen Frenkel (1998), 'Managing people in China: perception of expatriate managers', *Journal of World Business*, **33**(1), 17–34.

Sharma, D. Deo and Carolina Wallström-Pan (1997), 'Internal management of Sino-Swedish joint ventures', in Ingmar Björkman and Mats Forsgren (eds), *The Nature of the International Firm*, Copenhagen, Denmark: Copenhagen Business School Press, pp. 363–90.

Shenkar, Oded (1990), 'International joint ventures' problems in China: risks and remedies', *Long Range Planning*, **23**(3), 82–90.

Shenkar, Oded (1996), 'The firm as a total institution: reflections on the Chinese state enterprise', *Organization Studies*, **17**(6), 885–907.

Steensma, H. Kevin and Marjorie A. Lyles (2000), 'Explaining IJV survival in a transitional economy through social exchange and knowledge-based perspectives', *Strategic Management Journal*, **21**(8), 831–51.

Szulanski, Gabriel (2000), 'The process of knowledge transfer: a diachronic analysis of stickiness', *Organizational Behavior and Human Decision Processes*, **82**(1), 9–27.

Teece, D.J. (1977), 'Technology transfer by multinational firms: the resource cost of transferring technological know-how', *Economic Journal*, **87**, 242–61.

Tsang, Eric W.K. (1994), 'Human resource management problems in Sino-foreign joint ventures', *International Journal of Manpower*, **15**(9/10), 4–21.

Tsang, Eric W.K. (1997), 'Choice of international technology transfer mode: a resource-based view', *Management International Review*, **37**(2), 151–68.

Tsang, Eric W.K. (1998), 'Can *guanxi* be a source of sustained competitive advantage for doing business in China?', *Academy of Management Executive*, **12**(2), 64–73.

Tsang, Eric W.K. (1999a), 'The knowledge transfer and learning aspects of international HRM: an empirical study of Singapore MNCs', *International Business Review*, **8**(5/6), 591–609.

Tsang, Eric W.K. (1999b), 'A preliminary typology of learning in international strategic alliances', *Journal of World Business*, **34**(3), 211–29.

Tsang, Eric W.K. (1999c), 'Internationalization as a learning process: Singapore MNCs in China', *Academy of Management Executive*, **13**(1), 91–101.

Tsang, Eric W.K. (2001), 'Managerial learning in foreign-invested enterprises of China', *Management International Review*, **41**(1), 29–51.

Tsang, Eric W.K. (2002), 'Acquiring knowledge by foreign partners from international joint ventures in a transition economy: learning-by-doing and learning myopia', *Strategic Management Journal*, **23**(9), 835–54.

Tsang, Eric W.K. (2003), 'Resistance to restructuring in Sino-foreign joint ventures: toward a preliminary model', *Journal of Organizational Change Management*, **16**(2), 205–22.

Tung, Rosalie L. (1986), 'Corporate executives and their families in China: the need for cross-cultural understanding in business', *Columbia Journal of World Business*, **21**(1), 21–5.

Vanhonacker, Wilfried (1997), 'Entering China: an unconventional approach', *Harvard Business Review*, March–April, 130–40.

Villinger, Roland (1996), 'Post-acquisition managerial learning in Central East Europe', *Organization Studies*, **17**(2), 181–206.

Von Glinow, Mary Ann and Mary B. Teagarden (1988), 'The transfer of human resource management technology in Sino-U.S. cooperative ventures: problems and solutions', *Human Resource Management*, **27**(2), 201–29.

Walsh, James P. and Gerardo Rivera Ungson (1991), 'Organizational memory', *Academy of Management Review*, **16**(1), 57–91.

Wang, Pien, Tony W. Tong and Chun Peng Koh (2004), 'An integrated model of knowledge transfer from MNC parent to China subsidiary', *Journal of World Business*, **39**(2), 168–82.

Warner, Malcolm (1993), 'Human resource management "with Chinese characteristics"', *International Journal of Human Resource Management*, **4**(1), 45–65.

Westney, D. Eleanor (1991), 'International transfer of organizational technology', in Richard D. Robinson (ed.), *The International Communication of Technology: A Book of Readings*, New York: Taylor & Francis, pp. 167–81.

Winter, Sidney G. (1995), 'Four Rs of profitability: rents, resources, routines, and replication', in Cynthia A. Montgomery (ed.), *Resource-Based and Evolutionary Theories of the Firm: Towards a Synthesis*, Norwell, US: Kluwer Academic Publishers, pp. 147–78.

Zhao, Zheng, Jaideep Anand and Will Mitchell (2005), 'A dual networks perspective on interorganizational transfer of R&D capabilities: international joint ventures in the Chinese automotive industry', *Journal of Management Studies*, **42**(1), 127–60.

6.   Business organizations in China

Doug Guthrie and Junmin Wang[1]

For two-and-a-half decades, China's transition to a market economy has produced remarkable growth rates and fundamental changes in the organization of economic action. Though lacking the fundamental institutional shifts that have defined many transforming socialist economies around the world, China's gradualist reforms have nevertheless been radical and deep (Naughton, 1995; Guthrie, 1999, 2003, 2005; Nolan, 2004). The emergence of business organizations in China has played a key role in the transformation of the Chinese economy. In order to understand the emergence of the capitalist business organizations in China today, we must first examine the varieties and types of organizations that have come to function like business organizations. Once we have identified the organizational forms that fall under the rubric of business organizations in China, it is also crucial to examine the forces that have brought about this process of change. This chapter will take up both agendas.

In the Chinese context, it is far too simplistic to think of business organizations as only covering private enterprises in the economy; this sector, while important, comprises only one of the organizational types that are behaving like business organizations in China today. In this chapter, we focus our attention on four types of organizations that comprise the category mainland Chinese business organizations. State-owned enterprises (SOEs), township and village enterprises (TVEs), private enterprises and foreign-funded enterprises are all part of the group of Chinese organizations that behave, to varying degrees, like business organizations China. We also focus our attention on the institutional changes that have shaped business organizations in China today. Specifically, we look at (1) the evolution of government–enterprise relationships, (2) the impact of foreign direct investment (FDI), (3) the transformation of social relationships in China's market economy, and (4) the emergence of business associations. Through each of these areas of change, we address the question of the forces that have shaped the emergence of Chinese business organizations.

THE EMERGENCE OF BUSINESS ORGANIZATIONS IN CHINA

What are business organizations? How do we classify them? And which organizations in the Chinese context fit into this classification scheme? In the simplest terms, classical definitions of business organizations would posit that business organizations are (1) composed of relationships between owners and workers and (2) established for the purpose of pursuing profits in exchange for the provision of goods and/or services (Sparling, 1906). For example, Noble (1927: 232) defined a business organization as an 'association expressed in a variety of relationships – joint owners, joint operators, agent and principal, trustee and beneficiary, employer and employee. The history of efforts of these individuals or groups of individuals within the business unit to accomplish that purpose for which the business unit was formed, namely, the making of profit, is recorded in the accounts of the enterprise'. Dean (1917: 107) placed the concept squarely in the realm of property rights, positing the right that owners have as the residual claimant on revenues generated by the services. Business organizations are 'cooperative arrangements of men for the purpose of acquiring . . . property rights (quantitatively measured by the unit of value, the dollar) by producing some product or service exchangeable for some form of property, usually a right to money, which may be distributed as income to individuals'.

By these terms, only private enterprises and some foreign-funded enterprises in China would fall under the category of business organizations. However, strict classifications of business organization do not capture the rich variety of organizations that behave like capitalist firms in China. An analysis of business organizations must focus on what it means to operate like a business organization rather than on official categories or types. The evolution of the study of property rights is illustrative here. Where classical studies of property rights defined the institutional arrangements into basic categories (private, public or state-owned), more recent work in this area has focused on the specific practices that define property rights as a 'bundle' of rights, including (1) the right to residual income flows, (2) the right of managerial control, and (3) the right to transfer assets (Demsetz, 1967; Furubotn and Pejovich, 1974; Oi and Walder, 1999). The property rights issue is especially important in this case, because many firms in China have long operated *like* private firms while still occupying the status of being state-owned (Walder, 1995; Oi and Walder, 1999). The same is true for business organizations: in China today, beyond private and foreign-funded enterprises, SOEs and TVEs have also evolved to behave like business organizations in various ways.

As indicated in Figures 6.1 and 6.2, China had 46 767 state-owned and state-holding enterprises in 2001, occupying 27.3 per cent of the total enterprises; these organizations contributed 41 per cent of the output value to the total gross industrial output of the country. The 31 038 collective-owned enterprises (18.1 per cent of the total) contributed just over 8 per cent of the output value to the total gross industrial output; 31 423 foreign firms (18.3 per cent) contributed 28 per cent to the total output; and 36 218 private enterprises (21.1 per cent) contributed nearly 13 per cent to the total output.[2]

TVEs as Business Organizations

The earliest sector of the Chinese economy to surge in growth and output in China's reform era was that of the township and village enterprises. Indeed, the rapid growth of China's economy in the 1980s was largely due to the exceptional growth rates of the rural industrial economy, where the vast majority of TVEs reside. As the primary segment contributing to China's high economic growth in the 1980s, the TVE sector expanded to 24 529 in 1993, almost 15 times its size in 1978. By 1998, however, the number had dropped to 20 039, owing to the informal privatization processes led by the local governments in the 1990s.[3] These organizations are essentially state-owned: though not controlled by the national or provincial governments, they were still controlled by the state, as township and village governments owned the property. Local governments were the residual claimants, and controlled managerial decisions and the rights of transferring assets. However, after

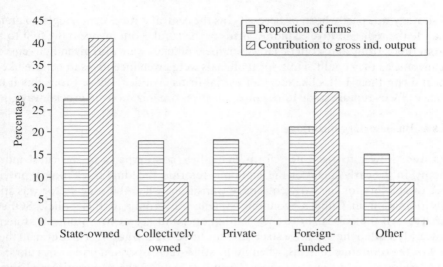

Source: *Statistical Yearbook of China* (2002).

Figure 6.1   Various organizational types in China, 2001

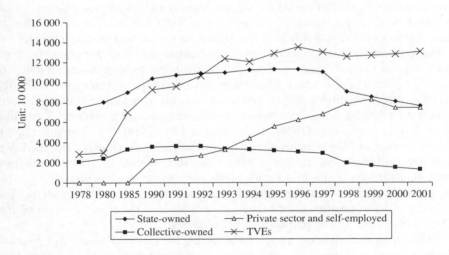

Source: *Statistical Yearbook of China* (2002).

Figure 6.2   Changing numbers of employees by sector, 1978–2001

the economic reforms began, TVEs faced few of the institutional and organizational legacies of the planned economy that larger state-owned organizations controlled by higher levels of government faced.[4]

As the economic reforms progressed, managerial and ownership control were quickly decentralized to give local officials direct control over the firms under their jurisdictions.

This strategy was partly born of necessity: as the central government sought to gradually dismantle the redistributive economy, firms in the rural economy were the first to be cut off from funds from state coffers. However, local officials were also given free rein to generate income as they could. Thus, local officials were given incentives to behave like managers and run their TVEs like local industrial firms (Walder, 1995). From this frame of reference, TVEs rapidly came to resemble business organizations in crucial ways.

SOEs as Business Organizations

SOEs were slower to see true reform than their counterparts in the rural industrial economy. In the early stages of the economic reforms, the 'dual track' policy provided a degree of stability for the early enterprise transitions when the state sector was still evidently dominant in China's economic system. According to this policy, SOEs were allowed to sell the goods above the 'plan' quotas and keep extra profits, a system that significantly shifted the incentive structures for these organizations. Thus, even in the early period of the economic reforms, when SOEs still largely operated under the rubric of the planned economy, managers were given incentives to direct their enterprises to behave like business organizations in the emerging market economy.

In 1992, the Chinese government made clear its market-driven reform direction and shifted its policy making towards creating the rules, laws and institutions that govern a market economy. From this point forward, the 'dual track' system was phased out.[5] Since then, substantial restructuring of state-owned industry has been central to the reform agenda. By the mid-1990s, SOEs were increasingly being pushed to restructure their operations in fundamental ways, causing them to be treated and to behave more and more like business organizations in practice, if not in legal form. Firms were placed on independent budgetary systems (*duli hesuan*). Many were cut off completely from the redistributive funds of central government coffers; and many were given full latitude to make decisions over how they would govern themselves in China's emerging markets. Laws like the Enterprise Bankruptcy Law (1986), the Enterprise Law (1988), the Company Law (1994) and the Labour Law (1995), established a framework for these changes. But the key point here is that, although the transition away from the planned economy was a gradual process, managers in many of China's SOEs were increasingly being handed the key responsibilities that fit the management of a business organization. Although they did not possess the right to transfer assets, they increasingly had the rights to residual income flows, and the power and responsibility of managerial control.[6]

In addition to the declining scale of the SOEs, their contributions to China's gross domestic product and total industrial output have also significantly decreased. In 1978, the SOEs generated about 80 per cent of China's gross domestic product. By 2003, the contribution of the SOEs had dropped to 17 per cent and the collective, private and joint-venture sectors generated over 70 per cent. In 1978, the state sectors contributed over 75 per cent of China's industrial output and collective sectors accounted for about 22 per cent (Naughton, 1995). In 1995, the state sectors' portion in the industrial output had declined to 35 per cent, while collective sectors contributed over 36 per cent of the industrial output values and private sector and other non-state sectors produced the rest (National Statistical Bureau of China, 1996). By 2001, the shares of gross industrial output being produced by the private firms, combined with foreign-funded enterprises, had risen to 38 per cent, while the share of the SOEs was only 18 per cent and the share of collective sectors was down to 10 per cent (National Statistical Bureau of China, 2002). It is very clear that, through the reform era, the non-state firms have been growing at a strikingly faster rate than the state sector.

Even today, however, the SOEs still remain a massive force in China's economy. They provide basic employment and social welfare for the majority of urban workers and the bulk of fiscal revenues for most levels of government. They still control more than half of China's industrial assets and dominate vital industries such as financial services, power, telecommunications, steel and petrochemicals, among others. China cannot accomplish its market reform and business revolution in the near future without successfully further restructuring and reforming its state sector. In the era of economic reform, however, the entry and booming of large numbers of collectives, private firms, joint ventures and foreign firms have significantly driven China's market reforms and sharply overshadowed the status and roles of SOEs in the industrial sector and the national economy.

Private and Foreign-funded Enterprises as Business Organizations

In the Chinese context, the organizations that populate these two categories of economic organization are the closest to the classic definitions of business organizations. Private firms, for their part, are fairly clear-cut; they are organized around relationships between principals (owners) and agents (managers and workers) and they are basically oriented toward the pursuit of profits in exchange for the production of goods and the provision of services. There is one key distinction among types of organizations within this sector, namely, that between household businesses (*getihu*) and private enterprises (*siying qiye*). Household businesses employ a maximum of seven employees, whereas private enterprises employ eight or more workers. In addition, private enterprises are subject to the Enterprise Law (or the Company Law, depending on whether the organization has made this transition), while household businesses are not.

Foreign-funded organizations are a little more complicated. In general, these organizations come in two primary forms. First, wholly owned foreign enterprises (WOFEs) are private organizations that are funded by a foreign parent or benefactor. However, these organizations are different from private business organizations in that they are largely extensions of the parent organizations that formed them. Thus, while these organizations may appear to be the most similar to private organizations in the Chinese economy in terms of property rights, they are most often closely tied subsidiary organizations. Further, especially for larger organizations in this category, their operation in the economy depends in part on their relationships with other organizations and with the local or national government (depending on their scale and scope).

The second form that appears within this category is the joint venture (JV) firm. Joint ventures (*hezi qiye*) are usually entities fully independent from the parent organizations that have contributed resources to their formation. However, these parent organizations may control their business decisions to varying degrees. In some cases, JVs operate as fully independent entities, exercising managerial control and control over residual income. In other cases, parent companies from both the foreign and the Chinese partner sides can exercise significant managerial control over these entities (see also Chapter 9 in this volume).

Table 6.1   Comparison of state-owned and foreign-funded firms, 2002

	Foreign-funded	SOEs w/no foreign funds
Ratio of output to assets (%)	9.83	8.17
Ratio of profits to cost (%)	5.85	5.75
Labour prod. (yuan/person-year)	75 913	54 772

Note: 'Foreign-funded' refers to those firms that are Sino-foreign joint ventures or Sino-foreign cooperative projects.

Source: Statistical Yearbook of China (2003: 446, 456).

In the 1990s, private and foreign-funded firms replaced TVEs as the most dynamic sectors of the economy (see Table 6.1). With respect to foreign-funded firms especially, these organizations have seen the highest levels of labour productivity, ratio of output to assets, and ratio of profits to cost (Guthrie, 2005). In contrast to the decline of the SOEs, the non-state sectors have become the key driving force of China's market-led reforms and the most competitive force supporting the high-speed growth of the national economy during the past 25 years.[7]

THE EVOLUTION OF GOVERNMENT–ENTERPRISE RELATIONSHIPS

One of the key goals of China's economic reforms since 1979 has been to transform the relationships between enterprises and the state. Under the planned economy, almost all of China's enterprises were state-owned and state-run (here again, 'state-run' includes collectives and TVEs). Enterprises varied in terms of the level of government under which these enterprises resided (from central to local) and in terms of the resources they were able to extract from the government (Walder, 1992). However, there was no question that the state was the residual claimant, exercised managerial control and exercised control over the transfer of assets. There were a small number of collective enterprises, but their managerial system was not essentially different from that of state-owned enterprises (Walder, 1995). These organizations (state- and collectively owned enterprises alike) served not only as production units of the governmental system, but also as redistribution units for the goods of social welfare. Enterprises before economic reform were essentially inseparable from the government and highly dependent on it.

An observable degree of separation of enterprises from the state during the 1980s was actually a direct result of the state-initiated enterprise reforms, rather than the emergence of 'civil society' in urban China, as some scholars have argued (for example Whyte, 1992; White, 1996; White *et al.*, 1996; Deng, 1997; Deng and Jing, 1992). Deng's reforms transformed enterprises in two significant ways: (1) relieving them of the responsibility for social benefits and (2) turning economic autonomy over to both economic organizations and the managers that ran them. During the 1980s, the decentralization of economic responsibilities for TVEs and the local officials that governed them had transformed the responsibilities and rights of both governments and the enterprises they governed.

In similar ways, the 'dual track' policy rebuilt the incentive structures of the SOEs and the responsibilities and rights of both the government and enterprises, though, as discussed above, this process occurred in a much more gradual fashion. Thus these enterprises obtained, in many cases, enough financial control and freedom from the burden of social welfare costs to transform their practices in the market economy. In addition, as the party and the administrative arm of the government, the administrative bureaus receded from direct control over enterprise behaviour; managers throughout the Chinese economy have become the key decision makers of TVEs and SOEs, along with their counterparts in the private and foreign-funded economy.

Market Transition, Enterprise Reforms and the Rule of Law

Over the course of the reforms, the central government has transformed its role from the country's economic decision maker into the macroeconomic policy maker, passing a battery of key laws and regulations that changed the practices of organizations. For example, in 1979, the Chinese government passed the Joint Venture Law, allowing foreign firms to enter the Chinese economy for the first time since 1949. Decollectivization policies in rural areas and the creation of the categories of household business (*getihu*) and private enterprise (*siying qiye*) stimulated the emergence of private enterprises. The entry of these start-up firms quickly gave rise to increasing market pressure on the state sector. In 1986, the State Council passed regulations that changed the nature of employment relationships, essentially marking a formal end to the institution of lifetime employment (Guthrie, 1998b, 1999, 2002a).[8] Also in 1986, the Chinese government passed the Enterprise Bankruptcy Law that for the first time established that insolvent enterprises might apply for bankruptcy. Two years later, with the passage of the Enterprise Law, the state not only underscored the government's policies toward hardening budget constraints for SOEs, but also stipulated the government's policies and legal guaranty for protecting the non-state sector, through regulations such as the *Rules of Foreign Invested Enterprises* and the *Provisional Regulations of Private Enterprises*.[9]

In 1992, coinciding with Deng's tour of southern China, the State Council further specified that enterprises were entitled to up to 14 rights: decision making in production and operation, price-setting for products and labour, selling of products, material purchasing, import and export, investment decision, disposition of retained bonuses, disposition of property, decision on joint operation or mergers, labour employment, personnel management, distribution of wages and bonuses, internal structuring and refusing apportioning. Since then, SOEs have been expected to operate independently in the market, according to law and be responsible for their own profits and losses. Two years later, the Company Law was passed. This law governed the process of converting enterprises into shareholding companies and stipulated that companies funded by investing bodies of different ownerships were all equal under the law. More importantly, the Company Law encouraged enterprises to build new corporate structures and standardize organizational bodies (mainly with regard to shareholder meetings, corporate boards and managers), in order to block further political interventions in the decision making of enterprises. By the mid-1990s, the government would formally define its role in the economy as 'creat[ing] the conditions for all sectors of the economy to participate in the market competition on an equal basis, and guarantee enterprises from all sectors to be treated indiscriminately'.[10]

Coinciding with these legislative changes was the founding of the Shanghai and Shenzhen Stock Exchanges in the early 1990s. Since 1993, the number of listed companies has risen from 10 to 1160, with a total market capitalization of 525.6 billion US dollars (Gao, 2002). Following the gradualist model, the Chinese government's construction of the institutions that govern public ownership has been spread across the period. After a series of regulations such as 'the Opinions on Standardizing the Joint Stock Limited Companies' and 'the Provisional Regulations on the Administration of Issuing and Trading of Stocks', the Securities Law was passed in 1998, forming legal guaranty for the standardized operation of the listed companies. Yet, even in the area of public ownership of listed companies, we must acknowledge the complexities of enterprise–state relations in the Chinese model, as the government's withdrawing from control over publicly listed state enterprises, like every other institutional change in the Chinese economic reforms, has been a gradual process.[11]

Since 1979, the non-state sectors have also been increasingly entitled to the legal acknowledgment and protection from the capricious whims of the state. In 1997, at the Fifteenth National Congress, the government issued the significant formal statement that 'the non-state sector is an important component part of this country's socialist market economy', and the statement was incorporated into the Constitution in 1999. At this point, the status of the non-state sector, especially the private sector, in China's economic system was officially legitimated. In 2004, the government further amended the constitution to protect private property rights for the first time since the People's Republic of China was founded in 1949. Over the course of China's market transition, the law-building process of the central government, especially since the 1990s, has gradually rationalized the institutions that govern autonomous business practice in China. These changes have brought about the rapid growth of the non-state sectors and intensified the transformation of the state sector in the reform era. They have also codified the autonomy of organizations operating as businesses in China. As a result, all types of China's business organizations have been more or less driven towards independent market behaviour, with diminishing reliance on the government system.

Fiscal Reforms and the Rise of Local States

While it is certainly true that the state has gradually withdrawn itself from economic management and control of enterprises in the reform era, nevertheless, it is premature to conclude that the Chinese state has become insignificant in its relationships with the business organizations. In particular, it is important to note that, in the reform era, local governments have arisen to play important roles in the development of local enterprises and economic development of their regions more generally (Huang, 1995; Walder, 1995; Lee, 1991). This process has occurred at varying rates, depending on a given locality's relationship to the central government (Li, 1997). Since the beginning of the reform era, policies of economic decentralization have gradually transferred most economic decision-making power from the central government to localities by a series of tax and fiscal reforms.

In 1980, the fiscal reforms started with the implementation of a fiscal responsibility system, under which the central government and provincial-level governments signed revenue-sharing contracts. According to this contract, taxes collected by local governments were to be divided into two parts: (1) central fixed revenues to be remitted to the central government; and (2) local revenues to be shared by the central and local governments in terms of various standards across regions. This revenue-sharing system provided local governments with both strong incentives and institutional means to increase their revenue base, allowing them to retain more when they collected more revenues and guaranteeing the rights of localities to income from their assets. The direct outcome of these reforms was an explosion of local revenues in the 1980s that lasted until 1994 when the central state was forced to enforce new fiscal reforms (Wang, 1995; Wang and Hu, 2001). In addition, economic decentralization policies have involved local governments in a number of responsibilities for carrying out national social policies and a variety of economic activities. For instance, the governments at the city level are responsible for 100 per cent of expenditures for social security, unemployment insurance and social welfare, and the governments at the county and township levels account for 70 per cent of education and 55–60 per cent of health expenditures.[12]

The increasing responsibilities in the reform era have made local governments actively involved in economic activities and business affairs in the localities. Lower levels of local governments have played significant roles in the development of TVEs that became the most dynamic sector in China's transitional economy during the 1980s and the early 1990s. By the early 1990s, the TVEs were contributing to between 40 and 50 per cent of the tax revenues collected by local governments. As noted above, local governments, in many cases, actually came to behave like 'industrial firms' themselves during the rural industrialization process (Walder, 1995). Other studies (Lin, 1995; Oi, 1992) have examined how local governments at the township and village levels have engineered the development of collective enterprises and formed corporate structures to govern them.

The fiscal reforms of 1994 put more duties on the localities and required the lower levels of local governments to be responsible for expenses and social welfare. At the same time, the early 1990s' liberalization policy of foreign investment and foreign trade increased local government's responsibility for managing the foreign sector in localities. These conditions created both fiscal pressure and incentives for local states to be more involved in the local–global business activities for capital accumulation. Aside from dealing directly with foreign capital, local governments were given the authority to relax the rules governing foreign exchange balances, power and water fees, land prices for factory buildings, restrictions on hiring non-local workers and other policies related to foreign investors.

Local governments often interpret Beijing's policies flexibly and implement them strategically in localities for their own good. For example, Hsing (1998) found that local governments in Guangdong Province manipulated the central state's policies of land leasing and foreign investment in a variety of informal ways.[13] As a result, foreign investors have begun to realize that favourable investment policies issued by Beijing are not nearly as advantageous as the 'special deals' that can be crafted with local officials (ibid.). Rather than dealing with the central government, foreign investors often prefer to build up long-term alliances with local officials for more stable and favourable investment conditions and cheaper local resources.

In addition to directly developing enterprises for more revenues and dealing with the foreign investors for more capital, local governments have formed various relationships with local business organizations, including the non-state sectors. Accounting for the higher rates of productivity in smaller industrial jurisdictions, Guthrie (2005) has argued that local officials (former agents of the planned economy) became 'the teachers or collaborators of capitalism' to the local managers in their gradual adaptation to the rules of the market. Wank's study (1999) of the private sector reveals how private entrepreneurs have established patron–client networks with local state agents to maximize revenues and security. These clientelist networks in localities have evolved from personal links between entrepreneurs and individual officials and face-to-face *guanxi* practice to broad institutionalized localistic networks on an organizational basis (Wank, 2002). The result of these macro-level policies is that the state has established the conditions under which a variety of organizational types, including those that are still state-owned, have the latitude to behave like business organizations in China today.

FDI, GLOBAL BUSINESS AND ORGANIZATIONAL CHANGE AT THE FIRM LEVEL

At the same time that it was embarking on the domestic reforms that transformed the economy during the 1980s and the 1990s, China was opening itself to the global community. The 1979 Joint Venture Law was the first of a series of regulations allowing the flow of foreign capital into China. In 1980, China enforced its opening-up policies in a small part of the coastal region where four 'special economic zones' (SEZs) in Fujian province (Xiamen) and Guangdong province (Shenzhen, Shantou and Zhuhai) were established. After witnessing the rapid growth of these SEZs, former Premier Zhao Ziyang implemented 'the coastal development strategy' in the mid-1980s to accelerate the flow of FDI and expand foreign trade to a wider region, including eastern and southern provinces in coastal areas.

Since the early 1990s, China has become a major recipient of FDI that represents the major part of total foreign capital received by China (including foreign loans, FDI and other investments). Beginning in 1991, the amount of FDI in China rose precipitously.[14] In 1993, China received more FDI than any other country and, since then, has been the second largest recipient in the world, behind only the US. By early 1999, FDI in joint ventures and wholly foreign-owned companies had exceeded one-quarter of a trillion US dollars, several times larger than cumulative FDI since World War II received by Japan, South Korea and Taiwan combined (Lardy, 2002). In 2002, China's total inflows of FDI reached US$400 billion, making it the world's largest recipient of FDI. And the investment trend is, at this point, accelerating, reaching US$13.4 billion in the first quarter of 2005, up about 9.5 per cent over the first quarter figure for 2004 (Meyer, 2005).

Explosive growth trends have also occurred in the area of foreign trade, one of the most significant indicators signifying that China has emerged as a major player in the global economy. China's foreign trade grew from US$20 billion in the late 1970s (about the thirtieth in the world) to US$510 billion in 2001, making it the sixth largest trading nation in the world, behind the US, Germany, Japan, France and the UK. The total volume of exports increased four times from 1978 to 1990, and almost five times from 1990 to 2000. The total imports had increased four times from 1978 to 1990, and more than four times from 1990 to 2000.[15]

With China's rapid economic growth in GDP and its explosive growth in foreign trade, business organizations have experienced dramatic changes. The nation's economic architects aspired to forcing rational economic actions and organizational structures onto the development agenda of business organizations through initiating several waves of enterprise reforms at different time periods. From Zhao Ziyang in the 1980s to Zhu Rongji in the 1990s, the Chinese leaders have clearly focused on the creation of rational account-ability and the embracing of international standards. The enterprise reforms in the reform era have concentrated on building a 'modern enterprise system' (*xiandai qiye zhidu*) and forcing enterprise restructuring in terms of all of the accounting practices based on inter-national models and standards of firm managements.

There has been some debate over the impetus behind the dramatic investment in China. On the one hand, Huang (2003) has recently argued that FDI has been attracted to China because of a distorted institutional environment: the artificial suppression of the private sector in order to protect the state sector has created an opportunity for extraordinary growth in the FDI sector. Others (for example Fu, 2000) have argued that the state has purposefully set in place the institutions to attract FDI, because of the variety of positive externalities that come along with it. Both the government and the enterprises recognized the need for foreign capital, advanced management experience and technology. In either case, the impact on Chinese business organizations has been significant. Coupled with the reformers' intentions, the inflows of foreign capital and global corporations into China have exerted significant pressure on the evolution of Chinese business organizations to adapt to the rules of the global market. The desire to attract foreign investment and tech-nology, in turn, has led to institutional accommodations that support legal–rational accountability and the rule of law within the firm. These influences from foreign investors and global corporations are evident in not only the nation's macroeconomic policies, but also organizational changes at the firm level. From the perspective of foreign investors, many of them are more interested in long-term investments to capture market share than in cheap labour. They generally seek Chinese partners that are predictable, stable, and knowledgable about modern business practices and negotiations.[16] Pressure from inter-national organizations and foreign investors has accelerated the rationalization of China's economic system both at the state level and within firms.

As a result, significant organizational learning has occurred on both sides of the joint venture equation in China. Several scholars have examined the issue of organizational learning as the central theme of organizational change (March, 1981, 1991; Levitt and March, 1988; Cohen and Levinthal, 1990), with many focusing on the issue of interorgan-izational transfers of knowledge, specifically with regard to strategic alliances between firms (Child, 2001; Hamel, 1991; Kogut and Zander, 1992). Within this line of research, organizational learning has been defined as the practices that organizations adopt as rou-tines to guide behaviour (Levitt and March, 1988) or the acquisition of knowledge that is recognized as useful to the organization (Huber, 1991). A number of scholars have focused specifically on organizational learning in joint venture alliances (Kogut, 1988, 1989; Kogut and Singh, 1988; Lane and Lubatkin, 1998) and this is a key issue for the development of Chinese business organizations. On the foreign side, Luo and Peng (1999) have shown the importance of organizational learning, as intensity and diversity of experience for foreign firms operating in China are both important predictors of perfor-mance (see also Chapter 5 in this volume).

Luo *et al.* (2001) have raised the issue that the JV literature has overwhelmingly focused on the experience and learning of the foreign partner. However, significant organizational

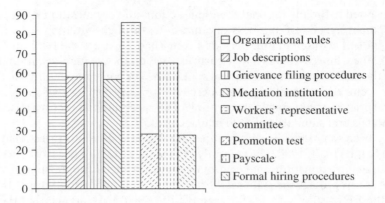

Source: Guthrie (1999: ch. 3).

Figure 6.3   Percentages of firms in Shanghai institutionalizing formal labour reforms, 1995

learning has occurred on the Chinese side of the JV dyad. On the Chinese side, a process of rationalization is occurring in the Chinese workplace as well, where Chinese companies are adopting a number of the rational bureaucratic systems that are mostly found in Western organizations, such as grievance filing procedures, mediation committees, formal organizational rules and guidelines, and many others. Guthrie's (1999, 2002a, 2005) studies of urban industrial firms in Shanghai provide concrete evidence that Chinese factories and companies have been experimenting with a number of formal institutions in the workplace. Figure 6.3 shows that more than 60 per cent of workplaces in industrial Shanghai have adopted formal organizational rules, formal grievance filing procedures and formal pay scales. About 85 per cent of workplaces have institutionalized Worker Representative Committee meetings. And more than 50 per cent have institutionalized formal job descriptions and mediation institutions within the firm.

Foreign investment, specifically joint venture relationships between foreign firms and their Chinese business partners, has played a crucial role in this process of change. Guthrie (1999) found that joint venture relationships have a statistically significant and consistent effect on the rationalization of organizational decisions and practices of Chinese factories. Chinese factories and companies that have formal relationships with foreign firms are significantly more likely to have formal organizational rules. They are about 17 times more likely to have formal grievance filing procedures, five times as likely to have worker representative committee meetings and twice as likely to have formal hiring procedures. In addition, these companies that have foreign partners are more likely to adopt the laws and regulations the Chinese government has constituted to create a rational–legal economic system, for example the Company Law. This binds them to the rules of the international community. This relationship amounts to a significant positive effect of foreign joint ventures: pushing partner organizations in China to adopt stable rational–legal structures and systems. More importantly, the Chinese partner companies in these joint venture relationships are also changing as a result of the joint venture negotiations.

While these stable, rational–legal systems are adopted more often to attract foreign investors than they are for the good of workers, nevertheless, they have radical implications for the structure of authority relations and, therefore, for the lives of individual Chinese citizens. Compared to the state sector and urban collectives, the average wages in the foreign sector and joint ventures are significantly higher and have increased much faster, especially after 1993. The visible internal structure changes in Chinese workplaces are affecting millions of Chinese citizens on a daily basis. The workers in those business organizations have greater bargaining power within their own workplaces and now are entitled to numerous human rights (except for the right to independent unionization), guaranteed by the Labour Law (1994). Examples in this realm include the right to file grievances with Labour Arbitration Commissions (LAC), the right to a fair hearing at the LAC, and the right to a minimum wage. With respect to grievances filed with the LACs, by 2000, workers were winning, on average, about 60 per cent of the cases brought before the LACs.[17]

GUANXI: CHINESE BUSINESS CULTURE?

One cannot write about business organization in China today without touching on the issue of the role of *guanxi* (social relationships) in Chinese business (see also Chapter 4 in this volume). *Guanxi* is widely noted to be one of the key aspects of Chinese culture and plays important roles in business activities in China. Many scholars have examined the role of *guanxi* in Chinese business (for example Bhattacharya *et al.*, 1998; Bian, 1997; Boisot and Child, 1999; Fahr *et al.*, 1998, Gold *et al.*, 2002; Guthrie, 1998a; Hamilton, 1991; Luo, 1997, 2001a, 2001b; Pearce *et al.*, 2000; Peng and Heath, 1996; Salk and Shenkar, 2001; Xin and Pearce, 1996; Yeung, 1997). In general, China scholars have agreed on the centrality of *guanxi* in Chinese society, culture and everyday life, but there are disagreements on the extent to which *guanxi* is something unique to China and how it is changing in China's reform era.[18] Some scholars have stressed the increasing roles of *guanxi* and social networking in doing business and attributed the practices of the gift economy in contemporary China to the cultural characteristics of Chinese society (for example Yang, 1994, 2002; Bian, 1997). A large body of work on East Asia generally supports this view, providing evidence on how social relationships can serve business goals, forming Chinese-style business practices and organizations (for example Redding, 1990; Hamilton, 1991; Fields, 1995; Solomon, 1999; Boisot and Child, 1999). This cultural perspective offers important insights for understanding the ways in which *guanxi* and *guanxi* practices function in Chinese business.

However, some scholars have also argued that *guanxi* is a system that emerged from the institutional structure of the command economy (for example, Walder, 1986; Oi, 1991; Wank, 1999; Guthrie, 1998a, 2002b). According to this view, to understand the changing role of *guanxi* in Chinese business today, we must first examine the institutional changes occurring in Chinese society and the ways economic actors have responded to those changes through the changing use of *guanxi* in business activities. Moreover, the perspective that *guanxi* is a cultural element of being 'Chinese' regardless of time or place keeps us from understanding how specific institutional structures of Chinese society at certain time periods have defined, facilitated or decreased economic actors' reliance on networks to accomplish business tasks. The view from this body of work is that the empirical reality of the industrial and commercial economies in the era of China's economic reform suggests that practices and perceptions of *guanxi* are changing in important ways in the urban industrial economy. These changes suggest a trend that does not fully fit with theories that see an increasing role of *guanxi* and *guanxi* practice throughout China during the economic transition.

While important studies have shown the role of *guanxi* in reform-era China in such areas as obtaining jobs (Bian, 1997), in the vitality of the small-scale private sector (Wank, 1999; Hsing, 1998) and even in firm performance (Peng and Luo, 2000), other studies have shown that *guanxi* practice is diminishing in importance, especially for large-scale organizations, as markets become rationalized across China (Guthrie, 1998a, 2002b). In China today, powerful economic actors often pay more and more attention to the laws, rules and regulations that are part of the emerging rational–legal system that is being constructed by the Chinese state. Many managers of large industrial organizations increasingly view the practice of emphasizing *guanxi* to accomplish administrative tasks as unnecessary and dangerous in light of new regulations and prohibitions against such approaches to official procedures. However, this set of practices fits closely with the position economic actors occupy within the institutional structure of China's economy (Guthrie, 2002b). The higher a firm is in China's administrative hierarchy, the less likely the general or vice general manager of the firm is to view *guanxi* practice, that is using connections to get things done, as important in the economic transition. The lower a firm is in the administrative hierarchy, the more likely the firm's general manager is to view *guanxi* practice as important to success in the economic transition. Attitudes toward *guanxi* practice also vary with a number of organizational factors ranging from the background of the firm's general manager to whether or not the organization has a joint venture with a foreign company.

Of the two types of *guanxi* that shape action in China today (that is *guanxi* and *guanxi* practice), *guanxi* practice lies in conflict with the rational–legal system emerging at the state level (that is formal laws, policies and rational procedures), while *guanxi*, more broadly conceived, is often viewed as a necessary part of the market reforms and business transactions in a market economy. The importance of this distinction is increasing in the urban industrial economy, for two reasons. First, large industrial organizations are monitored by the state much more closely than individual actors in the economy are. Given that the official discourse surrounding *guanxi* practice is negative, it is not surprising that large-scale industrial organizations are more careful about the extent to which they engage in this institution. In addition to the fact that markets are becoming increasingly competitive, the very existence of markets changes the meaning and significance of *guanxi* in China's transitional economy.

In China today, emerging markets and the transition from a command to market economy allow actors the freedom to make economic choices in an open market. Previously, one element of *guanxi* practice for industrial managers under the command economy was the necessity of gaining access to distribution channels (input and output) that were controlled by state officials under that system. In China's transitional economy today, officials have no such control over the distribution of resources and products. Under the economic reforms, an open market increasingly distributes the flow of goods in many sectors. This change has profound implications for the transition away from a focus on *guanxi* practice to a more general focus on *guanxi* as business relationships. Industrial managers no longer need to curry favour with state officials to overcome bottlenecks or gain access to resources. As a result, they do not view *guanxi* practice as an important part of decision making in China's industrial economy.

Currently, the Chinese government is engaged in the project of constructing a rational–legal system that will govern the decisions and practices of economic actors. This is especially true for large-scale organizations that are more closely monitored by the state administrative offices than individuals or small-scale entrepreneurs. Through the construction of this rational–legal system, the state pushes actors (especially large-scale industrial firms) to approach economic activities in ways that are sanctioned by the rational–legal system. In addition, as the government continues to place economic responsibilities directly on the shoulders of firms, the constraints of the market force business organizations to consider many factors that make economic sense, many of which often lie in conflict with the use of social connections.

NEW FORMS OF SOCIAL CONTROL: BUSINESS ASSOCIATIONS AND COOPTATION

In 1988, the Chinese government began to impose control on social organizations, including various business associations, by creating an official registration system to be enforced by a newly established Social Organization Management Department within the Ministry of Civil Affairs. One year later, the 'Regulations on Registration and Administration of Social Organizations' was issued by the State Council, along with the 'Measures on Management of Foundations' and the 'Interim Rule on Management of Foreign Chambers of Commerce'. These guidelines essentially stipulate that all social organizations must be sponsored by a government or Party organization, even though they all have the right to independent legal status. After a period of rapid proliferation, by the end of 1992, the number of established and registered social organizations settled at around 40 000. In 1998, a new set of regulations was issued through the 'Regulations on Registration and Administration of Social Organizations' and the 'Interim Regulation on Registration and Management of Private Non-Profit Organization'.

The 1990s laws on social organization aimed to incorporate governmental supervision and control on the one hand, while transferring the function of governmental monitoring to a separate governing body on the other. A large body of work on China's reforms has emphasized the corporatist model of social organization and control (for example Pearson, 1994; Unger and Chan, 1995, 1996; Kang, 2002) or embedded relations (for example Foster, 2002) between social organizations and their governing agencies (*zhuguan bumen*). And, beyond the formal ties between business associations and the governing system stipulated by law, there are various informal ties between the entrepreneur group and the state officials that directly influence the way those business associations are run (for example Goodman, 1999; Parris, 1999; Wank, 1999, 2002).

It is still too early to draw conclusions about the degree of independence of entrepreneur groups and business associations that are emerging in China's reform era. The reality of China's position as a still authoritarian regime and the status of the Chinese Communist Party (CCP) as the most powerful organization in China suggest significant limitations on the relative autonomy of these groups. However, the emergence and growth of new social groups have brought about social and political implications that cannot be ignored in today's China. While the wealth attached to the economic elites running new business organizations has not led directly to democratic values or to pressure on the CCP for radical political reforms (Goodman, 1999; Parris, 1999), these economic elites have become one of the most important social groups and they have begun to exert pressure on China's political regime.[19]

Perhaps the most critical evidence of the importance of this social group comes from the government's embracing of Jiang Zemin's 'three representatives' policy that permits private entrepreneurs to be members of the CCP. Proposed by Jiang in 2001, this policy was incorporated into China's Constitution at the 16th Party Congress in 2002. This policy is a direct outcome of the rapid growth of private economy in the 1990s. Thus the cooptation model becomes clearly a major part of China's economic growth and trans-formation. By incorporating private entrepreneurs into its political camp, China's only ruling party is now announcing that it continues to represent not only the workers and peasants, but also all of the people's interests, including the capitalists, the so-called 'advanced social productive forces' (*xianjin shengchanli*). In doing so, the CCP has ended many years' exclusion policies directed toward private entrepreneurs during the past half a century. While these entrepreneur groups comprise only a small part of the Chinese pop-ulation, their inclusion is a clear statement by the CCP and the Chinese government that the business groups can no longer be ignored within the political community.

IMPLICATIONS FOR RESEARCH AND PRACTICE

The issues raised in this chapter cover a diverse range of themes all relating, in one way or another, to the evolution of business organizations in China. It is useful, at this point, to step back and assess the future of business organizations in China with regard to both research and practice. On the research side, scholarship must continue to walk the line between macro-level analyses and micro-oriented studies that reach deep inside the firm to understand the ways in which managerial decisions are made. Macro-level analyses will naturally continue to be important in the evolution of our understanding of business organizations in China. Studies in this area must be sensitive to the ways in which China's institutional environment is changing and the impact these changes have on the environ-ment for economic organizations. While a good deal of significant macro-level work has been done on foreign direct investment in China (Huang, 2003; Fu, 2000), productivity across sectors of the economy (Chen *et al.*, 1988; Woo *et al.*, 1993; Rawski, 1994, 1995) and the policy changes that have driven China's reforms forward (Naughton, 1995), research in this area will benefit from more deep thinking about the shape and construct of evolving institutions in China.

Of particular importance are the *mediating institutions* that govern business organiza-tions, but are often left out of strict macro-level analyses. For example, Walder's (1992, 1995) examination of the institutional hierarchy of the former command economy and its lingering impact on the operation of business organizations in China today was a crit-ical insight that changed the way many scholars thought about the operation of business organization in China.[20] We know that these types of mediating institutions are critical macro-level filters for the changes that are occurring throughout China. However, they are often left out of macro-level analyses, for two reasons. First, institutions such as these are outside the realm of usual suspects for the macro-level data that seem to matter the most. Thus, when macro-level studies are conducted, researchers often simply search for the data that are most often used in macro-level analyses, ignoring the critical institutions that have shaped variation in performance across sectors of the economy. Second, understanding and gathering data on these types of institutions often require in-depth qualitative research, a type of research that is frequently absent from macro-level studies of economic change in China. The main point here is that, in order truly to understand business organizations in China today, macro-level studies must extend beyond the types of data that have become the bread and butter for this field.

Against the backdrop of the macro-level changes occurring in China, it is also crucial that we continue to look deeply inside the firm to understand the mechanisms by which business organizations operate. In discussing these issues as they relate to our understanding of the impact of FDI (often treated as a macro-level variable), Meyer (2005: 307) recently articulated the research agenda in the following way: 'The challenge for management researchers, then, is to get inside firms . . . and understand the flows of resources, technologies, and know-how . . . the balance of power between parent companies and their joint venture partners. Until we understand these processes at the firm level, we will not fully understand the impact of FDI on the viability of Chinese firms and China's overall economic wellbeing.' Large-scale quantitative studies of business organizations in China are useful for understanding general trends, but they often obscure the ways in which decisions are made at the firm level. This is not a call to abandon large-scale quantitative analyses of firms in China, but rather to supplement these studies with detailed case analyses. There can be no substitute for sitting across the table from a Chinese manager and discussing with him/her the complex web of forces and relationships acting upon and shaping the decisions they face on a daily basis in China's rapidly changing economic landscape.

The implications of China's rapid evolution for practitioners are somewhat more complex, as they depend upon what the practitioners aspire to accomplish in China. However, there are basic principles that can be extracted from this analysis as lessons for practitioners. First, like academic scholars, practitioners must be highly sensitive to China's rapidly changing institutional environment, as well as the lingering effects of past institutions. In rapidly changing societies like China, accomplishing tasks not only is a matter of understanding the current rules of the system, but also requires an understanding of the institutions that governed China in the past.

Second, even as the institutional environment is still in flux, the legal system is stabilizing in a way that is predictable and rational. It is useful in this sense for practitioners to develop a solid understanding of the current legal system in China and how it operates. Scholars like Lo and Tian (2005) have effectively detailed the workings of the Chinese legal system, revealing that it is no longer a system run capriciously by a one-party government. Indeed, the Chinese legal system has evolved in significant ways, and it behoves all practitioners to have a good sense of how the legal system affects business organizations in China.

Third, sensitivity to local difference is perhaps one of the most important realities a practitioner must face. Recently, a local Chinese practitioner in Kunming recounted to us a story about the hits and misses of practitioners coming to visit China's southwest. In recounting a talk delivered to a group of SOE managers by Peter Senge, the Chinese consultant lamented: 'In the end, it was useless for him to come here. It doesn't matter how famous he is. If people don't understand how to translate the basic concepts, no one is going to get anything out of his expertise. If local people here have never heard of the concept of a "learning organization", the ideas are not going to mean anything to them'. Local conditions, the decentralization of the reform effort and variation in local policies all shape the challenges that practitioners face in a given locality, and it is crucial to understand the variation that exists across localities in China.

CONCLUSIONS

Business organizations in China are a thriving and fundamental part of the economic and social transformation that is occurring in that country. However, a narrow definition of business organization does not capture the rich variety of organizational forms that are behaving like business organizations in China today. State-owned enterprises, township and village enterprises, private enterprises and foreign-funded enterprises all, to varying degrees, behave like business organizations. TVEs and SOEs are not private businesses, but they operate like business organizations in key ways. TVEs have been governed by local officials who often treat these enterprises as their own industrial firms. Although they are agents of the state, they themselves behave like owners of industrial firms, and thus operate their organizations like business organizations. SOEs are in a different situation. These organizations are not as independent from central and provincial governments as TVEs are. However, they have come to operate like business organizations in the Chinese economy. Through being forced to compete with the non-state sector and through learning the behaviour of business organizations through joint ventures with foreign corporations over the course of the economic reforms, SOEs have come to behave more and more like business organizations in today's China.

Private enterprises and foreign-funded enterprises look much more like business organizations as they are typically defined in capitalist economies. Private enterprises are defined by relationships between owners and workers and they are free to operate in a way that maximizes the flow of revenues and profits. Foreign-funded firms are basically in the same position, however, many of them occupy positions of tightly controlled subsidiaries or agents of the corporations they represent. All of these organizational types operate like business organizations, and all are subject to the rapidly changing institutions that define China's transforming economy.

NOTES

1. We would like to thank Henry Yeung for thoughtful comments on earlier drafts.
2. Data from *Chinese Statistical Yearbook*, 2002, National Statistical Bureau of China Press. The figures include 'all the state-owned and non-state-owned industrial enterprises [with annual sales of over 5 million *yuan*]'. Foreign firms include 18 257 enterprises with funds from Hong Kong, Macao and Taiwan, and 13 166 foreign-funded enterprises.
3. See discussions in Oi and Walder (1999).
4. For example, according to Li's (1997) study on state enterprises in the 1980s, SOEs supervised by local governments were more likely to reduce workers' wages because of 'poor performance' than those supervised by the central state. Li's study also indicates the hardening budget constraints in local governments' supervision over SOEs.

5. In the spring of 1992, Deng Xiaoping took his 'southern tour' to Shenzhen and officially declared the Chinese economic system as a market economy with socialist characteristics, indicating a clear market-driven direction of China's economic reform.

6. There are obvious and famous exceptions here: state-owned enterprises like Baoshan Steel were still closely monitored and supported by the state (Steinfeld, 1998). However, while these organizations are often viewed as the markers of what is occurring in the Chinese reform process, this view is mistaken. Still important to the economy, these largest state-owned organizations are not representative of the economy as a whole. Thus, even though many scholars view these organizations as measures of the progress of China's reforms, they are more accurately the exceptions that prove the rule.

7. It is important to note the interdependence of these sectors here: as state-owned enterprises were placed on the dual track system, private firms were allowed to emerge in the economy, becoming a force that essentially forced the state sector to compete (Naughton, 1995). Similarly, the foreign sector has been a key factor in the teaching of management practices (Guthrie, 1999, 2005), as well as in the transfer of technology.

8. Although labour contracts officially afforded SOEs the opportunity to end lifetime employment, the practice continued for many years, though it has been declining steadily since the formal changes in 1986 (Guthrie, 1999, 2002a and 2002b).

9. As with all reforms adopted over the course of China's transition, these formal laws and regulations that governed enterprise behaviour were first experimented with in many venues over significant periods of time before becoming officially codified in formal laws and regulations.

10. See 'the Decision on Several Issues for Establishing a Socialist Market Economy System' passed in the Third Plenary Session of the Fourteenth National Congress of the CCP in 1993.

11. A typical ownership transformation for a state-owned enterprise would allow the state to retain between 40 per cent and 50 per cent of the company's shares; between 20 per cent and 30 per cent of the shares are designated for institutional shares; the remaining 30 per cent of shares are designated for public consumption.

12. For discussion see Wong (2002).

13. For example, in Hsing's book (1998), a city government divided the land for one foreign project into several small lots and granted land use permission individually. This method could satisfy the standard of the smaller size of land that this level of governments had the authority to grant. Similar strategies have been used more widely for foreign investment arrangements in regions throughout southern China.

14. According to Lardy (1996), four factors contribute to such dramatic increases in the FDI China attracted in the early 1990s: (1) the increasing magnitude of aggregate FDI flowing to developing countries in the 1990s; (2) China's political stability in the post-Tiananmen era, combined with the explosive growth of domestic economy, rebuilt the confidence of foreign firms and investors; (3) after one decade's economic liberalization and practice of the coastal developmental strategies, China's foreign investment regime had been systematically liberalized and more sectors had been opened to foreign investors; and (4) it is widely believed that Chinese firms have disguised their money as 'foreign investment' to take advantage of the special policies only provided to foreign invested enterprises. (This final point likely accounts for the high rates of FDI flowing in from Hong Kong.)

15. Although total Chinese exports have somewhat outpaced total imports since the early 1990s, the difference is relatively small compared to the overall level of trade.

16. Here again we are speaking of joint venture partnerships, as opposed to other types of foreign investment.

17. *Statistical Yearbook of China* 2002.

18. See the discussions in Gold *et al.* (2002: 3–20).

19. The Chinese Academy of Social Sciences (CASS) recently released a report on social stratification of contemporary China in 2004. It suggested that China's 'middle class' accounted for 19 per cent of the country's 1.3 billion population by 2003. According to the Academy's criteria, in their report, families with assets valued from 150 000 (US$18 137) to 300 000 *yuan* (US$36 275) can be classified as middle class.

20. Walder's work in this area conceptually overlapped with Wong's (1991, 1992) work on decentralization. However, Walder's work was very specific about identifying the key institutional constructs that have served as the filter of macro-level policies for individual firms.

REFERENCES

Bhattacharya, Rajeev, T. Devinney and M. Pillutla (1998), 'A formal model of trust based on outcomes', *Academy of Management Review*, **23**(3), 459–72.

Bian, Yanjie (1997), 'Bringing strong ties back in: indirect ties, network bridges, and job searches in China', *American Sociological Review*, **62**, 366–85.

Boisot, Max and John Child (1999), 'Organizations as adaptive systems in complex environments: the case of China', *Organization Science*, **10**(3), 237–52.

Chen, Kuan, H. Wang, Y. Zheng, G.H. Jefferson and T. Rawski (1988), 'Productivity change in Chinese industry: 1953–1985', *Journal of Comparative Economics*, **12**,570–91.

Child, J. (2001), 'Learning through strategic alliances', in M. Dierkes, A.B. Antal, J. Child and I. Nonaka (eds), *Handbook of Organizational Learning and Knowledge*, Oxford: Oxford University Press, pp. 657–80.

Cohen, W.M. and D.A. Levinthal (1990), 'Absorptive capacity: a new perspective on learning and innovation', *Administrative Science Quarterly*, **35**(1), 128–52.

Dean, Earl H. (1917), 'Economics and the science of business', *The Journal of Political Economy*, **25**(1), 106–10.

Demsetz, Harold (1967), 'Toward a theory of property rights', *Ownership, Control, and the Firm: The Organization of Economic Activity*, vol. 1, Oxford: Blackwell, pp. 104–16.

Deng, Zhenglai (1997), *The State and the Society (guojia yu shehui)*, China: Sichuan People's Press.

Deng, Zhenglai and Jing Yuejin (1992), 'Constructing China's civil society', *Chinese Social Sciences Quarterly*, **1**.

Farh, Jiing-Lih, A. Tsui, K. Xin and B. Cheng (1998), 'The influence of relational demography and guanxi: the Chinese case', *Organization Science*, **9**(4), 471–88.

Fields, Karl J. (1995), *Enterprise and State in Korea and Taiwan*, Ithaca, NY: Cornell University Press.

Foster, Kenneth W. (2002), 'Embedded with state agencies: business associations in Yantai', *The China Journal*, **47**, 41–65.

Fu, Jun (2000), *Institutions and Investments: Foreign Direct Investment in China During an Era of Reform*, Ann Arbor, MI: University of Michigan Press.

Furubotn, Eirik and S. Pejovich (eds) (1974), *The Economics of Property Rights*, Cambridge, MA: Ballinger.

Gao, Sheldon (2002), 'China stock market in a global perspective', Research Report published by Dow Jones & Company, Inc.

Gold, Thomas, D. Guthrie and D. Wank (eds) (2002), *Social Connections in China: Institutions, Culture, and the Changing Nature of Guanxi*, New York: Cambridge University Press.

Goodman, David (1999), 'The new middle class', in M. Goldman and R. MacFarquhar (eds), *The Paradox of China's Post-Mao Reforms*, Cambridge, MA: Harvard University Press.

Guthrie, D. (1998a), 'The declining significance of guanxi in China's economic transition', *The China Quarterly*, **154**, 254–82.

Guthrie, D. (1998b), 'Organizational uncertainty and labor contracts in China's economic transition', *Sociological Forum*, **13**(3), 457–94.

Guthrie, D. (1999), *Dragon in a Three-Piece Suit: The Emergence of Capitalism in China*, Princeton, NJ: Princeton University Press.

Guthrie, D. (2002a), 'The transformation of labor relations in China's emerging market economy', *The Future of Market Transition*, **19**, 137–168.

Guthrie, D. (2002b), 'Information asymmetries and the problem of perception: the significance of structural position in assessing the importance of *Guanxi* in China', in T. Gold, D. Guthrie and D. Wank (eds), *Social Connections in China: Institutions, Culture, and the Changing Nature of Guanxi*, New York: Cambridge University Press, pp. 37–56.

Guthrie, D. (2003), 'The quiet revolution: the emergence of capitalism in China', *Harvard International Review*, **25**(2), 48–53.

Guthrie, D. (2005), 'Organizational learning and productivity: state structure and foreign investment in the rise of the Chinese corporation', *Management and Organization Review*, **1**(2), 165–95.

Hamel, G. (1991), 'Competition for competence and interorganizational learning within international strategic alliances', *Strategic Management Journal*, **12**, 83–103.

Hamilton, G.G. (1991), *Business Networks and Economic Development in East and Southeast Asia*, Centre for East Asian Studies, Hong Kong: University of Hong Kong Press.

Hsing, You-tien (1998), *Making Capitalism in China: The Taiwan Connection*, New York: Oxford University Press.

Huang, Yasheng (1995), 'Administrative monitoring in China', *The China Quarterly*, **143**, 828–43.

Huang, Yasheng (2003), *Selling China: Foreign Direct Investment during the Reform Era*, New York: Cambridge University Press.

Huber, G. (1991), 'Organizational learning: the contributing processes and the literatures', *Organizational Science*, **2**(1), 88–115.

Kang, Xiaoguang (2002), 'A study of China's political stability in the 1990s', *Twenty-First Century*, **72**, 33.

Kogut, B. (1988), 'Joint ventures: theoretical and empirical perspectives', *Strategic Management Journal*, **9**, 319–32.

Kogut, B. (1989), 'The stability of joint ventures: reciprocity and competitive rivalry', *The Journal of Industrial Economics*, **38**, 138–98.

Kogut, B. and H. Singh (1988), 'The effect of national culture on the choice of entry mode', *Journal of International Business Studies*, **19**(3), 411–32.

Kogut, B. and U. Zander (1992), 'Knowledge of the firm, combinative capabilities, and the replication of technology', *Organization Science*, **3**(3), 383–97.

Lane, P. and M. Lubatkin (1998), 'Relative absorptive capacity and interorganizational learning', *Strategic Management Journal*, **19**(5), 461–77.

Lardy, N. (1996), 'The role of foreign trade and investment in China's economic transition', in A. Walder (ed.), *China's Transitional Economy*, New York: Oxford University Press.

Lardy, N. (2002), *Integrating China into Global Economy*, Washington, DC: Brookings Institution Press.

Lee, Hong Yung (1991), *From Revolutionary Cadres to Party Technocrats in Socialist China*, Berkeley, CA: University of California Press.

Levitt, B. and J. March (1988), 'Organizational learning', *Annual Review of Sociology*, **14**, 319–40.

Li, Linda Chelan (1997), 'Provincial discretion and national power: investment policy in Guangdong and Shanghai, 1978–93', *The China Quarterly*, **152**, 778–804.

Lin, Nan (1995), 'Local market socialism: local corporatism in action in rural China', *Theory and Society*, **24**, 301–54.

Lo, Vai Io and X. Tian (2005), *Law and Investment in China: The Legal and Business Environments after China's WTO Accession*, London: RoutledgeCurzon.

Luo, Yadong (1997), 'Partner selection and venturing success: the case of joint venturing firms in the People's Republic of China', *Organization Science*, **8**(6), 648–62.

Luo, Yadong (2001a), 'Toward a cooperative view of MNC-host government relations: building blocks and Performance Implication', *Journal of International Business Studies*, **32**(3), 401–19.

Luo, Yadong (2001b), 'Antecedents and consequences of personal attachment in cross-cultural cooperative ventures', *Administrative Science Quarterly*, **46**(2), 177–201.

Luo, Yadong and M. Peng (1999), 'Learning to compete in a transition economy: experience, environment, and performance', *Journal of International Business Studies*, **30**(2), 269–95.

Luo, Yadong, O. Shenkar and M. Nyaw (2001), 'A dual perspective on control and performance in international joint ventures: lessons from a developing economy', *Journal of International Business*, **32**(1), 41–58.

March, James (1981), 'Footnotes to organizational change', *Administrative Science Quarterly*, **26**(2), 563–77.

March, James (1991), 'Explorations and exploitation in organizational learning', *Organization Science*, **2**(1), 71–87.

Meyer, Marshall (2005), 'Is China for sale?', *Management and Organization Review*, **1**(2), 303–7.

National Statistical Bureau of China (1996), *Chinese Statistical Yearbook*, National Statistical Bureau of China Press.

National Statistical Bureau of China (2002), *Chinese Statistical Yearbook*, National Statistical Bureau of China Press.

Naughton, Barry (1995), *Growing out of the Plan: Chinese Economic Reform 1978–1993*, New York: Cambridge University Press.

Noble, Howard S. (1927), 'The relation of business organization to accounting', *The Accounting Review*, **2**(3), 232–6.

Nolan, Peter (2004), *Transforming China: Globalization, Transition and Development*, London: Anthem Press.

Oi, Jean C. (1991), *State and Peasants in Contemporary China*, Berkeley: University of California Press.

Oi, Jean C. (1992), 'Fiscal reform and economic foundations of local state corporatism in China', *World Politics*, **45**(1), 99–126.

Oi, Jean C. and Andrew Walder (eds) (1999), *Property Rights and Economic Reform in China*, Stanford, CA: Stanford University Press.

Parris, Kristen (1999), 'The rise of private business interests', in M. Goldman and R. MacFarquhar (eds), *The Paradox of China's Post-Mao Reforms*, Cambridge, MA: Harvard University Press.

Pearce, Jone, I. Branyiczki and G. Bigley (2000), 'Insufficient bureaucracy: trust and commitment in particularistic organizations', *Organization Science*, **11**(2), 148–62.

Pearson, Margaret (1994), 'The Janus face of business associations in China: socialist corporatism in foreign enterprises', *Australian Journal of Chinese Affairs*, **31**, 25–46.

Peng, Mike and P. Heath (1996), 'The growth of the firm in planned economies in transition: institutions, organizations, and strategic choice', *The Academy of Management Review*, **21**(2), 492–528.

Peng, Mike and Y. Luo (2000), 'Managerial ties and firm performance in a transitional economy: the nature of a micro–macro link', *Academy of Management Journal*, **43**(3), 486–501.

Rawski, Thomas G. (1994), 'Progress without privatization: the reform of China's state industries', in V. Milor (ed.), *Changing Political Economies: Privatization in Post-Communist and Reforming Communist States*, Boulder, CO: Lynne Reinner Publishers, pp. 27–52.

Rawski, Thomas G. (1995), 'Implications of China's reform experience', *China Quarterly*, **144**, 1150–73.

Redding, Gordon S. (1990), *The Spirit of Chinese Capitalism*, Berlin and New York: Walter de Gruyter.

Salk, Jane and O. Shenkar (2001), 'Social identities in an international joint venture: an exploratory case study', *Organization Science*, **12**(2), 161–78.

Solomon, Richard H. (1999), *Chinese Negotiating Behavior: Pursuing Interests through 'Old Friends'*, Washington DC: United States Institute of Peace Press.

Sparling, Samuel E. (1906), *Introduction to Business Organization*, New York: The Macmillan Co.

Statistical Yearbook of China (various years), Beijing: National Statistical Bureau of China Press.

Steinfeld, Edward (1998), *Forging Industrial Reform in China: The Fate of State-Owned Industry*, New York: Cambridge University Press.

Unger, Jonathan and A. Chan (1995), 'China, corporatism and the East Asian model', *The Australian Journal of Chinese Affairs*, **33**, 29–53.

Unger, Jonathan and A. Chan (1996), 'Corporatism in China: a developmental state in an East Asian context', in Jonathan Unger (ed.), *China after Socialism: In the Footsteps of Eastern Europe or East Asia*, Armonk: NY: M.E. Sharpe.

Walder, Andrew G. (1986), *Communist Neo-Traditionalism: Work and Authority in Chinese Industry*, Berkeley, CA: University of California Press.

Walder, Andrew G. (1992), 'Property rights and stratification in socialist redistributive societies', *American Sociological Review*, **57**, 524–39.

Walder, Andrew G. (1995), 'Local government as industrial firms: an organizational analysis of China's transitional economy', *American Journal of Sociology*, **101**, 263–301.

Wang, Shaoguang (1995), 'The rise of the regions: fiscal reform and the decline of central state capacity in China', in Andrew Walder (ed.), *The Waning of the Communist State: Economic Origins of Political Decline in China and Hungary*, Berkeley, CA: University of California Press.

Wang, Shaoguang and Angang Hu (2001), *The Chinese Economy in Crisis: State Capacity and Tax Reform*, Armonk: M.E. Sharpe.

Wank, David (1999), *Commodifying Communism: Business, Trust, and Politics in a Chinese City*, New York: Cambridge University Press.

Wank, David (2002), 'Business–state clientelism in China: decline or evolution?', in T. Gold, D. Guthrie and D. Wank (eds), *Social Connections in China: Institutions, Culture, and the Changing Nature of Guanxi*, New York: Cambridge University Press.

White, Gordon (1996), 'The dynamics of civil society in post-Mao China', in Brian Hook (ed.), *The Individual and the State in China*, Oxford: Clarendon Press.

White, Gordon, J. Howell and S. Xiaoyuan (1996), *In Search of Civil Society: Market Reform and Social Change in Contemporary China*, Oxford: Clarendon Press.

Whyte, Martin King (1992), 'Urban China: a civil society in the making?', in A.L. Rosenbaum (ed.), *State and Society in China: The Consequences of Reform*, Boulder, CO: Westview Press.

Wong, Christine (1991), 'Central–local relations in an era of fiscal decline: the paradox of fiscal decentralization in post-Mao China', *China Quarterly*, **128**, 691–715.

Wong, Christine (1992), 'Fiscal reform and local industrialization: the problematic sequencing of reform in post-Mao China', *Modern China*, **18**, 197–227.

Wong, Christine (2002), 'China's provincial public expenditure review', World Bank Workshop on Decentralization and Intergovernmental Fiscal Reform, Washington, DC, 13–15 May.

Woo, Wing Thye, W. Hai, Y. Jin and G. Fan (1993), 'How successful has Chinese enterprise reform been? Pitfalls in opposite biases and focus', *Journal of Comparative Economics*, **18**, 410–37.

Xin, Katherine and J. Pearce (1996), 'Guanxi: connections as substitutes for formal institutional supports', *The Academy of Management Journal*, **39**(6), 1641–58.

Yang, Mayfair (1994), *Gifts, Favors and Banquets: the Arts of Social Relationships in China*, Ithaca, NY: Cornell University Press.

Yang, Mayfair (2002), 'The resilience of guanxi and its new deployments', *The China Quarterly*, **170**, 459–76.

Yeung, H.W.C. (1997), 'Business networks and transnational corporations: a study of Hong Kong firms in the ASEAN region', *Economic Geography*, **73**(1), 1–25.

PART II

Business and Marketing

7. Challenges of marketing to Asian consumers: exploring the influence of different cultures, life styles and values on consumer behaviour in Asia

Piyush Sharma, Cindy M.Y. Chung, M. Krishna Erramilli and Bharadhwaj Sivakumaran

The last quarter of the twentieth century witnessed many monumental events including the splintering of the former Soviet Union into several independent nations, demolition of the Berlin wall, opening up of erstwhile closed economies in Asia, and the emergence of globalization. As a result, the early 1990s was abuzz with the news of the arrival of global consumers who were supposed to share a common set of consumption-related symbols such as product categories, brands and consumption activities (Terpstra and David, 1991). Mass-media programming, flowing primarily from the US, was supposed to have played a major role in the creation, learning and sharing of such consumption symbols (Appadurai, 1990).

In the last decade or so, however, companies around the world seem to have faced a reality check. The notion that global thinking would gradually break the wall of economic nationalism and chauvinism seems no longer to be taken for granted (Suh and Kwon, 2002). It is argued that globalization may not be able to obliterate cultural differences and standardize consumer behaviour around the globe (Schütte and Ciarlante, 1998). Rather, consumer behaviour may well become more heterogeneous because of cultural differences. As consumer incomes converge across countries, the manifestation of value differences may become even stronger (de Mooij and Hofstede, 2002). This phenomenon makes it increasingly important to understand values of national cultures and their impact on consumer behaviour in different countries.

Nowhere is this heterogeneity better illustrated than in Asia, a huge continent with diverse countries such as those in the Middle East (Iraq) and in the Far East (Japan). Over the last decade or so, there has been a tremendous focus on two of the largest economies in the world, India and China – both in Asia. The rapid economic progress and burgeoning 200–300 million strong middle-class populations in both of these countries have attracted multinational companies to their doorstep (Batra, 1997; Manrai and Manrai, 2001). However, the going has been tough and most of these companies have faced hurdles like poor infrastructure, bureaucratic controls and cultural differences (Batra, 1997). With the liberalization of trade and the opening up of their respective economies over time, the first two hurdles may well soon be things of the past. However, cultural differences may well persist. Therefore, it is important for these companies to understand the sociopsychological reasons for the underlying differences among Asian consumers and incorporate these in their strategies (see also chapters in Part I of this volume).

Prior research shows that Asian consumers prefer products made in Western countries (Bandyopadhyay, 2001; Bandyopadhyay and Banerjee, 2002; Cui and Liu, 2001). They are also becoming more materialistic (Tse *et al.*, 1989; Zhou and Hui, 2003a, 2003b), but are still distinctly different from their Western counterparts (Alpert *et al.*, 1997; Kaynak *et al.*, 2000; Lundstrom *et al.*, 1998). Yet there is little consensus on the exact nature and role of the underlying sociopsychological processes for these differences in consumer behaviour between Asian countries (also within Asian countries) and the West. While there are several areas in international marketing, we focus in this chapter on three broad ones and discuss some important conceptual issues in (1) the segmentation of Asian consumers, (2) the similarities and differences of decision-making styles among Asian consumers, and (3) the role of culture, social values and life style in shaping consumer behaviour in Asia.

We organize this chapter in the above order. In each of the above areas, we critically review the existing literature and point out specific research gaps and problems. Finally, we offer some broad directions for future research.

INTERNATIONAL CONSUMER SEGMENTATION AND ASIAN CONSUMERS

International consumer segmentation has become an important issue in cross-border marketing, helping companies target international customers more effectively (Steenkamp and Hofstede, 2002). One of the key challenges in international marketing is to develop segments of consumers in different countries that are likely to exhibit similar responses to marketing efforts. This is not a major problem for multinational companies that adopt a multi-domestic strategy, where each country represents a separate segment and marketing strategies are developed separately for each country. These firms tend to rely on standard segmentation techniques developed for their domestic markets (Jeannet and Hennessey, 1998). On the other hand, international segmentation is a particularly challenging issue for companies adopting a global/regional strategy, where they use the same marketing strategies across national borders in an attempt to benefit from cost reductions.

Despite its importance, international market segmentation had received little attention in the marketing literature, with only about 1 per cent of the published papers in the international marketing area that deal directly with the topic during the 1980–90 period (Aulakh and Kotabe, 1993). Recently, there has been an upsurge in interest in this area, although most research has focused on the Triad countries, namely the US, the European Union and Japan (Steenkamp and Hofstede, 2002). Based on the unit of analysis, empirical studies in this area can be categorized into two types.

1. Group-level, including information on countries (or regions) or on individual consumers aggregated at the country (or region) level, such as a combination of economic, political, geographic and demographic information (Helsen *et al.*, 1993; Huszagh *et al.*, 1986) or cultural variables (Hofstede, 1980; Steenkamp, 2001).
2. Individual-level that uses disaggregate, individual-specific information about consumers, ranging from domain-specific characteristics such as attribute evaluations

(Moskowitz and Rabino, 1994, 1999; Moskowitz and Greene, 2000), attitudes (Verhage *et al.*, 1989), risk and brand loyalty ratings (Yavas *et al.*, 1992) to intermediate constructs such as means–end chains (Ter Hofstede *et al.*, 1999) and general characteristics such as values (Kamakura *et al.*, 1994).

However, most of these studies are exploratory and very few test specific hypotheses or base their work on a theoretical or conceptual framework, limiting their generalizability. Moreover, most of these studies have been restricted to the Triad countries. It has been more difficult and costly to collect data in other countries, especially in Asia, because of limited infrastructure and access. Interestingly, most of these studies have identified consumer segments that span multiple countries even with data related to individual consumers and their characteristics (Ter Hofstede *et al.*, 1999; Wedel *et al.*, 1998; Yavas *et al.*, 1992).

Consumer behaviour in Asian countries has been researched for several years, and much of this learning has been integrated into the global marketing strategies of multinational corporations (Bandyopadhyay, 2001; Batra, 1997; Belk, 1988; Cui and Liu, 2001; Manrai and Manrai, 2001; O'Cass and Lim, 2002; Suh and Kwon, 2002). De Mooij and Keegan (1996) provide a good overview of life style research in Asia, describing studies conducted in countries like Japan, Malaysia, Singapore, Taiwan and Thailand (as summarized in Table 7.1).

In Japan, the Dentsu Consumer Value Survey found four life-models among consumers (Suzuki, 1990). 'Achievers' are enterprising individuals who attach importance to

Table 7.1   Empirical studies of Asian consumer segmentation

Country (reference)	Consumer segments
Japan (Suzuki, 1990)	Four Achievers, Intelligent, Group Merit and Membership-dependent
Malaysia (Kiu, 1989)	Seven Yesterday People, Village Trendsetters, Chamaeleons, Loners, New breed, Yuppies and Sleepwalkers
Singapore (Kiu, 1989)	Chinese Singaporean (Four) Brat Pack, Possession Paraders, Comfortable Careerists and Traditional Malay Singaporean (Six) Modern, Jing Di Wa (Frogs in a well), Disaffected, Hard-pressed Providers, Bo-Chaps and Dependent Matriarchs
Singapore (NBS, 2005)	Singaporean Resident Females (Six) Novices, Rebels, Experimenters, Conformists, Veterans and Retired
Taiwan (Kiu, 1989)	Eight Traditional Homebodies, Confident Traditionalists, Family-centred Fatalists, Lethargic, Middle-Class Hopefuls, Discontented Moderns, Rebellious Young and Young Strivers
Bangkok (Kiu, 1989)	Nine Today's Women, Comfortable Middle Class, We Got the Blues, Mainstream Belongers, Young Achievers, Young at Heart, Trying to Make it, The Left Outs and Almost There
China (Cui and Liu, 2001)	Four Yuppies, Little Rich, Salary Class and Working Poor

individuality and to human relationships, whereas the 'Intelligent' segment attaches importance to individuality in the area of intelligence, culture and arts, and to nature. The 'Group Merit' segment makes full use of the organization to its own advantage, attaches importance to human relationships and shows a great interest in art and culture. Finally, the 'Membership-dependent' group is highly loyal to the organization, family centred, and has a deep interest in nature. There are several other interesting trends found among Japanese consumers, such as a shift from homogeneity to variety, adherence with social expectations to personal preferences, work-driven existence to a more balanced life, and acquiring things to seeking new experiences (Wilk, 1990).

The Survey Research Group (SRG) has conducted several such studies among consumers in Malaysia, Singapore, Thailand and Taiwan (Kiu, 1989). They found seven psychographic segments in Malaysia where the 'Sleepwalkers' were predominantly ethnic Chinese, relatively more family minded, moralistic, introvert, conforming, socially and physically inactive, followers, non-doers and neurotic. These consumers were not religious, adventurous or house-proud, and were less community spirited or patriotic. They also appeared to be more price-sensitive, and interested in the functional rather than emotional benefits of the products. They bought to fit in and not to stand out, in direct contrast with the 'Trendsetters'. Interestingly, they had negative perceptions towards most packaged foods including refrigerated milk, branded biscuits, and even tomato sauce, because these were thought to be less fresh and bad for health. In fact, most rural consumers across Asia are likely to fit the description for this category.

In Singapore, ten segments emerged in the SRG study: four among ethnic Chinese Singaporeans and six among Malay Singaporeans. On the other hand, Taiwan had eight psychographic clusters and Thailand had nine. More recently, Cui and Liu (2001) analysed China's urban consumers in seven regional markets, based on a 1997 national survey. They discovered four segments – Yuppies, Little Rich, Salary Class and Working Poor – that were distinctive in their demographics, psychographics, life styles, media usage and consumption patterns. These findings dispute the notion of Asia as a homogeneous market and suggest that multinational corporations need to adapt to local market conditions in different regions in China and other Asian countries.

A recent study conducted by the Nanyang Business School in Singapore on contraceptive methods adopted by women has thrown up some interesting findings. Six segments have emerged in this study. Since they seem to be quite different from those found in earlier studies, we briefly report them. The first segment, the 'Novices', consisted of sexually inactive singles in the 21–30 age group who exhibited very low knowledge about contraception, but had an overall positive attitude and behavioural intentions. Interestingly, contrary to the popular perception about Singapore being a very modern nation, most of these novices seemed to come from very conservative families. Most of them were embarrassed talking about sex and contraception, and very concerned about what their parents, other family members and friends would think, if they found out that they were sexually active. On the other hand, 'Rebels' were sexually active singles in the 21–35 age group. Unlike the 'Novices', they were quite knowledgable about contraception and very concerned about it. They were also more likely to use the Internet, women's magazines and ask their friends and colleagues for advice. Surprisingly, many of them relied on the so-called 'unsafe' contraceptive methods such as withdrawal and rhythm methods.

'Experimenters' were mostly newly married women who were neither very knowledgable, nor interested in knowing more about contraception. They did not have any strict preference for any particular contraceptive methods and tried many options or even none. 'Conformists' were older married women who were still sexually active and relied more on the opinion of doctors and their spouse to decide whether to use contraception or not, and the choice of method. 'Veterans' and 'Retired' were older married women who were not very sexually active, less educated compared to the other segments, and more likely to use relatively more permanent contraceptive methods such as intra-uterine devices and sterilization. These segments also sharply differ from Western studies, where, for example, the 'Novices' are almost non-existent, most young singles are sexually active, and they use some form of contraception. Thus, despite being economically developed, Singapore differs considerably from economically comparable Western countries in terms of contraceptive usage, suggesting strongly that culture matters a great deal. To summarize the above discussion, we find the following:

1. Most of these studies, by and large, use psychographic segmentation or incorporate psychographics in their segmentation process. Is this reflective of the real corporate world where psychographics is doubtless used, even though demographic and behavioural segmentation is possibly used to a greater extent? For example, Toyota has modelled Corolla for the low-income group, Camry for the middle road and Lexus for the high end. Why is there the inconsistency between theory and practice?
2. Most of these studies report many segments that are similar in their definition and characteristics across different countries, with only a few unique elements relevant to the culture of each country. For example, each country has segments like 'Young Achievers', 'Traditionalists' and 'Providers'. These segments are similar in terms of demographics, but there are few differences in their expectations and perceptions. However, there are also some stark differences across countries and, sometimes, across ethnic groups even in the same country. For example, the 'intelligent' segment and the 'chameleon' segment seem unique. Besides, even in tiny Singapore, there seem to be differences between the Malays and ethnic Chinese. But do the marketing managers of MNCs identify these differences as well? *Prima facie*, it does not seem so. For instance, a McDonald's in Singapore may seem similar to the one in Bangkok, except for slight adaptations in the menu to suit local tastes. The earlier question about the inconsistency between theory and practice arises here again.
3. We can clearly see that, despite the massive wave of globalization through massmedia, international tourism, multinational marketing and the resulting proliferation of consumerism throughout Asia, Asian consumers are still quite different in their attitudes and perceptions, tastes and preferences, and even values, as compared to their Western counterparts (Suh and Kwon, 2002).
4. Are the segments stable over time? For instance, 16 years have passed since 1989 and there has been a sea change socially, economically and politically in some of these countries, for example Malaysia, Thailand and even Singapore, not to speak of India and China. Thus longitudinal or periodic tracking studies are absolutely essential. Indeed, they can even be used for predictive purposes. For instance, it is widely accepted that India is economically ten to 15 years behind China. Does this then mean that India will look like China today in ten to 15 years?

5. The segments that have emerged from the contraceptive study in Singapore are quite different from those in earlier studies. Is this due to the unique nature of the product or is it because of history and maturation? If the former, does this mean that product-centric segmentation is the answer or does it mean that psychographic segmentation has been too widely used, at least by academics? If the latter, again, it lends strength to our call for longitudinal studies.

Notwithstanding the above, some researchers have also found the emergence of a uniform global consumer culture among the younger Asian consumers (O'Cass and Lim, 2002; Wee, 1999). Teenagers in Asia are shown to be heavily influenced not only by the West, but also by more affluent Asian countries. For example, Japan is seen as the fashion centre for many Asian teenagers (in Thailand, Hong Kong and Singapore in particular), and as the starting point for trends such as Pokémon and Hello Kitty. These teens seem to be influenced by a complex mix of East Asian, Western and their own cultures. Owing to a combination of the strong family ties in Asian societies with the independent values acquired from the Western media, Asian teens are emerging as a unique market (Wee, 1999).

SIMILARITIES AND DIFFERENCES AMONG ASIAN CONSUMERS

Although we have touched upon similarities and differences among consumers in different Asian countries in the preceding section, we delve deeper into these now. Here, we look at some of the 'big picture' issues. Asia is the home of the world's most dynamic markets, representing nearly 25 per cent of the world economy and 50 per cent of the world population (Schütte and Ciarlante, 1998). Researchers have long realized the need to establish specific theories for consumer behaviour in Asia, but their efforts have been thwarted by the wide variation in economic, industrial and social development across the various Asian countries. Researchers have explored similarities among Asian consumers, using several perspectives classified below.

1. *Economic perspective*:   Groups of Asian countries are shown to possess some common characteristics, based on their geographic proximity that is coupled with similarities in their economic goals and state of development, such as emergence of regionalization in South Asia (Siddiqi, 1991). Other researchers have focused on the developing countries in Asia and termed them 'transitional economies' (Batra, 1997), developing countries (Batra *et al.*, 2000) and emerging markets (Manrai and Manrai, 2001) based on their similar economic characteristics. For instance, countries like Thailand and Malaysia are bunched up, whereas the two Koreas, though culturally similar, are not, owing to economic diversity.
2. *Sociopsychological perspective*:   Asian countries are shown to possess similar social characteristics such as life styles, attitudes, interests and opinions (Tai and Tam, 1996), psychographics (Ewing, 1999), demographics (Cui and Liu, 2001) and a trend towards greater consumerism, materialism and symbolic consumption (Tse *et al.*, 1989; Zhou and Hui, 2003b). These researchers suggest that there is a gradual shift in

the traditional values and attitudes in Asian societies, because of various influences resulting in the development of a more homogeneous group of Asian consumers who share similar values and life styles. For instance, India and China are often spoken of in the same breath, for reasons explained above.

3. *Cultural perspective*:   Cross-cultural differences are used to explain the differences between Asians and Westerners in their consumer behaviour: attitudes and perceptions on the one hand (Luna and Gupta, 2001; Maheswaran and Shavitt, 2000) and their needs and values on the other (Kim *et al.*, 2002). These researchers argue that most Asian consumers have a collectivistic orientation, compared to the predominantly individualistic orientation of Western consumers. This is why 'East is East and West is West and never the twain shall meet', as Kipling famously put it.

Most Western marketers perceive Asian countries to be relatively similar, whereas the reality is quite different (Jevons, 2000; see also Chapters 8 and 10 in this volume). In recent years, researchers have begun to explore several important differences among consumers in different Asian countries, and even within the same country, because these differences often present a great challenge to the creation and implementation of regional marketing strategies (Phau and Chan, 2003). We next review the literature that investigates some key differences among consumers in different Asian countries. Phau and Chan used the national identity (NATID) framework developed by Keillor and Hult (1999) to compare consumers in six Asian economies namely, South Korea, Taiwan, Thailand, Singapore, Hong Kong and Japan. They found Thailand to be the country with the strongest national identity and Singapore with the weakest. Further analyses of the various dimensions of national identity construct revealed that Thai consumers scored high on all the four dimensions, namely national heritage, cultural homogeneity, belief system and consumer ethnocentrism. Singapore was the weakest in terms of national heritage (not surprising in view of its relatively short history); Hong Kong scored lowest on cultural homogeneity and belief system, whereas Japan had the lowest score on consumer ethnocentrism.

These researchers suggested that these NATID scores can be a useful tool for companies planning to invest in Asian markets. Specifically, countries with a relatively weak sense of national identity and low ethnocentric tendency, such as Singapore, can be used as a 'springboard' market for entering Asia. They also suggested that similarities and differences in the various dimensions of national identity may provide an indication of how much standardization or customization may be needed in each of these economies. Moreover, the relatively high cultural homogeneity and national heritage scores in countries like Japan, South Korea and Thailand may need strong 'localization' of advertising and promotional themes to overcome any negative backlash.

Prior researchers like Rostow (1960) attempted to differentiate countries on the basis of their degree of economic development. Similarly, Dichter (1962) grouped countries according to their size and the development of their middle class, whereas others have proposed more complex typologies involving many micro and macro variables (Samli and Hassan, 1992). However, most of these segmentation schemes are either too general and overly simplistic or very specific and complicated (Phau and Chan, 2003). Therefore, there is a need for a more practical and, yet, conceptually rigorous typology that academic researchers as well as managers in multinational organizations may use to understand the differences among consumers in different countries. Researchers have found that three factors shape consumption values: economic development, political ideology, and business training and philosophy (Tse *et al.*, 1989). However, it is also observed that developing countries are acquiring hedonistic consumption attitudes in a different sequence and much more rapidly than was the case in Western Europe and the US (Belk, 1988).

Moreover, other researchers have suggested that theories developed from research into Western consumers may not be exactly applicable to Asian consumers. For example, it is shown that Maslow's hierarchy of physiological, safety, social, self-esteem and self-actualization needs may not be followed by mainland Chinese in this sequence (Nevis, 1983; see also Chapter 10 in this volume). Instead, they may progress from social to physiological and from safety to self-actualization in the service of society (rather than individual aggrandizement). To sum up, there is a dearth of research in this area and this is quite surprising given its managerial importance. For instance, KFC is successful in China while it has not set the Ganges on fire in India. Likewise, even P&G and Coca-Cola have failed to make a significant impact in India so far. It is reasonable to think that this relative failure is due to more than just legal or economic reasons; clearly, there are some important conceptual differences. Hence there is a need to explore more deeply the underlying sociopsychological factors that influence consumers in general, and Asian consumers in particular, such as culture, life styles and social values.

INFLUENCE OF CULTURE, LIFE STYLES AND VALUES ON ASIAN CONSUMERS

Several researchers have explored the role of life style and values on consumer behaviour across different cultures, especially in Asian countries (Yau, 1994). Tai and Tam (1996) found some significant differences in a comparative study of ethnic Chinese consumers in two Asian economies with a dominant population of ethnic Chinese descent, namely, Singapore and Hong Kong. Singapore residents were generally more home-oriented, placed a higher value on education, and were more concerned about the environment. They also showed a positive attitude towards advertising and were more concerned about the quality of a product rather than its price. Hong Kong respondents were generally more traditional and conservative, adhering more strongly to cultural values such as face (*mien tze*) and tended to have a stronger belief in fate (*yuan*). They were also more fashion-conscious and less optimistic about the future. However, both groups exhibited similar activity patterns and buying practices. These findings indicate a significant influence of the original Chinese culture, moderated by the distance from mainland China and exposure to other cultures. While ethnic Chinese in Hong Kong have largely remained isolated from other cultures, those in Singapore have been influenced greatly by their interaction with people from Indian, Malay, British and many other cultures. One can surmise that some even more interesting differences may emerge in a study of ethnic Chinese in other parts of Asia, such as Malaysia, Indonesia and Myanmar.

Gorn (1997) explored Japanese consumers and concluded that many research findings in the US do not simply hold up in Japan because of its interdependent culture. For example, unlike the Americans, the Japanese do not take credit for success and blame others for failure, because the Japanese culture emphasizes integration with the group rather than self-enhancement (Kashima and Triandis, 1986). They also do not view themselves as better than others in the society around them, nor do they seem to want to stand out in the crowd (Markus and Kitayama, 1991). The Japanese also tend to be overly pessimistic about their own performance and focus on their negative characteristics in order to integrate better with their groups (Heine and Lehman, 1995). These findings have major implications for companies planning to enter countries with similar interdependent cultures, such as South Korea, China and many countries in Southeast Asia.

Individualism and instrumental rationality, the cornerstones of Western societies, have undermined the social values that used to hold these societies together. As argued by Lal (1999), this results in the breakdown of family structures and the rise of a hedonistic consumer culture. However, he claimed that such dysfunctional consequences may not arise in Asian societies. This is because, unlike the 'guilt' cultures in the West, Asian consumers have 'shame' cultures. The cultural mores are enforced by social pressure, irrespective of their belief systems or religions, such as Islam, Hinduism or even Buddhism. Hence consumer values in these Asian societies are likely to be heavily influenced by 'a sense of shame' or 'loss of face'. Nowhere is this more evident than in the traditional extended family system prevalent in most Asian countries. In this system, older parents and even married siblings live under the same roof and share common facilities and infrastructure. Of course, rapid urbanization and resource constraints are putting this system to the test and nuclear families are becoming increasingly common in most large Asian cities.

Kim *et al.* (2002) examined the relationship of consumer values, needs and purchase behaviour in two Asian consumer markets, China and South Korea. They found some interesting similarities and differences among consumers in the two countries. First, self-directed values were found to be the underlying determinant of needs to be satisfied, not social affiliation values in both the countries. This finding is in stark contrast to the conventional understanding that the consumers in these so-called 'collectivistic' countries consider relationship or social affiliation values as more important than individual or self-directed values. Moreover, the authors also found some interesting differences among the Chinese and the Korean consumers. Specifically, brand-loyal Chinese consumers considered experiential image the most important aspect of the appeal of branded apparel, whereas for Korean consumers it was the social image with performance quality assurance. These findings show that cultural values may interact with socioeconomic status in different societies and result in such differences in consumer behaviour. Therefore culture alone may not be a sufficient predictor of the differences in consumer values and attitudes across the different countries.

More specifically, Gong (2003) explored the impact of Chinese culture on Chinese consumers' decision-making process in the context of infusion of Western life style in China. This study is set in the context of Chinese cultural values that have formed a clear and consistent system for generations. This research suggests that Chinese consumers' tastes and values are shifting, as they become more affluent, mobile and media accessible. This is evident in their increasing emphasis on individualism, self-fulfilment and internationalism. However, deep-rooted Chinese cultural values still remain distinct and continue to exert great influence on the Chinese consumers. These predominantly Confucian values include frugality, greater introspection, group orientation, low risk taking, high uncertainty avoidance, and the suppression of desires for instant gratification. These values are manifested in consumer behaviour in the form of a greater reliance on word-of-mouth, a narrower price range for price/value trade-off, higher importance attached to brand name, manufacturer and country-of-origin, and less trust in product warranties.

These findings reflect the emergence of the Asian version of the 'Yuppie' phenomenon. These young high achievers across Asia seem to be hedonically motivated, highly brand-conscious, and individualistic in their orientation. However, they still seem to retain many of their traditional cultural values, such as low risk taking and uncertainty avoidance. This has major implications for multinational companies trying to target this highly affluent and lucrative consumer segment. They cannot simply take their advertising campaigns from Western countries and transplant them in Asia. In fact, companies like DaimlerChrysler seem already to have realized this and changed the tone of their recent TV advertising campaigns, released all over Asia, from an individualistic, indulgent tone to one based on group harmony and reliable performance.

Tsutsumi and Chung (2003) analysed the eating-out behaviour of consumers in two countries, Japan and South Korea, over the 1976–98 period. They found many similarities in their behaviour. Specifically, the relative price and habit formation effect had a direct influence and income had an indirect influence on eating-out expenditure. These were explained by the similarity in the dietary styles in both countries and similar concomitant changes in their dietary styles with their economic growth. However, they also found South Korean consumers' behaviour to be more complex and variable, as compared to the Japanese. This difference was put down to the more rapid economic growth in South Korea, as compared to Japan, that may have introduced more variability in the behaviour and choices of South Korean consumers.

These findings once again demonstrate the interaction of cultural, social and economic factors in shaping consumer attitudes and behaviours in different societies. Fast-food chains such as McDonald's, KFC and Pizza Hut are discovering this increase in eating-out trend among Asian consumers, but they are also realizing that the Asian palate seeks much more variety than the usual fare that their menus used to offer. As a result, they have been forced to include local flavours and variants such as the tandoori chicken pizza in North India and laksa sauce in Southeast Asia, as reported in the popular media.

Clammer (2003) examined the relationship between class, consumer values, consumer culture and civil society in several contemporary Southeast Asian cities, including Singapore, Bangkok, Manila and Kuala Lumpur. He argued that the relationship between class and civil society participation creates the primary cultural context in which new middle classes in Asia operate, and provides the linkage between globalization and local urban cultures. In simpler terms, he suggested that urban middle classes in these growing Southeast Asian cities have a strong desire for development and participation in ever-widening circles of consumption opportunity, such as shopping, travelling and entertainment. Hence it seems that modern Asian consumers have certainly evolved in the face of globalization. They are, however, still busy with relatively more existential issues and, hence, are yet to achieve the level of emancipation reached in many Western societies.

This throws down a big challenge to marketers in Asia, in terms of segmenting their markets, targeting the most profitable segments and positioning their products accordingly. For example, the combined rural population in India and China exceeds one billion and, at present, it may present a bigger market opportunity to a black and white TV or a motorcycle manufacturer, as compared to the relatively smaller market for luxury automobiles or home appliances in the urban parts of these countries. Companies that are able to position clearly their products in each of these segments and their various subsegments are likely to be able to capitalize on the consistently high growth experienced by these economies. In summary, the key issues from the above discussion are the following:

1. Asian consumers seem to be quite collectivistic as compared to their individualistic Western counterparts.
2. While there has been some cultural change, this appears to be on the surface rather than deep-rooted. For instance, certain core values like group harmony and loss of face still appear to be quite strong and resistant to change in Asia.
3. There are some significant differences between countries in Asia and this seems to be the result of the interaction between social, economic and cultural factors.

However, the research into the factors responsible for these similarities and differences is quite scattered. Researchers have used several perspectives to explain why the Asian consumers behave the way they do, including culture, life style, social values, attitudes and belief systems. We next examine another rich body of knowledge in this area, namely the consumer decision-making styles literature in the context of Asian consumers. This discussion may help us understand these differences better.

CONSUMER DECISION-MAKING STYLES IN ASIA

The Consumer Style Inventory (CSI) was first developed to determine the basic characteristics of consumer decision-making styles among young consumers in the US (Sproles and Sproles, 1990; Sproles and Kendall, 1986). Researchers have identified the following eight consumer styles:

1. perfectionist high quality conscious;
2. brand conscious;
3. novelty and fashion conscious;
4. recreational or shopping conscious;
5. price conscious;
6. impulsive and careless;
7. confused by too much choice; and
8. habitual and brand loyal.

According to these researchers, the identification of these characteristics among consumers helps to profile an individual consumer style and educate consumers about their specific decision-making characteristics. Such a typology based on consumer decision-making styles may even be useful for companies to segment their consumers and it has been recommended that this inventory (CSI) be used in different population groups to determine its general applicability (Walsh *et al.*, 2001). Several researchers have attempted to validate Sproles and Kendall's (1986) CSI in different countries around the world to explore the cross-cultural differences in consumer decision-making styles. We next review some of these studies conducted in Asian countries and discuss their findings (see also Table 7.2).

Table 7.2   Empirical studies of consumer decision-making styles

Country (reference)	Consumer decision-making styles
United States (Sproles and Kendall, 1986)	Eight Perfectionist, high quality conscious; Brand conscious; Novelty and fashion conscious; Recreational or shopping conscious; Price conscious; Impulsive, careless; Confused by too much choice; and Habitual, brand loyal
South Korea (Hafstrom *et al.*, 1992)	Eight Brand-consciousness; Perfectionist, high quality conscious; Recreational-shopping; Confusion (too much choice); Time–energy conservation; Impulsive careless shopping; Brand-loyal shopping; and Price-value consciousness
China (Fan and Xiao, 1998)	Five Brand conscious, Time consciousness, Quality consciousness, Price consciousness, Information utilization
China (Siu *et al.*, 2001)	Four Perfectionist, Brand Conscious, Novelty-Fashion Conscious and Recreational
China (Tai, 2005)	Ten Price and value consciousness; Fashion enthusiasm; Brand consciousness; Quality consciousness; Personal style conscious; Environmental and health consciousness; Convenience and time consciousness; Brand and store loyalty; Shopping influences; Reliance on the mass media
India (Canabal, 2002)	Five Brand Conscious, High Quality Conscious / Perfectionist, Confused by too much choice, Impulsive / Brand Indifferent, and Recreational Shopper

In some of the early empirical studies in this area in Asia, Hafstrom *et al.* (1992) used the CSI to identify the decision-making styles of South Korean students, whereas Fan and Xiao (1998) used a modified CSI with mainland Chinese students. These researchers found several differences among young mainland Chinese, American and South Korean consumers, despite the similarities with respect to the major dimensions and item loading (Fan and Xiao, 1998). Specifically, the 'novelty and fashion-conscious consumer' identified by Sproles and Kendall (1986) was not found in the South Korean study. Instead, a new factor of 'time–energy conserving' was observed (Hafstrom *et al.*, 1992). In a similar study with South Indian consumers in the city of Coimbatore, Canabal (2002) found five reliable decision-making styles, as compared to the eight styles in the original CSI.

The 'brand-conscious' style was number one in the list of factors for the South Korean, Chinese and Indian students and second for the US sample. The 'perfectionists' or 'high quality-conscious' consumer was also identified among the top three factors for all four samples. However, a factor such as 'confused by too much choice' was relatively more common among the Indian young consumers than it was for the South Korean, Chinese or US samples. It should be noted that, for the Chinese sample (Fan and Xiao, 1998), the components of the 'confused by too much choice' were similar to what they identified as 'information utilization' style. Furthermore, it seems that the 'price/value-conscious' style was more important for American and Chinese students than for Indians and South Koreans. As a factor, it did not reach a significant alpha level in the analysis.

On the other hand, the 'impulsive/careless' factor for the South Korean sample included some of the components that loaded in the 'dissatisfied/careless' for the Indian sample. It seems that, for South Korean students who scored high in this factor, there was an association between being careless and being impulsive. It may be that those young consumers with high scores in a similar factor in India, on the other hand, make careless decisions, not out of impulsiveness, but out of brand indifference. The Indian consumers identified carelessness as a factor in itself, a trait with which they were dissatisfied, rather than one that made them buy on impulse. Finally, the 'fashion conscious' style, reported for American consumers by Sproles and Kendall (1986) and not found by Hafstrom *et al.* (1992) for the South Korean students, was loaded with some of the items in the 'recreational shopper' style for the Indian sample. It could be interpreted that young Indian consumers who are fashion-conscious derive pleasure from their shopping trips, and devote time to such activity that they consider recreational. A similar correlation between 'time-conscious' style components and the 'fashion-conscious' style was reported by Fan and Xiao (1998) for Chinese students.

In a large survey of 357 students and 387 adult consumers in China, Siu *et al.* (2001) found only four relatively stable decision-making styles for Chinese consumers, 'perfectionist', 'brand-conscious', 'novelty fashion-conscious' and 'recreational'. They also suggested that the 'price-conscious' factor needs to be redeveloped, if the CSI is to be applied to different cultures. Recently, Tai (2005) used the CSI with Chinese working females in Shanghai and Hong Kong. She found ten shopping style dimensions, four of which were not found in the original CSI: 'personal style consciousness', 'environment and health consciousness', 'reliance on mass media', and 'convenience and time consciousness'. She also identified four distinct shopping styles and termed them 'active fashion chaser', 'rational shopper', 'value buyer' and 'opinion seeker'. Despite their exploratory nature, the key findings from the above studies can be summarized as below:

1. There seems to be a remarkable similarity in decision-making styles, not just between one Asian country and another, but also between Asian countries in general and the US. For instance, the 'perfectionist' and the 'brand-conscious' styles seem to be found in all markets. Again, this seems inconsistent, not just with corporate wisdom that stresses cross-country differences, but also with academic research. For instance, Kacen and Lee (2002) showed cross-cultural differences in impulse buying. Likewise, Sharma and Sivakumaran (2004) found that impulsiveness itself means different things to Western consumers vis-à-vis Asian ones. Is the inconsistency due to some missing moderator constructs? Or is it an artefact or the exploratory nature of research in this area?

2. While there are some differences in decision-making styles (for example South Korean versus mainland Chinese), most studies provide very little by way of theoretical explanation for these differences. This could be due to the exploratory nature of the studies.

3. Most studies have been conducted at different times in different countries by a different set of researchers. Studies conducted in *two different countries simultaneously by the same set of researchers* are the need of the hour. In this way, a common conceptual framework would be ensured, thereby potentially leading to more rigorous research, deeper understanding and greater generalizability.

In general, there is a need for more theory-based and rigorous research in this area.

CONCLUSION

In this chapter, we have reviewed a large body of literature exploring consumer behaviour in Asia and identified several important issues. First, we highlight that globalization may be able neither to break the wall of economic nationalism and chauvinism (Suh and Kwon, 2002), nor to obliterate cultural differences and standardize consumer behaviour around the globe (Schütte and Ciarlante, 1998). Rather, consumer behaviour will probably become more heterogeneous because of cultural differences. As consumer incomes converge across countries, the manifestation of value differences will become stronger (de Mooij and Hofstede, 2002). Hence it is increasingly important to understand values of national cultures and their impact on consumer behaviour.

Next, we have identified the emergence of multicultural markets in which consumers and marketers from different cultures coexist, interact and adapt to each other. Hence it may not be useful to apply traditional ethnic segmentation schemes, because such consumers may no longer conform to any one specific set of cultural values (Jamal, 2003; Lindridge and Dibb, 2003). International segmentation should help firms in structuring the heterogeneity that exists among consumers and nations, by identifying segments that transcend national boundaries and yet can be targeted in an effective and efficient manner (Steenkamp and Hofstede, 2002).

We have further reviewed several studies exploring similarities and differences among consumers in various Asian economies, including Japan, China, South Korea, India, Singapore, Malaysia, Thailand and Taiwan. Most of these studies found that Asian consumers are becoming more affluent, materialistic and discerning in their tastes and preferences. Interestingly, however, they are still heavily influenced by their deeper cultural values and traditions, such as 'face' for the Chinese or 'shame' for the South Asians, just as 'guilt' is an important element of the Western cultures.

Finally, we have reviewed several empirical studies investigating differences in decision-making styles among Asian consumers that used Sproles and Kendall's (1986) consumer-style inventory (CSI). Once again, we found several similarities across different Asian countries. Specifically, we found strong consensus on a few decision-making styles such as brand consciousness, quality consciousness and recreational shopping. Interestingly, these styles seem to represent the basic characteristics of a growing consumer society, wherein consumers begin to expect good quality and show preference for specific brands. Moreover, consumers start enjoying shopping as an activity on its own rather than as a means to an end, that is to buy things. All these trends are quite visible in most Asian countries today, with the growth in the number and size of shopping malls and the availability of top quality and well-known brands across most product categories.

However, we did notice several differences as well. On the one hand, we find many consumers in India and South Korea who are confused by too much choice, as well as indulging in careless impulsive shopping. These findings place them very close to the American consumers reported in the original studies by Sproles and Kendall (1986). On the other hand, many Chinese consumers tend to be more novelty/fashion-conscious, price-conscious or concerned about convenience and time/energy conservation. These styles are not observed among the American, South Korean or Indian consumers, hence these differences are probably a reflection of the relatively recent growth in consumerism

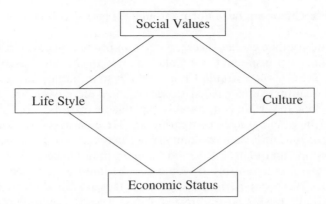

Figure 7.1   Understanding Asian consumers: a conceptual framework

in China (more novelty/fashion-conscious) coupled with their relatively more conservative life styles (little time or resources for shopping).

As indicated in Figure 7.1, we propose a four-pronged approach to conceptualize and explore differences among Asian consumers and between them and the Western consumers. The four aspects in this framework are social values, life style, culture and economic status. We suggest that all these four factors interact with each other and shape the Asian consumers' attitudes and behaviour. Researchers in the past have used one or at best two of these factors for segmenting consumers. However, our review of research conducted in different Asian countries shows that there are many similarities among Asian consumers because of similar cultural and social values. There are also significant differences due to socioeconomic and life style factors. Hence, it may be more useful to incorporate all these four factors in future attempts to segment the Asian consumers.

Research on international marketing with an Asian focus is of paramount importance, not just because of the vastness and diversity of the continent. It is also crucial because of the rapid economic strides made by countries like India and China that result in vast consumer markets for MNCs. Here, using our synthesis of the above literature review, we offer some pointers for future research. First, while there is a considerable body of work on market segmentation in the B2C (Business to Consumer) sector, the B2B (Business to Business) sector is yet to be explored as comprehensively. For instance, for a company like Cisco or Caterpillar, does it make sense to segment their respective markets similarly in India and China? *Prima facie*, it appears that B2B purchases, being relatively more rational ones, would mean that cultural differences would matter less. Empirical support for this notion is a sore need. If it is not supported, that would be a startling finding as well.

Second, while there is work on segmentation based on psychographics or demographics within countries, there is little work on regional differences within the same country. This may well be extremely important for large countries like India and China. For instance, in India, there are 25 states and at least 14 different official languages, and there is a lot of anecdotal evidence suggesting differences between regions and states. It is widely believed that southern Indians are more conservative, more frugal and prudent money-wise than their northern Indian counterparts. Empirical support for this and similar notions is, again, the need of the hour. What is more, it boggles the mind that a land as diverse as India or China can be uniform throughout (see also Chapters 8 and 10 in this volume).

Third, there are companies that succeed in certain product markets in Asia and struggle in certain others. For instance, Coca-Cola is a hit in the Middle East, while in India it is not. Likewise, KFC is successful in China and not so in India. Further research, both qualitative and quantitative, is needed to see whether these cases are just random or whether they are due to certain conceptually explainable reasons.

Fourth, while there are studies comparing similar countries like South Korea and Japan, there is precious little data on comparisons between, say, India and Iran, or even India and China, for that matter. It would be interesting to see if there are significant differences between such countries. It would also be interesting to see whether the so-called 'core values' like group harmony and loss of face are found throughout Asia.

Finally, the Middle East is largely treated as one bloc. It would be interesting to see whether, in fact, this is correct. Anecdotally, Iraq and Saudi Arabia, Jordan and Saudi Arabia, are supposed to be different. Since the Middle East is rich, it is all the more important to study it, at least from a managerial viewpoint.

In conclusion, we see that, despite numerous efforts to understand the Asian consumers and develop a simple segmentation scheme for them, there is still little clarity or consensus on this matter. However, the current research seems to be moving towards integrated conceptual frameworks that may incorporate culture, values and consumer life styles along with several relevant demographic and psychographic variables as the determinants of consumer behaviour, mediated by important constructs such as consumer decision-making style. Future research in this area would help academics, as well as managers in multinational companies, to understand better the sociopsychological processes underlying the similarities and differences in the behaviour of their international consumers, especially in Asia, and develop suitable marketing strategies to identify and tap consumer segments that transcend national boundaries.

REFERENCES

Alpert, Frank, Michael Kamins, Tomoaki Sakano, Naoto Onzo and John Graham (1997), 'Retail buyer decision-making in Japan: what US sellers need to know', *International Business Review*, **6**(2), 91–112.

Appadurai, Arjun (1990), 'Disjuncture and difference in the global economy', in Mike Featherstone (ed.), *Global Culture: Nationalism, Globalization and Modernity*, London: Sage Publications, pp. 295–310.

Aulakh, Preet S. and Masaaki Kotabe (1993), 'An assessment of theoretical and methodological development in international marketing: 1980–1990', *Journal of International Marketing*, **1**(2), 5–28.

Bandyopadhyay, Soumava (2001), 'Competitiveness of foreign products as perceived by consumers in the emerging Indian market', *Competitiveness Review*, **11**, 53–64.

Bandyopadhyay, Subir and Bibek Banerjee (2002), 'A country of origin analysis of foreign brands by Indian consumers', *Journal of International Consumer Marketing*, **15**(2), 85–104.

Batra, Rajeev (1997), 'Marketing issues and challenges in transitional economies', *Journal of International Marketing*, **5**(4), 95–114.

Batra, Rajeev, Venkatram Ramaswamy, Dana L. Alden, Jan-Benedict E.M. Steenkamp and S. Ramachander (2000), 'Effects of brand local and nonlocal origin on consumer attitudes in developing countries', *Journal of Consumer Psychology*, **9**(2), 83–95.

Belk, Russell (1988), 'Third world consumer culture', in Erdogan Kumcu and A. Fuat Firat (eds), *Marketing and Development*, Greenwich, CT: JAI, pp. 103–27.

Canabal, Maria E. (2002), 'Decision making styles of young South Indian consumers: an exploratory study', *College Student Journal*, **36**(1), 12–19.

Clammer, John (2003), 'Globalization, class, consumption and civil society in South-east Asian cities', *Urban Studies*, **40**(2), 403–19.

Cui, Geng and Qiming Liu (2001), 'Emerging market segments in a transitional economy: a study of urban consumers in China', *Journal of International Marketing*, **9**(1), 84–106.

de Mooij, Marieke K. and Geert Hofstede (2002), 'Convergence and divergence in consumer behavior: implications for international retailing', *Journal of Retailing*, **78**(1), 61–9.

de Mooij, Marieke K. and Warren Keegan (1996), 'Lifestyle research in Asia', in Siew Meng Leong, Swee Hoon Ang and Chin Tiong Tan (eds), *Marketing Insights for the Asia–Pacific*, Singapore: Heinemann, pp. 87–98.

Dichter, E. (1962), 'The world customer', *Harvard Business Review*, **40** (July–August), 119–21.

Ewing, Michael T. (1999), 'Affluent Asia: towards a cross-national psychographic typology', *Journal of International Consumer Marketing*, **11**(6), 25–37.

Fan, J.X. and J. Xiao (1998), 'Consumer decision making styles of young-adult Chinese', *The Journal of Consumer Affairs*, **32**(2), 275–94.

Gong, Wen (2003), 'Chinese consumer behavior: a cultural framework and implications', *The Journal of American Academy of Business*, **3**(1/2), 373–80.

Gorn, Gerald J. (1997), 'Breaking out of the North American box', *Advances in Consumer Research*, **24**, 6–8.

Hafstrom, J.L., J.S. Chae and Y. Chung (1992), 'Consumer decision-making styles: comparison between the United States and Korean young consumers', *Journal of Consumer Affairs*, **26**, 146–58.

Heine, S.J. and D.R. Lehman (1995), 'Cultural variation in unrealistic optimism: does the West feel more invulnerable than the East', *Journal of Personality and Social Psychology*, **68**(4), 595–607.

Helsen, Kristiaan, Kamel Jedidi and Wayne S. DeSarbo (1993), 'A new approach to country segmentation utilizing multinational diffusion patterns', *Journal of Marketing*, **57** (October), 60–71.

Hofstede, Geert (1980), *Culture's Consequences: International Differences in Work-related Values*, Beverly Hills, CA: Sage.

Huszagh, S., R.J. Fox and E. Day (1986), 'Global marketing: an empirical investigation', *Columbia Journal of World Business*, **21**, 31–44.

Jamal, Ahmad (2003), 'Marketing in a multicultural world: the interplay of marketing, ethnicity and consumption', *European Journal of Marketing*, **37**(11/12), 1599–1620.

Jeannet, Jean-Pierre and Hubert David Hennessey (1998), *Global Marketing Strategies*, 4th edn, Boston: Houghton Mifflin.

Jevons, Colin (2000), 'Misplace marketing: international marketing with marketing misplaced, it's often not international', *Journal of Consumer Marketing*, **17**(1), 7–8.

Kacen, Jacqueline J. and Julie Anne Lee (2002), 'The influence of culture on consumer impulsive buying behavior', *Journal of Consumer Psychology*, **12**(2), 163–76.

Kamakura, W.A., T.P. Novak, Jan-Benedict E.M. Steenkamp and T. Verhallen (1994), 'Identifying pan-European value segments with a clusterwise rank-logit model', *Recherche et Applications en Marketing*, **8**(4), 29–55.

Kashima, Y. and H.C. Triandis (1986), 'The self-serving bias in attributions as a coping strategy: a cross-cultural study', *Journal of Cross-Cultural Psychology*, **17**, 83–97.

Kaynak, Erdener, Orsay Kucukemiroglu and Akmal S. Hyder (2000), 'Consumers' country-of-origin perceptions of imported products in a homogeneous less-developed country', *European Journal of Marketing*, **34**(9/10), 1221–41.

Keillor, Bruce D. and G. Thomas M. Hult (1999), 'A five-country study of national identity: implications for international marketing research and practice', *International Marketing Review*, **16**(1), 65–82.

Kim, Jai-Ok, Sandra Forsythe, Qingliang Gu and Sook Jae Moon (2002), 'Cross-cultural consumer values, needs and purchase behavior', *The Journal of Consumer Marketing*, **19**(6), 481–502.

Kiu, Victor (1989), 'How advertising people in Asia interpret psychographic data', Paper presented at AdAsia Advertising Congress, 18–23 February, Lahore, Pakistan.

Lal, D. (1999), *Unintended consequences: the Impact of Factor Endowments, Culture, and Politics on Long-run Economic Performance*, Boston, MA: MIT Press.

Lindridge, Andrew and Sally Dibb (2003), 'Is "Culture" a justifiable variable for market segmentation? A cross-cultural example', *Journal of Consumer Behavior*, **2**(3), 269–86.

Luna, David and Susan Forquer Gupta (2001), 'An integrative framework for cross-cultural consumer behavior', *International Marketing Review*, **18**(1), 45–69.

Lundstrom, William J., Oscar W. Lee and D. Steven White (1998), 'Factors influencing Taiwanese consumer preference for foreign-made white goods: USA versus Japan', *Asia Pacific Journal of Marketing and Logistics*, **10**(3), 5–29.

Maheswaran, Durairaj and Sharon Shavitt (2000), 'Issues and new directions in global consumer psychology', *Journal of Consumer Psychology*, **9**(2), 59–66.

Manrai, Lalita A. and Ajay K. Manrai (2001), 'Marketing opportunities and challenges in emerging markets in the new millennium: a conceptual framework and analysis', *International Business Review*, **10**, 493–504.

Markus, H.R. and S. Kitayama (1991), 'Culture and the self: implications for cognition, emotion and motivation', *Psychological Bulletin*, **98**, 224–53.

Moskowitz, Howard R. and J. Greene (2000), 'Creative segmentation: a new approach to direct marketing', Annual Meeting of the National Center For Direct Marketing, Orlando, Florida.

Moskowitz, H. and S. Rabino (1994), 'Sensory segmentation: an organizing principle for international product concept generation', *Journal of Global Marketing*, **8**(1), 73–93.

Moskowitz, H. and S. Rabino (1999), 'Segmentation, optimisation and database mining', *Journal of Database Marketing*, **7**, 31–45.

NBS (2005), 'A study of contraceptive usage and attitude among Singaporean women', Singapore: Nanyang Business School.

Nevis, Edwin C. (1983), 'Cultural assumptions and productivity: the United States and China', *Sloan Management Review*, **24**(3), 17–29.

O'Cass, Aron and Kenny Lim (2002), 'Understanding the younger Singaporean consumers' views of Western and Eastern brands', *Asia Pacific Journal of Marketing and Logistics*, **14**(4), 54–79.

Phau, Ian and Kor-Weai Chan (2003), 'Targeting East Asian markets: a comparative study on national identity', *Journal of Targeting, Measurement and Analysis for Marketing*, **12**(2), 157–72.

Rostow, Walt Whitman (1960), *The Stages of Economic Growth: A Non-communist Manifesto*, New York: Cambridge University Press.

Samli, A. Coskun and Salah S. Hassan (1992), 'International segmentation options: getting away from conventional wisdom', *Developments in Marketing Science*, **15**, 185–8.

Schütte, Helmut and D. Ciarlante (1998), *Consumer Behavior in Asia*, New York: New York University Press.

Sharma, Piyush and Bharadhwaj Sivakumaran (2004), 'Self-indulgence or loss of self-control? Or, is it a bit of both? Investigating cross-cultural aspects of impulse buying behaviour', *Asia-Pacific Advances in Consumer Research*, **6**, 151–2.

Siddiqi, M.M. Shahid (1991), 'An overview of the economies in the Southern Asian Association of Regional Cooperation', *The Mid-Atlantic Journal of Business*, **27**, 55–6.

Siu, Noel Y.M., Charlie C.L. Wang, Ludwig M.K. Chang and Alice S.Y. Hui (2001), 'Adapting consumer style inventory to Chinese consumers: a confirmatory analysis approach', *Journal of International Consumer Marketing*, **13**(2), 29–48.

Sproles, Elizabeth Kendall and George B. Sproles (1990), 'Consumer decision-making styles as a function of individual learning styles', *The Journal of Consumer Affairs*, **24**(1), 134–47.

Sproles, G.B. and E.L. Kendall (1986), 'A methodology for profiling consumers' decision making styles', *The Journal of Consumer Affairs*, **20**(2), 267–79.

Steenkamp, Jan-Benedict E.M. (2001), 'The role of national culture in international marketing research', *International Marketing Review*, **18**(1), 30–44.

Steenkamp, Jan-Benedict E.M. and Frenkel Ter Hofstede (2002), 'International market segmentation: issues and perspectives', *International Journal of Research in Marketing*, **19**, 185–213.

Suh, Taewon and Ik-Whan G. Kwon (2002), 'Globalization and reluctant buyers', *International Marketing Review*, **19**(6), 663–80.

Suzuki, Hiroe (1990), 'Japanese life-style, life models and applications to creative concepts', ESOMAR Conference on America, Japan and EC '92: The Prospects for Marketing, Advertising and Research, Venice, Italy.

Tai, Susan H.C. (2005), 'Shopping styles of working Chinese females', *Journal of Retailing and Consumer Services*, **12**(3), 191–203.

Tai, Susan H.C. and Jackie L.M. Tam (1996), 'A comparative study of Chinese consumers in Asian markets – a lifestyle analysis', *Journal of International Consumer Marketing*, **9**(1), 25–42.

Ter Hofstede, Frenkel, Jan-Benedict E.M. Steenkamp and Michel Wedel (1999), 'International market segmentation based on consumer–product relations', *Journal of Marketing Research*, **36** (February), 1–17.

Terpstra, Vern and Kenneth David (1991), *The Cultural Environment of International Business*, 3rd edn, Cincinnati, OH: South-Western.

Tse, David K., Russell W. Belk and Nan Zhou (1989), 'Becoming a consumer society: a longitudinal and cross-cultural content analysis of print ads from Hong Kong, the People's Republic of China, and Taiwan', *Journal of Consumer Research*, **15** (March), 457–72.

Tsutsumi, Nobuko and Yong-Sun Chung (2003), 'A comparative study of eating-out behavior between Japan and Korea by fuzzy regression', *International Journal of Consumer Studies*, **27**(1), 40–46.

Verhage, B.J., L.D. Dahringer and E.W. Cundiff (1989), 'Will a global marketing strategy work? An energy conservation perspective', *Journal of the Academy of Marketing Science*, **17**(2), 129–36.

Walsh, Gianfranco, Thorsten Henning-Thurau, Vincent Wayne-Mitchell and Klaus-Peter Wiedmann (2001), 'Consumers' decision-making style as a basis for market segmentation', *Journal of Targeting, Measurement and Analysis for Marketing*, **10**(2), 117–31.

Wedel, Michel, Frenkel Ter Hofstede and Jan-Benedict E.M. Steenkamp (1998), 'Mixture model analysis of complex samples', *Journal of Classification*, **15**(2), 225–44.

Wee, Thomas Tan Tsu (1999), 'An exploration of a global teenage lifestyle in Asian societies', *The Journal of Consumer Marketing*, **16**(4), 365–73.

Wilk, Robert (1990), 'The new rich: a psychographic approach to marketing to the wealthy Japanese Consumer', ESOMAR Conference on America, Japan and EC '92: The Prospects for Marketing, Advertising and Research, Venice, Italy.

Yau, O.H.M. (1994), *Consumer Behavior in China: Customer Satisfaction and Cultural Values*, New York: Routledge.

Yavas, Ugur, Bronislaw J. Verhage and Robert T. Green (1992), 'Global consumer segmentation versus local market orientation: empirical findings', *Management International Review*, **32**(3), 265–73.

Zhou, Lianxi and Michael K. Hui (2003a), 'Foreign products in China retain symbolic value for consumers', *Marketing News*, **37**(13), 22–3.

Zhou, Lianxi and Michael K. Hui (2003b), 'Symbolic value of foreign products in the People's Republic of China', *Journal of International Marketing*, **11**(2), 36–58.

8. Marketing practice 'crossvergence' in post-crisis Asia: an illustrative case analysis

Tim G. Andrews

INTRODUCTION

This chapter draws together a stream of research detailing the emergence of 'crossvergent' strategic marketing practices within the Southeast Asian subsidiaries of a host of Western-headquartered multinational corporations (MNCs). In addition to the initial havoc wrought on local corporate balance sheets, the 1997/98 Asian financial crisis was to trigger the imposition of a series of convergence programmes from Western corporations anxious to 'rein in' the traditionally high levels of autonomy afforded to their hitherto successful local subsidiaries. However, such attempts to try and harmonize indigenous marketing methods in line with core corporate norms and values were met by an often hostile spate of divergent counter-implementation measures undertaken by local management teams, resentful of what they perceived to be unwarranted Western 'meddling' in their domestic affairs. In the ensuing stand-off – for as long as 18 months in certain cases (for example Andrews and Chompusri, 2001) – corporate envoys and incumbent expatriate executives gradually came to acknowledge the importance of local business mores, and practices and the contextual rationale that underpin them. The ethnic Chinese ties and long-held business values that cross-weave much of the regional customer base led a substantial number of MNCs to re-evaluate their initial change programmes, blending headquarters-oriented marketing ideology synergistically with the more sales-based Asian approach.

Using the term 'crossvergence' to depict this fusion of marketing approaches stems from the underpinning work values on which both UK corporate and Thai subsidiary approaches to marketing strategy were held to be founded. Conceived as the final, albeit transitory, resolution of a process comprising convergence (that is in the form of Western-oriented change initiatives) and divergence (in the form and rationale of indigenous resistance), the crossvergence of the values, which underpin these opposing forces, essentially marks the recomposition of the subsidiary corporation's organizational culture. Within the small, but growing, body of literature examining the relative influence of corporate and national forces on the overall cultural make-up of the subsidiary organization (for example Mead, 2005; Neal, 1998; Nohria and Ghoshal, 1994; Hofstede, 1991; Burack, 1991) any significant shifts in the working values of a subsidiary organization would, in the short space of 18 months, be almost inconceivable. Certainly within the small body of research exploring the convergence–divergence–crossvergence of work values, the course of evolutionary change is to be measured in decades, generations, centuries, or even millennia (for example Ralston *et al.*, 1997).

However, the unprecedented pace and severity of the Asian financial crisis, set alongside the elevated cultural distance involved (Lim, 1999), triggered externally imposed business convergence programmes of such revolutionary magnitude (in terms of both organizational and strategic precedents) that the length of the entire convergence–divergence–crossvergence (CDC) process was effectively accelerated from the decades or even centuries, suggested by Ralston *et al.* (1997), to between two to five years (Andrews and Chompusri, 2001; see also Barker and Duhaime, 1997; Gersick, 1991; Greenwood and Hinings, 1996 for related discussion). Furthermore, this compression of the habitual timescale associated with strategic change forces derived from the work values that undergird them (for example Giacobbe-Miller *et al.*, 2003; Heuer *et al.*, 1999) provided my colleagues and I with a unique opportunity to observe the CDC construct *holistically* and *in process*, allowing us to clarify facets of the framework previously misdiagnosed, hidden, or simply incomplete – a classic case of catalytic change facilitating the formation of critical insight (Andrews and Chompusri, 2005; Gersick, 1991). As a programme of study, the longitudinal, multi-case analysis of emerging crossvergent marketing practices began in the summer of 1997 and continued as the corporate response to the crisis unfolded in a series of Southeast Asian subsidiary organizations until the end of 2000. What had begun as the fieldwork phase of a research programme into total quality management implementation within the marketing departments of a number of UK-headquartered multinationals in Thailand metamorphosed opportunistically into a far wider programme of study into the strategic and processual changes taking place across a host of Southeast Asian subsidiaries in a range of industries.

The use of case studies as a research strategy is frequently criticized, typically on the grounds that it is impossible to produce either statistical generalizations or theories that are generalizable to all populations, and with this we concur. However, throughout the course of this project, the regional corporate environment was in a state of transformation and uncertainty that rendered unsatisfactory our adopting a more positivist 'closed lab' approach. Our chosen field of organizational *change* necessitated a *dynamic* research design. The traditional 'snapshot', point-in-time study based on cross-sectional data is thus patently inappropriate (Greenwood and Hinings, 1996; Eisenhardt, 1989). Static by nature, such an approach would have underestimated the key dimension of dynamism embedded in the concept of change, especially where the phenomenon delineated (marketing practice crossvergence) was at an embryonic stage of analysis and relatively unexamined (Andrews and Chompusri, 2001; Khiliji, 2002). Moreover, the locus of study was atypical, illustrative of an extreme situation the analysis of which has been traditionally associated with the case study method (for example Eisenhardt, 1989). Finally, whereas a great deal has been written about the macro-management implications of the Asian regional collapse, there has been little attempt to explore the situation 'in the trenches'. The case studies utilized in this stream of research helps to redress this balance.

For the purposes of this chapter, in order to summarize adequately research into the phenomenon of post-Asian crisis marketing crossvergence, I have opted to keep intact the rich contextual grounding of the process by focusing on one particular case illustration (the SAC corporation)[1] that formed the core case for the initial spate of research and afforded us largely unhindered access to internal documentation and respondent interviews, as well as, crucially, observation in both participant and direct guises. The empirical data traced below, specifically as regards the formation of crossvergent brand development strategies, are therefore taken from an amalgamation of published research (Andrews and Chompusri, 2001; Andrews, 2001; Andrews *et al.*, 2003), in addition to hitherto unpublished fieldwork providing additional textual richness.

The Thai business context forms the ideal contextual backdrop for the exploration of crossvergent marketing practices. First, by the mid-1990s, Thailand had become the regional headquarters of choice for many multinational companies for Southeast Asia and China (for example Powpaka, 1998). Second, in terms of business culture, Thai senior managers tend to share the ethnicity and attendant values of the ethnic Chinese and thus provide us with a fairly representative sample for the Asia Pacific region as a whole. Third, concerning our focus on work values variance, in terms of economic ideology on the one hand and national culture on the other, Thailand also emerges as a suitable contextual base for the successful reception of Western management norms, with an established constitutional monarchy, and a democratic, relatively stable and pro-business political system. However, ethnically much less diverse than most of its neighbours, Thailand has been able to retain its language, culture and tradition almost entirely intact, being the only Southeast Asian country never to have been colonized by the forces of 'Western imperialism' throughout a national history spanning over 800 years (Infothai, 1998; Nivatpumin and Sivasompoon, 1997; Lawler, 1996).

Fourth, within the confines of cross-national cultural theory, Thais are depicted as being relatively homogeneous and 'non-confrontational', expressing high needs to avoid uncertainty, a high level of power distance and an agrarian-based, highly collectivist group orientation, and in particular contrast to the highly individualist, self-oriented nations of the US and the UK (for example Hofstede, 1980, 1991). Finally, Thailand suffered the full severity of the Asian economic meltdown of 1997–8, playing host to the initial wave of business collapse and reacting to post-crisis Western 'interference' with a characteristic wave of culturally insular, nationalistic anti-Western feeling. In this context, SAC corporate changes apparently successfully imposed in the former Western colonies of Malaysia, Singapore and Vietnam were demonstrably inappropriate in Thailand, not only through the actions of senior sales management, but also by their key portfolios.

The rest of the chapter is organized as follows: the second section details the convergence–divergence–crossvergence construct from its origins at the macro-level force, delineating shifting work values to an organization-level force in the wake of the Asian financial crisis. We then provide the empirical backdrop to the marketing operations and organization at SAC (Thailand) Ltd as the conduit through which the organization interacted in the pre-crisis 'boom' years of the 1990s. The fourth section then interweaves the observed cultural variations in working values behind the resistance and subsequent compromise of corporate marketing revision within the development of crossvergent marketing solutions, specifically in terms of branding strategy practice within the Thai post-crisis environment. We then outline the implications of intracorporate crossvergence for future research, focusing on a number of contributions to the theory and practice of cross-national management and marketing strategy.

THE CONVERGENCE–DIVERGENCE–CROSSVERGENCE FRAMEWORK

Developed decades ago as contrasting explanations of values formation (Webber, 1969), the dynamics of convergence and divergence within organizations and managerial practices worldwide have attracted attention in a range of management disciplines (for example Adler, Doktor and Redding, 1986; Sparrow, Schuler and Jackson, 1994; McGaughey and De Cieri, 1999). Partly as a response to the increasing internationalization of corporate strategy, international companies have continued to grapple with the diverse value systems of their multidomestic operational workforces, as they explore the possibilities of creating a common corporate culture deemed necessary in the creation of a 'seamless global organization' (Ralston *et al.*, 1997: 189). Depicted as 'concepts or beliefs about desirable end states or behaviours that transcend specific situations, guide selection or evaluation of behaviour and events, and are ordered by relative importance', individual work values are held to play a crucial role in a manager's decision-making process (Schwartz and Bilsky, 1987, cited in Ralston *et al.*, 1993: 250). Aggregated to the organizational level, a key factor for multidomestic companies aspiring to design and develop a universal corporate culture (Ralston *et al.*, 1997: 184) is ascertaining whether the diverse work values of the various local operations are capable, when exposed to external influences, of evolving (that is converging) toward the common set of values held by the corporate centre (Ralston *et al.*, 1997: 178; 1999; Dunphy, 1987).

Implicit in studies exploring the interaction of Western MNCs with diverse societal cultures is the respective impact of two primary forces that influence the formation of individual work values, namely economic ideology – as the force for convergence – and national culture as the divergent anchor (Ralston *et al.*, 1993, 1997; Khiliji, 2002; Ronen, 1986). Economic ideology may be defined as the 'workplace philosophy' that pervades the sociopolitical systems within which a corporate subsidiary must function in the normal course of business (Ralston *et al.*, 1993, 1997). Since MNCs stem from the industrialized nations that, until very recently, have been equated to Western capitalistic countries, convergence has meant assimilating the ideological values of Western capitalistic economies (Dunphy, 1987; Webber, 1969).

But while both economic ideology and societal culture may influence managerial values, the question drawing much attention in the current literature is one of *significance* (Ralston *et al.*, 1993; Neghandi, 1983): when indigenous employees are exposed to Western management practices at the workplace (for example at the branch subsidiary of a US multinational in Thailand), do they also take on the values assumed in the West to be a part of a capitalistic system? This is of particular importance to Western MNCs operating in the emerging markets of East Asia, not least because of the important constants within the Eastern and Western cultures that differentiate them from one another (Ralston *et al.*, 1997: 180). These appear to centre on the relative focus on the good-of-the-group (collectivism) in the East – based on the primary influences of Confucianism, Taoism and Buddhism – versus the good-of-the-individual (individualism) in the West, grounded in the tenets of the Judaeo-Christian religion (ibid.: 179).

The convergence view posits that economic ideology drives values and that exposure to Western ways of engaging in business will result in the value systems of indigenous managers responding more strongly to the common requirements of management, discounting the importance of cultural differences (McGaughey and DeCieri, 1999: 236; Ralston *et al.*, 1993, 1997; Ronen, 1986). McGaughey and DeCieri (1999: 236) neatly summarize Kerr *et al.*'s (1960) arguments. They suggest that the logic of industrialism generates economic and technological imperatives that mould the development of national institutional frameworks in industrialized societies towards a common pattern or convergence, in spite of disparate politics, ideology and cultures. In this manner, the multidomestic branch operations of Western MNCs will converge over perhaps 'ten, twenty years or perhaps generations' (Ralston *et al.*, 1997: 183) towards utilizing similar sets of practices (Rowley and Benson, 2002), grounded in the progressive indigenous shift towards the external values introduced into the workplace (Giacobbe-Miller *et al.*, 2003; Andrews and Chompusri, 2005).

Against a backdrop of increasingly global communications, regional economic integration and internationalization (Rowley and Benson, 2002: 91–2), Western management techniques, behaviour and business systems would comprise the force for this change (Ralston *et al.*, 1997: 182). They seek to homogenize the various business functions – of which marketing forms a prime example – under the auspices of global industry 'best practices', around which organizations would have to converge, or else be at a competitive disadvantage. As Rowley and Benson (2002: 92) argue, an implicit assumption is that the effects of 'best practice' are not firm specific, but rather universal and transferable.

Such notions of convergence, and its modern variant, universalism, have permeated a cross-section of debates within the disciplines of organization and management for decades. Yet recent research has begun to question the underlying tenets of convergence as being too simplistic: for example, in the assumption that all organizations compete in the same ways (Rowley and Benson, 2002). Moreover, just as there is evidence suggesting that the global business environment, in terms of economic forces and technology, has a converging effect on values held by managers, there is other evidence to suggest that culture is a sufficiently powerful force to resist the impact of Western-style industrialization (Ralston *et al.*, 1993; Rowley and Benson, 2002). Proponents of the divergence approach argue that indigenous differentials drive managerial value systems (Robertson *et al.*, 2001; Khiliji, 2002; Ralston *et al.*, 1997) and that individuals will retain their diverse, culturally determined values regardless of economic ideology (Ralston *et al.*, 1997: 183; Ricks *et al.*, 1990). Local customs, institutions and labour forces provide serious constraints on the degree of convergence rendered possible within the MNC branch subsidiary, and may well lead to increasing levels of divergence in the form and content of functional specialization (Hofstede, 1991; McGaughey and DeCieri, 1999: 237). This is often reflected in turn at the level of practices and policies (Rowley and Benson, 2002: 90).

However, an increasing body of recent research suggests that deterministic arguments of economic ideology-driven convergence on the one hand and culture-driven divergence on the other are simply inadequate to explain the dynamic and often complex interactions between organizations and their environments (Khiliji, 2002; Andrews and Chompusri, 2005). This is especially the case, given the increasing cross-pollination of culture and ideology within a cross-section of emerging Eastern economies (Ralston *et al.*, 1997: 184; George, 1992; Ohmae, 1990; Ralston *et al.*, 1993).

At the broad level, simultaneous evidence for both convergence and divergence within the individual organization may be found within relevant empirical research, with convergence studies concentrating on macro-level variables (structure/technology) and divergence studies concentrating on micro-level variables to account for culturally based dissimilarities (Rowley and Benson, 2002: 96; McGaughey and DeCieri, 1999: 235). Yet even remaining focused within the confines of a micro-level focus (that is in accounting for individual-level work values composition), there has been a marked deficiency of work to account for the way managerial values change over time (Rowley and Benson, 2002). As Ralston *et al.* (1993: 260) note, 'some values may change while others do not. Some values may change more rapidly than other values. Other unique values may evolve from a combination of influences'.

A more recent perspective, developed by Ralston and associates through the 1990s (for example Ralston *et al.*, 1993, 1997, 1999) seeks to address this caveat, utilizing the anthropological roots of acculturation theory. These authors posit that an integrative alternative exists that might be characterized as the melting pot philosophy of values formation (Ralston *et al.*, 1997: 184). Crossvergence denotes a unique set of individual work values formed when an individual incorporates both national culture influences and economic ideology influences synergistically to create a unique value system that is different from the value set supported by either national culture or economic ideology (ibid.: 183). Centred on the relative contribution of national culture and economic ideology to the overall work values equation (Ralston *et al.*, 1997: 178), crossvergence, as a temporal, transitional state between convergence and divergence, reflects more accurately the composition of individual work values, when Western MNCs interact with indigenous employees in emerging East Asian markets.

In the wake of the Asian financial crisis, Andrews and associates (Andrews *et al.*, 2003; Andrews and Chompusri, 2001; Andrews, 2001) re-emphasized the contribution of organizational variables to the convergence–divergence–crossvergence (CDC) debate, reconceptualizing the CDC framework as a *dialectical* process at the intracorporate level. This work draws from the opposing forces of corporate culture on the one hand and societal culture on the other. In line with previous studies into corporate versus national cultures (Laurent, 1986; Mead, 2005; Schein, 1985; Schneider and Barsoux, 1997), the initial reascendance of corporate culture in the wake of the Asian financial crisis (specifically in the form of MNC strategic audits of their regional subsidiaries) was conceived as the force for *convergence* (the 'glue' that holds corporations together), societal cultural variables as the resisting force for *divergence*, and a subsequent compromise of the two to mark *crossvergence*, the blended integration of working values and practices to emerge synergistically at the corporate–subsidiary interface (see also Khiliji, 2002; Rowley and Benson, 2002; McGaughey and De Cieri, 1999; Ralston *et al.*, 1997; Chapter 18 in this volume).

EMPIRICAL BACKGROUND

Corporate Asia, Pre- and Post-crisis

Through the pre-crisis growth years of the 1980s and the early 1990s, the majority of foreign multinationals in Southeast Asia adhered to all the implicit guidelines of business process adaptation. In the context of unparalleled market growth and prosperity, multinational corporations of the era tended to pride themselves on their 'multidomestic approach' towards the region, with each domestic unit responsible for a given domestic territory enjoying considerable autonomy (see also Chapter 2 in this volume). With the onset of the Asian economic collapse in 1997, however, these same Western corporations began to question the extent of these adaptation strategies, as the sharp and unexpected decline in local market demand took hold that punctured almost overnight the myth of never-ending growth in the region (Lim, 1999). Business units in Thailand – as the precursor of the regional collapse – and elsewhere were suddenly confronted with a collapse in domestic purchasing power, rising production costs and excessive staffing levels (*Bangkok Post*, 1998; Bardacke, 1998). External bodies and local analysts together were quick to emphasize the fact that, in light of the economic crisis, increasing competition, global trading pressure and computerization, the region's domestic private sectors and governments were now being effectively compelled to reprioritize their attitudes to business, finally coming to grips with the importance of product quality, innovation, worker productivity and internal cost structures (Godement, 1999; Yuthamanop, 1999; Toews and MacGregor, 1998).

In effect, the crisis had served to demystify the *cultural* facets of Asian business, reasserting the rationalism of 'Western', essentially Anglo-Saxon, approaches to business management and strategy (Bhopal and Hitchcock, 2001; cf. Chapters 4 and 17 in this volume). Against this backdrop, the domestic subsidiaries of formerly indulgent Western parents were being placed under an increasingly critical microscope from corporate headquarters. In order to facilitate the implementation of corporate strategic objectives (Andrews and Chompusri, 2001), sustained programmes of rationalization and stabilization followed the initial defensive efforts designed to halt deterioration and gain control of the firm's cash flow (Hoffman, 1989; Robbins and Pearce, 1992; Hofer, 1980). Many multinationals felt compelled to streamline and re-evaluate radically their local Southeast Asian operations, a development that was to result in the local imposition of a stream of organizational restructuring programmes. Indigenous business practices and values once prized for their flexibility during the boom years (Bhopal and Hitchcock, 2001) were now being deemed suspect and even unprofessional now that the bubble had finally burst.

The rapid convergence of global business practices and values, enacted through the direct intervention of Western parent corporations, was aimed at strengthening the central steerage of corporate control in order to deal with this sudden upheaval of short-to-medium-term strategic direction. In cultural terms, parent corporations sought to maximize control via the overwhelming of ethnic differences across diverse cultural contexts (Entrekin and Chung, 2001; Giacobbe-Miller *et al.*, 2003; Adler and Jelinek, 1986; Khiliji, 2002). They reimposed parent corporate values in order to tilt the constituent organizational culture away from its hitherto indigenous predominance and more in line with globally acknowledged business process norms (Reade, 2001; Andrews and Chompusri, 2001; Young, 2000; Legewie and Meyer-Ohle, 2000), a classic utilization of parent corporate culture as the 'hidden adhesive' to control and hold geographically dispersed units in line (Gupta and Govindarajan, 2000; Kim *et al.*, 2003). Functionally, the changes encompassed both organizational change processes (for example global business streaming – Andrews *et al.*, 2003), marketing standardization strategies (Theodosiou and Katsikeas, 2001; Jain, 1989) and human resource management practices (Rowley and Benson, 2002; Entrekin and Chung, 2001).

Such convergent forces for change, notably in the guise of Western corporate investors as well as the IMF controlled programme of economic recovery, were stigmatized locally, however, as the twin destroyers of the indigenous economy, notably, by political and industrial elites across the region. These elites sought to enhance the notion of an Asian cultural identity that was utilized as a cohesive force for the resistance of alien Western values (Bhopal and Hitchcock, 2001). Within the corporate environment, many of the post-crisis restructuring initiatives and their attendant value criteria were deemed as representing 'concepts from another galaxy', when imposed in the Thai environmental context (Mead, 2005; Kind, 1997; Nivatpumin and Sivasompoon, 1997). Against this backdrop, a sustained distinction between globally handed down policy and local practice emerged across the region, whereby centrally diffused guidelines were agreed to by local managers, but then either ignored or adapted *in practice* to fit local norms and values (Andrews and Chompusri, 2001; Rowley and Benson, 2002; Legewie and Meyer-Ohle, 2000).

SAC (THAILAND) LTD

A successful marketer of premium grade motor lubricants, SAC International was established in 1938, currently holding operations spanning 85 countries across the globe. With its focus turning exclusively to the premium end of the motor oils market, SAC has traditionally competed on product differentiation and innovation as its route to competitive advantage. Its core values are built upon the premium quality tag to embrace the valued notions of technology and performance. SAC lubricants were first introduced to the Thai market as part of an agency agreement in 1968. Initial growth levels soon prompted head office to upgrade the Thai unit into a fully-fledged corporate subsidiary, complete with manufacturing operations, a move previously only attempted in the former British colony of Singapore. With the rapid expansion of the Thai economy in the decade from 1985, the company enjoyed unprecedented sales and profitability growth. In the face of such performance, SAC home office progressively relaxed its control over local marketing strategy, notwithstanding traditional attention to meticulous maintenance of the company's strong corporate heritage and centrally ordained brand values. Grounded in detailed local market research in order to 'live, breathe and feel' each market territory on a day-to-day basis, a major thrust of SAC's locally-inspired business philosophy was that, concurrent to centrally conceived corporate brand values, their Thai division responsible for their Thai operations should be run the 'Thai way'.

In the wake of the region-wide business collapse, however, motor oil consumption (traditionally a mirror to economic activity) shrank by some 40 per cent over two years, as companies struggled to cope with tightening marketing margins and increased competition (Bardacke, 1998; Siamwalla and Sobchokchai, 1998; Stiglitz, 1998). In this context, and along with the majority of Western-based corporations, SAC sought to reverse its traditional focus on marketing adaptation. It utilized the crisis, along with a host of other key multinationals, as a timely catalyst for strategic and organizational change, as the 'engine of reform'.

MARKETING STRATEGY CROSSVERGENCE

Departmental Organization: Roles and Reform

In organizational and strategic terms, the extant consumer marketing department was highly idiosyncratic for a SAC marketing division, encompassing both marketing and sales functions, but with a marked emphasis on the latter. The Bangkok-based senior sales manager effectively doubled as the department's strategist and second-in-command to the marketing director himself, also an ethnic Chinese Thai national. These two local managers drafted all necessary planning and strategic documents, including those for departmental advertising and promotion campaigns. The label of 'marketing' was applied to just two of the ten departmental managers, both of whom were responsible merely for signage, stock control and the loan of equipment. In the Western sense of the word, the marketing function as such has been given barely even a backseat in the strategic hierarchy, perceived as little more than a backroom administrative function in support of the core sales team. Departmental power thus resided within the closely knit ranks of the remaining eight senior sales managers, a state of affairs not uncommon within the Asia-based subsidiaries of West-headquartered multinationals.

Asian business culture has traditionally tended to give more weighting to the sales function that, acting at the front-line of customer acquisition and management, was deemed to comprise the key to local market success in an environment where successful trading traditionally depends upon the qualitative nature of external relationships with customers and suppliers. Operating within intricate and often very influential 'bamboo networks', local sales representatives were held to possess an 'ear' for the genuine needs of their customer base. This is grounded in an understanding of dealer behaviour at a level far deeper than their marketing counterparts could ever hope to emulate (Andrews, 2001; Andrews and Chompusri, 2001; Andrews *et al.*, 2003).

In seeking to converge local sales and marketing practice towards corporate norms and practices, the region-wide programme of restructuring and strategic reorientation was imposed upon the Thai consumer marketing department in November 1997. A major thrust of the changes imposed was to strengthen the marketing function within the unit, initially by creating a new consumer marketing unit, separated from sales and placed under the control of a new, externally selected managerial recruit of Thai origin yet with a Western education. The newcomer was then charged with recruiting three new managers who, on the back of a streamlined sales reorganization, were to act as counterparts for the three remaining senior sales managers for each of Thailand's main upcountry commercial regions.

Operationally, the creation of this separate marketing nexus was partly in response to corporate calls for more regulated strategic planning documentation, grounded in a series of detailed criticisms of the traditional lack of proactive bias and ad hoc, incoherent organization, seemingly thought out no more than a single month in advance. In the weeks to follow, however, corporate head office was to admit surprise at the sustained hostility of indigenous reaction to the revised directives. The Thai sales managers viewed these initiatives as an inappropriate use of resources in Thailand, where the local sales teams were deemed to possess a natural, longstanding feel for the market. The apparent desire by corporate executives to wish to bind themselves – and others – in plans and graphs was considered to be a mark of naïveté in a business context where flexibility had served the unit so well and for so long. Instinctive decision making was traditionally considered as the local prerequisite for marketing success in a domestic environment perceived as both unknown and unknowable. Senior local management reiterated their preference for gathering market data through informal channels and personal cum familiar customer/supplier relationships. This subjective grassroots information would then be interpreted through intense face-to-face discussion in the belief that, only via multiple perspectives, broad involvement and extensive data sharing, would the comprehension of external market ambiguity be attainable. This level of understanding – albeit intrinsically imperfect – was claimed to reside only in those of a Thai – specifically Thai–Chinese – cultural heritage (see also Schneider and Barsoux, 1997).

Progressive corporate acknowledgment of these cultural mores, and in particular those concerning ethnic Chinese ties, led to the compromising of the desired convergence programme toward the traditional customer-led values of the sales-oriented Thai business environment. While maintaining the desire for more documented strategy plans, the reporting lines of the newly separated departments were split, with both subunits enacting both *direct* and *indirect* lines of communication with both local customers on the one hand and the incumbent Western CEO on the other. A direct line of working between the sales team and its customers was then established, a move viewed with particular satisfaction by weary sales managers with their traditional emphasis upon business relationships. By contrast, the customer lines to the new marketing team were of an almost exclusively indirect nature. All contact with the company's customers was henceforth to emerge exclusively via their sales counterparts, effectively shielding them from the customer interface. To offset this imbalance, the sales team was to hold but a dotted-line or indirect working rapport with incumbent (predominantly Western) chief executives, as opposed to the direct line given over to 'new marketing'. This was judged by our respondents to be a satisfactory, if not optimal, compromise solution for the companies involved, permitting them to take advantage of both group and subsidiary best working practices. Local managers felt that they were supported now in what they performed best: the maintenance of relational networks among their indigenous clientele. The new marketing teams, usually similarly satisfied, were keen to stress that the new structure provided them with a new base of power, via their direct line to the respective country manager, a factor that would in practice make the sales team wary of crossing them.

Viewed in the context of the crossvergence dialectic of corporate versus societal cultural values, SAC's corporate culture is viewed as finding expression and promotion within the push for convergence expressed in the formation of the new consumer marketing department. The Thai societal culture, by contrast, formed the force for divergence through the resistance of consumer sales managers. The eventual emergence of compromise working arrangements suitable to both camps comprises the blending of these value profiles within the evolution of the agreed re-organization and reporting lines, binding sales and marketing to the corporate directorate on the one hand and the indigenous customer base on the other.

Brand Development

A key plank of marketing revisions at SAC Thailand concerned the re-enforcement of brand development strategies in line with core corporate values. The traditional focus among SAC subsidiaries in Southeast Asia was on short to medium returns, tending to push any notions of brand building way down their list of priorities. Top Asian executives were therefore largely dismissive of a soft, fuzzy concept perceived as a fanciful and excessive drain on limited resources. During the boom years of the 1980s and the early 1990s, it had seemed that this local resistance to global branding methods was entirely justified, with the local units of some of the world's foremost multinationals reporting record sales and profitability growth levels on the back of traditional, relations-based working practices. In this context, the specific attention to brand development could, within reason, be kept on a backburner (along with notions of regional coordination and even economies of scale) on the strength of rocketing domestic sales. The local execution of mandatory marketing induction courses was therefore centred on the marketing process, bypassing much of the corporate-oriented material in the sales-driven emphasis on the motor lubricant metaphor as an expression of the informal and inflexible nature of the local company–customer rapport (Andrews *et al.*, 2003).

Initial SAC corporate measures centred on the strict and immediate incorporation of global branding guidelines to be disseminated in all domestic marketing training programmes, both to new and existing departmental managers, specifically in order to take fuller advantage of what was centrally perceived as the company's key global competitive assets. Perceived as a key strategic asset, SAC corporate had become increasingly concerned with the perceived debasement of its master brand positioning in Thailand. A 'brand protection' initiative was imposed in order to converge perceived disparate brand imaging and standardize corporate market communication. This was to include the duplication of the corporate 'brand portfolio analysis' framework used in the West to divide competitor positioning policy into top-end, premium and best value. The Thai unit itself was instructed largely to avoid the latter economy/volume category in future, corporate strategy being to specialize only in small-volume, high-margin trade.

Home office management were increasingly concerned that the Thai marketing team were competing on price and promotion discounts in the mass-market, thereby placing the master brand at a perceivably lower level than in Malaysia or Singapore, or even Vietnam. The fear was that this disparate positioning would result in the erosion of brand premiums gained elsewhere, as the entire region gravitated towards the lowest common denominator. Senior Thai marketing executives were thus advised to assist in rebuilding domestic SAC brand strength by devoting a higher proportion of domestic resources to targeting prestige, imported car and motorcycle manufacturers, and franchise holders as part of a continuing regional goal to attain a 'dominant state of mind' among *quality* consumers. Stated future objectives were to concentrate on making local consumers *aspire* to buying SAC lubricants, rather than persuading them to switch or maintain their brand of choice on the basis of cost (Andrews and Chompusri, 2001).

In the wake of the economic collapse, however, these revisions were met with sustained and hostile resistance. Whatever loyalty customers had shown to the international motor oil brands, among the likes of Shell, Mobil and Caltex, this was rapidly being eroded as the year wore on, with traders across the board placing greater emphasis on attaining maximum volume returns. As the recession deepened through 1998, price effectively surpassed brand as a deciding factor in product choice among hard-hit motorists, notwithstanding the sharp increase in available brands among increasingly savvy consumers through much of the 1990s. The flood of cheaper mineral brands to find their way into the Thai market in the immediate post-crisis period effectively ensured that low-cost, often illegal, local distributors were the only suppliers to gain market share as the downturn wore on. Against this backdrop, local managers vehemently opposed the new corporate training guidelines, berating notions of brand development as a risky, intangible, untimely exercise in an environment where the traditional emphasis on price marketing was now, more than ever before, the only way to maintain long-established relations with hard-hit but loyal trading customers. SAC's restated aim of seeking to 'trade up' local consumers into buying premium and top-end motor lubes was therefore criticized as nonsensical, in an environment where the reality of consumer demand recentred the 'bread and butter' mid-range products as the core focus of consumer interest.

Again, over time, however, a compromise was struck regarding the provision of appropriate training in corporate brand values for both new and existing marketing/sales personnel. Crisis notwithstanding, local senior sales managers became receptive to the notion that strengthening SAC brand awareness among local teams *now* would have important beneficial knock-on effects for the long-term future of respective master brands within the region. To this end, agreement was made for a series of region-wide 'refresher courses' that focused on core corporate values, instanced by the stated values of being marketing-led, technology-focused and of premium quality calibre. Local managers were to be allowed some measure of autonomy in the preparation and dissemination of such training, however, with both marketing and sales managers working in conjunction with corporate requirements through regional human resources envoys sent for the purpose.

The emerging dialectic of intracorporate forces, whereby initial corporate convergence measures were resisted before a series of compromise strategic practices were to emerge, is typified here in the case of *Si-Flow*, the locally conceived flagship product sold exclusively in Thailand since its launch in 1995. In the desire to strengthen their top-end brand positioning in the Thai market, corporate envoys informed the indigenous managers of the plan to replace Si-Flow altogether with a higher-positioned regional alternative already in use through much of the region, including Malaysia and Singapore. Immediate opposition to these plans was vociferously expressed, based upon the understandably emotional attachment to a product brand they had developed and packaged internally and free from UK interference. Si-Flow, they insisted, was SAC's premium product in the market, conceived and marketed by the local operations team 'for the Thai people' and jealously guarded as such.

Furthermore, the corporate aim of having locals aspiring to buying the planned alternative was roundly dismissed as being wholly unrealistic in the local crisis-torn economic environment. As the general preference for Western goods continued to decline in light of the government-sponsored 'buy Thai' campaign, the comment that one cannot eat aspirations or images appeared especially persuasive. Using their leverage gained through their detailed knowledge of the domestic market, the local sales and marketing team were able virtually to quash this corporate initiative. Via an invisible, but very powerful, network of sales representatives, close – often related – Bangkok customers and a sympathetic accounts receivable team, wild swings in sales of Si-Flow from one week to the next were sent as a message to the UK headquarters to abstain from tampering with this prized domestic product.

The lengthy standoff concerning Si-Flow was eventually resolved in a compromise gradually adhered to, so that, by mid-1999, a perceivable set of crossvergent positioning practices had arisen. To begin with, the renewed corporate emphasis upon the top-end market segment was partly diluted to adhere to the local stress upon the shrinkage in purchasing power. Corporate guidelines for Thailand were to amalgamate local areas of emphasis, devoting more resources to the mass-market, 'bread-and-butter' segments traditionally served by the internationally perceived low-end standard products (instanced by

Super 2T for motorcycles and LT40 for automobiles). Recognizing Si-Flow as an unusu-
ally sensitive case, SAC headquarters again struck a deal with the local marketing team.
Minor repositioning facets were incorporated along with a higher-quality blend, although
the local name was kept in adapted form so that New Si-Flow entered the market in mid-
1999, backed by a centrally funded, heavily promoted relaunch campaign.

CONCLUSIONS AND IMPLICATIONS

This chapter has sought to provide a timely synopsis of the crossvergence construct,
drawing from the original spate of studies into crossvergent managerial work values progressed by Ralston and Associates during the 1990s. Against the immediate backdrop of
the Asian financial crisis, these studies were conducted prior to the tentative reconceptualization of the CDC dynamic as an organizational variable. The dynamics of CDC as a
dialectic process are illustrated within the sphere of cross-national brand development
strategy, tracing the intracorporate forces for convergence (that is in the shape of corporate homogenization programmes), divergence (in the explicit forces for indigenous resistance and attendant rationale) and, finally, crossvergence as the medium-term resolution
(or synthesis) of the headquarters–subsidiary standoff.

In seeking to conserve the contextual richness necessary to explicate the progressive
emergence of crossvergent marketing practices, we have grounded the empirical delineation of the construct within one particularly revelatory case study organization – among
the many utilized in the series of studies – selected for the extreme nature of the dialectic
witnessed, helpful in clarifying the underlying processes involved. The marketing illustra-
tions presented in this chapter, in centring on the fortunes of one single Western parented
Southeast Asian subsidiary organization, must be viewed, along with the series of studies
as a whole, with considerable caution as regards their generalizability beyond the contextual boundaries denoted. Nonetheless, as indicative of a much broader phenomenon, this
summary of the post-Asian crisis crossvergence studies, although context-specific, does
identify important implications for strategic and organizational management within the
region based on a series of theoretical and practical conclusions identified below.

Contribution to Theory

In broad theoretical terms, by operationalizing the unique and invaluable insights into the
CDC process afforded us by the Asian crisis, we have presented an analysis that recon-
ceptualizes – and ultimately redefines – the construct of 'crossverging' managerial work
values. In incorporating the cross-national, intracorporate tensions to emerge between
headquarters and subsidiary units within the context of the Asian financial crisis, the construct of crossvergent managerial practices and values to emerge is viewed as *less* a matter
of economic ideology versus societal culture, and *more* a question of the relative influence
of global corporate versus national/societal cultures, expressed in this context through the
working solutions to emerge at the corporate–societal interface. In the case presented
above, the origins and development of such resolutions were rendered explicit under the
clarifying light of a sensitive programme of cross-national organizational restructuring
catalysed by the Asian financial crisis. In this manner, the shifts in organizational culture

composition traced at the Thai subsidiary were dramatically compressed into a very short time span. These shifts made it easier for the CDC process underpinning shifting work values to be witnessed in its entirety, and clarified facets of the construct previously misdiagnosed, hidden, or simply incomplete – a classic case of 'catalytic change' facilitating the formation of critical insight (Gersick, 1991).

In this context, crossvergence is reconceived as forming the transitory stage of resolution in a dialectical process of organization-level cultural change. Use of the dialectic dynamic to depict the forces for convergence versus divergence is not without precedent (for example Fombrun, 1986; Benson, 1977), even within the context of the post-financial business environment in Asia (Ng and Warner, 2002; see also Chapter 18 in this volume). Yet, in incorporating notions of crossvergence, Andrews and associates build on this work, formalizing corporate homogenization programmes provided for an enforced period of convergence as the 'thesis', the diverging backlash of Asian indigenous management resistance as 'antithesis' and, critically, transitory resolution of subsidiary management practices (crossvergence) as the underutilized 'synthesis', specifically through the compromised fusion of these opposing forces (Andrews and Chompusri, 2001, 2005).

Depicted in terms of the underlying forces for corporate culture homogeneity on the one hand and national culture diversity on the other, the crossvergence framework delineated above also informs the small, but growing, body of literature examining the *relative* influence of corporate and national cultures upon the overall cultural make-up of the subsidiary organization (Neal, 1998; Nohria and Ghoshal, 1994; Hofstede, 1991; Burack, 1991). In particular, the conceptualization of corporate and national cultures as competing forces operationalized as a dialectical progression (specifically in the wake of cataclysmic exogenous upheaval) suggests that future research into these variables, at least within the context of the multinational corporation, should be mindful of their essentially dynamic nature, a characteristic often hidden within studies conducted against a relatively stable backdrop.

Moreover, portrayed at the level of shifting work values, the dialectic of convergence–divergence–crossvergence above contains suggestions for future studies of organizational turnaround (Pearce and Robbins, 1993) within similar type-contexts (Bruton *et al.*, 2001). Specifically, where the relative success of corporate-instituted programmes of change depends on cultural congruency, as was so obviously the case above, the usual multi-stage framework comprising cost and then strategic-level recovery measures (for example Bibeault, 1982; Hambrick and Schecter, 1983; Hoffman, 1989), although necessary, appears manifestly incomplete. Specifically, in incorporating the CDC dialectic as a framework for cultural level shifts, the studies summarized above point the way to the temporal and content extension to this process. Against the backdrop of crisis in Asia – reconceptualized as part of a CDC dialectic – the attempted reimposition of parent corporate values at the strategic/recovery stage formed not the end, but merely the beginning, of the process that was to engender prolonged and costly periods of confrontation and upheaval, primarily on the basis of cultural incongruence (Andrews and Chompusri, 2001). To this end, we posit the reconfiguration of turnaround as a longer process to include, in addition to the convergence measures of cost reduction and strategic reorientation, the subsequent indigenous, culture-based period of resistance, as well as the eventual parent corporate–subsidiary compromise, facets deemed as both important (Bruton and Rubanik, 1997) and in need of further research (Kim *et al.*, 2003; Andrews and Chompusri, 2005).

Finally, as a marketing concern, the studies empirically illustrated in this chapter add textual richness to our current understanding of how the business values of a developing economy have an impact upon Western corporate marketing strategy. Ostensibly a marketing-led corporation, SAC International can learn from Thai notions of sales-led business process flexibility, by emphasizing the informal mechanics of indigenous customer relationships as the cornerstone of any future change initiative within the qualitatively distinct Thai market context. In his study on market orientation in Thailand, Powpaka (1998) suggests that, instead of seeking to 'iron-out' the other's cultural differences, moves should be initiated to establish a balanced, two-way process to mould the marketing practices adopted at the corporate–subsidiary interface. Further to bridging the inherent cultural tensions in the headquarters–subsidiary dynamic, this would also provide a flexible base on which to conduct organic tactical modification, in order to suit the changing needs of progressively unstable markets.

Contribution to Practice

The delineation of marketing practice crossvergence made in the post-crisis Thai environmental context of a British multinational may provide broader insights for corporate strategists operating in the emerging territories of Southeast Asia. Certainly the resilience of traditional Thai business practice in the face of Western corporate ideology at SAC bodes ill for simplistic notions of seamless global corporate cultures underpinning standardized sets of marketing strategies. Accordingly, in seeking to understand the shifting value systems of their worldwide operations – and in particular the extent to which the cross-societal managerial values of their workforces are becoming more alike or not (Mead, 2005; Ralston *et al.*, 1997; McGaughey and De Cieri, 1999) – the conceptualization of relative shifts in the composition of subsidiary organizational culture as a dialectical progression of competing forces may provide insight into the way the constituent elements of corporate versus national culture may be identified, disentangled and, crucially for multinational corporations operating in the context of high cultural distance, *foreseen*.

Within the multinational corporation, it is notoriously difficult to determine the relative degree to which crossvergence is influenced by divergent, sociocultural elements, and convergent, macro-level elements. This problem is compounded by the inherently dynamic nature of the forces in question (McGaughey and De Cieri, 1999; Ralston *et al.*, 1997). Previous studies have even provided evidence for both convergence *and* divergence acting simultaneously within the single organization (Khiliji, 2002; Rowley and Benson, 2002). However, the conceptualization of the CDC process progressed throughout this chapter provides a temporal road-map of the opposing dynamics; a guide to the aggregate relative influences of corporate culture versus societal culture upon the branch subsidiary organization at any one point. In this way, the CDC dialectic can assist parent corporations in determining the appropriate time and (should this not be possible) manner in which convergence programmes are implemented. Through this implementation, of course, they can seek to reoptimize their headquarters–subsidiary relationships. Within the Southeast Asian region, this is especially important, imbuing Western MNCs with a timely resource for managing the plethora of diverse and rapidly changing economies within its borders (Andrews and Chompusri, 2005).

Finally, it is hoped that our in-depth empirical observations might shed new light upon the ongoing debate on the 'standardization/adaptation' of international marketing strategy (for example Jain, 1989; Lazer and Shaw, 2000). We aim a light at the culturally bound perception of a corporation's international marketing values. In practical terms, they might also serve as a source of valuable practical data for international business executives seeking to negotiate the conflicting needs of integration and differentiation within the complex post-crisis Asian business environments (McGaughey and De Cieri, 1999). In this manner, it is anticipated that a reduction, and even elimination, of the year-long performance lag experienced by SAC (Thailand) Ltd in post-crisis Thailand may in the future be feasible.

NOTE

1. Corporate, individual and product brand identities are protected by the use of pseudonyms.

REFERENCES

Adler, Nancy and Mariann Jelinek (1986), 'Is "organization culture" culture bound?', *Human Resource Management*, **25**, 73–90.

Adler, Nancy J., R. Doktor and S.G. Redding (1986), 'From the Atlantic to the Pacific century: cross cultural management reviewed', *Journal of Management*, **12**(2), 295–318.

Andrews, Tim G. (2001), 'Downsizing the Thai subsidiary corporation: a case analysis', *Asia Pacific Business Review*, **8**(2), 150–70.

Andrews, Tim. G. and N. Chompusri (2001), 'Lessons in crossvergence: restructuring the Thai subsidiary corporation', *Journal of International Business Studies*, **32**(1), 77–93.

Andrews, Tim G. and N. Chompusri (2005), 'Temporal dynamics of crossvergence: institutionalizing MNC integration strategies in post-crisis ASEAN', *Asia Pacific Journal Management*, **22**(1), 5–22.

Andrews, Tim G., Nartnalin Chompusri and Bryan J. Baldwin (2003), *The Changing Face of Multinationals in Southeast Asia*, London: Routledge.

Bangkok Post (1998), *Foreign Investment: The World in Thailand*, Bangkok: Post Publications.

Bardacke, Ted (1998), 'Asia's great depression', *Financial Times*, 1 July.

Barker, Vincent L. and I.M. Duhaime (1997), 'Strategic change in the turnaround process: theory and empirical evidence', *Strategic Management Journal*, **18**, 13–38.

Benson, J.K. (1977), 'Organizations: a dialectical view', *Administrative Science Quarterly*, **22**, 1–21.

Bhopal, Mhinder and M. Hitchcock (2001), 'The culture and context of the ASEAN business crisis', *Asia Pacific Business Review*, **8**(2), 1–19.

Bibeault, D.G. (1982), *Corporate Turnaround: How Managers Turn Losers into Winners*, New York: Doubleday.

Bruton, G.D. and Y.T. Rubanik (1997), 'Turnaround of high technology firms in Russia: the case of Micron', *Academy of Management Executive*, **11**(2), 68–80.

Bruton, G.D., D. Ahlstrom and J.C.C. Wan (2001), 'Turnaround success of large and midsize Chinese owned firms: evidence from Hong Kong and Thailand', *Journal of World Business*, **36**(2), 146–65.

Burack, E. (1991), 'Changing the company culture – the role of human resource development', *Long Range Planning*, **24**(1), 88–95.

Dunphy, D. (1987), 'Convergence/divergence: a temporal review of the Japanese enterprise and its management', *Academy of Management Review*, **12**, 445–59.

Eisenhardt, K (1989), 'Building theories from case study research', *Academy of Management Review*, **14**(4), 532–50.

Entrekin, L. and Y.W. Chung (2001), 'Attitudes towards different source of executive appraisal: a comparison of Hong Kong Chinese and American managers in Hong Kong', *International Journal of Human Resource Management*, **12**(6), 965–87.

Fombrun, C.J. (1986), 'Structural dynamics within and between organizations', *Administrative Science Quarterly*, **31**, 403–31.

George, Robert L. (1992), *The East–West Pendulum*, Englewood Cliffs, NJ: Prentice-Hall.

Gersick, C. (1991), 'Revolutionary change theories: a multilevel exploration of the punctuated equilibrium paradigm', *Academy of Management Review*, **16**(1), 10–36.

Giacobbe-Miller, J.K., D.J. Miller, W. Zhang and V.I. Victorov (2003), 'Country and organizational-level adaptation to foreign workplace ideologies: a comparative study of distributive justice values in China, Russia and the United States', *Journal of International Business Studies*, **34**(4), 389–406.

Godement, François (1999), *The Downsizing of Asia*, London: Routledge.

Greenwood, R. and C.R. Hinings (1996), 'Understanding radical organizational change: bringing together the old and the new institutionalism', *Academy of Management Review*, **21**(4), 1022–54.

Gupta, A. and V. Govindarajan (2000), 'Knowledge flows within multinational corporations', *Strategic Management Journal*, **21**, 473–96.

Hambrick, D.C. and S.M. Schecter (1983), 'Turnaround strategies for mature industrial product business units', *Academy of Management Journal*, **26**(2), 231–48.

Heuer, Mark, J.L. Cummings and W. Hutabarat (1999), 'Cultural stability or change among managers in Indonesia?', *Journal of International Business Studies*, **30**(3), 599–610.

Hofer, C.W. (1980), 'Turnaround strategies', *Journal of Business Strategy*, **1**(1), 19–31.

Hoffman, R.C. (1989), 'Strategies for corporate turnarounds: what do we know about them?', *Journal of General Management*, **14**(3), 46–66.

Hofstede, G. (1980), *Culture's Consequences: International Differences in Work-Related Values*, Beverly Hills, CA: Sage.

Hofstede, G. (1991), *Cultures and Organisations: Software of the Mind*, London: McGraw-Hill.

Infothai Co. (1998), 'The Thai attitude to work', *Infothai CM*, 18 June.

Jain, S.C. (1989), 'Standardization of international marketing strategy: some research hypotheses', *Journal of Marketing*, **53**, 70–79.

Kerr, C., J.T. Dunlop, F. Harbison and C.A. Myers (1960), *Industrialism and Industrial Man*, Cambridge, MA: Harvard University Press.

Khiliji, S.E. (2002), 'Modes of convergence and divergence: an integrative view of multinational practices in Pakistan', *International Journal of Human Resource Management*, **13**(2), 232–53.

Kim, K., J.-H. Park and J.E. Prescott (2003), 'The global integration of business functions: a study of multinational businesses in integrated global industries', *Journal of International Business Studies*, **34**(4), 327–44.

Kind, S. (1997), 'Please hammer don't hurt me', *Bangkok Post*, 18 September, Post Publications, Bangkok.

Laurent, A. (1986), 'The cross-cultural puzzle of international human resource management', *HR Management*, **25**, 91–102.

Lawler, J.L. (1996), 'Diversity issues in South-East Asia: the case of Thailand', *International Journal of Manpower*, **17**, 152–68.

Lazer, W. and E. Shaw (2000), 'Global marketing management: at the dawn of the new millennium', *Journal of International Marketing*, **8**(1), 65–77.

Legewie, J. and H. Meyer-Ohle (2000), 'Economic crisis and transformation in Southeast Asia: the role of multinational companies', in Jochen Legewie and H. Meyer-Ohle (eds), *Corporate Strategies for Southeast Asia after the Crisis*, Houndmills: Palgrave, pp. 231–50.

Lim, L. (1999), 'An overview of the Asian financial crisis', *Journal of Asian Business*, **15**(1), 79–81.

McGaughey, S.L. and H. de Cieri (1999), 'Reassessment of convergence and divergence dynamics: implications for international HRM', *International Journal of Human Resource Management*, **10**(2), 235–50.

Mead, R. (2005), *International Management*, 3rd edn, Oxford: Blackwell.

Neal, M. (1998), *The Culture Factor: Cross-National Management and the Foreign Venture*, London: Macmillan.

Neghandi, Arant R. (1983), 'Cross-cultural management research: trends and future directions', *Journal of International Business Studies*, **14**(2), 17–28.

Ng, S.H. and M. Warner (2002), 'Strategic convergence or divergence: comparing structural reforms in Chinese enterprises', in Usha C.V. Haley and Frederich Jurgen Richter (eds), *Asian Post-crisis*

Management: Corporate and Governmental Strategies for Sustainable Competitive Advantage, Houndmills: Palgrave.

Nivatpumin, C. and B. Sivasompoon (1997), 'Corporate focus: making layoffs the last resort', *Bangkok Post*, 5 June, Post Publications, Bangkok.

Nohria, N. and S. Ghoshal (1994), 'Differentiated fit and shared values: managing headquarters–subsidiary relations', *Strategic Management Journal*, **15**, 491–502.

Ohmae, Keniche (1990), *The Borderless World: Power and Strategy in the Interlinked Economy*, New York: Harper Business.

Pearce, J.A. and K.D. Robbins (1993), 'Toward improved theory and research on business turnaround', *Journal of Management*, **19**(3), 613–36.

Powpaka, S. (1998), 'Factors affecting the adoption of market orientation: the case of Thailand', *Journal of International Marketing*, **6**(1), 33–55.

Ralston, D.A., Nguyen V. Thang and Nancy K. Napier (1999), 'A comparative study of the work values of North and South Vietnamese managers', *Journal of International Business Studies*, **30**(4), 655–72.

Ralston, D.A., D.J. Gustafson, F.M. Cheung and R.H. Terpstra (1993), 'Differences in managerial values: a study of US, Hong Kong and PRC managers', *Journal of International Business Studies*, **24**(2), 249–75.

Ralston, D.A., D.H. Holt, R.H. Terpstra and Y. Kai-Cheng (1997), 'The impact of national culture and economic ideology on managerial work values: a study of the United States, Russia, Japan and China', *Journal of International Business Studies*, **28**(1), 177–207.

Reade, C. (2001), 'Dual identification in multinational corporations: local managers and their psychological attachment to the subsidiary versus the global organization', *International Journal of Human Resource Management*, **12**(3), 405–24.

Ricks, David. A., Brian Toyne and Zaida Martinez (1990), 'Recent developments in international management research', *Journal of Management*, **16**(2), 219–53.

Robbins, D.K. and J.A. Pearce (1992), 'Turnaround: retrenchment and recovery', *Strategic Management Journal*, **13**, 287–309.

Robertson, C.J., M. Al-Habib, J.A. Al-Khatib and D. Lanoue (2001), 'Beliefs about work in the Middle East and the convergence versus divergence of values', *Journal of World Business*, **36**(3), 223–44.

Ronen, Simcha (1986), *Comparative and Multinational Management*, New York: Wiley.

Rowley, C. and J. Benson (2002), 'Convergence and divergence in Asian human resource management', *Californian Management Review*, **44**(2), 90–109.

Schein, E.H. (1985), *Organizational Culture and Leadership*, CA: Jossey-Bass.

Schneider, S.C. and J. Barsoux (1997), *Managing Across Cultures*, London: Prentice-Hall.

Schwartz, S.H. and W. Bilsky (1987), 'Toward a universal psychological structure of human values', *Journal of Personality and Social Psychology*, **53**(3), 550–62.

Siamwalla, A. and O. Sobchokchai (1998), 'Responding to the Thai economic crisis', Thailand Development Research Institute Conference, 22 May, UNDP, Bangkok.

Sparrow, Paul, R.S. Schuler and S.E. Jackson (1994), 'Convergence and divergence: human resource practices and policies for competitive advantage worldwide', *The International Journal of Human Resource Management*, **5**(2), 267–99.

Stiglitz, J. (1998), 'Lessons of the Asia crisis', *Financial Times*, 3 December, Pearson, London.

Theodosiou, M. and C.S. Katsikeas (2001), 'Factors influencing the degree of international pricing strategy standardization of multinational corporations', *Journal of International Marketing*, **9**(3), 1–19.

Toews, B. and R. MacGregor (1998), *Culture Shock! Succeed in Business – Thailand*, Singapore: Times Books.

Webber, Ross H. (1969), 'Convergence or divergence', *Columbia Journal of World Business*, **4**(3), 75–83.

Young, S. (2000), 'The multinational corporation: the managerial challenges of globalization and localization', in Jochen Legewie and H. Meyer-Ohle (eds), *Corporate Strategies for Southeast Asia after the Crisis*, Houndmills: Palgrave, pp. 3–24.

Yuthamanop, P. (1999), 'Client–driven strategy essential', *Bangkok Post*, 23 July, Post Publishing, Bangkok.

9. Entry and marketing strategies of FDI firms in China

Tung-lung Steven Chang

The recent influx of foreign direct investment (FDI) firms into China is a development of the growing concern of multinationals for competitiveness in the global market. Such FDI inflows have led to China's recent dramatic growth in exports. According to the UNCTAD, China received US$53.5 billion of inward FDI (that is 9.6 per cent of the world's total inward FDI and 12.4 per cent of China's gross fixed capital formation) in 2003. In the same year, with a trade surplus of US$25.53 billion, China's total foreign trade (imports/exports) reached US$851.21 billion, an increase of US$230.4 billion (or 37.1 per cent) from 2002. Its total exports reached US$438.37 billion, with an increase of 34.6 per cent from the previous year. More than two-thirds of its exports were generated by foreign-funded collective and private sectors in which foreign multinationals have participated significantly.

China provides foreign multinationals with opportunities to exploit their core competencies. As its economy continues to grow, China has become not only an offshore low-cost manufacturing site, but also a promising market for both consumer and industrial goods. Recent studies reveal that multinationals view China as a core component in their approach to globalization (BCG, 2003; BCG and KW, 2004). However, owing to its unique business and legal environment, oppressive political system and underdeveloped infrastructure, it is necessary to overcome some difficulties in order to capitalize fully on the 'China opportunity'. Among the major challenges, multinationals have found the following issues to be crucial: (1) matching entry strategies with the right business approach, (2) finding the right joint venture partners for penetrating China's market (see also Chapter 5 in this volume), and (3) implementing effective local marketing (see also Chapter 10 in this volume).

In this chapter, we first examine the differences between export-oriented and domestic-oriented FDI firms in China. The motive for a firm to enter a foreign market is either to exploit cost advantage or to develop its firm-specific advantage (Dunning, 1993; Erramilli and Rao, 1990; Madhok, 1997). First, by comparing export-oriented with domestic-oriented FDI firms, we will observe the primary business approaches such firms employ in order to match their motives for China entry. Second, we study a subset, the international joint ventures (IJVs), of such FDI firms and examine the characteristics of export-oriented and domestic-oriented IJVs. Whether or not the choice of IJVs is forced by the host government, joint venture partners have found that it is important for them, first, to match each other's needs with complementary capabilities and resources, and, second, to balance each other's powers with mutual commitment in order to succeed in foreign markets (Beamish, 1993; Chang *et al.*, 1998; Pan and Tse, 2000). We will examine the partnerships of our sample IJVs in order to understand the difference between export- and domestic-oriented

IJVs in China. Third, we focus on domestic-oriented FDI firms and further review the differences in marketing strategies adopted by such firms with different entry modes, namely wholly-owned and joint ventures. Finally, we review several Taiwanese firms in order to trace the transition of their business from export orientation to domestic orientation and to study their marketing strategies that enable their business success in China.

MARKET ENTRY CHALLENGE TO FDI FIRMS IN CHINA

As a dynamic fast-growing emerging market, China has shown major disparities in economic performance, infrastructure and standard of living. In order to make a successful entry into China, multinationals have to overcome barriers and constraints such as market diversity, local protectionism, relationship development and competitive context (Walters and Samiee, 2003). China has evolved into a nation of 'two countries' that consist of a coastal urban megalopolis of 400 million people who can afford luxuries, and a vast 'Third World' interior of 900 million people who can hardly make a living (Powell, 2002). Domestic-oriented FDI firms repeatedly discover that provincial and city authorities impose numerous protection mechanisms to support local firms in competing with their rivals based in other regions of China (see also Chapter 6 in this volume). In addition, the fragmented regional distribution network makes penetration of outside goods especially difficult, since outside firms do not have *guanxi* with local distribution players (Su and Littlefield, 2001). Furthermore, markets in China are characterized by intense competition and, more often than not, the toughest competitors are locally owned enterprises (Walters and Samiee, 2003).

Until recently, foreign firms have been restricted from using distribution services in China both for their own proprietary operations and for third parties (Jiang and Prater, 2002). As a result, supply chain-related costs can be 30 to 40 per cent of wholesale prices in China, compared with 5 to 20 per cent in the US (Tanzer, 2001). Such a problem exists not only with foreign FDI firms, but also with well-known Chinese companies. After UPS and MAERS were granted their operation licences in 2001, foreign export-oriented FDI firms could utilize more efficient distribution services in China to improve product delivery for their global customers. Domestic-oriented FDI firms, such as Coca-Cola, IKEA and McDonald's, may outsource their distribution and logistics to either foreign partners (for example EAC logistics) or local partners (for example Sinotrans). In addition, a few foreign FDI firms such as Wal-Mart and Carrefour have received permission to establish distribution networks in China to serve better their target consumers (Jiang, 2002; Jiang and Prater, 2002). Therefore, in order to succeed in China, export-oriented and domestic-oriented FDI firms should consider different models for the distribution and logistics development in the country.

MARKET ENTRY, MARKETING STRATEGY AND PARTNERSHIP

To capitalize on the China opportunity, multinationals need to develop appropriate entry and marketing strategies that can effectively serve the need of the growing middle class.

A review of the international business literature reveals that key factors in the success of foreign FDI firms in emerging markets are (1) early entry, (2) strong commitment to technology transfer, (3) adaptive product strategy, and (4) a proper distribution network. Although early movers into foreign markets tend to bear a high risk of failure, as opposed to followers that benefit from the experience of early movers (for example Shaver *et al.*, 1997; Yan, 1998), studies of entry strategies in China have shown that foreign FDI firms enjoy early mover advantages for achieving higher performance in profitability, market share and sales growth (Isobe *et al.*, 2000; Luo and Peng, 1998; Pan and Chi, 1999; Pan *et al.*, 1999). Such advantages can be attributed to less competition in the local market, strong brand loyalty among local consumers, and more support from local governments.

In order to compete in the global market, multinationals require a set of core competencies that are rooted in a firm, industry, or country (Cantwell, 1991; Porter, 1990). As firms entering foreign markets for business expansion, they are concerned with the utilization of resources and core competencies that ought to be cultivated effectively and efficiently. The inability of a firm to develop all of the needed resources and core competencies forces it to acquire them from outside (Madhok, 1997; Mutinelli and Piscitello, 1998). As resources and core competencies are spread out, multinationals have to deal with constraints that become more crucial as they enter into unfamiliar markets and areas of activity.

Previous studies suggest that a strong resource commitment to technology transfer is necessary for ensuring superior subsidiary performance in the local market (Isobe *et al.*, 2000; Mishra and Gobeli, 1998; Morck and Yeung, 1991). In order to establish a strong competitive position in foreign markets, FDI firms tend to transfer newer and more advanced technologies that are related to their core business (Kogut and Chang, 1991). However, the cost of technology transfer has never been trivial. Teece's study (1977) of 20 international technology transfer projects, for instance, shows that the average cost of such projects accounted for 19 per cent of total costs. The learning capability of FDI firms is a significant factor for such knowledge acquisition from the parent companies (Szulanski, 1996; Lyles and Salk, 1996; see also Chapter 5 in this volume). This capability is especially important for entering emerging markets like China, where technical specifications and established distribution networks rarely exist (Yan, 1998; Mitchell, 1991). The success of a firm's foreign market entry results from its capability to integrate technology into the systems of local production and commercialization (Chang, 1996). In fact, foreign FDI firms tend to employ capability building through joint ventures, and conduct capability exploitation with wholly owned entry mode in order to enhance their chance of success in China (Luo, 2002).

A firm's selection of entry modes is not based upon a gradient that reflects its international involvement, but rather upon its ability to internationalize business operations subject to host country regulations. The driving force underlying market entry strategy is an issue of the management of a firm's capabilities (Kogut and Zander, 1993). A firm's market entry strategy should, therefore, match its existing stock of resources, core competencies and motives in order to succeed in foreign markets. International business literature (for example Dunning, 1993; Erramilli and Rao, 1990) reveals that firms go international for different reasons:

1. Resource seeking: in order to compete effectively with their rivals, multinationals must learn to exploit cost advantage.

2. Oligopolistic interaction: to help maintain their competitive position in the global market, multinationals have to follow their competitors as they develop business in foreign countries.
3. Follow-the-client: by entering the same foreign country, multinationals can better serve clients who conduct substantial businesses in it.
4. Market seeking: using their ownership advantages, firms can easily expand their businesses into foreign markets.

It is imperative for multinationals to form joint ventures in emerging markets in order to tailor their products to consumer tastes, and gain national distribution networks for market access. Prahalad and Lieberthal (1998) suggest that multinationals should rethink their price/performance equation, brand management, product design, packaging, market building cost and capital efficiency to guarantee better their success in emerging markets like China. Adaptive Korean FDI firms, focusing on product improvement and differentiation, have demonstrated a strong financial performance in China (Han and Kim, 2003). However, the localization of their distribution and promotion strategies may be excessive, making it difficult for those Korean firms to achieve a differentiated advantage over local competitors, as well as Western multinationals. Previous study shows that access to distribution networks is critical for foreign FDI firms in emerging markets, and cannot be taken for granted (Prahalad and Lieberthal, 1998).

According to the resource-based theory, the firm is a collection of the productive resources and assets, built through ongoing learning processes. In a country where local business practices and social or legal systems restrict a wholly-owned entry mode, multinationals tend to use collaborative governance modes, such as joint ventures and strategic alliances, teaming up with competent local partners in order to enter the market successfully. Such partnerships serve as an important means for multinationals to acquire and cultivate necessary resources, including market knowledge and management know-how (Chang *et al.*, 1998; Hamel, 1991). In China, it is especially crucial for foreign multinationals to find savvy and trustworthy partners, according to the local and/or global markets they intend to serve (BCG, 2003).

THE SAMPLE AND DATA

This chapter uses the survey data collected by the Chung-Hua Institution for Economic Research in 1999 (Kao and Wang, 1999). The sample firms were drawn from China's National Industry Census Data of 1995 that reported 59 311 foreign firms doing business in China by means of wholly-owned subsidiaries, joint ventures and collaborations. An adequate sample size was determined by using stratified sampling in terms of the means of market entry, size of investment, industry and country of origin. Using structured questionnaires, well-trained interviewers were sent out to collect data from top managers of randomly selected foreign multinational firms in the coastal provinces of China. This survey was conducted from February to April 1999 and information was collected from 1303 responding firms. Among them there were 495 wholly-owned subsidiaries, 708 international joint ventures and 100 collaborative businesses. The profile of our sample is presented in Table 9.1.

Table 9.1   Profile of the sample FDI firms

Country of origin	Wholly-owned	Joint venture	Collaboration
Hong Kong	110	262	47
Taiwan	252	195	38
Japan	33	78	3
Rest of Asia	16	24	0
Europe and N. America	22	71	7
Others	62	78	5
Total	495	708	100

As shown in Table 9.1, significantly fewer FDI firms from Europe and North America were included in our sample. US direct investment in China has been very small as a result of American multinationals' preference for direct market access and China's export-promotion FDI regime (Zhang, 2000). Another reason may be the elusive cost advantage many Western companies have found in China. As of July 2003, the direct sourcing of industrial goods from China accounted for only 3 per cent of the US market (see also Chapter 11 in this volume). According to a BCG study (Hout and Hemerling, 2003), most of the US industrial goods (about 70 per cent) came primarily from domestic production, while imports from Japan and Western Europe accounted for another 20 per cent. Among the 10 per cent that came from low-wage economies, China contributed less than one-third, shipping fewer goods than Mexico. Therefore our sample is an accurate represent-ation of reality.

The variables used in this chapter are the following:

1. Motive: '1' (resource seeking); '2' (operational incentives); '3' (follow-the-client); '4' (market seeking).
2. Export experience: '1' ($\geq$ 20 yrs); '2' (16–20 yrs); '3' (11–15 yrs); '4' (6–10 yrs); '5' (1–5 yrs); '6' (0 yr).
3. Export orientation: export-oriented if (exports/total sales) $>$ 50%; Domestic-ori-ented if (exports/total sales) $<$ 50%.
4. Supervisory authority: '1' if foreign parent; '0' otherwise.
5. Business approach: '1' if OEM/ODM; '0' if OBM.
6. Partnership: '1' (SOE), '2' (COE), '3' (TVE), '4' (PE).[1]
7. Chairmanship: '1' if foreign Chairman; '0' otherwise.
8. Business risk: coefficient of variances of annual sales by industry.
9. Psychic distance: '1' (Hong Kong), '2' (Taiwan), '3' (Asia), '4' (others).
10. Channel control: '1' (high), '2' (medium), '3' (low), '4' (no channel).
11. Upgrade or new product launch: '1' (none), '2' (once a year), '3' (2 or 3 times a year), '4' ($\geq$3 times a year).
12. Technology change: '1' if there has been a big change; '0' otherwise.
13. R&D expenditures: 5 point scale, from '1' (very low) to '5' (very high).
14. Corporate/brand image: 5 point scale, from '1' (very low) to '5' (very high).

EXPORT VERSUS DOMESTIC ORIENTED FDI FIRMS IN CHINA

In this chapter, we applied logit regression analysis to examine the differences between export-oriented and domestic-oriented FDI firms in China. The logit regression equation is as follows:

$$Y = \exp(-BX)/[1 + \exp(-BX)],$$

where $Y = 1$ if the FDI firm is export-oriented, and $-BX = B_0 + B_i X_i$; B_i ($i = 0, 1, 2, \ldots, n$) are regression coefficients. X_i ($i = 0, 1, 2, \ldots, n$) represent five independent variables. The results are shown in Tables 9.2 and 9.3.

As shown in Table 9.2, the chi-square statistic of the likelihood ratio for this model is 474.82 (with a p-value < 0.001), indicating that the logit regression model can satisfactorily predict the kinds of FDI firms that tend to be export-oriented or domestic-oriented. Our findings indicate that export-oriented FDI firms are those that seek low-cost resources from the local market, prefer to do business with OEM or ODM, accept management and marketing advice from foreign parent companies, and have many years of export experience. Their counterparts, domestic-oriented FDI firms, are those who seek demand in local markets, prefer to develop their own brands (OBM), utilize the market knowledge of Chinese partners and usually have little export experience.

Table 9.2   Logit regression on export orientation of all FDI firms

Variables	Coefficient	Chi-square
Intercept	1.637	
OEM/ODM business	0.845	7.472**
Supervisory authority	0.887	8.262**
Export experience	−0.532	18.862***
Resource vs market-seeking motive	−0.378	21.486***
−2 Log (L)		474.82***

Notes: **: $p < 0.01$; ***: $p < 0.001$.

Table 9.3   Logit regression on export orientation of IJV firms

Variables	Coefficient	Chi-square
Intercept	−1.049	−2.39*
Chairman of the board	0.370	2.38*
Partnership	0.419	4.87***
Business risk	0.258	2.87**
Psychic distance	−0.456	−4.37**
Resource vs market-seeking motive	−0.468	−4.48***
−2 Log (L)		187.69***

Notes: *: $p < 0.0$; **: $p < 0.01$; ***: $p < 0.001$.

Among the sample FDI firms, it is noted that the number of IJVs is greater than that of wholly-owned firms. The major reasons for forming joint ventures in China are (1) government requirement or pressure as a condition of market entry, (2) a need for the other partner's skills, such as technological, managerial or the knowledge to work with the local market, and (3) a need for either the other partner's key assets, like capital, patents and raw material sources, or its attributes, such as the use or manufacturing of certain products or services (Beamish, 1993).

Since joint venture partners always strive to match each other's objectives and resources in order to succeed, foreign partners of IJVs tend to seek access to the Chinese market and labour, while Chinese partners seek access to foreign technology, management know-how and capital (Pan, 1996).

There has been a tendency for foreign firms to team up with a Chinese partner owned by a central or provincial government since the mid-1990s (Pan, 1997). Under China's unique political economy, the level of government is closely related to the level of control over resources (see also Chapter 6 in this volume). Thus state-owned enterprises (SOEs) tend to enjoy better access to resources than private or township/village enterprises (P/TVEs). With the ability to access more local resources, SOEs are in a better position than P/TVEs to establish large-scale IJVs with foreign firms that possess the appropriate technology and management know-how.

In our sample, export-oriented IJV firms tend to team up with P/TVEs, while domestic-oriented firms tend to team up with SOEs. A review of the influence of foreign partners in the business operations of our sample IJV firms suggests that the P/TVE partners have a tendency to adjust themselves towards Western practices of property rights and agent control systems. If the desired technology and management know-how are acquired, IJVs that partner with P/TVEs will eventually perform better than those partnered with SOEs. We expect that foreign multinationals with a focus on global demand will prefer to team up with P/TVEs in order to respond to the dynamic changes in the global market.

Previous studies suggest that the equity distribution among joint venture partners has strategic implications (Contractor, 1990; Pan, 1996). Given China's political economy, a variety of government regulations, protection mechanisms, Chinese business practices and local networking could create substantial market barriers to foreign firms. Local partners with an understanding of native cultural and consumption behaviours will help foreign firms penetrate their markets easily (Beamish and Banks, 1987; Hennart, 1991). However, conflicts of interest and management styles could occur between foreign and local partners that might hinder the success of such joint ventures (Vanhonacker and Pan, 1997). In order to increase the financial performance of IJVs in the host country, foreign firms tend to increase management control by adopting a majority share (Woodcock *et al.*, 1994). In general, the partner who is the majority shareholder will have a greater control over and influence upon the IJVs, in keeping with its responsibility as the majority shareholder (Harrigan, 1985). In addition, previous studies indicate that foreign partners of IJVs in China tend to possess better corporate governance systems and ownership advantages, such as technology and capital resources. Thus those foreign partners who are the majority shareholders of IJVs have clearer goals and the ability to ensure superior profitability.

In order to understand the differences between export-oriented and domestic-oriented IJVs, this chapter examines the motives, partnerships and nationalities of foreign parent firms (that is psychic distance) of our sample IJVs in China's dynamic market environment. As shown in Table 9.3, the results of logistic regression indicate that export-oriented IJVs tend to be foreign resource-seeking firms from Hong Kong and Taiwan not headed by local Chinese chairmen, and partner with Chinese collective firms and private enterprises in dynamic and challenging industries. In general, domestic-oriented IJVs are formed by American and European market-seeking multinationals headed by Chinese chairmen, and partner with Chinese state-owned enterprises in less risky industries.

FACTORS INFLUENCING THE EXPORT INTENSITY OF FDI FIRMS

In this chapter, we are also interested in knowing the determinants of export intensity of such FDI firms. As shown in Table 9.4, export intensity labour intensity and capital intensity are used as independent variables. In the following analyses, export intensity is calculated by the ratio of export sales to total sales, labour intensity by the ratio of number of workers to total number of employees, and capital intensity by the ratio of actual investment amount to total number of employers. We conduct the OLS multiple regression analysis in order to examine how the export intensity of our sample firms is influenced by the variables considered in this research. The OLS multiple regression analysis is explained by the following equation:

$$Y_{(n\times1)} = X_{(n\times q)} \, b_{(q\times1)} + e_{(n\times1)},$$

$$q = k + 1,$$

where n represents the number of observations, k represents the number of predictors, and e is an error term. Y is the export intensity and export performance score of the sample firm. X is an ($N \times q$) matrix that specifies the sample firms' scores for all of the study variables representing governance structure, motive, business approach, supervisory authority, export experience, labour intensity and capital intensity; b is a ($q \times 1$) column vector that represents an intercept plus all of the regression coefficients. The results are shown in Table 9.4.

As shown in Table 9.4, six variables studied in the OLS regression model very well explain (about 21 per cent of adjusted R^2) the export intensity of FDI firms in China. All of the six variables contribute significantly to the export intensity of our sample FDI firms. According to the beta coefficients, OEM and ODM business approach (0.309) is the most important factor in boosting export sales of our sample FDI firms. Although capital and labour are usually considered important factors in a firm's business expansion, it is interesting to see that the more labour-intensive and the less capital-intensive those FDI firms are, the more export sales they generate. Supervisory advice from foreign parent companies is important for the FDI firms in China to generate more exports. With international marketing skills and experience of international business operations, foreign parent companies can help FDI firms in China to bring their products to the global market. By utilizing low-cost resources in China, as those FDI firms accumulate more experience of exporting business, their chance of enhancing export intensity will be higher.

Table 9.4   OLS multiple regression on export intensity of FDI firms

Variables	Beta	B	(t-value)
Intercept		99.81	(10.80)***
Capital intensity	−0.052	−0.11	(−2.12) ***
OEM/ODM business	0.309	33.28	(12.41) ***
Labour intensity	0.056	2.65	(2.28) ***
Supervisory authority	0.185	19.20	(7.39) ***
Export experience	−0.149	−9.76	(−6.03) ***
Resource vs market-seeking motive	−0.157	−8.78	(−6.38) ***
$R = 0.4639$; Adjusted $R^2 = 0.2116$; $F (6,1296) = 59.226$, $p < 0.0000$			

Note: ***: $p < 0.001$.

CHINA ENTRY AND LOCAL MARKETING STRATEGIES OF TAIWANESE MULTINATIONALS

China continues to represent an enormous market for both consumer and industrial products. It has become the largest market for washing machines, the second largest for beer, and the third largest for carbonated soft drinks. By volume as of June 2003, China accounted for about 31 per cent of the world consumption of televisions, 24 per cent washing machines, 16 per cent steel and 14 per cent synthetic rubber (BCG, 2003). In the auto industry, global automakers have pursued successful joint venture strategies by investing heavily in assembly plants operated by Chinese partners. Only 15 years after Volkswagen entered the market, more than half (53.4 per cent) of the passenger cars sold in China rolled out of VW's Chang-chun and Shanghai joint ventures in 2000, while other foreign joint ventures accounted for nearly all the rest – a further 43 per cent (Gao, 2002). In 2003, GM enjoyed a pre-tax profit of US$2300 per car, with a market share of about 5 per cent in China (Farrell *et al.*, 2004).

Multinationals have tried to penetrate the mass market by using various marketing strategies over the last few years. The challenge lies, however, in China's unique market conditions and underdeveloped marketing infrastructure. When companies expand into new locations and product categories, they typically run into the following problems: (1) fragmented markets and channels, (2) low prices in non-urban areas, (3) many competitors in different regions with diverse approaches, (4) immature distribution infrastructures and intermediaries, and (5) extraordinary strains on marketing and organizational capabilities. As a result, foreign multinationals entering China often find themselves caught in the value trap: the more they invest, the more they seem to lose as shareholder value drains away. The multinationals that accelerate quickly out of such traps pay close attention to scale, costs/prices and marketing insights in order to deploy resources effectively (Hsu and Hemerling, 2003).

To understand the marketing strategies employed by our sample domestic-oriented FDI firms in China, we conducted a logistic regression to examine the differences of marketing practices between domestic-oriented, wholly-owned and IJV firms. The advantages of wholly-owned FDI are full control over such business ventures, timely responses to

Table 9.5   Logit regression on wholly-owned, domestic-oriented FDI firms

Variables	Coefficient	Chi-square
Intercept	0.662	
Channel control	−0.317	5.41*
Upgrade or new product launch	0.540	9.88**
Technology change	−0.758	11.22***
R&D expenditures	0.178	4.74*
Corporate/brand image	−0.279	5.79**
−2 Log (L)		513.1***

Notes: *: $p < 0.0$; **: $p < 0.01$; ***: $p < 0.001$.

market changes and quick decision-making processes for strategic actions. As shown in Table 9.5, compared to IJVs, wholly-owned FDI firms in China tend to utilize a tighter control over their distribution channels, upgrade or launch new products more often, use more mature and stable technology and spend more on R&D, but pay less attention to building corporate/brand image. It has been noted that there is extreme localism in marketing in China, due to the many markets on provincial and subprovincial levels that are often closed to foreign firms (BCG and KW, 2004). Because of this localism, local brands in various markets may have a better effect upon their target consumers. Consequently, there are a limited variety of national brands. Such a phenomenon may explain why wholly-owned, domestic-oriented FDI firms pay less attention to image building. However, brands that are globally known will be recognized at the local markets in China.

As shown in Table 9.5, such wholly-owned firms tend to adopt effective channel control for launching upgraded or new products to their target markets in China. By using a vertical marketing system with its own sales and distribution network, Tingyi, a Taiwanese multinational, has captured the market for packaged noodles in the premium segment (Hsu and Hemerling, 2003). Leveraging its scale, it has established its own sales and distribution network that includes more than 300 sales offices across China and serves nearly 34 000 retailers directly. In addition, Tingyi services the remaining retail outlets through distributors that provide logistics, and wholesalers that sell to remote locations. Such a tight control over its distribution channels has allowed Tingyi to build strong relationships with its retailers and, as a result, dominate as much as half of the total shelf space allocated to the category. In order to attract value-conscious consumers, Tingyi often upgrades and embarks upon new product launches through value improvement (larger package sizes), product extensions (an economy-priced noodle brand) and category expansions (beverages and snacks ready for consumption).

China Entry of Taiwanese FDI Firms

In this chapter, we examine four Taiwanese FDI firms in order to review their competitive advantage and marketing practices in China. The analysis of these four firms is based on secondary data including corporate annual reports, corporate websites, public information websites, books and newspaper/magazine reports. The first three from our sample

Table 9.6   Profiles of Taiwanese firms' entry into China

Company / Category	Pou Chen Corporation	Cheng Shin Rubber Ind., Co., Ltd.	Giant Manufacturing Co., Ltd.	Johnson Health Tech. Co., Ltd.
Year of China entry	1988	1991	1992	2000
Initial investments (1998)	492 383	3 576 824	1 039 459	2 632[a]
Total investments (2004)	3 180 055	8 946 766	2 387 095	620 418
No. of subsidiaries in China	26	8	5	2
Global sales (2004)	125 460 658	31 609 621	21 781 520	6 701 138
Advertising expenditures	4 413 443 (4%)	2 775 077 (8%)	1 517 054 (7%)	1 708 766 (25.5%)
R&D expenditures	4 057 595 (3.2%)	570 075 (1.8%)	174 364 (0.8%)	193 760 (2.9%)
Vertical integration	Back/Forward	Back/Forward	Back/Forward	Forward
Entry mode	WO & JV	WO & JV	WO & JV	WO
JV partner	China	Japan, China	China (SOE)	n/a
Business approach	OEM/ODM	OEM/ODM; OBM[e]	OEM/ODM (35%); OBM (65%)	OEM/ODM (10%); OBM (90%)
Customer focus	Industry & consumer	Industry & consumer	Industry & consumer	Industry & consumer
Market focus	Domestic/Export	Domestic/Export	Domestic/Export	Export
Sales percentage by region 2004 (1998)[b,c]	America 2.52 (10.81)%	America 34.77 (56.60)%	America 47.62 (43.23)%	America 65.81 (57.23)%
	Europe 1.12 (4.39)%	Europe 28.56% (18.82)	Europe 28.24 (28.35)%	Europe 17.75 (17.04)%
	Asia 95.52 (82.94)%	Asia 36.67[d] (24.58)	Asia 16.69 (13.06)%	Asia 10.50 (24.23)%
	Others 0.84 (1.86)%		Others 7.45 (5.34)%	Others 5.93 (1.5)%
Sales % of China market	n/a	n/a	8.52%	2.01%

Notes:
(1) Sales are in NT$1000.
(2) (a) investments of year 2000; (b) year 2000 data for Cheng Shin Rubber Ind., Co., Ltd; (c) year 1999 data for Johnson Health Tech Co., Ltd; (d) other than America and Europe; (e) ratios for Cheng Shin are not available.

Source: Taiwan Economic Journal data bank and various corporate annual reports.

entered China around 1990. The fourth is a more recent FDI firm that entered China in 2000. The profile of these FDI firms is shown in Table 9.6. In terms of entry modes, the first three firms used IJV to enter China at the beginning. As China adjusted its policy to allow foreign multinationals to enter the market with full control over their direct investments, they then established wholly owned subsidiaries. The global sales of these firms range from NT$6701 to NT$125 461 million, with 2004's cumulative direct investments in China ranging from NT$620 to NT$8947 million. All firms substantially increased their direct investments in China from 1998 to 2004. As of December 2004, the first three firms had gradually changed their focus from export-oriented to domestic-oriented, and adopted an integrated Chinese strategy by viewing China as both a market and a sourcing location. Johnson Health Technology still exports substantially from China by using a comprehensive sourcing strategy.

Three out of the four companies employ both OEM/ODM and OBM in China. Johnson Health Technology relies most heavily upon OBM (90 per cent). Giant Manufacturing is second (65 per cent), while Pou Chen always employs OEM/ODM for its shoe business. This phenomenon is reflected in the company advertising expenditures, with Johnson spending NT$1709 million, or 25.5 per cent of its global sales, while Pou Chen spends the least, only 4 per cent. As shown in the American sales percentage by region (see Table 9.6), those employing more OBM (Giant and Johnson) enjoyed an increase in sales from 1998 to 2004, in comparison to Pou Chen and Cheng Shin, whose sales decreased during that period. This increase is due to Johnson and Giant's concentration on OBM to gain brand recognition. However, Johnson, an export-oriented FDI firm in China, did not give such focus to the Asian market, as its Asian sales percentage fell by nearly 14 per cent from 1998 to 2004. In contrast, Pou Chen, Cheng Shin and Giant increased Asian sales. As a proxy, this trend indicates the previously noted shift in their focus from export-oriented to domestic-oriented in the three companies.

Prior to 2003, the majority of Pou Chen's income came from the shoe business. In 2003, 88.1 per cent (NT$9.48 billion) of its total annual revenue (NT$10.76 billion) came from selling shoes to a large account, Nike, revealing its primary business approach as OEM/ODM. In 1999, Pou Chen diversified its business into computer electronics and telecommunications, but it was not until 2004 that the business for consumer electronics rolled in and shoe sales dropped to 54.7 per cent (NT$9.38 billion) of the total annual revenue (NT$17.14 billion). Through drastic diversifications, Pou Chen has established 26 subsidiaries in China, whereas Giant Manufacturing and Cheng Shin have fewer subsidiaries because of the continuing of their original core businesses.

The first three companies have already had both backward and forward vertical integrations, in contrast with Johnson Health Technology, a manufacturer of cardiovascular equipment and treadmills, which has employed only forward vertical integration. Via backward vertical integration, these companies have obtained benefits such as improved supply chain coordination, differentiation by means of increased control over inputs, and increased entry barriers to potential competitors. Through forward vertical integration, they have also obtained otherwise inaccessible downstream distribution channels. Such integrations, visible in all four firms, will strengthen their competitive positions and ability to capture upstream/downstream profit margins.

By comparing their R&D expenditures, it becomes apparent that these companies also spend a substantial amount to ensure product quality and consumer satisfaction. If the products integrate more technology, the R&D expenditure is far higher: Pou Chen and Johnson spend the highest percentage of their sales in R&D (3.2 per cent and 2.9 per cent, respectively). Such practices reflect the fact that China offers a vast and inexpensive talent pool that compels foreign multinationals to establish research and development centres or subsidiaries in the country.

Case Studies of Competitive Advantage and Local Marketing in China

Pou Chen Corporation

Founded in 1969, Pou Chen became an OEM vendor for Adidas in 1980, and upgraded its design and manufacturing capabilities to be an OEM/ODM supplier for name-brand shoemakers in 1983. The competitive advantage of Pou Chen lies in its technological capability, with which the company efficiently conducts R&D, product design and commercialization. In general, Pou Chen has been able to complete a process and launch a new product within three to six months. In 2004, Pou Chen obtained 22 patents in its shoe business, including those for improved sole structure, leather processing methods and digitally designed shoe moulds. Furthermore, by using CPC, an e-commerce system, Pou Chen can easily share details concerning materials, design, product development, delivery and marketing information with its strategic partners, and stabilize the seasonal fluctuations in its production process to reduce costs and improve product quality. By using the OEM/ODM business approach, Pou Chen has developed lock-in relationships with name brands such as Nike, Adidas, Timberland and Rockport. In 2005, the European Union removed all quota limitations on its shoe imports from China. Via Pou Chen's unrestricted connections under this new policy, name-brand shoe manufacturers in its lock-in relationships will be able to further expand their businesses into the European market.

As of 2004, Pou Chen had established 170 assembly lines in China and over 130 others throughout Southeast Asia. By 2005, the company planned to expand this number to 329 lines in total, an estimated production capacity of 200 million pairs of shoes per year. Having concentrated on China's market, Pou Chen has received exclusive rights to sell athletic products by Converse, Hush Puppies, Wolverine and Asics in China. Its retail stores, totalling 350 in 2004, rose to 600 in 2005, and are projected to reach 1000 by 2008. It has also entered the niche of women's shoes, having acquired 50 per cent of the former leading company, B.V.I., by 2003. Through utilization of B.V.I.'s competitive advantage in women's shoe design and manufacturing, Pou Chen expects to become the world's largest supplier in the business.

Cheng Shin Rubber

Founded in 1967, Cheng Shin produced tyres for various vehicles through OEM. Thanks to technology improvements, Cheng Shin began to shift to an ODM approach by using product differentiation strategies to launch new high-quality products in the 1980s. In 1982, through international collaborations with Toyo (Japan), it built a plant to produce radial tyres in Taiwan. Seven years later, in 1989, Cheng Shin targeted the American market by creating its own brand, Maxxis. By 1991, it had set up a wholly owned subsidiary in Xiamen, China, for the manufacture and export of bicycle and motorcycle tyres. In 1995, it established a joint venture company with Toyo in Kunshan and later developed two more subsidiaries: Tian-jin and Hai-yen. In 2004, Cheng Shin exported 30 per cent of Xiamen's output, 45 per cent from Kunshan, but almost nothing from the Tian-jin and Hai-yen factories. Its total sales in China that year reached NT$18.5 billion, with NT$11.5 billion (62 per cent) for domestic consumption.

As the earliest Taiwanese tyre company to enter China, Cheng Shin enjoyed a first-mover advantage. Its subsidiaries are dispersed along the coastline, with at least one in each region of China (North, Central and South). This locational pattern gives the company an extra location advantage, first to export its products, and later to sell domestically. Currently, Cheng Shin is the largest tyre manufacturer in both Taiwan and China. It has become a key supplier of General Motors in North America and the main supplier of Shanghai General Motor, as well as Ford, Toyota, Nissan and Fiat in China. In addition to its building partnerships with major car companies, Cheng Shin has also formed strategic alliances to expand further its business in China. It has formed a joint venture of $150 million with China's Hai-Yen Industrial Co., a state-owned enterprise, and Toyo of Japan to produce steel radial tyres for cars and trucks.

As an early entrant, Cheng Shin has cultivated its marketing strengths with effective distribution channels in China. Over the years, Cheng Shin has developed a vertical marketing system that consists of 138 distributors, ten warehousing centres and 1500 retailers across coastal provinces and major cities in China. Beginning by selling tyres to local bicycle and motorcycle companies in the mid-1980s, Cheng Shin's business has grown with the pace of China's economic development for the past two decades. As the demand for passenger cars and trucks emerges, Cheng Shin gradually shifts its market focus to capitalize on such opportunities. It has created multiple brands with a large variety of products to address various market segments. Maxxis and Cheng-Shin brands are for the high-end and middle segments using skimming pricing, while Ying-Hua and Performance brands are for the low-end segment using the penetration pricing strategy. Cheng Shin has spent a substantial amount to promote its high-end brands, especially Maxxis, through event marketing campaigns and sponsoring individuals and teams, such as the Houston Rockets and the Los Angeles Lakers of the NBA. In 2004, it spent NT$2.78 billion on advertising that accounted for 8 per cent of its annual global sales.

Giant Manufacturing Co.

Giant started its bicycle business as an OEM vendor in 1972 and then developed its own brand in 1981. Over the years, Giant has expanded its product lines for a variety of target segments, including leisure, mountain, racing, ladies', children's, and electric bikes. Through its global configuration, Giant has developed a value chain that performs R&D, manufacturing and marketing activities in various countries in order to conduct ODM and OBM businesses. Currently, it has manufacturing centres stationed in Taiwan, Canada, Australia and China, with 48 agents and more than 10 000 retailing outlets selling its products in the global market. In order to lead fashion, Giant has formed an 'A-Team' with 20 upstream and downstream strategic partners in Taiwan's bicycle industry. Such collaborations in research and product development have enabled Giant to launch high value-added new products for its global target consumers. With its fluid-form and press-form technology, Giant has developed various new products, such as TCR Advanced and TCR Time Trial racing bikes, the XtC mountain bike, Trance/Reign/Faith series, Suede, Revive and Bella/Areva/Vida/Gloss fashion bikes.

Giant entered China in 1992, as a result of a global reconfiguration, in order to reduce costs, improve price competitiveness, capitalize on local demand, and respond quickly to the dynamic changes in China's market. Giant has established two manufacturing centres in China: a wholly owned subsidiary, Giant (Kunshan), which produces high-end and average products, and a joint venture, Giant-Phoenix (Shanghai), which manufactures average and low-end products.

Giant has effectively implemented local market campaigns in China, based on its global experience in market segmentation, product positioning and marketing strategy formulation. By 2003, Giant had developed an efficient vertical marketing system to penetrate the China market that consisted of 18 direct factory outlets, 20 dealers, 370 specialty stores, and 1458 retailing stores throughout the country. By using skimming pricing, Giant has successfully differentiated its products from local competitors and become the number one brand. Like Cheng Shin, Giant has also spent a substantial amount of money to sponsor sports and conduct event-marketing campaigns. As shown in Table 9.6, Giant spent NT$1.52 billion in 2004, or 7 per cent of its global sales, on global marketing, as well as local promotions in China. Consequently, Giant sold 130 million bicycles in China, thus accounting for about 36 per cent of the total shipments of its two local manufacturing centres in 2004. In 2004, the third manufacturing centre was completed in Chengdu, focusing on the production of electric bikes.

Johnson Health Technology

Johnson Health Technology was founded in 1975 as a manufacturer of exercise machines. By using OEM, Johnson provided products for Universal, Tunturi, Schwinn, Omron and Mizuno, and had become the world's major supplier in about ten years. By the late 1980s, Johnson had upgraded its R&D capability and became an ODM vendor for the name-brand companies. It then acquired Epix in 1996, an American marketing firm, created its own brands, Vision, Matrix and Horizon, and began to design its own cardiovascular machines. Through its global configuration, Johnson established a Taiwan-based R&D centre, manufacturing facilities of key components in Shanghai, and marketing subsidiaries in target country markets, such as the US, Germany, the UK, France, Spain and so on. This arrangement has helped the company to launch new products much faster than its competitors, and has thus strengthened Johnson's competitive edge in the global market. Johnson employs effective product positioning through four different brands: Matrix that targets a commercial market and premium country clubs, such as Hyatt with a price up to US$10 000; Johnson that targets commercial high-end markets with a price up to US$6000; Vision that targets specialty stores and is priced at US$3500 to US$5000; and Horizon that is supplied to large chain stores, such as Sports Authority and Dick's Sporting Goods, at a selling price of US$599–US$1500.

In 2000, Johnson established a wholly-owned subsidiary in China to improve its price competitiveness through low-cost sourcing and to manufacture key components for high-end products, as well as low-end machines. Its key suppliers also entered China. Together, they developed an effective supply chain to support Johnson's production. By the first season of 2005, Johnson imported 74 per cent of its parts from its subsidiary in Shanghai that improved its price competitiveness by about 20 per cent. In addition, because the market for exercise equipment in China had been steadily increasing, Johnson established a second subsidiary to handle the marketing and sales of its four brands in China. In 2003,

Johnson sold about 50 of its Vision and Horizon products through dealers and its 32 direct retail outlets. Matrix products were sold directly to local clubs in China. Among its four brands, Matrix enjoyed the highest profit margins, Vision generated the most profits, and Horizon produced the highest sales volume for Johnson in China. However, the sales in China accounted for only 2 per cent of its global sales.

In summary, these four firms benefit from an early-mover advantage. Pou Chen, Cheng Shin and Giant entered with international joint ventures before China reinstated its open-door policy in 1992, and abandoned its planned economy in favour of a market economy in 1993. Such an early entry gave these firms a great advantage over their later arriving rivals, by allowing them to enjoy low cost production and to develop a strong value delivery system. This system is part of a competitive vertical marketing system, comprising key suppliers and competent intermediaries, as well as themselves in their distribution channels. Although Johnson entered China with a wholly-owned subsidiary in 2000, it is considered an early entry of its own field.

In addition, these four Taiwanese FDI firms have successfully incorporated China as an important strategic location in their global configuration and have adapted their business strategies to the market demand in China. As customers in China gradually increase their demand for their products, these firms have changed their marketing focus from a predominantly export orientation to a more domestic orientation. The evolution of such strategies can be seen from their respective marketing approaches that have been shifting from OEM/ODM toward OBM. With relevant business strategies, as illustrated previously, their successes in China can be attributed to their competitive advantage in technology, marketing, and lock-in relationships.

CONCLUSION

As a dynamic, fast-growing, emerging market, China has become not only an offshore low-cost manufacturing site, but also a promising market for both consumer and industrial goods. Multinationals around the world have viewed China as a core component in their approach to globalization. In order to make a successful entry into China, however, foreign multinationals must overcome barriers and constraints such as competitive context, relationship development and local protectionism. We have found that markets in China are characterized by intense competition. Frequently, the toughest competitors are locally owned enterprises. The fragmented regional distribution network makes penetration of outside goods especially difficult, since outside firms do not have connections with local distribution players. In addition, provincial and city authorities impose numerous protection mechanisms to support local firms in their competition with rivals based in other regions of China.

Analysing the survey data collected by the Chung-Hua Institution for Economic Research in 1999, this chapter examines (1) the characteristics of export-oriented and domestic-oriented FDI firms in China, in terms of their motives, business approaches, export experience and supervisory authority; (2) the choice of partnership of the export-oriented and domestic-oriented IJVs; and (3) the marketing practices adopted by wholly owned and joint-venture FDI firms. Our findings indicate that export-oriented FDI firms are those that seek low-cost resources in China, prefer to do business with OEM or

ODM, rely on management and marketing support from foreign parent companies and have more experience in exporting business. Their counterparts, domestic-oriented FDI firms, are those that seek demand in China, prefer to develop their own brands (OBM), and utilize the market knowledge of Chinese partners who usually have little export experience.

In our analysis, export-oriented IJV firms tend to team up with P/TVEs, while domestic-oriented firms tend to team up with SOEs. A review of the influence of foreign partners in the business operations of our sample IJV firms suggests that the P/TVE partners have a tendency to adjust themselves towards Western practices of property rights and agent control systems. If the desired technology and management know-how are acquired, IJVs that partner with P/TVEs will eventually perform better than those partnered with SOEs. The results of logistic regression indicate that export-oriented IJVs tend to be foreign resource-seeking firms from Hong Kong and Taiwan not headed by local Chinese chairmen. Such IJVs are usually partnered with Chinese collective firms or private enterprises in dynamic and challenging industries. However, in general, domestic-oriented IJVs are formed by American and European market-seeking multinationals headed by Chinese chairmen. Such IJVs tend to partner with Chinese state-owned enterprises in less risky industries.

By comparing IJVs and wholly-owned FDI firms in our sample, we find that wholly owned FDI firms, as opposed to IJVs, are able to exercise a tighter control over their distribution channels, upgrade or launch new products more often, use more mature and stable technology and spend more on R&D, but pay less attention to building corporate/brand image. Although brands that are globally known will be recognized at the local markets in China, it has been noted that there is extreme localism in marketing in China, at provincial and sub-provincial levels. Many markets are often closed to foreign firms. Because of this localism, local brands in various markets may have a better effect upon their target consumers. This explains why wholly owned, domestic-oriented FDI firms care less about building a national brand.

Multinationals can now source almost anything from China (see also Chapter 11 in this volume). The nation has long been the world's leading manufacturer of products such as air conditioners, motorcycles and televisions. Wal-Mart, for instance, has established a sourcing division in Shenzhen to buy directly from Chinese factories. But, in recent years, the opportunity to source in China has expanded to include extremely high-tech products, as well as components that are part of a more complex logistics pattern, like automobile parts. Further evidence is readily seen in the huge new industrial parks outside Shanghai and Beijing. There Intel is making semiconductors, General Electric is producing sophisticated medical equipment and Nokia is building next-generation mobile phones. Taiwanese information and communications manufacturers have already capitalized on the 'China Opportunity' through FDI over the years. Experts estimate that such Taiwanese FDI firms contribute 40 per cent to 80 per cent of China's exports in information and communications hardware (Einhorn *et al.*, 2005).

Hemerling and his colleagues suggest that multinationals adopt various distinctive sourcing strategies for their China entry (Hemerling *et al.*, 2003). Our study confirms that it is crucial for multinationals to develop a comprehensive sourcing, by building strong relationships with key Chinese suppliers and by attracting talented R&D engineers/staff to lock in a competitive advantage. Such a strategy significantly reduces not only costs, but also time for product development. Consequently, this makes it difficult for competitors to keep up. Our case study reveals that the four Taiwanese FDI firms have gradually employed an integrated China strategy that views China both as a principal supply base and as an important market. With a high commitment to the local market, foreign multinationals design their businesses to outsource components for products to be sold abroad and to produce others to be sold in China. Economies of scale will be reached if products are configured to meet both local and global requirements. For further growth, foreign multinationals will need to capture global advantage by integrating low-cost sourcing into a business model that can be managed across many country markets. With this strategy, the economics of globalization will be unstoppable through the development of a real global business that leverages both scale and lock-in relationships.

ACKNOWLEDGMENT

The author acknowledges the kind assistance of Dr Wen-Thuen Wang, Research Fellow of Chung-Hua Institution for Economic Research, and her permission to use her IJV survey data for this research.

NOTE

1. Foreign multinationals can form international joint ventures with various local partners in China, including state-owned enterprises (SOEs), collective enterprises (COEs), township and village enterprises (TVEs) and private enterprises (PEs).

REFERENCES

Beamish, P.W. (1993), 'The characteristics of joint ventures in the People's Republic of China', *Journal of International Marketing*, **1**(2), 29–48.
Beamish, P.W. and J.C. Banks (1987), 'Equity joint ventures and the theory of the multinational enterprise', *Journal of International Business Studies*, **18**, Summer, 1–16.
The Boston Consulting Group (BCG) (2003), *China: The Pursuit of Competitive Advantage and Profitable Growth*, Shanghai: The Boston Consulting Group.
The Boston Consulting Group (BCG) and Knowledge Wharton (KW) (2004), *China and the New Rules for Global Business*, Shanghai: The Boston Consulting Group.
Cantwell, J.A. (1991), 'The theory of technological competence and its application to international production', in D. McFetridge (ed.), *Foreign Investment, Technology and Economic Growth*, Calgary: University of Calgary Press.
Chang, T. (1996), 'Cultivating global experience curve advantage on technology and marketing capabilities', *International Marketing Review*, **13**(6), 22–42.
Chang, T., C. Chuang and W. Jan (1998), 'International collaboration of law firms: modes, motives and advantages', *Journal of World Business*, **33**(3), 241–62.
Contractor, F.J. (1990), 'Ownership patterns for U.S. joint ventures abroad and the liberalization of foreign government regulations in the 1980s: evidence from the benchmark surveys', *Journal of International Business Studies*, **20**(1), 55–73.
Dunning, J.H. (1993), *The Globalization of Business*, London: Routledge.
Dunning, J.H. (1995), 'Reappraising the eclectic paradigm in an age of alliance capitalism', *Journal of International Business Studies*, **26**(3), 461–91.

Einhorn, B., M. Kovac, P. Engardio and D. Roberts (2005), 'Why Taiwan matters?', *Business Week*, 16 May, 76.

Erramilli, M.R. and C.P. Rao (1990), 'Choice of foreign entry modes by service firms: role of market knowledge', *Management International Review*, **30**, 135–50.

Farrell, D., P. Gao and G.R. Orr (2004), 'Making foreign investment work for China', *McKinsey Quarterly*, Special Edition, 24–33.

Gao, T. (2002), 'The impact of foreign trade and investment reform on industry location: the case of China', *Journal of International Trade & Economic Development*, **11**(4), 367–86.

Hamel, G. (1991), 'Competition for competence and interpartner learning within international strategic alliances', *Strategic Management Journal*, Winter Special Issue, **12**, 83–103.

Han, C.M. and J.M. Kim (2003), 'Korean marketing in China: an exploratory analysis of strategy–performance relationship', *Journal of International Marketing*, **11**(2), 79–100.

Harrigan, K.R. (1985), *Strategies for Joint Ventures*, Lexington: MA: D.C. Heath.

Hemerling, J., H. Hsu, P. Cotte and H. Sirkin (2003), 'Aim high, act fast: the China sourcing imperative', in *China: The Pursuit of Competitive Advantage and Profitable Growth*, Shanghai: The Boston Consulting Group.

Hennart, J.F. (1991), 'The transaction costs theory or joint ventures: an empirical study of Japanese subsidiaries in the United States', *Management Science*, **37**: 483–97.

Hout, T. and J. Hemerling (2003), 'China's next great thing', *Fast Company*, March (80), 31–2.

Hsu, H. and J. Hemerling (2003), 'Breaking out of China's value trap', *China: The Pursuit of Competitive Advantage and Profitable Growth*, Shanghai: The Boston Consulting Group.

Isobe, T., S. Makino and D.B. Montgomery (2000), 'Resource commitment, entry timing, and market performance of foreign direct investments in emerging economies: the case of Japanese international joint ventures in China', *Academy of Management Journal*, **43**(3), 468–84.

Jiang, B. (2002), 'How international firms are coping with supply chain issues in China', *Supply Chain Management*, **7**(3/4), 184–8.

Jiang, B. and E. Prater (2002), 'Distribution and logistics development in China. The revolution has begun', *International Journal of Physical Distribution & Logistics Management*, **32** (9), 783–98.

Kao, C. and W. Wang (1999), *A Comparative Study of Foreign Investment in Mainland China*, Taipei, Taiwan: Chung-hua Institution for Economic Research Press.

Kogut, B. and S.J. Chang (1991), 'Technological capabilities and Japanese foreign direct investment in the United States', *The Review of Economics and Statistics*, **73**(3), 401–13.

Kogut, B. and U. Zander (1993), 'Knowledge of the firm and the evolutionary theory of the multinational corporation', *Journal of International Business Studies*, **24**(4), 625–46.

Luo, Y. (2002), 'Capability exploitation and building in a foreign market: implications for multinational enterprises', *Organization Science*, **13**(1), 48–63.

Luo, Y. and M.W. Peng (1998), 'First mover advantages in investing in transitional economies', *Thunderbird International Business Review*, **40**(2), 141–63.

Lyles, M.A. and J.E. Salk (1996), 'Knowledge acquisition from foreign parents in international joint ventures: an empirical examination in the Hungarian context', *Journal of International Business Studies*, **27**(5), 877–903.

Madhok, A. (1997), 'Cost, value and foreign market entry mode: the transaction and the firm', *Strategic Management Journal*, **18**(1), 39–61.

Mishra, C.S. and D.H. Gobeli (1998), 'Managerial incentives, internalization, and market valuation of multinational firms', *Journal of International Business Studies*, **29**(3), 583–97.

Mitchell, W. (1991), 'Dual clocks: entry order influences on incumbent and newcomer market share and survival when specialized assets retain their value', *Strategic Management Journal*, **12**(2), 85–100.

Morck, R. and B. Yeung (1991), 'Why investors value multinationality', *Journal of Business*, **64**(2), 165–87.

Mutinelli, M. and L. Piscitello (1998), 'The entry mode choice of MNEs: an evolutionary approach', *Research Policy*, **27**(5), 491–505.

Pan, Y. (1996), 'Influences on foreign equity ownership level in joint ventures in China', *Journal of International Business Studies*, **27**(1), 1–26.

Pan, Y. (1997), 'The formation of Japanese and U.S. equity joint ventures in China', *Strategic Management Journal*, **18**(3), 247–54.

Pan, Y. and P.S.K. Chi (1999), 'Financial performance and survival of multinational corporations in China', *Strategic Management Journal*, **20**, 359–74.

Pan, Y. and D.K. Tse (2000), 'The hierarchical model of market entry modes', *Journal of International Business Studies*, **31**(4), 535–54.

Pan, Y., S. Li and D.K. Tse (1999), 'The impact of order of entry and mode of market entry on profitability and market share', *Journal of International Business Studies*, **30**, 81–104.

Porter, M. (1990), *The Competitive Advantage of Nations*, New York: Free Press.

Powell, B. (2002), *Fortune*, 4 March.

Prahalad, C.K. and K. Lieberthal (1998), 'The end of corporate imperialism', *Harvard Business Review*, **76**(4), 68–79.

Shaver, J.M., W. Mitchell and B. Yeung (1997), 'The effect of own-firm and other-firm experience on foreign direct investment survival in the United States, 1987–97', *Strategic Management Journal*, **18**, 811–24.

Su, C. and J.E. Littlefield (2001), 'Entering guanxi: a business ethical dilemma in mainland China?', *Journal of Business Ethics*, **33**(3), 199–211.

Szulanski, G. (1996), 'Exploring internal stickiness: impediments to the transfer of best practice within the firm', *Strategic Management Journal*, **17**(winter), 27–43.

Tanzer, A. (2001), *Forbes*, **168**, 74–6.

Teece, D.J. (1977), 'Technology transfer by multinational firms: the resource cost of transferring technological know-how', *Economic Journal*, **87**, 242–61.

Vanhonacker, W.R. and Y. Pan (1997), 'The impact of national culture, business scope, and geographic location of joint venture operations in China', *Journal of International Marketing*, **5**(3), 11–30.

Walters, Peter G.P. and S. Samiee (2003), 'Marketing strategy in emerging markets: the case of China', *Journal of International Marketing*, **11**(1), 97–106.

Woodcock, C.P., P.W. Beamish and S. Makino (1994), 'Ownership-based entry mode strategies and international performance', *Journal of International Business Studies*, **25**(2), 253–73.

Yan, R. (1998), 'Short-term results: the litmus test for success in China', *Harvard Business Review*, **76**(5), 61–9.

Zhang, K.H. (2000), 'Why is U.S. direct investment in China so small?', *Contemporary Economic Policy*, **18**(1), 82–94.

10. China marketing

Ying Ho and Kam-hon Lee

China is emerging as an economic giant no one can ignore. It is rapidly transforming itself from a centrally controlled economy into a market-based economy. The integration of China into the global economy has been among the most dramatic economic developments of recent decades (International Monetary Fund, 2004). China achieved annual GDP growth of 9.3 per cent in 2003 (World Bank, 2005). Its exports and imports have grown at an average rate of 15 per cent each year since 1979, compared with a 7 per cent annual expansion of world trade over the same period (International Monetary Fund, 2004). China's strong economic growth, huge market potential, and low-cost labour force have attracted much foreign investment. In the past years, many international firms moved into the China market and achieved mixed business results. Nowadays, multinational corporations (MNCs) recognize that China's marketing may not be the same as that in Western countries. China's unique political, economic and social environments evoke much complexity in marketing activities.

There is a clear need for marketing research to provide better understanding of the intricate marketing environment in China. In past decades, we witnessed a proliferation of China-related marketing research. Despite the large collection of literature available, there has not yet been a comprehensive review of existing work. This chapter attempts to review contemporary China marketing research, synthesize literature findings and identify future research directions. We searched through 36 English language, referred marketing and management journals, covering the period of 1986 to 2005. The 36 journals represent a collection of top-tier journals in the marketing and management disciplines. The journals are listed in Appendix 10.1. We identify a total of 118 articles related to China marketing research. Since this chapter focuses on current theoretical developments in China marketing, we have excluded studies that are descriptive in nature.

This chapter begins by outlining the exchange view of marketing and the metatheoretical perspective in studying China marketing issues. We then examine and synthesize extant literature based on two dimensions: (1) research topic (that is customer-related, firm-related or exchange-related), and (2) research approach (that is developmental, cross-cultural or comparative). This chapter consists of three main elements, namely customer, firm and customer–firm interaction. In the customer section, we discuss Chinese customers' buying behaviour, in terms of their mental processing relevant to a purchase decision (that is the perceptual and learning constructs). In the firm section, we examine companies' strategic decisions regarding entry mode, product, distribution and communications in China. In the customer–firm interaction section, we study relationship management and negotiation in the context of China marketing. The chapter ends by presenting the limitations of the existing China marketing studies and an agenda for future research.

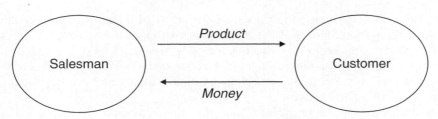

Source: Bagozzi (1974).

Figure 10.1   The customer–salesman dyad

MARKETING AS EXCHANGE

The exchange concept has been proposed by a number of marketing scholars as a funda-mental framework for viewing marketing (Bagozzi, 1974). Marketing is connoted as a dynamic relationship between parties (that is buyer and seller) within an exchange. This relationship is depicted in Figure 10.1. Major actors in a marketing exchange relationship are the firm and the customer. These two parties are not isolated actors responding to market stimuli. Through market interactions, the firm and the customer jointly determine outcomes of a market exchange. These two parties interact in such a manner so as to max-imize their rewards and minimize their costs. Typical rewards may include desired phys-ical objects, psychological pleasure or social gain. Costs are usually classified as noxious objects or psychological and social punishments (Bagozzi, 1974).

To examine systematically the China marketing literature, we categorize existing research according to whether they are customer-related, firm-related or exchange-related. Firm-related research accounts for the majority (88 studies) of the China mar-keting literature. Customer-related research is also popular (26 studies). Exchange-related research (four studies) is receiving disproportionately less attention from marketing researchers.

A METATHEORETICAL PERSPECTIVE

Researchers employ different approaches when they study marketing issues in China. These approaches can be classified as developmental, cross-cultural and comparative from a metatheoretical perspective (Lee, 2000). The developmental approach embraces a universalistic stand and assumes that independent variables are necessary and sufficient to explain marketing situations in all economies. In terms of theory development, it posits that the same theory is appropriate to explain marketing issues in all economies, includ-ing China. China marketing is considered as one datum point to substantiate the prevail-ing theory.

The cross-cultural approach postulates that marketing situations in two economies can be similar or different. A marketing theory formulated in developed countries may or may not be applicable to developing countries. Therefore researchers may need to modify the-ories generated in the developed economies, and to incorporate moderating variables to explain the marketing situation in the Chinese context. Although many marketing theories are originally developed in Western countries, they can, after moderation, incorporate and explain the marketing situation in China. There is a transfer of learning if we can identify regional differences and variables that moderate the situations. In terms of theory development, the cross-cultural approach uses China as a context for testing moderating variables and expanding theories.

The comparative approach explains China marketing in terms of the unique features of Chinese society. It advocates that China marketing can be self-sufficient as a subject of investigation. What is known, based on Chinese materials, would be directly relevant and applicable to China. What is learned from other economies, for example a developed economy, can be totally irrelevant and thus misleading as regards understanding the marketing situation in China. Nevertheless marketing researchers can allow the possibility to contrast and integrate similarities and differences from various cultures in a comparative framework. In terms of theory development, this approach explains the China marketing situation, with unique variables in the Chinese context not studied in developed economies before.

We employ this metatheoretical perspective to review systematically extant China marketing research. We classified the 118 studies according to two dimensions, research topic (that is customer-related, firm-related or exchange-related) and research approach (that is developmental, cross-cultural or comparative). Table 10.1 shows that China marketing research predominantly adopts the developmental approach (95 studies). The cross-cultural approach (21 studies) and comparative approach (two studies) are substantially less popular.

The popularity of the developmental and cross-cultural approaches is expected. The developmental approach adopts a universal stand and is simple to understand. It is a powerful tool to analyse China's position on a great map of the world. Since marketing issues of various economies are going to be explained by the same identified dimensions (for example GNP per capita, power distance, and so on), it is possible to explain and predict the marketing situations in China. Marketing researchers also frequently use the cross-cultural approach. As the political, economic and cultural environments in China are vastly different from those in the developed countries, China presents a rich context for testing and moderating marketing theories developed in Western countries. It is a natural extension for researchers to validate what they learnt from Western countries in China. In comparison, the comparative approach is much less popular. The marketing discipline has a long history of research activities based on Western economies. Most of the existing theories are constructed in developed countries. Studies employing a unique Chinese perspective are rather scant. This is probably due to the difficulty for marketing researchers of identifying unique and novel Chinese variables to explain China marketing issues.

Table 10.1   Categorization by research topic and approach

	Developmental	Cross-cultural	Comparative	Total
Customer-related	11	14	1	26
Firm-related	80	7	1	88
Exchange-related	4	0	0	4
Total	95	21	2	118

Only two studies employ the comparative approach to examine the China market. A firm-related study explains advertised prices in terms of the unique superstitious beliefs in Chinese society (Simmons and Schindler, 2003). Superstitious meanings attached to certain digits in traditional Chinese culture correspond to the use of those digits at the end of advertised prices. Digit 8, associated with prosperity and good luck in Chinese, is overrepresented among the price endings used in Chinese advertising. Digit 4, associated with death, is underrepresented among price endings in Chinese advertisements. In addition, a customer-related study identifies Chinese consumers' animosity toward Japan as a unique Chinese variable (Klein *et al.*, 1998). Chinese consumers' attitude toward Japanese products is negatively affected by the historical background (for example the Nanjing Massacre) and the resultant feelings of animosity toward Japan. This effect is independent of product quality judgment. These two studies illustrate how researchers may study China marketing from a comparative perspective. They suggest that the dominant tendency to apply Western theories in China may not be the only way of learning. China can be self-sufficient as a subject of investigation for marketing researchers.

Since most research employs the developmental and cross-cultural approaches, we focus on the 95 developmental and the 21 cross-cultural studies. For cross-cultural studies, we identify the moderating variables and list them in Appendix 10.2. In the following sections, we summarize and integrate what we have learnt from the literature in relation to the customer, the firm and the customer–firm interaction.

THE CUSTOMER

The theory of buyer behaviour describes a buying process in terms of three interrelated sets of variables: input variables, output variables and learning and perceptual constructs (Howard and Sheth, 1969). Input variables are the marketing stimuli (for example significant and symbolic attributes of the brands) from a buyer's environment. Output variables are buyer behaviours, such as attention, brand comprehension, attitude, intention and purchase. The central constructs of the theory are the learning and perceptual subsystems. They describe a buyer's mental state in relation to a purchase decision. The perceptual subsystem serves the function of information processing. The learning subsystem serves the function of concept formation. This section examines customers' mental processing (that is the perceptual and learning constructs) related to their buying behaviours.

Perceptual Subsystem

The perceptual subsystem delineates a customer's information procurement and processing related to purchase decisions. Examples of perceptual constructs include attention, stimulus ambiguity, perceptual bias and overt search. Chinese customers' brand recall is associated with brand-name suggestiveness (that is characters that are suggestive of product-linked benefits) (Lee and Ang, 2003). Chinese brand-names that incorporate character-level and/or radical-level suggestiveness evoke better memory and more favourable attitudes toward the ad and the brand. Nevertheless, the effects of radical suggestiveness on ad and brand attitudes were found only under unfamiliar conditions.

   Moreover, the effectiveness of brand-name translation techniques on brand evaluation depends on (1) the degree of emphasis of the original English name, as compared with the Chinese name, and (2) the type of prior translation method for brand names within the product category (Zhang and Schmitt, 2001). Furthermore, language proficiency determines the type of processing bilingual consumers engage in when they evaluate brand-name information. Highly proficient Chinese–English speakers activate both lexical–semantic and phonological representations of Chinese and English, placing weight on both the sound and meaning–name components. Less proficient speakers activate primarily the representations of Chinese, placing more weight on meaning than on sound (Zhang and Schmitt, 2004). In addition, differences in language structure (that is presence/absence of classifier) affect the perceived similarity between objects (Schmitt and Zhang, 1998). Chinese speakers perceive objects that share a classifier as more similar than objects that do not share a classifier.

   Difference in linguistic structure between Chinese and English is the major moderating variable of consumer information processing. Chinese is based on a system of ideographs, whereas English is based on alphabets. This dissimilarity in scripts, which determines the relation between spoken and written words, is likely to affect perception, mental representations (for example the degree of phonological and visual encoding) and memory (Schmitt *et al.*, 1994). This linguistic difference has a moderating effect on the way consumers process different modes of brand and advertising information (for example visual and auditory presentations). Chinese words are processed more contextually and rely to a greater degree on visual and/or semantic codes (Tavassoli, 1999). Mental representation of verbal information in Chinese is coded primarily in a visual manner (Schmitt *et al.*, 1994). As a result, visual brand identifiers are integrated in memory more easily with Chinese brand names (Tavassoli and Han, 2002). Non-verbal visual elements are also better retrieval cues for Chinese than for English ad copy. However, they interfere more with the cognitive responses to Chinese than English ad copy (Tavassoli and Lee, 2003). Owing to contextual processing of information, Chinese consumers rely more on inter-item semantic association in their retrieval of words from memory (Tavassoli, 1999).

Learning Subsystems

The learning subsystem describes a customer's concept formation relating to purchase decisions. Learning constructs include motives, brand apprehension, choice criteria, attitude, purchase intention, confidence in judgment, and satisfaction with purchase.

Attitude toward advertisement

Surveys of Chinese customers' attitude toward advertisement show that more educated and richer urban Chinese enjoy advertising more than the less educated or lower-income Chinese. The more educated Chinese also find advertising more informative and a better aid in their purchasing decisions (Zhou *et al.*, 2002b). Moreover, Chinese consumers' reaction to advertising appeals is driven by both the desire for global cosmopolitanism and a nationalistic desire to invoke local cultural values (Zhou and Belk, 2004).

   From a developmental perspective, advertisement design characteristics have an impact on customers' response to corporate identity visual systems (Henderson *et al.*, 2003). In terms of *feng shui* (Chinese geomancy) perception, Asians (such as Chinese) prefer organic and nature-based features, as well as curved elements, as opposed to angular features. In addition, Chinese customers' attitude toward advertisements is shaped by customer characteristics (for example information need and involvement). In the context of web advertising, Chinese users are more receptive to banner advertisements that match their information needs and navigation goals (Gong and Maddox, 2003). Customers' situational and enduring involvement with the product also positively affects their recall and attitude toward banner advertisements.

From a cross-cultural perspective, cultural factors have significant moderating effects on the impacts of advertising appeals on customers' attitude toward advertisements. Ego-focused (for example pride and happiness) rather than other-focused (for example empathy and peacefulness) emotional appeals lead to more favourable attitudes for members of a collectivist culture (for example China) (Aaker and Williams, 1998). Moreover, difference in self-construal (that is independent self versus interdependent self) also has a moderating effect on customers' attitudes toward advertising framing methods (that is differentiation versus assimilation) (Aaker and Schmitt, 2001). Chinese customers have higher preference levels for brands in the assimilation frame than in the differentiation frame.

Attitude toward brand

From a developmental perspective, Chinese customers' attitude toward a foreign brand (for example McDonald's) is related to societal norms and values evoked in various usage situations (Eckhardt and Houston, 2002). Meaning attached to foreign brands is largely dependent on cultural values evoked in the specific usage situation. Cultural factors (that is food attitude, linguistic difference and self schema) remain the major moderating variables of customer attitude formation. First, cultural difference in food attitude significantly moderates the relationship between a customer's affective and cognitive evaluative bases (Cervellon and Dube, 2002; Dube *et al.*, 2003).

Second, linguistic difference between logographic writing system (for example Chinese) and alphabetic writing system (for example English) has a moderating effect on the relationship between peripheral cues (for example script and sound cues) and brand attitude (Pan and Schmitt, 1996). Chinese native speakers' attitudes are affected primarily by script matching, whereas English native speakers' attitudes are affected primarily by sound matching.

Third, self-schema difference also moderates the effectiveness of advertising appeals on customers' brand attitude (Wang *et al.*, 2000). Connected appeal results in more favourable brand attitude than separated appeal for the Chinese audience. The result is reversed for those customers from the US. In addition to cultural factors, market efficiency has a moderating effect on the relationship between Chinese customers' price and quality perception. Owing to an inefficient market environment (that is less ascertainable and credible product information), Chinese customers possess a weaker price–quality schema than American consumers (Zhou *et al.*, 2002a).

Choice criteria

Decision-making behaviour of Chinese customers is influenced by society-level, firm-level and individual-level factors. On the society-level, the less egalitarian and more patriarchal

Chinese society significantly affects decision-making mode in Chinese families (Ford *et al.*, 1995). Mainland Chinese report significantly fewer joint decisions and significantly more husband-only decisions. At the firm level, an organization's marketing variables (such as product quality, promotional effort and service) are important factors in winning sales in China's industrial machinery market (McGuinness *et al.*, 1991). Moreover, symbolic benefits (such as modernity, prestige and association with foreign life style) of foreign food products constitute one of the primary driving forces of Chinese customers' purchases (Zhou and Hui, 2003). At the customer level, situation-specific felt ethnicity drives a person's ethnic food purchases (Stayman and Deshpande, 1989).

Similar to attitude formation, cultural factors serve as the major moderating variables of consumers' choice behaviour. Cultural orientation (independent versus interdependent) moderates the effect of subjective norms on intentions and behavioural expectations (Bagozzi *et al.*, 2000). This relationship is generally greater for Chinese than for Americans and Italians. Moreover Bian and Keller (1999) suggest that risk aversion and individualism/collectivism orientation have moderating effects on the relationship between people's fairness judgments and their subsequent decisions. Fairness judgment of Chinese does not necessarily coincide with their decisions in the same health and safety situations, whereas Americans tend to make decisions consistent with their fairness judgments (Bian and Keller, 1999). In the context of service encounters, Keillor *et al.* (2004) suggest that physical good quality positively affects behavioural intentions in China's fast-food industry. However, researchers find no such relationship in the Netherlands and Sweden. The Chinese long-term latent demand for consumer products is postulated as the moderating variable, but this remains speculative.

Overall Observation

Generally speaking, the number of consumer studies in China is still small, when compared with that of Western countries. This is probably due to the difficulty in obtaining high-quality consumer data in China. These studies cover two important mental processes in buyer behaviour (that is perceptual and learning subsystems). Researchers address some important issues of consumer behaviour, including information processing, attitude formation and choice behaviour. They provide a rough sketch of buyer behaviour in the China market. Nevertheless, extant customer-related literature is relatively silent on other consumer topics, such as information search, purchase motivation, judgment process and post-consumption satisfaction. These concepts are also central to our understanding of Chinese customers' purchase behaviours.

In addition, the cross-cultural approach (14 studies) is more popular than the developmental (11 studies) and the comparative (one study) approaches. A number of researchers perceive that Chinese consumers behave differently from their counterparts in developed countries. Cross-cultural variations in consumer behaviours are explained in terms of linguistic structure and cultural orientations (for example individualism/collectivism, self-construal). It is not surprising that a large number of studies adopt the cross-cultural approach in examining Chinese consumer behaviours. According to Hofstede (1993), culture is the collective programming of the mind that distinguishes the member of one group or category of people from another. In other words, a person's consumption behaviour is likely to be influenced by his/her dominant cultural environment. China is different from Western countries in terms of cultural dimensions such as power distance, uncertainty avoidance, individualism/collectivism, masculinity/femininity and long-term orientation (ibid.). Therefore cultural factors are valuable in explaining differences of consumption behaviours between the Chinese and Westerners.

THE FIRM

Once multinational firms decide to enter China, they need to make a number of strategic decisions in order to achieve marketing success. These strategic decisions include the entry mode choice and the marketing mix design (Bagozzi *et al.*, 1998, p. 648; see also Chapter 9 in this volume). They are the means by which a firm defines and supports its competitive position in its target market. The entry mode decision refers to the institutional arrangement to be used to sell and support products and services in the China market. The marketing mix decision determines product strategy, pricing strategy, distribution strategy and marketing communications strategy.

It is important to understand how marketing executives make decisions. Chinese cultural values (that is face saving, long-term exchange relationships and restricted competition, unquestioned respect for leaders, and pan-ethical view) significantly affect Chinese executives' market entry and product decisions (Tse *et al.*, 1988). For example, Chinese executives make fewer adjustments of their environment when they make international marketing decisions. Their tendencies to hold dichotomous and fatalistic views of their environment are also evident in their decision process. From a cross-cultural perspective, developmental differences have moderating effects on mainland Chinese executives' risk-taking behaviour in international marketing activities (Lee *et al.*, 2005). When facing ethically questionable business proposals, mainland Chinese executives are less sensitive to moral and legal risk, make fewer risk adjustments and are more inclined to engage in questionable business practices than their Hong Kong counterparts.

MNCs' performance in China is determined by a number of environmental and organizational factors. Firm performance is shaped by environmental factors, such as marketized and munificent environments (Davies and Walters, 2004), cooperative MNC–host government relations (Luo, 2001c) and organizational collaboration with partners (Luo, 1997). Firm performance is also affected by organizational factors such as corporate entrepreneurship (Liu *et al.*, 2002), organizational innovativeness (Deshpande *et al.*, 2004; Zhou *et al.*, 2005a), organizational culture (Deshpande *et al.*, 2004), host-country experience (Luo, 1999; Luo and Peng, 1999), parent–affiliate trust, control and integration (Child *et al.*, 2003) and parent–subsidiary links (Luo, 2003b). The effect of parent–subsidiary links (that is a parent firm's control flexibility, resource commitment and local responsiveness) is moderated by regulatory interference and industrial opportunity (Luo, 2003b).

A firm's marketing strategy is also a major factor that affects its performance in the China market. Firm strategies are shaped by organizational capabilities and transactional costs (White and Liu, 2001). Strategic orientations may include analyser orientation (Luo and Park, 2001), pioneering (Song *et al.*, 1999), defensive strategies (Tan and Litschert, 1994), environmental strategies (Chan, 2005), internal capability development and international diversification (Yiu *et al.*, 2005), product quality orientation (Lin and Germain, 2003), product competitiveness (Han and Kim, 2003), customer orientation and learning orientation (Liu *et al.*, 2002) and relationship marketing orientation (Sin *et al.*, 2005). Various components of stakeholder orientation (customer orientation, competitor orientation and employee orientation) have robust interaction effects on company performance (Luk *et al.*, 2005).

Nevertheless, the cultural dimension of collectivism affects the perceived importance of various pioneering advantages (Song *et al.*, 2000). Environmental uncertainty (that is technological turbulence and perceived market dynamism) has moderating effects on the association between product quality orientation and firm performance (Lin and Germain, 2003). Globalization (that is global partnership, market seeking and product sourcing) also moderates the link between a firm's marketing resources and firm performance (Luo *et al.*, 2005). Effects of relationship marketing orientation and marketing orientation on business performance are moderated by economic ideology and industry type (Sin *et al.*, 2005).

We have identified 88 firm-related marketing studies from the literature. These studies predominantly use the developmental approach (80 studies). Only seven studies employ the cross-cultural approach and one study uses the comparative approach. The following section examines firm strategies, in terms of entry mode choice and marketing mix decisions.

Entry Mode Strategy

Entry mode choice (wholly owned subsidiary, joint venture, franchise, and so on) is a major decision made by international marketers when they enter the China market. Peng (1997) discusses the advantages and problems of strategic choices for growth (for example generic expansion, acquisitions, interorganizational relationships). For many years, the Chinese government has placed ownership restrictions on private enterprises. Most MNCs have chosen joint venture (JV) as the entry mode. JVs in China are characterized by high frequency of association with government partners, investment from ethnically related countries, low realization rate of intended JVs, predetermined JV duration and lack of relationship between stability and performance (Beamish, 1993). In terms of equity JV (EJV), there are substantial differences between Japanese and American EJVs with respect to selection of Chinese partner and the foreign partner, foreign equity ownership, foreign capital contribution, EJV business scope, and EJV location (Pan, 1997; see also Chapter 9 in this volume). Key difficulties identified for EJVs include local sourcing, recruitment of skilled Chinese managers, and the clarity of laws and regulations (Vanhonacker and Pan, 1997).

Most researchers use the developmental approach in studying MNCs' entry mode strategy. Entry mode choice is determined by host-country factors, home-country factors, industry-specific factors and operational-related factors (Tse *et al.*, 1997). Examples of host-country factors include perceived governmental intervention, environmental uncertainty and protection of intellectual property rights (Luo, 2001b). In terms of home-country factors, equity ownership of a JV is influenced by the source-country's currency exchange rate, cost of borrowing, export capability and management orientation (Pan, 2002). A firm's country of origin also affects its location and industry selection (Schroath *et al.*, 1993). At the industry level, firms of the same industry mimic each other's choice of wholly-owned plants. Technology-intensive firms are more likely to abandon JV entry modes, owing to contractual hazards (Guillén, 2003).

At the firm level, firm size influences equity JV characteristics (for example equity stake, alignment with foreign partners and industry choice) (Pan and Li, 2000). Cultural distance between partners is associated with entry mode choice of US-based MNCs (Tihanyi *et al.*, 2005). Entry timing can also be explained by firm capabilities (that is internationalization, size and scope) and entry mode (Gaba *et al.*, 2002). Moreover, EJV is the suitable choice for firms seeking transfer of tacit, embedded knowledge (Shenkar and Li, 1999). Last but not least, a study of South Korean firms in China shows that a firm's rate of foreign expansion can be predicted by its business group experience and imitation among firms from the same home-country industry (Guillén, 2002).

Entry mode choice has a major influence on firm performance. Non-Chinese MNCs generate technological and international market access spillover benefits for Chinese firms, while ethnic Chinese investors from outside China confer only market access benefits (Buckley *et al.*, 2002). Venture performance in an international market is determined by a firm's strategic decisions including entry timing (Isobe *et al.*, 2000; Luo, 1998; Pan and Chi, 1999; Pan *et al.*, 1999) mode of entry (Pan *et al.*, 1999), location advantages (Pan and Chi, 1999) and resource commitment to technology transfer (Isobe *et al.*, 2000). Performance of large, established US–China manufacturing JVs can be explained by strategic factors, such as controlling decision making, establishing a sales network, retaining inter-partner learning, and influencing government officials (Osland, 1994).

In addition, JV performance is influenced by partnership characteristics, such as cultural diversity in management (Li *et al.*, 2002), product relatedness with parents (Luo, 2002c) and cooperation (Luo, 2002b). Osland and Cavusgil (1996) provide a detailed review of performance issues in US–China JVs. In addition to performance, a firm's choice of entry mode influences a number of operational issues. Ownership type influences a firm's environment–strategy configuration (Tan, 2002), capability exploitation and building (Luo, 2002a). Both source and recipient networks (Zhao *et al.*, 2005) and overseeing effort and management involvement (Tsang, 2002) determine knowledge transfer in a JV (see also Chapter 5 in this volume).

Inter-partner relationship management is a critical issue for partnership success. A firm's willingness to cooperate with a second foreign firm can be predicted by the level of risk in China, the level of control and home-country's trade relationship with China (Pan and Tse, 1996). Inter-partner consensus has a strong and positive relationship with the achievement of strategic objectives for both partners (Yan and Gray, 2001). Relationship commitment positively predicts JV performance (that is interaction frequency) (Lin and Germain, 1999). Moreover, environment-level factors (market disturbance, regulatory deterrence), organization-level factors (goal congruity, cultural distance) and individual-level factor (accumulated tenure overlap) determine the level of personal attachment between JV partners (Luo, 2001a). Personal attachment and structural attachment in turn significantly contribute to JV performance, but their rates of contribution to JV profitability diminish as the attachments increase (Luo, 2002d).

Managerial control of JV partners is also significantly related to venture performance (Ding, 1997). However, the perceived control–performance relationship between foreign and Chinese firms is contingent on equity stake, committed resources and cultural distance (Luo *et al.*, 2001). The pattern of control is influenced by partners' bargaining power (Yan and Gray, 1994), firms' strategic intentions, and familiarity with the local culture and market (Calantone and Zhao, 2001). Foreign equity ownership in Chinese JVs is related to advertising intensity, foreign capital input, EJV investment amount, contractual duration, local and foreign partner alignment, and JV location (Pan, 1996).

In terms of conflict resolution, hostility is identified as a common dimension of intracultural and intercultural conflict situations (Doucet and Jehn, 1997). Inter-partner credible threat and partners' relative control significantly affect partners' relative payoffs (Zhang and Rajagopalan, 2002). In addition, conflict resolution strategies have a partial mediating effect on the relationship between JV context (cultural similarity and relationship duration) and JV satisfaction (Lin and Germain, 1998). Tse *et al.* (1994) employ the cross-cultural perspective in examining joint project conflicts. They postulate that the Chinese collectivist culture affects executives' reactions to person-related versus task-related conflicts. Because of their emphasis on collectivism and group harmony, Chinese executives react more positively to task-related conflict, but more negatively to person-related conflict. The order is reversed for Canadian executives.

Product Strategy

New product success in China is affected by such factors as relative product advantage (Parry and Song, 1994; Song and Parry, 1994), marketing's influence (Li and Atuahene-Gima, 1999) and market orientation (Wei and Morgan, 2004). Supportiveness of organizational climate also has an indirect positive effect on new product performance, via its impact on market orientation (Wei and Morgan, 2004). Nevertheless, environmental factors (environmental turbulence and institutional support) have a moderating effect on the relationship between product innovation strategy and firm performance (Li and Atuahene-Gima, 2001). Environmental uncertainty (technology uncertainty and demand uncertainty) also moderates the effectiveness of strategic decision comprehensiveness on new product performance (Atuahene-Gima and Li, 2004). From a cross-cultural perspective, characteristics of Chinese firms (that is low proficiency of marketing activities and varied quality of industrial products) have moderating effects on the association of marketing proficiency and product quality with new product success (Calantone *et al.*, 1996). The relationships are stronger in China than in the US.

Regarding new product diffusion, macroenvironmental variables (such as international trade or urbanization level) affect the penetration potential of new products (Talukdar *et al.*, 2002). The average penetration potential for developing countries (such as China) is about one-third of that for developed countries. Average time to peak sale for developing countries is 17.9 per cent longer than that for developed countries.

In terms of marketing influence in new product development, the efficacy of marketing's influence tactics is contingent upon the degree of functional interdependence in the new product development stages, and the degree of interdepartmental conflict (Atuahene-Gima and Li, 2000). Goal incongruity among marketing, research and development, and manufacturing functions impairs cross-functional integration in China (Xie *et al.*, 2003).

Distribution Strategy

All distribution studies employ the developmental approach. These studies discuss retail format choice, managerial networking, and alliance among channel members. A firm's retail format choice is shaped by host country conditions, the retailers' global position and global strategy (Goldman, 2001). Expected limitations in the China market include consumer-side factors (for example purchasing power, preference and mobility), supply-side factors (supplier reliability, product quality and availability), restrictive laws and regulations, undeveloped distribution, technological and legal infrastructures, government intervention and lack of adequate retail sites.

In terms of managerial networking, *guanxi* represents the Chinese system of doing business on the basis of personal relationships (Lovett *et al.*, 1999; see also Chapter 4 in this volume). *Guanxi* is important for business executives' trust in their connections (Farh *et al.*, 1998). The extent of *guanxi* utilization is determined by institutional, strategic and organizational factors (Park and Luo, 2001). A firm's propensity to engage in agency business activity depends on environmental uncertainty, perceived industry growth, venture size and product development alliance (Li and Atuahene-Gima, 2002). The use of managerial networking (such as *guanxi*) also depends on ownership type (that is private, state-owned and collective–hybrid companies) (Xin and Pearce, 1996; see also Chapter 6 in this volume), structural uncertainty, competitive pressure, industrial regulation and capacity utilization (Luo, 2003a). The relationship between industry dynamics and networking is moderated by a firm's strategic proactiveness (Luo, 2003a).

An exporter's relationships with a distributor (such as prior *guanxi*, personal friendships, trust and satisfaction) positively affect its performance (Ambler *et al.*, 1999). Nevertheless, the effect of relationship resources on venture performance is moderated by time (ibid.). Personal friendships appear to have a significant influence in the first three years of business operation. Long-term and market commitment, and prior *guanxi* (prior business relationship) are important success factors throughout the venture life. In addition, managers' micro interpersonal ties with top executives at other firms and with government officials help improve macro organizational performance (Peng and Luo, 2000). Nonetheless, industry type moderates the relationship between managerial ties and firm performance. For low-growth industries, impact of personal ties with managers at other firms on market share is stronger. Small firms that are not state-owned and in the service industry are more likely to reap the benefit of government connections (Peng and Luo, 2000; see also Chapter 3 in this volume).

Communications Strategy

Nowadays, advertising has become an important promotional tool in the China market. Survey studies indicate that a Chinese commercial is a melting pot of Eastern and Western cultural values (Cheng and Schweitzer, 1996). Chinese advertisements emphasize utilitarian appeals (Tse *et al.*, 1989), traditional cultural values (Ji and McNeal, 2001; Lin, 2001) and contain a large amount of information (Rice and Lu, 1988). A predominant majority of companies use a combination of standardization and localization advertising strategy (Yin, 1999). Relative to television and newspapers, a magazine is an effective vehicle for reaching upscale and status-seeking targets (Hung *et al.*, 2005).

Market communications literature identifies a number of independent variables that explain firms' advertising strategy in China. Cultural values promoted in Chinese advertising are predicted by product type and media type (Zhang and Shavitt, 2003). Modernity and individualism values are more pervasive in magazine advertisements, while collectivism and traditional values are more pervasive on television commercials (Zhang and

Shavitt, 2003). Cultural differences (for example individualism/collectivism, high-context/ low-context) are manifested more apparently in traditional storytelling techniques, such as story line, comparison and identification, than cinematographic variables, such as subjective camera, direct address and pacing (Zhou *et al.*, 2005b). In terms of advertising effect, cultural congruity predicts effectiveness of advertising appeals, but this effect is moderated by product use conditions (Zhang and Gelb, 1996). Moreover, the effect of advertising expenditure on long-term sales of products is contingent on the product type (Zhou *et al.*, 2003). Significant marketing persistence is found in sales of consumer durables, whereas there are mixed results in sales of non-durables.

Management and motivation of sales employees is another important element of communication strategy. Sales force and frontline employees are valuable company resources. Their effective marketing efforts directly determine a firm's success. Employees' normative commitment to a firm is shaped by the culture dimension of collectivism (Cheng and Stockdale, 2003). Chinese employees have a higher level of normative commitment than Canadian employees. Moreover, procedural and performance-based distributive justice is a significant predictor of employee job satisfaction (Leung *et al.*, 1996).

From a cross-cultural perspective, cultural variables moderate the effects of motivational factors on sales force performance. Chinese collectivist orientation and high uncertainty avoidance have moderating effects on the impact of process control and supervisor accessibility on supervisee trust (Atuahene-Gima and Li, 2002). Collectivism/ individualism orientation also moderates the impact of customer request legitimacy on employees' compliance intention (Hui *et al.*, 2004b). Chinese subjects are less reluctant than American subjects to break the organization's rule, when the customer's special request is deemed legitimate. Moreover, communication culture (that is high-context versus low-context) has moderating effects on the association between goal specificity and selling efforts (Fang *et al.*, 2004). Furthermore, power distance moderates the impact of employee empowerment on job satisfaction (Hui *et al.*, 2004a). In addition to the cultural variables, successful implementation of the empowerment approach in Chinese organizations also depends on employees' desire to satisfy customer needs.

Overall Observation

China marketing researchers have devoted considerable efforts to studying firm behaviour during the past two decades. The amount of firm-related research (88 studies) is substantially larger than that of customer-related research (26 studies) and exchange-related research (four studies). A majority of firm studies concentrate on the use of strategic alliances (for example managerial networking and JV) to adapt to China's uncertain market environment. China has been in a state of flux since its adoption of the 'open door policy' in the late 1970s. Current findings help us to understand how MNCs adapt themselves in a rapidly evolving, transitional economy such as China. Despite the large number of studies, many firm-related topics remain under-researched. Examples include product strategy (for example product life cycle management), pricing strategy (market forces affecting price setting, effectiveness of pricing tactics, and so on), distribution strategy (channel design and effectiveness and so on) and communications strategy (effect of message content and structure, media selection, and so on).

A dominant share of firm research employs the developmental approach (80 studies). Many researchers treat firm behaviour in the China market as an additional data point to validate marketing models developed in Western countries (cf. Chapter 3 in this volume). Firm studies employing the cross-cultural perspective mainly focus on employee management issues such as compliance intention, trust and job satisfaction. These studies pay a great deal of attention to cultural factors (for example individualism/collectivism, power distance and uncertainty avoidance) that may affect Chinese employee behaviour. Results suggest that many established models in developed countries are also applicable to China. This helps international marketers to better understand the China situation and formulate strategic directions.

CUSTOMER–FIRM INTERACTION

A market exchange system may be defined as a set of actors and their interactions with each other. While previous sections deal with individual actors in the market exchange (that is customer and firm), this section examines the customer–firm interaction. We have identified only four such studies in the literature. These studies adopt the developmental approach in studying market exchange activities. They cover two critical issues in market exchange: relationship management and negotiation.

Relationship Management

China is going through a transition from a centrally directed to a market-based economy (see also Chapters 3 and 6 in this volume). As a result, relationship building and maintenance is becoming increasingly important in China. Relational resources (that is customer relationships, business–partner social capital and governing-agency social capital) have a positive impact on a firm's performance (Luo *et al.*, 2004). Among the three types of relationship resources, customer relationships have the strongest influence on a firm's performance (ibid.). Nevertheless, influences of these resources are moderated by domestic or international firm ownership. Performance implications of customer relationship and business-partner social capital are stronger for an international JV than domestically owned firms (ibid.).

Another important issue is the relative influence of different parties in a marketing relationship. In the context of an advertising agency–client relationship, relative power of the firm and the client depends on the decision-making process (bottom-up, top-down, and so on) (Prendergast *et al.*, 2001). Agency power is the weakest in the bottom-up decision-making process.

Negotiation

Business negotiation in China involves complicated and delicate considerations. Western businessmen regard negotiations with Chinese executives as a daunting task. Roots of Chinese culture (that is agrarianism, morality, Chinese pictographic language and Chinese people's wariness of foreigners) underpin the major elements in the Chinese negotiation style (that is personal connections, the intermediary, social status, interpersonal harmony, holistic thinking, thrift, face or social capital, and endurance) (Graham and Lam, 2003). In the context of negotiating with the Chinese government, Chinese negotiators are influenced by national–ethnic culture, organizational culture and professional culture (Chen and Faure, 1995).

Culture serves as the independent variable to explain Chinese negotiation styles. Cultural orientations such as collectivism, power distance and uncertainty avoidance significantly influence the cognitive moral development and negotiation style of Chinese executives (Ford *et al.*, 1997). Chinese executives tend to be more concerned about organizational norms than their American counterparts (ibid.). Moreover, negotiator attractiveness and negotiators' problem-solving approach have an impact on partners' satisfaction (Adler *et al.*, 1992).

Overall Observation

Exchange-related topics receive the least attention from marketing researchers. The amount of research does not correspond to its importance in contemporary marketing management. Extant exchange literature covers two important areas in market exchanges (that is relationship management and negotiation). While the findings give us some preliminary understanding, there is much room for future research. For example, customer–firm interaction is especially important in service encounters, where exchange outcomes are jointly determined by the customer and the service employee. Customer–firm exchange at the 'moment of truth' largely determines consumers' exchange satisfaction and post-consumption behaviour (for example complaint, word-of-mouth and exit).

With the proliferation of service firms (such as restaurants, hotels and airlines) in China, marketing practitioners need to understand the dynamics of firm–customer exchange in order to make wise business decisions. It is unfortunate that there are not many customer–firm interaction studies conducted in the service industry in China. Various factors (social norms, political and economic environment and so on) that may affect market exchanges in the service industry are unexplored in China. Therefore, there is a need to validate Western knowledge of market exchange with China data, and/or to explore moderating variables to explain different exchange phenomenon in the China market.

CONCLUSION AND FUTURE RESEARCH DIRECTIONS

In this chapter, we review current research of China-related marketing. A number of China marketing studies were published in top-tier marketing and management journals during the period 1986–2005. Research findings enhance our understanding of the current marketing situation in China. These studies cover a wide range of customer-related, firm-related and exchange-related marketing topics. Firm-related issues (such as decision making, entry mode choice and marketing mix strategies) attracted the most research attention, while customer-related issues (such as information processing and attitude formation) are also popular among researchers. There is substantially less research that focuses on customer–firm exchange activities. This indicates that there is an imbalance of research topics. Marketing exchange is a dynamic process in which exchange outcomes depend on bargaining, negotiation, power, conflict and the shared meanings existing between buyer and seller (Bagozzi, 1978). Therefore exchange-related topics are as important as firm-related and customer-related research. A more complete view of the dynamic process of marketing requires future studies to fill in this research gap. Moreover, the 118 articles cover a wide range of research topics. This means that, for each topic, we can only identify a small number of studies. In order to have an in-depth understanding of a marketing issue, we need to accumulate a certain amount of research work in that area. It is important for future research efforts to be more focused on certain areas in order to generate research synergy.

In terms of research approach, most China marketing literature employs the developmental (81 per cent) and cross-cultural (18 per cent) approaches. Meanwhile, researchers rarely use the comparative approach. There are merits and limitations for all three approaches. The developmental approach is powerful in drawing a big picture to position a particular economy on a grand map. However, when an established theory is not directly applicable to a new economy, the conclusion is misleading. The cross-cultural approach brings in what one learned from modern business practices in the developed countries in a carefully articulated way. When an appropriate moderating variable is identified, there is effective transfer of learning. However, an overemphasis on this approach may still be dangerous, because researchers can be blind to the uniqueness of the Chinese marketing situation. The comparative approach recognizes the uniqueness of the China market. However, it may fail to see how to learn from what is known and established in the developed economies, and it may 'reinvent the wheel'. Therefore it is important to integrate all these approaches in future research attempts in order to get a more comprehensive understanding of China marketing.

In the future, we expect a further increase in the number of developmental studies. Western marketing knowledge is getting increasingly popular in China, as is evident in the rapid growth of MBA education programmes in recent years. Our literature review suggests that marketing models developed in Western countries are largely applicable to China. Therefore marketing researchers need to continue validating Western marketing knowledge in order to enhance an understanding of the China market. China data and business cases serve as valuable data points to confirm what we have learnt from Western countries in the China marketplace. While developmental studies contribute great application value to marketing practitioners, these studies have limited publication value or theoretical contribution.

The amount of cross-cultural research will also escalate. Marketing is about people (consumers, employees, marketers, and so on) and culture is an important factor in shaping people's mindset and behaviours. Cultural variables (such as linguistic structure, value orientations, and so on) will continue to serve as necessary factors that moderate the effects and relationships postulated by Western models. Our review shows that marketing studies related to people mostly use the cross-cultural approach (for example information processing, attitude formation and empowerment effect). For instance, in terms of employee/sales force management, researchers demonstrate that Chinese collectivist orientation moderates (1) the relationship between process control and supervisor accessibility on supervisee trust (Atuahene-Gima and Li, 2002), and (2) the association between customer request legitimacy on employees' compliance intention (Hui *et al.*, 2004b). Moreover, power distance has a moderating effect on the impact of employee empowerment on job satisfaction (Hui *et al.*, 2004a). In addition, communication culture (that is high-context versus low-context culture) moderates the relationship between goal specificity and selling efforts (Fang *et al.*, 2004). These findings underscore the importance of cultural variables as moderators of human behaviour in marketing activities. Nevertheless, existing studies focus on a small number of cultural variables (linguistic difference, self construal, power distance, collectivism/individualism, and so on). Marketing researchers should remain sensitive to all cultural factors and their effects in China marketing issues.

Marketing researchers rarely use the comparative approach. This is understandable given the difficulty for researchers to identify explanatory variables that are unique to China. Nevertheless, the comparative approach should have a place in China marketing research. When the existing Western models cannot be applied in China, researchers should consider the possibility of unique Chinese factors in solving the research problems. Some marketing studies consider Chinese animosity toward Japan and superstitious beliefs as unique Chinese experience (Klein *et al.*, 1998; Simmons and Schindler, 2003). These studies demonstrate that it is possible to explain the China marketing phenomenon in terms of variables that are only applicable in China. Chinese culture contains many distinctive social customs, Confucian teaching and religious thoughts. These variables may be potentially valuable in explaining China marketing issues.

To sum up, there was a proliferation of China-related marketing research over the past two decades. While extant studies generate valuable information on China marketing, there is much room for researchers to validate and moderate further marketing models developed in Western countries. In the future, marketing researchers will be encouraged to integrate the developmental, cross-cultural and comparative perspectives in investigating China marketing issues.

REFERENCES

Aaker, Jennifer and Bernd Schmitt (2001), 'Culture-dependent assimilation and differentiation of the self: preferences for consumption symbols in the United States and China', *Journal of Cross-Cultural Psychology*, **32**(5), 561–76.

Aaker, Jennifer L. and Patti Williams (1998), 'Empathy versus pride: the influence of emotional appeals across cultures', *Journal of Consumer Research*, **25**(3), 241–61.

Adler, Nancy J., Richard Brahm and John L. Graham (1992), 'Strategy implementation: a comparison of face-to-face negotiations in the People's Republic of China and the United States', *Strategic Management Journal*, **13**(6), 449–66.

Ambler, Tim, Chris Styles and Xiucun Wang (1999), 'The effect of channel relationships and guanxi on the performance of inter-province export ventures in the People's Republic of China', *International Journal of Research in Marketing*, **16**(1), 75–87.

Atuahene-Gima, Kwaku and Haiyang Li (2000), 'Marketing's influence tactics in new product development: a study of high technology firms in China', *The Journal of Product Innovation Management*, **17**(6), 451–70.

Atuahene-Gima, Kwaku and Haiyang Li (2002), 'When does trust matter? Antecedents and contingent effects of supervisee trust on performance in selling new products in China and the United States', *Journal of Marketing*, **66**(3), 61–81.

Atuahene-Gima, Kwaku and Haiyang Li (2004), 'Strategic decision comprehensiveness and new product development outcomes in new technology ventures', *Academy of Management Journal*, **47**(4), 583–97.

Bagozzi, Richard P. (1974), 'Marketing as an organized behavioral system of exchange', *Journal of Marketing*, **38**(4), 77–81.

Bagozzi, Richard P. (1978), 'Marketing as exchange: a theory of transactions in the marketplace', *The American Behavioral Scientist*, **21**(4), 535–56.

Bagozzi, Richard P., Jose Antonio Rosa, Kirti Sawhney Celly and Francisco Coronel (1998), *Marketing Management*, Upper Saddle River, NJ: Prentice-Hall.

Bagozzi, Richard P., Nancy Wong, Shuzo Abe and Massimo Bergami (2000), 'Cultural and situational contingencies and the theory of reasoned action: application to fast food restaurant consumption', *Journal of Consumer Psychology*, **9**(2), 97–106.

Beamish, Paul W. (1993), 'The characteristics of joint ventures in the People's Republic of China', *Journal of International Marketing*, **1**(2), 29–48.

Bian, Wen-Qiang and L. Robin Keller (1999), 'Patterns of fairness judgments in North America and the People's Republic of China', *Journal of Consumer Psychology*, **8**(3), 301–20.

Buckley, Peter J., Jeremy Clegg and Chengqi Wang (2002), 'The impact of inward FDI on the performance of Chinese manufacturing firms', *Journal of International Business Studies*, **33**(4), 637–55.

Calantone, Roger J. and Yushan Sam Zhao (2001), 'Joint ventures in China: a comparative study of Japanese, Korean, and U.S. partners', *Journal of International Marketing*, **9**(1), 1–23.

Calantone, Roger J., Jeffrey B. Schmidt and X. Michael Song (1996), 'Controllable factors of new product success: a cross-national comparison', *Marketing Science*, **15**(4), 341–58.

Cervellon, Marie-Cecile and Laurette Dube (2002), 'Assessing the cross-cultural applicability of affective and cognitive components of attitude', *Journal of Cross-Cultural Psychology*, **33**(3), 346–57.

Chan, Ricky Y.K. (2005), 'Does the natural-resource-based view of the firm apply in an emerging economy? A survey of foreign invested enterprises in China', *Journal of Management Studies*, **42**(3), 625–72.

Chen, Derong and Guy Olivier Faure (1995), 'When Chinese companies negotiate with their government', *Organization Studies*, **16**(1), 27–54.

Cheng, Hong and John C. Schweitzer (1996), 'Cultural values reflected in Chinese and U.S. television commercials', *Journal of Advertising Research*, **36**(3), 27–45.

Cheng, Yuqiu and Margaret S. Stockdale (2003), 'The validity of the three-component model of organizational commitment in a Chinese context', *Journal of Vocational Behavior*, **62**(3), 465–89.

Child, John, L. Chung and H. Davies (2003), 'The performance of cross-border units in China: a test of natural selection, strategic choice and contingency theories', *Journal of International Business Studies*, **34**(3), 242–54.

Davies, Howard and Peter Walters (2004), 'Emergent patterns of strategy, environment and performance in a transition economy', *Strategic Management Journal*, **25**(4), 347–64.

Deshpande, Rohit, John U. Farley and Douglas Bowman (2004), 'Tigers, dragons, and others: profiling high performance in Asian firms', *Journal of International Marketing*, **12**(3), 5–29.

Ding, Daniel Z. (1997), 'Control, conflict, and performance: a study of U.S.–Chinese joint ventures', *Journal of International Marketing*, **5**(3), 31–45.

Doucet, Lorna and Karen A. Jehn (1997), 'Analyzing harsh words in a sensitive setting: American expatriates in communist China', *Journal of Organizational Behavior*, **18**(Supplement), 559–82.

Dube, Laurette, Marie-Cecile Cervellon and Jingyuan Han (2003), 'Should consumer attitudes be reduced to their affective and cognitive bases? Validation of a hierarchical model', *International Journal of Research in Marketing*, **20**(3), 259–72.

Eckhardt, Giana M. and Michael J. Houston (2002), 'Cultural paradoxes reflected in brand meaning: McDonald's in Shanghai, China', *Journal of International Marketing*, **10**(2), 68–82.

Fang, Eric, Robert W. Palmatier and Kenneth R. Evans (2004), 'Goal-setting paradoxes? Trade-offs between working hard and working smart: the United States versus China', *Journal of the Academy of Marketing Science*, **32**(2), 188–202.

Farh, Jiing-Lih, Anne S. Tsui, Katherine Xin and Bor-Shiuan Cheng (1998), 'The influence of relational demography and *guanxi*: the Chinese case', *Organization Science*, **9**(4), 471–88.

Ford, John B., Michael S. LaTour and Tony L. Henthorne (1995), 'Perception of marital roles in purchase decision processes: a cross-cultural study', *Journal of the Academy of Marketing Science*, **23**(2), 120–31.

Ford, John B., Michael S. LaTour, Scott J. Vitell and Warren A. French (1997), 'Moral judgment and market negotiations: a comparison of Chinese and American managers', *Journal of International Marketing*, **5**(2), 57–76.

Gaba, Vibha, Yigang Pan and Gerardo R. Ungson (2002), 'Timing of entry in international market: an empirical study of U.S. Fortune 500 firms in China', *Journal of International Business Studies*, **33**(1), 39–55.

Goldman, Arieh (2001), 'The transfer of retail formats into developing economies: the example of China', *Journal of Retailing*, **77**(2), 221–42.

Gong, Wen and Lynda M. Maddox (2003), 'Measuring web advertising effectiveness in China', *Journal of Advertising Research*, **43**(1), 34–49.

Graham, John L. and N. Mark Lam (2003), 'The Chinese negotiation', *Harvard Business Review*, **81**(10), 82–91.

Guillén, Mauro F. (2002), 'Structural inertia, imitation, and foreign expansion: South Korean firms and business groups in China, 1987–95', *Academy of Management Journal*, **45**(3), 509–25.

Guillén, Mauro F. (2003), 'Experience, imitation, and the sequence of foreign entry: wholly owned and joint-venture manufacturing by South Korean firms and business groups in China, 1987–1995', *Journal of International Business Studies*, **34**(2), 185–98.

Han, C. Min and Jung Min Kim (2003), 'Korean marketing in China: an exploratory analysis of strategy–performance relationships', *Journal of International Marketing*, **11**(2), 79–100.

Henderson, Pamela W., Joseph A. Cote, Siew Meng Leong and Bernd Schmitt (2003), 'Building strong brands in Asia: selecting the visual components of image to maximize brand strength', *International Journal of Research in Marketing*, **20**(4), 297–313.

Hofstede, Geert (1993), 'Cultural constraints in management theories', *Academy of Management Executive*, **7**(1), 81–94.

Howard, John A. and Jagdish N. Sheth (1969), *The Theory of Buyer Behavior*, New York: John Wiley & Sons.

Hui, Michael K., Kevin Au and Henry Fock (2004a), 'Empowerment effects across cultures', *Journal of International Business Studies*, **35**(1), 46–60.

Hui, Michael K., Kevin Au and Henry Fock (2004b), 'Reactions of service employees to organization–customer conflict: a cross-cultural comparison', *International Journal of Research in Marketing*, **21**(2), 107–21.

Hung, Kineta, Flora Fang Gu and David K. Tse (2005), 'Improving media decisions in China: a targetability and cost–benefit analysis', *Journal of Advertising*, **34**(1), 49–63.

International Monetary Fund (2004), 'China's growth and integration into the world economy: prospects and challenges', occasional paper No. 232, Washington, DC: IMF.

Isobe, Takehiko, Shige Makino and David B. Montgomery (2000), 'Resource commitment, entry timing, and market performance of foreign direct investments in emerging economies: the case of Japanese international joint ventures in China', *Academy of Management Journal*, **43**(3), 468–84.

Ji, Mindy F. and James U. McNeal (2001), 'How Chinese children's commercials differ from those of the United States: a content analysis', *Journal of Advertising*, **30**(3), 79–92.

Keillor, Bruce D., G. Tomas M. Hult and Destan Kandemir (2004), 'A study of the service encounter in eight countries', *Journal of International Marketing*, **12**(1), 9–35.

Klein, Jill G., Richard Ettenson and Marlene D. Morris (1998), 'The animosity model of foreign product purchase: an empirical test in the People's Republic of China', *Journal of Marketing*, **62**(1), 89–100.

Lee, Kam-hon (2000), 'Business ethics in China – a metatheoretical perspective', *Online Journal of Ethics*, **2**(4).

Lee, Kam-hon, Gong-ming Qian, Julie H. Yu and Ying Ho (2005), 'Trading favors for marketing advantage: evidence from Hong Kong, China and the United States', *Journal of International Marketing*, **13**(1), 1–35.

Lee, Yih Hwai and Kim Soon Ang (2003), 'Brand name suggestiveness: a Chinese language perspective', *International Journal of Research in Marketing*, **20**(4), 323–35.

Leung, Kwok, Peter B. Smith, Zhongming Wang and Haifa Sun (1996), 'Job satisfaction in joint venture hotels in China: an organizational justice analysis', *Journal of International Business Studies*, **27**(5), 947–62.

Li, Haiyang and Kwaku Atuahene-Gima (1999), 'Marketing's influence and new product perform-ance in Chinese firms', *Journal of International Marketing*, **7**(1), 34–56.

Li, Haiyang and Kwaku Atuahene-Gima (2001), 'Product innovation strategy and the performance of new technology ventures in China', *Academy of Management Journal*, **44**(6), 1123–34.

Li, Haiyang and Kwaku Atuahene-Gima (2002), 'The adoption of agency business activity, product innovation, and performance in Chinese technology ventures', *Strategic Management Journal*, **23**(6), 469–90.

Li, Ji, Leonard Karakowsky and Kevin Lam (2002), 'East meets East and East meets West: the case of Sino-Japanese and Sino-West joint ventures in China', *Journal of Management Studies*, **39**(6), 841–63.

Lin, Carolyn A. (2001), 'Cultural values reflected in Chinese and American television advertising', *Journal of Advertising*, **30**(4), 83–94.

Lin, Xiaohua and Richard Germain (1998), 'Sustaining satisfactory joint venture relationships: the role of conflict resolution strategy', *Journal of International Business Studies*, **29**(1), 179–96.

Lin, Xiaohua and Richard Germain (1999), 'Predicting international joint venture interaction fre-quency in U.S.–Chinese ventures', *Journal of International Marketing*, **7**(2), 5–23.

Lin, Xiaohua and Richard Germain (2003), 'Product quality orientation and its performance impli-cations in Chinese state-owned enterprises', *Journal of International Marketing*, **11**(2), 59–78.

Liu, Sandra S., Xueming Luo and Yi-Zheng Shi (2002), 'Integrating customer orientation, corpor-ate entrepreneurship and learning orientation in organizations-in-transition: an empirical study', *International Journal of Research in Marketing*, **19**(4), 367–82.

Lovett, Steve, Lee C. Simmons and Raja Kali (1999), 'Guanxi versus the market: ethics and efficiency', *Journal of International Business Studies*, **30**(2), 231–47.

Luk, Chung-leung, Oliver H.M. Yau, Alan C.B. Tse, Leo Y.M. Sin and Raymond P.M. Chow (2005), 'Stakeholder orientation and business performance: the case of service companies in China', *Journal of International Marketing*, **13**(1), 89–110.

Luo, Xueming, K. Sivakumar and Sandra S. Liu (2005), 'Globalization, marketing resources, and performance: evidence from China', *Journal of the Academy of Marketing Science*, **33**(1), 50–65.

Luo, Xueming, David A. Griffith, Sandra S. Liu and Yi-Zheng Shi (2004), 'The effects of customer relationships and social capital on firm performance: a Chinese business illustration', *Journal of International Marketing*, **12**(4), 25–45.

Luo, Yadong (1997), 'Partner selection and venturing success: the case of joint ventures with firms in the People's Republic of China', *Organization Science*, **8**(6), 648–62.

Luo, Yadong (1998), 'Timing of investment and international expansion performance in China', *Journal of International Business Studies*, **29**(2), 391–407.

Luo, Yadong (1999), 'Time-based experience and international expansion: the case of an emerging economy', *Journal of Management Studies*, **36**(4), 505–34.

Luo, Yadong (2001a), 'Antecedents and consequences of personal attachment in cross-cultural cooperative ventures', *Administrative Science Quarterly*, **46**(2), 177–201.

Luo, Yadong (2001b), 'Determinants of entry in an emerging economy: a multilevel approach', *Journal of Management Studies*, **38**(3), 443–72.

Luo, Yadong (2001c), 'Toward a cooperative view of MNC-host government relations: building blocks and performance implications', *Journal of International Business Studies*, **32**(3), 401–19.

Luo, Yadong (2002a), 'Capability exploitation and building in a foreign market: implications for multinational enterprises', *Organization Science*, **13**(1), 48–63.

Luo, Yadong (2002b), 'Contract, cooperation, and performance in international joint ventures', *Strategic Management Journal*, **23**(10), 903–19.

Luo, Yadong (2002c), 'Product diversification in international joint ventures: performance impli-cations in an emerging market', *Strategic Management Journal*, **23**(1), 1–20.

Luo, Yadong (2002d), 'Stimulating exchange in international joint ventures: an attachment-based view', *Journal of International Business Studies*, **33**(1), 169–81.

Luo, Yadong (2003a), 'Industrial dynamics and managerial networking in an emerging market: the case of China', *Strategic Management Journal*, **24**(13), 1315–27.

Luo, Yadong (2003b), 'Market-seeking MNEs in an emerging market: how parent–subsidiary links shape overseas success', *Journal of International Business Studies*, **34**(3), 290–309.

Luo, Yadong and Seung Ho Park (2001), 'Strategic alignment and performance of market-seeking MNCs in China', *Strategic Management Journal*, **22**(2), 141–55.

Luo, Yadong and Mike W. Peng (1999), 'Learning to compete in a transition economy: experience, environment, and performance', *Journal of International Business Studies*, **30**(2), 269–95.

Luo, Yadong, Oded Shenkar and Mee-Kau Nyaw (2001), 'A dual parent perspective on control and performance in international joint ventures: lessons from a developing economy', *Journal of International Business Studies*, **32**(1), 41–58.

McGuinness, Norman, Nigel Campbell and James Leontiades (1991), 'Selling machinery to China: Chinese perceptions of strategies and relationships', *Journal of International Business Studies*, **22**(2), 187–207.

Osland, Gregory E. (1994), 'Successful operating strategies in the performance of U.S.–China joint ventures', *Journal of International Marketing*, **2**(4), 53–78.

Osland, Gregory E. and S. Tamer Cavusgil (1996), 'Performance issues in U.S.–China joint ventures', *California Management Review*, **38**(2), 106–30.

Pan, Yigang (1996), 'Influences on foreign equity ownership level in joint ventures in China', *Journal of International Business Studies*, **27**(1), 1–26.

Pan, Yigang (1997), 'The formation of Japanese and U.S. equity joint ventures in China', *Strategic Management Journal*, **18**(3), 247–54.

Pan, Yigang (2002), 'Equity ownership in international joint ventures: the impact of source country factors', *Journal of International Business Studies*, **33**(2), 375–84.

Pan, Yigang and Peter S.K. Chi (1999), 'Financial performance and survival of multinational corporations in China', *Strategic Management Journal*, **20**(4), 359–74.

Pan, Yigang and Xiaolian Li (2000), 'Joint venture formation of very large multinational firms', *Journal of International Business Studies*, **31**(1), 179–89.

Pan, Yigang and Bernd Schmitt (1996), 'Language and brand attitudes: impact of script and sound matching in Chinese and English', *Journal of Consumer Psychology*, **5**(3), 263–77.

Pan, Yigang and David K. Tse (1996), 'Cooperative strategies between foreign firms in an overseas country', *Journal of International Business Studies*, **27**(5), 929–46.

Pan, Yigang, Shaomin Li and David K. Tse (1999), 'The impact of order and mode of market entry on profitability and market share', *Journal of International Business Studies*, **30**(1), 81–103.

Park, Seung Ho and Yadong Luo (2001), 'Guanxi and organizational dynamics: organizational networking in Chinese firms', *Strategic Management Journal*, **22**(5), 455–77.

Parry, Mark E. and X. Michael Song (1994), 'Identifying new product successes in China', *The Journal of Product Innovation Management*, **11**(1), 15–30.

Peng, Mike W. (1997), 'Firm growth in transitional economies: three longitudinal cases from China, 1989–96', *Organization Studies*, **18**(3), 385–413.

Peng, Mike W. and Yadong Luo (2000), 'Managerial ties and firm performance in a transition economy: the nature of a micro–macro link', *Academy of Management Journal*, **43**(3), 486–501.

Prendergast, Gerard, Yizheng Shi and Douglas West (2001), 'Organizational buying and advertising agency–client relationships in China', *Journal of Advertising*, **30**(2), 61–71.

Rice, Marshall D. and Zaiming Lu (1988), 'A content analysis of Chinese magazine advertisements', *Journal of Advertising*, **17**(4), 43–8.

Schmitt, Bernd H. and Shi Zhang (1998), 'Language structure and categorization: a study of classifiers in consumer cognition, judgment, and choice', *Journal of Consumer Research*, **25**(2), 108–22.

Schmitt, Bernd H., Yigang Pan and Nader T. Tavassoli (1994), 'Language and consumer memory: the impact of linguistic differences between Chinese and English', *Journal of Consumer Research*, **21**(3), 419–31.

Schroath, Frederick W., Michael Y. Hu and Haiyang Chen (1993), 'Country-of-origin effects of foreign investments in the People's Republic of China', *Journal of International Business Studies*, **24**(2), 277–90.

Shenkar, Oded and Jiatao Li (1999), 'Knowledge search in international cooperative ventures', *Organization Science*, **10**(2), 134–43.

Simmons, Lee C. and Robert M. Schindler (2003), 'Cultural superstitions and the price endings used in Chinese advertising', *Journal of International Marketing*, **11**(2), 101–11.

Sin, Leo Y.M., Alan C.B. Tse, Oliver H.M. Yau, Raymond P.M. Chow and Jenny S.Y. Lee (2005), 'Market orientation, relationship marketing orientation, and business performance: the moderating effects of economic ideology and industry type', *Journal of International Marketing*, **13**(1), 36–57.

Song, X. Michael and Mark E. Parry (1994), 'The dimensions of industrial new product success and failure in state enterprises in the People's Republic of China', *The Journal of Product Innovation Management*, **11**(2), 105–18.

Song, X. Michael, C. Anthony Di Benedetto and Lisa Z. Song (2000), 'Pioneering advantage in new service development: a multi-country study of managerial perceptions', *The Journal of Product Innovation Management*, **17**(5), 378–92.

Song, X. Michael, C. Anthony Di Benedetto and Yuzhen Lisa Zhao (1999), 'Pioneering advantages in manufacturing and service industries: empirical evidence from nine countries', *Strategic Management Journal*, **20**(9), 811–36.

Stayman, Douglas M. and Rohit Deshpande (1989), 'Situational ethnicity and consumer behavior', *Journal of Consumer Research*, **16**(3), 361–70.

Talukdar, Debabrata, K. Sudhir and Andrew Ainslie (2002), 'Investigating new product diffusion across products and countries', *Marketing Science*, **21**(1), 97–114.

Tan, Justin (2002), 'Impact of ownership type on environment–strategy linkage and performance: evidence from a transitional economy', *Journal of Management Studies*, **39**(3), 333–54.

Tan, J. Justin and Robert J. Litschert (1994), 'Environment–strategy relationship and its performance implications: an empirical study of the Chinese electronics industry', *Strategic Management Journal*, **15**(1), 1–20.

Tavassoli, Nader T. (1999), 'Temporal and associative memory in Chinese and English', *Journal of Consumer Research*, **26**(2), 170–81.

Tavassoli, Nader T. and Jin K. Han (2002), 'Auditory and visual brand identifiers in Chinese and English', *Journal of International Marketing*, **10**(2), 13–28.

Tavassoli, Nader T. and Yih Hwai Lee (2003), 'The differential interaction of auditory and visual advertising elements with Chinese and English', *Journal of Marketing Research*, **40**(4), 468–80.

The World Bank Group (2005), 'World Development Indicators database', The World Bank Group (available at http://www.worldbank.org/data/), reviewed 26 August.

Tihanyi, Laszlo, David A. Griffith and Craig J. Russell (2005), 'The effect of cultural distance on entry mode choice, international diversification, and MNE performance: a meta-analysis', *Journal of International Business Studies*, **36**(3), 270–83.

Tsang, Eric W.K. (2002), 'Acquiring knowledge by foreign partners for international joint ventures in a transition economy: learning-by-doing and learning myopia', *Strategic Management Journal*, **23**(9), 835–54.

Tse, David K., Russell W. Belk and Nan Zhou (1989), 'Becoming a consumer society: a longitudinal and cross-cultural content analysis of print ads from Hong Kong, the People's Republic of China, and Taiwan', *Journal of Consumer Research*, **15**(4), 457–72.

Tse, David K., June Francis and Jan Walls (1994), 'Cultural differences in conducting intra- and inter-cultural negotiations: a Sino-Canadian comparison', *Journal of International Business Studies*, **25**(3), 537–55.

Tse, David K., Yigang Pan and Kevin Y. Au (1997), 'How MNCs choose entry modes and form alliances: the China experience', *Journal of International Business Studies*, **28**(4), 779–805.

Tse, David K., Kam-hon Lee, Ilan Vertinsky and Donald A. Wehrung (1988), 'Does culture matter? A cross-cultural study of executives' choice, decisiveness, and risk adjustment in international marketing', *Journal of Marketing*, **52**(4), 81–95.

Vanhonacker, Wilfried R. and Yigang Pan (1997), 'The impact of national culture, business scope, and geographic location on joint venture operations in China', *Journal of International Marketing*, **5**(3), 11–30.

Wang, Cheng Lu, Terry Bristol, John C. Mowen and Goutam Chakraborty (2000), 'Alternative modes of self-construal: dimensions of connectedness–separateness and advertising appeals to the cultural and gender-specific self', *Journal of Consumer Psychology*, **9**(2), 107–15.

Wei, Yinghong (Susan) and Neil A. Morgan (2004), 'Supportiveness of organizational climate, market orientation, and new product performance in Chinese firms', *The Journal of Product Innovation Management*, **21**(6), 375–88.

White, Steven and Xielin Liu (2001), 'Transition trajectories for market structure and firm strategy in China', *Journal of Management Studies*, **38**(1), 103–24.

Xie, Jinhong, Michael Song and Anne Stringfellow (2003), 'Antecedents and consequences of goal incongruity on new product development in five countries: a marketing view', *The Journal of Product Innovation Management*, **20**(3), 233–50.

Xin, Katherine R. and Jone L. Pearce (1996), '*Guanxi*: connections as substitutes for formal institutional support', *Academy of Management Journal*, **39**(6), 1641–58.

Yan, Aimin and Barbara Gray (1994), 'Bargaining power, management control, and performance in United States–China joint ventures: a comparative case study', *Academy of Management Journal*, **37**(6), 1478–517.

Yan, Aimin and Barbara Gray (2001), 'Antecedents and effects of parent control in international joint ventures', *Journal of Management Studies*, **38**(3), 393–416.

Yin, Jiafei (1999), 'International advertising strategies in China: a worldwide survey of foreign advertisers', *Journal of Advertising Research*, **39**(6), 25–35.

Yiu, Daphne, Garry D. Bruton and Yuan Lu (2005), 'Understanding business group performance in an emerging economy: acquiring resources and capabilities in order to prosper', *Journal of Management Studies*, **42**(1), 183–206.

Zhang, Jing and Sharon Shavitt (2003), 'Cultural values in advertisements to the Chinese X-generation: promoting modernity and individualism', *Journal of Advertising*, **32**(1), 23–33.

Zhang, Shi and Bernd H. Schmitt (2001), 'Creating local brands in multilingual international markets', *Journal of Marketing Research*, **38**(3), 313–25.

Zhang, Shi and Bernd H. Schmitt (2004), 'Activating sound and meaning: the role of language proficiency in bilingual consumer environments', *Journal of Consumer Research*, **31**(1), 220–28.

Zhang, Yan and Nandini Rajagopalan (2002), 'Inter-partner credible threat in international joint ventures: an infinitely repeated prisoner's dilemma model', *Journal of International Business Studies*, **33**(3), 457–78.

Zhang, Yong and Betsy D. Gelb (1996), 'Matching advertising appeals to culture: the influence of products' use conditions', *Journal of Advertising*, **25**(3), 29–46.

Zhao, Zheng, Jaideep Anand and Will Mitchell (2005), 'A dual networks perspective on inter-organizational transfer of R&D capabilities: international joint ventures in the Chinese automotive industry', *Journal of Management Studies*, **42**(1), 127–60.

Zhou, Lianxi and Michael K. Hui (2003), 'Symbolic value of foreign products in the People's Republic of China', *Journal of International Marketing*, **11**(2), 36–58.

Zhou, Nan and Russell W. Belk (2004), 'Chinese consumer readings of global and local advertising appeals', *Journal of Advertising*, **33**(3), 63–76.

Zhou, Kevin Zheng, Chenting Su and Yeqing Bao (2002a), 'A paradox of price–quality and market efficiency: a comparative study of the US and China markets', *International Journal of Research in Marketing*, **19**(4), 349–65.

Zhou, Dongsheng, Weijiong Zhang and Ilan Vertinsky (2002b), 'Advertising trends in urban China', *Journal of Advertising Research*, **42**(3), 73–81.

Zhou, Nan, Dongsheng Zhou and Ming Ouyang (2003), 'Long-term effects of television advertising on sales of consumer durables and nondurables: the case of China', *Journal of Advertising*, **32**(2), 45–54.

Zhou, Kevin Zheng, Chi Kin (Bennett) Yim and David K. Tse (2005a), 'The effects of strategic orientations on technology- and market-based breakthrough innovations', *Journal of Marketing*, **69**(2), 42–60.

Zhou, Shuhua, Peiqin Zhou and Fei Xue (2005b), 'Visual differences in U.S. and Chinese television commercials', *Journal of Advertising*, **34**(1), 111–19.

APPENDIX 10.1   JOURNAL LIST

Table 10.2   Marketing journals

Name	Number of articles
International Journal of Research in Marketing	7
Journal of Advertising	5
Journal of Advertising Research	1
Journal of Consumer Psychology	4
Journal of Consumer Research	6
Journal of International Marketing	17
Journal of Marketing	4
Journal of Marketing Research	2
Journal of Product Innovation Management	6
Journal of Retailing	1
Journal of the Academy of Marketing Science	3
Marketing Letters	0
Marketing Science	2

Table 10.3   Management journals

Name	Number of articles
Academy of Management Journal	6
Academy of Management Review	0
Administrative Science Quarterly	1
California Management Review	0
China Quarterly	0
Harvard Business Review	0
Human Relations	0
Human Resource Management	0
Industrial and Labor Relations Review	0
Journal of Applied Psychology	0
Journal of Cross-cultural Psychology	2
Journal of International Business Studies	24
Journal of Management	0
Journal of Management Studies	10
Journal of Occupational and Organizational Psychology	0
Journal of Organizational Behavior	0
Journal of Vocational Behavior	1
Organizational Behavior and Human Decision Processes	0
Organization Science	4
Organization Studies	0
Personnel Psychology	0
Sloan Management Review	0
Strategic Management Journal	12

APPENDIX 10.2 MODERATING VARIABLES

Table 10.4 Moderating variables

Author(s)	Year	Journal	Research topic	Article title	Moderating variable(s)
Aaker and Schmitt	2001	Journal of Cross-cultural Psychology	Customer	Culture-dependent assimilation and differentiation of the self: preferences for consumption symbols in the United States and China	Self-construal
Aaker and Williams	1998	Journal of Consumer Research	Customer	Empathy versus pride: the influence of emotional appeals across cultures	Individualism/collectivism
Bagozzi et al.	2000	Journal of Consumer Psychology	Customer	Cultural and situational contingencies and the theory of reasoned action: application to fast food restaurant consumption	Independent/interdependent-based culture
Bian and Keller	1999	Journal of Consumer Psychology	Customer	Patterns of fairness judgments in North America and the People's Republic of China	Risk aversion, individualism/collectivism
Cervellon and Dube	2002	Journal of Cross-cultural Psychology	Customer	Assessing the cross-cultural applicability of affective and cognitive components of attitude	Food attitude
Dube et al.	2003	International Journal of Research in Marketing	Customer	Should consumer attitudes be reduced to their affective and cognitive bases? Validation of a hierarchical model	Food attitude
Keillor et al.	2004	Journal of International Marketing	Customer	A study of the service encounter in eight countries	Long-term latent demand for consumer products
Pan and Schmitt	1996	Journal of Consumer Psychology	Customer	Language and brand attitudes: impact of script and sound matching in Chinese and English	Linguistic structure
Schmitt et al.	1994	Journal of Consumer Research	Customer	Language and consumer memory: the impact of linguistic differences between Chinese and English	Linguistic structure
Tavassoli	1999	Journal of Consumer Research	Customer	Temporal and associative memory in Chinese and English	Linguistic structure

Tavassoli and Han	2002	Journal of International Marketing	Customer	Auditory and visual brand identifiers in Chinese and English	Linguistic structure
Tavassoli and Lee	2003	Journal of Marketing Research	Customer	The differential interaction of auditory and visual advertising elements with Chinese and English	Linguistic structure
Wang et al.	2000	Journal of Consumer Psychology	Customer	Alternative modes of self-construal: dimensions of connectedness-separateness and advertising appeals to the cultural and gender-specific self	Self-schema
Zhou et al.	2002a	International Journal of Research in Marketing	Customer	A paradox of price-quality and market efficiency: a comparative study of the US and China markets	Market information efficiency
Atuahene-Gima and Li	2002	Journal of Marketing	Firm	When does trust matter? Antecedents and contingent effects of supervisee trust on performance in selling new products in China and the United States	Individualism/collectivism, uncertainty avoidance
Calantone et al.	1996	Marketing Science	Firm	Controllable factors of new product success: a cross-national comparison	Low proficiency of marketing activities, varied quality of industrial products
Fang et al.	2004	Journal of the Academy of Marketing Science	Firm	Goal-setting paradoxes? Trade-offs between working hard and working smart: the United States versus China	high/low-context communication style
Hui et al.	2004a	Journal of International Business Studies	Firm	Empowerment effects across cultures	Power distance
Hui et al.	2004b	International Journal of Research in Marketing	Firm	Reactions of service employees to organization–customer conflict: a cross-cultural comparison	Individualism/collectivism
Lee et al.	2005	Journal of International Marketing	Firm	Trading favors for marketing advantage: evidence from Hong Kong, China and the United States	Developmental differences
Tse et al.	1994	Journal of International Business Studies	Firm	Cultural differences in conducting intra- and intercultural negotiations: a Sino–Canadian comparison	Individualism/collectivism, group harmony

11. Global retailers and Asian manufacturers

Gary G. Hamilton and Misha Petrovic

The principal thesis of this chapter is that the single most important driver of Asia's economic growth has been, and continues to be, the symbiotic relationship between large American and European retailers and brand name merchandisers, on the one hand, and Asian manufacturers, on the other hand.[1] In the past 40 years, East Asian countries have become the world's chief site for sourcing manufactured consumer goods. The most important firms that source goods from Asia are the large retailers and brand-name merchandisers. At first, many of these were American firms, but, since the 1980s, European retailers and merchandisers have also increasingly sourced goods from Asian manufacturers. As these American and European retail firms have become larger, more globally oriented and more competitive with each other, they have increasingly come to rely on Asian manufacturing to supply them with high-quality, but relatively inexpensive, goods.

Beginning in the late 1970s, Asian firms, although remaining very competitive with each other, gradually worked out a division of labour, so that some economies in the region developed large vertically integrated conglomerates specializing in producing finished products, and other economies developed extensive inter-firm networks specializing in producing small to large batches of goods designed for niche markets. In the 1990s, responding to difficult market conditions, many of the leading manufacturers from throughout the region (namely, from Taiwan, Hong Kong, South Korea and Japan) began to relocate some of their factories to China, leading to extraordinarily rapid growth in both the Chinese economy and in the exports from China to the US and Europe. This chapter will describe and explain these underlying trends. The first step in the explanation is to outline the transformation of retailing in the US that begins after World War II.

THE NATIONAL ORGANIZATION OF US RETAILING BETWEEN 1945 AND 1965

The consolidation and concentration in retailing in the US occurred at different times and for different reasons than had been the case in manufacturing. In the decades before World War II, the manufacturing sectors of the American economy had already gone through several periods of mergers and massive consolidations that not only resulted in vertical and horizontal control over processes of production, but, by virtue of the economic power of manufacturing firms, also allowed them to control the distribution and retailing of their products as well (Chandler, 1977; Perrow, 2002). For instance, the automobile manufacturers developed franchised retail outlets, as did some consumer appliances makers (for example RCA and GE). More often, manufacturers dealt directly with wholesalers that in turn distributed products to many small retail stores, most of which were independently owned.

Despite the preponderance of small independently owned retailers, there were a number of large retail chains that began to emerge before World War II. The mail-order mass retailers, such as Sears and Roebuck and Montgomery Wards, were very prominent before World War I, and in the 1920s, with the growth of cities and the decline of rural America, these same firms began to establish chain stores in urban cores throughout the US. Also the largest retailer before World War II was A&P (Atlantic and Pacific) that had established a national chain of grocery stores early in the twentieth century. These chain stores, however, were important exceptions to the rule, as most retail firms, whatever the type of product they sold, continued to be small, regionally concentrated and privately owned. Clothing, shoes, groceries, hardware and building supplies, household appliances, as well as most other consumer products, were sold through such locally or regionally owned stores. These stores obtained their goods through supply lines that they neither directly controlled, nor could indirectly influence through their buying power. Therefore, with only a few exceptions before World War II, there was a stark contrast between the relative concentration of manufacturers in their respective sectors, and the relative lack of concentration of retailers in their respective sectors.

Immediately after World War II, therefore, the large-firm model of corporate capitalism predominated (Perrow, 2002; Chandler, 1990). In the US, the position of General Motors, Ford, IBM, General Electric, Westinghouse, Boeing and a long list of other large corporations in nearly every economic sector seemed unassailable. Likewise in the early postwar years, mammoth business groups in Europe and Japan, such as Daimler-Benz, Volkswagen, Mitsubishi and Mitsui, re-emerged stronger than they were before the war, and new giants, such as Toyota and Sony, suddenly entered the scene.

THE GLOBALIZATION OF SUPPLIER MARKETS FOR US RETAILERS AFTER 1965

In 1965, the US ran its first postwar trade deficit with Japan. The deficit was rather small, US$334 million, and did not represent a major cause for concern, especially in comparison with the massive US$6.3 billion trade surplus with the rest of the world. In retrospect, however, the beginning of the US trade deficit with Japan could easily be interpreted as a telling, even if only symbolic, indicator of the new era in the evolution of the US economy, characterized by persistent trade deficits with Asian economies and the flooding of domestic markets by foreign manufactures. In sharp contrast with the previous period, the structure and dynamics of the post-1965 US economy have been profoundly affected by its rapidly developing links with the global economy. In 1965, the ratio of total US international trade (imports and exports) to its GDP stood at a relatively modest 10 per cent, a little bit over half of what it was at its all-time high in 1919, and still lower than in the years before the Great Depression. Fifteen years later, in 1980, it reached 24 per cent. In the same period, the US economy changed from a net exporter, the position it had held since the 1870s, to a net importer, with a trade deficit in 1980 approaching US$20 billion.

Trade figures from 1965 on show that imports in most major categories of manufactured goods constituted a growing percentage of US consumption (Feenstra and

Hamilton, 2006). In 1965, imports accounted for less than 10 per cent of total US consumption in all major categories of manufactured consumer goods, but import penetration in all categories of consumer (non-grocery) goods rose rapidly after that. Where did these imports come from? The answer is that East Asian economies (Japan, South Korea, Taiwan, Hong Kong and China) accounted for over 50 per cent in almost all categories of imports from 1975 on. We will now disaggregate these trends decade by decade to show the dramatic shifts that occurred from 1965 to the present time.

1965–1975: CREATING ASIAN SUPPLIERS FOR AMERICAN RETAILERS

Beginning around 1965, US imports of foreign goods from Asia begin to rise abruptly. If we examine the detailed data from US Customs, some clear trends begin to emerge (Feenstra and Hamilton, 2006). First, Taiwan and South Korea joined Japan and Hong Kong as the principal Asian economies exporting to the US, with Singapore coming somewhat later and providing smaller quantities of a narrower range of US imports than the other Asian newly industrialized economies (NIEs). In 1965, imports from Taiwan and South Korea were almost non-existent. Starting around 1968 for Taiwan and 1970 for South Korea, their exports jumped suddenly.

Second, from a US perspective, during the first decade (1965–75), these economies contributed only a very small percentage of total US consumption, even in the fastest growing categories. But from the perspective of the exporting economies, these goods exported to the US accounted for a very large percentage of the total growth of these economies. This was especially true for Hong Kong, Taiwan and South Korea, all of which maintained low levels of domestic consumption during the first several decades of industrialization.

The third trend is a very rapid increase in the number of categories of items being exported. Assuming that the pattern of US imports in 1972 reflects emerging trends that started a few years earlier, we see a very rapid increase in the number of seven-digit custom classifications for items exported from South Korea and Taiwan between 1972 and 1988. Already by 1972, Taiwan exported to the US over 2000, and Korea over 1000, categories of goods. These totals rapidly rise and peak in 1985 and 1986, at levels approaching 6000 categories for Taiwan and 5000 for South Korea.

The fourth trend shows that, throughout the period, despite the wide variety of exported goods, a very high percentage of their total value was concentrated in only a very few product categories. The highest concentration for both countries occurs in the earliest period, with nearly 50 per cent of the value of South Korea's exports to the US and 25 per cent of the value of Taiwan's exports contained in only ten categories of seven-digit classifications. Indeed, in 1972, nearly 90 per cent of the value of South Korean exports, and nearly 80 per cent of the value of Taiwan's exports was in the top 100 categories.

For the period before 1975, what explains these four emergent trends? Instead of the usual inchoate supply-side stories used to explain the 'Asian miracle', most often in terms of developmental states (see chapters in Part III of this volume), smart and trusting entrepreneurs and free trade regimes, we should see that these particular trends are the direct results of the emergence of global intermediaries and their abilities to create supplier markets, often including suppliers themselves, for retail products to be sold in the US.

Therefore, rather than simply asking what comparative advantages these few Asian economies had in this period (Gereffi and Wyman, 1990), we should ask instead why most of the major US retailers began to source products in East Asia between 1965 and 1975.

First of all, we know that most of the major retailers did begin to source during this period (for example Jung, 1984; Gereffi, 1994; Gereffi and Korzeniewicz, 1994). They developed networks of buying offices (or contracted with major sourcing firms) in Hong Kong, Taiwan and South Korea in the late 1960s and early 1970s, and they quickly ramped up their orders from these countries in the following years. For example, Sears established its buying office in Taiwan in 1967, Kmart and J.C. Penney in 1971, and Associated Merchandising Corporation (which bought for Dayton-Hudson, Federated Department Stores and Target, among many others) and Mast Industries (a wholly owned subsidiary of The Limited) in 1973. At about the same time, most of these US retailers opened offices in South Korea (Jung, 1984; Rhee *et al.*, 1984).

The reason they came to Asia in the first place was their rapid expansion and intense competition in the US during the late 1960s and early 1970s (Bluestone *et al.*, 1981; Bucklin, 1972; Hanchett, 1996). In response to Fair Trade laws, many of the largest department stores began to develop private labels clothing that they could use to undercut their brand-name competitors. The department stores first bought their private label clothing from American-based manufacturing companies located in the South. When orders rapidly expanded, these Southern manufacturers began to arrange for a portion of their manufacturing to be done in Asia. Their ability to source goods in Asia was facilitated by Japanese trading companies, especially Mitsui, that served as intermediaries between American firms that ordered the goods and the Asian firms that manufactured them (Kojima and Ozawa, 1984; Bonacich *et al.*, 1994; Yoshino and Lifson, 1986; Tsurumi, 1984).

With the initial success of Japanese trading companies in creating competent suppliers, it soon became apparent to all concerned that neither the Japanese trading companies nor other types of go-betweens were needed any longer to match US retailers to non-Japanese Asian manufacturers. The general department stores and, more importantly, the new generation of discount and specialty retailers, especially those specializing in fashion apparel and footwear, eliminated the middlemen and began directly to arrange their own contracting relationships in Asia. They were helped in this matchmaking effort by local firms and business groups that established their own trading companies to represent local manufacturers and to negotiate with US retailers.

By 1975, Asian supplier markets had been created, partly by Japanese multinationals and partly by local efforts, and a model of how to do contract manufacturing in Asia (and elsewhere) was in the process of being developed and institutionalized. From the beginning, contract manufacturing spawned a relationship between retailers and manufacturers that did not exist in the US: beginning on a small scale in the early 1960s, but then accelerating rapidly after that, retailers started to source directly batches of differentiated goods specially ordered for sale in niche markets. The standard reason given for the early contract manufacturing in East Asia is the cheap labour that of course was a factor. But even more important was that American-based retailers, engaged in hot competition in their home markets, began to develop and organize manufacturing directly without owning factories, and without the corporate and labour negotiations that would be involved in subcontracting with American-based firms. This model of brand-name merchandising blurred the distinction between retailing and manufacturing, so much so that many manufacturing firms, such as The Gap, The Limited, Nike and, later, Dell Computers, began to appear that did not actually manufacture anything. These firms rather focused almost entirely on building and assessing consumer demand, designing products for consumer niches, merchandising those products to the target markets, and building relationships with Asian manufacturers that would supply their goods (Gereffi, 1994).

During this same decade when the American retail sector was beginning its transformation, the East Asian economies were developing the capacity to respond quickly to the needs of intermediary buyers for reliable infrastructures for international trade. The East Asian NIEs founded extensive trade and manufacturing associations and built world trade centres, all to facilitate the matching process between buyers and potential manufacturers. At the same time, these economies began rapidly to establish the physical and financial infrastructure that would facilitate international trade (for example ports, shipping, containerization, fast freight forwarding, railways, highways, as well as banking, credit markets, stock markets and corporate insurance). These infrastructure projects and market institutions allowed global intermediaries to develop the industries and to create competitive supplier markets throughout East Asia and allowed Asian manufacturers to become increasingly more responsive to big buyer demands.

1975–1985: DIVERSIFICATION OF SUPPLIER MARKETS FOR US RETAILERS

The rapid expansion and growing diversity of retailing in the US and the equally rapid expansion of Asian manufacturing during the period from 1965 to 1985 are two aspects of the same economic phenomenon. After the first ten years, by 1975, the retailers, the various sets of intermediaries (trading companies) and the Asian manufacturers had, provisionally, worked out the basic method of contract manufacturing. Moreover, the governments and industrialists in the key areas (Japan, Hong Kong, Taiwan, South Korea and Singapore) had built sufficient economic infrastructures to facilitate this type of long-distance manufacturing.

At this moment, around 1975, the US slipped into a severe recession. The Vietnam War had ended precipitously and the first oil shock had occurred. A few years later, in 1980, a second oil shock happened. The traditional retailing sector and US manufacturers both declined rapidly during the period. As occurs in most economic downturns, in this recession, many American consumers saved money by shopping where they could find the lowest prices. It was in this period that competition between the new discount and specialty retailers, on the one hand, and the older, more traditional retailers, on the other hand, came to a head, and set off a wave of mergers and acquisitions, resulting in even greater consolidation within the US retail sector (Bluestone *et al.*, 1981). The number of mass discounters dwindled from over ten to four major chains. Moreover, the major department stores, such as Macy's and the Bon Marché, curtailed their in-store brands and began to build mini-boutiques within their stores, featuring such brand name apparel manufacturers as Polo, Ralph Lauren and Anne Klein. In addition, many of the same brand-name manufacturers began to open factory outlet stores in scattered locations around the US and elsewhere (Cohen, 2002).

The rise of the new retailers stocked with many items manufactured in Asia contributed to a reorganization of US manufacturing that occurred in the late 1970s and the early 1980s. Many analysts of the period began to worry that American firms were no longer competitive (Bluestone and Harrison, 1982). Many older and well-established manufacturing firms were forced into bankruptcy, and many survivors, including IBM, among many others had to restructure. The Upper Midwest, formerly renowned as the industrial heartland of America, became widely known as the 'Rustbelt'. An important cause of this crisis in American manufacturing was that many traditional retailers had maintained their American-based supply lines and stocked their shelves with more traditional types of products. As these retailers lost customers, because of their competitors' low prices and the availability of new products carried by other retailers, the orders with American manufacturers declined even as the imports of foreign products surged.

The need to cut costs and to restructure led once-powerful manufacturers to join the ranks of the factory-less brand-name merchandisers. Beginning in the late 1970s and continuing through the 1990s, such firms as Schwinn (bicycles), Eddie Bauer (specialty outdoor clothing), General Electric and Westinghouse (household appliances) and Compaq (computers) closed all or most of their consumer product factories in the US, and began to contract all or a large part of their products overseas, mostly in East Asia. In making the move to Asia, many American firms actually invested in and helped to organize the Asian production of their branded goods. Others played a more passive role, letting the Asian manufacturers perform the primary entrepreneurial functions. In both regards, these businesses simply followed in the footsteps of the earlier firms, copying the first-comers' techniques of contract manufacturing and direct sourcing of component parts and finished goods (Appelbaum and Smith, 1996). What started in textiles had, by 1985, spread to almost every category of consumer goods, including a full range of high-technology products, most of which were never mass-produced in the US. In fact, the Asian supply lines for high-technology products had been sufficiently developed by the early 1980s for Dell Computer Corporation and Gateway to owe their successes entirely to contract manufacturing, much of which centred in Taiwan (see also Chapter 16 in this volume). These firms started their businesses, respectively, in 1984 and 1985.

From 1975 on, the general trend has been for these Asian economies to specialize, and therefore to diverge in what they produce (Feenstra and Hamilton, 2006; Orrù *et al.*, 1997). The reason for this divergence is the system of production that emerges in each economy in response to repeat orders from big retail buyers that, in turn, reinforce what was ordered there. South Korea, for example, started the industrialization process in the late 1960s with a few large and competitive business groups and, as the orders began to come in, these large groups, known locally as *octopi*, gobbled up most of the opportunities presented by foreign buyers. The result was that the big business groups, the *chaebol*, controlled the flow of orders and vertically integrated to prevent other *chaebol* from obtaining the orders.

By contrast, Taiwan began the industrialization process with many small firms competing for the early orders and no major players that could monopolize the opportunities. The Taiwanese businesspeople began from the outset to specialize in products that small firms, interlinked in small networks, could produce profitably. As the orders began to flow, the Taiwanese small and medium-sized manufacturers became experts at producing a wide variety of products in batches, and the largest private-sector enterprises, usually family-owned business groups, became suppliers of intermediate goods (for example plastics, synthetic yarn, textiles, chemicals) and business services (for example shipping, insurance).

The big buyers in those locations quickly became sophisticated in sourcing their products with those entrepreneurs who could best produce them. For instance, Nike ordered very large runs of low-end standardized running shoes from South Korea, and their high-end and more specialized shoes from Taiwan. In the industrializing economies of East Asia, the ordering system reinforced the competitive dynamics that drove the divergence in the industrial structure of each country, quite apart from anything that the government of that country did (see also Chapter 12 in this volume). By 1985, the basic organizational trajectories of these economies were firmly in place and dependent on their continuing linkages with US retailers and merchandisers.

1985–1997: RATIONALIZATION OF GLOBAL SUPPLY LINES

Two developments occurred in the mid-1980s that would forever restructure the organization of Asian economies. The first was the Plaza Accords signed in 1985 and the second was the global implementation of 'lean retailing', a development that started in the previous decade, but was only gradually implemented in Asia in the late 1980s and the 1990s. On 22 September 1985, at the Plaza Hotel in New York City, after years of running trade deficits with South Korea, Japan and Taiwan, the US completed negotiations on a currency reform measure that all parties signed. The Plaza Accord, as this currency reform became known, removed the pegged trading range of East Asian currencies with the US dollar and allowed the Asian currencies to appreciate by as much as 40 per cent.

The second development was a comprehensive reorganization of global supply lines that resulted from the US retailers' implementation of what is known as 'lean retailing' (Abernathy *et al.*, 1999). Barcodes, scanners and more generally electronic data interchange (EDI) became the medium to continue the trend towards the globalization of supply lines that was already well under way in the late 1960s and the 1970s (Brown, 1997). A core principle of value merchandising – for discount retailers, brand-name merchandisers and specialty retailers – is to match as closely as possible the number and types of goods on hand to the number and types of goods that consumers will actually buy. This involves a precise calculation of consumer demand. In the 1960s and the 1970s, however, value merchandisers and department stores could only anticipate consumer demand, and to hedge their risks they would buy limited quantities of a limited range of each type of differentiated good.

The development of high-powered mainframe computers and database software suitable for inventory control, both of which did not become widely available until the early 1980s, quickly made barcodes and scanners the preferred instruments for assessing consumer choice at the place and time of purchase. By the late 1980s, these innovations allowed retailers and merchandisers to rationalize their supply chains. Other types of retailers in the 1980s commandeered these innovations first designed for grocery stores. At first, however, the adoption of UPC codes was uneven. Many of the older retail firms, such as Sears, not only had predominantly American supply lines, but also had already made large capital investments in developing proprietary, automated inventory systems, and were reluctant to make additional and even larger investments to adopt universal product codes and standardized scanning devices. But after Kmart and Wal-Mart both adopted the technology in the early 1980s and required their vendors to do so as well, most other retailers had to follow suit.

This push into lean retailing occurred at the very time currencies in the leading export economies in Asia were being re-evaluated upwards relative to the US dollar (except for Hong Kong that remained pegged to the US dollar). In the span of just a few years, the Japanese, Taiwanese and, to a lesser degree, South Korean economies went through a momentary period of jubilation, a period when everyone felt much richer and many began to make extravagant purchases at home and abroad. The period of jubilation ended quickly, however, when domestic manufacturers realized that they could no longer meet the price points that the US retailers and merchandisers required.

The currency revaluation stopped the Japanese economy in its tracks, but not its main exporting firms. By the late 1980s, Japanese industries were major OEM suppliers in just a few products (for example microwaves, computers). Instead, many of the largest Japanese business groups had gone to considerable effort to build their own globally rec-ognized brand names (for example Sony, Panasonic and Toyota), or to use their technol-ogy to develop upstream products, such as Toshiba's LCD panels and Shimano's bicycle gears, that they could then sell to all makers of the respective products. In order to remain competitive in terms of price and quality, many major Japanese companies transferred their final assembly sites, along with some production, to other countries. The effect of these foreign direct investments on the domestic economy was widely reported in Japan as the 'hollowing out' of the Japanese economy.

Unlike Japan, South Korea and Taiwan were able to escape severe recessions, and they were even able to increase their exports, but they did so in quite different ways. By 1985, the four largest South Korean *chaebol* (Hyundai, Samsung, Lucky Goldstar and Daewoo) dwarfed all the other business groups in South Korea in size and sales, and virtually monopolized exports from South Korea. After the currency evaluations, these behemoths began to follow the precedent set by the largest Japanese business groups, establishing global brand names and developing higher quality, up-market products.

In the wake of the Plaza Accords, many of Taiwan's export manufacturers faced a serious dilemma (Kao and Hamilton, 2000; Gereffi, 1999). They had OEM contracts for goods that they needed to deliver to US retailers, but they could not produce those goods profitably. If they failed to honour their contracts, the retailers and brand-name mer-chandisers would easily find other manufacturers to make the products. If they stayed in Taiwan and honoured their contracts, they would likely go bankrupt, and lose the con-tract anyway. After several years of hesitation, those small and medium-sized firms making garments, bicycles, footwear and other types of similar consumer goods moved their manufacturing operations to China (see Hsing, 1998). The move occurred suddenly, like a stampede, in a matter of just a couple of years.

The period between 1985 and 1997 was characterized, then, by further divergence of national development strategies, initiated in response to the reorganization of American demand for consumer goods. At the same time, however, the whole region was rapidly becoming more integrated, and was beginning to show an increasingly elaborate pattern of intraregional trade, investment and production (Dicken, 1998). By the mid-1990s, any attempt to classify national economies in East Asia as to the level of their industrial development would be of little use. While Japan may still be a clear leader in advanced consumer electronics, as well as in the automotive sector, sizeable portions of its production and assembly are organized outside its borders. South Korea and Taiwan both managed to reshape their economies after the Plaza Accords, although in very different ways.

1997 TO THE PRESENT DAY: CONVERGENCE IN CHINA

By the mid-1990s, many of the Japanese, South Korean, Hong Kong and Taiwanese manufacturers had re-established their labour-intensive export businesses in new locations. At home, new businesses had been started, often manufacturing products that had been unknown only a few years earlier and rarely manufactured in the US: cell phones, digital cameras, laptop computers and DVD players. Although many Asian firms continued to hold contracts with US retailers and brand-name merchandisers, they also worked diligently to obtain new orders from retailers and merchandisers in Europe and Latin America, as well as all across Asia. The US share of total exports has declined throughout the period, although the absolute values of exports continue to rise. Also by the mid-1990s, US big box retailers no longer simply purchased goods in Asia; they began actively to integrate Asian manufacturers into their supply chains. Again, American manufacturers continued their long, gradual decline, driven in large part by the eagerness of American retailers to unify and simply their supply lines around the least-cost producers, mostly Asian ones in all areas of consumer goods, except for food and cosmetics.

What seemed, momentarily, like an endless expansion, like a Pacific Century dawning, came to an abrupt halt in 1997. Starting in Thailand in the summer of 1997, the financial underpinnings of economies all across Asia crumbled. The financial and property markets in Indonesia, Malaysia, Singapore, the Philippines, Hong Kong and South Korea were all deeply shaken, each for slightly different reasons; all of these countries also suffered sudden and serious declines in exports and domestic production (see also Chapter 8 in this volume).

When the financial crisis occurred in Asia, the US was in the buoyant years of the dot.com boom and the run-up to the Y2K scare, which led computer owners to upgrade their computers for fear that their internal clocks would be unable to register the new millennium. These were the years when high-technology merchandisers, such as Dell, Gateway and Hewlett Packard, cemented their ties with Taiwanese manufacturers, and when the Taiwanese manufacturers began to relocate their low-end PC production to China. These were also the years that Wal-Mart and Target began establishing superstores across the US and that Wal-Mart was beginning its global expansion (Petrovic and Hamilton, 2006). US demand for the full range of consumer goods was at an all-time high, and outside of those areas most affected by the crisis, global demand was also picking up, especially in China.

First the Asian financial crisis and then the 2001 bursting of the dot.com bubble in the US led businesses worldwide to reconsider their Asian strategies. In 2001, US demand for high-technology consumer goods suddenly and precipitously declined, which also led to an economic slowdown in Taiwan. But China's economy continued to grow. Encouraged by the Chinese government and by China's membership of the World Trade Organization, businesses around the world began to look to China as both its manufacturing platform and its next big market. The largest investors in China were its closest neighbours: Hong Kong and Taiwan continued their large-scale investments in the mainland, but now they were joined by large investments from Japan and South Korea; the four economies together account for 70 per cent of the total direct foreign investment in China. The convergence of Asian firms developing manufacturing sites in China prompted retailers to establish buying offices there as well. As one Wal-Mart buyer explained, retailers followed their Taiwanese suppliers: 'The only reason [manufacturing] moved from Taiwan was China's low level of wages. "We didn't have any trouble in China, because the Taiwanese went into China and built their factories. We were dealing with the same people"' (quoted in Hornblower, 2005).

Recognizing the potential of China as the single best low-cost provider of goods, and as representing a huge domestic market in its own right, Wal-Mart executives established, in 2001, their direct buying office (that later turned into Wal-Mart's global sourcing headquarters) in Shenzhen, China, just across the border from Hong Kong and, in 2003, another buying office in Tianjin. In 2004, Wal-Mart exported over US$18 billion of goods purchased in China, amounting to 10 per cent of all US exports from China. Wal-Mart alone accounted for 30 per cent of all foreign buying in China. Besides exporting from China, Wal-Mart is also in the midst of a huge expansion of retail stores in China, where it will be opening dozens of stores in the next few years. Wal-Mart is not the only major retailer to combine foreign buying with a domestic presence in China. The giant French firm, Carrefour, the second largest retailer in the world, is the largest foreign retailer in China, and is well ahead of Wal-Mart. Not far behind the frontrunner are German retail chains Metro and Ahold.

China is now emerging as the world's premier manufacturing platform for a large range of consumer goods (Lardy, 2003). It is also one of the world's largest consumer markets. Some large US manufacturers, such as General Motors, are making considerable investments in joint ventures producing for China's domestic market. But the largest US investments in China are likely to be made by America's largest companies, the retailers, and, in particular, Wal-Mart, a firm that has now become one of the few truly global marketmakers.

CONCLUSION

Along with many other firms, Wal-Mart has invested in China's manufacturing capacity, and, on the basis of this investment, Wal-Mart has consolidated its global chain, reducing the number of principal suppliers, and forming a global alliance with the top 50. These investments having been made, will Wal-Mart and other retailers and merchandisers soon or easily abandon China for some other locations, such as India or Southeast Asia? Even if China's prices rise, perhaps through an upward re-evaluation of its currency, will China's manufacturing platform become less important than it is today? Of course, these questions are for the future to answer. But one thing should be clear from the above narrative: neither the comparative advantage of locations in global markets nor the competitive advantage of nations in international trade is decided by the impersonal workings of costless markets. Real firms, creating and maintaining real markets, competitively determine both comparative and competitive advantage in the global economy today. As the global retail sector consolidates, as it has been doing for the past 50 years, there is every reason to conclude that a relatively small number of very large retailers will become the hub of the global economy, and the makers of both consumer and supplier markets throughout the world (also see Reardon *et al.*, 2003).

There is much yet to understand about the role of retailers in the global economy. We therefore conclude with two propositions that we hope will fuel future research, as well as two policy implications that may become more pressing as time passes. First, we conclude that markets do not emerge spontaneously, in order to ensure the match between global demand and global supply; they are rather created and shaped by real economic players. The most prominent players making markets in the global economy today are retailers and trade-name merchandisers.

This leads us to our second major proposition. Global markets cannot be reduced to the operation of an abstract, costless price mechanism. Instead, they consist of a rich, increasingly complex, patchwork of institutions that shapes and enables international trade (see also Chapter 3 in this volume). Market mechanisms are made and reproduced by large business firms that typically dedicate a substantial amount of their organizational resources to such 'market-making' activities, not for the universal benefit of all or to approximate the economist's model of perfect competition, but rather to maximize their own trading opportunities.

Given the accuracy of our general interpretation, as well as of these specific propositions, we offer two sets of policy implications that derive from our research. The first set of implications applies to firms trying to locate themselves in the global economy. Our research suggests that global markets do not, and should not be expected to, balance firms, regions and nations in a state of productive equilibrium. How economies actually develop depends on many factors, not the least of which are the accumulated results of many choices that result in increasing returns in some locations, and decreasing returns in other locations. Although institutionalized markets do generate a fair amount of stability and predictability, that fact alone does not necessarily ensure optimal, efficient or universally beneficial outcomes. However, rather than viewing such outcomes as examples of market failure, as distortions of the ideal form of competitive market, we should understand these outcomes as the result of many knowledgable actors making successive choices about how to position themselves in global markets. Our research implies that, increasingly, such choices will involve working with one or more of the global market makers or finding a niche where one can grow one's own business apart from their influence. And increasingly those niches are becoming harder and harder to find; increasingly all consumer-oriented firms get drawn into spheres of activity shaped by global retailers. This implication suggests that, going forward, the business strategies of firms will be ever more tightly linked to the strategies of market makers and their competitors (see also Chapter 2 in this volume).

The second set of implications suggests that officials charged with developing national economic policies can no longer rest blithely on the assumption that, in the long run, the so-called 'law of comparative advantage' will result in a global equilibrium, with all nations being rewarded for efforts in creating transparent economic institutions, building efficient infrastructures and investing in human capital. Our research implies that economic planners will soon face untenable alternatives between promoting protectionism to preserve a nation's industries or allowing those industries to fall victim to the intense global competition among fewer and fewer huge retailers whose cost-cutting choices drive the geographical location of their rootless suppliers. The world economy that appears to some to be 'flat' today (Friedman, 2005) may end up being very lopsided in the not too distant future.

NOTE

1. This chapter is a much shortened version of Chapter 6 in Gary G. Hamilton, *Commerce and Capitalism in Chinese Societies* (2006). This version was presented before the US-China Commission on 20 May 2005. The longer version contains a more developed discussion and a full set of references. The sources given here are those that most pertain to the retail revolution in the US and to the links between US retailers and Asian manufacturers.

REFERENCES

Abernathy, Frederick H., John T. Dunlop, Janice H. Hammond and David Weil (1999), *A Stitch in Time: Lean Retailing and the Transformation of Manufacturing – Lessons from the Apparel and Textile Industries*, New York: Oxford University Press.

Appelbaum, Richard P. and David Smith (1996), 'Governance and flexibility: the East Asian garment industry', in Frederic C. Deyo, Richard F. Doner and Eric Hershberg (eds), *Economic Governance and the Challenge of Flexibility in East Asia*, Lanham, MD: Rowman & Littlefield, pp. 79–106.

Bluestone, Barry and Bennett Harrison (1982), *The Deindustrialization of America*, New York: Basic Books.

Bluestone, Barry, Patricia Hanna, Sarah Kuhn and Laura Moore (1981), *The Retail Revolution: Market Transformation, Investment, and Labor in the Modern Department Store*, Boston: Auburn House Publishing Company.

Bonacich, Edna, Lucie Cheng, Norma Chinchilla, Nora Hamilton and Paul Ong (eds) (1994), *Global Production: The Apparel Industry in the Pacific Rim*, Philadelphia: Temple University Press.

Brown, Stephen A. (1997), *Revolution at the Checkout Counter*, Cambridge, MA: Harvard University Press.

Bucklin, Louis P. (1972), *Competition and Evolution in the Distributive Trades*, Englewood Cliffs, NJ: Prentice-Hall Inc.

Chandler, Alfred D., Jr (1977), *The Visible Hand: The Managerial Revolution in American Business*, Cambridge, MA: Harvard University.

Chandler, Alfred D., Jr (1990), *Scale and Scope: The Dynamics of Industrial Capitalism*, Cambridge, MA: Harvard University.

Cohen, Nancy E. (2002), *America's Marketplace: The History of Shopping Centers*, Lyme, CT: Greenwich Publishing Group.

Dicken, Peter (1998), *Global Shift: Transforming the World Economy*, 3rd edn, New York: The Guilford Press.

Feenstra, Robert C. and Gary G. Hamilton (2006), *Emergent Economies, Divergent Paths: Business Groups and Economic Organization in South Korea and Taiwan*, New York: Cambridge University Press.

Friedman, Thomas L. (2005), *The World is Flat: A Brief History of the Twenty-First Century*, New York: Farrar, Straus and Giroux.

Gereffi, Gary (1994), 'The international economy and economic development', in Neil Smelser and Richard Swedberg (eds), *The Handbook of Economic Sociology*, Princeton: Princeton University Press, pp. 206–33.

Gereffi, Gary (1999), 'International trade and industrial upgrading in the apparel commodity chain', *Journal of International Economics*, **48**(1) (June), 37–70.

Gereffi, Gary and Miguel Korzeniewicz (eds) (1994), *Commodity Chains and Global Capitalism*, Westport, CT: Praeger.

Gereffi, Gary and Donald Wyman (eds) (1990), *Manufacturing Miracles: Paths of Industrialization in Latin America and East Asia*, Princeton, NJ: Princeton University Press.

Hamilton, Gary G. (2006), *Commerce and Capitalism in Chinese Societies*, London: Routledge.

Hanchett, Thomas W. (1996), 'US tax policy and the shopping-center boom of the 1950s and 1960s', *American Historical Review*, **101**(October), 1082–1110.

Hornblower, Sam (2005), 'Wal-Mart and China: a joint venture' (http://www.pbs.org/wgbh/pages/frontline/shows/walmart/secrets/wmchina.html).

Hsing, You-tien (1998), *Making Capitalism in China: The Taiwan Connection*, New York: Oxford University Press.

Jung, Ku-Hyun (1984), 'Trade channel evolution between Korea and the United States', in Karl Moskowitz (ed.), *From Patron to Partner: The Development of US–Korean Business and Trade Relations*, Lexington, MA: Lexington Books, pp. 97–122.

Kao, Cheng-shu and Gary G. Hamilton (2000), 'Reflexive manufacturing: Taiwan's integration in the global economy', *International Studies Review*, **3**(1), June, 1–19.

Kojima, Kiyoshi and Terutomo Ozawa (1984), *Japan's General Trading Companies: Merchants of Economic Development*, Paris: Development Centre of the Organisation for Economic Co-operation and Development.

Lardy, Nicholas R. (2003), 'United States–China Ties: reassessing the economic relationship', testimony before the House Committee on International Relations, US House of Representatives, Washington DC, 21 October, found at http://www.iie.com/publications/papers/lardy/1003.htm.

Orrù, Marco, Nicole Woolsey Biggart and Gary G. Hamilton (1997), *The Economic Organization of East Asian Capitalism*, Thousand Hills: Sage Publications.

Perrow, Charles (2002), *Organizing America: Wealth, Power, and the Origins of Corporate Capitalism*, Princeton, NJ: Princeton University Press.

Petrovic, Misha and Gary G. Hamilton (2006), 'Making global markets: Wal-Mart and its suppliers', in Nelson Lichtenstein (ed.) *Wal-Mart: Template for 21st Century Capitalism*, New York: The New Press.

Reardon, Thomas, C. Peter Timmer, Christopher B. Barrett and Julio Berdegue (2003), 'The rise of supermarkets in Africa, Asia, and Latin America', *American Journal of Agricultural Economics*, **85**(5), 1140–47.

Rhee, Yung Whee, Bruce Ross-Larson and Garry Pursell (1984), *Korea's Competitive Edge: Managing the Entry into World Markets*, Baltimore, MD: The Johns Hopkins University Press.

Tsurumi, Yoshi (1984), *Sogoshosha: Engines of Export-Based Growth*, Montreal: The Institute for Research on Public Policy.

Yoshino, M.Y. and Thomas B. Lifson (1986), *The Invisible Link: Japan's Sogo Shosha and the Organization of Trade*, Cambridge, MA: The MIT Press.

PART III

Business–State Relations

12. The state and transnational capital in adaptive partnership: Singapore, South Korea and Taiwan

Christopher M. Dent

The relationship between transnational capital and the state has stirred much interest and debate within the international political economy literature. The analysis presented here makes a comparative case study analysis of this relationship in the foreign economic policy (FEP) calculus of three East Asian newly industrialized economies: Singapore, South Korea and Taiwan (the NIE-3).[1] While each of the NIE-3's own path of economic development has differed significantly, there nevertheless exist important similarities. This relates not just to being a constituent of the East Asian regional economic dynamic, but also to their shared developmental state tradition.

The relationship between the state and transnational capital is also a key to understanding the NIE-3's foreign economic policy formation, yet this too differed significantly across the group. In Singapore, the state has forged close working relations with the hosted foreign transnational corporations (TNCs) that dominate the economy. In South Korea, the state has cultivated a home-grown transnational capital capacity, as seen in its developmental alliance forged with the *chaebol* conglomerates. Furthermore, an arm's-length relationship with foreign TNCs was traditionally maintained, although this changed after the cataclysmic events of South Korea's 1997/1998 financial crisis. The Taiwanese state's own relationship with transnational capital has, meanwhile, concentrated on the transborder economic space being created by intensifying commercial interactions with mainland China (see also Chapters 9 and 16 in this volume). The NIE-3's foreign trade, investment and finance policies are also shaped to some considerable degree by these respective relationships, as is the conduct of their economic diplomacy.

This chapter is organized along the following lines. It first considers different conceptual and theoretical aspects of the state's relationship with transnational capital, and then briefly introduces a macro-framework of FEP analysis, before progressing to examine case studies of Singapore, South Korea and Taiwan. The core argument made here is that states can work in an 'adaptive partnership' with transnational capital in meeting various foreign economic policy objectives, these being broadly oriented by the pursuit of economic security in the international system – and a new conceptual perspective of economic security is also presented by this chapter.

Here 'adaptive partnership' refers to the way states seek to adapt to the fast-changing conditions of a globalizing world economy in various forms of conjunction with transnational capital. Both states and TNCs – the main organizational representation of transnational capital – can gain from entering into such an arrangement, working with each other to respond to new challenges presented by globalization. The strong techno-cratic capacities and corporatist relations with business enjoyed by developmental states place them in an ideal position to cultivate such adaptive partnerships. However, as we discuss in relation to the NIE-3, the nature of this partnership can vary significantly and, moreover, there exist numerous problems with maintaining it.

TRANSNATIONAL CAPITAL AND THE STATE

The notion of transnational capital adopted by this chapter relates to functionally inte-grated business capital that transcends national borders, and hence primarily concerns, and may collectively refer to, TNC activities. More specifically, 'functionally integrated business capital' implies different organizational components of a business enterprise that operate in a concerted and commonly purposeful manner, and its configuration across national borders makes this 'transnational' in character. Hence transnational capital and TNCs, its main organizational representation, are extant between relatively localized (that is involv-ing just two or three countries) or highly internationalized (that is globalized) scales. Furthermore, transnational capital is distinguishable from foreign capital in relation to a specific nation-state in that it also includes indigenously originating or 'home' TNCs.

Many discourses on globalization centre on the state–transnational capital relation-ship. Hyperglobalists such as Ohmae (1990, 1995) posit TNCs as powerful, independent and stateless organizations in a world where national borders and nation-states them-selves are becoming increasingly redundant. According to this view, globalization is grad-ually delegitimizing the 'national' economy and the 'nation' state as purposeful economic and political unitary referents. Moreover, transnationalizing processes significantly undermine the effectiveness of the state's national economic management policies (Cable, 1995; Horsman and Marshall, 1994; Ohmae, 1995; Vernon, 1971). Other analysts that subscribe to the irresistible rise of global neoliberalism further contend that the state's economic managerial role generally is in decline, deferring to the logic of freer markets in a transnationalizing age (Huntington, 1991; Fukuyama, 1992).

While these views found both widespread expression and a willing audience during the early post-Cold War period, when 'globalization fever' seemed to grip many, various counter-opinions and perspectives emerged in the latter 1990s. For instance, Dicken (1998) reminded us that globalization is a *process*, not an end-state, and, moreover, glob-alizing forces were evidently working to a highly asymmetric pattern. Meanwhile, Mann (1997) stressed the global variety of nation-states in terms of size, form, power, geography and centralization, and it therefore followed that the impact of globalization and transna-tional capital upon them depended upon both what manifestation of the state was being examined, and its actual engagement with economic globalizing processes. Although Mann identified transnational capitalist formation as a major threat to nation-state integrity, he argued that transnational capital and the state often work in a complemen-tary and coordinative fashion. From a somewhat different perspective, Shaw (1997) con-tended that globalization is not undermining the state, but rather working to transform it into new forms, and that the state had demonstrated its adaptive nature when confronted by the challenge of globalization. These are important premises on which adaptive part-nerships between states and transnational capital are founded.

More generally, TNCs are embedded in networks of relations with various state and non-state actors, comprising various tiers of government, suppliers and clients, financial institutions, trade unions, industry associations, universities and research institutes (Sally, 1994). These represent the institutional underpinnings of the political economy in which transnational capital operates. They are part of a broader complex interdependence of relationships and linkages between different agents and structures in the contemporary international system that has become closely associated with the concept of globalization itself (Keohane and Nye, 1977; Jones, 1995). The extent to which TNCs are, though, free from state governments and other forms of political authority is a highly contentious debate (Dicken, 1998; Drucker, 1997). This chapter is more specifically concerned with the relationship between transnational capital and national state political authority that, in turn, mainly relates to government agencies and their cultivated relationships with business and society. Thus, in relation to state–TNC adaptive partnerships, the work of state capacity theorists, such as Evans (1995) and Weiss (1995, 1998), is highly relevant in that they highlight the state's potential to develop mutually beneficial relations with business in meeting the economic challenges posed by globalization.

Just as firms must adapt to changing international economic circumstances so, of course, must state governments. In charting the adaptive course of the state's economic role, and drawing upon the analytical perspectives of the regulationist school, Jessop (1993, 1997) plots the shift from Keynesian welfare statism, as the mode of social regulation (MSR) that underpinned the Atlantic Fordist capitalist accumulation regime up to the 1970s, to the post-Fordist MSR of Schumpeterian workfare statism that focuses on the state's move away from passive welfare measures towards a more activist approach in which the state seeks to optimize the competitive potential of labour and capital. Along similar conceptual lines, Cerny (1997, 2000) notes the rise of the competition state as one embracing the challenge of intensifying global economic competition, and whereby the consequent commodification of the state aims to make 'economic activities located within the national territory, or which otherwise contribute to national wealth, more competitive in international and transnational terms' (Cerny, 2000: 30).

Invariably, the competitive state engages in certain collaborative interactions with transnational capital, this occurring in the broader context of state–firm diplomacy (Stopford and Strange, 1991). One aspect of this concerns how states bargain with foreign TNCs to assimilate their propriety assets (for example capital, technology) into the national economy: the higher value-added these assets the better. Thus a prime economic policy function of the state in the global era is to capture and retain value-added activities from various sources of transnational capital. Yet there is a conflictual, as well as cooperative, dimension to state–TNC diplomacy in which clashes of interest can arise over various regulatory issues, such as local content regulations and environmental standards (Grosse and Behrman, 1992; Pitilis, 1991). As Gordon (1988: 61) generally observed, TNCs and governments 'operate in a fully dialectical relationship, locked into unified but contradictory roles and positions, neither the one nor the other partner clearly or completely able to dominate'. With these two last points in mind, the integrity of the state–TNC adaptive partnership is obviously more difficult to maintain when new conflicts of interest emerge between the state and transnational capital. This is discussed later in more particular detail in relation to the recent FEP developments of South Korea and Taiwan.

Issues of extraterritoriality add a further dimension to the state–transnational capital relationship, wherein the inclusion of third party states can bring additional complications. This may arise when the state plays some role in the transnationalization of capital itself, a key area of our analysis on the NIE-3. As Cerny (2000) argued, the imperative of international competitiveness can lead to pressures upon the state to create or expand transnational regimes, transnational neocorporatist structures of policy bargaining and transgovernmental linkages. We later discuss this in relation to Taiwan's engagement with the mainland China economy and the Singapore government's regionalization strategy. In both cases, the state has sought to manage the expanded formation of home-based transnational capital within their respective subregional locales in accordance with economic security objectives.

A state's ability to conduct an effective diplomacy with foreign TNCs, however, very much depends on its own power-base, technocratic capacities, general adaptive qualities and the development level of the economy over which it presides. Indeed, the relationship between transnational capital and developing states has been long debated in the development studies literature. Modernization theories have contended the generally positive impact of TNCs upon developing country growth and development by the diffusion of new and more advanced capital, technology and other value-adding proprietary assets that accompany their inward investments. Hosted TNCs can also help stimulate local entrepreneurship through competition effects and joint venture arrangements, as well as promote stronger forward and backward industrial linkages within the host economy (see also Chapter 13 in this volume). In contrast, dependency theories claim that TNCs can stunt developing-country development through their predatory corporate practices (Cardoso and Faletto, 1979). As developing countries often maintain a critical dependence on foreign TNCs in terms of capital, technology and production, their governments are sometimes forced to make policy and regulatory compromises in accordance with TNC demands, for example lowering environmental standards.

The dependency theory view of the predominantly hierarchical and exploitative nature of the global political economy, in which autonomous transnational capital remains dominant within the world economic structure, is closely associated with neoMarxist theories on the transnational capitalist class, or TCC (Robinson and Harris, 2000; Van der Pijl, 1998).[2] In comparison, statist theories of development offer a different and more optimistic view by emphasizing how strong states can develop and harness transnational capital to meet transformative developmental objectives. This developmental statist view is thus closely associated with the work of the aforementioned state capacity theorists (Johnson, 1982; Amsden, 1989; Wade, 1990; Evans, 1995; Weiss, 1998; Woo-Cumings, 1999). Drawing mainly upon examples from East Asian NIEs, Clark and Chan (1995) contend that national political cultures and the synergistic relation between the state and society therein can exercise a decisive influence in regulating foreign TNC access, and in orchestrating foreign TNC contributions to national development. For example, the state can develop society's absorptive capacity to take advantage of a TNC's conferred assets (for example technology and management skills) on the host economy. As we elaborate further below, Singapore, South Korea and Taiwan have all been exemplars of developmental statism, and this has proved a key determinant of both their respective state–transnational capital relationships and foreign economic policies.

Commenting on the developmental state tradition in the NIE-3, Haggard and Cheng (1987: 102) observed in the mid-1980s that 'South Korea, Taiwan and Singapore all have *dirigiste* bureaucracies capable of extracting and channelling resources to targeted industries and selectively altering and sequencing the system of industrial incentives, including to foreign investors.' In more specific relation to the debate on the state and transnational capital, Evans (1985: 195) commented that 'the challenges of dealing with transnational linkages in general and contests with transnational capital in particular may, under certain circumstances, stimulate the development of new state capacities and may legitimate the expansion of the state's role into areas that would otherwise be the preserve of private capital. Furthermore, transnational capital may, under certain circumstances, prefer dealing with a "stronger", more bureaucratically capable state apparatus'. These factors constitute the origins of developmental states' adaptive partnerships with transnational capital, albeit then somewhat state-coercive in approach.

Many analysts, however, now argue that developmental statism represented a historic phase in Japan and the East Asian NIEs' economic development, owing to the gradual retreat of the state's authoritarian-styled guidance of the economy over the last two decades. This trend, it is argued, owed much to the twin eroding forces of democratization and neoliberal advocacy, the latter infiltrating via both domestic and external sources (Jomo, 2000; Kim, 1999; Kuo, 1998). Moreover, earlier acknowledged arguments concerning the difficulties of sustaining national economic management projects and neomercantilist policies in the contemporary global era are also used to qualify this view. Other analysts, though, contend that the developmental state is not becoming extinct, but is rather evolving within the broader context of state adaptation, responding to the fast-changing economic and technological environment of a globalizing world economy (Dent, 2004; Evans, 1997; Low, 2001; Weiss, 2000; Woo-Cumings, 1999) – a key theme of this chapter's core argument.

For instance, while the policy tools and means may have changed, developmental states still preside over various adaptive-cum-transformative economic projects that increasingly involve a partnering with transnationalized capital. More specifically, such policy tools and means are underpinned by the developmental states' strong technocratic capacities (for example effective bureaucracy, strategic planning and implementation capabilities, market intelligence infrastructure) and relational resources (for example negotiative and collaborative links with business and society) that provide the fundamental basis of its adaptive capabilities per se. These capacities and resources are still possessed by the NIE-3 in varying degrees and forms and will be examined in detail later. Moreover, without such attributes, most states would find it difficult to establish and develop an adaptive partnership with transnational capital.

Our case analysis on the NIE-3 indicatively argues that development statism remains strongly evident in Singapore and Taiwan, but now relatively less so in South Korea. This has important implications for the NIE-3's respective foreign economic policies and the state's adaptive partnership with transnational capital. In addition, we show in our case study analyses how, by their very nature, these adaptive partnerships are themselves evolving within the mercurial conditions of the contemporary international economic order, and that their integrity is significantly tested by frequently arising conflicts of interest between states and TNCs.

FOREIGN ECONOMIC POLICY: A NEW MACRO-FRAMEWORK OF ANALYSIS

The macro-framework of FEP analysis briefly presented here is taken from conceptual modelling I have developed elsewhere (Dent, 2000, 2002). There I contend that the constituent elements of foreign economic policy, or FEP conduct, fall into two broad domains. The first of these is technical policy realms, which themselves can be subcategorized into a core element (trade, FDI, international finance, and foreign aid policies) and an associative element (for example industry policy). The former possesses a more overt and cognitive international focus, while the latter is generally allied to the former in some functionally supportive, often competitiveness-enhancing manner. The second domain is economic diplomacy, which broadly concerns the means and parameters within which trade, investment, and other international economic relations are conducted between representative agents of different FEP powers. Economic diplomacy can be generally viewed from different levels of engagement, modalities, exercises of power and bargaining processes.

This macro-framework of FEP analysis also incorporates three orienting interactive dimensions into the model. First, cognitive–ideological approaches relate to key ideological nodes of thought (for example liberalism, mercantilism), value-system traditions, the accommodation of economic culture and other ideational or value-based factors that shape the thinking behind FEP formation. This closely interacts with a second orienting dimension, namely the set of generic economic security objectives that in turn broadly delineate pursued FEP interests. In the FEP context, we can venture a working definition of economic security as safeguarding the structural integrity and prosperity-generating capabilities and interests of a politico-economic entity in the context of various externalized risks and threats that confront it. Here, 'politico-economic entity' broadly equates with an FEP power (a nation-state or some other state-form[3]) with respect to its own territorial economy and extraterritorial economic interests. Hence, FEP protagonists[4] may work, insofar as they are able, to safeguard the transnational commercial interests of their home-based or hosted foreign TNCs. The structural integrity aspect essentially relates to maintaining the internal construction of the economy during its interactions in the global economy, and its ability to meet the basic demands of economic agents located therein. The prosperity-generating capabilities aspect broadens the conventional boundaries of the economic security concept beyond its usual attention to minimizing direct and immediate economic vulnerabilities. In addition, eight typologies of economic security interest are developed that build on this working definition.

- *Supply security*: relating to securing key supply chains involving foreign sources. This is especially important for import-dependent or foreign technology-dependent economies that respectively lack natural resources and indigenous techno-industrial self-sufficiency.
- *Market access security*: concerns securing the best access possible to key foreign markets. This is particularly crucial for export-oriented economies with small domestic markets, like the NIE-3.
- *Finance-credit security*: ensuring the financial solvency of the FEP power in the international system, as well as its maintenance of access to, or influence or control over, sources of international credit.

- *Techno-industrial capability security*: preserving and developing the ability of the economy to generate prosperity, productivity and other welfare-creating factors; also involves maintaining the economy's position as close as possible to the technological frontier. This may derive from indigenous or foreign sources, and relate to issues of access and acquisition of foreign technology.
- *Socioeconomic paradigm security*: the defence of a society's preferred socioeconomic paradigm and its welfare goals where defined. This often entails the resistance of foreign pressure to adapt to new international norms that are associated with a counter-paradigm.
- *Trans-border community security*: regionalized concerns that may either precipitate trans-border economic crises or concern localized interdependence issues, for example subregional economic integration. These often centre on trans-border spillovers or externalities that require market failure correction policies, and hence the management of a shared trans-border economic space.
- *Systemic security*: upholding the integrity of the international economic system, entailing cooperative and concessionary acts to uphold multilateral regimes of systemic governance, facilitate inter-state bargains and maintain overall systemic stability.
- *Alliance security*: maintaining and developing international economic partnerships with state and non-state actors in pursuance of the above interests. This may take various forms, ranging from donor–client alliance relationships to looser cooperative or coordinative arrangements between relatively equal partners.

We apply these economic security typologies throughout our case analysis on the NIE-3 states' relationship with transnational capital regarding FEP objectives. It is also noted how economic security challenges are changing all the time, presenting a constant test to the adaptive capabilities of the NIE-3 developmental states, and to their adaptive partnerships fostered with transnational capital. The third orienting interactive dimension concerns contesting actor-based influences that examine how different domestic actors (for example trade unions, industrial associations), international actors (for example foreign governments, international economic organizations) and transnational actors (for example TNCs, transnational civil society) interact within the model to shape FEP formation. We now examine the varied and changing nature of the NIE-3 states' adaptive partnerships with transnational capital in their respective FEP contexts.

SINGAPORE

Singapore is an entrepôt city-state in the Venetian tradition that has maintained a strong commercial *raison d'être* since its British imperial origins, consequently having the most historic relationship with transnational capital of the NIE-3. In the early independence period, the new Peoples' Action Party government sought to expand Singapore's commercial functionality by developing industrial estates as satellite platforms for hosted foreign TNC export production. The Economic Development Board (EDB) was created as the state's key partner agency working with foreign TNCs to these ends, both acting as their service-provider and as a developmental pilot by strategically planning the infusion of increasingly higher value-added investments (Huff, 1995; Low, 2001; Schein, 1996). Central to this was the Pioneer Industries Ordinance, still administered by the EDB and that enables the Singapore state to continue channelling investment capital to prioritized sectors for development through various incentive-based measures, for example subsidized funding and tax breaks. American electronics manufacturers were particularly courted for their inward investment in initial phases of Singapore's developmental strategy, the reasons being partly politico-military security-motivated: embedding American capital interests in Singapore through FDI significantly enhanced the US's stake in the city-state's own political survival and stability, and hence created a deterrent to invasion from either Malaysia or Indonesia.[5]

Singapore's engagement with foreign transnational capital developed and diversified in subsequent decades and, by the 1990s, its economy had become comprehensively based upon it. By 2000, foreign TNCs accounted for well over half of the city-state's production, employment and investment, and around 80 per cent of its exports. Over this time, though, the Singapore state's adaptive partnership capacities vis-à-vis foreign transnational capital have similarly developed and diversified. With respect to (economic) alliance security objectives, this close state–transnational capital relationship undergirds Singapore's economic diplomacy ties with key partners. For example, the US's choice of Singapore as the first Asian state with which to negotiate a free trade agreement (FTA) was partly based on long-founded American corporate interests in the city-state.[6]

The Singapore state's regionalization strategy, principally driven by the twin objectives of further internationalizing Singapore's indigenous firms, and assisting the transnational restructuring and cost-competitive endeavours of hosted foreign TNCs in an adaptive context, also met certain alliance security objectives by helping to cultivate more positive relations with the city-state's immediate economic partners. The Indonesia–Malaysia–Singapore Growth Triangle (IMSGT) project laid the cornerstone of this strategy from the late 1980s onwards, whereby state-initiated moves aimed to foster development of a localized transnational economy, with Singapore at its commercial hub. New policy measures stemming from the project were designed to engage more deeply Malaysia and Indonesia in a transnational division of labour, in which relatively labour-intensive production of Singapore's hosted TNCs was relocated to the neighbouring foreign provinces of Johor (Malaysia) and Riau (Indonesia). Centrepieces of the IMSGT were the new industrial parks established in the Riau Islands of Batam and Bintan, co-managed by Jurong Town Corporation International (JTCI), a Singapore government-linked company, and local Indonesian authorities, and attracting a mix of both Singapore's home and foreign transnational capital (see Table 12.1). The IMSGT also makes an important contribution to Singapore's trans-border community security interests. Stronger transnational capital linkages with Malaysia and Indonesia, and the more common economic space created thereby, have provided a firmer basis for interdependence cooperation on such issues as freshwater and natural gas resources, and piracy in the Malacca Straits.

Out of the IMSGT project developed the Singapore state's more comprehensive and extensive foreign industrial park (FIP) policy, whereby JTCI and other government-linked companies organized and co-managed transnational capital activities into the deeper East Asian hinterland. This in turn formed a key objective aspect of the government 'Regionalization 2000' programme, formally introduced in 1995, and founded on

Table 12.1 Summary profile of selected Singaporean foreign industrial parks (FIPs)

FIP	Start-up year	Size	No. of investors	Investments ($m)	Nationality of investors
Batam, Indonesia	1991	500 ha	87	306	Japan 48%, S'pore 26%, Europe 13%, US 5%, others 8%
Bintan, Indonesia	1992	4 km^2	25	88	S'pore 74%, Japan 22%, others 4%
Suzhou, China	1994	70 km^2	85	2860	US 34%, S'pore 27%, Europe 15%, Japan 14%, others 10%
Wuxi, China	1995	1 km^2	48	585	Japan 37%, Asia 31%, Europe 17%, US 15%
Ho Chi Min City, Vietnam	1997	500 ha	25	312	S'pore 56%, Japan 16%, Europe 12%, others 16%
Bangalore, India	1997	100 ha	16	167	Europe 43%, India 28%, S'pore 18%, Japan 10%, US 1%

Source: Singapore Investment News, May 1998.

two other main objectives: (1) enhancing Singapore's role as a value-adding gateway to the Asia Pacific for foreign TNCs; (2) establishing stronger linkages with regional economies to develop further its manufacturing and service sectors. The shift from the subregional to the pan-regional was fundamental to the Singapore state's endeavours to develop a second or external wing to the domestic economy, and also in understanding the regional–global interface in the state's adaptive partnership with transnational capital (Low, 2001; Pereira, 2000; Yeoh and Willis, 1997; Yeung, 2000). Southeast Asia's financial crisis of 1997/98 further confirmed opinions within the Singapore government concerning the risks and constraints of focusing simply on the regional. In the crisis aftermath, the state made greater efforts to promote Singapore as a prime regional node in *global* circuits of transnational capital. This new going global strategy aimed to promote more specifically Singapore as below:

- *High-tech export production centre*: marking a continuation of the developmental state's ongoing transformative economic project. Efforts to further upgrade Singapore's techno-industrial capacity, in order to attract increasingly technology-intensive FDI, centred on creating a knowledge-based economy (KBE).[7]
- *Regional operations centre for TNCs*: especially as a regional headquarters location and distribution hub for transnational capital in Southeast and East Asia. Hong Kong remains Singapore's main rival here.
- *Regional research and development (R&D) centre in niche sectors*: the newest component in this strategy. Foreign TNCs working in the biotechnology and life science fields have been particular targets of the Singapore state.[8]

The last of these objectives marked the Singapore state's attempts to avoid the so called 'truncation' problem, deriving from an overdependence on inward FDI and an important predicament of Singapore's techno-industrial capacity security. Dicken (1998: 263) describes a truncated plant as one 'which concentrates mainly or exclusively on production activities and which, therefore, lacks the higher-level administrative and R&D functions'. The city-state's recession of the mid-1980s raised fears of foreign capital flight and spurred the government to form the Singapore Economic Review Committee (SERC) that mainly comprised state and foreign TNC representatives, and was charged with recommending new directions for the economy's development. To further avert the 'truncation' problem, the SERC recommended the cultivation of Singapore's home TNC capacity and improved incentives to attract industrial complex FDI, whereby new investment in production is accompanied by supporting value-added activities, for example research, design and marketing. The embedding of such activities in the city-state helps further realize Singapore's techno-industrial capacity security objectives by the city-state economy's broader assimilation of key functions of foreign TNCs, and thus further broadening the nature of this state–TNC adaptive partnership (see also Chapters 13 and 15 in this volume).

Singapore's recently initiated venture into the biotechnology sector provides a good example of its KBE developmentalism and attention to continually techno-industrial capacity security objectives in partnership with transnational capital. In 2001, the government established two funds amounting to S$1 billion (approx. US$580 million) each as part of financing this transformative project. The first was budgeted to the Biomedical

Research Council (BMRC) with the aim of developing new public research capabilities in the biomedical subsector. The second was budgeted to the EDB's new Biomedical Sciences Investment Fund (BMSIF) that provides support for biotechnology-related R&D activities undertaken by leading companies located in Singapore. The Biomedical Sciences Executive Committee is charged with coordinating the different state agencies involved. Under this, the Ministry of Education has strengthened the life sciences curriculum in the city-state's schools, and worked with universities in the introduction of new life science degree programmes. In addition, the former National Science and Technology Board (NSTB)[9] launched a S$500 million National Science Scholarships programme in July 2001 to nurture local research talent for science and technology with particular emphasis on the biomedical sciences. Meanwhile, the EDB has worked on improving other areas of biotechnology skills-base through various training programmes.

The EDB is also responsible, in partnership with the Jurong Town Corporation (the parent statutory agency of the JTCI), for developing and managing the Biopolis industrial estate complex, where Singapore's biotechnology sector activities are clustered. At the cost of S$500 million and located near the National University of Singapore and the National University Hospital, the Biopolis complex was opened in October 2003, consisting of seven buildings spread over eight hectares that provides facilities for 2000 scientists. Here, personnel from its public research institutes and private biotechnology companies work alongside each other in production and R&D activities.[10] The Singapore government aims to double its biomedical output to S$20 billion by 2010, or about 12 per cent of the city-state's economy, and raise its share of manufacturing from 7 per cent in 2003 to 15–20 per cent by 2005.[11]

The Singapore government purposely selected the biotechnology sector as an area where it could develop a competitive advantage over rivals such as China and India. These emerging economies have eroded Singapore's competitive advantage in other technology sectors such as electronics. Philip Yeo, EDB chief from 1986 to 2001, commented on the launch of Singapore's biotechnology development project, 'We cannot compete with America. We cannot compete with Europe, so we look for areas where we have an advantage. An advantage is that we are in Asia. We can develop a niche.'[12] The EDB continues to promote niche industry development in other high-tech sectors, such as photonics, a key enabling technology in next-generation Internet and high-speed wireless connectivity.[13]

Part of Singapore's wider going global strategy entails the government's foreign talent policy. Securing the stream of foreign human capital required to sustain the emerging KBE paradigm is integral to the current stage of Singapore's transnational capital development and, as such, has become a core supply security objective. The Contact Singapore scheme is designed to attract foreign TNC cadres and technopreneurs to the city-state. In addition, the government has negotiated contracts with foreign business schools to establish Singapore-based campuses intended to act as a regional magnet for the best young managerial and technical talent from Southeast Asia to study first in Singapore, and thereafter, hopefully, settle.

Another important recent development in Singapore's foreign economic policy is its bilateral FTA strategy that emerged mainly in response to recent institutional failures by the WTO and Asia-Pacific Economic Co-operation (APEC) forum to progress with their respective trade liberalization agendas (Dent, 2001). By October 2005, Singapore had either operationalized or signed bilateral FTAs with Australia, the European Free Trade Agreement (EFTA) group, India, Japan, Jordan, New Zealand, South Korea and the US, and also a quadrilateral FTA with Chile, Brunei and New Zealand, making Singapore Asia's most active FTA protagonist. The association with Singapore's alliance security objectives was previously noted. Moreover, in the context of transnational capital and market access security interests, Singapore's FTA strategy is also seen to support critically its entrepôt and regional export platform functionalities, by maintaining and developing Singapore-based access to key international markets.

Furthermore, the importance of Singapore's trade–FDI nexus means that compromised market access, whether actual or threatened, could undermine its ability to attract foreign transnational capital. Retaining and luring further foreign TNC export production is generally vital to Singapore's economic security interests, and hence ensuring access to Asia-Pacific export markets is a priority FEP objective. In addition, this strategy is part of maintaining Singapore's demonstrative advocacy of transnational economic liberalism: the government has vehemently stressed how its bilateral FTA policy is WTO/APEC-consistent, keeping the momentum of trade liberalization going during a period when these multilateral and transregional regimes have experienced some significant inertia. Furthermore, the Singapore state's quick and effective implementation of its new FTA diplomacy demonstrated its keen adaptive reflexes to critical changes in the regional and global market order.

SOUTH KOREA

In contrast to Singapore, the South Korean state opted to cultivate a long-term adaptive partnership with domestic corporate power in the form of the *chaebol* big business groups, such as Samsung, Hyundai, LG and Daewoo. From the 1950s and the 1960s, the state itself actively promoted the *chaebol*'s conglomerated development with the intention of exploiting various economies of scale and scope that had been demonstratively achieved by Japan's pre-war template: the *zaibatsu*. South Korea also closely imitated Japan's ardent neomercantilism founded on a strong strategic trade policy in sectors especially selected for capital development, for example automobiles. It was arguably the most *dirigiste* developmental state of the NIE-3 group. Past South Korean governments drew extensively upon production subsidies, financial credit allocation, tariff protection, export quotas and tax rebates to steer the concomitant course of *chaebol* business and national economic development. In this sense, the *chaebol* were close developmental partners of the South Korean state, and both very much worked together in meeting new international economic challenges.

The South Korean developmental state's fostering of indigenous enterprise and the country's non-reliance on inward FDI would seem to question the relevance of the dependent development thesis to South Korea's case (Bradshaw *et al.*, 1993). Nevertheless, the *chaebol*'s heavy reliance on foreign loan capital and the propriety technology assets of foreign TNCs has been a defining feature of the country's development (Smith, 1997; Smith and Lee, 1990). Over the 1967–71 period, foreign capital accounted for 39.5 per cent of South Korea's total savings, and 90 per cent of the former comprised loan capital. This trend continued, albeit to a less extreme degree, into the 1970s and the

1980s (Haggard and Cheng, 1987). The state's preference for foreign debt finance over inward FDI provided it with considerable leverage over the *chaebol*, and also constituted a very different approach to finance-credit security, in comparison to its Singaporean counterpart. State-mediated foreign loans were offered at comparatively lower rates of interest than from domestic loan capital, and the finance relationship within the state–*chaebol* nexus was the lynchpin of the state's investment coordination strategy that shaped key aspects of structural economic development.

In addition, the state's proclivity for a more arm's-length relationship with foreign transnational capital was underwritten by a fervent economic nationalism that pervaded both the state bureaucratic cadres and the South Korean society, bred partly by a post-colonial mistrust of foreign capital incursions into the domestic domain. However, the accelerated liberalization of South Korea's international finance policy through the 1990s enabled the *chaebol* to acquire foreign loans more directly from external sources and with progressively diminishing state mediation. The consequent expansion of the *chaebol*'s foreign debts was principally responsible for precipitating South Korea's chronic financial crisis in 1997, and bringing finance-credit security to the fore of the country's FEP object-ives. It could also be argued that this partial dismantling of the developmental state's tech-nical apparatus (that is economic policy instruments associated with it) ultimately compromised South Korea's finance-credit security position with regard to foreign capital, as well as unravelling key aspects of the state's adaptive partnership with the *chaebol*. In contrast to both Singapore and Taiwan, South Korea had embarked on financial liberalization without first properly institutionalizing financial market order, a task subsequently undertaken after the crisis (Heo and Tan, 2003; Thurbon, 2001).

Up to the 1997/1998 crisis, South Korea was perceived as one of the economies most impermeable to foreign investment. Very strict controls were imposed on inward FDI in terms of technology transfer, local content and export quota stipulations. Where such foreign investment was permitted, it was often guided into specific sectors with the aim of cultivating the *chaebol*'s own techno-industrial learning and other adaptive-related capacities (Mardon, 1990). Once this was achieved, foreign TNCs were frequently encour-aged to divest, as perhaps best exemplified in the petroleum-refining sector (Clark and Chan, 1995). We note later how this FEP approach to techno-industrial capability secu-rity was to change after the crisis.

Meanwhile, the state began to promote the early transnational development of the *chaebol* from the late 1960s onwards, especially in resource-intensive outward FDI pro-jects, for example oil and mining. This FEP imperative arose in accordance with South Korea's supply security interests: sustaining the rapid pace of industrialization required an increasing demand for raw materials that a natural resource-poor South Korea chron-ically lacked. In the 1980s, the state became particularly active in developing the *chaebol*'s global reach and ability to better adapt to global market competition, and hence their more comprehensive transnationalization. For example, the Korean Trade Promotion Agency (KOTRA) worked closely with the *chaebol* in areas of export market intelligence, whilst the EPB provided technical assistance on many logistical aspects of *chaebol* over-seas investment.

The motives behind this policy were broadly twofold, namely: *domestic push* factors, including rising labour costs and a low small and medium-sized enterprise (SME) sup-plier ratio in the South Korean economy; and *global pull* factors, centring on the need to develop a strategic global position in the big Triad markets of North America, East Asia and Europe, which could be best achieved by insider locations (Dent and Randerson, 1996). This latter aspect relates directly to the evolution of South Korea's market access security interests, and the country's structure of economic diplomacy ties more generally. The country progressed beyond its unipolar clientistic links with the US (1950s–1960s), and then a bipolar economic dependency upon the US and Japan (1970s–1980s), to a tripolar framework by the early 1990s, in which the Single European Market became the new target of *chaebol* transnational strategy.

The South Korean state's wider promotion of *chaebol* transnationalization became more formulated by the mid-1990s, as part of Kim Young-sam government's *segyehwa* (globalization) policy. Formally introduced in 1994, *segyehwa* was a broader programme for liberalizing South Korea's trade, international finance and FDI policies (Gills, 1996; Kim, 2000; Rowley and Bae, 1998). As it transpired, the imperative of supporting the *chaebol*'s global strategies and their constant adaptation to global market competition was prioritized over economic liberalization during this period (Gills, 1999). From 1993 to 1997, South Korean outward FDI expanded between two to three times faster than inward FDI entering the economy.[14] Indeed, to many outsiders, *segyehwa* was perceived as a one-way globalization strategy of primarily seeking to improve South Korea's export competitiveness and extending *chaebol* transnationalization.[15]

The advent of the 1997/98 financial crisis, though, brought dramatic changes to South Korea's political economy. For instance, the crisis had both catalysing and accelerating effects on various processes of economic liberalization, now forced through by neoliberal critics of developmental statism within the country's political and bureaucratic ranks. This brought significant change regarding the *cognitive–ideological approach* to South Korea's FEP formation. Domestic neoliberal advocacy was fortified by the IMF's bailout programme, whereby funds were provided on the condition of implementing widespread neoliberal economic reforms in finance, trade and FDI policy, labour markets and corporate governance. The new Kim Dae-jung government (1998–2002), installed during the early crisis aftermath, heartily embraced the IMF's policy prescriptions, and added its own dose of neoliberal reform, thus leading to further diminishment of technical developmental state practices. In keeping with the established ritual of newly incumbent South Korean presidents, Kim Dae-jung further announced his resolve to decouple the state–*chaebol* nexus, as part of fostering a new economic and corporate paradigm, and thus seek to break further with the adaptive partnership with domestic transnational capital (Cherry, 2005).

These post-crisis reforms had important implications for South Korea's FEP, with the state endeavouring to rebrand the country as an open trading nation, and as a new attractive base for foreign TNC investment. Trade and inward FDI policy liberalization duly ensued. Furthermore, the new economic policies of the Kim Dae-jung government intended to change the calculus of the state's relationship with transnational capital, essentially switching priorities from promoting *chaebol* transnationalization to domestic economy transnationalization. In the crisis aftermath, South Korea's outward FDI had collapsed, symptomatic of the *chaebol*'s global overreach: in short, the conglomerates had expanded their transnational capital too fast and too ambitiously under the circumstances of poorly managed financial liberalization, resulting in chronic overcapacity problems and creating mountains of non-performing loans (Thurbon, 2001). Weiss (1998,

2000) argued that this arose as a direct consequence of the state's curtailment of the afore-mentioned investment coordination strategy, representing both a vital retraction of South Korean developmental statism during the 1990s and a critical loosening of the state's adaptive partnership with the *chaebol*. In the meantime, inward FDI rose sharply: in 1996, South Korea attracted just US$3.2 billion of FDI. By 2000, it had reached levels of over US$15 billion per annum, although these levels dipped during the early 2000s before recovering to US$12.8 billion in 2004.

It was the 1998 Foreign Investment Promotion Act (FIPA) that primarily reshaped South Korea's new inward FDI regime, from one of investment regulation to that of invest-ment promotion,[16] introducing new legislation designed to create 'an investor-oriented policy environment by streamlining foreign investment procedures, strengthening invest-ment incentives and establishing an institutional framework for investor–relationship management'.[17] By August 2000, 99.6 per cent of all South Korea's business sectors were open to foreign investment. Under FIPA, the number of FDI restricted industries was reduced from 42 (fully 18, partially 24) to 31 (fully 13, partially 18) from a total classified number of 1148 industries. It also made the country's administrative procedures for FDI more simplified and transparent, as well as creating new tax incentives and a new institu-tional infrastructure for attracting inward FDI. The latter centred on two new agencies, these being the Korea Investment Service Centre[18] (a 'one-stop-shop' for foreign firms), and the Office of Investment Ombudsman (dealing with foreign firm grievances). In addi-tion, FIPA introduced new incentives for factory site lease and a new Foreign Investment Zone initiative, conferring greater policy management and control on local governments in this area. Various capital and financial market policy reforms were designed to under-pin the Act, such as the elimination of and raising ceilings on foreign ownership[19] (includ-ing land purchases) and the liberalization of foreign borrowing. This permitted much greater scope for acquisition-related FDI, including that of a hostile nature, and foreign investment in South Korean real estate.

Foreign takeovers of *chaebol* divisions included Renault's buy-out of Samsung Motors, while Volvo acquired Samsung's Heavy Industry division for US$300 million in June 1998. In other high-profile examples, Daimler Chrysler also bought a 15 per cent stake in Hyundai Motors, and LG Electronics signed a new joint venture deal with Philips in June 1999, whereby the latter invested a 50 per cent stake in a newly established company that was a spin-off of a subdivision of the former. More generally, this denoted a reorienta-tion of techno-industrial capability security thinking within South Korea's FEP. There was a marked shift away from arm's-length methods of inducing foreign technology trans-fer to that whereby inward FDI is proactively courted by the South Korean state, with the aim of assisting the techno-industrial restructuring of the economy and making its indus-tries more globally competitive. To some extent, this also demarcated the state's switch in adaptive partnership preference from the *chaebol* to foreign TNCs. For example, the post-crisis infusion of foreign investment was hoped to inculcate new management thinking into South Korea's corporate culture, and help Korean firms better adopt leading-edge methods of foreign corporate practice.

Also in a techno-industrial capability security context, and in relation to South Korea's trans-border community security interests, the more recent Roh Moo-hyun government (2003–7) implemented a new Free Economic Zone (FEZ) policy with the aim of pos-itioning the country as Northeast Asia's regional hub for transnational business activities.

The FEZs were specifically devised to attract high value-added FDI based on high-tech infrastructure provision, low taxes, an FDI-friendly regulatory environment, and other incentives. Three FEZs were planned around Incheon, Busan and Gwangyang. This took advantage, not only of existing infrastructural hubs (sea ports and airports) within South Korea, but also of the country's geographic centrality and connections within the Northeast Asian region, for example Incheon's position in the Yellow Sea and Busan's in the Sea of Japan.

More specifically, the Incheon FEZ – due to be completed by 2008 – involves the creation of an international financial services district and the Songdo 'intelligent city'. The district will include a 60-storey world trade centre, 60 office buildings and a technology complex comprising research centres and venture start-ups alongside the Korean Institute of Science and Technology, a state-funded agency and part of the government's industrial intelligence network of agencies. Biotechnology and information and communications technology (ICT) sectors were particularly earmarked for development here, and the entire complex should be complete by 2008. At the Busan-Jinhae FEZ, a high-tech industrial and logistics hub will be established, including a logistics park around the port, an industrial and R&D park, and a leisure resort that capitalizes on the city's beachfront. In November 2004, Renault-Samsung Motors announced plans to build a new US$600 million automobile engine production plant in the Busan-Jinhae FEZ, and the FEZ had in total attracted US$3.7 billion worth of inward FDI in its first year of operations (March 2004 to March 2005).[20]

Meanwhile, the third FEZ, at Gwangyang Bay, would concentrate on maritime logistics, distribution and manufacturing, involving 24 complexes, the first to be completed by 2006, all linked by new high-tech rail, road and airport infrastructures. There has been high-level political backing for the FEZ policy, and generally applied financial incentives across all three zones include tax exemptions, increased from eight to ten years, with a 100 per cent reduction in corporate and income taxes for seven years and a 50 per cent reduction for a further three years; simplified administrative procedures; heavily subsidized land leases on government-owned land; more flexible labour laws; and tariff-free imports. The development of these FEZs over forthcoming years will further transnationalize South Korea's economic linkages within Northeast and East Asia.

While recent South Korean governments may have thus brought considerable change to the technical policy realms of South Korea's post-crisis FEP, a resilient neomercantilism and developmental statism nevertheless remains deeply embedded within the domestic political economy, thus ensuring a significant degree of paradigmatic continuity (Dent, 2000, 2002). In the context of contesting actor-based influences over FEP formation, much of this has centred on the struggles within both South Korea's state bureaucratic cadres and societal strata over embracing the globalism eagerly peddled by the higher political ranks of the Kim Dae-jung administration. The economic nationalist backlash against various representations of foreign capital – be it the IMF, newly investing foreign TNCs or the increase of foreign imports into South Korean markets – has often proved severe. There was uproar, for instance, in the country's media when total imports of foreign cars increased by an alarming 100 per cent over 1999–2000, from around 2000 to 4000 units.[21] While the crisis had made the public more appreciative of the benefits of inward FDI (for example as a new source of employment), there remains a significant discrepancy between the government's willingness to embrace foreign investment and a persisting view within South Korean society that equates foreign ownership with colonialism. As one interviewed official from the Ministry of Foreign Affairs and Trade (MOFAT) commented, 'selling Daewoo to Ford, GM or any other foreign company to many Koreans equates to selling your country' (interview with MOFAT official, November 2000).

Paradigmatic struggles between globalism and economic nationalism have also been played out between different government ministries. For example, during the late 1990s, MOFAT and the Ministry of Culture and Tourism (MOCAT) feuded over South Korea's 'screen quota' system, designed to insulate the domestic film industry from foreign competition, where officials from the latter strongly opposed calls to scrap the system.[22] This dispute over South Korea's 'screen quota' persisted into the mid-2000s, and increasingly involved the US government and film industry that were calling for the quota to be scrapped. A similar conflict arose between MOFAT and the Ministry of Agriculture and Forestry (MOAF) over the former's plans to liberalize partially the country's agricultural trade regime in accordance with MOFAT's bilateral FTA strategy.

This economic nationalist backlash against global neoliberalism and foreign capital revealed the sociocultural underpinnings or relational aspects of the South Korean developmental state. In addition, the difficulties experienced by recent South Korean governments over decoupling the state–*chaebol* nexus, as demonstrated by its financial bailout of Hyundai's Engineering and Construction division in March 2001,[23] are a further indication of the structural relations on which developmental statism is based (that is between the state and business, the state and society), and how their interlocking nature makes them especially resilient. In other words, the technical apparatus (that is economic policy instruments) of the developmental state can be dismantled, yet its embeddedness within the domestic political economy is not so easily eradicated.

Moreover, South Korea's economic nationalism underpins persistently strong socioeconomic paradigm security interests within the country. The Kim Dae-jung government sought to bring about a paradigm shift in this respect, but has been thwarted by societal counter-pressures to maintain paradigm continuity in both foreign and domestic economic policy matters. The more recent Roh Moo-hyun government has experienced similar difficulties. Thus the calculus of the South Korean state's relationship with transnational capital remains in limbo, not being able to withdraw completely from its once close adaptive partnership with home TNCs, while simultaneously being constrained by a resilient economic nationalism that hinders the more direct infusions of foreign transnational capital into the domestic economy.

TAIWAN

Taiwan too has emulated aspects of the Japanese developmental statism, and has pursued an essentially neomercantilist FEP over recent decades. Unlike South Korea, though, Taiwan is a predominantly SME-based, atomistic structured economy that has subsequently made state–business relations relatively more difficult to develop. Nevertheless, a greater institutionalization of state–business policy networks was increasingly evident from the mid-1980s onwards, seeing the formation of joint industry task forces, regularized policy consultations, and other organizational arrangements (McBeath, 1998).

Taiwan's SME sector is highly internationalized, and has traditionally performed a sub-servient original equipment manufacture (OEM) role within international subcontracting networks in the service of core TNCs. The more recent shift from OEM subservience to original design manufacture (ODM) and to original design logistics/global logistics (ODL/GL) in transnational value-chains is an evident advance in Taiwan's development position (see also Chapter 16 in this volume).

In comparative terms, Taiwan's FDI policy has traditionally lain between Singapore's open, proactive approach, and South Korea's past closed, reactive approach to foreign investment. Huang (1989) has argued that the Taiwanese state initially adopted a moder-ate-to-conservative style of regulating inward FDI, preventing the domination of foreign TNCs in most manufacturing sectors. On FDI promotion, the 1960 Statute for the Encouragement of Investment (applied to domestic and foreign investment alike) first defined Taiwan's investment incentive and promotion system. This initially had a strong sectoral focus, with information technology, industrial machinery and other strategic industries receiving special attention by and during the 1980s. In addition, Taiwan's pion-eering EPZ policy initiated during the mid-1960s played a vital role in inducing inward FDI, emphasis here being placed on integrating complementary and not competing foreign capital with respect to Taiwan's domestic capital interests.

Somewhat mirroring developments in South Korea at the time, Taiwan embarked on a new round of trade and FDI policy liberalization during the latter 1980s. Most import-antly, towards the end of the decade, the Taiwanese state began to remove restrictions on trade and investment with mainland China. This was to have enormous consequences for Taiwan's transnational economic development and FEP. The liberalization of cross-straits commerce led to a rapid expansion of Taiwan's trade and FDI linkages with the Peoples' Republic of China (PRC), with Hong Kong playing a vital intermediating role due to Taipei's retained restrictions on direct transport links. For Taiwan's SMEs, this change in policy allowed them to exploit low production costs and new market opportun-ities across the straits, as well as further internationalizing their operations. Shared lin-guistic, sociocultural and often kinship links with their PRC commercial partners naturally proved conducive to this transnationalization (Hsing, 1996).

At first, Taiwan's central bank, the Central Bank of China (CBC), a key state agency in Taiwan's FEP formation, actively supported the process, seeing this as an opportunity for the developmental state and Taiwanese companies to adapt better to new regional and global competitive pressures. The CBC programmatically lent US dollars to Taiwanese enterprises via the Bank of Communications, the Export–Import Bank, the International Commercial Bank and China, and the China Development Corporation to cover up to 80 per cent of individual investment project costs. In effect these small, PRC-investing firms became highly localized, micro-TNCs that in turn were creating a transnational eco-nomic space between Taiwan and China's neighbouring coastal provinces, particularly incorporating Fujian, Jiangsu and Guangdong. By 2005, between 40 000 and 50 000 Taiwanese firms were operating in China with a collectively amassed FDI stock of around US$80 billion that represented between 60 and 70 per cent of Taiwan's total outward FDI.

On the one hand, the growing embeddedness of Taiwanese capital in China helped realize certain economic security objectives of Taiwan's FEP. In terms of supply security, it has significantly diversified the range of resources and products made available to Taiwanese firms at a competitive cost price and from a localized 'foreign' source. Concerning market access security, China has become Taiwan's second largest country export market, generating annual trade surpluses currently approaching US$20 billion in this bilateral trade alone. Without this bilateral surplus, Taiwan would be in overall trade deficit, substantially reducing the scope to accumulate the foreign exchange reserves on which Taiwan so depends to meet a prime finance-credit security objective. Furthermore, expanding transnational capital linkages across the straits have greatly assisted the techno-industrial restructuring of the Taiwanese economy, and thus helped advance certain of Taiwan's techno-industrial capacity security interests, especially where this has led to the competitive upgrading of key industries such as electronics. In this respect, then, the adaptive opportunities presented to Taiwan's TNCs have been significantly enhanced. On the other hand, the deepening development of a cross-straits economic space poses a broader security dilemma for policy makers in Taipei. This particularly relates to the various economic dependency risks associated with Taiwan's increasing reliance on China for the above.

Aware that these factors conferred on Beijing significant potential leverage over the Taiwanese state, Taipei adopted a two-pronged approach. It first stopped the liberalization of cross-strait commercial exchange and actively promoting any trade and investment links with China. Second, a 'Go South' policy was launched around the same time (1993–4) that aimed to promote Taiwan's transnational capital expansion into Southeast Asia as an alternative location to mainland China (see also Chapter 13 in this volume).[24] While this became a major component of Taiwan's FEP, it was more reactive to events than a catalyst of them, as it was generally perceived to follow behind the substantive overseas investments Taiwanese firms had made in Southeast Asia from the late 1980s onwards. The policy framework did, however, extend important supporting measures to these firms' operations in the region, including tax incentives and special credit lines. Moreover, according to one research interviewee closely analysing these trends, this constituted a function of developmental statism, where the government sought to cultivate its adaptive partnership with Taiwanese business in a transformative economic context.[25]

While the Taiwanese state nevertheless continued to promote home firms' transnational development into Southeast Asia, it was simultaneously trying to restrain its expansion into mainland China, and thus attempting to steer the path of Taiwanese transnationalizing capital down a particular adaptive route. In August 1996, the government called upon Taiwan's companies to scale back their investments in China. At the same time, the Council for Economic Planning and Development – the main pilot agency of the Taiwanese developmental state – withdrew a proposal relaxing certain constraints on cross-straits investment. In July 1997, the government released new guidelines for investment and technological cooperation with mainland China that widened the sectoral scope of prohibited investments, banned infrastructure projects, and limited individual project investments to a US$50 million ceiling (Deng, 2000).

Interestingly, it was a proposed large-scale investment project by Formosa Plastics that prompted the then Kuomintang government into introducing this so-called 'no haste, be patient' policy, which in turn led to the restrictions noted above. The US$3.8 billion project had been announced in May 1996, based on initial plans to construct thermal power plants in Fujian province. If state-endorsed, the investment would have been 22 times bigger than the second largest ever made by a Taiwanese company in China, and undoubtedly led to a marked acceleration of cross-straits investment by the precedent set.

As one of Taiwan's largest TNCs, it could source funds from its overseas subsidiaries (intended mainly from the US) to bypass government finance-related regulations on China-bound investments.[26] This appeared a classic globalization predicament of state power being circumvented by transnational capital.

However, the Taiwanese government were able to persuade Formosa Plastics' boss, Wang Yung-ching, to abandon the project, convincing him of the political and security risks for Taiwan this would create.[27] As McBeath (1998) notes, the state retained sufficient powers to deny the company use of Taiwanese assets to construct such projects in China, yet further argued that, while Wang was not able to change state policy on investment, his actions did lead to the clarifying of it. In this sense, it also helped clarify key problem areas in the Taiwanese developmental state's adaptive partnership with transnational capital that were to come to a head in 2000 and 2001, as we discuss next.

As the 1990s progressed, deepening financial globalization opened up increasing opportunities for Taiwanese firms to reroute capital via third countries to mainland China (Yang and Hung, 2003; Zhang *et al.*, 2003). However, the regulations and measures embodied in the 'no haste, be patient' policy still frustrated the Taiwanese business community to the extent of galvanizing growing pressure upon the government to change it. After the inaugural Economic Development Advisory Conference held in August 2001, this policy was replaced by the 'active liberalization, effective management' approach of the new Democratic Progressive Party (DPP) government under Chen Shui-bian. However, the ensuing liberalization of cross-strait commerce was undertaken in a strong reregulatory context. For example, the US$50 million ceiling on mainland investment projects was replaced by an annual ceiling on total corporate investment in China, thus constituting a shift from firm-specific, micro-controls to macro-controls. The government also retained many of its product-specific and industry-specific bans on cross-strait commerce, and individual mainland investments over US$50 million would continue to be reviewed for approval by state officials.

Nevertheless, these were important concessions that demonstrated how ultimately the Taiwanese state was compelled to establish a firmer adaptive partnership with Taiwan's transnationalizing companies. The imperative to help these companies better compete and adapt in challenging regional and global market conditions proved too great, and the Taiwanese state and its foreign economic policy too had to adapt accordingly. Yet this episode is also illustrative of how the Taiwanese developmental state continues to shape the course of the economy's transnational development, albeit under the stronger partnering influence of Taiwan's business community in the post-authoritarian era.

Whilst there has been a substantive flow of Taiwanese investment to mainland China, the core of Taiwanese business high valued-added activity remains firmly rooted in Taiwan itself. The Taiwanese state continues to operate a well-defined high-tech industrial policy framework, based around various state agencies charged with cultivating adaptive partnerships with business (for example the National Science Council, Industrial Technology Research Institute and the Science and Technology Advisory Group), and also Taiwan's high-tech industrial parks, where many of these adaptive partnership interactions take place. The most important of these is the Hsinchu Science-based Industrial Park, established in 1980, host to over 360 firms and the cradle of Taiwan's ICT hardware industry. A similar high-tech park was established at Tainan in the late 1990s, and a third is under development near the city of Taichung.

Many innovative new developments in the global ICT industry occur within these high-tech industrial parks. For example, while Taiwan Semiconductor Manufacturing Corporation (TSMC) received government approval to build a US$900 million 8-inch silicon wafer chip plant investment in Shanghai in 2004, TSMC also announced in the same year plans to construct a US$7.5 billion state-of-the-art 12-inch silicon wafer chip plant at Taichung. Foreign TNCs, such as Dell and Hewlett Packard, also have multi-billion dollar subcontracting interests in these parks, linked with small and large Taiwanese firms alike. There are obviously links here to the way Singapore and South Korea have sought to create designated geoindustrial spaces to work in adaptive partnership with transnational capital, and this forms an increasingly critical aspect of the NIE-3's pursuit of techno-industrial capacity security.

Returning to the matter of Taiwan's cross-strait commerce policy, we should consider both present and future developments in the context of socioeconomic paradigm security and transborder community security. To some, the growth of transnational capital linkages between Taiwan and mainland China is not transnational at all, given special unifying ties between the two territories; that is both are essentially ethnic Chinese-based economies. Yet Taiwan and China represent two strongly distinguishable politico-economic entities, and China continues to represent a counter-paradigm threat to Taipei. Whilst Beijing currently states that Taiwan's capitalist enclave and associated socioeconomic paradigm can continue in perpetuity under its aforementioned 'one country, two systems' model, Taiwan's government and its people remain highly suspicious of China's longer-term intentions. Moreover, the deepening democratization heralded by the DPP electoral victory in March 2000 has meant to many that Taiwan has, at least in principle, further politico-economic achievements to defend against China's irredentist intentions. Hence the further merging of the Taiwan economy into that of China through transnational capital linkages presents a challenge to the former's socioeconomic paradigm security interests.

This very same merging, however, simultaneously necessitates Taiwan paying greater attention to the expanding trans-border community security interests it shares with China, for example economic migration. To help manage issues therein, the Taiwanese government established in 1990 the Straits Exchange Foundation (SEF) as its principal unofficial cross-strait representative body to deal with its Chinese counterpart, the Association for Relations Across the Straits (ARATS). The re-initiation of SEF–ARATS dialogue after its breakdown in the early 1990s will become increasingly critical, as these interests develop in salience. Given the lack of official diplomatic recognition between the two sides, the Taiwanese state is likely to continue depending upon the use of chief representatives from Taiwan's TNCs to serve as quasi-diplomats in this respect.[28] Indeed, their use in other aspects of international economic relations has arisen from the circumstances of Taiwan's contested statehood, and this arrangement demonstrates how both the state and transnational capital interests may be effectively allied to realize common commercial objectives within an adaptive partnership context.

CONCLUSION

Various discourses and debates on the state–transnational capital relationship have emerged within the international political economy literature. This chapter has focused on this relationship in three East Asian developmental states (Singapore, South Korea and Taiwan – the NIE-3) through the lens of foreign economic policy (FEP) analysis. In different ways, their respective state governments have all worked closely alongside various forms of transnational capital in sustained, and yet evolving, adaptive partnerships, and in overall accordance with largely state-determined FEP objectives that themselves are generally oriented by the pursuit of economic security in the international system. As the preceding analysis has shown, a developmental state's ability to cultivate links with both home-originating and foreign TNCs is very much based on their own capacities to adapt within a fast-changing, globalizing world economy, and to meet the economic and technocratic challenges arising therein. We have argued that this can depend on the extent to which such states develop an adaptive partnership with transnational capital, with both seeking ways, often mutually, to adapt and prosper in a globalizing world economy.

While TNCs seek to extract policy concessions from states, and influence state economic policy-making processes, they also view those states endowed with sufficient technocratic capacities as adaptive partners, whereby both agents gain by working in conjunction to respond to the mutual challenges presented by globalization. In this case analysis of the NIE-3's foreign economic policies, it has been argued both that developmental states make particularly good adaptive partners for TNCs, and that they also demonstrate a strong proclivity themselves to forging adaptive partnerships with transnational capital. The NIE-3 developmental states (especially Singapore and Taiwan) have generally retained strong technocratic capacities that have adapted and evolved in the face of globalization challenges, and thus continue to provide the basis on which these partnerships can operate.

In Singapore, the state has long fostered an adaptive partnership with the hosted foreign TNCs that now dominate the economy. More recently, it has nurtured the TNC capacity of indigenous companies. Both their internationalization and the transnational restructuring of hosted foreign TNCs have been assisted by the state's regionalization strategy. This has further progressed to where the state has intensified efforts to promote Singapore as a prime regional node in *global* circuits of transnational capital, aiming more specifically to develop Singapore's capacities as a high-tech export production centre, a regional operations centre for TNCs and a regional R&D centre in niche sectors. These all dovetail into the Singapore government's current transformative economic project, namely developing a knowledge-based economy in the city-state. More generally, the Singapore state combines an activist managerial role in its own economy's transnational capital development, with a vocal advocacy of transnational economic liberalism, as revealed in its recent bilateral FTA strategy. In sum, the state's adaptive partnership with transnational capital is a central factor in Singapore's FEP calculus, and is consequently instrumental in the city-state's pursuit of economic security.

South Korea, in significant contrast to Singapore, based its developmental state strategy on a strong corporatist alliance forged between government and domestic big business groups (that is the *chaebol* conglomerates), and on an arm's-length relationship with foreign capital. While the South Korean state actively supported the *chaebol*'s transnational capital development, it strictly mediated foreign transnational capital's contribution to national economic development. The country's 1997/98 financial crisis, however, brought dramatic change. As part of the post-crisis economic and corporate paradigm advocated by the then newly incumbent Kim Dae-jung government, the more neoliberal-minded state switched priorities from promoting *chaebol* transnationalization to domestic economy transnationalization. The subsequent eradication of many remaining neomercantilist policies and measures has been accompanied by a vigorous government campaign to attract inward FDI. However, the state–transnational capital relationship in South Korea is undergoing a protracted transition, owing to the state–*chaebol* nexus proving as resilient as ever. However, the reasons for this persisting linkage are more political than policy-functional, and much of the adaptive partnership between the state and the *chaebol* has broken down. The *chaebol* still work with South Korean government agencies in various trade and industry policy domains, but not as intimately.

Taiwan's SME-based economy has long been plugged into a wide range of international subcontracting networks, where its small dynamic firms perform various production services for foreign TNCs. As the 1990s progressed, Taiwanese companies increasingly used both mainland China and Southeast Asia as an overseas base for their own transnational capital development. The Taiwanese state played an instrumental role here in both supporting this development and, then, in the case of PRC trade and investments, restraining the ensuing expansion of transnationalized economic linkages that posed serious potential threats to Taiwan's national security. Moreover, it was further noted how the transnational economic space expanding across the straits caught Taiwan's FEP between conflicting economic security interests, which in turn created tensions in the state's adaptive partnership with Taiwanese TNCs. While the government's reins over Taiwan's transnational capital development into mainland China have slackened somewhat, a developmental statist combination of smart regulation and effective corporatist relations fostered with business still confers on the state significant influence over decisions made by Taiwan's home TNCs. In addition, recent policy changes on cross-straits commerce have led to a de facto firming of the Taiwanese state's adaptive partnership with Taiwan's transnationalizing firms, as both now more openly and conjunctively seek to use the mainland China economy to enhance Taiwan's economic and corporate competitive positions. What is more, the state's continued use of Taiwanese TNC representatives to serve as quasi-diplomats in international economic relations provided an illustration of congruent commercial interests that often arise between the state and transnational capital.

The special development context of the NIE-3 admittedly makes the transposition of their state strategies towards transnational capital to other states inherently difficult. Various elements made the generally successful relationship between the state and transnational capital in Singapore, South Korea and Taiwan possible. These included the state's impressive technocratic capacities, sophisticated corporate relations fostered with business per se, helpful sociocultural factors and situational imperatives of a geopolitical and geoeconomic nature that initially compelled the state to seek a developmental adaptive partnership with certain forms of transnational capital. From a different perspective, it should also be conceded that these adaptive partnerships must deal with constantly arising conflicts of interests between the state and TNCs. Moreover, TNCs generally now enjoy more influence over the (foreign) economic policy process, as our discussions on Taiwan particularly revealed. Notwithstanding such points, this chapter has analysed one of many contemporary examples where both the state and transnational capital are working to congruent ends in their respective adaptations to the challenges posed by globalization.

NOTES

1. This chapter is a substantially revised version of Dent (2003).
2. To a TCC analyst such as Robinson (1996), the state–transnational capital relationship is posited within a global capitalist framework, organized by a set of interlocking institutions that mainly comprise TNCs that own and manage the world's resources and appropriate its wealth; international financial agencies that shape the conducive conditions for global capital accumulation; state governments that create the local and global political, administrative and legal environment that permits the whole system to function; and formal and informal transnational elite fora (for example the Trilateral Commission) that develop strategies and ideas for the maintenance and reproduction of the system.
3. These can include substate units (for example states within a federated union such as the US), supranational or intergovernmental units (for example the EU), or city-states like Singapore. Notwithstanding Taiwan's contested statehood, it still possesses state-like capacities that enable it to conduct a viable FEP.
4. These relate to actors that are responsible for the directing (political or quasi-political leadership) or managing (bureaucratic leadership) of FEP.
5. This was a distinct possibility during the turbulent mid-1960s, when military tensions in the regional locale reached near boiling point.
6. Interviews with US Embassy and AmCham officials in Singapore, September 2000. The US–Singapore FTA was signed in 2003.
7. In the late 1990s, the EDB actively courted and succeeded in getting Hewlett-Packard, SGS-Thompson, Hitachi, and Nippon Steel to set up high-tech wafer and integrated circuit fabrication plants in Singapore (Poon and Thompson, 2001).
8. Some initial success has been achieved here. In March 2001, two high-profile biotechnology firms, SurroMed and Affymetrix, announced their intentions to establish multi-million dollar research and production centres in Singapore, developing leading-edge techniques for identifying and measuring genetic material and proteins. Later that year, the Singapore government announced plans to develop a Biopolis industrial park to attract further foreign investment from biotechnology firms.
9. Now known as the Agency for Science, Technology, and Research (A*STAR).
10. Amongst these is British biotech scientist Alan Colman, who famously cloned 'Dolly' the sheep, and moved to Singapore in 2001 after his European funding slowed.
11. While Singapore does have relatively liberal laws on stem cell research, in November 2003 it introduced tough penalties in this area, including ten years in prison and S$100 000 (US$58 000) in fines, for scientists who try to clone humans (*Financial Times*, 20 November 2003).
12. *Reuters News*, 18 November 2003.
13. *Electronic Engineering Times*, 11 November 2003.
14. Between 1994 and 1996 more specifically, South Korean outward FDI grew at an average annual rate of around 36 per cent.
15. As at least implicitly contended by most interviewed foreign representatives in Seoul (May 1998, November 1998, October 1999).
16. MOFAT Report, 'Korea's new economy: recovery, reform, liberalization, and the road ahead', 3 June 2000.
17. *Recent Trends and Policy Directions in Foreign Investment Policy*, 12 October 2000, MOCIE, p. 5.
18. Created in April 1998 and staffed by experts from various agencies, including representatives from MOFE, MOCIE, Korea Customs Service, and local governments.
19. Earlier, under the conditions of an IMF bailout programme, the limit on foreign ownership was raised from 26 per cent to 50 per cent by the end of 1997. FIPA raised this further to 55 per cent by the end of 1998.
20. *Korea Times*, 9 October 2005.
21. Over the same period, South Korea had exported well over 100 times this number.
22. *Korea Times*, 18 August 1998.
23. *Asian Wall Street Journal*, 6 March 2001.
24. In 1994, the Executive Yuan passed the 'Guidelines for Strengthening Economic and Trading Relations with Southeast Asia', intending to promote and manage the growing economic interdependence between Taiwan and the region.
25. Interview with an analyst at the Taiwan Institute of Economic Research, April 2000.
26. The rules of the government's Economic Screening Committee then permitted a Taiwanese company's foreign subsidiaries to invest freely in China without reporting it, so long as the parent company's stock share did not exceed 20 per cent. In the Formosa Plastics case, the parent company held only 10.5 per cent (Deng, 2000).
27. In the 1950s, Wang (then a rice merchant) had been chosen by the state to establish Taiwan's first PVC factory.
28. For example, the late Dr Koo Chen-fu of Taiwan Cement had chaired the SEF since its inception, and nine of the organization's 27 directors are also Taiwanese business leaders.

REFERENCES

Amsden, A. (1989), *Asia's Next Giant: South Korea and Late Industrialisation*, Oxford: Oxford University Press.

Bradshaw, Y.W., Y.J. Kim and B. London (1993), 'Transnational economic linkages, the state and dependent development in South Korea, 1966–1988: a time series analysis', *Social Forces*, **72**(2), 315–45.

Cable, V. (1995), 'The diminished nation-state: a study in the loss of economic power', *Daedalus*, **124**(2), 44–6.

Cardoso, F.H. and E. Faletto (1979), *Dependency and Development in Latin America*, Berkeley, CA: University of California Press.

Cerny, P.G. (1997), 'Paradoxes of the competition state: the dynamics of political globalisation', *Government and Opposition*, **32**(2), 251–74.

Cerny, P.G. (2000), 'Structuring the political arena: public goods, states and governance in a globalising world', in R. Palan (ed.), *Global Political Economy: Contemporary Theories*, London: Routledge.

Cherry, J. (2005), 'Big deal or big disappointment? The continuing evolution of the Korean developmental state', *Pacific Review*, **18**(3), 327–54.

Clark, C. and S. Chan (1995), 'MNCs and developmentalism: domestic structures as an explanation for East Asian dynamism', in T. Risse-Kappen (ed.), *Bringing Transnational Relations Back In: Non-State Actors, Domestic Structures and International Institutions*, Cambridge: Cambridge University Press.

Deng, P. (2000), 'Taiwan's restriction of investment in China in the 1990s: a relative gains approach', *Asian Survey*, **40**(6), 958–80.

Dent, C.M. (2000), 'Continuity and change in South Korea's foreign economic policy', *Journal of the Asia Pacific Economy*, **5**(3), 275–302.

Dent, C. M. (2001), 'Singapore's foreign economic policy: the pursuit of economic security', *Contemporary Southeast Asia*, **23**(1), 1–23.

Dent, C.M. (2002), *The Foreign Economic Policies of Singapore, South Korea and Taiwan*, Cheltenham, UK and Northampton, MA, USA: Edward Elgar.

Dent, C.M. (2003), 'Transnational capital, the state and foreign economic policy: Singapore, South Korea and Taiwan', *Review of International Political Economy*, **10**(2), 246–77.

Dent, C.M. (2004), 'The new international political economy of East Asia and the developmental state', in L. Low (ed.), *Developmental States: Relevancy, Redundancy or Reconfiguration?*, New York: Nova Science.

Dent, C.M. and C. Randerson (1996), 'Korean foreign direct investment in Europe: the determining forces', *The Pacific Review*, **9**(4), 531–52.

Dicken, P. (1998), *Global Shift: Transforming the World Economy*, London: PCP.

Drucker, P.F. (1997), 'The global economy and the nation-state', *Foreign Affairs*, **76**(5), 159–71.

Evans, P. (1985), 'Transnational linkages and the economic role of the state: an analysis of developing and industrialised nations in the post-World War II period', in P.B. Evans, D. Rueschmeyer and T. Skocpol (eds), *Bringing the State Back In*, Cambridge: Cambridge University Press.

Evans, P. (1995), *Embedded Autonomy: States and Industrial Transformation*, Princeton: Princeton University Press.

Evans, P. (1997), 'The eclipse of the state? Reflections on stateness in an era of globalisation', *World Politics*, **50**(October), 62–87.

Fukuyama, F. (1992), *The End of History and the Last Man*, New York: Free Press.

Gills, B.K. (1996), 'Economic liberalisation and reform in South Korea in the 1990s: a coming of age or a case of graduation blues?', *Third World Quarterly*, **17**(4), 667–88.

Gills, B.K. (1999), 'Globalisation, crisis and labour in South Korea', paper given at the International Political Economy Group Workshop, University of Hull, 13 March.

Gordon, D.M. (1988), 'The global economy: new edifice or crumbling foundations?', *New Left Review*, **168**, 24–64.

Grosse, R. and J.N. Behrman (1992), 'Theory in international business', *Transnational Corporations*, February, 93–125.

Haggard, S. (1986), 'The newly industrialising countries in the international system', *World Politics*, **38**(2), 343–70.

Haggard, S. and T.J. Cheng (1987), 'State and foreign capital in the East Asian NICs', in F. Deyo (ed.), *The Political Economy of the New Asian Industrialism*, Berkeley, CA: University of California Press.

Heo, U. and A.C. Tan (2003), 'Political choices and economic outcomes – a perspective on the differential impact of the financial crisis on South Korea and Taiwan', *Comparative Political Studies*, **36**(6), 679–98.

Horsman, M. and A. Marshall (1994), *After the Nation-State: Citizens, Tribalism and the New World Disorder*, London: Harper Collins.

Hsing, Y. (1996), 'Blood, thicker than water: interpersonal relations and Taiwanese investment in Southern China', *Environment and Planning A*, **28**, 2241–61.

Huang, C. (1989), 'The state and foreign investment: the cases of Taiwan and Singapore', *Comparative Political Studies*, **22**(1), 93–121.

Huff, W.G. (1995), 'The developmental state, government, and Singapore economic development since 1960', *World Development*, **23**(8),1421–38.

Huntington, S. (1991), *The Third Wave: Democratisation in the Late Twentieth Century*, Oklahoma: University of Oklahoma Press.

Jessop, B. (1993), 'Towards a Schumpeterian workfare state? Preliminary remarks on post- Fordist political economy', *Studies in Political Economy*, **40**(1), 7–39.

Jessop, B. (1997), 'Capitalism and its future: remarks on regulation, government and governance', *Review of International Political Economy*, **4**(3), 561–81.

Johnson, C. (1982), *MITI and the Japanese Miracle*, Stanford, CA: Stanford University Press.

Jomo, K.S. (2000), 'Comment: crisis and the developmental state in East Asia', in R. Robison, M. Beeson, K. Jayasuriya and H.R. Kim (eds), *Politics and Markets in the Wake of the Asian Crisis*, London: Routledge.

Jones, R.J.B. (1995), *Globalisation and Interdependence in the International Political Economy: Rhetoric and Reality*, London: Pinter.

Keohane, R.O. and J.S. Nye (1977), *Power and Interdependence*, Boston: Little, Brown.

Kim, S.S. (2000), 'Korea and globalisation (*Segyehwa*): a framework for analysis', in S.S. Kim (ed.), *Korea's Globalisation*, Cambridge: Cambridge University Press.

Kim, Y.T. (1999), 'Neo-liberalism and the decline of the developmental state', *Journal of Contemporary Asia*, **29**(4), 441–61.

Kuo, C.T. (1998), 'Private governance in Taiwan', in S. Chan, C. Clark and D. Lam (eds), *Beyond the Developmental State: East Asia's Political Economies Reconsidered*, London: Macmillan.

Low, L. (2001), 'The Singapore developmental state in the new economy and polity', *Pacific Review*, **14**(3), 411–42.

Mann, M. (1997), 'Has globalisation ended the rise and rise of the nation-state?', *Review of International Political Economy*, **4**(3), 472–96.

Mardon, R. (1990), 'The state and effective control of foreign capital: the case of South Korea', *World Politics*, **43**, 111–38.

McBeath, G.A. (1998), *Wealth and Freedom: Taiwan's New Political Economy*, Aldershot: Ashgate.

Ohmae, K. (1990), *Borderless World: Power and Strategy in the Interlinked Economy*, London: Collins.

Ohmae, K. (1995), *The End of the Nation-State: The Rise of Regional Economies*, London: Harper Collins.

Pereira, A. (2000), 'State collaboration with transnational corporations: the case of Singapore's industrial programmes (1965–1999)', *Competition and Change*, **4**(4), 1–29.

Pitilis, C. (1991), 'Beyond the nation-state? The transnational firm and the state', *Capital and Class*, **43**, 131–52.

Poon, J.P.H. and E.R. Thompson (2001), 'Effects of the Asian financial crisis on transnational capital', *Geoforum*, **32**, 121–31.

Robinson, W.I. (1996), 'Globalisation: nine theses of our epoch', *Race and Class*, **38**(2), 13–31.

Robinson, W.I. and J. Harris (2000), 'Towards a global ruling class? Globalisation and the transnational capitalist class', *Science and Society*, **64**(1), 11–54.

Rowley, C. and J. Bae (eds) (1998), *Korean Business: Internal and External Industrialisation*, London: Frank Cass.

Sally, R. (1994), 'Multinational enterprises, political economy and institutional theory: domestic embeddedness in the context of internationalisation', *Review of International Political Economy*, 1(1), 161–92.

Schein, E.H. (1996), *Strategic Pragmatism: The Culture of Singapore's Economic Development Board*, Cambridge, MA: MIT Press.

Shaw, M. (1997), 'The state of globalisation: towards a theory of state transformation', *Review of International Political Economy*, 4(3), 497–513.

Smith, D.A. (1997), 'Technology, commodity chains and global inequality: South Korea in the 1990s', *Review of International Political Economy*, 4(4), 734–62.

Smith, D.A and S.H. Lee (1990), 'Limits on a semi-peripheral success story? State dependent development and the prospects for South Korean democratisation', in W.G. Martin (ed.), *Semi-peripheral States in the World Economy*, New York: Greenwood Press.

Stopford, J. and S. Strange (1991), *Rival States, Rival Firms: Competition for World Market Shares*, Cambridge: Cambridge University Press.

Thurbon, E. (2001), 'Two paths to financial liberalisation: South Korea and Taiwan', *The Pacific Review*, 14(2), 241–68.

Van der Pijl, K. (1998), *Transnational Classes and International Relations*, London: Routledge.

Vernon, R. (1971), *Sovereignty at Bay*, Harmondsworth: Penguin.

Wade, R. (1990), *Governing the Market: Economic Theory and the Role of Government in East Asian Industrialisation*, Princeton: Princeton University Press.

Weiss, L. (1995), 'Governed interdependence: rethinking the government–business relationship in East Asia', *Pacific Review*, 8(4), 589–616.

Weiss, L. (1998), *The Myth of the Powerless State: Governing the Economy in a Global Era*, London: Polity.

Weiss, L. (2000), 'Developmental states in transition: adapting, dismantling, innovating, not normalising', *Pacific Review*, 13(1), 21–56.

Woo-Cumings, M. (ed.) (1999), *The Developmental State*, Ithaca: Cornell University Press.

Yang, C. and S.W. Hung (2003), 'Taiwan's dilemma across the strait: lifting the ban on semiconductor investment in China', *Asian Survey*, 43(4), 681–96.

Yeoh, B. and K. Willis (1997), 'The global–local nexus: Singapore's regionalisation drive', *Geography*, 82, 355(2), 183–6.

Yeung, H.W.C. (2000), 'State intervention and neoliberalism in the globalising world economy: lessons from Singapore's regionalisation programme', *Pacific Review*, 13(1), 133–62.

Zhang, Z., X. Xu and W.B. Zhang (2003), 'The dynamics of political and economic interactions between mainland China and Taiwan', *Papers in Regional Science*, 82, 373–88.

13.   Capital's search for order: foreign direct investment, models and hybrid models of social order in Southeast Asia

Nicholas A. Phelps[1]

There may be good reasons why, in economic theory, nations should not compete with one another for capital (Krugman, 1996). The reality, however, is rather different, since 'the combination of structural dependence and capital mobility means that governments at all levels . . . must compete with each other for investment' (Thomas, 2000: 26). Reading much of the recent advocacy regarding foreign direct investment (FDI) policy and promotion, especially that circulating in the US and the UK, one might be forgiven for thinking that multinational enterprises (MNEs) entertain a remarkably limited set of criteria, when considering locations for their international investments. The sorts of policy advocacy emanating from Western oriented international organizations (IOs) and governments stress the establishment of open, stable, transparent and secure business environments within which the transaction costs facing MNEs are minimized. This is precisely the sort of macroeconomic stance adopted in the UK, where interventions on the micro scale of industrial policy have been avoided (Hood and Young, 1997), with the expectation that the UK economy could be opened up as a competitive space within the global economy (Wilkinson, 2000). The recent record regarding the contribution of FDI to UK's economic performance is, however, disappointing, most of all in those subnational territories now most dependent on FDI (Phelps et al., 2003).

At the other side of the world stand a set of East Asian national economic models, where the transactions costs facing FDI are rarely minimized, while additional costs are imposed as a result of seemingly less open, less transparent, sometimes less stable or secure, environments in which investment decisions are mediated by the visible hand of active industrial policies (MacIntyre, 1994; Wade, 1990; Whitley, 1992a, 1992b). On the face of it, these environments ought to be considerably less attractive to FDI and engender fewer host country economic impacts, yet, for various reasons, many East Asian nations are successful in attracting FDI and, crucially, obtaining wider benefits, while some are even regarded as models of FDI-led economic growth and investment promotion practice.

In juxtaposing these two broad West–East policy stances at the outset, what this chapter attempts to make clear is that the 'market for capital' is more differentiated than is entertained in much of the academic literature and Western policy advocacy. Not only is there a supply of markedly different FDI policy environments, but also these are met and, indeed, it stands to reason, sustained by markedly different demands emanating from MNEs in respect of their individual investment decisions. It is not just governments that compete, but also TNCs, for a favourable host economy (Chang, 1998: 233–5). The diversity of supply and demand in the market for capital, their complex interaction (including signals other than price) and their generative effects, in terms of the economic impacts of FDI on host economies, arguably remain underexamined from an analytical as well as a policy perspective (see also Chapters 12 and 14 in this volume). Consideration of capital's search for order not only focuses analytical attention on the market for capital, but also draws attention to the policy latitude open to governments in an increasingly integrated international economy.

THE UNEVEN SUPPLY OF SOCIAL ORDER

Whilst, in very broad terms, it is possible to discern a degree of homogenization of state regulatory stances toward business (Strange, 1997), global business regulation has proceeded relatively slowly by virtue of multiple mechanisms and often conflicting principles (Braithwaite and Drahos, 2000). Consequently, it is also clear that national business systems continue to vary considerably even within similar regional contexts (Whitley, 1992a, 1992b). In light of the failed Multilateral Agreement on Investment (MAI), variety also persists in the more specific sphere of the FDI regulatory environment. Here, 'what exists comprises a patchwork of bilateral treaties, regional arrangements, and limited plurilateral or multilateral instruments. This patchwork . . . weakens the bargaining power of countries vis-à-vis TNCs, which have learned how to exploit the absence of a transparent and harmonized FDI regulatory environment' (Young and Tavares, 2004: 11).

At the very least, 'the regulatory asymmetry created by different states . . . constitutes an uneven surface of transaction costs' facing MNEs (Yeung, 1998: 298). But, as Young and Tavares imply, the engagement of MNEs with this uneven regulatory terrain is something that goes beyond purely economic considerations, let alone those centred on the minimization of production or transaction costs. Thus, although ASEAN (Association of South East Asian Nations) countries have operated similar incentives to overseas investors, there has been quite pronounced variation among them in terms of bureaucratic efficiency, the sectors restricted to foreign ownership, and performance measures (Harianto and Safarian, 1997). This is most apparent in the East Asian setting, where a number of factors conspire to present a business environment very different from the arm's-length liberal orders of the US and UK.

In the most general terms, the prevalence of state intervention in various forms necessitates a distinctively politicized set of MNE–state interactions across virtually all nations in East Asia. Moreover, intertwined colonial histories coupled with the ethnic Chinese diaspora have, for example, created important fissures running through the business systems and wider society of Southeast Asian states (Bornschier and Trezzini, 2001; see also Chapters 15 and 18 in this volume). The main orchestrators of regional divisions of labour have been Japanese and Chinese MNEs, both of which are bearers of distinctive cultural and political–economic practices to host nations across the region (Whitley, 1992b). Yet 'differences in Southeast Asian states contribute to spatial variations of ethnic Chinese business. In Singapore, Chinese firms tend to engage more in western management practices because of alliances with western TNCs. But in Indonesia, Thailand and

Malaysia, Chinese firms tend to be more engaged with patron–client relationships needed to secure business niche' (Yeung, 1999: 111).

Following Bornschier and Trezzini's line of argument, we can identify a 'market for social order' represented by national modes of social regulation. 'Governments produce "order" and "sell" this public utility to capitalist undertakings as well as to citizens which they rule . . . By means of supplying this utility, governments affect the locational quality of their territory in the framework of the world economy' (Bornschier and Trezzini, 2001: 212–13). The growing resources spent on the likes of investment promotion provide confirmation of the significant signalling costs of selling such models of social order to capital. It is not the purpose of this chapter to propose a classification of models of social order, but a casual inspection suggests there to be at least four broad models within which there is further variation in terms of national business systems (Whitley, 1992a and b).[2] Paradoxically, rapid international economic integration actually means that it is the most immobile factors of production that have become important in determining the competitive position of nations vis-à-vis the attraction of FDI.

This is particularly the case regarding sources of technology (Cantwell, 1995) composed of the created assets of systems of innovation. However, it would also include skilled labour and even the rarely acknowledged role of the quality of the built environment and transport and communications infrastructure, and the institutions that deliver these (Berry and McGreal, 1995). The key word here is *quality*, in that the notion of a market for social order directs our attention away from an exclusively economistic view of MNEs' search for suitable host environments. For example, whilst firms' power to engage in regulatory arbitrage has increased in the context of rapid international economic integration, the resultant regulatory competition that exists among states need not result in a competition for laxity or the minimization of costs facing potential investors, since companies remain attracted to environments that provide effective regulation and, indeed, are often prepared to pay a premium for regulatory efficiency and created assets, such as labour skills.

National Models of Social Order

Nation states then, clearly, represent different offerings to potential investors in terms of their macroeconomic stability and size, the specifics of their business system and the specifics of their FDI policies. It is these different offerings that match up to the different requirements of international investors. Some of the similarities and differences between national modes of social order are heavily imbued with intertwined colonial histories and subsequent postcolonial insecurities. In general terms, the sorts of coalitional politics necessitated by these and other considerations have resulted in a mix of liberal and illiberal economic policies.

Moreover, it would be as well to remember that these national models of social order are not passive or static offerings to potential inward investors. So, in the case of Malaysia for example, 'while broadly liberalising entry conditions, Malaysian policy-makers sought to capitalise on the regional strategies of MNCs in order to upgrade the industrial sector. In this regard the globalisation of manufacturing offered the Malaysian state a role and rationale for continued discretionary intervention' (Felker, 2001: 130). Even so, there was an element of serendipity regarding this interventionist role, since the active pursuit of

FDI by Malaysia coincided with a first wave of Western MNEs' search for lower-cost locations, and has subsequently proved obstructive to the creation of new stocks of FDI (Ritchie, 2005).

Within the Southeast Asian setting, for example, there are clear gradations in existence that, in the minds of the Western-oriented business community, are often caricatured in terms of social order. So, for example, Singapore is sometimes referred to as 'Asia-lite', as one interviewee described it (Interview 1 in Appendix 13.1) – a logical first point of entry into the Southeast Asia region, in light of its approximation to Western business systems. Indeed, Ong (1999) suggests that Singapore's model of social order may, in important respects, be in the vanguard of neoliberalism (commonly associated with Western nations), since the 'practical rationalities of liberalism' are already deeply ingrained in the psyche of citizens. So, according to the managing director of Reuters, the continued attractiveness of Singapore to MNEs within the region entails 'comparing infrastructure quality and cost to the US and Europe, not other Asian cities' (Chellam, 1998).

There is also economic competition that exists between neighbouring countries in the region. As Felker (2003: 265) has observed, 'Singapore's FDI-led, yet highly interventionist, growth pattern has furnished an influential template for emulation by its less-proficient neighbours.' Malaysia and Singapore would be cases in point. The common colonial history and subsequent tensions over Singapore's separation from Malaysia have set in train significant elements of competition for FDI and in terms of government funded projects (Phelps, 2004a). Something of this competition derives from the close mimicking by Malaysian institutions of practices, with the impression being that 'Malaysia doesn't do it quite as well' (Interview 1).

Indonesia, the other leg of the Indonesia–Malaysia–Singapore Growth Triangle (IMS-GT), has seen the competitiveness of its model of social order decline somewhat. In Suharto's New Order era (1967–97), overseas investors had adjusted to the additional transactions costs of KKN practices in Indonesia (*Korupsi, Kolusi, Nepotisme* in Indonesian). Although potentially quite considerable, these additional costs were relatively predictable, as a result of highly centralized bureaucratic government, and seemed to be outweighed by the profits to be gained by investors operating in the economy. Some sense of this is implied in one interviewee's observation that 'The trade delegations that come here, they keep saying, "well why should I get involved in here?" And the guy sitting next to them, who has been here for ten years, just smiles' (Interview 2).

Indonesia used to see itself as a competitor with Malaysia, crystallized in the IMS-GT context. Since the 1997/1998 Asian economic crisis, however, it has one of the poorest performances in terms of UNCTAD's (2002) FDI Competitiveness Index, and now competes with countries at least an echelon below Malaysia and Singapore such as Cambodia, Laos and Nigeria (Interview 3), and seeks trade and investment agreements with such countries (Interview 4). In the newly devolved post-New Order era in Indonesia, the transaction or 'hassle' costs facing overseas investors have risen further, since KKN practices have become decentralized and less predictable (Phelps, 2004b). Moreover, unlike some Latin American countries (Maxfield and Schneider, 1997), overseas investors have played no significant role in stabilizing neoliberal reforms.

> Many foreign business interests have decided to defend the privileges they gained under the old regime rather than play any active part in pressing for political reform. . . . It is clear . . . that

such groups have less of an interest in liberal democratic reforms than they do in social order, predictability and the protection of property rights – all of which could be accommodated within a range of political regimes other than a liberal democratic one. (Hadiz and Robison, 2005: 237)

Therefore, deeply entrenched political interests have hijacked neoliberal reforms, producing a paradoxical predatory neoliberalism (Hadiz and Robison, 2005).

Coexisting with elements of competition between nation states and their distinctive models of social order are elements of cooperation that have produced zones of economic integration or 'graduated sovereignty', as Ong (1999) describes them: 'In Southeast Asia, governments seeking to accommodate corporate strategies of location have become flexible in their management of sovereignty, so that different production sites offer institutional domains that vary in terms of their mix of legal protections, controls and disciplinary regimes' (ibid.: 215). A prime example here would be the well-documented example of the IMS-GT. It is no surprise that a small city state like Singapore is closely associated with instances of extraterritorialization, since, as one interviewee indicated, it represents too small a territory to reap the full spillover advantages of a knowledge economy, the simple fact being that Singapore has rarely been host to a collectivity of major businesses in the same product sector (Interview 5). The stitching of several overseas industrial estates into a web of economic relations centred on Singapore, therefore, represents an important means of accessing such externalities. It is to a consideration of these hybrid models of social order that I now turn.

Hybridity in the Supply of Social Order

There is a small, but growing, number of instances of hybrid models of social order. At a mesogeographic scale, these are constituted through the likes of government-to-government agreements to create special zones of economic integration in which there is a degree of regulatory harmonization (Ong, 1999; Rimmer, 1994). Southeast Asia appears to be *the* case in point, where a number of such growth triangle agreements have been made with varying degrees of success and of regulatory interaction and policy transference. For Ong, these represent important instances of transnationalism, yet the sensitivities of newly created post-colonial states also belie the rhetoric of these, still quite shallow, instances of transnational economic integration. The most celebrated examples have been driven by strategies of extraterritoriality (Ruggie, 1993) associated with the most dominant states in the region (notably Singapore), and, as a result, have been associated with significant international conflict (Phelps, 2004b). Some indication of the fragility of these zones of economic integration is provided by the lack of economic convergence in the territories included in these zones, sensitivities over ethnic divisions, the lack of supporting new transnational institutions, and even the fragility of government-to-government relations themselves. A more sober assessment indicates an unwillingness to integrate beyond the isolated projects that we consider below (Perry and Yeoh, 2000).

At least in rhetorical terms, if not in other ways, an element of competition exists between such zones, despite the large distances that separate them. Despite its early success, concern was raised over streamlining procedures between the members of the IMS-GT, with Indonesia's Dr Habibie arguing that 'we have to do this as quickly as possible because we have competition, we're not the only triangle' (Koh, 1991). In the

IMS-GT, for example, the Singapore–Indonesia leg of the GT is strong. In the past, it was by and large embodied in the Batamindo industrial estate, but it is now increasingly spilling over into other privately developed estates on Batam. The Singapore–Malaysia leg, which has not been underpinned by any specific Singapore–Malaysia government-sponsored industrial estate, has typically involved more politics, as we have mentioned above (Interview 7). Things have also evolved in that the closer political connections between central governments in Singapore and Indonesia, which also helped cement the Batam–Singapore leg of the IMS-GT, have become clouded in uncertainty in the post-Suharto era (Interview 8). In another instance, however, the Singapore government and its linked companies withdrew from a proposed industrial estate development in Thailand. The Singapore government's commitment to the proposed estate endured, despite protests by local community and environmentalists (Low, 2000) and in the face of a downturn in the FDI inflows. It was finally severed after Thailand's Board of Investment (BOI) decision reduced the financial incentives associated with the estate to those operating at other estates (Thongrung, 2000).

At a microgeographic scale, such hybrid models appear in the case of offshore financial centres (Hudson, 2000) and industrial estates (Perry and Yeoh, 2000; Phelps, 2004b) that embody enclaves within given national modes of social regulation. The Singapore government and its linked companies have been the main instigators of such instances of hybrid social order. These enclaves embody distinctive hybrid models of social order in the sense that they have necessarily been formed as joint ventures between Singapore government-linked companies, such as SembCorp and Ascendas on the one hand, and the host government and its linked companies. These enclaves necessarily embody a model of social order different to that on offer on industrial estates elsewhere in host economies (Interview 6). The Batamindo industrial estate on the Indonesian island of Batam, for example, stands apart in terms of its security, labour supply and relations, and physical and communications infrastructure, from Indonesia. Indeed, by virtue of developments such as Batamindo, Batam represents a model or template for industrialization and institutional development elsewhere in Indonesia (Phelps, 2004b). As one interviewee of a major MNE with operations throughout Southeast Asia noted, 'It's no secret. It's a fact that it's different from the rest of Indonesia' (Interview 7).

The process of creating these enclaves of hybrid social order are magnified when we consider that major elements of the model of order being exported from Singapore have been designed, orchestrated and implemented from within a city-state, as opposed to large nations with internal territorial administrations. In the case of the Vietnam–Singapore Industrial Park (VSIP) in Vietnam, as in the case of Batam and Bintan in Indonesia, this has worked to the advantage of Singapore's extraterritorialization, since good relations between park management and provincial government have set VSIP apart from other enclaves in Vietnam, in terms of the quality and efficiency of administrative procedures and government–business interactions (Bao, 2004; Hien and Hiep, 2003). However,

> Many initiatives spearheaded by the Singapore government in China have focused their negotiations and agreements . . . with the central or national government. Little effort is made by the government-linked companies to address the concern and agenda of local government in China. . . . Their projects in China subsequently face implementation problems because this mismatch of scale politics results in conflicts of interests with local authorities and officials. (Yeung, 2000: 812)

Although Singapore's overseas industrial estates in China (at Wuxi and Suzhou) have been developed as joint ventures, where the physical, utility, communications and commercial infrastructure represents something of a departure from that elsewhere in China, the variable success of these two experiments is a product of the variable relations among tiers of government and government-linked and private companies (Interview 14).

Significant competition between separate developments has plagued the export of Singapore's model of social order to China. Whilst the industrial estate in Wuxi has proved successful, there has been competition between the Suzhou industrial park officially sanctioned by central government in Singapore and China, and a neighbouring park in Suzhou promoted by the provincial government. There has been competition for the same foreign investors, some of which have been diverted from the joint venture industrial estate to the provincial funded estate, whilst differences in working methods between Singapore and Chinese bureaucrats are claimed to have slowed development by 50 per cent (Hoong, 1997; Yin, 1997), so much so that Singapore's Senior Minister Lee Kuan Yew was quoted as saying, 'I wish Wuxi was placed in Suzhou and Suzhou was in Wuxi' (Yin, 1997). These specific conflicts highlight a broader incompatibility of the Singapore model of social order with that prevailing in China despite the connections presumed to exist via the ethnic Chinese diaspora. So it was recently claimed that Singaporeans' knowledge of Western business environments is greater than their knowledge of the Chinese business environment (Chen, 1999).

In contrast to the emphasis on the formative role of hegemonic national states and international organizations (such as the World Bank and International Monetary Fund) in much of the literature, which stresses the role of politics and public policy in the harmonization of business regulation, the private sector itself is, and has always been, influential in processes by which global regulation of business is constructed. MNEs, being significantly more internationalized than states and being potential conduits of a kaleidoscope of various national and local models of social order, are in a unique position to effect the transfer of business-regulatory practices. Their location and relocation decisions come to shape incentives-based and rules-based competition directly, in terms of regulatory arbitrage at point of entry or reinvestment, but also indirectly. Elements of 'modelling' are closely implicated in this competition between enclaves, as is the case on Batam where at least one privately developed industrial estate has sought to model itself on the original Batamindo Singapore–Indonesia joint venture (Interview 8).

Along with many other MNEs, the US company Seagate, which manufactures disk drives for the computer industry, has several factories spread across the Southeast Asia region. It is this spread of operations and division of labour within MNEs that sensitizes them to local conditions and, of course, permits a degree of regulatory arbitrage. So, for example, an interviewee at Seagate's Penang factory noted how the cheaper labour-cost option of China now open to MNEs has prompted renewed activity on the part of local institutions to provide other competitive advantages with which to retain MNEs (Interview 9). Seagate has long had a presence in Southeast Asia, but has recently expanded with encouragement from Singapore's EDB (Economic Development Board) into China on the Wuxi industrial estate. Undoubtedly, a measure of this estate's distinctiveness in China stems from the export of Singapore social order via government-linked companies, as we have already seen, but it also represents a response to model practices channelled via MNEs themselves. An interviewee at the company described the sorts of changes in institutional practices regarding the processing of imports and exports made locally: 'They have put in a tremendous amount of work in changing the infrastructure . . . They changed it drastically to accommodate us' (Interview 10).

Moreover, MNEs frequently seek to overlay and further modify existing models or hybrid models of social order by their collective actions. Though less applicable to our interests in this chapter, this can apply to the case of physical and communications infrastructure in the least developed business environments (Fisman and Khanna, 2004). But, in the case of Batam discussed above, it has extended into the spheres of business advocacy, and even health and social amenities (Interview 8). Therefore, as Braithwaite and Drahos observe, 'globalization of business regulation sometimes occurs through globalization of rules followed by globalization of compliance . . . Conversely, globalization often occurs first through globalization of business practice via the mechanism of modelling, that then becomes codified and solidified as globalized rules' (Braithwaite and Drahos, 2000: 551). Yet this is itself a subject worthy of consideration, since capital's search for order is not simply a matter of selection among fixed and competing national and hybrid models of social order; these are themselves, at least partly, modelled in capital's own image.

CAPITAL'S DEMAND FOR SOCIAL ORDER

In general terms, MNEs are risk-averse creatures that tend to avoid uncertain host economy environments (Safarian, 1993: 53) and have long been interested in the transparency and efficiency of host state regulatory environments. There are strong arguments to the effect that a reasonably common element of governments' competition for capital rests on the efficient creation of a certain minimum of social order, such as legal stability and justice (Julius, 1997: 466). However, MNEs have quite differentiated requirements of potential host environments over and above this minimum. Indeed, there are a variety of strategies to government relations adopted by MNEs, from exit and avoidance to partnership and voice (see also chapters in Part I of this volume). The latter entail significant search costs on the part of MNEs, while it is clear that an important minority of FDI flows remain destined for risky host economy environments. Thus 'the architecture of global production is not, in fact, driven by an immutable economic logic of intensifying cost competition, but rather involves crucial strategic dimensions' (Felker, 2003: 256). Capital's demand for social order remains variegated, according to investment type, strategic objectives of investments, and corporate culture, to name but three.

Firm Investment Type

As we have already alluded to, the market for capital is in fact highly differentiated. Alongside longer established flows of horizontal FDI, it is now well recognized that different types of investment associated with different parts of the division of labour for a product or service (vertical FDI) – administration, research and development, design, manufacture, and sales and marketing – present different locational requirements. As a result, broad and distinctive spatial divisions of labour have become apparent within national territories (Massey, 1984) and at the global scale (Frobel *et al.*, 1980). Such

specialization and differentiation have long been apparent in connection with the production of goods and services, in the form of, for example, prototype production, component manufacture and final assembly.

It has long been recognized that the division of labour is also related to the life cycle of
the product concerned, with mature products being relocated to developing countries
with lower costs (Vernon, 1966). Much has changed and continues to change in the international economy in a way that might undermine the applicability of product cycle considerations (Vernon, 1979). However, it should be noted that such considerations remain
apparent within the division of labour developed by Japanese MNEs in Southeast Asia
(Hayter and Edgington, 2004). Furthermore, the indeterminacy of the product cycle
model itself serves to highlight MNEs' variegated demand for social order, since there are
different capital–labour combinations open to investments at the same stage of the life
cycle (Taylor, 1986).

Moreover, the process of specialization and differentiation is increasingly a feature of
parts of the division of labour commonly regarded as indivisible, such as research and
development and design. There is then growing evidence that the working out of the division of labour is now producing increased specialization and differentiation *within* these
parts of the division of labour. Such developments are open to interpretation, but it is
clear that one scenario implies increased desire of MNEs to tap into pre-existing clusters
of technological activity, at the same time as their reduced commitment to developing new
capabilities in other shallow or 'contingent clusters' of production, such as those developed in Southeast Asia (Felker, 2003: 271).

Firm Strategy

Differentiation in capital's demand for social order also exists in terms of firm strategies
that need not revolve around the minimization of production or transaction costs. In very
general terms, it may be fair to argue that international economic integration has
increased the sensitivities of MNEs to transaction costs facing them in international production (Dunning, 1997) and that, as a result, such investors look to host environments
in which such costs are at their lowest. Yet, where cost considerations are apparent, they
can also involve quite different logics. On the one hand, Black and Decker's switch from
Singapore to China is part of an inexorable logic of cutting costs in the price-sensitive
product market of power tools, involving other similar shifts from the UK to Eastern
Europe and from the US to Mexico (Phelps and Waley, 2004). On the other hand, Dyson's
shift from the UK to Malaysia has taken place against a backdrop of a buoyant market
for its premium brand-name vacuum cleaners. Its premium brand product coupled with
the youthfulness of the company and the need to expand its product portfolio has determined a strategy whereby the lower costs of production in Malaysia form a solution to
generating a cash surplus for reinvestment in research and development of new products
rather than simple cost cutting per se (Interview 11). Moreover, Dyson's presence here was
driven partly by personal connections of company directors at a high level in the
Malaysian government.

In an increasingly integrated international economy, there are relatively few national
territories that require a direct presence in order for an MNE to service the market. The
sizeable markets of Brazil, India and Indonesia would be such instances, but China would

be the example par excellence. A major element of FDI flows into China has been stimulated by the need for a presence in this vast market, regardless of the present costs of production. Furthermore, national and subnational governments have typically been more concerned to utilize the bargaining power conferred by market size in their negotiations with prospective investors (Yeung and Li, 1998).

Related to this are two well-known principles of competition that are actually quite far removed from the minimization of costs. The first of these is the idea of first mover advantages, whether this be entry into a specific geographical or a particular product market. The second, and closely related, competitive principle is that of oligopolistic reaction (Knickerbocker, 1973) in which major MNEs commonly follow their competitors into particular host economies on the basis that they must retain competitive parity. An element of FDI flows into China is surely driven by such motives. So, for example, one interviewee of a major MNE with operations across the Southeast Asia region noted of China how 'you have to be there with the others and preferably be early' (Interview 7).

The principle of oligopolistic reaction also draws attention to a broader strategic consideration, namely, that some firms are able to compete politically by shaping the non-market environment (Boddewyn, 1993) and, to a degree, that participation in many host country environments necessitates some degree of political influence. Seagate Technology is one of a number of disk drive manufacturers that developed a division of labour in Southeast Asia, with factories in Singapore, Malaysia and Indonesia. Their presence in at least some of these locations (including the touted IMS-GT) has been significantly mediated by, if not developed from their relationship with, the Singapore government in the shape of the EDB. As one interviewee said of their former facility on Batam island in Indonesia:

> We went to Batam . . . and that was a sponsorship from the EDB. . . . We chose to come out in that we didn't really have that strong a relationship with the Indonesian government – didn't mean it was bad – we just didn't have any because we were there at the invitation of the EDB. (Interview 10)

Conscious of the need to retain cost competitiveness in a price-sensitive product market, Seagate has recently established manufacturing in Wuxi, China, again at the instigation of the EDB. What we see here is the manner in which supply and demand for social order interacts, and, in particular, how capital's search for order has been managed by states.

Firm Culture

The matter is further complicated by the possibility of competing centres of strategy within major MNEs. Much recent literature has focused on the possibilities for subsidiary autonomy and initiative within parent company MNE organizations (Phelps and Fuller, 2000). Such autonomy and initiative derives in no small measure from multinationality per se. Thus 'the multinational firm provides a culture within which identities are constituted and interests constructed from the perspective of membership of at least two states and of one firm' (Tetrealt, 1999: 71). Multinationality necessarily entails that the economics of location choice become to a greater or lesser extent adulterated by political considerations (Boddewyn, 1993).

Whilst MNE organizational structures have evolved from the international division prevalent until the 1960s and the 1970s, there remains a case for arguing that 'firms are able to be much more idiosyncratic in their approach to dealing with business partners abroad than at home' (Whitley, 2001: 74). The point here is that, whilst MNEs in general and particular MNEs in the round are risk-averse creatures, the picture may be more complicated with regard to particular parts of MNEs. Thus it has been suggested that 'the larger TNCs are able and often willing to accommodate a lot of "restrictive" policy measures, as far as they are stable and the changes in them are predictable' (Chang, 1998: 225).

Whether nationality matters in terms of the impact of FDI on host economies remains an open question (cf. Reich, 1990; Pauly and Reich, 1997). On a priori grounds, Dunning's eclectic framework suggests that the home economy of an MNE significantly shapes its ownership advantages and hence the mode of entry. The evidence from Southeast Asia suggests that there are indeed apparently different responses. One interviewee referred to unpublished surveys conducted by AMCham and JETRO in Malaysia that revealed US MNEs to have a greater disposition toward training and appointing Malay staff to senior positions than their Japanese counterparts (Interview 12).

Moreover, Asian MNEs coming from their home developmental state environment have arguably also shaped the terms of competition for long-established Western MNEs. Schoenberger (1997) has recently identified time-based competition as a key ingredient in the cultural crises facing major companies in an era of rapid international economic integration. Such time-based competition has at least two facets. On the one hand, following the just-in-time logic pioneered by the likes of Japanese MNEs, Western MNEs have adapted to the faster pace of product development and production. On the other hand, it is also clear that coming from their home environment of developmental states – underpinned by favourable government loans and 'patient capital' – Asian MNEs have been able to forgo profitability in the short term, in order to pursue longer-term goals of generating increased market share. An extreme example of this is provided by the internationalization of South Korean *chaebol*, such as LG, for whom rapid internationalization has been necessary in order to generate revenues to service major debts accrued by virtue of favourable government-underwritten loans (Phelps *et al.*, 1998).

Naturally, MNEs from the Asian setting (notably, Japanese MNEs) have established a division of labour engaging with the variety of models of social order apparent in the Southeast Asian region, yet the difficulties of engaging with models of social order should not be underestimated. So, for example, although private sector Singapore MNEs have enjoyed greater flexibility (by virtue of being able to deploy *guanxi* relations) than their government and its linked company counterparts in dealing with the business and administrative system in China (Yeung, 2000), the specificity of the Singapore model of social order may make it rather difficult to export. In light of the difficulties of getting Singaporean firms to internationalize, it has been observed that 'the Singapore company is good in a very mature environment but not good in emerging markets' (*The Straits Times*, 1999).

In general terms, there is undoubtedly some dynamic matching of the demand for social order with supply of that order. So, for example, one MNE was outspoken about similarities between the Indonesian culture and its own business culture or philosophy, when locating on Batam within the IMS-GT: 'The Indonesian staff have proved to be self-motivated and controlled. Their attitude stems from the state ideology, Pancasila, which is similar to AT&T's Shared Values . . . the Indonesians, although culturally different, share AT&T's philosophy towards business (*Straits Times*, 1992).

Yet it may not be possible to link any sort of dynamic equilibrium of demand and supply for social order to ownership or industry characteristics of the investors concerned. As one interviewee explained in the case of investments drawn to the likes of the Batamindo industrial estate,

> If you go to Batam . . . you can see the environment is very different from Singapore . . . it's quite chaotic but it's booming. There are some companies who go there and try, some companies go there and just don't make it and they can be from the same country or from the same industry. . . . I guess they have different personalities . . . Some companies are more street-smart so they are comfortable in an environment like Indonesia where there are a lot of things you have to do under the table just to survive. And that type of environment is chaotic but it lets them grow. Whereas other companies look for a lot more transparency and want a stable environment, they are nervous when things are a bit chaotic. (Interview 13)

Capital's search for order in terms of the functions and strategies associated with particular investments and broader issues of corporate culture remains an important analytical issue.

CONCLUSION

What this brief consideration of capital's search for order highlights is the continued legitimate role for government to shape the market for capital at a time when 'the "development space" for diversification and upgrading policies in developing countries is being shrunk behind the rhetorical commitment to universal liberalisation and privatization' (Wade, 2003: 622). The social order that MNEs seek can clearly be provided under conditions well removed from the Western (Anglo-American) business system model. What is more, in light of the inability of the Washington consensus template to deliver sustained economic growth and poverty reduction in a range of settings, variety is important. Indeed, it is the East Asian experience in particular (with its fully politicized MNE–state relations) that suggests that 'there is clearly an important role for institutional diversity in rapid catch-up growth' (Crafts, 2004: 56).

Moreover, it is clear that, despite the emphasis in Western policy discourse and much academic literature, the demand for social order emanating from MNEs is diverse. We have been able to give just a flavour of this in the present chapter. However, this is a subject worthy of further investigation not only for its intrinsic economic–geographical interest, but also for its value in shedding light on potential points of leverage for governments concerned to shape processes of economic globalization. The global market for capital is one that is coordinated by a more or less visible hand. On the supply side, nation states spend resources signalling their models of social order to MNEs. On the demand side, MNEs are implicated in the search costs associated with finding suitable homes for their various investments.[3] Therefore, there remains considerable scope for national and subnational governments to shape the manner in which their economies participate in, and draw benefits from, processes of international economic integration.

NOTES

1. I would like to thank the British Academy (SG-39277) for funding the research upon which this chapter is based, and Henry Yeung for comments made on a previous draft of this chapter.
2. There is the neoliberal or competition state model represented by the UK and the US (Cerny, 1997); the social welfare model of mainland Europe (although here again there are important variations; see Dunford, 1996); the developmental state model of East Asia (Wade, 1990), and what might be termed the 'predatory' state model found in some Asian countries (for example, Indonesia) and many African nations.
3. In the middle, although not the subject of this chapter, are a range of market intermediaries, including international organizations, but also location, management and political risk consultants (see Phelps, Power and Wanjiru, 2006).

REFERENCES

Bao, G. (2004), 'An investor friendly destination', *Saigon Times*, 15 April.

Berry, J. and S. McGreal (1995), 'European cities: the interaction of planning systems, property markets and real estate investment', in J. Berry and S. McGreal (eds), *European Cities, Planning Systems and Property Markets*, London: Spon Press, pp. 1–16.

Boddewyn, J. (1993), 'Political resource and markets in international business: beyond Porter's generic strategies', in A. Rugman and A. Verbeke (eds), *Research in Global Strategic Management: Global Competition – Beyond the Three Generics*, London: JAI Press, pp. 83–99.

Bornschier, V. and B. Trezzini (2001), 'World market for social order: embedded state autonomy and third world development', *Competition and Change*, **5**, 201–44.

Braithwaite, J. and P. Drahos (2000), *Global Business Regulation*, Cambridge: Cambridge University Press.

Cantwell, J. (1995), 'The globalisation of technology: what remains of the product cycle model', *Cambridge Journal of Economics*, **19**, 155–74.

Cerny, P. (1997), 'Paradoxes of the competition state: the dynamics of political globalization', *Government & Opposition*, **32**, 251–74.

Chang. H.J. (1998), 'Transnational corporations and strategic industrial policy', in R. Kozul-Wright and R. Rowthorn (eds), *Transnational Corporations and the Global Economy*, London: Macmillan, pp. 225–43.

Chellam, R. (1998), 'Singapore still attractive to MNCs', *Straits Times, Business Times*, 22 March, p. 13.

Chen, K. (1999), 'Singaporean's "don't know China as well as they think"', *Straits Times*, 11 June.

Crafts, N. (2004), 'Globalization and economic growth: a historical perspective', *The World Economy*, **27**, 45–58.

Dunford, M. (1996), 'Disparities in employment, productivity and output in the EU: the role of labour market policies and welfare regimes', *Regional Studies*, **30**, 339–57.

Dunning, J. (1997), 'How should national governments respond to globalisation?', *The International Executive*, **39**, 55–66.

Felker, G. (2001), 'The politics of industrial investment policy reform in Malaysia and Thailand', in K. Jomo (ed.), *Southeast Asia's Industrialisation: Industrial Policy, Capabilities and Sustainabilty*, Basingstoke: Palgrave, pp. 129–82.

Felker, G. (2003), 'Southeast Asian industrialisation and the changing global production system', *Third World Quarterly*, **24**, 255–82.

Fisman, R. and T. Khanna (2004), 'Facilitating development: the role of business groups', *World Development*, **32**, 609–28.

Fröbel, F., J. Heinrichs and O. Kreye (1980), *The New International Division of Labour*, Cambridge: Cambridge University Press.

Hadiz, V. and R. Robison (2005), 'Neo-liberal reforms and illiberal consolidations: the Indonesian paradox', *Journal of Development Studies*, **41**, 220–41.

Harianto, F. and A.E. Safarian (1997), 'MNEs and technology diffusion: a Southeast Asian example', in P. Buckley and J.L. Muchielli (eds), *Multinational Firms and Industrial Relocation*, Cheltenham, UK and Lyme, US: Edward Elgar, pp. 189–219.

Hayter, R. and D. Edgington (2004), 'Flying geese in Asia: the impacts of Japanese MNEs as a source of industrial learning', *Tijdschrift voor Economishe en Sociale Geografie*, **95**, 3–26.

Hien, L. and B. Hiep (2003), 'Big inflow to Binh Duong', *Saigon Times*, 1 January.

Hood, N. and S. Young (1997), 'The United Kingdom', in J.H. Dunning (ed.), *Governments, Globalization and International Business*, Oxford: Oxford University Press, pp. 244–82.

Hoong, C.L. (1997), 'SM Lee unhappy over Suzhou park progress', *Straits Times*, 5 December.

Hudson, A. (2000), 'Offshoreness, globalization and sovereignty: a postmodern geopolitical economy?', *Transactions of the Institute of British Geographers*, **25**, 269–83.

Julius, D. (1997), 'Globalization and stakehokder conflicts: a corporate perspective', *International Affairs*, **73**, 453–68.

Knickerbocker, F.T. (1973), *Oligopolistic Reaction and Multinational Enterprise*, Boston, MA: Harvard University Press.

Koh, E (1991), 'Harmonise rules to speed up growth triangle, says Habibie', *Straits Times*, 31 May.

Krugman, P. (1996), *Pop Internationalism*, Cambridge MA: MIT Press.

Low, E. (2000), 'JTCI pressing on with Thai project despite protests', *Straits Times, Business Times*, 5 April.

MacIntyre, A. (ed) (1994), *Business and Government in Industrialising Asia*, Melbourne: Allen and Unwin.

Massey, D. (1984), *Spatial Divisions of Labour*, London: Macmillan.

Maxfield, S. and B.R. Schneider (eds) (1997), *Business and the State in Developing Countries*, Ithaca: Cornell University Press.

Ong, A. (1999), *Flexible Citizenship: The Cultural Logics of Transnationality*, London: Duke University Press.

Pauly, L. and S. Reich (1997), 'National structures and multinational corporate behaviour: enduring differences in the age of globalisation', *International Organization*, **51**, 1–30.

Perry, M. and C. Yeoh (2000), 'Singapore's overseas industrial parks', *Regional Studies*, **34**, 199–206.

Phelps, N.A. (2004a), 'Archetype for an archipelago? Batam as model of industrialisation in *reformasi* Indonesia', *Progress in Development Studies*, **4**(3), 206–29.

Phelps, N.A. (2004b), 'Triangular diplomacy writ small: the political economy of the Indonesia–Malaysia–Singapore growth triangle', *The Pacific Review*, **17**(3), 341–68.

Phelps, N.A. and C. Fuller (2000), 'Multinationals, intracorporate competition and regional development', *Economic Geography*, **76**(3), 224–43.

Phelps, N.A. and P. Waley (2004), 'Capital versus the districts: the story of one multinational company's attempts to disembed itself', *Economic Geography*, **80**(2), 191–215.

Phelps, N.A., J. Lovering and K. Morgan (1998), 'Tying the firm to the region or tying the region to the firm? Early observations on the case of LG in South Wales', *European Urban and Regional Studies*, **5**, 119–37.

Phelps, N.A., M. Power and R. Wanjiru (2006), 'Learning to compete: the investment promotion community and the spread of neoliberalism', in K. England and K. Ward (eds), *Neoliberalization: States, Networks, Peoples*, Oxford: Blackwell.

Phelps, N.A., D. MacKinnon, I. Stone and P. Braidford (2003), 'Embedding the multinationals? Institutions and the development of overseas manufacturing affiliates in Wales and North East England', *Regional Studies*, **37**(1), 27–40.

Reich, R. (1990), 'Who is us?', *Harvard Business Review*, **68**, 53–64.

Rimmer, P. (1994), 'Regional economic integration in Pacific Asia', *Environment & Planning A*, **26**, 1731–59.

Ritchie, B.K. (2005), 'Coalitional politics, economic reform, and technological upgrading in Malaysia', *World Development*, **33**(5), 745–61.

Ruggie, J. (1993), 'Territoriality and beyond: problematizing modernity in international relations', *International Organization*, **47**, 139–74.

Safarian, A.E. (1993), *Multinational Enterprise and Public Policy: A Study of the Industrial Countries*, Aldershot, UK and Brookfield, US: Edward Elgar.

Schoenberger, E. (1997), *The Cultural Crisis of the Firm*, Oxford: Blackwell.

Straits Times (1992), 'Quick off the mark', 15 April, *Business Times*.

Straits Times (1999), 'China losing its lustre for Singapore firms', 18 September, *Business Times*.

Strange, S. (1997), 'The future of global capitalism: or, will divergence persist for ever?', in C. Crouch and W. Streeck (eds), *Political Economy of Modern Capitalism*, London: Sage, pp. 182–91.

Taylor, M. (1986), 'The product cycle theory – a critique', *Environment & Planning A*, **18**, 751–61.

Tetrealt, M. (1999), 'Out of body experiences: migrating firms and altered states', *Review of International Political Economy*, **6**, 55–78.

Thomas, K. (2000), *Competing for Capital: Europe and North America in a Global Era*, Washington, DC: Georgetown University Press.

Thongrung, W. (2000), 'Jurong set to abandon Rayong estate project', *The Nation*, 9 November.

UNCTAD (2002), *World Investment Report: Transnational Corporations and Export Competitiveness*, Geneva: United Nations.

Vernon, R. (1966), 'International trade, international investment and the product cycle', *Quarterly Journal of Economics*, **80**, 190–207.

Vernon, R. (1979), 'The product cycle hypothesis in a new international environment', *Oxford Bulletin of Economics and Statistics*, **41**, 255–68.

Wade, R. (1990), *Governing the Market: Economic Theory and the Role of Government in East Asian Industrialisation*, Princeton: Princeton University Press.

Wade, R.H. (2003), 'What strategies are viable for developing countries today? The World Trade Organisation and the shrinking of "development space"', *Review of International Political Economy*, **10**, 621–44.

Whitley, R. (1992a), *European Business Systems*, London: Sage.

Whitley, R. (1992b), *Asian Business Systems*, London: Sage.

Whitley, R. (2001), 'The institutional structuring of business transactions', in R. Appelbaum, W. Felstner and W. Gessner (eds), *Rules and Networks: The Legal Culture of Global Business Transactions*, Oxford: Hart Publishing, pp. 73–99.

Wilkinson, R. (2000), 'New labour and the global economy', in D. Coates and P. Lawler (eds), *New Labour in Power*, Manchester: Manchester University Press, pp. 136–48.

Yeung, H.W.C. (1998), 'Capital, state and space: contesting the borderless world', *Transactions of the Institute of British Geographers*, **23**, 291–309.

Yeung, H.W.C. (1999), 'The internationalization of ethnic Chinese businesses from Southeast Asia: strategies, processes and competitive advantage', *International Journal of Urban and Regional Research*, **23**, 103–27.

Yeung, H.W.C. (2000), 'Local politics and foreign ventures in China's transitional economy: the political economy of Singaporean interests in China', *Political Geography*, **19**, 809–40.

Yeung, Y.M. and X.J. Li (1998), 'Bargaining with transnational corporations: the case of Shanghai', *International Journal of Urban and Regional Research*, **23**, 513–33.

Yin, L.H. (1997), 'SM Lee airs frustrations over Suzhou project', *Straits Times, Business Times*, 5 December.

Young, S. and A. Tavares (2004), 'Multilateral rules on FDI: do we need them? Will we get them? A developing country perspective', *Transnational Corporations*, **13**, 1–29.

APPENDIX 13.1   LIST OF INTERVIEWEES

(Interview 1) Executive Director, American Chamber of Commerce in Singapore, Singapore, 5 September 2002.

(Interview 2) Deputy Director, Indonesia Resident Mission, Asian Development Bank, 19 September 2002.

(Interview 3) Executive Director, American Chamber of Commerce in Indonesia, 19 September 2002.

(Interview 4) Director, Bilateral Cooperation, Indonesian Ministry of Industry and Trade, Jakarta, 20 September 2002.

(Interview 5) Deputy Director, Jurong Island Development Department, JTC Corporation, Singapore, 23 September 2002.

(Interview 6) Senior Marketing Manager, SembCorp Parks Management, Singapore, 23 October 2002.

(Interview 7) Chairman and CEO, Phillips Group of Companies in Malaysia, Petaling Jaya, Malaysia, 3 October 2002.

(Interview 8) President Director, Ciba Vision, Batam, Indonesia, 22 October 2002.

(Interview 9) Senior Manager, Corporate Communications, Penang Seagate Industries, Bayan Lepas, Penang, 9 October 2002.

(Interview 10) Vice President, Business Process, Seagate Technology International, Ang Mo Kio, Singapore, 9 September 2002.

(Interview 11) Head of Operations Far East, Dyson Ltd., Senai Industrial Estate, Johor, Malaysia, 16 October 2002.

(Interview 12) Research analyst, American Malaysian Chamber of Commerce, Kuala Lumpur, Malaysia, 18 October 2002.

(Interview 13) Officer, Economic Development Board of Singapore, Singapore, 25 October 2002.

(Interview 14) European Regional Director, Economic Development Board of Singapore, London, 26 June 2002.

14. Government policies towards FDI across East and Southeast Asia: move towards business policies encouraging inter-firm relationships between MNEs and local firms

Axèle Giroud

Over the past two decades, levels of foreign investment flows worldwide have risen exponentially to reach a peak of US$1388 billion in 2000. In 2003, Asia attracted US$96.9 billion out of the world total of US$559.5 billion foreign direct investment (FDI) inflows worldwide (UNCTAD, 2004). Specifically, countries across East and Southeast Asia have become major recipients of world FDI, with the notable emergence of China as the world's biggest host for foreign investment. Total FDI inward stocks in China soared from US$63.6 billion in 1993 to US$501.5 billion in 2003.

The experience of China has been unmatched elsewhere. Still, other countries in the region have also witnessed a sharp increase in inward FDI stocks. These increased from US$213.5 billion in Hong Kong in 1993 to US$375.0 billion in 2003; from US$41.6 billion to US$147.3 billion in Singapore; and from US$20.6 billion to US$59.0 billion in Malaysia (UNCTAD, 2004). In 2003, the major recipients of inward FDI stocks in the region were China, Hong Kong, Singapore, Malaysia, Indonesia, South Korea, Thailand, Taiwan and Vietnam. While levels of stocks do differ widely, from US$501.5 billion in China to US$18.6 billion in Vietnam, all countries, bar Indonesia, have witnessed a steady increase in FDI stocks, encouraging governments to adapt and develop appropriate policy frameworks to attract FDI and to maximize the benefits to be gained from foreign investment.

Countries encourage inward FDI flows as a means to enjoy growth and development. Growth rates across East Asia are high, with exports, consumption and investment fuelling such steady rates of growth (World Bank, 2005). Foreign firms contribute to the development of host economies through a variety of channels, directly or indirectly. Initially, they contribute to the level of investment in host economies. For instance, FDI flows accounted for 43.8 per cent of gross fixed investment in Singapore over the 2001–2003 period. Foreign firms also help to boost employment levels and increase competition. They often bring superior technology, management and quality control systems, particularly in less developed economies. In Asia, multinationals have contributed to the export potential of host economies, thereby contributing to the balance of payment positions of countries. Indirectly, multinationals have also generated positive spillovers through inter-firm linkages with suppliers, customers and competitors. Such linkages constitute a predominant means of enhancing local firms' capabilities in less developed economies, and governments need to generate policies to support and encourage positive linkages within their national borders.

The role of government in creating assets is considerable in the 21st century and, in many countries, there are arguments in favour of treating foreign investors on the same basis as local firms. Host countries' policy framework plays a critical role in determining the effects of FDI on the economy. For developing countries, especially, the challenge lies in the use and maximization of capabilities within their national borders. As traditional means of encouraging positive impacts from foreign firms, such as encouraging the formation of joint ventures, are becoming less favourable with the increasing liberalization of policies, governments are striving to create a conducive environment within which inter-firm relationships can flourish, and the superior capabilities of foreign firms are transferred to local companies.

To be attractive to FDI, governments across Asia have adapted their policies to facilitate, encourage and develop the activities of MNEs across the region and within national boundaries. The purpose of this chapter is to examine the various systems of business policy models adopted across East and Southeast Asian countries as regards the activities of MNEs (see also other chapters in Part III of this volume). This comparative analysis follows a historical perspective, and considers two major recent turning points that have had an impact upon the policy orientation of governments across the region, namely the Asian economic crisis in 1997, and the opening-up of China to foreign investment. Despite a relaxation of government policies towards foreign firms' activities, governments are nonetheless trying to adopt soft policies aimed at encouraging foreign firms to establish and develop business relationships with locally owned firms, for these two strengthen their competitive advantage. The aim of the chapter is therefore twofold: to compare policies towards FDI across the region from a historical perspective, and take a critical view of the way governments promote inter-firm relationships to strengthen local endogenous capabilities.

FOREIGN DIRECT INVESTMENT: TYPES AND IMPACT

Types of FDI

One must distinguish between various ways through which foreign investors may invest abroad; in foreign direct investment, we include the process through which foreign investors acquire ownership of assets for the purpose of controlling the production, distribution and other activities of a firm in another country (Moosa, 2002). In the case of a joint venture, or an acquisition, many researchers consider that a minimum of a 10 per cent shareholding allows foreign firms to exert a significant influence over the key policies of the foreign affiliate. The relationship established between the foreign parent and its affiliates overseas matters, inasmuch as FDI often involves shifting part of the company's assets, production or sales, and this transfer may benefit the host economy.

Transfer will differ, whether the investment is horizontal, with the intention to produce the same or similar kinds of goods abroad as at home, or vertical, whereby the foreign firms' aims are exploiting raw materials, acquiring suppliers or being nearer to the consumers through acquisition of distribution outlets. When the investor does conduct FDI for opportunistic acquisitions of foreign assets, the parent may be a pure holding company, and the investment will be integrated within a conglomerate. FDI entry generally takes one of two forms: greenfield investments (the assets established are entirely new), or cross-border mergers and acquisitions (M&A). The entry can be wholly owned by the foreign company or a joint venture. FDI often occurs in order to maximize profit and reduce costs by taking advantage of differences in cost structures, due to factor productivity and remuneration differentials across countries.

There are four principal types of FDI motivation. These are natural resource-seeking, market-seeking, efficiency-seeking and strategic asset (capability)-seeking activities. Undoubtedly, there is a variety of factors explaining each investment, and the reasons why firms invest abroad change over time and according to circumstances (Sun *et al.*, 2002). Apart from reasons for overseas expansion that are internal to the firms, there are two key types of determinants related to the host economy. The first type includes the institutional features of the host economy (features such as political stability, macroeconomic policies, government policies in terms of the general business environment, labour conditions, intellectual property protection, and so on) (UNCTAD, 1998). The second type covers business facilitation measures, such as FDI incentives, reducing costs of running subsidiaries, and providing a good environment with amenities for expatriates (UNCTAD, 1998, Holland *et al.*, 2000). The key challenge for governments is not only to attract foreign investors, but also to encourage them to remain in the country and invest further, as well as creating linkages with indigenous companies.

In the new globalized world, MNEs do not simply resort to integration strategies with stand-alone foreign affiliates, relatively independent from parent companies and without links to other affiliates of the same firm (UNCTAD, 1998: 109), they adopt complex integration strategies whereby firms select locations to combine their firm-specific advantages with country-specific resources in the most efficient manner. This may lead firms to separate individual functions and locate them in the most appropriate host economies. As a result, MNEs are increasingly searching for specialized clusters to benefit from a dynamic knowledge-generating and knowledge-enhancing environment, within which they are also more likely to participate and contribute to the local economy. In this context, host governments in Asia and elsewhere need not only to address the issue of attracting foreign firms, but also to ensure that they provide a dynamic business environment for firms to operate in, as well as encouraging foreign firms to create linkages with local firms.

From the above discussion, we conclude that the benefits brought by FDI depend on a number of factors, some being country-specific (such as government policies), some being related to the firm itself and the type of technology transferred. Still, there is evidence in the literature that FDI has played an important role in the development of many Asian countries (Jomo, 2001; Thorpe and Little, 2001; Yusuf, 2002).

MNEs, Inter-firm Linkages and Benefit to Host Economies

MNEs benefit host economies on a macroeconomic basis, for instance, through their impact on economic growth (Li and Liu, 2005) and the balance of payments. On a microeconomic basis, these benefits also depend upon the type of activities conducted by the foreign affiliates and relationships with other businesses (Scott-Kennel, 2004). One key impact, particularly for developing economies, results from the transfer of technology (Ernst *et al.*, 1998; Kumar, 1998; UNCTAD, 1999; Takatoshi and Krueger, 2000; Lall, 2002; Chen, 2005). As recipients of foreign technology, host economies need to provide a conducive environment, where technology can be absorbed. Borenzstein *et al.* (1998) looked at FDI flows from industrial countries to 69 developing countries, and found that FDI did contribute somewhat more to growth than domestic investment, essentially through technology transfer.

Depending on the host economy in Asia, some industries are almost entirely dominated by foreign firms, such as the electronics industry in Malaysia or the automobile industry in Thailand. The type of inter-firm linkages established will vary, depending upon the competitive environment, the technological environment and, to some extent, facilitation measures provided by the host government. Foreign firms may establish linkages with local suppliers, provided that the local supply industry is sufficiently developed. They may also develop links with their customers and contribute to the technological development of the latter. Finally, they have an impact on competitors or companies that might be in a position to cooperate with the foreign firms on specific projects. Such linkages are illustrated in Table 14.1, and reflect the variety of inter-firm linkages that can be created by MNEs in host economies.

The most common source of transfer from foreign firms is linked to the technical support related to the production process and the product. Indeed, it is found that, even in the transfer of business and organizational know-how, or in the case of training, transfers are often related to technical management and knowledge or involve support by the foreign firm in technical production and quality control (Giroud, 2003: 89). As an example, buyer–supplier technology transfer spans product-related technology, transfer of process technology, and organizational and managerial know-how transfer. Technology transfer is not the only link between foreign firms and local firms. Foreign firms may also provide training and managerial support (UNCTAD, 2001; Giroud, 2003).

MNEs, Government Policies and Inter-firm Linkages

The sharp increase in international investment worldwide has taken place, in part, as a result of relaxation of government policies towards foreign investment, and the endeavour by governments worldwide to attract an increasing share of foreign investment within their national boundaries. FDI-friendly policies have proliferated in the 1990s, as part of governments' broader efforts to create attractive policy environments, and this is notable in Asia (Brook and Hill, 2004; Lall and Narula, 2004; Yusuf *et al.*, 2004b). Key national policies related to FDI focus on attracting foreign investment, encouraging positive impact and addressing concerns of foreign investors. Countries can attract FDI in many ways. They can liberalize the conditions for admission and establishment of foreign investors, they can promote FDI inflows in general, or they can promote FDI more selectively, focusing on activities, technologies or investors (UNCTAD, 2003: 86).

Across East and Southeast Asia, governments have used selected measures both to attract foreign investors and to try and influence their activities. All countries have aimed at creating favourable business and investment environments. The second step consists of promoting a competitive environment (Asian Development Bank, 2003; Uchida and Cook, 2005) and, to do so, some governments have encouraged inter-firm linkages,

Table 14.1 Linkages between foreign affiliates and local enterprises and organizations in host economies

Form	Relationship of foreign affiliate to local enterprise			Relationship of foreign affiliate to non-business institution
	Backward (sourcing)	Forward (distribution)	Horizontal (cooperation in production)	
'Pure' market transaction Short-term linkage	'Off-the-shelf' purchases Once-for-all or intermittent purchases (on contract)	'Off-the-shelf' sales Once-for-all or intermittent sales (on contract)		
Longer-term linkage	Longer-term (contractual) arrangement for the procurement of inputs for further processing Subcontracting of the production of final or intermediate products	Longer-term (contractual) relationship with local distributor or end-customer Outsourcing from domestic firms to foreign affiliates	Joint projects with competing domestic firms	R&D contracts with local institutions such as universities and research centres Training programmes for firms by universities Traineeships for students in firms
Equity relationship	Joint venture with supplier Establishment of new supplier affiliate (by existing foreign affiliate)	Joint venture with distributor or end-customer Establishment of new distribution affiliate (by existing foreign affiliate)	Horizontal joint venture Establishment of new affiliate (by existing foreign affiliate) for the production of same goods and services as it produces	Joint public-private R&D centres/training centres/universities

'Spillover'

Demonstration effects in unrelated firms
- Spillover on processes (incl. technology)
- Spillover on product design
- Spillover on formal and on tacit skills (shop-floor and managerial)

Effects due to mobility of trained human resources

Enterprise spin-offs

Competition effects

Source: UNCTAD (2001: 131).

271

Table 14.2   Mixed technology strategies towards inter-firm linkages

Policy	Policy instrument	Condition
Promote linkages with domestic economy	Business incubators Information clearing houses	Institutions able to bargain with MNEs
Build local technological capabilities	Industrial parks Supporting R&D	Institutions able to plan strategically
Encourage deepening of MNE activity	Supporting joint ventures, licensing and collaboration Supporting training of domestic labour force	Ability to integrate skills, financial markets infrastructure and technological capability development

Source: Adapted from Table IV.2 in UNCTAD (2003: 132).

particularly between MNEs and local firms, leading to a set of policies tackling various aspects of businesses, as shown in Table 14.2. Governments adopt soft policy provisions, whereby MNEs are not operating under mandatory rules, but rather are encouraged to conduct business in a particular way. These policies are part of mixed strategies adopted by governments, and it is difficult to assess their efficiency.

This section has highlighted the types of investment undertaken by foreign firms in host economies, the impact of MNEs' activities and related government provisions to attract and maintain foreign investment, as well as encouraging inter-firm linkages. In the following section, we consider specifically policies adopted within East and Southeast Asian economies.

GOVERNMENT POLICIES TOWARDS FDI IN EAST AND SOUTHEAST ASIA

This section aims to present, firstly, some issues related to the Asian economic crisis and its impact upon policy regimes of Asian economies. It then discusses FDI policy regimes adopted by governments, and the way they encourage and promote linkages through various means, namely, setting up and developing special industrial zones, encouraging technology transfer, using tax incentives as an incentive for MNEs to operate in predetermined business areas. Finally, this section covers recent policies adopted to foster backwards linkages.

Financial Crisis and its Impact on Policies

The financial crisis that took place in East Asia in 1997–8 has had an impact upon the way local government perceived and dealt with FDI (Choi *et al.*, 1999; Ahn, 2001). One major outcome from the Asia economic crisis was the realization that FDI is less volatile

Table 14.3   East Asia economic growth (per cent)

	2003	2004	2005	2006
East Asia	5.9	7.2	6.0	5.9
Dev. E. Asia	7.9	8.2	7.2	6.8
S.E.Asia	5.6	5.9	5.3	5.6
Indonesia	5.0	5.1	5.5	6.0
Malaysia	5.3	7.1	5.3	5.3
Philippines	4.7	6.1	5.0	5.0
Thailand	6.9	6.1	5.2	5.6
Trans. eco.				
China	9.3	9.5	8.3	7.5
Vietnam	7.3	7.7	7.5	7.5
Small eco.	4.2	5.0	3.5	3.9
N.I.E	3.0	5.9	4.3	4.6
Korea	3.1	4.6	4.2	4.8
3 Others	3.0	6.9	4.3	4.4
Japan	1.4	2.6	0.8	1.9

Note: World Bank East Asia Region, April 2005; consensus forecasts for NIEs other than Korea.

Source: World Bank (2005: 4).

than other forms of capital or portfolio flows. Countries that relied more on foreign investment showed greater stability in the face of the financial crisis. In addition, host governments voluntarily implemented new policies to aggressively attract FDI. They eliminated or relaxed policies towards foreign equity ownership, and generally governments moved towards greater liberalization (Haley and Richter, 2002). For instance, Stoever (2005) shows the case of South Korean government policies after the crisis. Key sectors were liberalized, such as trading and financial services. New foreign investment promotion acts were introduced to enhance the investment climate, so that overall greater transparency for both government and firms was achieved. As a result, post-crisis FDI policy reforms resulted in an enhanced policy environment more favourable for foreign firms.

Comparing the policy environment in Thailand, South Korea, Indonesia, the Philippines and Malaysia, Chung and Beamish (2005) showed that although policy restriction on FDI has loosened from the pre-crisis period to the post-crisis period, policy uncertainty has increased in parallel. Indicating how the environment influences the characteristics and performance of firms, they then demonstrated that firms reacted to a changing environment by favouring specific modes of entry, specifically wholly owned or majority-owned ventures. Clearly, numerous key determinants of FDI, including natural resources, supply of low-cost or highly skilled human capital, solid and reliable infrastructure, and access to regional or other markets, were not disrupted by the crisis. The five worst-hit countries have recovered quickly and still show high growth rates (see Table 14.3), except for Indonesia, that was also affected by political disturbances and uncertainty over economic policies.

Overall, although firms' strategies have changed, they have benefited since production costs were reduced; as a result of substantial exchange-rate depreciation, domestic assets fell, providing attractive investment opportunities, and corporate restructuring took place

Table 14.4   FDI flows before and after the Asian crisis (millions of dollars)

	1996	1997	1998	1999	2000	2001	2002	2003
Korea	2 325	2 844	5 412	10 598	9 283	3 528	2 941	3 752
China	40 180	44 237	43 751	40 319	40 772	46 846	52 743	53 505
Taiwan	1 864	2 248	222	2 926	4 928	4 109	1 445	453
H.Kong	10 460	11 368	14 776	24 591	61 939	23 775	9 682	13 561
Singapore	10 372	12 967	6 316	7 197	12 464	10 949	5 730	11 409
Malaysia	7 296	6 513	2 700	3 532	3 788	554	3 203	2 474
Thailand	2 271	3 627	5 143	3 562	3 350	3 813	1 068	1 802
Philippines	1 520	1 249	1 752	737	1 345	982	1 792	319
Vietnam	2 519	2 824	2 254	1 991	1 289	1 300	1 200	1 450
World	384 910	481 911	686 028	1 079 083	1 392 957	823 825	678 751	559 576

Source: http://www.unctad.org/en/subsites/dite/FDIstats_files/FDIstats.htm.

throughout the region, making local firms attractive to foreign firms. As a result of the crisis, East Asian economies further liberalized their economies and provided low-inflation environments, with favourable investment climates where cheap assets were available. This explains why FDI levels were sustained (see Table 14.4).

FDI Regimes in the Region

It would be impossible to depict a single policy prescription for all East and Southeast Asian economies. Historically, the most open economies towards FDI have been Hong Kong, Singapore and Malaysia. While China, the Philippines, Indonesia and Thailand have concentrated on actively attracting FDI, South Korea has adopted a cautious and conservative approach and, together with Taiwan, encouraged outward investment rather than inward flows. Generally, all economies in the region have adopted a panel of measures, spreading from sound economic policies and human capital strengthening to attract FDI while improving foreign firms' economic impact. The type of FDI promotion adopted by host economies depends predominantly upon the level of economic development and the role played by foreign investment, as part of the development strategy of the host economy.

Host governments address foreign investors' concerns by reducing obstacles to FDI,[1] granting foreign investors non-discriminatory treatment compared to domestic investors, providing protection in case of litigation, and promoting and encouraging inflows. Governments across East and Southeast Asia have recently paid increasing attention to investment facilitation. All countries have established strong independent investment promotion agencies[2] that work with the government to improve the investment environment, conduct international marketing and facilitate investment. Table 14.5 shows the various agencies that foreign investors need to approach in East and Southeast Asian countries, when they wish to engage in an investment activity. The nature and balance of policies applied vary, and locational advantages differ, and firms generally pay attention to the overall cost of investment.

A smooth investment process until the company is granted the right to investment is essential, and governments throughout the region have eased this process. Table 14.6

Table 14.5   Key foreign investment agencies

	FDI agency	Useful information
China	Ministry of Commerce (MOFCOM)	http://www.mofcom.gov.cn/
Hong Kong	Invest HK	http://www.investhk.gov.hk/
Taiwan	Investment Commission, Ministry of Economic Affairs (MOEA)	http://www.moeaic.gov.tw/
Republic of Korea	Korea Investment Service Centre (KISC)	http://www.kisc.or.kr
Singapore	Economic Development Board	http://www.sedb.com/
Malaysia	MIDA	http://www.mida.gov.my/
Thailand	BOI	http://www.boi.go.th/
Indonesia	Investment Coordinating Board of Indonesia (BKPM)	http://www.bkpm.go.id/
Vietnam	Ministry of Planning and Investment	http://www.mpi.gov.vn

Table 14.6   Starting a business in East and Southeast Asian countries

	Number of procedures	Time (days)	Cost (% of income per capita)	Min. capital (% of income per capita)
China	12	41	14.5	1 104.2
Hong Kong	5	11	3.4	0.0
Taiwan	8	48	6.3	224.7
Republic of Korea	12	22	17.7	332.0
Singapore	7	8	1.2	0.0
Malaysia	9	30	25.1	0.0
Thailand	8	33	6.7	0.0
Indonesia	12	151	130.7	125.6
Vietnam	11	56	28.6	0.0
Regional average	8	51	48.3	100.5
OECD average	6	25	8.0	44.1

Source: http:www.doingbusiness.org/.

shows the number of procedures and time needed in Asia to open a business, indicating that the most favourable environments are Hong Kong and Singapore, where the number of procedures is five and seven, respectively, within fewer than 11 days, at a cost equal to as low as 1.2 per cent of gross national income per capita, with no minimum deposit to obtain a business registration number.

When devising policies relating to the promotion of FDI inflows, governments also need to establish policies to ensure that the host economy derives the full economic benefits from FDI. Investment promotion and incentives are devised not solely to attract investment, but also to encourage foreign firms in specific industries, in selected investment locations and towards higher value-added-type activities, such as incentives encouraging foreign firms to establish R&D activities or regional headquarters. Key policies will be divided between mandatory measures aimed at enhancing the impact of foreign affiliates in host countries, and non-mandatory measures aiming to increase the contribution of foreign affiliates that encourage them to act in a desired way.

Industrial Zones as a Means to Promote Linkages

Governments in Asia have established a special industrial zone to attract foreign investors since the late 1960s. Singapore (Pereira, 2005) and Hong Kong were the first to encourage such zones, followed by Malaysia, then Indonesia and Thailand. More recently, China and Vietnam have also been very active in developing such zones, providing favourable conditions for foreign investors. In Malaysia, the government has to date established 14 free trade zones (FTZs), over 200 industrial estates throughout the country,[3] three specialized parks equipped with modern and up-to-date facilities for high-tech manufacturing activity and R&D companies, and a biotechnology park.

A distinct and widespread type of industrial zones developed across Asia includes export-processing zones (EPZs).[4] Although Singapore and Hong Kong have adopted this approach since the 1960s, and Malaysia and Thailand since the 1980s, the generalization of export-oriented policies occurred across Asia in the early 1990s. One major tool used across several Asian countries is that of EPZs. Firms located in EPZs normally export the majority of all of their production. In return, they benefit from favourable import duties, tax and incentives, and enhanced infrastructure. Such zones allow foreign firms to reduce production costs so that they can produce for the global market and achieve economies of scale. EPZs are successful in attracting export-oriented FDI. In some countries, they have generated entire industries, such as the electronics industry in Malaysia.

While these policies have resulted in the fast growth of manufactured exports and an export-led growth, critics have expressed concerns as foreign firms in these zones typically import a large share (or all) of their components, generate minimal linkages with the host economy, the jobs created involve minimal skills, and the transfer of technology by these firms may be minimum. Still, across East Asia, rapid development patterns are partly associated with the creation of EPZs, although this needs to be combined with other factors, such as sound macroeconomic and social policies. Most Asian countries, however, combine the development of export-oriented zones with specific industrial parks[5] and technology parks,[6] thus fostering industrial development and technological development in parallel with export-oriented development. This has led to regional production networks linking MNEs across Asia (Borrus *et al.*, 2000; Yusuf *et al.*, 2004a).

Each Asian country has adopted different economic development strategies, all aimed at the deepening of the industrial base and, in many cases, governments have targeted specific industries. Singapore and Malaysia have, for instance, used foreign firms to launch their electronics industries. As part of its second Industrial Master Plan, launched in 1995, Malaysia embraced a cluster-based approach strategy aiming at the development of specific industry clusters. The Master Plan continued earlier strategies of promoting reinvestments, industrial linkages, export and training; but it added new objectives, such as the facilitation of international linkages amongst the electronics and electrical appliances, and textiles industries.[7]

The new cluster-based approach and a stronger concern for local linkage creation indicated the willingness of the government to move away from mere incentives to attract foreign firms. This move demonstrates how countries initially focus on attracting foreign investors, as is the case still mostly for China or Vietnam, before paying increasing attention to further integration of such foreign firms within the host economy. Malaysia combines its industrial development policy with its foreign investment policy. Since 2001, ten key industry task forces aim to enhance the cluster-based industrial development and manufacturing activities.

The effectiveness of such policies, however, is not empirically proven. While investment inflows to target sectors are positively encouraged by governments, to date, cluster-based policies, such as the one implemented in Malaysia, have not yet been shown to be successful. In the less developed countries of the region, the development of a sound industrial base takes precedence over a cluster-based approach to economic development. Foreign firms will influence positively local firms once these have achieved a sufficient level of competitiveness.

Benefit from Linkages through Technology Transfer

One of the key benefits to be drawn from inter-firm linkages is that of technology sharing and absorption. Governments have developed distinct technology strategies, aiming at the maximization of technology transfer and dissemination. Governments actively encourage innovation to maximize the benefits of MNEs' activities within their national boundaries. Without doubt, foreign firms represent a dominant source of innovation, particularly in less developed countries in Southeast Asia, such as Malaysia, Thailand or Vietnam. First, governments aim at attracting MNEs with the most suitable technologies, before encouraging them to transfer technologies with the best potential for local development.

Depending upon the level of development of the host economy, MNEs will either transfer simple technologies suited to the low wage and low skill setting or the technology development process itself, with more design and R&D located within host countries. Among the developing world, Asia is the preferred destination for R&D activities within MNEs (UNCTAD, 2005).[8] The development impact of technology transfer extends to increasing technological capabilities of local suppliers and buyers, as well as contributing to local innovation capacity. This is why governments place much emphasis on it. For instance, Hong Kong has set up an innovation and technology fund that supports projects contributing either to innovation and technology upgrading in local industry or to the upgrading and development of the local industry.[9]

The issue of technology transfer is important for all Asian countries, but the means of transfer and emphasis varies. South Korea and Taiwan have relied heavily on licensing, machinery imports and reverse engineering. With more competitive domestic firms, technological capabilities can be assimilated by importing know-how and machinery. A different approach was adopted in Singapore, Hong Kong and, more recently, Malaysia, Thailand and Indonesia. Direct investment was used to acquire foreign technical and managerial know-how that was subsequently transferred to the domestic firms.

While Singapore, Hong Kong and Taiwan have long encouraged foreign technology transfer, newly industrializing economies in the region are in the process of facilitating such transfers. The latest attempt towards hi-tech development in Malaysia arose from the Multimedia Super Corridor (MSC). The MSC is 15 kilometres wide and 50 kilometres long, including Cyberjaya, an intelligent city that aims to attract multimedia industries, R&D centres, a multimedia university and operational headquarters for multinationals.[10] The Chinese government offers a tariff exemption policy for the importation of equipment, in order to encourage the flow of foreign advanced technology and equipment, promoting the industry structural adjustment and technological advancement, as well as maintaining a continuous, rapid and healthy development of the national economy.[11]

As mentioned above, developing Asia is attractive for foreign firms to relocate their R&D activities. Hence host governments must further refine their policies to meet individual needs of foreign firms; a strategic fit needs to be designed to combine the FDI policy objectives with each MNE's objectives, with the aim to encourage high-technology activities, R&D and the process of innovation within individual countries.

Tax Incentives and Linkages

While it has been shown that tax incentives only have a moderate role in attracting FDI to host economies, they can be a useful tool for governments to encourage firms' activities. Initially, MNEs typically select host economies by scanning a variety of factors, such as market size, access to raw materials or availability of skilled labour. Tax incentives then play a role inasmuch as they may influence the final location decisions made by firms.

Tax incentives or tax break are frequently used by governments across Asia to induce firms to invest in particular projects, sectors or activity considered crucial for development, to direct investment to selected geographical areas, to encourage higher value-added activities (such as regional headquarters) or indeed specifically inter-firm activities. Malaysia and China use tax incentives to direct investment towards less developed regions. For instance, China offers preferential income tax of 15 per cent in economic zones, high-tech industrial zones, economic and technological development zones, and a rate of 24 per cent in coastal opening areas and provincial capital cities.[12]

Hong Kong, Taiwan, Singapore and Malaysia have introduced a specific set of incentives directed towards R&D activities and technology projects (pioneer industries). In Singapore, incentives are used both for the promotion of new investments in industries and services and for encouraging existing companies to upgrade through mechanization and automation and through the introduction of new products and services. Table 14.7 illustrates some key incentives provided by the Singaporean government as part of the planning and promotion of industrial and commercial development.

Policies towards Encouraging Linkages with Suppliers

Asian governments have recently paid increasing attention to linkages with local suppliers. Most governments promote the creation of backward linkages using soft voluntary incentives rather than compulsory policies. Some programmes target initial purchase of equipment, while others go further and encourage a higher share of local content in production, not necessarily through using local content requirements, as these have not been found to be very effective (Hackett and Srinivasan, 1998). Local content is encouraged in

Table 14.7   FDI programmes and incentives in Singapore

Programme	Nature of incentive
Pioneer status	Exemption of corporate tax on profits arising from pioneer activity for up to 10 years
Venture capital fund	Exemption of corporate tax on income from approved venture capital funds
Technopreneur investment	Deduction from taxable income for losses incurred from investments into high-tech start-ups
Development & expansion	Corporate tax rate of 13%
Investment allowance	Exemption of taxable income of an amount equal to a specific proportion, not exceeding 50% of new investments in productive equipment
Operational headquarters	Income arising from the provision of approved services in Singapore taxed at 10%
Approved royalties	Full or partial exemption of withholding tax on royalty payments
Approved foreign loan	Full or partial exemption of withholding tax on interest payments
Double deduction for R&D expenses	Double deduction of qualifying R&D expenses against income

Source: APEC, *Guide for Investment Regimes* (2003: 536).

Taiwan by means of low-interest loans for the procurement of domestically produced automation equipment.[13] In China, foreign firms enjoy tax credit towards purchases of domestically made equipment within the volume of the total investment made.[14]

Malaysia has devised a complex framework and has initiated special programmes that work closely with both foreign investors and domestic suppliers in promoting mutually beneficial linkages between the two parties. The Malaysian example reflects a move by most developing countries in the region away from traditional types of import restrictions and content requirements, in favour of more interactive policies where the government intervenes in the upgrading process of the local supporting industries (Battat *et al.*, 1996). The Malaysian government promotes inter-firm linkages by way of its Industrial Linkages Programme (ILP), whereby large firms receive incentives to foster and develop local vendors. Such linkages promotions are encouraged by using market-friendly incentives, such as tax incentives, specific institutional arrangements, vendor development schemes, local content requirements, subcontracting exchange schemes and information provision and exchange.

On a regional basis, countries in Southeast Asia are joining up to generate linkages across the region through its ASEAN Industrial Cooperation Scheme (AICS) initiative.[15] This initiative has encouraged and supported existing activities performed by MNEs on a regional basis, with companies such as Toyota, Denso, Volvo, Sony, Matsushita, Goya and Nestlé, Mitsubishi, Isuzu, Honda, Nissan, Samsung and Yamaha Motor benefiting from the scheme. Southeast Asian countries have now demonstrated only the wish to generate and deepen industrial linkages within their own boundaries. They have acknowledged the need to coordinate policies on a regional basis to maximize opportunities for foreign firms, as well as the benefits to be gained from MNEs' activities for individual host countries of the region.

We would conclude from this section that governments have only just begun to consider the issue of backward linkages. They need to encourage foreign firms to supply direct parts and components locally, by providing incentives to those firms and support to local suppliers to become more competitive. The local entrepreneurship potential must be in place for the full benefit of backward linkages to take place; this will differ according to the level of economic development of the Asian country. The issue of technology and knowledge transfer between firms has not yet been fully tackled by governments, and there is a lack of coherent policies addressing this important issue. While emphasis is placed on intra-firm technology transfer to host economies, governments need to consider inter-firm technology transfer more specifically, and, for this, they need to pay greater attention to the global and regional strategies adopted by MNEs. The role played by the subsidiary and its level of independence will determine the type of relationships it will establish with local suppliers. Host governments should look into providing additional incentives for MNEs to create close links with their local suppliers.

CONCLUSION

In this chapter, we have discussed the recent change in governments' attitudes in Asia towards foreign direct investment, with a distinct move from establishing policies merely aiming at attracting FDI towards more encompassing measures and actions aiming at maximizing the benefits to be gained from foreign firms' activities in host economies. Governments have realized that different policy regimes for foreign firms are not a sufficient means to attract FDI and maximize the benefits to be drawn from such investment. In fact, foreign firms are attracted to dynamic business environments or locations offering comparative advantages that will enhance their own capabilities and competitiveness. Importantly, Asian governments have realized that the benefits from FDI are uneven, and they can be maximized by adopting sound policy regimes and institutional capacities (see also other chapters in Part III of this volume).

We have discussed in this chapter how policy regimes towards the enhancement of inter-firm linkages vary in Asia according to the level of economic development in host countries, and upon the development strategy adopted by the government and played by FDI within this strategy. Thus differentiation can be made between Hong Kong and Singapore, arguably the economies most open towards FDI. Singapore and Malaysia have undoubtedly developed some of the most selective and complete policies towards encouraging inter-firm linkages. China and Vietnam are still at the stage where governments concentrate their efforts on attracting foreign investment, while in parallel working towards offering more business-oriented environments for firms to operate in.

The current trend across all countries is that of moving away from mere policies aiming at attracting FDI, towards more complex policies aiming at upgrading local capabilities and increasing the role of MNEs in supporting this upgrading. Governments across the region adopt *voluntary* policies, thereby providing incentives to encourage inter-firm linkages. The key challenge, particularly for host economies in Southeast Asia, is not merely to attract new investments. But it is specifically important to enhance MNEs' embeddedness within host economies. One could point at the lack of empirical evidence about the efficiency of such voluntary policies, yet the move towards policies supporting MNEs' linkages needs analysing in the context of governments' endeavour to generate competitive business environments. In this context, both domestic and foreign firms can operate, often applying directive and selective policies aiming at enhancing the competitiveness of specific sectors of activities such as high-tech sectors. All fall within the long-term development objectives of host governments.

It has been argued that 'host governments that seek to enhance the advancement of their national industrial structures by attracting MNEs with cutting-edge technology and creating value-added capability need to implement fiscal incentives in which the value of incentives offered is proportional to the MNEs' ex-post performance' (Lim, 2005: 74). Our chapter reinforces this point. Asian governments adapt incentives to their specific development and industrial policies and objectives. They, in parallel, need to refine their policies further by paying more attention to what each MNE can bring and the particular strategy adopted by an MNE (Brook and Hill, 2004). Governments should not only continue to emphasize inter-firm linkages, but also customize their FDI incentives to individual firms.

Overall, we find evidence that FDI policies have been successful in attracting foreign investors, and many Asian governments have launched policies aimed at deepening linkages between foreign and local firms. However, we also find that governments should pay more attention, and adapt their incentives, to the individual objectives and strategies of foreign firms. Finally, inasmuch as FDI policies are linked to economic development policies, these must be considered in the wider regional and global contexts (Yusuf *et al.*, 2004b). The creation of linkages takes place beyond national borders, and regional initiatives will further facilitate foreign firms' regional activities.

From a business perspective, MNEs will welcome efficient tax breaks and a better environment to operate in, which will enhance their own competitive advantages. MNEs have much to gain in Asian environments, and much to gain from operating in more competitive industries. We find that it is at the time of the investment proposal that firms can lay out a clear proposal of activities for the host economy, in order to benefit from additional support and tailor-made incentives from host governments in Asia. With a better understanding of the benefit they can generate in the context of each government's industrial objectives, MNEs gain a strong bargaining power and they should take advantage of incentives offered across Asia.

As a final comment, we find that governments have paid attention to the type and form of investment in their wish to maximize the economic benefits of FDI, yet, to date, few studies have been conducted on the strategies adopted on a national, regional and global basis by MNEs (see chapters in Part I of this volume). Future research, therefore, ought to look into the assessment of the economic impact of MNEs on host countries' development trajectories in light of their overall strategy. Two avenues would be open: first, more empirical studies are needed to link firms' goals and strategies to the impact they have on host economies; second, more studies are needed to develop policy instruments that would enable governments to aim their incentives more precisely at the specific strategies adopted by MNEs.

NOTES

1. Such as restrictions on admission, establishment of operations through to the way they can be run.
2. For a global comparison of key investment promotion agencies, see MIGA (2005).
3. Some zones were developed by government agencies, namely, the State Economic Development Corporations (SEDCs), Regional Development Authorities (RDAs), port authorities and municipalities, and others by private developers in certain states.
4. An export-processing zone is an industrial zone specializing in the production of exports, and the provision of services for the production of exports and export activities with specified boundaries established, or permitted to be established, by the government.
5. An industrial zone specializes in the production of industrial goods, and the provision of services for industrial production established, or permitted to be established, by the government.
6. A technology park (also called high-tech parks) is a park for high-tech industrial enterprises, and enterprises providing services for high-tech development, including scientific–technological research and application and training and related services. These parks would typically have fixed geographical boundaries, and may have export-processing firms located within their boundaries.
7. http://www.mida.gov.my.
8. For instance, the share of developing Asia in American MNE's overseas R&D rose from 3 per cent to 10 per cent between 1994 and 2002.
9. There are four programmes under the fund: innovation and technology support programme, university–industry collaboration programme, general support programme and small entrepreneur research assistance programme (APEC, 2003: 180).
10. http://www.mdc.com.my.
11. http://english.mofcom.gov.cn/aarticle/topic/chinainvest/governmentalpolicies/200501/20050100013227.html.
12. http://english.mofcom.gov.cn/aarticle/topic/chinainvest/governmentalpolicies/200501/20050100013227.html.
13. MNEs receive loans for the procurement of domestically produced automation equipment by general productive enterprises, and warehousing enterprises are available at an interest rate 2.125 percentage points below the Chiao Tung Bank's prime rate (APEC, 2003: 569).
14. http://english.mofcom.gov.cn/aarticle/topic/chinainvest/governmentalpolicies/200501/20050100013227.html.
15. 'The Ministers noted that as of 6 August 2004, 126 out of 183 AICO applications have been approved. These approved AICO arrangements are estimated to generate US$1,482 million trade transactions per year. The Ministers agreed to extend the waiver on the 30 percent national equity requirement for AICO applications until 31 December 2005' (http://www.aseansec.org/16363.htm).

REFERENCES

Ahn, C.Y. (2001), 'A search for robust East Asian development models after the financial crisis: mutual learning from East Asian experiences', *Journal of Asian Economics*, **12**(3), 419–43.

APEC (2003), 'Guide for investment regimes for APEC member economies', (http://www.apecsec.org.sg/).

Asian Development Bank (2003), *Competitiveness in Developing Asia: Taking Advantage of Globalization, Technology, and Competition*, Manila: ADB (http://www.adb.org).

Battat, J., I. Frank and X. Shen (1996), *Suppliers to Multinationals: Linkages Programs to Strengthen Local Companies in Developing Countries*, Washington, DC: World Bank, Foreign Investment Advisory Service.

Borenzstein, E., J. De Gregorio and J.-W. Lee (1998), 'How does foreign direct investment affect economic growth?', *Journal of International Economics*, **45**(1), 115–35.

Borrus, M., D. Ernst and S. Haggard (2000), *International Production Networks in Asia: Rivalry or riches?*, London and New York: Routledge.

Brook, D.H. and H. Hill (2004), 'Divergent Asian views on FDI and its governance', *Asian Development Review*, **21**(1), 1–37.

Chen, S.-F. (2005), 'Extending internalization theory: a new perspective on international technology transfer and its generalization', *Journal of International Business Studies*, **36**(2), 231–45.

Choi, C.J., C. Millar and K.J. Choi (1999), 'Asian economic success and crisis: knowledge and financial capital', working paper, The Judge Institute of Management Studies, University of Cambridge.

Chung, C.C. and P.W. Beamish (2005), 'The impact of institutional reforms on characteristics and survival of foreign subsidiaries in emerging economies', *Journal of Management Studies*, **42**(1), 35–62.

Ernst, D., T. Ganiatsos and L. Mytelka (1998), *Technological Capabilities and Export Success in Asia*, London and New York: Routledge.

Giroud, A. (2003), *Transnational Corporations, Technology and Economic Development: Backward Linkages and Knowledge Transfer in South East Asia*, Cheltenham, UK and Northampton, MA: Edward Elgar.

Hackett, S.C. and K. Srinivasan (1998), 'Are there spillovers from direct foreign investment? Evidence from panel data for Morocco', *Journal of Development Economics*, **42**, 51–74.

Haley, U.C.V. and F.-J. Richter (2002), *Asian Post-Crisis Management: Corporate and Governmental Strategies for Sustainable Competitive Advantage*, Basingstoke/New York: Palgrave.

Holland, D., M. Sass, V. Benacek and M. Gronicki (2000), 'The determinants and impact of FDI in Central and Eastern Europe: a comparison of survey and econometric evidence', *Transnational Corporations*, **9**(3), 163–212.

Jomo, K.S. (2001), *Southeast Asia's Industrialization: Industrial Policy, Capabilities and Sustainability*, Basingstoke/New York: Palgrave.

Kumar, N. (1998), *Globalization, Foreign Direct Investment and Technology Transfers: Impacts on and Prospects for Developing Countries*, London/New York: Routledge, in collaboration with the United Nations University, and INTECH: Institute for New Technologies.

Lall, S. (2002), 'Linking FDI, technology development for capacity building and strategic competitiveness', *Transnational Corporations*, **11**(3), 39–88.

Lall, S. and R. Narula (2004), 'Foreign direct investment and its role in economic development: do we need a new research agenda?', *The European Journal of Development Research*, **16**(3), 445–62.

Li, X. and X. Liu (2005), 'Foreign direct investment and economic growth: an increasingly endogenous relationship', *World Development*, **33**(3), 393–407.

Lim, S.-H. (2005), 'Foreign investment impact and incentive: a strategic approach to the relationship between the objectives of foreign investment policy and their promotion', *International Business Review*, **14**, 61–76.

MIGA (2005), '2005 IPA Performance Benchmarking Program: Investor Inquiry Handling Study' (http://www.miga.org).

Moosa, I.A. (2002), *Foreign Direct Investment: Theory, Evidence and Practice*, Chippenham: Palgrave.

Pereira, A. (2005), 'Singapore's regionalization strategy', *Journal of Asia Pacific Economy*, **10**(3), 380–96.

Scott-Kennel, J. (2004), 'Foreign direct investment: a catalyst for local firm development?', *The European Journal of Development Research*, **16**(3), 624–52.

Stoever, W.A. (2005), 'Restructuring FDI policy in emerging economies: the Republic of Korea case', *Thunderbird International Business Review*, **47**(5), 555–74.

Sun, Q., W. Tong and Q. Yu (2002), 'Determinants of foreign direct investment across China', *Journal of International Money and Finance*, **21**(1), 79–113.

Takatoshi, I. and A.O. Krueger (2000), *The Role of Foreign Direct Investment in East Asian Economic Development*, Chicago: National Bureau of Economic Research (NBER).

Thorpe, R. and S. Little (2001), *Global Change: The Impact of Asia in the 21st Century*, Basingstoke/New York: Palgrave.

Uchida, Y. and P. Cook (2005), 'The transformation of competitive advantage in East Asia: an analysis of technological and trade specialization', *World Development*, **33**(5), 701–28.

UNCTAD (1998), *World Investment Report 1998: Trends and Determinants*, New York/Geneva: United Nations.

UNCTAD (1999), *World Investment Report 1999: Foreign Direct Investment and the Challenge of Development*, New York/Geneva: United Nations.

UNCTAD (2001), *World Investment Report 2001: Promoting Linkages*, New York/Geneva: United Nations.

UNCTAD (2003), *World Investment Report 2003: FDI Policies for Development: National and International Perspectives*, New York/Geneva: United Nations.

UNCTAD (2004), *World Investment Report 2004: The Shift Towards Services*, New York/Geneva: United Nations.

UNCTAD (2005), *World Investment Report 2005: TNCs and the Internationalization of R&D*, New York/Geneva: United Nations.

World Bank (2005), *East Asia update: East Asia's dollar influx – signal for change*, East Asia and Pacific Region (http://www.worldbank.org).

Yusuf, S. (2002), 'Remodelling East Asian development', *ASEAN Economic Bulletin*, **19**(1), 6–26.

Yusuf, S., A.M. Altaf and K. Nabeshima (eds) (2004a), *Global Production Networking and Technological Change in East Asia*, Washington, DC: World Bank, Oxford University Press.

Yusuf, S., M.A. Altaf and K. Nabeshima (eds) (2004b), *Global Change and East Asian Policy Initiatives*, Washington, DC: World Bank, Oxford University Press.

15. Change and continuity in business organization: the roles of the state and regional ethnicity in Singapore

Lai Si Tsui-Auch

The past few decades have witnessed an ascent of Asian enterprises as important players in the global economy. The extraordinary growth of these enterprises has sparked much research into their management and organization (Clegg and Redding, 1990; Orrú, Biggart and Hamilton, 1997; Yeung, 1998). Among the contending perspectives, the institutional perspective is the most holistic in explaining the emergence, forms of, and practices in these enterprises (see also Chapter 3 in this volume). Drawing upon research into business organizations in Singapore, this chapter argues that the explanatory power of the institutionalist perspective can be strengthened by explaining the roles of the state and regional ethnicity in shaping organizational change amid continuity.

Singapore is suitable for revealing organizational change amid continuity, the role of the state, and regional ethnicity. First, Singapore, like many other Asian countries, has undergone political, economic and sociocultural transformations over the past few decades. The research into how its businesses have dealt with rapid development and change will shed light on the experience of their counterparts elsewhere in Asia. Second, the state of Singapore constitutes the major capital in the economy,[1] creating and nurturing government-linked corporations (GLCs) to spearhead industrial and infrastructural development. The country is far from exceptional in the paramount role of the state: both South Korea (especially before 1997, see Chang, 2003; Tsui-Auch and Lee, 2003) and China (see *The Economist*, 2005; Chapter 6 in this volume) have been in the same league. An examination of the role of the state in influencing Singaporean business organization will pave the way for cross-national comparison. Finally, Singapore, like many other Southeast and South Asian countries, has an ethnically mixed population, and hence provides a suitable context for comparative studies of ethnic groups and their subgroup structures.

This chapter consists of five sections. The next section reviews contending perspectives of Asian business organization and identifies the gap in the existing literature. The second section outlines the Singapore context, whereas section three analyses how local enterprises (GLCs and ethnic Chinese and Indian businesses) dealt with state-driven institutional change. In the final section, I analyse the roles of the state and regional ethnicity in shaping organizational change amid continuity of different groups of enterprises, and conclude with suggestions of future research directions.

THEORETICAL PERSPECTIVES: MARKET, CULTURE AND INSTITUTION

Numerous authors have identified Asian businesses as being organized around families and personal relationship-based networks (Redding, 1990; Whitley, 1996; Yeung, 1999). There are largely three contending perspectives on Asian business organization, namely the market, cultural and institutional perspectives. From a market perspective, Chandler (1962, 1977, 1995) argued for the inevitability of the managerial enterprise replacing the family enterprise. He explained that changes in the market environment of the firm bring about changes in its strategy that in turn lead to the changes in the internal structure of the firm. The Chandlerian perspective presupposes that the more extensive the market, the more complex the technology, and the bigger the firm size, the more crucial will be the professional skills that are needed to sustain the profitability and growth of the enterprise. Hence the reliance on professional managers to run businesses will be greater, and the role of family members will be lessened.

The cultural perspective, however, rejects the rationalistic assumptions of the market perspective. The authors claim that organizations are not just products of the pursuit of economic benefits, but symbolic expressions of the cultural values of a society. Culture provides values and rewards through which organizations can be maintained (for a summary, see Child, 2000). In the East Asian context, Confucianism defines an ethical order in which people are born, not with rights, but with obligations to hierarchically arranged authorities, starting with the family and extending to the state. Redding (1990) emphasized that cultural values are enduring, and continue to exert influence in society, despite technological and economic modernization (see also Chapter 17 in this volume).

Parallel to the culturalists, who argue for the effects of the ideological roots of society, the institutionalists of Asian capitalism stress the institutional foundations of management and business (Orrú, Biggart and Hamilton, 1997). Key institutions include the family structure, authority relations, communal networks and the inheritance system (Hamilton and Biggart, 1988; Whitley, 1996). Institutional theorists emphasize the historical embeddedness of social structures and processes in which distinct transactional logics evolve, for example, the logic of patrilineality and personal trust that has been expounded by Confucians. This institutionalized logic shapes a society whose transactional order rests on obligation to higher authority in the family, community and state, rather than on rules that were developed to protect the individual (Orrú, Biggart and Hamilton, 1997). Hence the business organization of Asian enterprises is intrinsically different from that of Western enterprises.

Institutionalist authors are critical of the market perspective for its 'undersocialized' view, and the cultural perspective for its 'oversocialized' view of economic action. They regard economic action, not as an atomistic, individual decision, but as an action that is embedded in ongoing patterns of social relations and inter-actor ties. Whereas the market perspective presupposes that actors pursue efficiency alone, the institutional perspective argues that actors often aim at legitimacy, by seeking the understanding of other actors. While acknowledging the role of cultural values, the institutional perspective rejects a deterministic, oversocialized view that actors are culturally conditioned to comply with cultural values. Rather, it assumes that actors, though acting under institutional constraints, make choices to fit their purposes. They apply institutionalized norms with the intention of gaining legitimacy. They further argue that action in conformity with institutional norms yields not only legitimacy, but also efficiency. In their view, actors who disregard institutional norms encounter social friction that renders their actions inefficient. Actors who apply those norms are easily accepted by other actors, thus rendering their actions more legitimate, conflict-free and efficient. As Asian businesses are embedded in closely-knit business networks forged by family and personal ties, in which insiders (family and friends) are trusted and outsiders are distrusted, a reliance on kin, friends and long-serving employees in running businesses yields, not only legitimacy, but also efficiency.

While cultural theorists tend to see culture as static, institutional theorists recognize that institutions and cultural norms that they support do change in the face of economic and technological advances, though often slowly and with great difficulty (Biggart, 1997). The institutional perspective offers a holistic perspective to account for the roles of market, culture and institution in shaping business organizations. As Child (2000) acknowledged, the institutional perspective contextualizes culture and takes into account the influences both of systems of ideas and of material forces, yet he highlighted that the perspective emphasizes institutional constraints and continuity, and plays down institutional and organizational changes. In view of the rapid institutional change, especially since the Asian economic crisis (Yeung, 2000b; see also Chapter 18 in this volume), I concur with Child's view that it is timely to take stock of change amid continuity in business organization.

The state has been instrumental in shaping institutional change. Rapid institutional change has been witnessed in Singapore and other Asian countries that have been increasingly integrated into the world economy, through state-led or state-supported export-oriented industrialization, Western cultural imports, modern education and foreign direct investment since the 1960s. Institutionalists studying Asian economic organization, as with the political economists and development studies authors (Amsden, 1989; Johnson, 1982; Hill and Fujita, 1996; Tsui-Auch, 1998, 1999; Wade, 1990), generally accredit the role of government policies in shaping the organization of business systems, but rarely identify the role of the state in influencing business organization.

DiMaggio and Powell (1983) identified three categories of institutional isomorphism, of which the concept of coercive isomorphism appears to be the most relevant in the analysis of the role of the state in fostering organizational imitation. Coercive isomorphism is the process whereby organizational patterns are imposed by a powerful authority, usually the state. The other two concepts are mimetic isomorphism, whereby organizations respond to environmental uncertainties by imitating those organizations that are perceived as 'successful' in that kind of environment, and normative isomorphism, whereby 'appropriate' organizational patterns or the 'best practice' are championed by professional organizations. In this chapter, I will use the Singapore case to illustrate how the state has exerted, not only coercive isomorphism, but also mimetic isomorphism and normative isomorphism toward particular business organization models.

Institutions are often analysed at the national level. As many Asian societies are ethnically heterogeneous, there is a need to deconstruct the unitary notion of ethnicity. Recently, several authors have highlighted intraethnic diversity and explained how different groups structure their communities and foster solidarity (Markovits, 2000; Wang, 1996). However, they have offered no explanation for certain markers of intraethnic identification continuing to exert influence on the business organization of some groups, but not on that of other groups. A comparative study of ethnic subgroups, as reported in this chapter, represents an initial step to fill the gap in the existing literature.

STATE-LED ECONOMIC AND SOCIOCULTURAL DEVELOPMENT IN SINGAPORE

As early as the nineteenth century, the Southeast Asian region became the focus of multilateral trade that was dominated by Chinese and Indian traders (Brown, 1994). From 1819 under British rule, the colonial government groomed Singapore to be a major import/export centre that would absorb traders from China and British India, and immigrants already settled in British Malaya. When the British colonists departed, the Chinese entrepreneurs, who constituted the majority in the business community, took over the dominant economic interests of Singapore (Chan and Chiang, 1994).

Prior to the self-government of Singapore in 1959, the ethnic Chinese business community had become an important economic and political force. After the Peoples' Action Party (PAP) came to power in 1959, however, it attempted to forge a multiethnic and multicultural society, de-emphasizing the 'Chineseness' of Singapore in response to the 'internal ethnic imperatives as well as the regional geographical compulsions' (Vasil, 1995: 34). The ethnic Chinese business community came into conflict with the PAP, and openly backed the opposition, Socialist Front, that was sympathetic to the promotion of Chinese culture and education (Rodan, 1989).

Economic Development: 1963–1997

Following the separation of Singapore from Malaysia in 1963, the PAP government adopted a 'two-legged' policy that relied on multinational corporations and GLCs for industrialization (Rodan, 1989; see also Chapter 12 in this volume). The ruling elite regarded the local traders as rentiers who did not engage in real production activities (Low, 2001a). Consequently, it was not interested in assisting local businesses in industrialization, and did not identify the local private sector as a central object of either policy or patronage (Chalmers, 1992). Although the state was not attentive to the interests of local firms, the large family-controlled Chinese banks constituted a partial exception.[2] In contrast to other countries in the region, state intervention in the banking sector was particularly strong. The Banking Act of 1970 stipulated that banks and insurance companies had to seek approval from the Monetary Authority of Singapore for the appointment of their chief executive officers, directors and principal officers (Mak and Li, 1999).

Only after the 1985 recession did the state realize the danger of the overdependence on footloose multinational corporations and the need to nurture small- and medium-sized local businesses (Low, 2000a). It stepped up efforts at regionalizing its economy, and aimed at increasing the competitiveness of local businesses through professionalizing their management structures. Lee Kuan Yew (Prime Minister from 1965 to 1991, since then Senior Minister up to 2004, and now Minister Mentor) once remarked: 'The old family business in Singapore is one of the problems in Singapore. . . . business is kept in the family. And the idea of sinking money into an anonymous corporation run by professionals over whom they have no direct personal control is foreign to them. . . . So we have to accelerate this process' (Kwang *et al.*, 1998: 187).

Economic Restructuring since the Asian Economic Crisis of 1997

Like most countries in the region, Singapore consistently enjoyed high economic growth rates until the onset of the Asian economic crisis. The crisis led to an economic slowdown in the region. It devastated the property sector and the banks in which the ethnic Chinese businesses had an important stake. The crisis has given further impetus for the Singaporean state to restructure its economy, in order to make it appear more competitive in the eyes of key actors in international financial markets. Among others, there were three major initiatives. First, in light of the débâcles of the *keiretsu* and the *chaebol*, the government urged the GLCs to divest their non-core assets (Low, 2002). By so doing, it hoped to help these groups raise funds for further foreign acquisitions and create new investment opportunities for the domestic private sector (US Embassy of Singapore, 2001).

Second, the state urged domestic firms to undertake globalization rather than regionalization business strategies, thus moving beyond the crisis-ridden Southeast Asian region to China and the West for overseas investment. Third, to discourage the family rule of local banks, the Monetary Authority of Singapore required them to establish nominating committees for board and top management positions and to obtain its approval for the personnel selection. Lee Kuan Yew warned that the local family-controlled banks were 'going downhill' without foreign talent and competition (Low, 2001a). His criticism of the reliance on family ties was later reiterated by his eldest son, Brigadier-General Lee Hsien Leong (then Deputy Prime Minister and Finance Minister, and now Prime Minister and Finance Minister): 'World-class companies needed to be led by the best man for the job and . . . a founding family was unlikely to produce such a person generation after generation' (*The Straits Times*, 2001).

Sociocultural Change and Continuity

The state's commitment to economic growth and multi-ethnicity after independence led to the severing of ties with religions that might interfere with capitalist economic development and nation building (Tamney, 1995). As in other rapidly modernizing, export-oriented economies such as Hong Kong and Taiwan, Singapore emphasized Western education over classical or religious doctrines. The English-educated ruling elite designated English as the sole language of instruction in 1983, in light of the difficulties in achieving bilingualism (Borthwick, 1988). English-educated locals became liberal individuals with diverse cultural values and a high exposure to Western technology and management models.

Being alarmed at the persuasive influence of Western culture and rapid demographic and sociocultural change, the state sought to counteract it by initiating public campaigns. In 1979, the government embarked on a language and cultural campaign, aiming to persuade Singaporean Chinese to identify with their cultural heritage and values. In 1984, the government attempted to revive religious commitment through a Religious Knowledge Program, but recognized it as ineffective and finally abandoned it. Yet the metaphor of the family has remained in use, as the means to mobilize citizens to support the state's imperative for economic development, and to rally the multiethnic population to maintain social and political order in a disordered region (Tsui-Auch, 2004).

BUSINESS ORGANIZATION OF LOCAL ENTERPRISES

Table 15.1 summarizes the basic data of 20 large listed companies in 1997 and 2003. They are GLCs and ethnic Chinese enterprises. The GLCs are controlled by Temasek Holdings Limited (THL) and Singapore Technologies Holding Limited (STHL), whereas the private corporations are controlled by several ethnic Chinese families, such as the Wees, the Lees and the Kweks.

Government-linked Corporations (GLCs)

According to the Department of Statistics (2001), government-linked corporations are entities in which a holding company, wholly owned by the Singapore government (through the Ministry of Finance, Inc.), has an equity interest of 20 per cent or more. THL was founded in 1974 as a private limited investment holding company to manage the state's investments in GLCs. It owns stakes in most of the country's largest companies, including Singapore Airlines, SingTel and DBS Group Holdings. In total, it controls more than 200 first-tier and second-tier subsidiaries that cover a wide spectrum of industries, including transportation and logistics, ship repair and engineering, power and gas, telecommunications, media, financial services, manufacturing and property. As for the first-tier corporations, it has not only proposed broad strategies, but also preferred to appoint former politicians, civil servants and high-ranking military officials to positions as chairmen, directors and senior management (Low, 2001b).

Singapore Technologies Holdings Limited (STHL) was founded in 1989 to manage national defence-related entities. For national security reasons, the Ministry of Finance holds special shares in some of these corporations, including Singapore Technologies Engineering, Singapore Airlines and SingTel. The Health Corporation of Singapore has equity holdings in seven government-linked hospitals only, according to the Directory of Government-Linked Corporations 1994. The Ministry of National Development Holding has mainly dormant company shares in government-linked corporations. The Government Investment Corporation has only three operations and ten offices worldwide, and most board members are unknown (US Embassy of Singapore, 2001). There are also cross-holdings between government-linked investment holdings companies, as in the case of the Development Bank of Singapore (DBS) group. Temasek Holdings owned 12.6 per cent and the MND Holdings owned 13.9 per cent of its shares in 2002.

The GLCs are unusual hybrids of state and private enterprises. They compete with private firms, including multinational corporations, and sometimes with each other. They have generally been well-managed and run like private businesses, with a focus on bottom-line performance and professional management (US Embassy of Singapore, 2001; Singh and Ang, 1998). Whereas the GLCs prompted industrialization and economic development in Singapore, critics have asserted that (1) these corporations rely on ex-civil servants for management, who tend to be risk-averse; (2) they receive special privileges because of their links to the government; (3) they use capital less efficiently than private firms do;

Table 15.1 Large Singaporean listed companies

Ranking in SG 1000 for 2003	Companies	Types of sector (G/P)	Group control	Total assets 1997	Total assets 2003	Total subsidiaries 1997	Total subsidiaries 2003	Total associates 1997	Total associates 2003
1	DBS Group Holdings Limited	G	THL	43 103 059	159 595 000	18	14	17	25
3	United Overseas Bank Limited	P	Wee Fam.	40 565 426	113 446 399	70	77	4	21
4	Overseas Chinese Banking Corporation	P	Lee Fam.	45 468 851	84 497 426	68	70	0	16
9	Singapore Telecommunications Limited	G	THL	6 841 000	33 670 500	46	122	16	19
10	Singapore Airlines Limited	G	THL	13 194 700	19 184 000	19	22	19	29
15	Pacific Century Regional Developments	P	Li	402 771	1 783 885	18	23	3	4
16	Keppel Corporation Limited	G	THL	15 850 660	10 082 733	353	358	73	77
17	City Developments Limited	P	Kwek Fam.	7 108 122	13 059 053	168	256	30	4
19	Fraser & Neave Limited	P	Lee	4 457 495	7 730 146	84	149	5	13
20	Neptune Orient Lines Limited	G	THL	3 615 518	4 063 737	100	132	56	37
24	Hong Leong Finance Limited	P	Kwek Fam.	3 615 518	6 173 374	6	3	0	0
26	Sembcorp Industries Limited	G	THL, STHL	2 431 191	6 622 114	204	177	86	73
30	Keppel Land Limited	G	THL	4 059 905	4 362 162	112	135	28	33
32	Singapore Technologies Engineering	G	THL, STHL	2 113 304	4 253 102	44	80	21	28
36	United Industrial Corporation Limited	P	Wee Fam.	4 774 122	3 512 613	48	40	11	13
37	Singapore Land Limited	P	Wee Fam.	4 173 776	3 148 424	12	19	7	8
39	Singapore Press Holdings Limited	G	THL	1 994 524	3 368 245	29	25	8	6
46	United Overseas Land Limited	P	Wee Fam.	2 990 546	3 059 700	36	46	0	0
52	Wing Tai Holdings Limited	P	Cheng Fam.	1 982 317	2 258 792	51	41	19	12
55	Cycle & Carriage Limited	P		2 159 700	1 726 200	51	49	15	14

Notes: G = government, P = private; Fam = family. Associated companies are entities in which the Group generally has between 20% and 50% of the voting rights, and over which the Group has significant influence, but does not control these companies' financial and operating policy decisions. A subsidiary is a company in which the Group, directly or indirectly, holds more than half of the issued share capital, or controls more than half of the voting power, or controls the composition of the board of directors.

Sources: Lim *et al.*, 2005; Tsui-Auch, 2006.

(4) they have crowded out private investment and usurped entrepreneurial activity; and (5) their unrelated diversification makes them 'jacks of all trades, but masters of none' (US Embassy of Singapore, 2001; Webb and Saywell, 2002; Worthington, 2003). The government began pressurizing these groups to diversify their non-core holdings even before the Asian economic crisis, when it became clear that highly diversified business groups provided less potential long-term shareholder value than did the less diversified groups.

Although the overall policy is to divest non-core assets, the change seems to be more in form than in substance, indicating a superficial attempt to accede to the government's advice. In a study of large Singaporean enterprises, Lim *et al.* (2005) found that, although eight GLCs divested their non-core subsidiaries, only four reduced the number of non-core associates that they owned. One possible reason is that the GLCs sold only a portion of the shares held in that subsidiary, instead of making a complete sell-off, thereby turning the subsidiary into its associate. This strategy is deployed especially for subsidiaries that are seen as crucial to the national security of the country. The fundamental belief that GLCs are instruments for nation building and safeguards of national security is likely to inhibit their full divestment (Webb and Saywell, 2002). For example, SingTel reduced its ownership of SingPost from 100 per cent to 31 per cent, leading to a change of SingPost status from its subsidiary to its associate under the Financial Reporting Standards. Hence SingTel's number of non-core associates increased, whereas its non-core subsidiaries decreased. A lack of fundamental change in government ownership and control is also seen in the Development Bank of Singapore's divestment of DBS Land. The DBS group sold its stake in equity investments and some properties, notably, DBS Land. Nevertheless, DBS Land was acquired by Pidemco, a Singapore Technologies group subsidiary, and has since been renamed CapitalLand (US Embassy of Singapore, 2001).

In line with the government's policy to go global after the Asian economic crisis, GLCs prompted the pace of foreign acquisitions and shareholding beyond the region. Foreign acquisition can be an instrument to test unfamiliar markets. However, the link with the government might have hindered them from investing more aggressively, as other countries in the region resisted their attempts to acquire domestic firms. For instance, SingTel's failure to acquire Hong Kong Telecom from Britain's Cable & Wireless was attributed primarily to China's reluctance to permit a Singaporean government-owned entity to control Hong Kong's telecom assets (Mauzy and Milne, 2002). An alternative strategy deployed to circumvent such obstacles is to make foreign acquisition in the form of an associate rather than a subsidiary, hence reducing the discomfort of host country governments. For instance, SembCorp made foreign acquisition in the form of an associate in Switzerland, Spain and four other countries.

As the GLCs are increasingly commercially driven and involved in joint ventures with private firms, they have increased their hiring of top executives from the private sector. For example in DBS, a former JP Morgan banker, John Olds, was recruited to be the CEO. He is believed to have led DBS to make stunning profits and recover from the crisis, but he departed after serving only three years (*The Straits Times*, 2002b). The increased hiring of outsiders into senior management positions indicates that GLCs are subject to normative pressures that advocate professional managers. Nonetheless, trusted insiders still remain prominent in these corporations. In a study of the largest GLCs (Tsui-Auch, 2006), the majority of the positions of CEOs and chairmen remained in the hands of the state sector.

Ethnic Chinese Enterprises

It is often reported that ethnic Chinese formed webs of personal, business and political relationships in the region (Gomez and Hsiao, 2001; Yeung, 2000b; see also Chapter 18 in this volume). Facing a lack of support from their home government, and anti-Chinese movements in Southeast Asian countries, Singaporean Chinese business owners were keen to reduce risks. Geographically, they extended their businesses beyond Singapore to Asia and Australasia. In terms of business lines, they diversified from trading to manufacturing, banking, finance and insurance, and hotel and property development. As Hamilton (1997) succinctly described it, ethnic Chinese family businesses usually do not develop a vertically integrated firm when it expands. Rather, it develops into a business group, consisting of independent firms loosely linked to a mother or core company that often pursues conglomerate accumulation rather than vertical integration, and resembles a web structure rather than a unitary organization.

To finance their expansion, large firms increasingly resorted to listing some of their companies on the stock market. To meet the mandatory requirements on reporting and auditing that were imposed by the regulatory authority, they recruited professional managers from the external labour market. Given the state-driven normative isomorphic pressure on professionalism, and the presence of multinational corporations, ethnic Chinese business families perceived the professionalization of management as a means to gain legitimacy from regulatory authorities, international customers, employees and shareholders. This recognition of the importance of professional management led to a higher degree of formalization, including the implementation of systems of financial control and bureaucratic rules that covered recruitment, promotion and dismissal. However, decisions about personnel for top management positions continued to be made by family managers. This strategy of maintaining corporate rule, while coopting outside talent for management, resembles that of GLCs and the state sector at large.

Like the GLCs, ethnic Chinese enterprises have exhibited both stability and change since the Asian economic crisis. Despite yielding a better performance than DBS in general, the overcapitalized UOB group and OCBC group had to untangle cross-shareholdings with affiliated non-banking companies by July 2006, in line with government mandates. In fact, the Wee family, through UOB and its private investment vehicle, remained holding over 50 per cent of UOL and about 20 per cent of UIC, two large property groups (*The Straits Times*, 2005). In the non-banking sectors that encounter state intervention to a lesser extent, many large ethnic Chinese enterprises did not divest their non-core subsidiaries. Rather, some acquired more non-core companies (Wing Tai, C&C, and F&N), as they saw a need to diversify beyond their traditional business lines that have low potential for growth.

As compared to the GLCs, ethnic Chinese enterprises tended to acquire more subsidiaries and fewer associates beyond the region. Unlike the GLCs that are constrained by their government-linked status, private enterprises do not generate discomfort in host countries when acquiring foreign subsidiaries, and do not need to circumvent such an obstacle by turning the form of acquisition from subsidiary to associate (Lim *et al.*, 2005).

Compared to the GLCs, ethnic Chinese enterprises were less willing to incorporate outsiders for corporate rule. The infusion of professional managers into ethnic Chinese groups has not always proceeded smoothly. Drawing upon a study of 23 large ethnic

Chinese businesses in Singapore (Tsui-Auch, 2004),[3] I advanced two arguments. First, Chinese businesses in sectors that are under the supervision of the developmental state, that face increasing competition from Western corporations, and that lack offspring who are competent and interested in running family enterprises, have loosened family rule.

Second, businesses in sectors that are free from the direct intervention of the state, that seek survival in negative market situations, and that have trusted and competent offspring to harness the advantage of the family enterprise, have maintained family rule (Tsui-Auch, 2004). In the banking sector that was subject to strong state intervention, the Lee family of OCBC, which did not have any offspring who were competent and interested in taking up the baton (according to my interviewee and local media analysis), eventually hired a former Hong Kong banker as its CEO in 1999. After his sudden resignation in 2002, the OCBC hired an American banker (*The Straits Times*, 2002a). In 2003, Lee Seng Wee, who had served as the chairman for years, stepped down, and the former CEO of Singapore Airlines took over the post. UOB, however, insisted on family rule. In response to the criticism that the bank was still family-ruled after the Asian economic crisis, Wee Ee Cheong (UOB's current deputy chairman and president and son of the controlling shareholder, Wee Cho Yaw) argued that 'if the person running the bank happens to be a well-qualified family member, then we also have the added advantage of long-term commitment in the business' (*The Straits Times*, 2001).

Ethnic Indian Businesses

The 2001 annual report of the Singapore Indian Chamber of Commerce and Industry shows a total of 439 member companies. As compared to the 4000 member companies that the Chinese Chamber of Commerce has, the ethnic Indian business community constitutes a minority group in Singapore's economy. As shown in Table 15.1, there is no large company controlled by ethnic Indians. In my study of 13 ethnic Chinese and 13 Indian entrepreneurs (who began as traders) in Singapore and their businesses as of the early 1990s (Tsui-Auch, 2005), I report that they differed in the structures of operational management and business expansion: 11 out of the 13 ethnic Chinese incorporated outsiders into their operational management over time, whereas all the 13 Indians maintained family management; ten Chinese pursued unrelated diversification, whereas only one Indian did so.

This finding supports those reported in the few existing studies. In a study of entrepreneurs in Southeast Asia from 1870 to 1941, Brown (1994) observed that the longevity of ethnic Indian traders in their specializations was much greater than that of ethnic Chinese traders, who would diversify into any profitable area. Haley and Haley (1999) provided a list of the 15 most prominent ethnic Indian and 20 most prominent ethnic Chinese businesses in Southeast Asia. All of the ethnic Chinese businesses undertook unrelated diversification, but only nine ethnic Indian businesses did so. PuruShotam (1992) noted that the heavy reliance on family and communal networks often led to the postponement of plans for diversification and other improvements or developments in which the family members did not have expertise.

In addition, two phenomena in my comparative study are particularly intriguing. First, there existed an intraethnic division in business structure among the ethnic Indians: all the Sindhis maintained their trade specialization, and all the three entrepreneurs who undertook related diversification were Gujaratis. The only one who undertook unrelated diversification was a Tamil. At the time of the oral history interviews in 1991, a number of the ethnic Indian traders were experiencing business difficulties and considerable decline, whereas ethnic Chinese businesses expanded in scale and business lines, and some listed their companies on the stock exchanges in Singapore and elsewhere.

DISCUSSION

The overview of the GLCs and ethnic Chinese and Indian enterprises shows not only striking similarities, but also vast differences. Generally speaking, the GLCs and ethnic Chinese enterprises expanded in scale and diversified in business lines, professionalized their management, but retained corporate rule in the hands of the trusted insiders. Since the Asian economic crisis, the GLCs have divested superficially, and made a limited foray into both geographical diversification beyond Asia and Australasia, and the professionalization of their governance structure. Ethnic Chinese enterprises in sectors under strong state intervention have begun to divest incrementally, but the rest have not acceded to the government's advice. As compared to the GLCs, they made acquisition of foreign subsidiaries to a greater extent, but that of associates to a lesser extent. They were more reserved in terms of recruiting outsiders for the topmost managerial positions than the GLCs. Like the GLCs and their ethnic Chinese counterparts, ethnic Indian enterprises showed a preference for control and trust in insiders. However, they were less responsive to environmental change and continued to rely on family managers even in operational management. What is particularly intriguing is the intraethnic division in business structures. The following subsections will analyse the roles of the state and regional ethnicity in shaping the management and business structure of different groups and subgroups.

State-driven Institutional Isomorphism

Assuming the role of a developmental state in building a strong economy, the Singaporean government worked to guide their markets (Yeung, 2000a). It created GLCs to spearhead industrial and infrastructural development, and to compete with MNCs and local private enterprises. To mobilize its citizens to support the state's imperative for economic development and to offset the persuasive Western influence, the state harnessed traditional cultural values and institutional norms. In particular, it emphasized hierarchical control, loyalty to the family and the government, and trust in insiders. Long-serving, loyal ex-civil servants were employed to run the GLCs.

The state exerted institutional isomorphic pressure on local enterprises for the organizational imitation of the managerial enterprise. Coercive isomorphism is seen in the regulation of listed companies and in the Monetary Authority of Singapore's regulation of, and intervention in, the managerial personnel composition of banks and financial companies. The state's strategy of enticing multinational corporations led to the presence of a critical mass of professionally managed corporations that enhanced mimetic isomorphism. Owing to the distant state–capital relationship, ethnic Chinese businesses (except the banks) were left to fend for themselves, which averted the tradition of cronyism and patronage politics in government–business relations (Low, 2000b). Often they needed to gain legitimacy in the eyes of regulatory authorities and the public, and hence tended to take the state's imperative for professionalism seriously.

Since the Asian economic crisis, the Singaporean state has exerted institutional isomorphic pressure on the GLCs and banks for divestment, geographical diversification and professional governance. Coercive isomorphism is seen in the government mandate for banks to divest their non-core assets and the Monetary Authority's requirement for banks to seek its approval for the selection of board members and top executives. Mimetic isomorphism is further exemplified in the Overseas Chinese Banking Corporation's imitation of the government-linked corporation, the Development Bank of Singapore, in recruiting professional managers from outside the founding family for the position of CEOs and senior management. In addition, the state, through the ruling elite, state-controlled media and agencies, enhanced normative isomorphism by promoting professional management and governance as the best practice in managing large enterprises, and criticizing the reliance on family and network ties in running businesses.

Nevertheless, the state did not intend to copy the models of vertically integrated enterprise and managerial enterprise, but to adapt them to local cultural and institutional contexts. This is seen in the seemingly contradictory moves (1) to foster divestment in policy, but maintain sustained control in the GLCs in practice, and (2) to discourage family control and corporate rule in the private sector, but remain reliant on trusted insiders or the larger political family in the state sector (Low, 2000b). The government has relative autonomy to ignore market pressures to divest its equity in these corporations. Ex-civil servants are likely to resist divestment and greater competition from the private sector (US Embassy of Singapore, 2001; Saywell and Plott, 2002). So far, the limited change in the management leadership has led to a limited change in business structure.

Despite a focus on state-driven institutional isomorphism, my analysis is by no means deterministic. I acknowledge that private enterprises (banks, to a lesser extent) are freer to disregard government pressure. Hence different pathways on divestment, diversification and professional governance may emerge, although the overall directions are observed.

Regional Ethnicity and Strength of Ties

Why did ethnic Indian enterprises and their Chinese counterparts, which had shared similar patterns in business and management structures at foundation, differ vastly over time? Are there vast differences in the opportunity structure between the ethnic Chinese majority and ethnic Indian minority? Are there significant differences in culture and ethnic resources between them? Ethnic Chinese entrepreneurs, who constituted the majority in the business community, did enjoy greater access to local product and labour markets than their ethnic Indian counterparts. Nevertheless, one should not exaggerate the role of opportunity structure, given the government policies of economic and industrial development and ethnic management. During the British colonial rule, both groups were immigrants, who encountered colonial monopolies and regulations, and were limited to business niches left by the British and Western merchants. After Singapore's independence in 1959, both groups of traders were neglected by the developmental state, and were subjected to disadvantages in labour, product and financial markets. In terms of ethnic management, the ethnic Indian minority has encountered neither overt discrimination nor expulsion, such as the Nattukottai Chettiars in Burma and Gujaratis in East Africa experienced (Markovits, 2000). In fact, Singapore, being free from political turmoil and religious persecution, as well as enjoying economic viability as a free trading port, was particularly attractive to the Sindhis, who were virtually homeless after the partition of India.

Culturally, ethnic Indians and Chinese have much in common in terms of cultural attributes. They have followed to a great extent the model of the joint family, which originated from the early history of both countries, deriving primarily from the socioeconomic patterns of agricultural village life (Kotkin, 1993). Both cultures are characterized by patrilineality, patriarchalism and familialism. Given the roots of strong kinship and communal networks, one would expect ethnic businesses to maintain family management, and avoid diversification into areas in which the family members did not have expertise. Why did the ethnic Chinese diversify tremendously, as well as professionalize their management structure?

I argue that the difference in ethnic resource lies, not in cultural attributes of an ethnic group, but in the level of access to the homeland for labour and product markets. With the Communist takeover in 1949, mainland China became inaccessible for ethnic Chinese in Singapore, who wanted to follow capitalism or were sympathetic to the defeated Kuomintang that re-established its base in Taiwan. The inaccessibility of China and the broken cultural ties prevented Singaporean Chinese from capitalizing on their family and social ties in the homeland for labour and product markets. These ethnic Chinese could, however, gain access to the markets in Hong Kong and Taiwan, but they were much smaller than those of mainland China. In addition, they might not necessarily have relatives in these economies to help fill the managerial pool required for business expansion. Unlike ethnic Chinese who had severed their links with China, the Indians' links with India remained active. The flourishing relationships of trade, kinship and cultural contact enabled ethnic Indian traders to retain their original trades and to continue to rely on family and clan members for management.

Nevertheless, the difference in the level of access to the homeland should not be exaggerated, for three reasons. First, India pursued economic self-reliance and imposed import restrictions. Second, the entry of ethnic Indian workers into Singapore was restricted first by the British colonial government's Immigration Ordinance Act in 1952, and subsequently by the state that favoured the immigration of ethnic Chinese in the 1980s to compensate the rapidly declining fertility rate among Singaporean Chinese (Tamney, 1995; Saw, 1999). Third, the Sindhis were virtually homeless after the partition of India, like ethnic Chinese. They, however, maintained their trade specialization and family management, rather than diversify and professionalize their management, as did ethnic Chinese.

Ethnic resource and opportunity structure both play a major role in shaping the business and management structures of ethnic enterprises. Importantly, regional ethnicity must be taken into account. A number of authors have admitted that the term 'Indians' is very loose (Sandhu and Mani, 1993; PuruShotam, 1992). Many authors argued that India was never a nation until British colonization (Mehra, 2000). Kotkin (1993: 205) perceived Indians as 'tribes within tribes', and that there is 'no direct equivalent to the sense of a single racial and historic heritage that exists among the British, the Jews or the Chinese'. This intraethnic diversity resulted in the existence of 'a manifold frame of identification' among the Indians (Kothari, 1988: 155). Such a frame includes regional/linguistic identities, caste identity and religious identities, all of which overlap. Markovits (2000), however, argued that region and locality were much more important in structuring migrants' identities than religion and caste, as the latter two vary tremendously from one subgroup to another.

Regional differences were less significant in the social organization of traditional China than that of traditional India. China was established as a unified kingdom in 221 BC, despite periodic fragmentation and disintegration. The perception of 'the Chinese' as a single race is supported by beliefs held at both official and folk levels (Bolt, 2000). According to Woon (1984), even in the more culturally heterogeneous south China, which was exposed to successive waves of migration from the north, ethnic differences were perceived as cultural rather than racial, as inhabitants were primarily Han by the eighteenth century.

My comparative study of ethnic Chinese and Indian subgroups (Tsui-Auch, 2005), unravels the way in which the differential strength of regional ties shaped the differences in business and management structures of ethnic groups and subgroups. It argues that the differential strength of regional ties reflects the degree of intra-community homogeneity and inter-community heterogeneity. It surmises that a community is formed on the basis of regional identity: overlapping with dialect among the Chinese, and also with religious and/or caste identities among the Indians. The concept of intra-community homogeneity is concerned with the commonalities that members in the subgroup share in terms of language, trade specialization(s), religion, caste/class and geopolitical identity. The more commonalities people in a subgroup share, the higher the degree of intra-community homogeneity (see Table 15.2). The degree of inter-community heterogeneity indicates the extent of perceived difference among subgroups within a larger ethnic group. The more different the subgroups perceive themselves to be, the higher the degree of inter-community heterogeneity.

As indicated in Table 15.2, the ethnic Indian subgroups have a higher degree of intra-community homogeneity than the ethnic Chinese subgroups. Among the ethnic Indian subgroups, the Sindhis have the highest degree of intra-community homogeneity, whereas the Tamils have the lowest. The Sindhi Hindus share not only a language and religious beliefs (Hinduism), but also caste identity. The cultural ethos of the trading caste legitimized and encouraged economic success through trading. Engaging in the trade specialization of the communal trading networks enhanced the traders' chances of acquiring market information and customers, which are crucial for business survival and success. In addition, the Sindhis shared a geopolitical identity that was derived from the long history of foreign invasion and the loss of their homeland. Such a geopolitical identity reinforced the strong cohesion of the community.

As with the Sindhi merchants, the Gujaratis constituted a close-knit community, with commonalities in language and caste identity. Yet the Gujaratis were more diverse in religion (Hinduism and Islam) and trade specialization than the Sindhis. As shown in my oral history data analysis, some Gujaratis undertook related diversification, as compared to the Sindhis who maintained the original trades. The Tamil Muslim merchants had the lowest intra-community homogeneity among the ethnic Indian subgroups. While most had commonalities in language and religious beliefs, they differed in class and commercial experience. The entry into business was open. The merchants were not tied to any particular trade and tended to engage in a wide range of businesses on a small scale.

Table 15.2   Indicators of the intra-communal homogeneity among subgroups

	Sindhi	Gujarati	Tamil	Hokkien	Cantonese	Teochew
Language	Same	Same	Same	Same	Same	Same
Religion	Same	Varied	Same	Varied	Varied	Varied
Caste/class	Same	Same	Varied	Varied	Varied	Varied
Trade specialization(s)	Same	Same	Varied	Varied	Varied	Varied
Geopolitical identity	Same	N/A	N/A	N/A	N/A	N/A
Total number of commonalities	5	3	2	1	1	1

Source: Tsui-Auch (2005: 1206).

As with the Tamil entrepreneurs in Singapore, few ethnic Chinese came from trading families. The dialect-based communal networks, which had members from different economic classes and occupational backgrounds, were not as tightly knit as those of the Sindhis and Gujaratis. Ethnic Chinese traders were not bound to maintain a particular trade and were ready to diversify into any area. In addition, they appeared to be less tightly knit than the Tamil Muslims, as members had different philosophical or religious beliefs. Instead of relying solely on communal networks, ethnic Chinese developed heterogeneous, weak ties with loosely associated networks of friends and business contacts. These heterogeneous ties enabled them to tap information about industrial trends, potential business partners and managerial talent.

Why did ethnic Chinese recruit outsiders, whereas the Tamil trader maintained family management despite diversification? Inter-community heterogeneity must be considered an important factor. Regional, language, religious and/or caste differences gave rise to several distinctive cultural traditions and close-knit communal enclaves that divided the ethnic Indian subgroups. In Singapore, where each ethnic Indian community is a minority within a minority, the traders who would need to recruit outsiders might well have had to hire Indians from other communities. Perceiving a high degree of the inter-community heterogeneity, traders were reluctant to hire outsiders for management. On the other hand, ethnic Chinese found it easier to accommodate people from different communities. The degree of the inter-community heterogeneity is lower, with the differences stemming primarily from dialect. The dialect group identity was eroded and the Chinese identity increased with the government's fostering of the learning of Mandarin. Hence ethnic Chinese enterprises were willing to hire outsiders for operational management, and these outsiders constituted one of the key forces to push for changes in management and business structures.

CONCLUSION AND IMPLICATIONS

The above account of the change amid continuity in the business and management structures of Singaporean enterprises provides much support for the institutional perspective. First, social organization along family and network ties was constantly harnessed by both the state and family businesses. Second, the business leaders' modification of the models of vertically integrated enterprise and managerial enterprise to fit their local contexts demonstrates a capacity to change within the scope of cultural and institutional constraints. This provides support for the institutional perspective that adopts neither an oversocialized view nor an undersocialized view of actors.

However the institutional perspective reveals little of the role of the state in harnessing social organization and fostering institutional change, which in turn shapes the change and continuity in business organization. We need to take into account the state's capacities and strategies in guiding the market and harnessing culture and institutions. In explaining the state-driven institutional isomorphism toward professional management and divestment, DiMaggio and Powell's (1983) three categories of institutional isomorphism are useful. I agree with their view that the state imposes coercive isomorphism, but contend that the state can also enhance normative and mimetic isomorphism, as seen in the case of Singapore. Despite encountering similar policies and initiatives of the interventionist state, ethnic Chinese and ethnic Indians in Singapore pursued divergent pathways in business and management. My comparative study reveals the role of regional ethnicity and the strength of communal ties in shaping business and management structures of different subgroups. An understanding of regional ethnicity and the strength of communal ties is important in the study of business systems.

This chapter has used a holistic institutional framework that incorporates the state and regional ethnicity into the triad of market, cultures and institutions, in order to explicate the changing business organization in Singapore that has been increasingly integrated into the global production system through export-oriented industrialization since the 1960s (see Figure 15.1). Whether this framework is relevant to other Asian multiethnic economies that demonstrate state-driven integration into the work economy remains to be validated. Certainly, the context has to be taken into account, when the model is applied to a specific country, as country variables might exert influence on the management models of enterprises (Chang, 2006). Notable variables are the size of the economy, the state and economic development strategies. For example, the Singaporean state, which has adopted a foreign capital-dependent development model to spearhead economic development of a small economy, has taken professional management and governance more seriously than the states of Malaysia, Indonesia, Thailand and the Philippines.

My analysis of Singaporean business organization and the roles of the state and regional ethnicity also provides some directions for future research and practical implications. The role of the state in influencing the organizational and management models of firms merits further exploration. The existing knowledge gap can be filled by more comparative research into state-driven institutional isomorphism. Such research will serve to link the institutional perspective of Asian economic organization and neo-institutionalism in organization studies (see also Chapters 2 and 3 in this volume).

So far, most studies of business systems have focused on national and cultural factors. An exploration of regional ethnicity is especially important, as regionalism remains a strong force in many nations, such as China, India, Korea, Germany and Italy (Fukuyama, 1995). Such exploration can have practical implications. Many countries, including China and India, have increasingly attempted to attract overseas entrepreneurs to strengthen their economic development. To design an effective strategy in this area, governments need to assess the strength of ethnic and communal ties of potential over-

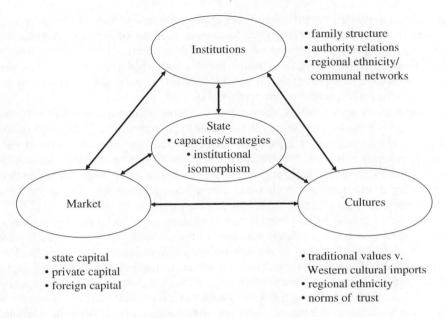

Figure 15.1   An integrated institutional framework

seas investors. Given the strong communal ties among the overseas Gujaratis and the Sindhis, the Indian government might well attract them by appealing to their communal loyalty.

However, in view of the decreasing significance of communal ties among ethnic Chinese abroad, the mainland Chinese government may have to reckon with the fact that ethnicity, community and culture play a limited role in their economic calculations. Nevertheless, these ethnic Chinese entrepreneurs do not constitute a homogeneous community (see also Chapter 18 in this volume). The Singaporean Chinese, who constituted the ethnic majority in Singapore and were led by a predominantly ethnic Chinese ruling elite, may have few sentimental links with mainland China. Ethnic Chinese minorities in other Southeast Asian countries, who encountered waves of anti-Chinese feeling, may have more sentimental links with mainland China. Ethnic Chinese of working-class origin may have more sentimental links with their homeland than those of the professional, middle class, who could assimilate quickly in the host country. To design an effective strategy, the Chinese government will need to deal with intraethnic diversity derived from nationality and class.

The research into Singaporean business organization also unfolds a paradox of institutional embeddedness that merits further exploration. Both the GLCs and private enterprises have been embedded in cultural preferences for control and norms of trusting insiders that are fundamental to the local institutional environment. Actions in tune with such cultural preferences and norms may have enhanced, not only legitimacy, but also efficiency in past operations, as tight control forges integration and economical use of resources (Mauzy and Milne, 2002), and close, personal connections make for good collaboration (Biggart, 1991). However, these preferences and norms have significantly constrained the growth and, perhaps, the long-term viability, of Singaporean enterprises. For instance, the insistence on government control over certain GLCs hinders them from seizing full investment opportunities in the rapidly changing world economy. The persistent reliance on ex-civil servants reinforces the 'lock-in' to past successful formulae, and renders the infusion of private sector professional managers difficult.

Like their government-linked counterparts, ethnic Chinese enterprises have had difficulty in recruiting and retaining outside talent. To expand, they will need fresh perspectives and resources beyond those offered by trusted insiders, regional network ties and traditional business activities. Nevertheless, one point to note is that the ethnic Chinese enterprises in this study typically engage in the service industry. Whether those that are involved more in the modern, higher-end manufacturing industry also demonstrate a 'lock in' (to family management) merits further exploration.

The reliance of ethnic Indian entrepreneurs on their communal ties for business and management had been economically rational, in the sense that it guaranteed high levels of support in terms of access to market information, capital and labour, and hence lowered transaction costs. However, such a 'lock in' to trading and family management negatively affected their economic performance, by making them vulnerable to economic structural change and insulating them from information beyond their communally based global networks. To chart the future pathways, all these enterprises will have to resolve the paradox of institutional embeddedness.

The study of Singaporean business organization can be a reference for that of mainland China. Interestingly enough, the business organization of China bears some resemblance to that of Singapore, reflecting commonalities in the political–economic and cultural traditions (see also Chapter 6 in this volume). The Chinese government, deeply suspicious of a politically independent private sector, implemented reforms that have given state-owned enterprises privileged access to capital, technology and markets. In order to spearhead industrial development, it attracted foreign direct investments from multinational corporations that now account for 85 per cent of the country's technology exports, maintain strong positions in the local markets, and control almost all the intellectual property in the country (*The Economist*, 2005). Like that of Singapore, China's economy is characterized by a dominance of large state-owned enterprises, increasingly powerful MNCs and a few large private companies. Some observers attributed China's failure to build world-class companies, such as Sony and Samsung, to the cultural bias for financial services over manufacturing and the pursuit of random, unrelated diversification with the aim of short-term profit generation, which also characterize Singaporean enterprises.

What merits further exploration through comparative studies is twofold: (1) how enterprises in Singapore and China deal with institutional change and resolve the paradox of embeddedness, and (2) whether these countries will create a distinct brand of capitalism anchored in short-term investments and random diversification, rather than long-term knowledge creation and related diversification, like that of Japan. Certainly, I am by no means arguing that the Singaporean model of business organization, which emerged out of its city-state status and history, can be generalized to that in such large countries as China. A contextualization of business organization in the historical, political–economic and sociocultural environment of each country will be of the utmost importance.

Finally, in the case of Singaporean business organization, the issue of organizational imitation is salient. The imitation of managerial enterprise by the GLCs and ethnic Chinese businesses has much in common with the imitation experiences of enterprises in many other countries. These include Japanese organizations' imitation of Western organizations during the Meiji restoration (Morikawa, 1992; Westney, 1987) and mainland Chinese and Eastern European firms' organizational imitation of foreign management models during the present institutional upheaval (Child and Markóczy, 1993; Geppert, 1996; Newman, 2000). In all of these cases, organizational imitation intensified with the rapid institutional and cultural changes that resulted from the state-led integration of national economies into the global economy. Comparative studies of these experiences will enhance the theorization of the circumstances in which, and the mechanisms by which, organizational imitation takes place.

NOTES

1. The Ministry of Finance (1993) estimated that the public sector and the GLCs accounted for 60 per cent of Singapore's GDP. The Ministry of Trade and Industry's Department of Statistics (2001) estimated that the GLCs contributed only 12.9 per cent of GDP in 1998, and that the non-GLCs, such as the statutory boards, accounted for another 8.9 per cent, for a total public sector share of 21.8 per cent. The latter estimate includes only the GLCs in which the government holds equity of at least 20 per cent, and hence the role of the state in the economy is seen as underestimated (Low, 2001b).
2. According to Low (2000a), this was perhaps due to their positive role in the entrepôt trade and the close working and personal relationships of the owners with the political leaders.
3. These two studies (Tsui-Auch, 2005; 2006) were based on an interpretive analysis of the oral history transcripts of personal interviews with prominent Chinese business owners that were recorded by the Oral History Centre of the National Heritage Board of Singapore, personal interviews with some business families, documentary research and historical–sociological analysis.

REFERENCES

Amsden, Alice H. (1989), *Asia's Next Giant*, New York and Oxford: Oxford University Press.

Biggart, Nicole W. (1991), 'Explaining Asian economic organization: toward a Weberian institutional perspective', *Theory and Society*, **20**, 199–232.

Biggart, Nicole W. (1997), 'Institutionalised patrimonialism in Korea', in M. Orrú, N.W. Biggart and G.G. Hamilton (eds), *The Economic Organization of East Asian Capitalism*, Thousand Oaks, London and New Delhi: Sage Publications, pp. 33–54.

Bolt, Paul J. (2000), *China and Southeast Asia's Ethnic Chinese: State and Diaspora in Contemporary Asia*, Westport, CT: Praeger Publishers.

Borthwick, S. (1988), 'Chinese education and identity in Singapore. Chinese identities in Southeast Asia: alternative perspectives', in J.W. Cushman and G. Wang (eds), *Changing Identities of the Southeast Asian Chinese since World World II*, Hong Kong: Hong Kong University Press, pp. 35–59.

Brown, Rajeswary Ampalavanar (1994), *Capital & Entrepreneurs in South-East Asia*, London: Macmillan.

Chalmers, Ian (1992), 'Loosening state control in Singapore: the emergence of local capital as a political force', *Southeast Asian Journal of Social Science*, **20**(2), 57–84.

Chan, Kwok-bun and Claire Chiang (1994), *Stepping out: the Making of Chinese Entrepreneurs*, Singapore: Prentice-Hall.

Chandler, Alfred D. (1962), *Strategy and Structure*, Boston, MA: MIT Press.

Chandler, Alfred D. (1977), *The Invisible Hand: the Managerial Revolution in American Business*, Cambridge, MA: Harvard University Press.

Chandler, Alfred D. (1995), 'Managers, families, and financiers', in M.B. Rose (ed.), *Family Business*, Aldershot, UK and Brookfield, US: Edward Elgar, pp. 20–48.

Chang, Sea-jin (2003), *Financial Crisis and Transformation of Korean Business Groups: the Rise and Fall of Chaebols*, Cambridge, UK and New York, US: Cambridge University Press.

Chang, Sea-Jin (2006), *Business Groups in East Asia*, Oxford: Oxford University Press.

Child, John (2000), 'Theorizing about organization cross-nationally', *Advances in International Comparative Management*, **13**, 27–75.

Child, John and L. Markóczy (1993), 'Host-country managerial behaviour and learning in Chinese and Hungarian joint ventures', *Journal of Management Studies*, **30**(4), 611–31.

Clegg, Stewart and G. Redding (eds) (1990), *Capitalism in Contrasting Cultures*, New York: Walter de Gruyter.

DiMaggio, P.J. and W.W. Powell (1983), 'The iron cage revisited: institutional isomorphism and collective rationality in organizational fields', *American Sociological Review*, **48**, 147–60.

Economist (2005), 'The struggle of the champions', 8 Jan., 57–60.

Fukuyama, Francis (1995), *Trust: the Social Virtues and the Creation of Prosperity*, Harmondsworth: Hamish Hamilton/Penguin.

Geppert, Mike (1996), 'Paths of managerial learning in the East German context', *Organization Studies*, **17**(2), 532–50.

Gomez, E.T. and H.H.M. Hsiao (eds) (2001), *Chinese Business in Southeast Asia*, Richmond, Surrey: Curzon Press.

Haley, G.T. and U.C.V. Haley (1999), 'Weaving opportunities: the influence of overseas Chinese and overseas Indian business networks on Asian business operations', in F.J. Richter (ed.), *Business Networks in Asia: Promises, Doubts, and Perspectives*, Westport, CT: Quorum Books, pp. 149–70.

Hamilton, G.G. (1997), 'Organization and market processes in Taiwan's capitalist economy', in M. Orrú, N.W. Biggart and G.G. Hamilton (eds), *The Economic Organization of East Asian Capitalism*, Thousand Oaks, London and New Delhi: Sage Publications, pp. 237–96.

Hamilton, G.G. and Nicole W. Biggart (1988), 'Market, culture, and authority: a comparative analysis of management and organization in the Far East', *American Journal of Sociology*, **92**, Special Supplement, 52–94.

Hill, Richard C. and K. Fujita (1996), 'Flying geese, swarming sparrows or preying hawks? Perspectives on East Asian industrialization', *Competition and Change: The Journal of Global Business and Political Economy*, **1**(3), 285–98.

Johnson, Chalmer (1982), *MITI and the Japanese Miracle*, Stanford, CA: Stanford University Press.

Kothari, R. (1988), *State against Democracy: in Search of Humane Governance*, Delhi: Ajanta Publications.

Kotkin, Joel (1993), *Tribes: How Race, Religion and Identity Determine Success in the New Global Economy*, New York: Random House.

Kwang, H.F., W. Fernandez and S. Tan (1998), *Lee Kuan Yew: The Man and His Ideas*, Singapore: Singapore Press Holdings and Times Editions.

Lim, Daixing, Wanzhen Ng and Ging Ng (2005), 'The state and business groups in Singapore', final year Project, Nanyang Business School, Nanyang Technological University, Singapore.

Low, Linda (2000a), 'State, politics and business in Singapore', Research Paper Series 2000-037, Faculty of Business Administration, National University of Singapore.

Low, Linda (2000b), 'Reinventing the Singapore development corporate state', Research Paper Series 2000-042, Faculty of Business Administration, National University of Singapore.

Low, Linda (2001a), 'The political economy of Chinese banking in Singapore', Research Paper Series 2001-015, Faculty of Business Administration, National University of Singapore.

Low, Linda (2001b), 'The Singapore developmental state in the new economy and polity', *The Pacific Review*, **14**(3), 411–41.

Low, Linda (2002), 'Rethinking Singapore Inc and government-linked corporations: from SOE-SOE to SOE-POE', Research Paper Series 2002-005, Faculty of Business Administration, National University of Singapore.

Mak, Yuen Teen and Y. Li (1999), 'Ownership structure and board independence', Research Paper Series 99-31, Faculty of Business Administration, National University of Singapore.

Markovits, Claude (2000), *The Global World of Indian Merchants, 1750–1947: Traders of Sind from Bukhara to Panama*, Cambridge, MA: Cambridge University Press.

Mauzy, Diane K. and R.S. Milne (2002), *Singapore Politics Under the People's Action Party*, London and New York: Routledge.

Mehra, Ajay K. (2000), 'Unity and diversity in India: two ends of a continuum or a converging horizon', in I. Ahmad, P.S. Ghosh and H. Reifeld (eds), *Pluralism and Equality: Values in Indian Society and Politics*, Thousand Oaks, London and New Delhi: Sage Publications, pp. 115–40.

Morikawa, H. (1992), *Zaibatsu: the Rise and Fall of Family Enterprise Groups in Japan*, Tokyo: University of Tokyo Press.

Newman, Karen L. (2000), 'Organizational transformation during institutional upheaval', *Academy of Management Review*, **25**(3), 602–19.

Orrú, Marco, Nicole W. Biggart and Gary G. Hamilton (eds) (1997), *The Economic Organization of East Asian Capitalism*, Thousand Oaks, London and New Delhi: Sage Publications.

PuruShotam, Nirmala (1992), 'The Singaporean Indian trader: the traditions of a modern economic sector', in M.C. Yong (ed.), *Asian Traditions and Modernization*, Singapore: Times Academic Press, pp. 163–203.

Redding, S. Gordon (1990), *The Spirit of Chinese Capitalism*, Berlin: De Gruyter.

Rodan, Garry (1989), *The Political Economy of Singapore's Industrialization: National State and International Capital*, Basingstoke: Macmillan.

Sandhu, Kernial Singh and A. Mani (1993), *Indian Communities in Southeast Asia*, Singapore: ISEAS and Times Academic Press.

Saw, Swee Hock (1999), *The Population of Singapore*, Singapore: Institute of Southeast Asian Studies.

Saywell, Trish and David Plott (2002), 'Re-imaging Singapore', *Far Eastern Economic Review*, 11 July, 44–7.

Singapore Department of Statistics (2001), *Contribution of government-linked companies to gross domestic product*, March, Singapore: Ministry of Trade and Industry.

Singh, Kulwant and Siah Hwee Ang (1998), 'The strategies and success of GLCs in Singapore', Research Paper Series 98-06, Faculty of Business Administration, National University of Singapore.

Straits Times (2001), 'UOB not looking at merger with local banks', 28 Feb., S21.

Straits Times (2002a), 'Alex Au exits from OCBC on a quiet note', 17 April, S17.

Straits Times (2002b), 'S'poreans must control S'pore banks: DPM', 3 July, A17.

Straits Times (2005), 'Wee Cho Yaw ups UOL stake to 10.97%', 5 April, H18.

Tamney, Joseph B. (1995), *The Struggle over Singapore's Soul: Western Modernization and Asian Culture*, Berlin: Walter de Gruyter.

Tsui-Auch, Lai Si (1998), 'Has the Hong Kong model worked? Industrial policy in retrospect', *Development and Change*, **29**(1), 55–78.

Tsui-Auch, Lai Si (1999), 'Regional production relationship and developmental impact: a comparative study of three production networks', *International Journal of Urban and Regional Research*, **23**(2), 346–60.

Tsui-Auch, Lai Si (2004), 'The professionally managed family-ruled business: ethnic Chinese business in Singapore', *Journal of Management Studies*, **41**(4), 693–723.

Tsui-Auch, Lai Si (2005), 'Unpacking regional ethnicity and the strength of ties in shaping ethnic entrepreneurship', *Organization Studies*, **26**(8), 1189–216.

Tsui-Auch, Lai Si (2006), 'Singapore business group: the role of the state and capital in Singapore Inc.', in S.-J. Chang (ed.), *Business Groups in East Asia: Financial Crisis, Restructuring, and New Growth*, Oxford: Oxford University Press, pp. 94–115.

Tsui-Auch, Lai Si and Y.-J. Lee (2003), 'The state matters: management models of Singaporean Chinese and Korean business groups', *Organization Studies*, **24**(4), 507–34.

US Embassy of Singapore (2001), 'Government-linked corporations face the future', March (http://singapore.usembassy.gov/ep/2001/GOVERNMENT-LINKED CORPORATIONS2000.html).

Vasil, Raj (1995), *Asianising Singapore: the PAP's Management of Ethnicity*, Singapore: Heinemann Asia.

Wade, Robert (1990), *Governing the Market: Economic Theory and the Role of Government in East Asian Industrialisation*, Princeton, NJ: Princeton University Press.

Wang, Gungwu (1996), 'Merchants without empire: the Hokkien sojourning communities', in S. Subrahmanyam (ed.), *Merchant Networks in the Early Modern World*, Aldershot, Hampshire: Ashgate Publishing Ltd., pp. 50–71.

Webb, Sara and T. Saywell (2002), 'Untangling Temasek', *Far Eastern Economic Review*, 7 Nov., 42–6.

Westney, Eleanor D. (1987), *Imitation and Innovation: the Transfer of Western Organizational patterns to Meiji Japan*, Cambridge, MA: Harvard University Press.

Whitley, Richard (1996), *Business Systems in East Asia: Firms, Markets and Societies*, London: Sage.

Woon, Y.-F. (1984), *Social Organization in South China, 1911–1949: the case of the Kuan Lineage of K'ai-p'ing County*, Ann Arbor: Center for Chinese Studies, University of Michigan.

Worthington, Ross (2003), *Governance in Singapore*, New York: RoutledgeCurzon.

Yeung, Henry Wai-chung (1998), *Transnational Corporations and Business Networks: Hong Kong Firms in the ASEAN Region*, London: Routledge.

Yeung, Henry Wai-chung (1999), 'Under siege? Economic globalisation and Chinese business in Southeast Asia', *Economy and Society*, **28**(1), 1–31.

Yeung, Henry Wai-chung (2000a), 'State intervention and neoliberalism in the globalizing era', *The Pacific Review*, **7**(3), 399–432.

Yeung, Henry Wai-Chung (2000b), 'Economic globalisation, crisis, and the emergence of Chinese business communities in Southeast Asia', *International Sociology*, **15**(2), 269–90.

16. How Taiwan built an electronics industry: lessons for developing countries today[1]

John A. Mathews

This chapter is concerned with the 'how to' of technological change, examining the steps followed by Taiwan in building its electronics industry, broadly defined, over the three decades from the 1970s to the 2000s. Taiwan was able to diversify away from primary products to manufactured products very quickly in its development trajectory, and established a series of industries in the 1960s that mopped up unemployment. By the 1970s, it was ready to pursue Japan and South Korea into knowledge-intensive sectors, like electronics. But it did not follow Japan and South Korea in every way, and, instead, built a distinct institutional system for managing and channelling technology diffusion, taking extraordinary measures to build technological competences.

Technological learning and acquisition is an instrument of economic development, and it involves both the micro-determinants of change, and the macro-benefits in terms of changing market shares and export performance. The analysis in this chapter builds on a broad foundation of literature that is concerned with development as competence enhancement, as a complement to macroeconomic stabilization.[2] Innovation is given a broad interpretation, covering not just the development of products and processes new to the world, but the adoption and adaptation of products and processes that are already in use in the advanced countries. It is this aspect of 'innovation' that is of critical relevance to developing countries, and was utilized to great effect by Taiwan in the creation and building of its electronics industry. The institutional innovations involved are all concerned with the capture of technologies in timely fashion: the building of capabilities in these technologies, such as in government-owned R&D institutes and the diffusion of these capabilities as rapidly as possible to the private sector, for example through a sequence of target R&D consortia. In view of these considerations, I suggest that it might be more accurate to refer to the system of institutions and policies not so much as a 'national system of innovation' as a 'national system of economic learning' – and the process involved, as one not of innovation, but as the management of technological diffusion, or technology diffusion management (Mathews, 2001; 2002b; 2003a; 2004c; see also Chapter 19 in this volume).

This chapter examines the case of electronics in Taiwan, but it is concerned to bring out most clearly the aspects of Taiwan's strategies that are most generalizable to, and applicable by, developing countries today. This is not to argue that there is an easy path for development, because there is no such path. But it is to argue that there are strategies that worked for Taiwan, and with appropriate institutional modifications, could work again for other countries – with the appropriate political will. The key lesson from the successful building of an electronics industry in Taiwan is that each developing country faces a complex world of bewildering variety. But with appropriate insights and strategies, the unprecedented flows of technology and capital available today can be tapped, and harnessed to accelerate the country's development (see UNIDO, 2002; UNCTAD, 2003). Temporary advantages in the form of low costs can be utilized by firms to insert themselves in global value chains, as Taiwanese firms have done consistently in the global electronics value chains. Insertion into global value chains involves finding strategic ways to complement the needs of established firms, and fashioning strategies and institutions accordingly. This is the task that each developing country needs to address in its own way. But there are lessons to be drawn from the way Taiwan transformed itself from a struggling country in poverty into a technology powerhouse.

The chapter proceeds by setting out the overall strategy and institutional drivers of the creation of the electronics industry in Taiwan, particularly in its early years, and providing the basic data on the development of the industry, and its contribution to GDP, exports and economic prosperity in Taiwan. The chapter then focuses more particularly on the specific technology-related initiatives undertaken, in sectors such as colour TV sets in the 1970s, semiconductors in the 1980s and 1990s, communications chips in the 1990s and, most recently, in flat panel displays. These cases bring into focus the changing balance between government and private sector initiative, with the government very much leading the way initially, as a 'collective entrepreneur', and handing over leadership to the private sector over time. The chapter closes with some hypotheses regarding the process through which Taiwan built a successful electronics industry, with an eye on the generalization of the process to other developing countries today, and the limits to its applicability by other countries.

INSTITUTIONAL SETTING OF THE ELECTRONICS SECTOR IN TAIWAN

Modern Taiwan dates its industrialization from the arrival of the Kuomintang (KMT) from China in 1949. The government, seeing itself as the government of the whole of China, but in exile, and hence styling itself as the Republic of China (ROC), set itself the task of rapidly building an industrial base in the island through guided development. The KMT government worked closely with a small group of industrialists who had escaped with it from the mainland. It appears that there was a commitment that the mistakes made on the mainland would not be repeated on Taiwan (see Figure 16.1).

The first decade of development followed a fairly conventional import-substitution strategy, combined with major land reform efforts to raise agricultural production. State-owned enterprises were established in key upstream sectors, such as oil, steel, electricity and gas, to ensure a supply of raw materials and feedstocks for the small- and medium-sized firms that were allowed to flourish in the consumer and intermediate goods sectors. It would appear that political ambitions to reunite China were at this point put on hold.

The second decade of the 1960s saw the emergence of a dual approach, with import substitution remaining for the domestic economy alongside the creation of an export sector, driven by export-promotion policies, both as a means of earning foreign currencies and as a means of supplying external discipline to government-led investment upgrading programmes. Thus a dual structure was created, with different policies

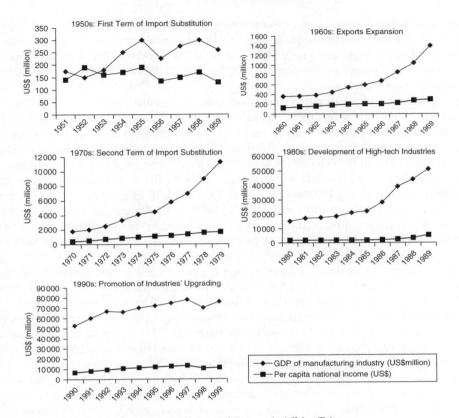

Source: Industrial Development Bureau, Ministry of Economic Affairs, Taiwan.

Figure 16.1   The growth and development of Taiwan, 1951–2000

applying to the domestic and export-oriented sectors. The *Statute for Encouragement of Investment* was passed in 1960, and served as the umbrella under which a variety of investment incentives were offered to enhance export performance and upgrade technology and performance. Institutional innovations, such as the creation of export processing zones, the manufacturing equivalent of nineteenth-century free ports, were introduced.[3] The GDP of manufacturing industry soared during this decade, from US$370 million in 1960 to just over US$1.4 billion by 1969, a fourfold expansion (see Figure 16.1). This pulled up per capita national income, which doubled during the decade, from just under US$200 in 1960 to just under US$400 in 1969.

The third decade of the 1970s saw several new industries established, through government guidance and an opening up to foreign investment, in order to secure the technologies needed for a further expansion of exports. The government established a major institution, the Industrial Development Bureau (IDB) in 1970, to act as coordinator of investment. Under its guidance, major improvements in the machinery, textiles, petrochemicals and motor industries were accomplished. This decade saw the government stimulate industrial development with major infrastructure projects (the Ten National

Construction Projects) that also stimulated domestic demand for industrial output. Electronics activities in Taiwan picked up during this decade, mainly in the form of joint ventures with foreign partners (from Japan and the US), and through foreign companies being required to source components locally, leading to the creation of a domestic parts and components industry.

In addition to investment vehicles already established, such as the National Chiaotung Bank, the government created technology diffusion vehicles as well, led by the Industrial Technology Research Institute (ITRI), in 1973. Its first laboratory, the Electronics Research Services Organization (ERSO), was dedicated to creating technological capabilities in the electronics sector. To further promote the use of computers in industry, and thereby stimulate a national IT industry, the government established the Institute for Information Industry (III) in 1979. The GDP of manufacturing expanded sixfold in this decade, from just under US$2 billion in 1970 to US$12 billion in 1979, driving per capita national income to a fivefold expansion, from just under US$400 in 1970 to US$2000 in 1979. The world was already on notice that a 'miracle' was happening in Taiwan.

The decade of the 1980s saw a further intensification of the guided national industrialization strategy, this time with the focus on electronics, information technology (IT) and other high-technology industries. Capital-intensive industries were established, and the government introduced major infrastructure innovations to accommodate them, including the new Hsinchu Science-based Industry Park (HSIP) established in 1980. The first semiconductor venture was spun off from ITRI/ERSO in 1980, as United Microelectronics Corporation (UMC) and many more followed, notably TSMC in 1986, created as a joint venture with Philips. This decade of the development of high-technology industries saw manufacturing GDP expand more than threefold, from US$15 billion in 1980 to just over $50 billion in 1989, pulling per capita national income up from US$2000 at the start of the decade to US$8000 at the end of the decade – a fourfold expansion. Taiwan was now on the brink of becoming a 'developed' nation.

The decade of the 1990s saw the flowering of high-technology industries in Taiwan; this was the decade when it became the 'Silicon Valley of the East' (Mathews, 1997). Continuing its guiding of the economy, the government enacted the *Statute for Upgrading Industries* in 1991, under which further incentives were offered to firms to enhance exports, upgrade technology, participate in ITRI-led R&D consortia (through which technology could be diffused to the private sector) and locate in new science-based industry parks, including extensions of Hsinchu, and new parks in Tainan in the south and Taichung in the centre. Target development was maintained through the IDB issuing its *Measures for Boosting Economic Development* and the *Strategies and Measures for Development of Ten Emerging Industries* in 1993, including IT, communications, flat panel displays and semiconductors as part of the electronics sector. The GDP of manufacturing industry further expanded from just under US$50 billion in 1990 to US$80 billion in 1997, and then recovered quickly following the 1997–8 Asian economic crisis, to reach just under US$80 billion again by 1999. Per capita national income was pulled above US$12 000 by 1994 and 1995, and had recovered to that level again by 1999 after the financial crisis.

By the end of the century, then, Taiwan had recorded the astonishing feat of raising national income nearly 100-fold, from just above US$100 in 1951 to just over US$10 000 in

2000, with manufacturing GDP being the primary engine of growth, expanding 400-fold, from under US$200 million in 1951 to just under US$80 billion in 2000. It had become the world's sixteenth largest economy, with worldwide trade totalling US$288 billion in 2000. It has become a major Information Technology (IT) manufacturer, producing 5.5 per cent of global semiconductor output and the majority of the world's computer terminals and peripherals. There is clearly a lesson here for all developing economies (see Wade, 1990; Amsden, 2001; Amsden and Chu, 2002; Tung, 2002).

The principal lesson is that to put such emphasis on manufacturing, as the engine of industrial development, a country has to go against the entrenched precepts of relying on 'comparative advantage', a doctrine formulated in the early nineteenth century by Ricardo, that was wrong at the time it was formulated, and is even more in error today, from the perspective of a developing country. Figure 16.2 shows how Taiwan utilized manufacturing industry (that was built on self-created competitive advantages, not any inherited comparative advantages) and used it to drive the development process. The figure shows how manufacturing traced 'industrial' value-added as the principal component of GDP. Of course, early on in the process, Taiwan utilized a competitive advantage in terms of low labour costs, just as any developing country today needs to seize such a short-lived competitive advantage. But the lesson is not to rely on such advantages forever, but to create an infrastructure and a set of institutions that will translate this temporary competitive advantage, based on low costs, into a more durable competitive advantage,

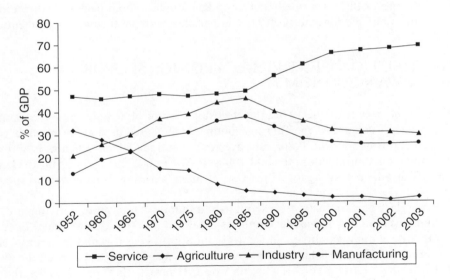

Notes:
(1) Industry includes Manufacturing, Construction, and Electricity, Gas and Water sectors.
(2) Services include Trade & Eating–Drinking Places, Transport, Storages and Communications, Government Services, and Finance, Insurance & Business Services.

Source: Industrial Development Bureau, Ministry of Economic Affairs, Taiwan.

Figure 16.2 Manufacturing as the engine of growth in Taiwan

based on manufacturing strength. The electronics industry, broadly defined, played a major role in this process in Taiwan.

The electronics industry provides another lesson, in that there has been a clear shift in the balance between government and the private sector as the industry has developed (see also chapters in Part III of this volume). In the early years, it was government initiatives that led to the stimulation of private sector involvement, where firms in the early years, such as Tatung, might have been reluctant to take what they saw as risky investments. Government interventions and the actions of agencies, such as the IDB and then ITRI, were designed to underwrite and reduce the risks of investment in such a demanding industry as electronics, followed by semiconductors and then IT generally. But as these industries became established, and the firms involved – such as UMC, TSMC and Winbond – became formidable competitors in their own right, so they gradually seized the initiative and were able to create their own investment strategies. By the time Taiwanese firms were electing to enter the flat panel display industry in the late 1990s, they were doing so purely as private initiatives. This changing balance between government and private sector initiative is characteristic of all developing countries' efforts to enter well-established global industries.

Finally, the point needs to be made that Taiwan was increasingly relying on mainland Chinese manufacturing activities, under contract, as the electronics industry matured. By the 1990s, mainland Chinese activities accounted for a significant proportion of Taiwanese electronics and IT exports. This has been, not just a business issue for Taiwanese firms, but a political issue, as the government in Taiwan has sought to hold back such direct investments in the mainland for fear of effective integration between the two political entities.

CONTRIBUTION OF THE ELECTRONICS SECTOR TO THE TAIWAN ECONOMY

Starting in the decade of the 1970s, the electronics sector grew to become the manufacturing and export engine of the Taiwan economy. It increased its share of manufacturing value-added throughout the 1980s, and overtook metal machinery, chemicals and food, textiles and related products, in the mid-1990s. By the year 2000, it was by far the leading sector in Taiwan, accounting for 35 per cent of manufacturing value-added, as shown in Figure 16.3.

Thus the electronics industry turned out to be a sound bet for Taiwan, driving its overall industrial development. It was the emphasis on electronics that differentiated East Asia from other developing countries, in Central and South America, in Africa and Central and South Asia. Figure 16.4a shows in graphic form just how great has been the disparity between these parts of the developing world. It reveals that, in the 1970s, the East Asian economies (South Korea, Taiwan mainly) still lagged behind the Latin American countries in terms of their share of world value-added in medium- and high-technology manufactures, the principal drivers of development. But by the late 1970s and early 1980s, they had rapidly caught up with and overtaken the Latin American countries, mainly through the agency of the electronics industry that was seen in East Asia as the passport to the future, but was overlooked in Latin America, or pursued, as in the Brazilian efforts with computers, in clumsy ways.

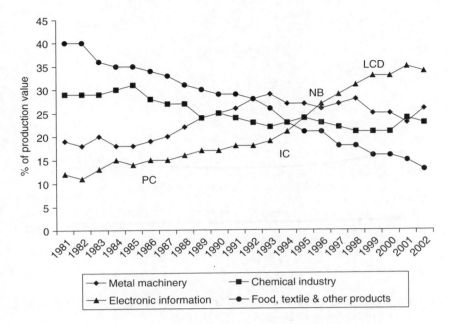

Source: Industrial Development Bureau, Ministry of Economic Affairs, Taiwan.

Figure 16.3 Electronics industry as the engine of manufacturing in Taiwan

In terms of production, the electronics sector passed through several important milestones, as shown in Figure 16.4b. By 1986, when electronics value-added accounted for more than 10 per cent of manufacturing value-added, it had already surpassed textiles in importance. Total production passed the US$25 billion mark in 1992. In that year, consumer electronics accounted for 13.1 per cent of output; IT products for 36.2 per cent; communication electronics for 6.9 per cent; and electronic parts and components (including semiconductors) for 43.8 per cent. As Figure 16.4b makes clear, the early predominance of consumer electronics gave way in the later 1980s and 1990s to IT and semiconductors/components. By 1998, electronics, broadly defined, accounted for over 25 per cent of manufacturing value-added: it had come to dominate Taiwan's manufacturing (and hence industrial) activity.

But the real strength of the electronics sector in Taiwan is revealed in the export figures. In terms of exports, electronics also emerged as the leading sector in Taiwan. If we divide the quarter-century from 1976 to 2001 into two periods, a first period from 1976 to 1988, and a second from 1989 to 2001, then we see from Table 16.1 that Taiwan's electronics exports made up an average of 16.1 per cent of total exports in the first period, rising to 32.2 per cent of total exports in the second period – as against the world situation, where electronics exports accounted for 7.3 per cent of world exports in the first period, and 13.3 per cent of world exports in the second period. Thus Taiwan's performance in both periods was more than twice as good as the rest of the world. In terms of imports, Taiwan was also a major importer of electronics

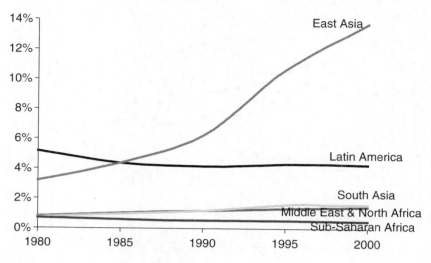

Source: Lall/UNIDO.

Figure 16.4a   *Developing regions: world market shares of medium- and high-tech manufacturing value-added, 1980–2000*

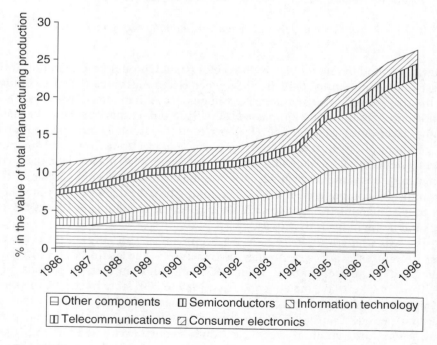

Source: Tung (2001).

Figure 16.4b   *Taiwan electronics production, 1986–98*

Table 16.1   Taiwan's export performance in electronics, 1976–2001 (per cent)

Share of export	1976–1988		1989–2001	
	Taiwan	World	Taiwan	World
Consumer electronics	2.5	1.2	1.8	1.1
IT products	2.9	1.4	8.5	2.8
Parts and components	2.1	1.9	9.6	3.4
Telecommunications	6.2	1.5	3.7	2.6
Semiconductors	2.4	1.3	8.6	3.4
Total electronics	16.1	7.3	32.2	13.3

Source: Author, based on data supplied by the World Bank.

goods, feeding into its IT and electronics consumer products. In the first period, its imports of electronics accounted for 10.9 per cent of total imports in Taiwan, and in the second period for 21.7 per cent of total imports, again exceeding world figures by a strong margin. Thus Taiwan had emerged, particularly in the 1990s, as a world trading power in electronics with exports and imports well exceeding world averages.

Moreover, Taiwan's performance was strong in all sectors of electronics. Its exports of consumer electronics, IT products, telecommunications and semiconductors all exceeded twice the world averages in the first period, from 1976 to 1988; only electronics parts and components were marginally above world averages for this period. This is the area where Japanese firms have been and remain dominant. In the second period, as shown in Table 16.1, Taiwan's export share in IT products grew to 8.5 per cent, as against the world average of 2.8 per cent, making Taiwan three times more export-competitive in these products, mainly IT products like PCs and motherboards. Its share of parts and components, including semiconductors, also rose dramatically during the second period.[4]

The comparison between a country's trade performance (exports and imports) compared with the world, for any specific product or group of products, can be captured using a variety of measures. The most widely recognized such measure is revealed comparative advantage (RCA).[5] Figure 16.5 shows the RCA for Taiwan's electronics exports, over the period 1976 to 2002, and Figure 16.6 shows the RCA for all East Asian economies, grouping them as Japan, as NIEs (Korea, Taiwan, Hong Kong and Singapore), the ASEAN countries, and China – for all electronics and for the major sub-sectors, including consumer electronics, IT products, telecommunications products, parts and components, and semiconductors. Figure 16.5 for Taiwan reveals that its exports for all electronics were consistently above an RCA of 1.0 throughout the period, meaning that its exports were above world averages.[6]

For East Asia as a whole, the figure for all electronics shows that Japan led the way, with its RCA curve rising and then falling in the 1990s as the other countries in East Asia were catching up with it. The NIEs had, by the late 1970s, already caught up with Japan in terms of RCA, and were still the leading group of countries in 2001 in terms of RCA.

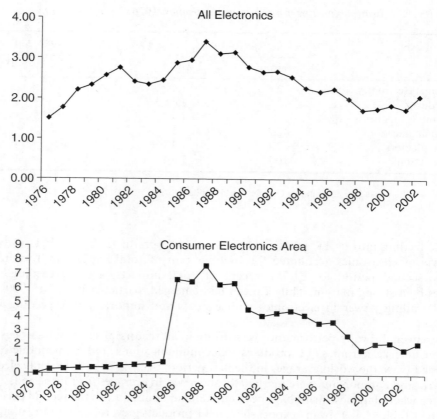

Source: Author, using data supplied by the World Bank.

Figure 16.5   *Revealed comparative advantage (RCA) in Taiwan's electronics trade, 1976–2002*

The ASEAN countries followed a few years later, with their RCA exceeding 1 in 1986, and exceeding that of Japan by the early 1990s. China follows on later still, with its RCA for all electronics reaching 1 by the year 1998, and then rapidly increasing.

As argued by Tung (2003) these patterns are very much in keeping with the patterns of distribution of trade competitiveness outlined by the Japanese economist Akamatsu, in his famous 'flying geese' metaphor.[7] We do not have to stick with a rigidly deterministic interpretation of this framework to see that countries gain an initial foothold in a new industry through a sequence of steps, from imports to domestic production and eventually to exports, and that they successively upgrade following their competitive advantages (Okita, 1985). Instead we may view Akamatsu's framework as an early – and profound – insight into the way that the developing economy needs to be linked to the advanced economies, in order to generate its own activities, utilizing its temporary competitive advantages of low costs. This is very much how Taiwan developed its own electronics sector, as we now examine.

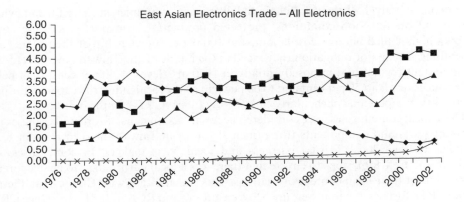

East Asian Electronics Trade – All Electronics

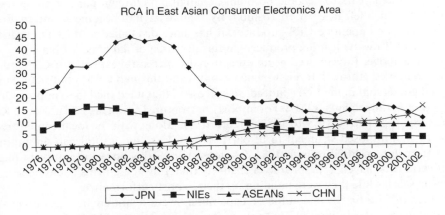

RCA in East Asian Consumer Electronics Area

—◆— JPN —■— NIEs —▲— ASEANs —✕— CHN

Source: Author, using data supplied by the World Bank.

Figure 16.6   East Asian exports of electronics: flying geese patterns

TECHNOLOGY DEVELOPMENT IN THE ELECTRONICS SECTOR

A comprehensive account of the development of the entire electronics industry in Taiwan is beyond the scope of this chapter, but four cases will be discussed, to give the background needed for the micro-focused discussion to come.

Taiwan's Success in Colour TV Sets (1970s)

Taiwan's successes in colour TV sets (CTVs) in the 1970s derived from its earlier experiences with black and white TVs and transistor radios in the 1960s. CTVs were considered extremely complex products in the 1970s, and were the issue for determined international competition between American and Japanese multinationals, as well as European firms, such as Philips and Grundig. It was this industry that saw a globalization of production, with American firms seeking a competitive edge over their Japanese and European rivals by outsourcing much of the value chain to lower-wage economies, such as Taiwan, where they could obtain good conditions: protected production in export-processing zones (EPZs), high-skilled but low-cost labour, and 100 per cent ownership of their plants and operations. The major obligation they faced at the hands of the Taiwan government was local content regulations, imposed initially in 1970 at a level of 40 per cent, then being raised successively to 50 per cent and to 60 per cent as the local industrial capacity for producing key components, particularly cathode ray tubes (CRTs), improved.

These local content rules were considered necessary as a means of forcing Japanese suppliers of parts and components (the principal source in Taiwan then) to transfer technologies to their local Taiwan partners and local parts makers. In some cases, the government itself took steps to ensure that there was a local parts maker to enable foreign firms to meet their local content obligations. This was the case with Chung-Hua Picture Tube (CPT), formed as a joint venture between Tatung and RCA in 1971 to produce CRTs. It took CPT ten years to become profitable, changing its foreign partner along the way from RCA, which left in 1976, to Toshiba. By 1980, CPT had become an internationally successful and competitive CRT producer; it has since diversified into LCD production, and is one of Taiwan's leading producers in this new area of flat panel displays.

As noted above, Taiwan became an exceptionally successful exporter of CTVs, mainly to the US market (through foreign-owned exports and through OEM contracting for US branded goods sold in the US) – indeed, so successful that it led the US to impose Orderly Marketing Arrangements (OMAs) or import controls on Taiwan, as well as South Korea, in the three-year period 1979 to 1982 (Figure 16.7). Along with the local content regulations, Taiwan imposed stringent tariff barriers on CTVs, and a total ban on imports of CTVs from Japan, lifted only in 1984. As noted above, this powerful intervention from the government played a major role in ensuring that Taiwanese firms could benefit from domestic sales, while they were building up their export performance.

In Taiwan, the first semiconductor capabilities were acquired by the public sector research agency, the Industrial Technology Research Institute (ITRI), founded in 1973.

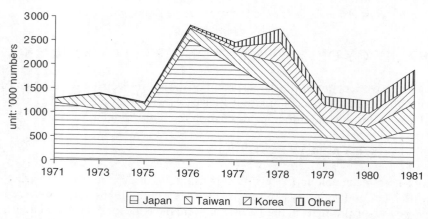

Source: OTA (1983).

Figure 16.7   Imports of CTVs into the US market, 1971–81

One of its laboratories entered into a technology transfer agreement with the US firm, RCA, in 1976, thereby acquiring initial semiconductor fabrication and design capabilities. The technology transferred was considered obsolete by RCA, but it served as a training ground for ITRI, which then diffused the skills to the private sector, by spinning off a new company, United Microelectronics Corporation (UMC) in 1980. UMC has since then repeatedly entered into new alliances with advanced firms, bringing itself up to world-class technological levels. In 1986, the public agency ITRI entered into a further technology transfer agreement with the European multinational Philips, to form a new VLSI spin-off, giving Philips's new fabrication capacity and privileged access to the Taiwan market. In order to avoid competing directly with Philips, this new company, Taiwan Semiconductor Manufacturing Corporation (TSMC) elected to produce chips only for third parties, thereby inventing the notion of the 'silicon foundry'. This has proved to be remarkably successful, and TSMC has continuously enlarged and deepened its technological capacities by transferring the technological specifications of its customer firms as it takes orders to produce their chips (see Mathews, 1997; Mathews and Cho, 2000).

Taiwan's Success in Communications Chips

Likewise in the communications chips sector, Taiwanese firms utilized various forms of technology leverage to become players in this most sophisticated segment of the IC market in the 1990s. Here, the technological challenge is to meet international standards for data transmission protocols. In the 1980s, before the industry's absorptive capacity had reached the appropriate level, some small firms tried to enter this industry as 'knock off' practitioners, taking US or Japanese products and copying them to sell for a lower price. Strict enforcement of property rights put a stop to this.

A new wave of Taiwanese ventures in this sector emerged in the 1990s, driven by technology leverage taking place through both the public and private sectors. In the private sector, firms, like Silicon Integrated Systems, entered the fast Ethernet data switching IC business by licensing technology from one of the leading US firms, National Semiconductor. In the public sector, ITRI's ERSO and CCL developed Ethernet switches and the ICs to drive them, and then formed R&D alliances with small firms to pass across the technology for rapid commercialization. Firms such as DLink and Accton have prospered through this process (see Mathews, 2002a).

Flat Panel Displays (LCDs) in Taiwan

Finally, consider the case of Taiwanese development of an LCD industry in the late 1990s. Taiwan grew in the second half of the 1990s to become the world's second largest supplier of notebook PCs, based partly on highly innovative developmental consortia in the 1980s, after Japan. But it was unable to penetrate into the key component segment of flat panel displays dominated by Japanese firms, including Sharp, Fujitsu, Toshiba and Matsushita. This meant that much of the value-added in notebook PCs was lost to Japan and represented a drain on Taiwan's balance of trade.

Efforts by ITRI/ERSO to launch a liquid crystal display (LCD) industry in Taiwan in the early 1990s were frustrated, partly owing to lack of sufficient absorptive capacity, and partly because of resistance from semiconductor incumbents. But in the second half of the 1990s, one Taiwanese firm after another committed itself to LCD production, as it became clear that thin-film transistor (TTF) LCDs were becoming the technological standard for notebook PCs, and as Japanese firms sought to outsource and 'second source' much of their LCD work to Taiwanese firms. By the late 1990s, through these several efforts, Taiwan was moving to establish itself as the world's third largest supplier of TTF LCDs, after Japan and South Korea – all of whom were considerably in advance of US and European firms in terms of mass production.[8]

Technological Learning: the Focus of Taiwan's Creation of an Electronics Industry

Since its founding in 1973, the Industrial Technology Research Institute (ITRI) has been an engine of Taiwan's high-tech development and, in particular, the engine for the electronics industry. It was founded by the country's leaders, including K.T. Lee, with the explicit aim of driving Taiwan's move up the technology ladder. ITRI has accomplished these goals by pursuing a sophisticated strategy of *fast followership*, through which ITRI staff identify key technologies and build expertise and capabilities in these technologies, before spinning off the technology and associated capabilities as rapidly as possible to the private sector. Thus ITRI has been the guiding engine that powers the technological component of Taiwan's development strategy. As such, it provides a model for all aspiring developing countries in the twenty-first century.

ITRI R&D now takes place at 12 campuses around Taiwan and focuses on such critical technological areas as semiconductors, flat panel displays, biomedical devices, broadband/mobile communications and nanotechnology. Since 2001, its research has generated more than 800 granted patents each year. At the end of 2003, ITRI employed almost 6200 staff, and had funding from the government and industrial contacts totalling US$500 million. Today, partly thanks to the research carried out at ITRI, Taiwan is a leading manufacturer of semiconductor chips, computers and optoelectronic products. More than 100 new firms have been spun out of ITRI, including well-known firms such as UMC, TSMC and MIRLE (in industrial automation), TEC (Taiwan Engine Company) and, most recently, Phalanx Biotech. ITRI is continuing with its programme of spinoffs from the R&D conducted within its laboratories, as well as sponsoring technology transfer through its formation of highly specific R&D alliances (Mathews, 2002a) and industrial consulting projects.

The business of ITRI is not research so much as technology transfer. It is arguably the most capable institution of its kind in the world in scanning the global technological horizon for developments of interest to Taiwanese industry, and then executing the steps required to import the technology (for example under licence, or through joint development), absorb and adapt it, involve Taiwanese firms in projects that utilize the new technology, and finally transferring products, equipment and know-how to Taiwanese firms, who will take over its further commercial development. This is not so much a 'national system of innovation' as a 'national system of economic learning' of prodigious effect.

Programmes are undertaken by ITRI both to facilitate the creation of new industries, as in the case of semiconductors, but also fine chemicals, pharmaceuticals, optoelectronics and aerospace, and to upgrade existing industries. In the latter case, a good example is ITRI's efforts to upgrade the technologies used in bicycle fabrication, such as carbon fibre, which resulted in Taiwan becoming a world leader in this sector. In the 1990s, ITRI sought to promote a series of technological collaborative alliances to make Taiwanese firms participants in current technological developments, in partnership with ITRI specialists. The submicron consortium formed in 1991 was one such project, which brought the consortium members into contact with the world's best DRAM process technology suppliers. A more recent one, which shows how ITRI stays abreast of technological developments, is the liquid crystal display consortium formed in 1993. ITRI maintains an extensive intellectual property portfolio, and operates its own venture capital fund, called the Industrial Technology Investment Corporation (ITIC).

A series of collaborative R&D ventures emerged in Taiwan in the 1980s and 1990s, within a quite distinctive institutional framework. Unlike the case of many of the collaborative arrangements between established firms in the US, Europe or Japan, where mutual risk reduction is frequently the driving influence, in the case of Taiwan it is technological learning, upgrading and catch-up industry creation that is the object of the collaborative exercises. The Taiwan R&D alliances were formed hesitantly in the 1980s, but flourished in the 1990s as institutional forms were found that encourage firms to cooperate in raising their technological levels. Most of these alliances have been in the information technology sectors, covering personal computers, work stations, servers and multi-media, as well as a range of consumer products, and telecommunications and data switching systems and products. But they have also emerged in other sectors, such as automotive engines, motor cycles, electric vehicles, and in the services and financial sector as well. Several such alliances could be counted in Taiwan in the late-1990s, bringing together firms and public sector research institutes, with the added organizational input of trade associations, and catalytic financial assistance from government.[9]

Taiwan and Patenting

One element still to be considered in this treatment is the passage from imitation to innovation, as measured by R&D expenditures and the rate of patenting in the electronics industry. While R&D expenditures are well covered in the existing literature, the recent astonishing performance of Taiwanese firms and institutions in taking out patents in the US Patent and Trademark Office (USPTO) is less well known. One of the clearest indications of innovation performance is the rate of take-up of patents issued by the USPTO.[10] Studies have recently been directed at linking the rate of patenting with economic variables, such as R&D expenditure and the proportion of scientists and technologists employed in a sector or country, in the notion of national innovative capacity (see Furman *et al.*, 2002). These studies have been extended to the East Asian case, where it is found that East Asian firms and institutions have made astonishing strides in recent years (see Hu and Jaffe, 2001; Jung and Imm, 2002; Hu and Mathews, 2005). Taiwan, in particular, has risen to third highest in the world in terms of per capita take-up of USPTO patents over the years 1997–2001.

The experience of East Asia in patenting with the USPTO is shown in Table 16.2, as compared with G7 countries and a reference group of comparable countries, including Finland, Israel and Ireland. The table reveals just how rapid has been the rise of East Asia as an innovative force, shifting from imitation to innovation. In terms of utility patents taken out in the US over the period 1997–2001 on a per capita basis, Taiwan ranks third in the world, behind the US and Japan. As can be seen, South Korea ranks eighth, with 6.6 patents per capita per year, averaged over the past five years, while

Table 16.2 Country statistics: averages for 5-year and 30-year periods (utility patent only)

Country	Patents per year			Patents per capita			Success rate			Annual growth rate		
	1968–97	1992–97	1997–2001	1968–97	1992–97	1997–2001	1968–97	1992–97	1997–2002	1968–97	1992–97	1997–2001
USA	44 850	56 683	79 717	15.5	21.5	28.6	58.9	52.2	53.2	4.9%	7.9%	9.7%
Japan	11 216	22 433	29 949	10.3	17.9	23.7	55.5	57.9	61.5	8.6%	6.5%	10.2%
Taiwan	437	1 535	3 778	2.3	7.3	17.2	35.5	39.3	45.7	26.2%	21.4%	27.8%
Israel	183	400	757	4.2	7.2	12.4	42.2	40.5	37.1	12.5%	15.4%	17.3%
Finland	181	370	609	4.2	7.2	11.8	48.6	51.3	47.0	11.4%	10.0%	13.6%
Germany	5 806	6 895	9 387	9.2	8.4	11.4	59.5	59.8	59.3	2.7%	4.3%	13.0%
Canada	1 380	2 119	3 121	4.9	7.2	10.2	50.7	49.3	48.6	6.5%	7.5%	11.2%
Korea	267	1 134	3 113	0.7	2.5	6.6	37.3	39.0	56.1	39.1%	36.1%	20.4%
France	2 432	2 881	3 662	4.3	5.0	6.2	66.5	61.9	60.4	16.4%	3.7%	8.5%
UK	2 492	2 427	3 469	4	4.2	5.9	53.5	50.2	50.6	2.7%	6.7%	10.8%
Singapore	16	59	174	0.6	1.7	4.4	40.2	41.5	33.3	44.9%	26.2%	33.7%
Italy	855	1 215	1 548	1.7	2.1	2.7	54.1	58.3	61.5	4.4%	4.5%	9.2%
Hong Kong	31	72	162	0.6	1.2	2.3	40.3	38.7	42.6	14.2%	23.0%	35.6%

Note: The data for Germany include West Germany before 1990.

Source: USPTO; World Development Indicators database (2003).

Table 16.3 *Patent numbers of top patenting firms and institutions: Taiwan, South Korea, Singapore, China (1997–2001)*

	1997	1998	1999	2000	2001	Total 1997–2001
Taiwan						
UMC	149	174	266	430	584	1 603
TSMC	130	218	290	385	529	1 552
ITRI	153	218	208	198	221	998
VISC	53	120	112	131	112	528
Winbond	24	59	115	115	126	439
Mosel-Vitelic	15	32	38	66	68	219
Korea						
Samsung Electronics	584	1 305	1 545	1 441	1 450	6 325
Hyundai Electronics	154	212	242	294	533	1 435
LG Electronics	113	215	229	220	248	1 025
Daewoo Electronics	215	319	273	120	54	981
LG Semicond.	119	235	311	255	42	962
ETRI	58	120	130	124	72	504
KIST	29	44	41	35	35	184
Singapore						
Chartered	30	39	44	79	135	327
China						
WSMC	0	0	6	61	37	104

Note: Company is included only for the total patent number more than 100.

Source: USPTO: patenting by geographic region (state and country), broken down by organization count, 1997–2001 utility patent grants by calendar year of grant.

Singapore is rising fast, to reach eleventh on a per capita basis. China has yet to make an impression.[11]

If we look at the firms and institutions involved, we gain a clearer idea of what has been happening in these latecomer catch-up countries. Table 16.3 shows the number of patents taken out in each of the five years from 1997 to 2001 by East Asian organizations (both firms and institutions) and the totals. Almost all of these firms and organizations operate in the electronics, IT, communications and, particularly, the semiconductor sectors. These are the advanced sectors where the East Asian firms have been making their mark, driving the overall totals reported above. South Korea has been more focused and concentrated in its patenting activities than other East Asian countries. In South Korea, the top five *chaebol* account for a large proportion of patents overall (69 per cent) from 1997 to 2001, whereas in Taiwan, the top five firms and organizations, all from the semiconductor sector, account for a smaller proportion overall (27.1 per cent). Patterns established in the realm of production appear to be carried across to the sphere of innovation.[12]

Of course, many of the patents created by Taiwanese and South Korean firms in the electronics and wider IT sector may be considered 'defensive' patents, in the sense that a patent portfolio is needed to find a seat at the table in negotiations between major players in the industry. Taiwanese firms, like TSMC and UMC, found that they needed such a patent portfolio to be able to strike cross-licensing deals with their customer firms, avoiding some of the intellectual property headaches that have plagued other Taiwanese firms. Overall, we may argue, on the basis of this prima facie evidence, that East Asian countries, led by Taiwan and South Korea, have developed the institutional foundations of *national innovation capacity*.[13] They are actively developing these foundations, as part of their strategy to move beyond imitation to innovation (Kim, 1997), like Japan.

HYPOTHESES REGARDING THE BUILDING OF AN ELECTRONICS INDUSTRY IN TAIWAN

Let us now draw back and generate some generalizable findings from this experience on the part of Taiwan in building a successful electronics industry. First, we need to consider the kind of 'innovation' that is involved in such industry building by a country that is a late-comer to the game. This can be expressed in the form of some hypotheses regarding the Taiwanese strategies and their effects. Innovation has been studied intensively, with theories of capitalist dynamics and competitive advantage being built on the role that innovation plays in unleashing Schumpeterian creative 'gales of destruction' through the economy (Schumpeter, 1942/1950). The reality is that economies as a whole benefit from innovations only as they spread, or diffuse, to a large number of firms.[14] This is certainly the case with the build-up of technological prowess in electronics in Taiwan. The processes of diffusion are generally held to follow two major pathways, namely market-induced imitation and organizationally induced technology transfer (usually within product cycle considerations).

Such a framework, however, fails to fit the reality of the achievements of Taiwanese late-comer firms that have integrated themselves into the high technology sectors of electronics. It fails to fit for three reasons. First, most of the successful firms have not been innovators in the usual sense of the word, nor have they been recipients of diffusion or technology transfer, but rather the instigators of the process. Second, the successful latecomer firms in Taiwan, such as UMC, TSMC and Acer, fashioned such sophisticated leverage devices for the acquisition and internalization of technology that in themselves become a source of competitive advantage. Third, institutional structures have been created in Taiwan to accel-erate the process of diffusion, taking over many of the functions of the market.

Diffusion as a Process

Technological diffusion was actively managed in Taiwan. From this perspective, diffusion is not a passive phenomenon, driven solely by strategic decisions and calculations taken by the originators of the novelty, but it is in fact a complex process, where technological leverage and strategic management play critical roles, as amply demonstrated in Taiwan's electronics industry. Thus diffusion is triggered as much by decisions of the adopters, who assimilate, accommodate, adapt and improve, as by the recipient or sources of the novelty. Diffusion, with its connotations of passive transfer, is thus a misnomer; what we are talking about is a multipolar process of active dissemination and leverage of resources, where the adoption and adaptation decisions are primary, and account for the extent to which diffusion (that is penetration) occurs. This is best described as a process of technology diffusion management (Mathews, 2001).

Diffusion Management as a Source of Competitive Advantage

The strategic calculations of the latecomer firm engaging in leveraging practices are quite different from those normally depicted in discussions of strategy and the enhancement of sustainable competitive advantages by firms.[15] The conventional discussion is couched in terms of the firm's identifying its sources of competitive advantage and then framing strategy so as to enhance and defend them. From the perspective of the latecomer firm, this makes no sense at all. For the latecomer, lacking resources and advantages, other than temporary cost advantages, the approach to strategy is to identify the resources that are most available and most susceptible to leverage, and then to implement a framework for actually tapping and incorporating these resources, and then improving on them. This is resource leverage in a developmental context – or what I have called developmental resource leverage (see Mathews and Cho, 2000).

Institutions of Diffusion Management

The Taiwan latecomers have found that the management of diffusion calls for quite different institutions than those that have been developed in the advanced countries to support R&D-led innovation. The institutions of diffusion management are concerned with accelerating the uptake of technologies by firms, with spreading the dissemination of new techniques and with hastening the processes of enhancement of organizational capabilities (organizational learning), through such devices as engineering research associations (Japan) and developmental consortia. The creation of such an institutional framework means that firms do not have to leverage and learn on their own. The results of earlier experiences with collaborative dissemination can be used to improve the outcomes, in a process that can be described as 'economic learning'. Such a process calls for an institutional framework that can accordingly be called 'a national system of economic learning', by contrast with the more conventional national system of innovation (see Mathews, 2003a).

Taken together, these three organizational innovations that are real innovations in Taiwan, whatever labels we wish to attach to them, represent a major departure in the understanding of innovation and its propagation, away from knowledge generation in individual firms, towards the management of technological diffusion as a strategic process of economic upgrading. The shift in theoretical perspective involved here really is profound. First, there is the issue that the industries being created cannot be conceived simply as firms, as in much industrial economics analysis, but as clusters of firms together with their institutional supports. Even where this is given due weight, a conventional view of industry evolution is concerned with patterns of innovation and their supporting institutional structures. By contrast, the approach pioneered in Taiwan is to see the process in terms of patterns and dynamics of diffusion and its management; the emphasis is on how innovations can be leveraged and turned into technological capabilities and competitive products as rapidly as possible.[16]

We capture the sense of these institutional frameworks that drive economic learning in Figure 16.8. On their own, these agencies and organizational innovations are not so remarkable, and can easily be replicated (as, for example, the economic development

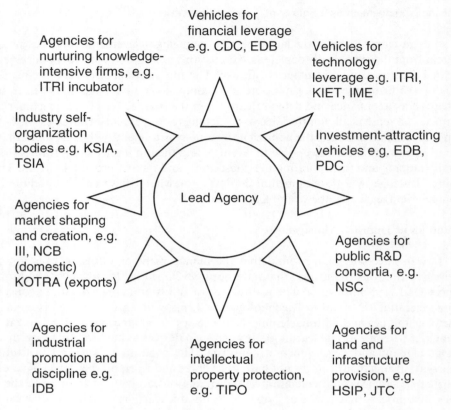

Vehicles for financial leverage e.g. CDC, EDB

Agencies for nurturing knowledge-intensive firms, e.g. ITRI incubator

Vehicles for technology leverage e.g. ITRI, KIET, IME

Industry self-organization bodies e.g. KSIA, TSIA

Investment-attracting vehicles e.g. EDB, PDC

Lead Agency

Agencies for market shaping and creation, e.g. III, NCB (domestic) KOTRA (exports)

Agencies for public R&D consortia, e.g. NSC

Agencies for industrial promotion and discipline e.g. IDB

Agencies for intellectual property protection, e.g. TIPO

Agencies for land and infrastructure provision, e.g. HSIP, JTC

Notes:
CDC = China Development Corporation (Taiwan), EDB = Economic Development Board (Singapore), HSIP = Hsinchu Science-based Industry Park, IDB = Industrial Development Bureau (Taiwan), III = Institute for Information Industry (Taiwan), IME = Institute for Microelectronics (Singapore), ITRI = Industrial Technology Research Institute (Taiwan), JTC = Jurong Town Corporation (Singapore), KIET = Korean Institute for Electronics and Telecommunications, KOTRA = Korea Overseas Trade Association, KSIA = Korea Semiconductor Industry Association, NCB = National Computer Board, NSC = National Science Council (Taiwan), PDC = Penang Development Corporation, TIPO = Taiwan Intellectual Property Organization.

Source: Mathews and Cho (2000).

Figure 16.8   National systems of economic learning in East Asia

agencies that have been emulated in Europe, such as the Welsh Development Agency, or Scottish Enterprise). What is remarkable is the total system formed by their interaction and mutual support. It is this systemic character of the elements that accounts for the capacity to learn. It is the adaptability of the total system that counts, with the facility to improve adaptation over time, as experience is gained and stored in appropriate institutional form, generating what might be called 'institutional capacity'.

Limits to Applicability of the Taiwan Model of Technology Diffusion Management

Finally, a discussion is in order on the limits to the applicability of the Taiwan model of 'technology diffusion management' – and hence to its generalizability to other developing countries in the twenty-first century. Taiwan has been less successful in some sectors of electronics, such as hard disk drives (HDDs) and, indeed, in other industrial sectors, such as the automotive industry. In the auto industry, for example, the Taiwanese established several motor vehicle companies, and linked them through technology leverage to Japanese automotive producers. But they have remained tied to these Japanese firms, producing under their brand for over two decades, with little prospect of breaking free to design and produce cars of their own, as would be the expected outcome of the leverage strategy. So, with certain qualifications, one might say that the leverage strategy has not served the Taiwanese particularly well in automotive products.[17]

Likewise in aerospace, the attempts by the Taiwanese to launch aircraft projects, through technology transfer from European and US producers, have yet to meet with success. The reasons for these shortcomings are many. While undoubtedly there were failings on the Taiwanese side, in terms of technological or marketing deficiencies, there were also powerful factors working against their success in the very nature of the industry. Whereas the semiconductor industry and electronics and IT generally are characterized by many competitors, fast product life cycles and rapid company turnover, none of these conditions applies in the cases of the automotive or aerospace sectors. The latter industries, on the contrary, are characterized by few players, huge investments in long product development cycles, and very low company turnover. All are factors mitigating against the prospects of securing technology through leverage, other than on the terms dictated by the incumbents for what they perceive to be their own interests (for example some technology transfer associated with OEM contracting) or, in aerospace, associated with defence and security issues. In other countries of Southeast Asia, such as Indonesia, attempts to enter high-technology sectors such as aerospace, without the accumulated technological capabilities and 'absorptive capacity' that Taiwan can demonstrate, have been even more controversial and problematic. The Indonesian case demonstrates quite vividly the limits and obstacles to catch-up by latecomers in technologically complex fields like aircraft manufacture (prior to the Asian economic crisis).[18]

Of all the countries in the developing world today, China and, to some extent, India, appear to be the most successful at applying the lessons of technology leverage. They are drawing thereby on the accumulated stock of knowledge of the advanced world and applying it in accelerated fashion to their own development agenda (see Hu, 2002; Zhao, 1995). China, in particular, seems to have studied the Taiwan model very closely, and – in spite of strident political denunciations – is applying it very successfully to its own case, in sector after sector in electronics and semiconductors, as well as in aerospace, advanced machine tools, and other knowledge-intensive industries. Of course, the East Asian models developed by Taiwan in particular need to be updated themselves, as discussed at some length in recent World Bank studies.[19]

The principal difference in the world faced by Taiwan in the 1960s and the world faced by Latin American or Central Asian countries today is that the world system today is tightly regulated by the World Trade Organization (WTO), and there are tightly-worded agreements associated with and forming part of the WTO system, such as the agreement on intellectual property rights (TRIPS: Trade Related Intellectual Property Rights) and on investment-related policies such as local content regulations (TRIMS: Trade Related Investment Measures). Current discussions of the prospects for developing countries today are concerned with the barriers created by such WTO instruments.[20]

CONCLUSION

Linkage, leverage and learning are strategies of innovation that are available to latecomer firms everywhere. They enable the firms to make connections with the wider global economy, and draw from these linkages skills, knowledge and technology resources that would otherwise lie well beyond the reach of the developing firm. These strategies are employed in pursuit of the strategic goal of industrial catch-up. This is an elusive goal that few countries so far from the non-Western world have achieved. Japan was the first, and it was followed by the Asian 'tigers', such as Taiwan, South Korea and Singapore. Of the developing countries today, probably China is most determinedly implementing strategies of linkage and leverage in the full pursuit of catch-up with the West, as an over-riding national goal.

The effect of applying strategies of linkage and leverage is that latecomers are enabled to overcome their disadvantages, and exploit their few advantages as latecomers to the full. It makes sense for latecomers to utilize all the resources from the advanced world that they can acquire, in return for providing services such as low-cost manufacturing. The trade-off can be exploited to the advantage of the latecomer only if there is a strategic choice to utilize the linkage for purposes of knowledge gain. This is the inescapable strategic choice that must be made by the latecomer itself.

Earlier theories of industrial development, such as the product life cycle theory, and early versions of global commodity chains, emphasized how firms in latecomer countries were caught up in decisions taken elsewhere, by firms in the advanced countries, and frequently trapped in positions from which they would not be able to extricate themselves (for example as low-cost contract producers without any hope of technological innovation). But the evidence is clear that latecomer firms do not have to adopt a passive stance in relation to global developments. They can make strategic choices like anyone else. But the point is that their choices are made within an institutional setting. Some institutions favour and facilitate firms' taking the risks of using innovation to build their technological capabilities. Other institutions leave them free to adopt the easy road of lowest-cost production. Some therefore drive the country up, while some let it sink down. Some institutions, such as the Economic Development Board in Singapore, have become famous for the unrelenting pressure they put on multinational corporations to upgrade continually the technological level of their operations, and expand the scope of their functions, to the benefit of domestic firms in Singapore. Complementary institutions provide incentives to local firms to become involved with multinationals, as local partners or suppliers. So the institutional framework biases the choices that firms make in certain directions.

In Taiwan, cooperative R&D consortia between competitor firms succeed because they are structured to enable participant firms to fence off their competitive efforts from their collaborative efforts. This is an outcome of institutional design. Countries on the development ladder, then, need to devote as much care to the growth and nurturing of these institutions, as they do to the firms operating within the context that they create. Institutional learning can take place, from country to country – and within countries, as the institutions created themselves adapt to new circumstances and acquire experience. Ultimately, technology leverage is only destined to succeed with the requisite preparation and investment in absorptive capacity, through institutions designed for the purpose, and this is precisely what characterizes Taiwan's experience, and makes it so eminently generalizable in the twenty-first century.

NOTES

1. This chapter is based on a World Bank project completed in 2004. Many thanks to Vandana Chandra for commissioning the study, and to the late Professor Sanjaya Lall for acting as mentor. For a complete version of the report, see Mathews (2004d) and for a more concise version see the chapter on Taiwan in Chandra (2006).
2. For a recent summary, see Lall and Urata (2002). For classic contributions to this literature, see Dahlman (1994), Lall (1990, 1992, 1997, 2000); Enos (1989, 1992); Lin (1994); Enos *et al.* (1997) or Hobday (1995). For a review of Lall and Urata, see Mathews (2004a).
3. The first Export Processing Zone, created under the guidance of Industry Minister K.T. Lee, was at Kaohsiung, opened in 1966. In such zones, companies could import components, and export finished products, free of duties. See Li (1988) for his own exposition.
4. Parts and components rose to account for 9.6 per cent of total exports, as against the world average of 3.4 per cent. Taiwan's share of semiconductors in the second period rose to 8.6 per cent of total exports, as compared with the world average of 3.4 per cent.
5. See Tung (2003) for a definition and discussion. In keeping with my remarks concerning the perniciousness of the doctrine of comparative advantage for a developing country, I propose to call RCA 'revealed competitive advantage', rather than the more passive-sounding 'revealed comparative advantage'.
6. The data for consumer electronics need to be adjusted for a statistical redefinition that occurred in 1985, redefining many goods that had been classified as communications products as consumer goods.
7. See Akamatsu (1962) for the original exposition in English of the 'flying geese' framework, and Ozawa (2003) for a recent authoritative Japanese exposition.
8. See Linden *et al.* (1998) for a description of the Taiwanese experience, and Wong and Mathews (1998) in the same special issue of *Industry and Innovation* for an Introduction that sets the scene for the analysis of this important global industry. For an historical overview, see Murtha *et al.* (2001) and, for a review of the book, Mathews (2004b). For an analysis that links strategies of entry with the cyclical industrial dynamics of the flat panel display industry, by Taiwanese and other East Asian firms, see Mathews (2005).
9. The evolution of Taiwan's R&D alliances and, in particular, their contribution to the technological learning within the electronics, semiconductor, IT and PC industries, is discussed in Mathews (2002a).
10. The USPTO is itself a product of American catch-up efforts; it was the first government agency established by the federal government in the eighteenth century, and its charter is embedded in the US Constitution.
11. See Hu and Mathews (2005) for an analysis of the patenting performance of five East Asian economies, in terms of their uptake of patents from the USPTO, based on the methodology applied by Furman *et al.* (2002) to a panel of 17 OECD countries with data covering the period from 1973 to 1996.
12. This is an important point and one that is neglected in many of the studies of 'national innovation systems'. See Park and Park (2003) for an exploration of this theme, where the intriguing claim is made (based on evidence from East Asian countries) that a threshold expenditure on R&D, amounting to 2 per cent of GDP, is needed before such systemic parallels start to exert themselves.
13. See Hu and Mathews (2005) for an econometric analysis of the national innovative capacity of five East Asian economies, including Taiwan.
14. See Rogers (1995) and Westney (1988) for pioneering studies of the processes of diffusion, and Schnaars (1994) for an analysis of how firms develop competitive advantages based on imitation rather than innovation.
15. On latecomer strategies generally, see Gerschenkron (1962). For the application of the concept to latecomer firms, see Hobday (1995) and Mathews (2002b).
16. Recent treatments of technological catch-up from this perspective include Lall (2000) and, for a closer focus on the firm level, Mathews (2003b).
17. There are important qualifications. In the mid-1990s, for example, the Taiwanese launched a collaborative R&D exercise to develop jointly a four-stroke automotive engine, after an earlier attempt in the 1980s to

develop a two-stroke engine had ended in failure. Technology in this instance was leveraged from the UK firm, Lotus, under the auspices of ITRI's Mechanical Engineering Laboratory. This has resulted in several participant Taiwanese automotive firms becoming engine producers, through a consortium, the Taiwan Engine Company, now a successful exporter of engines to China.

18. See McKendrick (1992) for an assessment of Indonesia's catch-up efforts in the aircraft industry, where the accumulation of impressive technological capabilities was not matched by managerial competences.
19. Yusuf (2003) is concerned in particular with the capacity of East Asia's economies to move towards a more open system of innovation, in transition from the imitation practices that have worked so well in the past.
20. On the situation facing Latin American and Caribbean countries, as seen by a group of World Bank economists, see De Ferranti *et al.* (2002).

REFERENCES

Akamatsu, K. (1962), 'A historical pattern of economic growth in developing countries', *The Developing Economies*, 1 (Mar.–Aug.), 3–25.

Amsden, A.H. (2001), *The Rise of 'The Rest': Challenges to the West from Late-Industrializing Economies*, New York: Oxford University Press.

Amsden, A.H. and W.W. Chu (2002), *Beyond Late Development: Taiwan's Upgrading Policies*, Cambridge, MA: MIT Press.

Chandra, V. (ed.) (2006), *Technology, Adaption, and Exports: How Some Developing Countries Got It Right*, Washington, DC: The World Bank.

Chang, Pao-Long, C. Shih and C. Hsu (1994), 'The formation process of Taiwan's IC industry – method of technology transfer', *Technovation*, **14**(3), 161–71.

Chen, T.-J. (1992), 'Technical change and technical adaptation of multinational firms: the case of Taiwan's electronics industry', *Economic Development and Cultural Change*, **40**(4), 867–81.

Chen, T.-J., B.-L. Chen and Y.-P. Chu (1998), 'The development of Taiwan's electronics industry', paper presented at a conference on Rethinking the East Asian Development Paradigm, Sasakawa Peace Foundation project, Tokyo.

Dahlman, C. (1994), 'Technology strategy in East Asian developing economies', *Journal of Asian Economics*, **5**, 541–72.

De Ferranti, D., G.E. Perry, I. Gill, J.L. Guasch and N. Schady with W.F. Maloney and C. Sanchez Paramo (2002), *Closing the Gap in Education and Technology*, World Bank Latin American and Caribbean Studies, Washington, DC: The World Bank.

Enos, J. (1989), 'Transfer of technology', *Asian–Pacific Economic Literature*, **3**(1), 3–37.

Enos, J. (1992), *The Creation of Technological Capacity in Developing Countries*, London: Pinter.

Enos, J., S. Lall and M. Yun (1997), 'Transfer of technology: an update', *Asian–Pacific Economic Literature*, **11**(1), 56–66.

Furman, J.L., M.E. Porter and S. Stern (2002), 'The determinants of national innovative capacity', *Research Policy*, **31**, 899–933.

Gerschenkron, A. (1962), *Economic Backwardness in Historical Perspective*, Cambridge, MA: The Belknap Press of Harvard University Press.

Hobday, M. (1995), 'East Asian latecomer firms: learning the technology of electronics', *World Development*, **23**(7), 1171–93.

Hu, A. (2002), 'Knowledge and development: the new catch-up strategy', in B. Grewal, L. Xue, P. Sheehan and F. Sun (eds), *China's Future in the Knowledge Economy: Engaging the New World*, Beijing: Tsinghua University Press; Melbourne: Victoria University, Centre for Strategic Economic Studies.

Hu, A.G.Z. and A.B. Jaffe (2001), 'Patent citations and international knowledge flow: The cases of South Korea and Taiwan', NBER working paper 8528, National Bureau of Economic Research, Cambridge, MA.

Hu, M.C. and J.A. Mathews (2005), 'National innovative capacity in East Asia', *Research Policy*, **34**(11), 1322–49.

Jung, S.C. and K.-Y. Imm (2002), 'The patent activities of South Korea and Taiwan: a comparative case study of patent statistics', *World Patent Information*, **24**(4), 303–11.

Kim, L.S. (1997), *Imitation to Innovation: The Dynamics of South Korea's Technological Learning*, Cambridge, MA: Harvard Business School Press.

Lall, S. (1990), *Building Industrial Competitiveness in Developing Countries*, Paris: Development Centre of the OECD.

Lall, S. (1992), 'Technological capabilities and industrialization', *World Development*, **20**(2), 165–86.

Lall, S. (1997), *Learning to Industrialize: The Acquisition of Technological Capability by India*, London: Macmillan.

Lall, S. (2000), 'Technological change and industrialization in the Asian newly industrializing economies: achievements and challenges', in L.S. Kim and R.R. Nelson (eds), *Technology, Learning & Innovation: Experiences of Newly Industrializing Economies*, Cambridge: Cambridge University Press.

Lall, S. and S. Urata (eds) (2002), *Competitiveness, FDI and Technological Activity in East Asia*, Cheltenham, UK and Northampton, MA, USA: Edward Elgar.

Li, K.T. (1988), *The Evolution of Policy behind Taiwan's Development Success*, New Haven: Yale University Press.

Lin, O. (1994), 'Development and transfer of industrial technology in Taiwan, ROC', in O. Lin, C.T. Shih and J.C. Yang (eds), *Development and Transfer of Industrial Technology*, Amsterdam: Elsevier.

Linden, G., J. Hart, S.A. Lenway and T.P. Murtha (1998), 'Flying geese as moving targets: are South Korea and Taiwan catching up with Japan in advanced displays?', *Industry and Innovation*, **5**(1), 11–34.

Mathews, J.A. (1997), 'Silicon Valley of the East: creating a semiconductor industry in Taiwan', *California Management Review*, **39**(4), 1–29.

Mathews, J.A. (2001), 'National systems of economic learning: the case of technology diffusion management in East Asia', *International Journal of Technology Management*, **22**(5/6), 455–79.

Mathews, J.A. (2002a), 'The origins and dynamics of Taiwan's R&D consortia', *Research Policy*, **31**(4), 633–51.

Mathews, J.A. (2002b), 'Competitive advantages of the latecomer firm: a resource-based account of industrial catch-up strategies', *Asia Pacific Journal of Management*, **19**(4), 467–88.

Mathews, J.A. (2003a), 'Competitive dynamics and economic learning: an extended resource-based view', *Industrial and Corporate Change*, **12**(1), 115–45.

Mathews, J.A. (2003b), 'Strategizing by firms in the presence of markets for resources', *Industrial and Corporate Change*, **12**(5), 1157–93.

Mathews, J.A. (2004a), 'Competitiveness, FDI and technological activity in East Asia (review of Lall and Urata, 2002)', *Research Policy*, **33**(6/7), 1060–62.

Mathews, J.A. (2004b), 'New perspectives on global industrial dynamics', *Academy of Management Review*, July, 506–9.

Mathews, J.A. (2004c), '*World industrial development in the 21st century: catch-up strategies and the latecomer effect*', MGSM working paper 2004–20, Macquarie Graduate School of Management, Sydney.

Mathews, J.A. (2004d), '*Understanding the "how to" of technological change: the case of electronics in Taiwan*', MGSM working paper 2004-21, Macquarie Graduate School of Management, Sydney.

Mathews, J.A. (2005), 'Strategy and the crystal cycle', *California Management Review*, **47**(2), 6–32.

Mathews, J.A. and D.S. Cho (2000), *Tiger Technology: The Creation of a Semiconductor Industry in East Asia*, Cambridge: Cambridge University Press.

McKendrick, D. (1992), 'Obstacles to "catch-up": The case of the Indonesian aircraft industry', *Bulletin of Indonesian Economic Studies*, **28**(1), 39–66.

Murtha, T.P., S.A. Lenway and J.A. Hart (2001), *Managing New Industry Creation: Global Knowledge Formation and Entrepreneurship in High Technology*, Stanford, CA: Stanford University Press.

Neely, A. and H. Hii (1999), 'The innovative capacity of firms', report commissioned by the Government Office for East of England, centre for Business Performance, Judge Institute of Management Studies, University of Cambridge.

Okita, S. (1985), 'Presentation: prospect of Pacific economies', *Pacific Cooperation: Issues and Opportunities*, report of the 4th Pacific Economic Cooperation Conference, Seoul, 29 April–1 May.

OTA (1983), *International Competitiveness in Electronics*, Washington, DC: Congress of the United States, Office of Technology Assessment.

Ozawa, T. (2003), 'Pax Americana-led macro-clustering and flying geese-style catch-up in East Asia: mechanisms of regionalized endogenous growth', *Journal of Asian Economics*, **13**(6), 699–713.

Park, Y.T. and G.M. Park (2003), 'When does a national system of innovation start to display *systemic* behavior?', *Industry and Innovation*, **10**(4), 403–14.

Rogers, E. (1995), *Diffusion of Innovations*, 4th edn, New York: The Free Press.

San, G. (1993), 'National systems supporting technical advance in industry: the case of Taiwan', in R. Nelson (ed.), *National Innovation Systems*, New York: Oxford University Press.

Sato, Y. (1997), 'Diverging development paths of the electronics industry in South Korea and Taiwan', *The Developing Economies*, **35**(4), 401–21.

Schnaars, S. (1994), *Managing Imitation Strategies: How Later Entrants Seize Markets from Pioneers*, New York: Free Press.

Schumpeter, A. (1942/1950), *Capitalism, Socialism and Democracy*, New York: Harper and Brothers.

Suarez-Villa, L. (1990), 'Invention, inventive learning, and innovative capacity', *Behavioral Science*, **35**(4), 290–310.

Tung, A.-C. (2001), 'Taiwan's semiconductor industry: what the state did and did not', *Review of Development Economics*, **5**(2), 266–88.

Tung, A.-C. (2002), 'Industrial targeting: lessons from past errors and successes of Hong Kong and Taiwan', *The World Economy*, **25**(8), 1047–61.

Tung, A.-C. (2003), 'Beyond flying geese: the expansion of East Asia's electronics trade', *German Economic Review*, **4**(1), 35–51.

UNCTAD (2003), *World Investment Report 2003: FDI Policies for Development – National and International Perspectives*, Geneva: United Nations Conference on Trade and Development.

UNIDO (2002), *Industrial Development Report 2002/2003: Competing through Innovation and Learning*, Vienna: United Nations Industrial Development Organization.

Wade, R. (1990), *Governing the Market: Economic Theory and the Role of Government in East Asian Industrialization*, Princeton, NJ: Princeton University Press.

Westney, E. (1988), *Imitation and Innovation*, Cambridge, MA: Harvard University Press.

Wong, P.K. and J. Mathews (1998), 'Competing in the global flat panel display industry: introduction', *Industry and Innovation*, **5**(1), 1–10.

Wu, R.-I. and M.-S. Tsen (1997), 'The development of information industry in Taiwan', paper delivered to the conference 'Foundation for Advanced Studies in International Development', Tokyo.

Yusuf, S. (2003), *Innovative East Asia: The Future of Growth*, Washington, DC: The World Bank.

Zhao, H. (1995), 'Technological imports and their impacts on the enhancement of China's indigenous technological capability', *Journal of Development Studies*, **31**(4), 585–602.

PART IV

Business, Development and Policy Issues

17. Cultural considerations of business and economic development in East Asia

F. Gerard Adams and Heidi Vernon

This chapter is concerned with the conflicting views about the role of culture in fostering the rapid economic development of East Asia. Some scholars have maintained that 'culture makes almost all the difference'.[1] Most of this work focuses on the influence of a stable and, perhaps, unique 'East Asian' cultural pattern, though some scholars emphasize the evolution of culture in an increasingly integrated world economy. Others have explained East Asian growth largely in non-cultural terms, on the basis of comparative advantage and trade, foreign direct investment flows, and economic development policy (see chapters in Part III of this volume). Still others have tried to combine cultural and economic considerations, for example seeing cultural factors as important ingredients in the absence of formal systems and legal remedies early in the development process, and as potential sources of difficulties as economic development matures or as it becomes more globalized.

In the next section, we review the relevant aspects of the history of economic development in East Asia and its current momentum. We then examine and synthesize the principal strands of literature, comparing cultural and economic development approaches to Asian business success. A synthesis of these views is highlighted. In the final section, we consider some survey studies, and relate the diverse views about the role of culture to East Asian managers' cultural perceptions and business practice. A brief concluding section evaluates the evidence and points to unanswered questions, emphasizing the informational gap between cultural attributes, business performance and economic development.

CULTURALLY IMPORTANT ASPECTS OF EAST ASIAN GROWTH PERFORMANCE

In the past 50 years, the record of economic advancement in East and Southeast Asia has been remarkable. Beginning close to the subsistence level, the countries of this region have entered on a rapid development path that has already taken some of them to advanced country living standards. A process that took two hundred years in the West is being accomplished in two generations in East Asia. This rapid development pattern is characteristic of countries located in the East Asian region, many of which are geographically adjacent to each other and have a common cultural heritage.

The rapid growth of East Asia is summarized in Table 17.1. Although growth was relatively slow in the early years of the second half of the century, since the 1970s growth has been very rapid. Only with maturity has there been a return to more moderate growth in the

Table 17.1   East Asian economic growth (per cent per year)

	1970–80	1980–90	1990–2002	2002–3
China	5.5	10.2	9.7	9.1
Hong Kong (China)	9.2	6.9	3.8	3.3
Indonesia	7.2	5.3	3.6	4.1
South Korea	10.1	8.9	5.6	3.1
Malaysia	7.9	5.3	6.2	5.2
Philippines	6.0	1.0	3.5	4.5
Singapore	8.3	6.7	6.7	1.1
Thailand	7.1	7.6	3.7	6.7
Vietnam	—	4.6	7.6	7.2
United States	2.8	3.5	3.3	2.9
Japan	4.3	4.2	1.3	2.7

Source: World Bank.

Table 17.2   East Asian per capita income, 2002, in US dollars per capita

	Exchange rate basis	PPP basis
China	960	4 520
Hong Kong (China)	24 690	27 490
Indonesia	710	3 070
South Korea	9 930	16 960
Malaysia	3 540	8 500
Philippines	1 030	3 322
Singapore	20 690	23 730
Thailand	2 000	4 300
Vietnam	430	2 300
United States	35 400	36 110
Japan	34 010	27 380

Note: PPP is Purchasing Power Parity.

Source: World Bank.

most advanced countries. Living standards and wages have risen rapidly. Some countries have already achieved advanced country income levels and status (South Korea, for example, is a member of the OECD), but others are still far behind (Table 17.2). At the same time there have been sharp increases in urbanization and in industrial development (Table 17.3).

It is not possible to measure how much these changes have been the result of cultural attributes or, in turn, how they have altered cultural perceptions of the populations in the East Asian countries. The impact on culture of population movement to the cities and of occupational change must be substantial. Note the sharp decline in the rural share of the population and the large and rapidly growing share of industrial output in most of the countries of the region (Table 17.3).

Table 17.3   Other country characteristics (2002)

	Population			Industrial Output		Exports (% of GDP)	Gross Capital Formation (% of GDP)	Foreign Investment (% of GDP)
	(million)	(% rural) 1990	(% rural) 2002	(% of GDP) 2002–3	(growth, % p.a.)			
China	1 280	80	62	53	11.9	29	40	11.7
Hong Kong	7	9	0	12	—	15	23	26.9
Indonesia	212	78	57	44	8.8	30	16	2.1
South Korea	48	43	17	34	7.6	35	29	1.0
Malaysia	24	58	41	47	8.8	114	24	5.8
Philippines	80	63	40	33	3.1	49	19	1.5
Singapore	4	0	0	35	6.9	141	21	11.7
Thailand	62	83	80	43	6.1	65	24	0.8
Vietnam	80	81	75	39	11.2	56	32	4.0

Source: World Bank.

East Asian development is generally seen as export-based, though high domestic rates of capital formation and internal development and investment-promoting public policies have played an important role. The countries in the region are at various points on a development track that can be termed a 'development ladder'. This evolution is based on an underlying product cycle process (Vernon, 1966). Starting with simple labour-intensive products, the East Asian developing economies have gone successively to more sophisticated and capital-intensive goods: first to clothing and apparel, athletic footwear, toys and electronic assembly, then to heavier mass production industries, like automobiles and parts, and, finally, to high tech and sophisticated services.

The stages of this pattern of development are shown in Figure 17.1. The changes in industrial structure over the years 1950–2010, shown in Figure 17.2, can be traced through to moves of specific industries between countries. For example, as labour costs rose, the production of athletics shoes moved successively from the US to South Korea, then to Taiwan and Thailand, and then to China, Indonesia and Vietnam. The essentials of this 'development ladder' process can be summarized as follows (Adams, 1998):

- countries take advantage of low labour cost to compete successfully in labour-intensive products;
- products become standardized and price becomes the most important factor in competitiveness;
- labour cost rises as labour becomes relatively more scarce and countries' living standards improve;
- labour-intensive industries are no longer competitive at home;
- industries migrate to countries where labour cost is lower;
- the more advanced countries seek more sophisticated capital-intensive and less standardized products.

Stage 1	Primary products	Abundant cheap land and labour
Stage 2	Labour-intensive manufactures	Low-cost labour
Stage 3	Hi-tech manufactures	Capital-intensive, technically sophisticated products
Stage 4	Services (high level)	Educated labour force

Figure 17.1   The development ladder

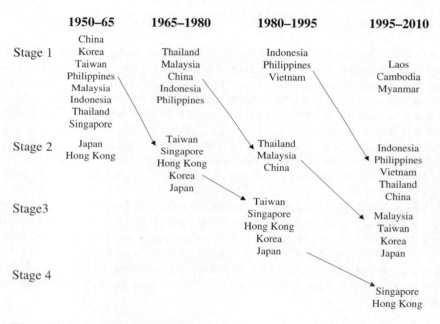

Figure 17.2   The stages of the product cycle process

This is a development process that closely links countries on lower rungs of the development ladder with more advanced countries. Ethnic networks of regionally oriented entrepreneurs and investors facilitate this process. In the case of China's export industries, for example, Taiwanese and Hong Kong-based business people have been extremely important.

While East Asian development has common features, as we have noted, in some important respects the East Asian countries are quite diverse. The leading countries and 'provinces', such as Singapore, Korea, Hong Kong (China) and Taiwan, are urbanized and focus on high-tech manufacturing or advanced financial and management services. Some countries, notably Malaysia and Indonesia, have substantial resource bases. Some, like China, are very large with potentially enormous geopolitical influence, while others, sometimes no less important, are very small, even city-states like Singapore. Some, including China, still have a large proportion of their population in subsistence agriculture. Some, like Singapore, have been organized as market economies since the colonial period, though government-owned and directed industries have played an important role, while others, like China and Vietnam, are still in transition from a history of economic planning and public ownership.

Finally, the ethnic and religious/cultural characteristics of the East Asian populations are quite diverse. Japanese, Chinese and Koreans share variants of a Confucian tradition, but Muslim, Christian and Hindu groups are also important in some countries in the area. However, the business world of much of the region has an ethnically Chinese overlay. As a result, despite their diversity, a common cultural and commercial influence ties the countries of the region together.

From an organizational perspective, East Asia represents a crossroads from the family business form prevalent among locally based firms in most of the region to the transnational European, American or Japanese corporations doing business there. In China and Vietnam, managers bring a still different background, since many of them have been employed by state or provincially owned enterprises (or large partially privatized firms). In China, only very small businesses can be said to be entrepreneurially owned and the large family business remains an exception (see also Chapter 6 in this volume). On the other hand, as we have noted in China, entrepreneurs from the ethnic Chinese community abroad, particularly from Hong Kong and Taiwan, have been very active in providing direct foreign investment and in building China's export industries.

Among these different settings, managers are likely to have very different experience and incentives. Business practices may also be different; they are less personal, and more routinized and formal in large public corporations and state-owned enterprises than in smaller business and family-owned firms. As economic development takes place and as East Asian countries become more integrated with the world economy, these different strains of management culture and practice learn from each other.

Finally, public policy has played in important role in promoting East Asian economic development.[2] Again, there are important common characteristics and some differences. The principal and most successful economic development policy has been the export orientation strategy of all the East Asian countries. This has been supported by investment promotion and in most countries, but not in all, by encouraging foreign direct investment. These policies have been the basis for the vast expansion of export manufacturing that has occurred in the East Asian countries, one after the other. In the process their domestic markets have also burgeoned. Government decision making has played an important role. Policies encouraging investment and growth are common to all the countries in the region.

But the role of the public sector relevant to private industry and the resulting structure of industry varies among the countries. In Singapore, for example, government has been a key player in fostering the development of a communications and IT-based economy. In some cases, nationally supported or state-owned companies have been a part of this process. Hong Kong, while now part of China, practises much more limited public sector intervention. For industrialization, South Korean policy has supported its large conglomerates, the *chaebol*, many of which operated heavy industry, whereas, in contrast, Taiwan encouraged small and medium-size firms in the electronics fields. Malaysia and Indonesia have attempted to advance technical progress by promoting technologically advanced projects. The Chinese case is particularly interesting. While state-owned enterprises (SOEs) are being de-emphasized, many of the most successful local firms and joint venture partners have a substantial share of public, often city or provincial, ownership.

As the World Bank's (1993) *The East Asian Miracle* and Robert Wade's (1990) *Governing the Market* demonstrate, there is no agreement among economists on whether or where industry-specific government direction has made a significant contribution to the growth process and whether it is likely to do so in the future. It is possible only to speculate on the importance of cultural factors in influencing the role of government in the development process. Singapore, a country where growth was led by a disciplined – one might even say Mandarin – government service, is a traditional example. By virtue of its small size and concentrated urban location, though, it is very much a special case. Looking over a broader range of countries in the region, it does not appear that cultural homogeneity, to the extent that it exists, can account for government development strategies or intervention.

CULTURAL APPROACHES AND ECONOMIC DEVELOPMENT

Culture as a basis for business and economic development has a long history, dating back to Weber's (1904) controversial thesis that the Calvinist work ethic lies behind the development of capitalist society.[3] The cultural approach has been revived to explain East Asia's rapid development (Huntington, 1996; Landes, 1998). Conflicting views are collected in Harrison and Huntington (2000). The thesis that Asian culture has been responsible for Asian success (we will refer to it as the AC-AS paradigm) has been largely a matter of historical and anthropological thinking. With reference to East Asia, the emphasis is on Confucian cultural values said to include the following:

- a strong sense of responsibility to the family, the group, and/or to the nation;
- reciprocal personal relationships, particularly to the same ethnic group (*guanxi*);
- a top-down view of control, with respect for elders, business leaders and government;
- acceptance of the prevailing system of social and enterprise governance;
- intense desire for harmony and stability; and
- a strong tradition of self-improvement and education, though not necessarily a work ethic (Pye, 2000).

These values are thought to apply to a broad East Asian region. Huntington (1998: 45), for example, writes that 'Chinese civilization is more than Confucianism and also transcends China as a political entity. The term "Sinic", which has been used by many scholars, appropriately describes the common culture of China and the Chinese communities in Southeast Asia and elsewhere outside of China as well as the related cultures.'

The AC-AS hypothesis is that Confucian values are a principal explanation of East Asia's rapid growth. The proponents of this view would argue that values interact with other considerations, like resources, investment, exchange rates, foreign direct investment and public policy, to account for successful economic development. Precisely which cultural dimensions are responsible is not always clear. The notion of allegiance to the group and reciprocal relationships between members of the ethnic family are the most relevant. The links among members of the ethnic Chinese group facilitate business relationships. On the other hand, Fukuyama (1995) fears that 'trust', the title of his book, will not be sufficient to enable East Asians to operate successfully in competition with worldwide multinational corporations. Paradoxically, as we have noted, the East Asian region is not as culturally homogeneous as one might imagine, and it may turn out to be more culturally flexible than some have supposed.

An interesting question is whether the issue is one of *culture* or one of *organizational structure*. In East and Southeast Asia, many businesses, even those organized as corporations, are owned and operated by a single extended family. Succession is usually to the next generation of family. In some countries, Malaysia and Indonesia, for example, close links, sometimes in return for financial considerations, between ethnic Chinese-dominated family businesses and government officials have played an important role. Outside top-level professional management (non-family) operates only in the largest firms and those that have significant European, American or Japanese participation or government ownership (Perkins, 2000; see also Chapters 15 and 18 in this volume). These issues of business organization confound the issue of cultural impact. It is frequently not possible to say whether the behaviours observed are culturally East Asian, or whether they are a reflection of family ownership and would occur in family firms anywhere in the world. A similar issue can be posed with regard to management technology. Are the interpersonal relationships observed in East Asian business reflective of traditional, in the meaning of 'old-fashioned', management rather than of East Asian culture?

Dimensions of Culture

An approach more firmly based on modern conceptual and empirical work in the organizational studies field is comprised in the work of Hofstede ([1980] 1984), Hofstede (1998), and of the many others who have followed similar theory- or survey-based work.[4] In contrast to the historians, the social scientists seek to identify the underlying dimensions of culture that distinguish among different societies. The methodology for this work has been based on questionnaire surveys and statistical factor analysis. Hofstede, for example, carried out surveys on the personnel of subsidiaries of IBM in more than 40 countries. On the basis of factor analysis of these data, Hofstede argues that national and regional cultural differences can be recognized along the following dimensions: power distance, uncertainty avoidance, masculinity/femininity and individualism/collectivism.

In his later work, Hofstede added Short- and Long-Term Time Orientation as another cultural dimension. In a study of China, Hofstede and Bond (1988) found still another category, Confucian dynamism, measuring work ethic and respect for tradition. Others have adopted similar cultural characteristic classification schemes, for example, Kluckhohn and

Strodtbeck (1961), Inkeles and Levinson (1969) and Trompenaars and Hampden-Turner (1998), and the Global Leadership Organizational Behavior Effectiveness programme (GLOBE), House *et al.* (2002). Their categories are not identical to Hofstede's, but one can see considerable overlap.[5] Trompenaars and Hampden-Turner, for example, build the following classification, drawing on classical work by Parsons:

- universalism versus particularism (rules versus relationships),
- communitarianism versus individualism (the group versus the individual),
- neutral versus emotional (the range of feelings expressed),
- diffuse versus specific (the range of involvement),
- achievement versus ascription (how status is accorded).

Some of the dimensions fit well the East Asian culture theme, for example the group versus the individual. Some fit closely with business practice, for example how status is accorded. The GLOBE studies add Performance Orientation and Humane Orientation and, finally, a dimension for Gender Egalitarianism, an important question from the perspective of values, as well as of business practice. We will consider below the difficulties of relating the cultural attributes to business practice and performance.

Economic Development Approaches

The economic development literature puts much less emphasis on cultural factors than on economic fundamentals and policies.[6] After all, cultural attributes have been characteristic of the East Asian region for much longer than its historically recent rapid economic development. The factors fundamental to economic growth in the economic development literature are savings and investment, exports, inflows of foreign direct investment, and macroeconomic stability.

Development economists are seldom in agreement about the 'what and when' of the initiation of the development process, but they are clear about the role of exports and investment, domestic and foreign. In contrast to the old import substitution ideas, they have witnessed the expansion of exports as an engine of industrialization and growth. This is not just a matter of textbook economics. Sachs (2000), for example, a very 'real-world' economist, emphasizes economic fundamentals. The 'flying geese' proponents (Akamatsu, 1962; Kojima, 2000) and the product cycle/development ladder views emphasize the links between countries, but they do so in terms of changing patterns of comparative advantage rather than common cultural orientations. As we have noted, development economists differ considerably about the role of government policies, in general, and about specific interventions. Cultural factors may have contributed to successful development, but, in the economic development literature, culture seems to play a role subsidiary to real economic endowments and policy.

Finally, some scholars have argued that economic and institutional changes influence culture and that divergent cultures tend to converge, as increasing international interaction takes place. Landes (2000: 3) argues that 'because culture and economic performance are linked, change in one will work back on the other'. Sachs (2000) endows the social system with positive feedback. Porter (2000: 27), who is a believer that culture can be modified rapidly, argues that 'What we are witnessing, in many ways, is the emergence of the core of an international economic culture that cuts across individual cultural divides and will increasingly be shared.' Inkeles (1998) also emphasizes the convergence thesis, entitling his book *One World Emerging*. One of the most current issues, in the rapidly changing global business context, is the response of business culture and of business practice when 'cultures meet'.[7]

Culture is not independent of economics, and cultural factors may be as much the result of economic change as its cause. Significantly for our discussion, Inkeles (ibid.: 345) says that 'Attitudes may change but behaviour may not, and the reverse pattern is also observed.' Moreover, the links between culture-based views and business behaviour are uncertain.

CULTURAL CONSIDERATIONS AND BUSINESS PRACTICES

Exactly what is meant by culture and how it affects business practices is an important issue. According to Porter (2000: 14), 'Economic culture is defined as beliefs, attitudes, and values that bear on economic activities.' Such a definition is overly broad and yet, also, overly narrow.[8] It encompasses views that relate to the society as a whole, like conformance to prevailing social norms. We will term them *social views*. It also includes individual aims, like the individual desire for high income or security. We will term these *personal objectives*. They may have very different implications for business interaction.

Porter's definition of economic culture also fails to recognize that culture is more than an assembly of diverse views. The cultural factors said to play a role in East Asia are not unrelated attitudinal dimensions. Rather, they are closely linked in a particular pattern of views about group (family, nation, ethnic group) allegiance and relationships between related individuals. This aspect of East Asian commercial culture serves as one explanation, though not the only one, for the emphasis on personal relationships and the top-down organization of many East Asian businesses.

With these exceptions, little is known about the way cultural values influence business practice in East Asia. A widespread view is that culture determines 'work values'. These are beliefs or attitudes about the cultural concepts that we have noted above, like *power distance* (Hofstede, [1980] 1984), Hofstede (1998), *machiavellianism* (Ralston *et al.*, 1993) or 'time is money' (Ralston *et al.*, 1999). But it is not clear how cultural considerations translate into values relevant to the job and, perhaps more importantly, into management practices and performance. Pye (2000) argues that culture works some times, but not in other circumstances. Cultural values are clusters that can be combined in different ways and produce different results.

Perkins (2000) argues that East Asian cultural arrangements in business represent an adaptation to the absence of laws and enforceable contracts at the early stages of East Asian development. But he also points out that they may be less important in a world that is increasingly internationalized, and uses a legal and formal contract system. Haider's (1999) similar position is that, in the early development stage, a family-based governance system (FBS) in Asian firms led to 'economically efficient use of limited entrepreneurial abilities', 'internal' financing and effective monitoring. At a more advanced stage of development, particularly when there is external financing, the FBS is not able to provide appropriate controls (see also Chapter 3 in this volume).

Fukuyama (1995) contrasts Asian business with multinational business practice, arguing that, in an increasingly global business world, 'trust' is not a sufficient basis for international business operations. Multinational firms rely instead on formal procedures and contracts, and are frequently organized in a horizontal committee management structure. It is precisely the reliance on informal relationships that may be partially responsible for the 1997 Asian economic crisis (and possibly current problems in China), where credit was extended without adequate evaluation of whether the debtors would be able to meet their obligations. The connection of cultural or organizational considerations with the crisis has had much discussion under the rubric of 'crony capitalism'. Krugman (1998), Corsetti *et al.* (1998a, 1998b), and Claessens *et al.* (2000) focus on concentrated ownership, insecure financial foundations and group affiliation as a basis for triggering the crisis, but one may want to dispute whether these are cultural or organizational factors.

The relationships between culture and business practices raise important and challenging issues. Even though Hofstede's work was done in a business setting, his original studies had little to say about the implications of culture for business practices. But the cultural concepts he developed have been basic, particularly to applications concerned with intercultural relationships in international business. In his 1998 study, Hofstede includes questions on business practices, but sees 'perception of practices to be entirely different from values and usually different from attitudes' and, in Hofstede (1997: 182), he notes that 'At the organizational level, cultural differences reside mostly in practices, less in values.'[9]

Others (Cox, 1994; Sackman *et al.*, 1997), however, have considered the interactions between organizational culture, individual attitudes and business practice as a complex, layered phenomenon. With the exception of 'relationship-based' business dealing and top-down management that we have noted above, studies that link business practices and micro-level cultural attributes tend to focus on particular disciplinary categories, like strategy (Kogut and Singh, 1988; see also Chapter 2 in this volume) and human resource management (Tung and Thomas, 2003; see also Chapter 5 in this volume) or on straightforward business practice issues encountered in a cross-cultural context, like intercultural teams, training, mergers and negotiations, international alliances, joint ventures, and so on (Bing, 2004; see also Chapter 5 in this volume).

Linking cultural attributes to business operations, ideally, linking them to business success or failure, poses many difficulties. There is the complexity of the influence of cultural factors at different levels of the organization. Different cultural attributes may make themselves felt in different settings: a 'top-down' orientation has very different consequences at the top than at the bottom. In addition, there is the complexity of business functions, some that may involve personal interactions among equals, like sales, and others that may require independent action like strategy or planning. The success of business operations depends on many factors besides culture. It is not always possible to take into account or hold constant for other issues, like the business climate, the stage of economic development, or the nature and organization of the industry. A complicating consideration is that business practices are closely linked to the organizational characteristics of the enterprise, whether it is a public corporation, a family-owned business or a state-owned enterprise, and to other factors, like the size of the firm or whether it is a national or transnational business, or whether it is a joint venture or wholly-owned enterprise. And, in turn, the organization of the business and its performance may depend on the cultural background of its founders.[10]

Do standardization and globalization mean that we are on the way toward a merged world culture and business practice, and/or can global competition influence business practice without changing the underlying cultural setting? The developing field of 'cross-cultural management' seeks to answer these questions and to develop appropriate practices (Tjosvold and Leung, 2003; see also Chapter 8 in this volume). Finally, returning to the question of economic development, the links between culturally determined business practices and the economic success of East Asia remain unclear. Even if we pick out culturally determined business practices that are specific to East Asia, we may not be able to say how they fit into the AC-AS hypothesis of East Asian development.

Survey Studies

Hofstede's ([1980] 1984) seminal empirical work on business-related culture made no attempt to relate business or economic performance to the cultural characteristics he identified. But, as we have noted, there have been numerous applications.[11] More recently, the Globe study (House *et al.*, 2002) also used worldwide data collection to identify cultural factors, in this case, those associated with business leadership. Table 17.4 shows indexes of cultural characteristics for East Asian countries, as compared to the US, drawn from Hofstede's work.[12] We note that, in terms of power distance, the East Asian countries average far above the US. In contrast, with respect to individualism and masculinity, the US is far above the East Asian average. For uncertainty avoidance, the range in East Asia is quite high, from very low in Singapore to high in South Korea. The US figure is close to the average for East Asia.

These results support the notion that East Asian cultures have much top-down distance, that is management by the owners or directors with little voice for the employees. American culture is seen to have more individuality and masculinity, which presumably means that US workers are more outspoken (participatory?) and assertive. Variations among countries are substantial. It is unfortunate that corresponding data are not listed for China, since that information might indicate the combined impact of culture and of the Chinese transition experience on these reported indexes.

A recent questionnaire study (Adams and Vernon, 2005) comparing Thai, Chinese and US managers gives a picture of the types of results that can be obtained. The objective of the study was to investigate the differences in cultural characteristics between East Asian (mainland Chinese and Thai nationals) and American managers, and, if possible, to relate them to business practices. A questionnaire survey of young managers was carried out in 2002 in China (Nanjing University Business School), Thailand (Sasin Graduate Institute of Business Administration, Bangkok), and the US (Northeastern University, College of Business Administration, Boston). The sample was small (59 in China, 53 in Thailand, and 44 in the US). Most of the respondents had work experience as managers or professionals in large firms. A notable fact is that only a small fraction of the Chinese respondents worked in private enterprises, with 60 per cent who worked in state-owned or collective organizations. Because the respondents were young and participants in an English language programme, there may be some bias toward international awareness that would not appear in a strictly native language group. On the other hand, the sample was not selective, in the sense that almost all of the participants in each class submitted a response. The questionnaire was adapted and expanded from one suggested by Hofstede

Table 17.4 Indexes of cultural characteristics

	Singapore	Hong Kong	Thailand	Taiwan	Philippines	Malaysia	Indonesia	S. Korea	E.A. average	USA
Power distance	74	68	64	58	94	104	78	60	75	40
Uncertainty avoidance	8	29	64	69	44	36	48	85	48	46
Individualism	20	25	20	17	32	26	14	18	22	91
Masculinity	48	57	34	45	64	50	46	39	48	62

Source: Drawn from tables in Hofstede (1997).

([1980] 1984, appendix I): 'Values Survey Module recommended for future cross-cultural survey studies'.[13]

The study made a distinction between personal aims, social objectives and business practices. While personal and social objectives may reflect cultural influences, they may have different implications for practice in the business environment. For example, *social objectives* may reflect the society's values, but may or may not translate into actions at the level of the enterprise. *Personal aims* may differ from the practices of the firm, where the respondent is employed. Moreover, in the case of personal aims, respondents may translate their objectives into the selection of their occupation or job, rather than simply into work practices. As we have noted, the questions concerned with *business practices* focus on such factual matters as the firm's organizational structure, personnel issues or the relations between managers and employees, and so on.

Within each of these categories there are various possible practice issues. The inevitable overlaps between these categories are apparent, but inescapable. For example, centralized governance may imply formal procedures and impersonal relationships, particularly in larger firms. Some business procedures may be universal or may be related to the characteristics of the business. Some practices are local customs that may or may not reflect cultural considerations. The questions posed in our questionnaire attempt to pick up some important aspects of each of the categories above.

Analysis of Survey Results

Survey results are summarized in Tables 17.5–17.7, dealing respectively with personal objectives, social objectives and business practices. In each case we show the mean value of the response (Likert Scale, 5 = most important, 1 = little importance), for the Chinese, Thai and US respondents. Chi-squared probabilities for differences between Chinese and US respondents, US and Thai respondents, Chinese and Thai respondents, and between all three groups are shown. For business practices, a 'yes, no, don't know' scale was used. We show the percentage answering 'yes', omitting 'don't knows'.

With regard to *personal objectives* (Table 17.5), the survey shows that, while all workers share the desire for accomplishment, there are significant differences between East Asian and American responses. This applies particularly with respect to the Americans' desire for personal rewards, high earnings (Q.2), and family time (Q.6), in contrast to Asian desire for job security (Q.4) and working for a prestigious organization (Q.5). Despite their common East Asian origin, there is also a significant difference between Chinese and Thai respondents, with respect to working for a prestigious organization, an objective that is much more important to the Chinese.

On *social values* (Table 17.6), traditional East Asian or Confucian values are readily apparent in the Asian responses. There are significant differences between East Asian and American managers concerning acceptance of differences in pay (Q.13), desire for harmony (Q.14), avoidance of uncertainty (Q.19), respect for government (Q.22) and for the prevailing hierarchy (Q.18 and Q.24). Asian managers, more than Americans, believe that firms should cooperate rather than compete (Q.15). Perhaps reflecting the socialist mentality, Chinese respondents, more than others, judge their government on the basis of whether it provides for the poor and the aged (Q.20). Finally, an important difference is the fact that the Chinese respondents believe that men are more capable than women, a view

Business, development and policy issues

Table 17.5   Survey of personal objectives

Personal objectives	Mean			Chi-squared probability			
	Ch	US	Th	Ch-US	US-Th	Ch-Th	Ch-US-Th
1. Have tasks at work that give a sense of accomplishment	4.03	4.25	4.02	0.265	0.50	0.239	0.190
2. Have opportunities for high earnings	3.85	4.36	3.96	0.008**	0.007**	0.367	0.009**
3. Have opportunities for promotion	4.03	4.22	3.77	0.459	0.116	0.418	0.267
4. Have employment security	3.41	3.89	3.11	0.035*	0.015*	0.362	0.015*
5. Work in a large prestigious company	3.38	2.71	2.63	0.004**	0.273	0.004**	0.004**
6. Have sufficient time for personal or family life	3.39	4.60	3.65	0.000***	0.004**	0.577	0.000***
7. Have little tension and stress on the job	2.61	3.16	2.89	0.060*	0.629	0.352	0.317
8. Have a good working relationship with one's direct superior	3.73	3.93	3.65	0.332	0.040*	0.146	0.212
9. Have considerable freedom to adopt one's own approach to the job	3.73	3.78	3.67	0.662	0.950	0.279	0.645
10. Work with people who cooperate well with one another	3.90	4.05	3.61	0.580	0.161	0.127	0.091*
11. Work in a well-defined job situation where expectations are clear	3.55	3.45	3.20	0.634	0.426	0.092*	0.289

Note: Statistically significant difference: *** at 0.001 level, ** at 0.01 level, * at 0.1 level.

that is not shared by Americans or Thais (Q.23). Other aspects of the workers' outlooks do not show East–West differences, for example the need to maintain good relationships with fellow workers, the need to follow company rules and the desire to participate in work-related decisions.

With regard to *business practices* (Table 17.7), it is more difficult to draw meaningful conclusions from responses. Inevitably, the responses reflect the impressions of the respondents, rather than objective measures of firm performance. Workers frequently do not know their enterprises' operating rules and practices, and are not likely to have an objective view of the firms' performance. Not surprisingly, in some important respects, business practice is the same worldwide. For example, most firms make regular reviews of employee performance and they make regular financial reports; managers can count on continued employment and will get preference over outsiders on promotions.

Allowing for the limitations of the questionnaire approach, there are nevertheless some clear differences in the responses. East Asian firms are characterized by top-down

Table 17.6   Survey of social values

	Mean			Chi-squared probability			
	Ch	US	Th	Ch-US	US-Th	Ch-Th	Ch-US-Th
12. A company's rules should not be broken even when the employee thinks it's in the firm's best interests	3.28	3.13	3.04	0.498	0.883	0.541	0.544
13. It is proper to have large differences in pay between low and high ranking members of an organization	4.00	3.42	3.45	0.001**	0.917	0.007**	0.014*
14. It is very important to maintain harmony within social and business groups	4.08	3.62	4.04	0.006**	0.027*	0.205	0.009**
15. Firms should cooperate with other firms rather than compete	3.55	2.58	3.21	0.000***	0.003**	0.031*	0.000***
16. Most business managers can be trusted	3.20	3.02	2.69	0.715	0.102	0.002**	0.011*
17. Quite a few employees dislike work and will avoid it if they can	2.92	3.40	3.22	0.122	0.681	0.350	0.276
18. In a well ordered society all have a rightful place, some high, some low	3.51	3.04	3.46	0.049*	0.023*	0.596	0.042*
19. The uncertainty inherent in life is a continuous threat that must be fought	3.41	2.64	3.43	0.002**	0.003**	0.746	0.007**
20. A society should be judged by how well it cares for its poor and elderly	3.92	3.31	3.50	0.006**	0.777	0.100	0.047*
21. Government officials usually know what is best for society and their orders should be followed	2.82	2.15	2.15	0.010*	0.039*	0.007**	0.001**
22. A strong government works best for a developing economy even if it is not a democratic government	3.30	2.73	3.07	0.071*	0.283	0.183	0.082*
23. On average, men are more capable of contributing to an organization's overall goals than women	3.63	1.67	2.08	0.000***	0.150	0.000***	0.000***

Table 17.6 (continued)

	Mean			Chi-squared probability			
	Ch	US	Th	Ch-US	US-Th	Ch-Th	Ch-US-Th
24. People act differently toward others depending on whether they are above or below in the organization's hierarchy	3.35	3.96	3.96	0.001**	0.569	0.001*	0.000***
25. Employees should have a lot of say in important work-related decisions	3.95	4.15	3.98	0.176	0.519	0.626	0.494
26. It is important to maintain polite relationships with people even if we strongly disagree with them	3.90	3.98	3.67	0.549	0.257	0.221	0.299

Note: Statistically significant difference: * at the 0.1 level, ** at the 0.01 level, *** at the 0.001 level.

management, delegating less authority to lower staff, and subordinates are more afraid to express disagreement than in American firms (Q.39 and Q.36). East Asian firms are less likely to use formal management procedures (Q.28, Q.33, Q.37 and Q.38). Even though Chinese enterprises are often publicly owned, 'relationship' culture is apparent, in that Chinese firms tend more to hire workers on the basis of family relationships, and place less emphasis on formal criteria for promotion (Q.29). Chinese traditional respect for education is also apparent in business practice, in hiring, for example (Q.30). Differences of dress (Q.40) and first-name basis (Q.43) reflect local custom, and may not have significance for business affairs. Again, the issue of the role of women is apparent, with Chinese (but not Thai) respondents saying that women have fewer significant possibilities for promotion (Q.35). There is no way, unfortunately, to gauge how or, indeed, whether the differences in business practices have impacts on business performance.

CONCLUSION

To summarize, there are clearly cultural differences between Asian and American managers. Our survey largely supports other recent thinking and surveys about East Asian business culture. In Asia, there is strong evidence of traditional values in the responses about personal and social objectives: job security, group cohesion, desire for harmony, avoidance of uncertainty, acceptance of existing hierarchy and relationship-based 'trust'. Despite the distinct history and organization of Chinese business, values in mainland China reflect traditional Asian characteristics. American respondents, on the other hand, are much more concerned with personal entitlements, and show far less consensus on group cohesion, hierarchy and cooperation. An especially interesting result is the sharp difference between Chinese and American managers (and, incidentally, also Thais) about

Table 17.7   Survey of business practices

	% yes responses			Chi-squared probability			
	Ch	US	Th	Ch-US	US-Th	Ch-Th	Ch-US-Th
27. The firm carries on regular formal reviews of the performance of key employees	75.0	83.4	73.4	0.296	0.556	0.326	0.377
28. The firm bases salary increases and/or promotions primarily on formal criteria	26.8	51.2	50.0	0.003**	0.065*	0.002**	0.001**
29. The firm hires new managers largely on the basis of family relationships or personal connections	44.3	30.3	23.4	0.069*	0.099*	0.062*	0.015*
30. The firm places heavier emphasis on the educational background than on experience of prospective new managerial employees	50.1	25.8	37.8	0.006**	0.127	0.421	0.024*
31. The firm tries to promote existing staff before seeking new managers from the outside	77.4	82.3	71.1	0.128	0.324	0.560	0.244
32. Management employees in the firm can count on continuing employment in the long term with little risk of termination	59.5	65.9	67.4	0.802	0.581	0.784	0.885
33. The firm has a formal retirement benefit plan for its employees	63.8	83.0	60.4	0.008**	0.077*	0.056*	0.028*
34. Managers in the firm consult their key employees before making most serious decisions	70.6	51.2	64.6	0.171	0.435	0.875	0.435
35. The firm offers significant possibilities for promotion to women as well as to men	57.6	84.5	83.0	0.021*	0.979	0.023*	0.019*
36. The top officers of the firm delegate a great deal of authority to managers at lower levels of the organization	46.1	70.3	56.9	0.068*	0.054*	0.135	0.062*
37. The firm has a formal organization chart to describe the structure of its management	78.9	90.2	74.0	0.081*	0.115	0.656	0.224
38. The firm makes regular financial reports of revenues, costs, and operating profits	75.5	90.0	78.2	0.168	0.364	0.793	0.432

Table 17.7   (continued)

	% yes responses			Chi-squared probability			
	Ch	US	Th	Ch-US	US-Th	Ch-Th	Ch-US-Th
39. In the firm important decisions are made largely from the top down with little employee participation	80.1	57.6	79.9	0.033*	0.040*	0.947	0.034*
40. In the firm, managerial employees dress for work in casual clothing	58.9	56.8	30.8	0.977	0.031*	0.012*	0.262
41. The firm provides expense accounts for many of its managerial employees	61.2	82.9	73.8	0.084*	0.631	0.427	0.132
42. In the workplace, subordinates are afraid to express disagreement with superiors	50.9	33.3	43.8	0.018*	0.508	0.250	0.000***
43. Long-term managers and workers are usually on a first name basis	59.6	95.3	80.6	0.000***	0.007**	0.090*	0.305
44. The firm rarely terminates employees even if their work is unsatisfactory	55.3	46.1	46.5	0.121	0.797	0.122	0.000***

Note: Statistically significant difference: * at the 0.1 level, ** at the 0.01 level, *** at the 0.001 level.

the role of women. Chinese managers take a decidedly more sceptical view of the potential of women in the workplace than Americans or Thais.

Cultural attributes appear to be reflected in business practices. There is evidence that Asian firms use less formal methods and rely more heavily on relationship-based practices than American enterprises. Asian firms are characterized by top-down management, but the links between cultural attributes, like personal objectives or social values and business practices, are not clear, if, indeed, they exist. As we have noted, the business practices reported in the surveys may reflect considerations other than culture. The way in which business is carried out may also be affected by the ownership/organization of the enterprise, its legal setting, its economic situation and the technological advancement of the organization's management practices. Most importantly, there is also still a gap between what is known about business practices and about business performance. It is not clear how culture influences business performance, and, in turn, how cultural forces affect aggregate economic development. These gaps pose some serious problems for the AC-AS hypothesis.

For the future, the increasing interaction between Asian and American and European business suggests that there will be some merging of management styles and, probably also, business practices. That may be necessary in a highly competitive and increasingly open world economy. As East Asian firms become larger and geographically more international, they are likely to assume many of the management systems that have become traditional in multinational corporations elsewhere in the world. Clearly, culture-based relationships are not sufficient to operate internationally on a large scale. It is less certain, however, whether convergence will extend to the managers' personal or social philosophies. These may continue to reflect their different cultural backgrounds.

NOTES

1. The title of an essay by Landes, in Harrison and Huntington (2000).
2. For a discussion, see Adams and James (1999).
3. While, today, Weber's view is accepted by many, it was widely criticized in historical circles (see, for example, Tawney, 1926). It is not clear, moreover, how the Calvinist work ethic thesis applies to East Asian development. Weber was apparently of the opinion that the Chinese virtue of patience would facilitate the assimilation of capitalism in the region (Pye, 2000).
4. For a summary, see Sackman *et al.* (1997: 18–21).
5. An unpublished 2005 paper, entitled 'Calling all cross-cultural enthusiasts: in search of a cultural dimension for change' (author unknown), attempts a comparison of these studies along 15 cultural dimensions. There is a great deal of overlap with Hofstede's factors. Some of the other factors may reflect differences in definition or naming, as much as clearly separate identifiable cultural dimensions.
6. Note that we are concerned here with mainstream economic views, not with the so-called *dependencia* theories. Note, also, that many textbooks on economic development do not show an index entry for 'culture', or cover the topic in only one or two pages (for example, Herrick and Kindleberger, 1983).
7. The difficulties of studying a diversity of cultures meeting at different levels of a business hierarchy are discussed in Sackman *et al.* (1997).
8. Other definitions of culture are more general and, somewhat less relevant to our purpose. For example, Triandis (1972: 4) defines culture as 'a cultural group's characteristic way of perceiving the man-made part of its environment'. To Hofstede (1980, 1984: 21), culture is 'the collective programming of the mind which distinguishes members of one human group from another'.
9. He contrasts this with the notion of popular literature (Peters and Waterman, 1982) that shared values represent the core of a corporate culture.
10. See, for example, Li *et al.* (2001), a study of Chinese joint ventures.
11. The recent applications are summarized in a massive survey in Schaffer and Riordan (2003) and Harzing and Hofstede (1996).
12. Hofstede (1997) develops the indexes as weighted combinations of appropriate questionnaire responses. These scores do not have meaningful absolute values, being primarily intended for ranking different countries along the desired dimensions.
13. The questions were based largely on those suggested by Hofstede, though we have specifically categorized them in line with our classification scheme. The detailed results of the questionnaire survey and a copy of the questionnaire are available from the authors on request.

REFERENCES

Adams, F.G. (1998), 'The East Asian development ladder: virtuous circles and linkages in East Asian development', in F.G. Adams and S. Ichimura (eds), *East Asian Development: Will the East Asian Growth Miracle Survive?*, Westport, CT: Praeger.

Adams, F.G., and W.E. James (eds) (1999), *Public Policies in East Asian Development*, Westport, CT: Praeger.

Adams, F.G. and H. Vernon (2004), 'Economic developments, business culture, and links to business practice: is there a Thai style of management?', *International Journal of Business*, **9**(2), 169–190.

Adams, F.G. and H. Vernon (2005), 'Business culture and management in China: a survey-based study', presented at the EAM International Conference in Cape Town, South Africa, June.

Akamatsu, K. (1962), 'A historical pattern of economic growth in developing countries', *The Developing Economies*, (March–August), 1–25.

Bing, John W. (2004), 'Hofstede's consequences: the impact of his work on consulting and business practice', *The Academy of Management Executive*, **18**(1), 80–87

Claessens, Stijn, S. Djankov and L.C. Xu (2000), 'Corporate performance in the East Asian Financial Crisis', *World Bank Research Observer*, **15**(1), 23–46.

Corsetti, G., P. Pesenti and N. Roubini (1998a, 1998b), 'What caused the Asian Currency and Financial Crisis?', Part I and II, NBER working papers W6833 and W6834, Cambridge, MA: NBER.

Cox, T. (1994), *Cultural Diversity in Organizations: Theory, Research and Practice*, San Francisco: Berret-Koehler.

Fukuyama, F. (1995), *Trust: The Social Virtues and the Creation of Prosperity*, New York: Free Press.

Haider, A. Kahn (1999), 'Corporate governance of family business in Asia', ADB Institute working paper no. 3, Manila: ADB.

Harrison, Lawrence E. and S.P. Huntington (eds) (2000), *Culture Matters: How Values Shape Human Progress*, New York: Basic Books.

Harzing, A.W. and G. Hofstede (1996), 'Planned change in organizations: the influence of national culture', in P.A. Bamberger, M. Erez and S.B. Bacharach (eds), *Research in the Sociology of Organizations*, vol.**14**, Greenwich, CT: JAI Press, pp. 297–340.

Herrick, Bruce and Charles R. Kindleberger (1983), *Economic Development*, New York: McGraw-Hill.

Hofstede, Geert ([1980] 1984), *Culture's Consequences*, Newbury Park, CA: Sage.

Hofstede, Geert (1997), *Culture and Organizations: Software of the Mind*, New York: McGraw-Hill.

Hofstede, Geert (1998), 'Attitudes, values and organizational cultures: disentangling the concepts', *Organizational Studies*, **19**(3), 477–94.

Hofstede, Geert and M. Bond (1988), 'The Confucian connection: from cultural roots to economic growth', *Organizational Dynamics*, **16**(4), 4–21.

House, R., M. Javidan, P. Hanges and P. Dorfman (2002), 'Understanding cultures and implicit leadership theories across the globe: an introduction to project GLOBE', *Journal of World Business*, **37**(1), 3–10.

Huntington, Samuel P. (1996), *The Clash of Civilizations and the Remaking of World Order*, New York: Touchstone. Reprinted by Simon & Schuster, 1998.

Inkeles, Alex (1998), *One World Emerging*, Boulder, CO: Westview.

Inkeles, A. and D. Levinson (1969), 'National character: the study of modal personality and socio-cultural systems', in G. Lindsay and E. Aronson (eds), *The Handbook of Social Psychology* vol. **4**, Reading, MA: Addison–Wesley.

Kluckhohn, F.R. and F.L. Strodtbeck (1961), *Variations in Value Orientation*, New York: HarperCollins.

Kogut, Bruce and H. Singh (1988), 'The effect of national culture on the choice of entry mode', *Journal of International Business Studies*, **19**(3), 411–32.

Kojima, K. (2000), 'The 'flying geese' model of Asian economic development: origin, theoretical extensions, and regional policy implications', *Journal of Asian Economics*, **11**, 375–401.

Krugman, Paul (1998), 'Saving Asia, it's time to get radical' (<http://www.pkarchive.org/crises/SavingAsia.html>).

Landes, David (1998), *The Wealth and Poverty of Nations*, New York: Norton.

Landes, David (2000), 'Culture makes almost all the difference', in L.E. Harrison and S.P. Huntington (eds), *Culture Matters: How Values Shape Human Progress*, New York: Basic Books, pp. 4–13.

Li, Ji, K. Lam and G. Qian (2001), 'Does culture affect behavior and performance of firms? The case of joint ventures in China', *Journal of International Business Studies*, **32**(1), 115–31.

Perkins, Dwight, H. (2000), 'Law family ties, and the East Asian way of business', in L.E. Harrison and S.P. Huntington (eds), *Culture Matters: How Values Shape Human Progress*, New York: Basic Books, pp. 232–43.

Peters, Thomas J. and Richard H. Waterman (1982), *In Search of Excellence: Lessons from America's Best-Run Companies*, New York: Harper & Row.

Porter, Michael (2000), 'Attitudes, values, and beliefs, and the microeconomics of prosperity', in L.E. Harrison and S.P. Huntington (eds), *Culture Matters: How Values Shape Human Progress*, New York: Basic Books, pp. 14–28.

Pye, Lucian W. (2000), 'Asian values from dynamos to dominoes', in L.E. Harrison and S.P. Huntington (eds), *Culture Matters: How Values Shape Human Progress*, New York: Basic Books, pp. 244–55.

Ralston, D.A., G.F. Cheung and R.H. Terpstra (1993), 'Differences in managerial values: a study of U.S., Hong Kong, and PRC managers', *Journal of International Business Studies*, **24**(2), 249–73.

Ralston, D.A., N.V. Thang and N.K. Napier (1999), 'A comparative study of work values of North and South Vietnamese managers', *Journal of International Business Management*, **30**(4), 655–72.

Sachs, Jeffrey (2000), 'Notes on a new sociology of economic development', in L.E. Harrison and S.P. Huntington (eds), *Culture Matters: How Values Shape Human Progress*, New York: Basic Books, pp. 29–43.

Sackman, S.A., M.E. Phillips, M.J. Kleinberg and N.A. Boyacigiller (1997), 'Single and multiple cultures in international cross-cultural management research: overview', in S.A. Sackman (ed.), *Cultural Complexity In Organizations: Inherent Contrasts and Contradictions*, Thousand Oaks, CA: Sage.

Schaffer, B.S. and C.M. Riordan (2003), 'A review of cross-cultural methodologies for organizational research: a best practices approach', *Organizational Research Methods*, **6**(2), 169–215.

Tawney, R.H. (1926), *Religion and the Rise of Capitalism*, New York: Harcourt Brace.

Tjosvold, Dean and K. Leung (eds) (2003), *Cross-Cultural Management*, Burlington, VT: Ashgate.

Triandis, H.C. (1972), *The Analysis of Subjective Culture*, New York: Wiley.

Trompenaars, F. and Charles Hampden-Turner (1998), *Riding the Waves of Culture*, New York: McGraw-Hill.

Tung, R.L. and D.C. Thomas (2003), 'Human resource management in a global world: the contingency framework extended', in D. Tjosvold and K. Leung (eds), *Cross-Cultural Management*, Burlington, VT: Ashgate, pp. 103–22.

Vernon, R. (1966), 'International investment and international trade in the product cycle', *Quarterly Journal of Economics*, May, 190–207.

Wade, Robert (1990), *Governing the Market: Economic Theory and the Role of Governance in East Asian Industrialization*, Princeton, NJ: Princeton University Press.

Weber, Max (1904), *The Protestant Ethic and the Spirit of Capitalism*, New York: Scribner's.

World Bank (1993), *The East Asian Miracle: Economic Growth and Public Policy*, New York: Oxford University Press.

18. The dynamics of Southeast Asian Chinese business[1,2]

Henry Wai-chung Yeung

For several centuries, tens of millions of ethnic Chinese people in Southeast Asia have engaged in a distinctive form of economic organization through which an informal array of Chinese entrepreneurs, traders, financiers and their closely-knit networks of family members and friends came to dominate the economic sphere of the very host countries they later considered 'home'. While deeply rooted in the cultural norms and social values of the traditional Chinese society in mainland China, this form of economic organization has evolved and adapted to dramatically different institutional contexts and political–economic conditions in the host Southeast Asian countries. In this chapter, I use the term 'Southeast Asian *Chinese capitalism*' as a heuristic device to describe this historically and geographically specific form of economic organization that refers to the social organization and political economy of the so-called 'overseas Chinese'[3] living outside mainland China, particularly in Southeast Asia (that is Singapore, Indonesia, Malaysia, the Philippines, Thailand and Vietnam).[4] Chinese capitalism has been a dominant mode of economic organization in Southeast Asia because of not only its economic significance in the host countries, but also its complex and yet intricate social organization and authority systems. The sheer diversity and prowess of economic activities controlled and coordinated by these ethnic Chinese has enabled some of them to become the very foundations of the economies in which they primarily reside and operate (see McVey, 1992; Brown, 1994; Hodder, 1996; Gambe, 2000; Gomez and Hsiao, 2001; Jomo and Folk, 2003).

While Chinese capitalism in Southeast Asia had experienced steady growth and development up to the late 1980s, its socioeconomic organization remained fairly stable and enduring. By the 1990s, the emerging contexts of accelerated economic globalization and the rise of mainland China had impinged quite significantly on this ethnic-centric form of economic organization. In particular, the 1997/1998 Asian economic crisis has fundamentally reshaped its contested nature and economic organization. In this chapter, I outline some of the most significant contextual changes that facilitated the reshaping and reconfiguration of Southeast Asian Chinese capitalism in recent years: the changing political–economic alliances in Southeast Asia, the interpenetration of globalization processes, and the rise of mainland China as a significant player in the global economy. I argue that these changes have led to a more *globalizing orientation* of Chinese capitalism in Southeast Asia. In making this case for globalizing Chinese capitalism, I am cognizant of the continual existence and discursive reconstitution of some historically distinctive elements of Chinese capitalism. This coexistence of both change and continuity in Chinese capitalism points to its growing hybridization, a transformative process in which traditional and new elements are continuously morphed and recombined into something that resembles neither traditional Chinese capitalism as we knew it nor the alleged universalism of global capitalism as most ultraglobalists would like it. Instead, a hybrid form of Chinese capitalism emerges as a distinctive feature in the political economic landscapes of Southeast Asia today (see Yeung, 2000a, 2004).

In making a strong case for Southeast Asian Chinese capitalism as a form of hybrid capitalism, I organize this chapter into two major sections. While detailed empirical data analysis and case studies have already been published elsewhere in Yeung (2004), this chapter serves as an avenue to bring together some broad threads for critical discussion and engagement. In this sense, I intend the chapter to be neither purely theoretical nor empirical in its focus. In the next section, I outline some of the most significant contexts for change and transformation in Southeast Asian Chinese capitalism, in particular the regionalization and internationalization of Southeast Asian Chinese capital and the rise of China as an important destination for this Chinese capital. In the penultimate section, I consider some of the broad changes occurring in Southeast Asian Chinese capitalism. These changes tend to reshape the social organization of Chinese family firms, their business networks and their reliance on political–economic alliances. Apart from these recent changes, I also consider how some of the historically distinctive features of Chinese capitalism in Southeast Asia either remain fairly stable or are discursively and strategically (re)constructed to constitute a new identity for Chinese capitalism. In the concluding section, I offer some tentative evaluation of the future of researching into Chinese capitalism in a global era.

GLOBALIZING SOUTHEAST ASIAN CHINESE CAPITALISM: CONTEXT FOR CHANGE

The relatively recent phenomenon of Southeast Asian Chinese capitalists going international and, in some specific cases, going global is arguably nothing very new (Yeung and Olds, 2000). After all, many first-generation ethnic Chinese entrepreneurs, described in Table 18.1, are themselves diaspora immigrants or, in the words of Wong (1988), 'emigrant entrepreneurs' from mainland China before the communist takeover in 1949. What is particularly important in this recent phenomenon is that these ethnic Chinese capitalists from Southeast Asia bring with them not just financial capital and business knowledge when they go international and global. More crucially, they also carry with them distinctive traits of social and economic organization that have been consolidated and enduring through several decades of evolutionary growth and development in their home countries in Southeast Asia. To some scholars of Chinese capitalism who subscribe to the role of culture (for example Redding, 1990; Whitley, 1992, 1999), these distinctive traits have been considered as *essentialized* ingredients and the 'spirit' of the so-called 'Chinese business system', for example the role of family in business organization and the role of ethnicity in business networks.

When these Southeast Asian Chinese capitalists enter into both new markets in Asia and beyond (for example North America and Western Europe), they necessarily encounter very different operating environments that prompt them to adapt and change in order to succeed in the host markets. This process of adaptation and change might not seem to be too different from the earlier historical period, when these ethnic Chinese had

Table 18.1   Major ethnic Chinese and their transnational corporations from East and Southeast Asia, 1997–2003

Company/group name	Major shareholder (ethnic Chinese)	Country of origin	Estimated net worth (US$billion) and *Forbes* world's richest billionaires ranking*						Major worldwide operations
			1997	Rank	2000	Rank	2003	Rank	
Hong Leong Group	Kwek Leng Beng / Quek Leng Chan	Singapore / Malaysia	5.8 / 2.9	45 / 112	2.0 / 1.8	207 / 224	1.7 / 1.5	236 / 278	CDL Hotels / Guoco (HK)
Goodwood Park Group	Khoo Teck Puat	Singapore	3.9	78	2.7	171	2.6	137	Goodwood Park Hotel Group (Asia)
Far East Organisation	Ng Teng Fong	Singapore	7.0	33	3.4	143	1.7	236	Sino Land (HK)
Sina Mas Group	Oei Widjaja	Indonesia	5.4	50	3.2	151	—	—	Asia Pulp and Paper and Asia Food
Salim Group	Liem Sioe Liong	Indonesia	4.0	75	1.0	312	—	—	First Pacific Group (HK)
Lippo Group	Mochtar Riady	Indonesia	1.8	183	—	—	—	—	Lippo Banks (worldwide)
Kalimanis Group	Bob Hasan	Indonesia	3.0	106	—	—	—	—	
Kerry Group	Robert Kuok	Malaysia/HK	7.0	33	4.6	84	3.4	97	Shangri-la Hotels and TVB (Asia)
YTL Group	Francis Yeoh	Malaysia	1.6	193	1.2	281	—	—	YTL Construction (Asia)
Charoen Pokphand Group	Dhanin Chearavanont	Thailand	1.7	184	1.2	281	1.3	329	CP Pokphand (Asia) / Telecom Asia (Asia)
Fortune Tobacco	Lucio Tan	Philippines	—	—	2.1	201	1.9	209	Eton Properties (HK)

* *Source:*   http://www.forbes.com, accessed on 1 March 2003.

arrived in Southeast Asia from the then mainland China. What strikes me, though, is how this latest round of adaptation and change has a rather rapid 'feedback' mechanism, such that these Southeast Asian Chinese capitalists are increasingly internalizing these new experiences and practices gathered through their international operations, and bring them back to their home countries in Southeast Asia. Through this iterative process of Southeast Asian Chinese adapting to new foreign markets and internalizing such new practices, the distinctive elements of their social organization of economic activities in their home countries in Southeast Asia also experience change and transformation. Couched in such terms, these Southeast Asian ethnic Chinese are both an embodiment of internationalization and an agent of change in their home countries.

What then are the changing contexts that prompt these Southeast Asian ethnic Chinese capitalists to go international, if not global, in their business operations? Here, I consider two important recent phenomena: (1) the changing domestic political–economic context in the aftermath of the 1997/1998 Asian economic crisis, and (2) the continual growth of mainland China as a major economic powerhouse in the global economy. My focus on these two recent phenomena does not imply that the changing contexts prior to the mid-1990s are not important, for example the increasing saturation of domestic markets, the continual hostility and discrimination in some Southeast Asian countries, and the growing competition from local and foreign firms in their home markets (see Yeung, 1999a, 1999b). Instead, the post-crisis Southeast Asia has witnessed significant contextual changes in terms of rising marketization, deregulation and liberalization in various sectors of the economies that threaten the cosy monopolistic positions of many leading ethnic Chinese capitalists (see also Chapters 8 and 15 in this volume). This growing domestic 'threat' continues to prompt the regionalization and internationalization of Southeast Asian Chinese capital, an ongoing process that finds its historical origins as early as in the late 1960s and the early 1970s (Chan and Chiang, 1994; Chan and McElderry, 1998).

In many ways, the Asian economic crisis has shifted our attention away from the Asian 'miracle' to the structural weaknesses of many Asian economies. Insofar as Chinese capitalism in Southeast Asia is concerned, one of the most significant transformative forces comes from the dissipation of what Yoshihara (1988) termed 'ersatz capitalism', a term that refers to the rent-seeking behaviour of Southeast Asian Chinese capitalists through political–economic alliances with dominant ruling elites (see also Jesudason, 1989; Gomez, 1999). This structural transformation in the political economy of Southeast Asian countries is likely to increase competition within and between ethnic Chinese and non-Chinese business communities (Yeung, 2000b; Menkhoff and Sikorski, 2002; Hewison, 2004). Several concurrent movements in the aftermath of the crisis have heralded the imminent demise or at least significant transformations of 'ersatz capitalism' in Southeast Asia.

In particular, social movements towards greater democratic participation by the people in the political process and a relatively more transparent governance system have been organized in Indonesia and Malaysia. In Indonesia, student movements in early 1998 not only brought down the Suharto regime, but also led to an early parliamentary election on 7 June 1999, after which the opposition party Democratic Party-Perjuangan (Struggle), led by Megawati Sukarnoputri, emerged as the winner. For the first time in its history, Indonesia has a democratically elected president. In Malaysia, the sacked former Deputy

Prime Minister Anwar Ibrahim, his wife and his supporters have established Parti Keadilan Nasional and reorganized the opposition to contest the dominant ruling party. These social and political movements have raised the political awareness of people in Southeast Asia in their quest for political and economic reforms which are necessary if these countries are to reap the full benefits of political change and economic development. These movements have also challenged the long existence of 'ersatz capitalism' and called for the demolition of unjust monopolies and special privileges held by certain ethnic Chinese and indigenous people.

This brings us to another type of movement that is primarily concerned with economic reforms in post-crisis Southeast Asia countries (see Low, 2001). These reform movements have important ramifications for Chinese capitalism, because of the loss of monopolistic positions and the collapse of political–economic alliances; two pre-crisis strategies aggressively pursued by ethnic Chinese in the economic realm of Southeast Asia. The structural reforms imposed by the International Monetary Fund (IMF) on Indonesia and Thailand have led to the loss of many monopolistic positions long held by ethnic Chinese elites. On 16 October 1998, the Indonesian parliament approved a landmark bill that allowed 100 per cent foreign ownership of banks. The move aimed at attracting foreign capital to strengthen its disaster-hit banking sector (*The Straits Times*, 17 October 1998). On 8 June 1999, the Indonesian government put in place regulations to make it easier for ailing companies to swap debt for equity (*The Straits Times*, 12 June 1999). Until then, Indonesian companies were saddled with over US$60 billion in foreign borrowings. The new laws allowed foreign creditors to take over new holdings companies or to acquire fully existing ones, lifting previous restrictions on foreign ownership. Despite these new initiatives legislated by the Indonesian government, foreign investors remained cautious in taking over failed Indonesian banks. In May 2000, for example, the government attracted only lukewarm interest among foreign investors to acquire a 22.5 per cent stake in Bank Central Asia, formerly the largest private bank in Indonesia, controlled by a powerful ethnic Chinese, Liem Sioe Liong (Hamilton-Hart, 2002: 158).

This reworking of Chinese capitalism in Indonesia explains why the net worth of several leading ethnic Chinese actors in Indonesia decreased so significantly after 1999 (see Table 18.1). By 2003, none of the ethnic Chinese elites in Indonesia made it onto the *Forbes* list of the world's richest billionaires. In Thailand, Hewison's (2004: 251) recent study has confirmed that the new accumulation regime in Thailand, while still emerging, will exhibit quite different features than the pre-crisis era: (1) a more significant role of foreign capital in the Thai economy; (2) export-orientation and internationalization as the key features of the business operations of most powerful Thai capitalists, ethnic Chinese or not, and (3) increasingly rules-based relationships between these capitalists and the Thai state.

Political shake-ups in some Southeast Asian countries have also contributed to the collapse of certain political–economic alliances between ethnic Chinese rent seekers and their political patrons. This phenomenon is best seen in the case of Malaysia. The Malaysian government has been pursuing an ethnic-biased *bumiputra* policy since the New Economic Policy inaugurated in 1971 to enable indigenous Malays to take control of the Malaysian corporate sector. Its logic rests in attempts at an 'ethnic bypass' through which the *bumiputra* can collaborate with foreign partners in order to avoid excessive dependence upon ethnic Chinese in Malaysia (Jomo, 1997; Gomez, 1999). The Asian economic crisis and the stock-market plunge, however, had crippled many Malaysian companies, particularly those owned by Malay *bumiputra* entrepreneurs. This unintended consequence of Malaysia's participation in the global economy forced the National Economic Action Council (NEAC), a high-powered council established by the prime minister to get the Malaysian economy back on track to high growth rates, to consider what previously was unthinkable: allowing non-*bumiputra* Malaysians and foreigners to own larger shares in local companies (*The Straits Times*, 21 February 1998; 24 July 1998).

The imposition of capital and foreign exchange controls on 1 September 1998 gave domestic banks some breathing space to recapitalize their reserves, but the same measure also backfired because foreign capital hesitated to invest in Malaysia's financial sector. On 29 July 1999, the central bank, Bank Negara, issued a directive to consolidate Malaysia's 21 commercial banks, 25 finance companies and 12 merchant banks into six major banking groups (*The Straits Times*, 31 July 1999). In this restructuring exercise, banks controlled by ethnic Chinese, mostly family-owned, lost favour with Bank Negara and were absorbed into other banking groups. As Ali A.H. Sulaiman, then Bank Negara governor, said, 'there was no place for family-run banks to survive in the long run in the face of globalization' (*The Straits Times*, 12 August 1999). By December 2000, 50 financial institutions had been consolidated into ten major banking groups, representing 94 per cent of the total assets of Malaysia's domestic banking sector (Hamilton-Hart, 2002: 165).

While the post-crisis Southeast Asia regional economy has been turned into a more competitive marketplace for ethnic Chinese capitalists, *the rise of mainland China* as a major economic powerhouse in the global economy represents an important challenge and opportunity for the continual international expansion of Southeast Asian Chinese capitalism. On the one hand, the emergence of mainland China as the world's largest recipient of foreign direct investment (FDI) in 2002 has undoubtedly diverted some of the foreign investment flows that might otherwise have gone to Southeast Asia (Wu and Puah, 2002). Although Table 18.2 shows that mainland China's inward FDI performance index over the periods 1988–90 and 1998–2000 remains fairly stable at respectively 53rd and 59th in rankings, it is clear that all five Southeast Asian countries (Singapore, Malaysia, Thailand, the Philippines and Indonesia) have experienced deteriorating inward FDI performance indexes and relative rankings during the same period.

Moreover, the relative shares of FDI in GDP in all five Southeast Asian countries between 1988–90 and 1998–2000 have decreased quite significantly, a reflection of both the rapid GDP growth of some countries (for example from 12.7 per cent to 2.2 per cent for Singapore) and the dramatic *net* decline in inward FDI (for example from 0.8 per cent to –0.7 per cent for Indonesia). Mainland China, on the contrary, has experienced an increasing share of FDI in GDP, from 1 per cent during the 1988–90 period to 1.3 per cent during the 1998–2000 period. This increase in relative share occurs in spite of its dramatic economic growth during the 1990s, underscoring the concurrent rapid influx of FDI during the same period.

This emerging *diversion effect* of mainland China as a major destination for worldwide FDI has posed two significant challenges for Southeast Asian economies. First, the post-crisis recovery of the Southeast Asian region is likely to be relatively slow and modest.

Table 18.2 The inward FDI performance index, 1988–90 and 1998–2000, for selected Asian countries and the US

	1988–90 FDI inflow share over:					1998–2000 FDI inflow share over:				
	GDP share	Employment share	Exports share	FDI Index	Rank	GDP share	Employment share	Exports share	FDI Index	Rank
Singapore	12.7	26.5	1.4	13.5	1	2.2	7.5	0.3	3.3	13
Hong Kong	5.0	11.8	0.7	5.9	4	6.3	24.5	1.1	10.6	2
United States	1.1	4.7	2.2	2.7	16	0.9	4.3	1.8	2.3	23
Malaysia	4.3	2.4	1.1	2.6	17	1.6	1.0	0.3	1.0	55
Thailand	2.4	0.6	1.4	1.5	37	0.9	0.3	0.4	0.5	86
Philippines	1.6	0.3	1.1	1.0	48	0.6	0.1	0.3	0.3	103
Taiwan	0.9	1.5	0.3	0.9	51	0.3	0.6	0.1	0.4	98
China	1.0	0.1	1.3	0.8	53	1.3	0.1	1.3	0.9	59
Indonesia	0.8	0.1	0.6	0.5	66	-0.7	-0.1	-0.4	-0.4	136
South Korea	0.4	0.5	0.3	0.4	75	0.6	0.9	0.3	0.6	81
Japan	0.0	0.0	0.0	0.0	101	0.1	0.3	0.1	0.2	120
Asia	1.1	0.2	0.6	0.6	—	0.9	0.2	0.6	0.6	—

Note: The index is based on an unweighted average of three ratios that reflect a country's propensity to attract FDI, taking into account the size and strengths of the economy. The three ratios are obtained by dividing the country's share of global FDI by its shares of global GDP, employment and exports.

Source: Wu and Puah (2002: Table 1, 47).

Table 18.3   Exchange rates per US dollar and real GDP growth rates of Southeast Asian economies, 1991–2002

Economy	1991–96	1997	1998	1999	2000	2001	2002
Indonesia							
Exchange rate	—	2 393	12 900	9 322	7 300	9 370	9 309
Real GDP growth	6.0	5.0	−13.2	0.9	4.8	3.4	3.7
*Malaysia**							
Exchange rate	—	2.49	4.50	3.80	3.80	3.80	3.80
Real GDP growth	8.9	7.3	−7.4	5.8	8.5	0.4	4.2
Singapore							
Exchange rate	—	1.41	1.76	1.69	1.68	1.73	1.79
Real GDP growth	8.4	8.5	0.1	5.9	9.9	−2.4	2.2
Thailand							
Exchange rate	—	25.81	54.22	36.98	37.15	42.99	42.99
Real GDP growth	8.2	−1.4	−10.8	4.2	4.3	1.9	5.2
The Philippines							
Exchange rate	—	26.33	42.16	38.85	40.46	49.25	51.7
Real GDP growth	2.7	5.2	−0.6	3.4	4.0	3.2	4.6

Note: * Malaysia introduced capital control in September 1998 and fixed the exchange rate against the US dollar at US$1 to RM$3.8.

Sources: Hamilton-Hart (2002: Tables 7.1 and 7.2) and 2001–2 GDP data from http://www.worldbank.org/data/countrydata/countrydata.html; accessed on 1 March 2004.

During the 1999–2003 period, the real GDP growth rates of most Southeast Asian countries remained fairly modest, a rather different picture as compared to the pre-crisis 1991–96 period (see Table 18.3). Much of the economic 'miracle' in the region prior to the 1997 crisis was underpinned by the rapid influx of FDI into Southeast Asia during the 1980s and the 1990s (see Lim and Fong, 1991; Dobson and Chia, 1997; Giroud, 2003; see also Chapters 12–14 in this volume).

FDI and technology transfer from Japan were particularly important in Southeast Asia, in view of the extensive presence of Japanese regional production networks in the region (Pongpaichit, 1990; Hatch and Yamamura, 1996; Encarnation, 1999; Edgington and Hayter, 2000; Hatch, 2000). The collaborative supplier relationships between ethnic Chinese manufacturers and Japanese firms in Southeast Asia were highly conducive to the development of Southeast Asian Chinese capitalism (Machado, 1997; Deyo and Doner, 2000). Aoyama (2000), for example, found that most Japanese electronics firms in Southeast Asia in 1992 did not purchase from their *keiretsu* firms. Instead, 98 per cent of the host-country purchases and 71 per cent of purchase in 'other areas' were made through non-*keiretsu* firms (mostly ethnic Chinese firms). While the diversion trend is not entirely clear yet, it is conceivable that new waves of FDI from Japan and other OECD countries will be more oriented towards penetrating the mainland China market and developing a major manufacturing base in mainland China. This in turn presents a significant challenge to the continual survival of ethnic Chinese manufacturers in Southeast Asia, who tend, in turn, to initiate defensive internationalization into

Table 18.4   *Leading Chinese business firms among the top 50 transnational corporations from Southeast Asia ranked by foreign assets, 1995 and 2000 (US$ million and number of employees)*

Ranking (foreign assets)		Name of TNC (founder or family)	Home economy	Industry	Foreign assets	
2000	1995				2000	1995
29	25	Fraser and Neave (Lee family)	Singapore	Food & beverages	1 318	957
34	37	Amsteel (William Cheng)	Malaysia	Diversified	1 143	209
40	—	WBL (Lee family)	Singapore	Electronics	879	—
43	—	Berjaya Group (Vincent Tan)	Malaysia	Diversified	832	—
50	—	Hume Industries (Quek Leng Chan)	Malaysia	Construction	593	—
—	35	Genting Bhd (Lim Goh Tong)	Malaysia	Properties	—	692
—	42	Creative Technology (Sim Wong Woo)	Singapore	Electronics	—	405

Note:
The table excludes government-linked corporations in Singapore (e.g. Neptune Orient Lines, Singapore Telecom and Keppel Corporation) and Taiwan (e.g. Chinese Petroleum and United Microelectronics).
[1] The index of transnationality is calculated as the average of foreign assets to total assets, foreign sales to total sales and foreign employment to total employment.

Source: UNCTAD (various years), *World Investment Report*, Geneva: UNCTAD.

mainland China to secure their existing customer base and to develop new market opportunities.

Second, the post-crisis diversion of FDI into mainland China and its rapid export-oriented industrialization also imply that ethnic Chinese firms in Southeast Asia will increasingly face formidable competition from mainland China's exports of manufactured goods.[5] This competition can present itself in two significant forms. Ethnic Chinese firms in Southeast Asia will experience a growing influx of manufactured goods from mainland China into their home turfs in Southeast Asia. This influx of cheaper imports can erode the steady profits long enjoyed by these ethnic Chinese manufacturers, via the monopolistic positions in their home countries. This competitive problem is less significant than the competition from mainland China in the exports market. Apart from those domestically oriented manufacturers, many ethnic Chinese-owned and controlled manufacturing firms in Southeast Asia are involved in regional production networks that export mainly to North America and, to a certain extent, Western Europe (for example Borrus *et al.*, 2000; Yeung, 2001). The growing competition from foreign- and domestic-owned manufacturers in mainland China can squeeze out a significant number of these

Total assets		Foreign sales		Total sales		Foreign employment		Total employment		Transnationality Index[1]	
2000	1995	2000	1995	2000	1995	2000	1995	2000	1995	2000	1995
4211	3199	944	1066	1551	1809	7826	8190	10750	10064	49.5	56.7
3453	1459	544	80	1416	1066	37094	7800	50218	28200	43.6	16.5
1106	–	338	–	534	–	12467	–	13374	–	70.8	–
3352	—	954	–	2052	–	5500	–	21783	–	29.0	–
1178	—	931	–	1341	–	6536	–	12545	–	51.6	–
–2283	–	62	–	982	–	–	–	–	–	18.3	
– 661	–	1175	–	1202	–	2048	–	4185	–	69.3	

Southeast Asian firms that are involved in relatively labour-intensive and low-tech production of manufactured goods. Even in the categories of high-tech and value-added manufactured products, such as hard disk drives, Southeast Asian suppliers are facing strong competition from mainland China (McKendrick *et al.*, 2000).

On the other hand, the rapid economic growth of mainland China represents a much welcomed opportunity to those ethnic Chinese firms from Southeast Asia that are well positioned and plugged into major global production networks (Fruin, 1998; Borrus *et al.*, 2000; McKendrick *et al.*, 2000; Henderson *et al.*, 2002). Their favourable articulation into global production networks can be explained by the early internationalization of these ethnic Chinese firms prior to the mid-1990s, such that they have already gained substantial operating experience and firm-specific knowledge in manufacturing for major brand-name producers in a variety of industries, for example consumer electronics and personal computers. The rise of mainland China thus presents a golden market opportunity for these ethnic Chinese capitalists from Southeast Asia to follow their lead-firm customers who have increasingly established and grounded their global production networks in mainland China.

In Table 18.4, some of the ethnic Chinese-owned and controlled TNCs from Malaysia and Singapore have quite successfully internationalized their operations, to tap into the business opportunities associated with selected global production networks (for example Hume Industries from Malaysia and Wearnes Electronics from Singapore). In some cases (for example Creative Technology), ethnic Chinese manufacturers from Southeast Asia have grown and/or leapfrogged from original equipment manufacturers (OEM) to original brand manufacturers (OBM) and original design manufacturers (ODM). The emergence of mainland China as a major market relatively unexploited by leading global firms has exerted a very attractive centrifugal force to induce these ethnic Chinese firms to establish their operations in mainland China. This centrifugal force has already operated very well on large manufacturing firms from Hong Kong, Taiwan and Singapore (Hsing, 1998; Magretta, 1998; Mathews, 2002; Yeung, 2002; Chen and Ku, 2004).

To sum up, the changing contexts during the post-crisis era present very significant challenges and opportunities for ethnic Chinese capitalists in Southeast Asia. The decline of political–economic alliances in their home countries and the rise of mainland China as both a competitor and a new market have reinforced the continual internationalization and globalization of Southeast Asian Chinese capitalism through both internal and external changes. Internally, more ethnic Chinese firms in Southeast Asia are experiencing management and structural transformations in order to professionalize and corporatize their business operations. Externally, these firms are less reliant on ethnic financial networks, and more on international financial markets, to secure access to capital in order to fuel their internationalization efforts (Yeung, 2003). It is important to point out that most of these internal and external changes had existed *before* the mid-1990s, although the 1997 economic crisis has clearly speeded them up. In the next section, I discuss some of these major changes and transformations and examine how they play an important role in the hybridization of Southeast Asian Chinese capitalism.

HYBRIDIZING SOUTHEAST ASIAN CHINESE CAPITALISM: CHANGE AND CONTINUITY

If the contexts for change in Southeast Asian Chinese capitalism have been made more favourable during the post-crisis era, what kind of change and transformations can we observe and analyse? In this section, I consider four major dimensions of change in Chinese capitalism: (1) less emphasis and reliance on political–economic alliances in the home country, (2) growing professionalization and bureaucratization of Chinese family firms, (3) tapping into non-ethnic sources of capital, and (4) reshaping 'Chinese' business networks.

This choice of changing dimensions represents my current understanding of the rather fluid and dynamic evolution of Chinese capitalism. It is intended to be neither comprehensive nor authoritative. Instead, I hope these dimensions will provide some important analytical clues for more detailed empirical research (cf. Yeung, 2004). More importantly, we should bear in mind that these changes by no means imply the convergence of Southeast Asian Chinese capitalism towards a particular capitalist model. Indeed, there are significant elements of continuity in Chinese capitalism that enable it to be sufficiently differentiated from the dominant mode of Anglo-American capitalism. Consequently, I consider some of these elements of continuity towards the last part of this section.

To begin our analysis of recent changes in Southeast Asian Chinese capitalism, we need to revisit Yoshihara's (1988: 3) characterization of Southeast Asian capitalism as a form of 'ersatz capitalism':

> What is ersatz about South-East Asian capitalism derives from the fact that the development of South-East Asian capital has been largely confined to the tertiary sector . . . South-East Asian

industrial capital cannot act as the vanguard of economic development because it does not have export capability. Any dynamism in this sense comes from the market economy, not from capitalism. This is because large industrial capitalists are comprador capitalists (acting as the agents of foreign manufacturers in their own countries), or they depend on foreign technology in a broader sense, or they are not efficient enough to compete in the international market.

This early assessment of Southeast Asian capitalism during the 1980s remains viable more than a decade later in the work of Brown (2000: 42) who concludes:

> the cultural embeddedness of Chinese capitalism is a product of historical cultural factors. Chinese capitalism in Southeast Asia, despite its heterogeneity, is not competitive. The accumulative, predatory tendencies of Chinese capitalism should not be mistaken for competitiveness. The Chinese links with the state, indigenous merchants, local elites and native technocrats, have varied from co-opting elites onto the boards of Chinese companies, to raising equity from indigenous sources, government capitals, to operating joint ventures with the state and with foreign multinationals and seeking technological alliances with foreign multinationals. The state has ranged from patron to partner, from investor to executor.

She further argues that 'links with the state and the exploitation of Chinese networks ensured the survival of Chinese family enterprises, irrespective of whether they were in labour intensive industries or in capital intensive sectors. Competition was not a determining factor in the survival of Chinese family enterprises' (p. 100).

Does Southeast Asian capitalism today continue to be ersatz and uncompetitive? How far does it depend on the role of ethnic Chinese capitalists as 'comprador capitalists' and on foreign capital for technology and market access? These are very substantial issues for further theoretical debates and empirical research. Without prejudicing Yoshihara's (1988) observation during the 1980s, I contend that the successful internationalization of a number of ethnic Chinese business firms from Southeast Asia (Yeung, 1999a, 2004) does entail more than the 'comprador-dependency' syndrome to include significantly new elements of organizational innovation, technological dynamism and financial management. My argument does not imply that most Southeast Asian countries, with perhaps the exception of Singapore, have moved well beyond ersatz capitalism as their preferred developmental trajectories. Rather, my argument of change and dynamism necessarily applies to the most important group of actors in Southeast Asian Chinese capitalism – the largest and most internationalizing Chinese business firms identified in Tables 18.1 and 18.4.

My previous work has shown that it is this group of internationalizing actors who are most likely to make a significant impact on the future trajectories of their home countries in Southeast Asia, through a variety of change and transformations in their own business organization and social practices during their international operations (Olds and Yeung, 1999; Yeung, 2000a, 2004; Gomez, 2004). Over time, these actors in Chinese capitalism are able to bring these new business and social practices back to their home countries, and to socialize other local firms into their increasingly global actor networks that are not necessarily based on ethnic or political–economic relationships. Southeast Asian Chinese capitalism, in its domestic context, does not have to be ersatz forever; it indeed evolves and is transformed over time into a form of hybrid capitalism that encapsulates both some elements of the past and new elements brought in through its globalizing actors.

In the first place, I argue that one of the most significant changes among the leading actors in Southeast Asian Chinese capitalism is the *decline in their reliance on pre-existing political–economic alliances* in the home countries. This reflects both the increasing pressures of international agencies (for example the IMF and World Bank during the 1997 Asian economic crisis) on these Southeast Asian countries to engage in economic reforms and corporate restructuring, and the higher standards of corporate governance and financial management required for these Southeast Asian firms to engage in international business operations. When these Southeast Asian Chinese firms operate internationally within and outside the Asia–Pacific region, they are often unable to transfer their political–economic alliances that are most likely to be embedded and bounded within their home countries. They are thus more likely to rely increasingly on their firm-specific expertise and advantage in establishing their international operations (see empirical case studies in Yeung, 2002, 2004; Gomez, 2004). This greater demand for firm-specific competitive advantages in turn may gradually induce these Chinese business firms to be less reliant on political–economic alliances even in their home countries, so that they can build and accumulate internationally transferable competitive advantages (for example cost and market advantages). They are critical agents of change in their domestic settings, for example, by transforming their home-based supplier networks and market channels that used to be solely based on either ethnic family relationships or political–economic alliances.

Second, the successful internationalization of Southeast Asian Chinese business firms also requires them to be less organized around the four highly stereotyped principles of paternalism, nepotism, personalism and fragmentation identified in earlier 'culturalist' studies of Chinese family firms (Silin, 1976; Redding, 1990, 2000; Whitley, 1992, 1999). Instead, I observe an emerging trend towards the *growing professionalization and bureaucratization* of Chinese business firms of both the family and non-family variants (see also Chapter 15 in this volume). While this trend was becoming more apparent during the first half of the 1990s, as ethnic Chinese firms were rapidly going international in their business operations, the 1997/1998 Asian economic crisis has hastened this transformative process, so that ethnic Chinese firms find it much harder to establish a competitive position in today's global economy on the basis of these ethnic-centric principles. After all, the founding patriarchs of most large-scale ethnic Chinese business firms are so overwhelmed by information and decisions that they have to delegate these information-processing and decision-making processes to a variety of trusted professional managers, who are neither necessarily ethnic Chinese nor personal friends. Their expanding business empire also implies that succession based on nepotism is becoming increasingly difficult. There may be a shortage of able or competent family heirs to take over some corporate decision making and responsibilities. As Fukuyama (1995: 64) once argued, 'a single family, no matter how large, capable, or well educated, can only have so many competent sons, daughters, spouses, and siblings to oversee the different parts of a rapidly ramifying enterprise'.

These founding patriarchs are thus hiring more professional managers to be the CEOs of their international operations in Asia and beyond. Well trained in top business schools elsewhere, and often equipped with considerable international business and industry experience, these professional managers are key players in an emerging transnational community of business elites, who are not only transferable in terms of their managerial skills, but also much more difficult to be 'controlled' in the traditional Chinese way of family-oriented business management. Sklair (2000) has coined the term 'transnational capitalist' to describe this group of highly dynamic and powerful executives. As Whitley (1999: 97) has noted, 'this mobility has become frequently based upon the possession of a general management credential such as the MBA degree . . . [And] "management" is seen more as a generalizable set of skills and competences than as a set of industry-specific functions linked to more technical competences'. Instead of reproducing 'highly personal and direct control over work processes and limited employer–employee trust' (ibid.: 93), we begin to find more competent professional managers being socialized into 'Chinese' capitalism so that over time, they become insiders and major movers in this increasingly reshaped form of hybrid capitalism.

Third, just as management and organizational structures of ethnic Chinese business firms are undergoing rapid change and transformations during the post-crisis era, their financial networks are also increasingly moving away from ethnic-centrism in their organization, so well described in the earlier studies of Chinese capitalism. In fact, these two processes of change – organizational and financial – go hand in hand in the sense that potential improvement in corporate governance through professionalization and bureaucratization is particularly welcome in developing Southeast Asian countries, in which many Chinese family firms thrive and shareholder protection and judicial efficiency are clearly inadequate. To ensure that global financial elites are comfortable with their financial positions and obligations, key actors in ethnic Chinese firms are required to follow certain accounting standards and business norms in global capital markets (see more empirical evidence in Yeung and Soh, 2000; Yeung, 2004).

As early as 1992, for example, Peter Woo – the successor to one of Hong Kong's most powerful Chinese family conglomerates, the Wharf Group – pronounced that 'There are no friends in finance. The world has changed. They [old style Chinese entrepreneurs] need to realize we are in a world market and need an international culture' (quoted in Clifford and Engardio, 2000: 70). Having received his MBA from Columbia University and developed his early career in Chase Manhattan Bank, Woo's attitude to the traditional norms in Chinese capitalism is not entirely surprising and inconsistent. The necessity for securing global finance provides a key force to effect dynamic changes in Chinese capitalism. The 1997/1998 Asian economic crisis has only made these changes even more apparent and necessary. Recent empirical studies in financial economics (Schmukler and Vesperoni, 2001; Mitton, 2002), for instance, have identified significant positive relationships between improved corporate governance (for example establishing credible investor protection provisions and appointing Big Six auditors) and lower cost of capital. Klapper and Love (2002) have also found that good corporate governance mattered a lot more in countries with weak shareholder protection and poor judicial efficiency. Schmukler and Vesperoni (2001) have reported that firms from emerging economies could benefit from accessing international bond markets, by securing long-term financing and extending their debt maturity structure. Raising capital in international financial markets, however, requires ethnic Chinese (family) firms to become increasingly 'credible' and 'transparent' in their management practices and systems of financial control, as defined by the gatekeepers of the global financial system (Ridding and Kynge, 1997).

Last but not least, this increasing tapping into non-ethnic sources of global financial capital necessarily implies the *reshaping* and *opening up* of what otherwise might be exclusively Chinese business networks. Reducing the reliance on internal (predominantly ethnic) capital within Chinese capitalism is attractive in an era of global competition, where investment outlays are becoming significantly larger and financial leverages have become the norm in most competitive industries. The threats of hostile takeover and acquisitions in deregulated Asian markets have also forced Chinese business firms to secure external finance to strengthen their financial positions. This shift from informal networks of credits and loans towards stock and capital markets in financing Chinese capitalism is not a recent phenomenon, though its extent has been significantly underestimated in the literature. For those ethnic Chinese firms and/or countries in search of financial resources from outside their 'home' economies and/or regions, it is important to secure the *consent* and recognition from global financiers for comparable standards of corporate governance and return to investments. These global financiers are leading bankers, fund managers, brokers, and so on, who are often based in major global cities, that in turn serve as their command and control centres of global investments (Sassen, 1991; Olds and Yeung, 2004).

The successful enrolment of ethnic Chinese actors into these global financial actor networks is imperative, in an era of more intensified competition, greater financial requirements for expansion and investments and higher risks associated with excessive reliance on domestic finance. This quest for global finance also requires actors in Chinese capitalism to come to terms with actors in international media and research institutions on business activities. This is because today's global financial system is increasingly characterized by a broader array of actors beyond just bankers and financiers (Harmes, 1998; Olds and Yeung, 1999; Yeung, 2003). Actors in international media and research houses play an increasingly critical role in producing reflexively texts, information and knowledge about Chinese capitalism that can significantly hinder or facilitate ethnic Chinese actors' access to global finance. A tentative outcome of this process of accessing global finance is the increasing reshaping and opening of ethnic Chinese business networks to include *non-Chinese actors*, who can bring in both international reputation and competitive advantage to the traditional organization of business activities in Chinese capitalism.

Whereas these four dimensions of change have undoubtedly exerted significant pressures for reshaping Southeast Asian Chinese capitalism, their collective impact does not necessarily lead to the demise of a form of economic organization that has taken many decades to evolve. Indeed, it is reasonable to argue for some degree of *continuity* and path dependency in Southeast Asian Chinese capitalism, such that a compromised scenario – a hybridized form of capitalism – is likely to emerge. What then are the likely dimensions of ethnic Chinese capitalism in Southeast Asia that remain relatively enduring either in their *structures* or in their *discursive reconstruction*? Here, I consider three particular dimensions of continuity in Southeast Asian Chinese capitalism: (1) the family firm as a central element in organizing Chinese capitalism, (2) strategic deployment of 'Chineseness' and Chinese identities, and (3) Chinese culture as discursive resources.

Although I have discussed above the likely recent changes to the ways in which ethnic Chinese organize their business and financial networks in a globalizing era, it must be cautioned that these changes do not necessarily erode the continual significance and viability of the *family firm* as the central organizing unit of Southeast Asian Chinese capitalism (Yeung, 2004). This predominance of the family firm, however, is clearly not unique to Chinese capitalism. In fact, more than 75 per cent of all registered companies in the industrialized economies today remain family businesses and a third of listed companies in the *Fortune 500* have families at their helm (Becht *et al.*, 2003); 43 of Italy's top 100 companies are family-owned and 26 of France's and 15 of Germany's are also family-owned. In the UK, where ownership was rapidly dispersed throughout the twentieth century, Franks *et al.* (2003) found that founding families retained board control well beyond the sale of their ownership stake (see also Chandler, 1990). According to a recent study of corporate ownership around the world (La Porta *et al.*, 1999: 481), even Microsoft Corporation can be classified as a family-owned firm since it is 23.7 per cent controlled by Bill Gates and his family.

In Southeast Asian Chinese capitalism, the family firm is likely to continue as the key organizational platform or 'mode of organizing', in the words of Hamilton (2000), for the accumulation of wealth by ethnic Chinese families that in turn defines the rationality of Chinese capitalism, albeit in culturally specific ways. As Weber ([1930] 1992: xxxi–xxxii; original italics) reminded us some time ago, '[modern] capitalism is identical with the pursuit of profit, and forever *renewed* profit, by means of continuous, rational, capitalistic enterprise'. While historically such 'rational' capitalistic enterprises might not have been developed in mainland China, Chinese capitalism – as I define it in this chapter – is organized around a particular social system of economic action and business activities that manifests itself through complex webs of family networks and personal relationships. It is embedded in a peculiar form of political economy in which the ethnic Chinese rule the 'host' economy and leave the political sphere to the reign of indigenous ethnic groups or colonial masters.

Chinese capitalism is thus organized and coordinated via neither market relations nor hierarchies of 'rational' firms (cf. Williamson, 1975, 1985; Powell, 1990; DiMaggio, 2001). Rather, it encompasses both markets and hierarchies, and configures these capitalist institutions through an informal system of social relationships and family obligations (see Hamilton, 2000). To Brown (2000: 6), 'The major institution within Chinese business has been the family. The family was the source of funds, contacts and managers. The primacy of the family has been maintained in recent decades, despite rapid diversification and international expansion. In many cases, the Chinese firm had no distinct existence outside the family.' While I argue in this chapter that the economic role and functions of the family in Southeast Asian Chinese capitalism are undergoing some significant changes, previous experience and evidence from research conducted on a variety of capitalisms point to the continual viability of the family firm as a central unit of organizing capitalism, irrespective of its ethnic variety and country of origin. While there is some evidence for the decreasing significance of the family firm in ethnic Chinese capitalism (for example Yeung and Soh, 2000; Wong, 2004), there is no convincing reason or evidence to expect the wholesale removal of the Chinese family firm from the Southeast Asian economic landscapes.

What is particularly challenging, though, to academic research into the dynamics of Southeast Asian Chinese capitalism is to understand and to appreciate the *changing ethnic identities*, associated with a whole new generation of ethnic Chinese in Southeast Asia. Decades of cultural assimilation and political integration of ethnic Chinese into most Southeast Asian countries have produced very significant outcomes in relation to their ethnic identities (see Wang, 1981, 2000; Lim and Gosling, 1983; Cushman and Wang, 1988; Suryadinata, 1995, 1997; Bolt, 2000; Yen, 2002; Ma and Cartier, 2003). In fact, most second and third generation ethnic Chinese in Southeast Asia are now considering themselves as Southeast Asians rather than 'overseas Chinese' who still have some romanticized allegiance to mainland China. This phenomenon of changing national identities among Southeast Asian-born ethnic Chinese differs very much from their ancestors who emigrated to Southeast Asia during the first half of the twentieth century.

Concurrent with this changing dimension of ethnic identities towards national identities, however, is the curious reconstruction of ethnic Chinese identities when these Southeast Asians operate in Asia and beyond. This reconstruction of ethnic identities is deemed necessary when Southeast Asian Chinese invest in mainland China and they need to tap into *guanxi*-based relationship networks by flashing their ethnic identities as 'Chinese'. The revival of Confucianism in Southeast Asia, particularly in Singapore, during the 1980s was very much founded on such belief that 'Chineseness' could help Southeast Asians to profit better from mainland China's opening and growth (see Berger and Hsiao, 1988; Tu, 1996). In fact, Singapore's former Prime Minister, Lee Kuan Yew, was one of the major proponents of such a Confucian revival. In his keynote address to the Second World Chinese Entrepreneurs Convention held in Hong Kong in 1993, Lee identified *guanxi* or personal relationships as an important advantage that 'overseas Chinese' should make use of in order to compete with their 'Western' rivals for capturing business in mainland China (see also Kotkin, 1992; Kao, 1993; Chang, 1995; Lever-Tracy *et al.*, 1996; Weidenbaum and Hughes, 1996). He argued that *guanxi* 'can make up for a lack in the rule of law, and transparency in rule and regulations. This guanxi capability will be of value for the next 20 years at least' (quoted in *Far Eastern Economic Review*, 2 December 1993, p. 17; see also *The Business Times*, 6 December 1993). Gomez (2004: 143–4) also reports that the former Malaysian Prime Minister, Mahathir Mohamad, was 'a vocal supporter of Malaysian Chinese tapping into transnational Chinese "networks" to develop their corporate base'.

In truth, while we find an interesting *strategic deployment* of 'Chineseness' and Chinese identities among Malaysian and Singaporean Chinese when they venture into mainland China (see Kong, 1999; Yeung, 2000c; Yang, 2002), we must recognize this form of strategic deployment as an *economic imperative* rather than a cultural revival among ethnic Chinese Southeast Asians. As Wang (1995: 26) points out succinctly, 'the profit basis of the present investments [by Southeast Asian Chinese] in China's development is a totally new basis for the relationship between Southeast Asian Chinese and China. That all investments should be placed on a rational and profitable basis is one to be encouraged and one that deserves very special attention.' Such a strategic deployment of ethnic identities helps to reinforce the continual 'cultural uniqueness' of Southeast Asian Chinese capitalism as distinctively 'Chinese', and yet it brings to the forefront a rather fragile and contingent sense of national identities among most ethnic Chinese Southeast Asians.

Increasingly, these Southeast Asians value their hybrid ethnic/national identities as a specific repertoire of *cultural resources* to be tapped into in different political–economic contexts (see also Ong and Nonini, 1997; Hsing, 2003). A Singaporean Chinese businessman in mainland China, for example, may identify himself as a Chinese when the local Chinese partner prefers to deal with an 'overseas Chinese'. In another context, this Singaporean businessman may prefer to use his Singaporean identity to fence off some requests for bribes and other unethical business practices. Such bicultural or multicultural identities are fairly handy for Chinese Southeast Asians to operate successfully in such a complex and changing business environment as mainland China. In short, the continual existence of 'Chineseness' in Southeast Asian Chinese capitalism owes much less to its ethnic identity than to the strategic deployment of this identity for economic purposes.

This continuity in Southeast Asian Chinese capitalism brings us to another side of the same coin, the *continual existence of hostility and discrimination* against ethnic Chinese in Southeast Asia. Ironically, the dramatic success of Chinese Southeast Asians in mainland China during the late 1980s and the 1990s was both an asset and a liability to these Southeast Asians and their families. Insofar as their success in mainland China was discursively and triumphantly constructed as the outcome of their reliance on their 'Chinese' identities and ethnic-centric business networks (for example Hamilton, 1991; East Asia Analytical Unit, 1995; Weidenbaum and Hughes, 1996), these Chinese Southeast Asians ran the looming danger of being the prime targets for such accusations as ethnic betrayal of national interest and ruthless exploitation of indigenous Southeast Asians to fuel their foreign ventures. During much of the 1980s and up to the mid-1990s, ethnic tension in Southeast Asia was largely eased through rapid economic development and some success in ethnic redistribution (particularly in Malaysia and Thailand).

The outbreak of the 1997/1998 Asian economic crisis, however, witnessed the ugly return of ethnic hostility and discrimination in Indonesia and, to a certain extent, Malaysia (see Yeung, 2000b). The May 1998 racial riots in Indonesia against ethnic Chinese serves as a serious reminder that ethnic tension remains a highly relevant issue in Southeast Asian Chinese capitalism. Elsewhere in Malaysia, some ethnic Chinese who had previously benefited from political–economic alliances were asked to bail out ailing companies controlled by politically well-connected *bumiputra* Malays. This was part of the state's recapitalization programme through which the state, represented by the National Economic Action Council (NEAC), intended to jump-start economic recovery under conditions of foreign exchange control and restricted global capital flows. Several well-connected Malaysian Chinese actors were specifically asked by Tun Daim Zainuddin, then NEAC Executive Director, to bail out debt-ridden *bumiputra* companies. Among them were Francis Yeoh, the beneficiary of the highly profitable power generating licence (YTL Group), and Lim Goh Tong, who depended heavily on the renewal of his lucrative casino licence to sustain his Genting casino and resort businesses (Gomez, 1999).

In rather ironic ways, the revival of 'Chineseness' among Southeast Asian Chinese in an era of rapid internationalization and the rise of mainland China has produced some unintended consequences that became apparent during and after the Asian economic crisis. More specifically, the continual existence of ethnic tension and hostility in post-crisis Southeast Asia has emerged as an important force in shaping how Chinese culture and identities continue to serve as significant discursive resources for ethnic Chinese in Southeast Asia. It may be rather exaggerated to claim that the kind of 'siege mentality' (Yoshihara, 1988; Redding, 1990), 'refugee mentality' (Kotkin, 1992), 'trader's dilemma' (Menkhoff, 1993) and 'stepping stone syndrome' (Yee, 1989) historically prompting the inward-looking orientation of Chinese capitalism in Southeast Asia may persist in the post-crisis era. But it is certainly possible that Chinese culture and identity will remain an important set of discursive resources for Chinese Southeast Asians, to engage in a form of economic organization that is neither entirely Chinese in its nature and ethnic composition, nor bounded within national political–economic institutional contexts like its counterparts elsewhere (see Hollingsworth and Boyer, 1997; Hall and Soskice, 2001).

CONCLUSION

In this chapter, I have shown how Southeast Asian Chinese capitalism is not a static form of organizing economic activities. While it is a relatively enduring and institutionalized structure, however, it is subject to contextual change and transformations. This claim may appear to be a moot point, but its significance really lies with the fact that much of the literature on the alleged success of 'overseas Chinese' in Southeast Asia – itself mushrooming like a cottage industry – tends to focus on its internal and often 'oversocialized' set of cultural norms in explaining empirical outcomes. This first wave of scholarship on Chinese capitalism was essentially predicated on theoretical constructs and empirical evidence available during the 1970s and the early 1980s. While some of their arguments and findings remain valid in today's globalizing era, it must be noted that the broader context in which Southeast Asian Chinese capitalism is embedded has changed very dramatically. The rapid interpenetration of globalization processes and the rise of mainland China during much of the 1980s and the 1990s have prompted both new theoretical insights and empirical work.

In particular, there is now a growing body of literature on Chinese capitalism that focuses on its *external* dimension (for example Hsing, 1998; Yeung and Olds, 2000; Mathews, 2002; Yao, 2002; Ma and Cartier, 2003; Gomez and Hsiao, 2004; Yeung, 2004). This literature builds on the earlier scholarship on Chinese capitalism and yet departs significantly in its theoretical foundations from its predecessors. Contrary to the earlier views of Chinese capitalism as a form of cultural artefacts that are permanent blueprints for Southeast Asian economies, this new literature seeks to identify the changing contexts of Chinese capitalism, and to analyse its dynamic transformations within these contexts. Taking an institutional and/or actor-network approach, these renewed studies of Chinese capitalism have pointed to its growing hybridization in terms of both economic organization around ethnic Chinese and multiple ethnic identities and mobilization strategies. They have collectively shown that, as a form of hybrid capitalism, Chinese capitalism does not have an essentialized core 'centre' that can be easily identified and explained. Instead, Chinese capitalism contains within itself a curious mixture and interpenetration of what previously were deemed distinctively Chinese elements, and a whole variety of non-Chinese capitalist practices and organizing principles.

One may ask, however, if Southeast Asian Chinese capitalism is really hybridized, what remains distinctive about it? Is it just about hybridity and hybridization? Are we witnessing an emerging and nascent form of Southeast Asian capitalism that is not organized around ethnicity? I have no doubt that these questions will demand very pressing research attention in the near future, and, therefore, cannot be satisfactorily answered here. Suffice it to say that the ongoing change in Southeast Asian Chinese capitalism does not entirely negate all of its distinctive attributes. There are still important features in Southeast Asian Chinese capitalism that sufficiently differentiate it from other forms of capitalism (for example Anglo-American capitalism). In particular, the *supranational organization* of Chinese capitalism, and the much more selective role of *personal and family relationships*, continue to underscore the uniqueness of such a regional form of capitalism. Whether it will survive the competitive and convergence pressures of economic globalization is a debatable issue. But there is no doubt that, as

Chinese capitalism is increasingly engaging with globalizing forces, its core features will be changed and reshaped and its viability depends very much on the usefulness of this mode of economic organization, both to its home countries and to the global economy. As Lim (2000: 12) concludes in her review of the past success, recent crisis and future evolution of Southeast Asian Chinese business,

> Whether Southeast Asian Chinese businesses will survive as independent entities in the long run will depend on their continued ability to be multi-cultural managers of and for others, providing sufficient value that multinationals will continue to see partnerships with them as necessary assets . . . In the long run, Southeast Asian Chinese companies will need to develop firm-specific competitive advantages that extend beyond their location-specific market knowledge, network assets and political connections to survive and prosper in the increasingly globally-integrated regional economy.

This conclusion no doubt carries the usual caricature of Southeast Asian Chinese capitalism as 'comprador capitalists', very similar to Yoshihara's (1988) notion of 'ersatz capitalism', but it also brings us a crucial message for future research into and understanding of Southeast Asian Chinese capitalism: we need to pay as much attention to its internal embeddedness in Southeast Asian countries as to its increasing articulation in the global economy that is both highly uncertain and transformative. These two elements of uncertainty and transformation are currently perhaps the best way to describe and characterize Southeast Asian Chinese capitalism.

NOTES

1. An earlier revised version of this chapter was published in *Asia Pacific Journal of Management*, **23**(3) in 2006. This chapter was first presented at the Symposium on 'China and Southeast Asia: Challenges, Opportunities and the Re-construction of Southeast Asian Chinese Ethnic Capital', 24–6 March 2004, City University of Hong Kong. I would like to thank Vivienne Wee and Kevin Hewison for inviting me to participate in the symposium. The NUS Academic Research Fund (R-109-000-050-112) supports the research underpinning this chapter. I am grateful to Angela Leung for her excellent research assistance. However, I am solely responsible for all errors and misinterpretations.
2. I use 'home' in inverted commas throughout this chapter, because many East and Southeast Asian economies might not be the birthplace for the first and, sometimes, second generations of many ethnic Chinese people.
3. The term 'overseas Chinese' may be contentious to some scholars or ethnic Chinese who are living outside mainland China. The term is related to the Chinese term *huaqiao* (Chinese national abroad) that has been sharply criticized in Southeast Asia for its implications that Chinese born abroad with status as a citizen in another nation are still Chinese in essence. *Huaren* (ethnic Chinese) has become more politically acceptable. In English, overseas Chinese is usually used to include *huaqiao, huaren* and residents of Taiwan, Hong Kong and Macau (*tong bao*), who are considered to be compatriots living in parts of the territory of China temporarily outside mainland Chinese control. See Wang (1991, 2000), Bolt (2000) and Ma and Cartier (2003) for the origin and status of ethnic Chinese living outside mainland China. Throughout this chapter, I will refer to 'ethnic Chinese' or to specific groups (for example Singaporean entrepreneurs), rather than 'overseas Chinese' in my discussions of change and continuity in Chinese capitalism. But references to the literature sometimes require the term 'overseas Chinese' to be clear. In such cases, I will use inverted commas to illustrate my discomfort with the term.
4. The term 'mainland China' will be used to denote the People's Republic of China.
5. Interestingly, one may argue that much of mainland China's exports is accounted for by foreign-owned manufacturing firms, some of which are managed and controlled by ethnic Chinese capitalists from East and Southeast Asia.

REFERENCES

Aoyama, Yuko (2000), 'Networks, keiretsu, and locations of the Japanese electronics industry in Asia', *Environment and Planning A*, **32**(2), 223–44.

Becht, Marco, P. Betts and R. Morck (2003), 'The complex evolution of family affairs', *The Financial Times*, 2 February.

Berger, Peter L. and Hsin-huang Michael Hsiao (eds) (1988), *In Search of an East Asian Development Model*, New Brunswick, NJ: Transaction Books.

Bolt, Paul J. (2000), *China and Southeast Asia's Ethnic Chinese: State and Diaspora in Contemporary Asia*, New York: Praeger.

Borrus, Michael, D. Ernst and S. Haggard (eds) (2000), *International Production Networks in Asia: Rivalry or Riches?*, London: Routledge.

Brown, Rajeswary Ampalavana (1994), *Capital and Entrepreneurship in South-East Asia*, London: Macmillan.

Brown, Rajeswary Ampalavana (2000), *Chinese Big Business and the Wealth of Asian Nations*, London: Palgrave.

Chan, Kwok Bun and See-Ngoh Claire Chiang (1994), *Stepping Out: The Making of Chinese Entrepreneurs*, Singapore: Simon and Schuster.

Chan, Wellington K.K. and A. McElderry (eds) (1998), 'Special issue on historical patterns of Chinese business', *Journal of Asian Business*, **14**(1).

Chandler, Alfred D. (1990), *Scale and Scope*, Cambridge, MA: Harvard University Press.

Chang, Maria Hsu (1995), 'Greater China and the Chinese "Global Tribe"', *Asian Survey*, **35**(10), 955–67.

Chen, Tain-Jy and Ying-Hua Ku (2004), 'Networking strategies of Taiwanese firms in Southeast Asia and China', in E.T. Gomez and H.M. Hsiao (eds), *Chinese Enterprise, Transnationalism, and Identity*, London: RoutledgeCurzon, pp. 151–71.

Clifford, Mark L. and Pete Engardio (2000), *Meltdown: Asia's Boom, Bust, and Beyond*, Paramus, NJ: Prentice-Hall Press.

Cushman, Jennifer W. and Gungwu Wang (eds) (1988), *Changing Identities of the Southeast Asian Chinese Since World War II*, Hong Kong: Hong Kong University Press.

Deyo, Frederic C. and Richard F. Doner (2000), 'Networks and technology development: a case study of a Thai autoparts manufacturer', *Journal of Asian Business*, **16**(1), 125–40.

DiMaggio, Paul J. (ed.) (2001), *The Twenty-First Century Firm: Changing Economic Organization in International Perspective*, Princeton, NJ: Princeton University Press.

Dobson, Wendy and S.Y. Chia (eds) (1997), *Multinationals and East Asian Integration*, Singapore: Institute of Southeast Asian Studies.

East Asia Analytical Unit (1995), *Overseas Chinese Business Networks in Asia*, Parkes, Australia: Department of Foreign Affairs and Trade.

Edgington, David W. and R. Hayter (2000), 'Foreign direct investment and the flying geese model: Japanese electronics firms in the Asia Pacific', *Environment and Planning A*, **32**(2), 281–304.

Encarnation, Dennis J. (ed.) (1999), *Japanese Multinationals in Asia: Regional Operations in Comparative Perspective*, Oxford: Oxford University Press.

Far Eastern Economic Review, 2 December 1993, p. 17.

Franks, Julian, C. Mayer and S. Rossi (2003), 'The origination and evolution of ownership and control', ECGI working papers, no. 09/203, European Corporate Governance Institute, Brussels.

Fruin, W. Mark (ed.) (1998), *Networks, Markets, and the Pacific Rim: Studies in Strategy*, New York: Oxford University Press.

Fukuyama, Francis (1995), *Trust: The Social Virtues and the Creation of Prosperity*, London: Hamish Hamilton.

Gambe, Annabelle R. (2000), *Overseas Chinese Entrepreneurship and Capitalist Development in Southeast Asia*, London: Macmillan.

Giroud, Axèle (2003), *Transnational Corporations, Technology and Economic Development: Backward Linkages and Knowledge Transfer in South-East Asia*, Cheltenham, UK and Northampton, MA, USA: Edward Elgar.

Gomez, Edmund Terence (1999), *Chinese Business in Malaysia: Accumulation, Accommodation and Ascendance*, Richmond, Surrey: Curzon.

Gomez, Edmund Terence (2004), 'Intra-ethnic cooperation in transnational perspective: Malaysian Chinese investments in the United Kingdom', in E.T. Gomez and H.M. Hsiao (eds), *Chinese Enterprise, Transnationalism, and Identity*, London: RoutledgeCurzon, pp. 109–47.

Gomez, Edmund Terence and Hsin-Huang Michael Hsiao (eds) (2001), *Chinese Business in South-East Asia: Contesting Cultural Explanations, Researching Entrepreneurship*, Richmond, Surrey: Curzon.

Gomez, Edmund Terence and Hsin-Huang Michael Hsiao (eds) (2004), *Chinese Enterprise, Transnationalism, and Identity*, London: RoutledgeCurzon.

Hall, Peter A. and D. Soskice (eds) (2001), *Varieties of Capitalism: The Institutional Foundations of Comparative Advantage*, Oxford: Oxford University Press.

Hamilton, Gary G. (ed.) (1991), *Business Networks and Economic Development in East and South East Asia*, Hong Kong: Centre of Asian Studies, University of Hong Kong.

Hamilton, Gary G. (2000), 'Reciprocity and control: the organisation of Chinese family-owned conglomerates', in Henry Wai-chung Yeung and Kris Olds (eds), *Globalization of Chinese Business Firms*, London: Macmillan, pp. 55–74.

Hamilton-Hart, Natasha (2002), *Asian States, Asian Bankers: Central Banking in Southeast Asia*, Ithaca, NY: Cornell University Press.

Harmes, Adam (1998), 'Institutional investors and the reproduction of neoliberalism', *Review of International Political Economy*, **5**(1), 92–121.

Hatch, Walter (2000), 'Regionalization trumps globalization: Japanese production networks in Asia', in Richard Stubbs and Geoffrey R.D. Underhill (eds), *Political Economy and the Changing Global Order*, New York: Oxford University Press, pp. 382–91.

Hatch, Walter and K. Yamamura (1996), *Asia in Japan's Embrace: Building a Regional Production Alliance*, Cambridge: Cambridge University Press.

Henderson, Jeffrey, P. Dicken, M. Hess, N. Coe and H.W.C. Yeung (2002), 'Global production networks and the analysis of economic development', *Review of International Political Economy*, **9**(3), 436–64.

Hewison, Kevin (2004), 'Pathways to recovery: bankers, business, and nationalism in Thailand', in E.T. Gomez and H.M. Hsiao (eds), *Chinese Enterprise, Transnationalism, and Identity*, London: RoutledgeCurzon, pp. 232–77.

Hodder, Rupert (1996), *Merchant Princes of the East: Cultural Delusions, Economic Success and the Overseas Chinese in Southeast Asia*, Chichester: John Wiley.

Hollingsworth, J. Rogers and Robert Boyer (eds) (1997), *Contemporary Capitalism: The Embeddedness of Institutions*, Cambridge: Cambridge University Press.

Hsing, You-tien (1998), *Making Capitalism in China: The Taiwan Connection*, New York: Oxford University Press.

Hsing, You-tien (2003), 'Ethnic identity and business solidarity: Chinese capitalism revisited', in Laurence J.C. Ma and C. Cartier (eds), *The Chinese Diaspora: Space, Place, Mobility and Identity*, Boulder, CO: Rowman and Littlefield Publishers, pp. 221–35.

Jesudason, James V. (1989), *Ethnicity and the Economy: The State, Chinese Business and Multinationals in Malaysia*, Singapore: Oxford University Press.

Jomo, K.S. (1997), 'A specific idiom of Chinese capitalism in Southeast Asia: Sino-Malaysian capital accumulation in the face of state hostility', in D. Chirot and A. Reid (eds), *Essential Outsiders: Chinese and Jews in the Modern Transformation of Southeast Asia and Central Europe*, Seattle: University of Washington Press, pp. 237–57.

Jomo, K.S. and Brian C. Folk (eds) (2003), *Ethnic Business: Chinese Capitalism in Southeast Asia*, London: RoutledgeCurzon.

Kao, John (1993), 'The worldwide web of Chinese business', *Harvard Business Review*, March–April, 24–36.

Klapper, Leora F. and Inessa Love (2002), 'Corporate governance, investor protection, and performance in emerging markets', policy research working paper no. 2818, World Bank, Washington, DC.

Kong, Lily (1999), 'Globalisation and Singaporean transmigration: re-imagining and negotiating national identity', *Political Geography*, **18**, 563–89.

Kotkin, Joel (1992), *Tribes: How Race, Religion and Identity Determine Success in the New Global Economy*, New York: Random House.

La Porta, Rafael, F. Lopez-de-Silanes and A. Shleifer (1999), 'Corporate ownership around the world', *Journal of Finance*, **54**(2), 471–517.

Lever-Tracy, Constance, D. Ip and N. Tracy (1996), *The Chinese Diaspora and Mainland China: An Emerging Economic Synergy*, London: Macmillan.

Lim, Linda Y.C. (2000), 'Southeast Asian Chinese business: past success, recent crisis and future evolution', *Journal of Asian Business*, **16**(1), 1–14.

Lim, Linda Y.C. and Pang-Eng Fong (1991), *Foreign Direct Investment and Industrialization in Malaysia, Singapore, Taiwan and Thailand*, Paris: OECD.

Lim, Linda Y.C. and L.A.P. Gosling (eds) (1983), *The Chinese in Southeast Asia*, Singapore: Maruzen Asia.

Low, Linda (2001), 'Asian crisis, corporate and financial restructuring, and transformation of traditional Chinese enterprises', in Leo Douw, Cen Huang and David Ip (eds), *Rethinking Chinese Transnational Enterprises: Cultural Affinity and Business Strategies*, Richmond, Surrey: Curzon, pp. 240–61.

Ma, Laurence J.C. and C. Cartier (eds) (2003), *The Chinese Diaspora: Space, Place, Mobility and Identity*, Boulder, CO: Rowman and Littlefield Publishers.

Machado, Kit G. (1997), 'Japanese transnational production networks and ethnic Chinese business networks in East Asia: linkages and regional integration', paper presented at the Chinese Business in Southeast Asia Conference, University of Malaya, Kuala Lumpur, 23–5 June.

Magretta, Joan (1998), 'Fast, global, and entrepreneurial: supply chain management, Hong Kong style: an interview with Victor Fung', *Harvard Business Review*, **76**(5), 103–14.

Mathews, John A. (2002), *Dragon Multinational: A New Model for Global Growth*, Oxford: Oxford University Press.

McKendrick, David G., R.F. Doner and S. Haggard (2000), *From Silicon Valley to Singapore: Location and Competitive Advantage in the Hard Disk Drive Industry*, Stanford: Stanford University Press.

McVey, Ruth (ed.) (1992), *Southeast Asian Capitalists*, Ithaca, NY: Cornell University Southeast Asia Program.

Menkhoff, Thomas (1993), *Trade Routes, Trust and Trading Networks – Chinese Small Enterprises in Singapore*, Saarbrucken: Verlag breitenback Publishers.

Menkhoff, Thomas and D. Sikorski (2002), 'Asia's Chinese entrepreneurs between myth-making and renewal', in T. Menkhoff and S. Gerke (eds), *Chinese Entrepreneurship and Asian Business Networks*, London: RoutledgeCurzon, pp. 23–42.

Mitton, Todd (2002), 'A cross-firm analysis of the impact of corporate governance on the East Asian financial crisis', *Journal of Financial Economics*, **64**, 215–41.

Olds, Kris and H.W.C. Yeung (1999), '(Re)shaping "Chinese" business networks in a globalising era', *Environment and Planning D: Society and Space*, **17**(5), 535–55.

Olds, Kris and H.W.C. Yeung (2004), 'Pathways to global city formation: a view from the developmental city-state of Singapore', *Review of International Political Economy*, **11**(3), 489–521.

Ong, Aihwa and D. Nonini (eds) (1997), *Ungrounded Empires: The Cultural Politics of Modern Chinese Transnationalism*, London: Routledge.

Pongpaichit, Pasuk (1990), *The New Wave of Japanese Investment in ASEAN*, Singapore: Institute of Southeast Asian Studies.

Powell, Walter W. (1990), 'Neither market nor hierarchy: network forms of organization', *Research in Organizational Behaviour*, **12**, 295–336.

Redding, S. Gordon (1990), *The Spirit of Chinese Capitalism*, Berlin: De Gruyter.

Redding, S. Gordon (2000), 'What is Chinese about Chinese family business? And how much is family and how much is business?', in H.W.C. Yeung and K. Olds (eds), *Globalization of Chinese Business Firms*, London: Macmillan, pp. 31–54.

Ridding, John and J. Kynge (1997), 'Empires can strike back', *The Financial Times*, 5 November, p. 13.

Sassen, Saskia (1991), *The Global City: New York, London, Tokyo*, Princeton, NJ: Princeton University Press.

Schmukler, Sergio and E. Vesperoni (2001), 'Globalization and firms' financing choices', IMF working paper WP/01/95, IMF,Washington, DC.

Silin, Robert H. (1976), *Leadership and Values: The Organization of Large-Scale Taiwanese Enterprises*, Cambridge, MA: Harvard University Press.

Sklair, Leslie (2000), *The Transnational Capitalist Class*, Oxford: Blackwell.

Suryadinata, Leo (ed.) (1995), *Southeast Asian Chinese and China: The Political–Economic Dimension*, Singapore: Times Academic Press.

Suryadinata, Leo (ed.) (1997), *Ethnic Chinese as Southeast Asians*, Singapore: Institute of Southeast Asian Studies.

The Business Times, various issues, Singapore.

The Straits Times, various issues, Singapore.

Tu, Wei-Ming (ed.) (1996), *Confucian Traditions in East Asian Modernity: Moral Education and Economic Culture in Japan and the Four Mini-Dragons*, Cambridge, MA: Harvard University Press.

UNCTAD (various years), *World Investment Report*, Geneva: UNCTAD.

Wang, Gungwu (1981), *Community and Nation: Essays on Southeast Asia and the Chinese*, Singapore: Heinemann.

Wang, Gungwu (1991), *China and the Chinese Overseas*, Singapore: Times Academic Press.

Wang, Gungwu (1995), 'The Southeast Asian Chinese and the development of China', in L. Suryadinata (ed.), *Southeast Asian Chinese and China: The Political–Economic Dimension*, Singapore: Times Academic Press, pp. 12–30.

Wang, Gungwu (2000), *The Chinese Overseas: From Earthbound China to the Quest for Autonomy*, Cambridge, MA: Harvard University Press.

Weber, Max ([1930] 1992), *The Protestant Ethic and the Spirit of Capitalism*, trans. Talcott Parsons, London: Routledge.

Weidenbaum, Murray and S. Hughes (1996), *The Bamboo Network: How Expatriate Chinese Entrepreneurs are Creating a New Economic Superpower in Asia*, New York: The Free Press.

Whitley, Richard (1992), *Business Systems in East Asia: Firms, Markets and Societies*, London: Sage.

Whitley, Richard (1999), *Divergent Capitalisms: The Social Structuring and Change of Business Systems*, New York: Oxford University Press.

Williamson, Oliver E. (1975), *Markets and Hierarchies: Analysis and Antitrust Implications*, New York: The Free Press.

Williamson, Oliver E. (1985), *The Economic Institution of Capitalism*, New York: The Free Press.

Wong, Raymond Sin-Kwok (2004), 'Chinese business firms and entrepreneurs in Hong Kong', in E.T. Gomez and H.M. Hsiao (eds), *Chinese Enterprise, Transnationalism, and Identity*, London: RoutledgeCurzon, pp. 39–71.

Wong, Siu-lun (1988), *Emigrant Entrepreneurs: Shanghai Industrialists in Hong Kong*, Hong Kong: Oxford University Press.

Wu, Friedrich and K.K. Puah (2002), 'Foreign direct investment to China and Southeast Asia: has ASEAN been losing out?', *Journal of Asian Business*, **18**(3), 45–58.

Yang, Mayfair M.H. (2002), 'The resilience of guanxi and its new deployments: a critique of some new guanxi scholarship', *The China Quarterly*, **170**, 459–76.

Yao, Souchou (2002), *Confucian Capitalism: Discourse, Practice and the Myth of Chinese Enterprise*, London: RoutledgeCurzon.

Yee, Albert (1989), *A People Misruled: The Chinese Stepping-Stone Syndrome*, Singapore: Heinemann Asia.

Yen, Ching-hwang (2002), *The Ethnic Chinese in East and Southeast Asia: Business, Culture and Politics*, Singapore: Times Academic Press.

Yeung, Henry Wai-chung (1999a), 'The internationalization of ethnic Chinese business firms from Southeast Asia: strategies, processes and competitive advantage', *International Journal of Urban and Regional Research*, **23**(1), 103–27.

Yeung, Henry Wai-chung (1999b), 'Under siege? Economic globalisation and Chinese business in Southeast Asia', *Economy and Society*, **28**(1), 1–29.

Yeung, Henry Wai-chung (2000a), 'The dynamics of Asian business systems in a globalising era', *Review of International Political Economy*, **7**(3), 399–433.

Yeung, Henry Wai-chung (2000b), 'Economic globalisation, crisis, and the emergence of Chinese business communities in Southeast Asia', *International Sociology*, **15**(2), 269–90.

Yeung, Henry Wai-chung (2000c), 'Local politics and foreign ventures in China's transitional economy: the political economy of Singaporean investments in China', *Political Geography*, **19**(7), 809–840.

Yeung, Henry Wai-chung (2001), 'Organising regional production networks in Southeast Asia: implications for production fragmentation, trade and rules of origin', *Journal of Economic Geography*, **1**(3), 299–321.

Yeung, Henry Wai-chung (2002), *Entrepreneurship and the Internationalisation of Asian Firms: An Institutional Perspective*, Cheltenham, UK and Northampton, MA, USA: Edward Elgar.

Yeung, Henry Wai-chung (2003), 'Financing Chinese capitalism: principal banks, economic crisis, and Chinese family firms in Singapore', Cornell Law School, East Asian Law and Culture Conference Series, working paper 1, 26 April (http://lsr.nellco.org/cornell/ealccs/caafm/1).

Yeung, Henry Wai-chung (2004), *Chinese Capitalism in a Global Era: Towards Hybrid Capitalism*, London: Routledge.

Yeung, Henry Wai-chung and Kris Olds (eds) (2000), *Globalization of Chinese Business Firms*, New York: Macmillan.

Yeung, Henry Wai-chung and Tse Min Soh (2000), 'Corporate governance and the global reach of Chinese family firms in Singapore', *Seoul Journal of Economics*, **13**(3), 301–34.

Yoshihara, Kunio (1988), *The Rise of Ersatz Capitalism in South East Asia*, Singapore: Oxford University Press.

19. Innovation policies for Asian SMEs: an innovation system perspective

Cristina Chaminade and Jan Vang

Among policy makers and academics, consensus suggests that innovation is a crucial factor in generating economic growth and development in the developed world (Lundvall, 1992; Von Hippel, 1988). Traditionally, the importance of innovations is ascribed to the new competitive landscape stemming from increased economic globalization, new types of regulation of international trade (Amin, 2004), improved ICT technologies, and lower prices on transportation (Fröbel *et al.*, 1980). In this structural explanation, firms in the developed world are forced to innovate to maintain their competitiveness, since firms located in developing countries can catch up by applying imitation-based strategies, and produce almost identical products to those manufactured in the developed world at a cheaper price (Vang and Asheim, 2006; see also the experience of Taiwan in Chapter 16 of this volume). Since firms in developing countries have been conceptualized as imitators it is not surprising that the importance of innovation for developing countries has only recently begun to be acknowledged.

Traditionally, growth, catching up and development in less industrialized countries has been considered a matter of exploiting their comparative advantage in terms of low factor costs (especially labour costs). We do not wish to debate the reasons for focusing on countries' comparative advantages. However, we argue that the models still suffer on several accounts. They tend to assume a mechanistic process that ignores the importance of firm's innovative practices in the process of upgrading in the value chain, the particularities of firms in developing countries and how the (lack of) systemic features in the institutional support system affects these innovative practices. Thus the increasing interest among governments in the Asian countries in innovation policies should be welcome. But before uncritically embracing these initiatives, some considerations need to be taken into account.

The problem is that, in developing countries, the general trend has been to follow the innovation policies of the developed world that, we will argue, might not be the most appropriate thing to do. In the developed world, innovation policy has been largely dominated by technology policy (Lundvall and Borrás, 2004), initially as a consequence of the so-called 'linear model of innovation' that places R&D in the centre of the innovation process, and primarily focuses on (radical) product innovations. Following this model, governments have supported mainly fast-growing and large firms in technology-intensive industries, such as information and communication technologies (ICT), biotechnology or Nanotechnology that showed rapid growth and high value added. Copying the innovation policy of the developed countries, many governments in the South also decided to implement large-scale programmes in high-tech industries dominated by large firms.[1]

However, most economic activity in developing countries remains outside these high-tech industries, and is based on small and medium-sized firms (SMEs).[2] For example, in Indonesia, Taiwan, India and Thailand, between 90 and 98 per cent of the establishments are SMEs, and employ between 70 and 80 per cent of the workforce. Clarysse and Uytterhaegen (1999) estimate that only 3 per cent of the SMEs are in high-tech industries and receive the attention of policy makers.[3] If the government wants to support innovation, a set of complementary policies is needed to address the main economic actors (SMEs) and most important industries (usually traditional and natural resource-based) in the economy. The point of departure for this chapter is that, in developing countries, SMEs are responsible for the largest part of employment and a significant share of value added, and that innovation policy supporting the particularities of SMEs has been widely ignored; occasionally, SMEs have even been discriminated against.

This chapter aims at shedding some light on the immensely complicated issue of innovation policy for SMEs in developing countries or, more specifically, Asian SMEs. In other words, one can say that the purpose of this chapter is to discuss the type of innovation policy needed to reach the 65 per cent of potential innovators that have been ignored by current policies (Clarysse and Uytterhaegen, 1999). Historical examples can also illustrate why the Asian SMEs should be targeted. The Asian SMEs have played a vital role in the development of the tiger economies in East Asia (Hong Kong and Taiwan) and their younger siblings in South East Asia (Malaysia, Thailand) and are among the most important sources of employment in the rest of Asia. Hence there are good reasons to look into the type of innovation policy that is needed to facilitate their growth and competitiveness. As the Asian innovation systems are primarily developed around supporting large firms or high-tech firms, there is also an urgent need to pay attention to redesigning the innovation systems to integrate the SMEs. Since these issues are, as said, immensely complicated and call for both theoretical and empirical novelty, the chapter will be explorative in nature, and cannot do full justice to the diversity of conditions shaping the innovation-based competitiveness of Asian SMEs.

Asian SMEs have traditionally tended to concentrate spatially with other SMEs operating in the same industry. This is especially clear in traditional industries and resources-based industries in Asian countries. The regional dimension is crucial, as SMEs tend to be dependent on regional conditions and regional support. This can partly be attributed to the fragmentation and the transitional character of the national innovation system in many Asian countries (Lundvall *et al.*, 2006).

The chapter applies the so-called 'regional innovation systems' (RIS) approach (cf. Chapter 16 in this volume). Regional innovation systems can be seen as a constellation of industrial clusters surrounded by innovation supporting organizations (Asheim and Coenen, 2005). In this sense, industrial clusters represent the production system/part of the regional innovation system. In the RIS approach, industrial clusters are defined as the geographic concentration of firms in the same or related industries (Porter, 1998; Pietrobelli and Rabellotti, 2004; for a critique, see Martin and Sunley, 2003). In well-functioning clusters, proximity facilitates the knowledge and information circulation. The recent adaptation of the RIS approach to the Asian context will be used as a departure point in the discussion (see also Vang and Asheim, 2006).

In the context of RIS, two important aspects need to be highlighted. Contrary to more traditional approaches to innovation and upgrading, an RIS approach stresses that supporting SMEs in their innovation-oriented upgrading process is a matter of not only facilitating the access to technology, but also providing what we later refer to as 'soft infrastructure' (increase qualification of the human resources, facilitate organizational change, support social capital). In contrast to other approaches stressing these variables, the RIS approach puts the emphasis on the systemic dimension. Most small firms will not be able to handle this process alone. They rely on interactive arrangements of a horizontal or vertical character that ensures the appropriate information and knowledge transfer. Arrangements such as subcontracting, clustering or collective support systems underpin the needed information and knowledge circulation (Berry *et al.*, 2002).[4] Furthermore collective arrangements facilitate the access to the resources needed in the innovation process (qualified human capital, technology, financial capital, and so on).

In this chapter, we analyse four clusters of SMEs that have been especially successful in entering the global market. Special attention is paid to the so-called soft infrastructure, the industry-specific needs for cluster (for example interaction) and RIS dynamics/policies (for example needs for devolution, industry-specific needs for building knowledge-creating institutions). By applying Pietrobelli and Rabellotti's (2004) SMEs typology of specialized suppliers, complex production systems, resource-based industries and traditional manufacturing industries, we strive towards providing some degree of totality of (relevant) industries; this typology adapts Pavitt's (1984) typology to developing countries. One case per industry is included. More specifically, Bangalore's software industry is presented as an example of specialized suppliers. The Thai automobile industry's clusters are examples of a complex production system. Taiwan's orchid industry is a case of a resource-based industry. The Jepara furniture cluster in Indonesia, represents a traditional manufacturing industry.

The rest of the chapter is structured as follows. After introducing stylized facts on SMEs' innovative performance, attention is turned to the theoretical framework. Taking into account the localized nature of SMEs' economic activity, our level of analysis is the regional system of innovation (RIS). We provide a general introduction, contextualize this to the Asian situation, and introduce the industry differences on the basis of Pietrobelli and Rabellotti's (2004) typology. We then turn to the empirical section, where special attention is paid to the four cases. Finally, we draw some general conclusions on innovation policies and the need for restructuring the Asian innovation systems.

REGIONAL INNOVATION SYSTEMS AND SMES

This section introduces the concept of regional innovation systems (RIS), and relates it to the Asian context. In innovation systems research, innovation is the result of an interactive learning process (Lundvall, 1992). The RIS approach stresses that regional clusters are crucial for Asian SMEs. Their interaction – at best – often takes place at the local level, with firms and other institutions located in the same geographical area. The extensive literature on regional innovation systems and clusters has long acknowledged the role of regional embedded networks in the innovation process of SMEs (Asheim *et al.*, 2003; Cooke and Morgan, 1998; Cooke and Will, 1999; Schmitz, 1992), and in developing countries (Albu, 1997; Bitran, 2004; Giuliani, 2004; Pietrobelli and Rabellotti, 2004; UNIDO, 1997, 2004; Giuliani and Bell, 2005). Moreover, this literature explicitly finds that mostly SMEs' external relations are more confined to the region than those of large firms (Cooke and Morgan, 1998; Asheim *et al.*, 2003). One of the reasons for this is that SMEs are more dependent on tacit knowledge and less capable of searching for and using codified knowledge. This forces them to rely more on personal ways of transferring (tacit) knowledge and on learning-by-doing and interacting.

According to Cooke and Morgan (1998), a RIS is defined as a system in which firms and other organizations are systematically engaged in interactive learning through an institutional milieu, characterized by embeddedness. The crux of this definition lies in the notion of embeddedness. This refers to the importance of personal relations and networks ingrained in local social and cultural institutions (Granovetter, 1985). Without it, the definition would equal the definition of a national innovation system written small. Additionally, a regional innovation system can be conceptualized as regional industrial clusters surrounded by supporting knowledge organizations (Asheim and Isaksen, 2002). This is the definition used in this chapter. Thus, the regional innovation system is boiled down to two main types of actors and the interactions between them. The first type of actors concerns the companies in a region's main industrial clusters, as well as their support industries (for example customers and suppliers). The second type of actors, backing up the innovative performance of the first type of actors, includes research and higher education institutes (universities, technical colleges and R&D institutes), technology transfer agencies, vocational training organizations, business associations, finance institutions, and so on. These knowledge-creating and diffusing organizations have considerable competence, train labour, provide necessary finance, and so on, to support regional innovativeness.

The notion of a well-functioning RIS involves a strategic institutionalization of innovation between the private and the public sectors in a systemic way, constituting an institutional infrastructure as a 'superstructure' to the production structure of a region. The systemic dimension of an RIS derives in part from this partner-based character, associated with innovation in networks. While, as Lundvall (1992) puts it, an innovation system is a set of relationships between entities or nodal points involved in innovation, it is really much more than this. Such relationships, to be systemic, must involve some degree of interdependence; not all relationships may be equally strong all the time, but some may be. Stressing interdependency is crucial in a developmental context, where, as we have explained above, the development model to a large extent is based on indigenous (at least in initial phases) capital and knowledge sources. The challenge is thus for most clusters in developing countries to attract TNCs and other capital influxes, and gradually develop a situation of interdependency between the TNC and the local/regional small firms, as well as between the TNCs and the institutional support system that is beneficial for both the TNC and the regional cluster of indigenous SMEs.

A developed and continuously developing absorptive capacity is a prerequisite for firms and regions to engage efficiently in interactive learning (Cohen and Levinthal, 1990; Zahra and George, 2002). Absorptive capacity, as conceptualized in this chapter, is considered as a dynamic capability that allows firms and/or regions to take advantage of knowledge and information in their environment, process it and commercialize it. Subsequently, organization change takes place to allow these firms to take advantage of the new information. We suggest, first, that a firm's absorptive capacity is a function of its prior internal knowledge, being tacit or codified, and the institutional setting, referring to, among other aspects, how social capital allows for knowledge to circulate and how public institutions serve this knowledge circulation. Second, a region has an absorptive capacity that is a function of individual firms' absorptive capacity, human capital (formal and tacit), social capital, and financial capital. Hence we oppose seeing regional absorptive capacity as simply an aggregate of the individual firms' absorptive capacity. Absorptive capacity building involves investing in training human capital and engaging in collaboration between firms and universities.

SMEs' potential to benefit from this regional or local system of innovation is more limited than that of large firms and, at the same time, they depend much more than large firms on the conditions of the RIS. Large firms usually have the resources to acquire the required technology, hire qualified human resources on their own, or introduce new managerial techniques. SMEs, especially in developing countries, on the other hand, usually need to engage in collective actions to share the costs of the acquisition of machinery that will be used by all, and find financial resources, as they will not be able to do it on their own. These collective actions usually take place between producers localized in a certain area and, in some cases, are based on existing longstanding social relationships or social capital. These are built on trust and based on the initiative of more qualified entrepreneurs, or the support of the government. Thus SMEs are very dependent on the local conditions, and the role of the RIS for clusters of SMEs in developing countries is crucial.

Since the acquisition and transformation of knowledge required for innovation and the learning processes differ significantly across industries (Pavitt, 1984; Asheim *et al.*, 2003; Asheim and Gertler, 2004; Tunzelmann and Acha, 2004), we emphasize that the interaction of and need for institutions providing knowledge support for SMEs in an RIS have also to account for industrial differences. One can differentiate between four categories of clustered Asian SMEs: traditional manufacturing, resource-based industries, complex product systems and specialized suppliers. Some of the clustered SMEs rely on indigenous capabilities, while others have to rely on exogenous sources, especially TNCs and – to a minor extent – members of transnational communities. The impact of the large firms on indigenous SMEs varies significantly across industries. Sometimes SMEs establish a cooperative agreement with large firms, in which the two groups are on even terms and share the technology, infrastructure, capital or knowledge available to the firms in the cluster. In other instances, SMEs are acting only as subcontractors of large firms, and the transfer of knowledge can be very limited. The role of large firms in a local cluster will be discussed and illustrated in the cases described later in this chapter. Table 19.1 summarizes the main characteristics of each cluster.

Traditional manufacturing and natural resources-based industries are the most common in most Asian countries (Dhungana, 2003). Food, beverages and textiles are the most important industries, in terms of employment and value added in manufacturing, at least in India, Indonesia, the Philippines, China, Sri Lanka and Thailand. With regard to the resource-based clusters in Asia, one can find convincing examples of their upgrading and insertion in the global value chains.[5] The upgrading in this type of industry is dependent on the development and acquisition of scientific knowledge, and its application to both product and processes. The linkages with basic and applied research institutions are crucial in the innovation of these industries. SMEs in complex product systems

Table 19.1   Main clusters of SMEs in Asia

Groups	Industries	Learning patterns	Description
Traditional manufacturing industries	Textile and garments, footwear, furniture, ceramic tiles	Mainly supplier dominated, labour-intensive firms	• Process innovation mainly and small incremental product innovation. Clustering facilitates organizational innovation • Most new techniques originate from machinery and chemical industries • Opportunity for technological accumulation is focused on improvements and modifications in production methods and associated inputs, and on product design • Competition based on costs • Externalities involve the access to workers' specialized skills, the linkages with specialized local supply of inputs and services, dissemination of specialized know-how and information, shared machinery and infrastructure and access to international markets • Information flows through informal channels facilitated by the local cohesion within the cluster as well as a result of the rotation of workers among the firms in the cluster
Resource-based industries	Sugar, tobacco, wine, fruit, dairy, mining	Supplier-dominated, science-based	• Importance of basic and applied research led by public research institutes owing to low appropriability conditions • Most innovation is generated by suppliers (machinery, seeds, chemicals, etc) • Most innovations and growth of these clusters are the result of the cooperation with scientific institutions • Increasing importance of international sanitary and quality standards and of patents • Upgrading of SMEs in these clusters can be with or without the intervention of a large firm. In some cases, upgrading is the result of joint technology development and coordinated actions

		between firms, business associations, universities and other actors. In some others, TNCs provide the technology and knowledge required for the upgrading of the local SMEs
Scale-intensive firms	Automobile and auto parts, aircraft, consumer electronics	• Technological accumulation is generated by the design, building and operation of complex production systems or products. • Process and product technologies develop incrementally (modular production systems). For consumer electronics, technological accumulation emerges mainly from corporate R&D labs and universities • Medium appropriability, high barriers to entry • Local SMEs are usually required to comply with international quality standards in order to participate in the network. Large assembler firms usually determine the scope of change of the local network of subcontractors • Externalities for geographical concentration are scarce, as both the leader firm and the assembler operate globally • Most knowledge needed in the production process is codified, thus the need to interact with local suppliers is limited
Specialized suppliers	Software	• Often small firms. Important user–producer interactions. Learning from advanced users • Low barriers to entry and low appropriability • High in-house R&D for development of cutting-edge technologies • Formal joint cooperation between firms is limited • Technological innovation is product innovation although upgrading is also the result of non-technological innovation such as joint marketing initiatives or changes in the organization • Mobility of human resources among the different firms is an important channel for knowledge diffusion across the cluster

Source: Adapted from Pietrobelli and Rabellotti (2004: 8).

(CoPS) are highly specialized firms, anchored to a large assembler that operates as the leading firm. Innovation in the network of CoPS is highly dependent on the strategy and the directions of the assembler. Specialized suppliers (for example in software) are very important in the most advanced countries in Asia (India, Singapore, South Korea) and are less relevant for the less developed countries.

RIS AND CLUSTERS OF SMES IN ASIAN COUNTRIES

The aim of this section is to apply the RIS framework to the Asian countries, in a way that highlights how systemic propensities differ across industries. In this section, we point to the stylized facts of constraints on economic development in Asian countries from an RIS perspective. The limited space in this chapter prevents us from paying too much attention to the different degrees of industrialization and development in the Asian countries. In accordance with most studies in development research, the RIS perspective stresses the importance of physical capital (hard infrastructure), social capital (soft infrastructure), human capital (education and training) and financial capital (Vang and Asheim, 2006). What the RIS perspective adds to this is the systemic propensities and an emphasis on interactive aspects in a territorial and industrial context. The hard infrastructure is considered more as a contingency than an actual part of the more theoretical aspects. Thus it will only be treated in this manner. Most attention will be paid to the other aspects (for example soft infrastructure). The importance of the different factors and the degree of interaction varies according to the dominating industrial activity in the region in question and, naturally, the already existing endowment of particular factors.[6] The discussion of each of the components of the RIS will particularize the four types of industries described above.

Human Capital (Soft Infrastructure) in the Asian Context

Human capital refers to 'the skills, education, health, and training of individuals' (Becker, 1998: 1). It is considered a corner stone in development (Romer, 1990). One of the most important drawbacks of developing countries is the poor supply of qualified general and, subsequently, industry-specific human capital. As a proxy for the lack of general human capital, one can use illiteracy rates. Adult illiteracy still reaches the double digits in some Asian countries, such as Indonesia and Malaysia (World Bank, 2003). Enrolment in secondary education is around 50 per cent,[7] while most of the developed world reaches 90 to 100 per cent. With the exception of some countries like South Korea, the enrolment in tertiary education is between 10 and 20 per cent. SMEs need to use human resources more intensively than large firms in their innovation process (Kaufmann and Tödtling, 2002).

As a consequence of the poorly developed educational system, SMEs in Asian countries have to rely on employing a significant portion of poor and low-skill workforce (Das, 2003) and rely much more on learning-by-doing, as opposed to formal training. The lack of qualification among the employees constrains the firms' absorptive capacity, that is the ability to utilize available information, and the information and knowledge that comes from interaction with users. Competencies, when it comes to incremental improvement, reorganization of production processes or cultivating craftsmanship knowledge, are highly limited. This means that firms have a limited prior knowledge of modern production, thus only limited absorptive capacity. In SMEs, almost all decisions are taken by the owners or the managing directors (Oyelaran-Oyeyinka and Lal, 2004). This implies that decisions made by small firms are highly influenced by the qualifications and skills of the manager directors.

The lack of qualified human resources, the poor managerial skills of the manager and the difficulties of gaining access to strategic information are considered to be the main obstacles to innovation in SMEs among Asian countries. The problems associated with the poor qualifications of human resources can be illustrated in the cases of the Jepara furniture cluster (Indonesia) and the Thai automotive cluster. In the Jepara cluster, as summarized in Table 19.2, knowledge creation is basically through apprenticeship and learning-by-doing in general. In the cluster, there are a limited number of highly skilled craftsmen, who are employed by joint ventures of SMEs or larger foreign firms (Sandee, 1998). Additionally, managerial and marketing skills are often lacking, which seriously limits the absorptive capacity of the firm. In the Thai automotive industry, owing to the lack of competition/incentives[8] and lack of opportunities, because of the global strategies on which the assemblers relied, the Thai SMEs were not stimulated to invest in their human capital and technological upgrading, nor did their profit margins allow for huge investments in human capital building. The central Thai government did not develop or implement competitiveness-oriented policies (the link to decentralization will be elaborated upon below). As a result, most Thai SMEs lack the human capital and organizational ability required to engage in innovation (and upgrading in the global value chain); that is, they lack the required absorptive capacity to acquire technology and knowledge generated elsewhere.

However, not all Asian RIS lack the required qualified human capital. For example, Taiwanese SMEs have undergone a tremendous upgrading in formal competencies in recent years, and the level of education among the population is very high. This is facilitating the upgrading process of the flower industry in Taiwan. The upgrading strategy for this industry has been based on creating links with biotech laboratories, which undertake research and development in new species of flowers. The high level qualification of the producers of the flowers facilitates the linkages between the scientific infrastructure provided by the RIS and the productive infrastructure. In the Bangalore software industry, there is also a sufficient supply of qualified human resources, as there are several universities, business schools and high schools located in the region that provide the cluster with the required supply of skilled labour.

Yet, even when the RIS provides the necessary supply of human capital, SMEs will only benefit from qualified human capital if the right organizational setting is in place. Investing in training is only one variable in the equation; if firms in the RIS do not have the ability to absorb skilled labour and use it to upgrade or move up in the value chain, all training efforts will be dismissed. In other words, the soft infrastructure of an RIS comprises both the provision of skilled human capital and the absorptive capacity of the firms, that in turn also depend on their employees and organizational issues. In sum, one of the key elements in the RIS in Asia is the provision of timely and qualified human capital to support the industries settled in the region. For Asian SMEs, being located in a 'human capital-rich region' is definitively an advantage, as the lack of skilled human capital is one of the main constraints on innovation and growth. But in order to benefit from these local

Table 19.2 *Comparison of the Asian cases*

	Traditional Jepara cluster	Resource-based Taiwan flower industry	CoPS Automotive Thailand	Specialized suppliers Software Bangalore
Stylized facts about the cluster	– Located on Java, Indonesia. – About 2000 small firms, 100 large and medium ones. – 40 000 permanent employees. – Firms are dispersed across 80 villages in the Jepara region. – 70% of production goes to international markets.	– Production dominated by small farms (1 ha per family). – Remarkable growth over the last decade as a consequence of increased domestic demand and increased exports (mainly Japan and the US). – Main competitors are Thailand or China. – Clear division of labour between the production and commercialization of flowers exists.	– Strongly dominated by TNC assemblers. Local SMEs are usually 2nd and 3rd tier, with very limited access to knowledge and technology. The first tier consists of more than 700 companies. 40% of these are owned by TNCs. Fully Thai-owned companies constitute 50%, but only 10% of the value. Second-tier suppliers are around 1000 firms. – Around 113 512 are employed in the industry. SME accounts for approximately 50% of the employees. – The Thai automobile industry is constituted by several clusters. – Diseconomies of agglomeration (ranging from increased wages, scarcity of workers to traffic congestion) have resulted in the emergence of new clusters scattered around Thailand.	– Most important IT cluster outside US. – Cluster with strong presence of multinational firms but dominated by SMEs. – Bangalore houses several high-tech clusters (defence, aeronautics and IT). It is the scientific and engineering centre of India. – India's best research university, Indian Institute of Science, is based in Bangalore. – Competitiveness is based on easy access to qualified and relatively cheap technical human capital; only 10–15% of the revenues of the sector are from SMEs.

				– Thailand is the most important hub for auto-motive production in Asia. – Most major assemblers are present in Thailand.	
Regional autonomy	High, due to geographical fragmentation and ethnical diversity. National policy is highly limited. Regional governments are responsible for designing and implementing policies in the region.	High: Taiwan is considered to be one region with complete de facto political autonomy from mainland China.	Low: the Thai innovation system is highly centralized (when it comes to the automotive industry). Policy-making, budget allocation is centralized in Bangkok. Regions do not hold any important decision-making powers, competencies or capacities.	Medium: while Bangalore has a certain degree of autonomy, the IT cluster is more shaped by the industrial development in the US than by local cluster effects and regional government bodies' policies. The state, apart from providing basic sound macroeconomic policies and other programmes, is not considered to be a main player in terms of regional policies.
Strategies for upgrading (role of TNC–SME)	Innovation is customer-driven, but most firms do not have direct access to the large international buyer. Joint actions to attend international trade fairs (supported by the government) have been very successful.	Innovation is science-driven. Growth of the industry is the result of interaction between biotech institutes and private industry. This is the result of deliberate policy initiatives generated by the Taiwanese government. High coordination between researchers and market producers is needed. Government can play a role in supporting the interaction between these institutions.	Innovation is TNC-driven. The TNC defines the scope of change and only SMEs that are 1st tier have access to knowledge and information on the market. SMEs that want to be part of the TNC network need to comply with international quality standards. Only 10% of the SMEs have an ISO certification. Government has a great role in	Innovation is customer-driven. but for many firms the customer is the TNC. They work on per job-work basis, as subcontractors, and their scope for upgrading and innovating is limited. Another group of SMEs have opted to be independent. They have better chances to enter international markets if they are able to gain

Table 19.2   (continued)

	Traditional Jepara cluster	Resource-based Taiwan flower industry	CoPS Automotive Thailand	Specialized suppliers Software Bangalore
			encouraging and supporting SMEs to obtain such quality standards.	recognition Support from the government to attend international trade fairs could have a positive impact.
Human capital	Craft industry. Knowledge acquisition is by learning-by-doing. There are a limited number of very qualified human resources that are shared by several SMEs and large firms. Managerial and marketing skills are needed.	Knowledge is very fragmented, in three groups: producers only know about production techniques, but nothing about the market; marketing of the flowers is dominated by 'marketing' firms; innovation in the cluster is driven by advances in biotechnology, with researchers in labs relatively isolated from producers and markets.	Production is dominated by blue-collar workers. Competition is based on costs, quality standards and to a lesser extent on *just in time*. Learning is limited as production is according to blueprints. Upgrading requires formal training in engineering and design.	Firms have easy access to qualified human resources. The region houses an important number of education and training institutions, so the technical skills are ensured. However managerial and marketing skills could be strengthened.
Social capital & networks	Social capital is strong, based on kinship and family ties. Collective action is common, both to use machinery and to attain economies of scale.	Social capital is strong, based on Chinese values and collective action is common. However, networks seem to be confined to one activity (production, research or commercialization).	Social capital is weak. Some initiatives like the Toyota's sponsored Automobile Industry Club only reach 1st tiers. Collaboration between the SMEs and collective action are almost non-existent, not even enough to achieve efficiency based on specialization.	Social capital is relatively weak, based on the alumni network and the mobility of workers. Collective action exists, especially for marketing purposes and, to a lesser extent, to share technological knowledge or gain economies of scale. However, collective action

			Government could support the introduction of quality standards to groups of complementary SMEs.	has been hampered by fierce competition between the firms. Cooperation is successful when based on specialization. Government could play a role supporting collective initiatives of complementary firms and providing information on the SMEs' core business.
Financial capital	Weak support by financial institutions. Cluster works on micro credits among the producers (based on social capital).	The upgrading of the cluster via investment in research and technology requires vast amounts of financial capital provided by the government and some large international firms.	Introducing quality standards is a costly process. Most of the SMEs in the cluster do not have any access to financial capital. Only SMEs in the 1st tier might benefit from some support from the TNC.	Venture capital market in India suffers from excessive regulations and bureaucracy. Funding is provided by some TNC and members of the transnational community returning from the US (or just setting up some business in India). Public procurement is non-existent.
Policy	The presence of the government in the cluster has been limited; however, some of the initiatives (like promoting attendance at international trade fairs) have been very successful. More support for the development of human capital, especially managerial and marketing skills, provision of information.	Success in this cluster is based on coordination of the different actors (producers, researchers and customers) as well as access to information on international opportunities and trends and the provision of infrastructure (scientific mainly). The government has a great role to play in setting the RIS	Latest Thai policy towards the sector has been quite detrimental for the SMEs as it eliminated the obligations of TNC to local manufacturers. Government has a role to play in the provision of soft and hard infrastructure for the cluster: qualification of human resources, introduction of quality standards, support of	Government has an important role fomenting collective actions among SMEs in the cluster, focusing on specialization and not competition. Assistance for international trade fairs could facilitate the insertion of these SMEs in the international market. Public procurement could

Table 19.2 (continued)

Traditional Jepara cluster	Resource-based Taiwan flower industry	CoPS Automotive Thailand	Specialized suppliers Software Bangalore
on international trends and facilitating direct access to the customer is needed.	infrastructure and connecting the relevant actors.	collective action and specialization (upgrading in the value change), encouraging a change of strategy from cost reduction to quality and specialization (knowledge based), and restoring the obligations of TNC towards indigenous SMEs.	also be a powerful incentive for the local SMEs. Finally, upgrading managerial skills to complement the high technical skills is needed.

Sources: Berry *et al.* (2002); Lecler (2002); NASSCOM (2005); Parthasarathy (2004); Sandee (1998), Sandee and Rietveld (2001); Taiwan Council of Agriculture (2003); Taiwan Ministry of Economic Affairs (2004); Techakanont and Terdudomtham (2004); Tsai (2001); Tsai and Wang (2002); Samart (2004).

conditions, Asian SMEs need to develop their absorptive capacity, creating organizations that nurture innovation.

Social Capital and Networks (Soft Infrastructure) in the Asian Context

Soft infrastructure varies significantly and is strongly dependent on the local culture. Its heterogeneity and dynamics might be measured in terms of value and behavioural regularities. Following the World Bank (1998: 8), 'Social capital refers to the institutions, relationships, and norms that shape the quality and quantity of a society's social interactions . . . Social capital is not just the sum of the institutions which underpin a society – it is the glue that holds them together.' Social capital refers both to *structural* social capital and to *cognitive* social capital (World Bank, 2002). Structural social capital refers to 'relatively objective and externally observable social structures, such as networks, associations, and institutions, and the rules and procedures they embody' (ibid.: 3). Cognitive social capital comprises 'more subjective and intangible elements such as generally accepted attitudes and norms of behaviour, shared values, reciprocity, and trust'.[9] Cognitive social capital can explain the rise in ethnic-based networks of SMEs in Asian countries (for example among Indians and Chinese) that provide the resources needed for the firm (see also Chapters 15 and 18 in this volume). Social capital thus consists of at least two dimensions (Paldam, 2000): (1) trust that can be divided into generalized trust and special trust, and the latter in turn into trust in the law enforcement system, trust in the political and administrative system, and local trust; and (2) cooperative ability, that is people's ability to work together. Moreover, it is crucial whether the trust is specific (that is limited to one group) or generalized (that is to society as such).

It is generally argued that social capital, and the related concepts such as trust, has implications for the interaction between agents and nodes in the Asian RIS. Contrary to that envisioned by mainstream economists, economic interaction is not primarily a market-based exchange of tangible goods by anonymous agents, regulated by a complete contract in the context of efficient contract enforcement. On the contrary, exchange relies on incomplete contracts, either because of the lack of possibilities for creating complete contracts, because of the disadvantages in terms of a low degree of flexibility built into complete contracts, or because of inefficient contract enforcement, depending on the mutual trust of the partners involved in the transaction.

However, our cases illustrate that strong social capital is not equally necessary for all industries. In clusters of SMEs operating in traditional sectors, where tacit knowledge is predominant and the institutional framework is weak, strong social capital might facilitate SMEs' access to human resources, machinery and information required to upgrade. This is clearly the case in the Jepara furniture cluster, where social ties support initiatives to hire collectively qualified human resources, to gain access to international markets, or to achieve economies of scale, when large orders coming from abroad to one firm are served by several SMEs linked to that firm. Social capital is also very important in the Taiwanese case. Small businesses form tight networks, encompassing personal and business relationships. These networks or *guanxi* are based on traditional Chinese social values, where human relationships are closely linked to families, relatives, friends, classmates and previous colleagues (Liu, 1998; see also Chapter 4 in this volume) and occasionally segmented along dialect groups (for example Hakka, mainlander and Taiwanese).

Social capital can also be exclusive. In contrast to other types of clusters, where horizontal knowledge spillovers are considered crucial, this is not the case for the Thai automobile clusters. Networks are limited to first tier suppliers.[10] Second and third-tier suppliers do not benefit from these business networks, as they do not meet the quality standards (Sevilla and Soonthornthada, 2000). As an example, only 10 per cent of the Thai suppliers have ISO 9000, 14000 or 18000 certification. That is, collaboration based on social capital between Thai SMEs is not yet of much relevance, as most Thai SMEs simply do not have the competencies, knowledge and information that can create synergetic relationships.

Unless there is a high degree of social capital, cooperation, communication and, thus, mutual learning is limited. In short, the absence of social capital in turn reduces the prospects among local firms of getting access to important knowledge, knowledge sharing and interactive learning, and, hence, entering a virtuous development circle. Low social capital is usually associated with a high degree of competition and a lack of trust. Trust is built when firms do not see the partner as a competitor, but as someone bringing complementary skills to the joint venture. That is, consortia of SMEs have often been prone to failure, owing to the competitive tendencies among group members. In the Bangalore software cluster, evidence suggests that they have been more effective when member firms are complementing, instead of competing against, each other. Joint action has often involved marketing of products and seldom the development of a product (Nadvi, 1995).

Brokering institutions, such as entrepreneurial associations or cooperatives, can support the development of social capital and trust among the clustered SMEs. In the Taiwanese flower industry, the distribution of flowers to the domestic and international markets is in the hands of cooperatives and cooperative marketing teams, who also set the quality standards that the farmers should meet (Hsieh, 2001). In the Bangalore software cluster, entrepreneurial associations are commonly used to provide information to international companies on the different SMEs in the cluster. Brokering institutions are also an important element of the soft infrastructure of an RIS, and an important instrument for policy interventions at the regional and industry level.

Social capital also underpins the development of a regional or local absorptive capacity. Through localized knowledge sharing and interactive learning, knowledge can be disseminated locally/regionally, and provide the crucial insight that local firms need to move up the global value chain. But social capital might also transcend the regional boundaries of the cluster, as the Bangalore case illustrates. The social capital of the Indian transnational community played a crucial role in establishing the IT industry. To get access to orders, capital and more sophisticated knowledge, the Indian firms were forced to concentrate on transnational corporations. This uncertainty allowed the Indian transnational community, who held important positions in American firms, to play a significant role in shaping the outsourcing decisions in American firms. Recently one has witnessed a significant growth in interaction between Bangalore firms and American and European firms, as well as a diversification of the profiles of firms investing in Bangalore. The Bangalore firms have developed a certain degree of autonomy from the lead firms in the US and Europe. The autonomy is a function of investments in human capital and new managerial strategies, hence they can now provide all types of services, from the highest end of the value chain to the bottom end. This has allowed several firms to move up the global value chain.

In summary, social capital constitutes one of the elements of the regional innovation system that can support the emergence and development of clusters of SMEs, and their upgrading. Social ties might facilitate access to the required hard and soft resources for innovation (machinery, capital, skills, knowledge and so on), as well as providing the required flexibility to cope with fluctuations in the market in terms of quantity.

Financial Capital (Hard Infrastructure) in the Asian Context

Financial capital, especially foreign capital, is a scarce resource in Asian countries, especially since the economic crisis of the late 1990s. Moreover, even when those funds reach the productive systems, SMEs usually find great difficulties in gaining access to them. Financial capital is crucial for investing in human capital, and might even work as a useful means for building up social capital. For SMEs, it is also the way to acquire more sophisticated technology or, in some cases, simply to introduce some machinery in their production processes.

In Asian countries, risk-seeking capital that deliberately aims at upgrading industrial production is crucial, but scarce. It is often a precondition for local firms to obtain possibilities for experimenting with new products or process innovation and, subsequently, reducing their dependency on the TNCs. Moreover, when capital is scarce, it is tempting to use the available capital for satisfying short-term needs, thus not investing in innovative projects, competence building and so on, that is needed for long-term growth. Additionally, SMEs usually do not fulfil the requirements, in terms of assets, posed by financial institutions to obtain a loan. They therefore have to rely on localized informal financial institutions.

Initiatives to build a venture capital community in Asian countries are rare and, in some cases, the results are not very satisfactory, as illustrated by the Bangalore case. Although the national government has made significant efforts in establishing a venture capital community in India, the results have been puzzling. The development of venture capital in India can be divided into two periods: 1986–95 and 1995 to the present (Avnimelech and Teubal, 2002). During the first period, the first set of guidelines for the emergence of venture capital firms was approved. The Indian government, with the support of the World Bank, financed the creation of four venture capital (VC) companies that were subsidiaries of state-controlled banks. One of them, the TDCI, was located in Bangalore. The results of this first phase were weak. Some of the reasons adduced to the failure were the high degree of bureaucracy and the state control of the VC. During the second period, the market was open to private VC. The first foreign-owned VC firm was established in the 1990s, as well as the first 100 per cent privately owned VC. During this second phase, non-resident Indians, who are members of the transnational community, have become significant investors. Nevertheless, the VC infrastructure in India remains weak, highly bureaucratized and over-regulated.

In the absence of an institutionalized financial structure, social capital can facilitate the access to financial resources, as some examples in Asia show. When there is not a reliable infrastructure to provide SMEs with risk capital, or when the SMEs do not fulfil formal demands from financial institutions, social networks might provide the access to micro-credits and loans. In the Jepara cluster, for example, immigrants are an important source of funding for the cluster (Supratikno, 2002; cf. Tambunan, 2005). This is also the case for the software cluster in Bangalore.

Lead firms in the cluster, suppliers or buyers can finance the acquisition of technology, or even the training of the human resources. But in most of the cases, access to funds provided by TNCs, for example, is limited to a number of SMEs, as shown in the Thai automotive cluster. Only SMEs in the first tier might benefit from some support by TNCs. As demonstrated by Ramachandran (1993) and Techakanont (2003), TNCs spend more resources on technology transfer to wholly owned subsidiaries than to joint ventures, while they spend the smallest quantity of resources on independent local firms (Techakanont, 2003).

The government can also play an important role in the provision of financial support for indigenous SMEs, as the Taiwanese case shows. SMEs in the cluster could not finance research activities, nor did the Taiwanese producers initially consider investing in these areas, as they did not realize the potential. Moreover, for financing R&D, the governmental financial support has been mainly in the form of loans at preferential rates for the construction of greenhouse facilities explicitly aimed at groups of SMEs. However, the RIS seems to be weak in the provision of funds for other purposes, such as upgrading of skills, participation in international trade fairs, and so on. That is, the amount of financial capital committed by the government for the upgrading of the cluster is high, but somewhat limited to the provision of hard infrastructure.

In summary, SMEs are bound by their local conditions, in particular their regional systems of innovation and their clusters. When discussing the role of the RIS in Asian countries and its impact on local SMEs, it is important to take into account different forms of capital and their relationships: social capital, human and organizational capital, financial capital and physical capital (infrastructure). Upgrading of SMEs in developing countries in general is possible when these four forms of capital are present, and the SME can find in the local milieu (RIS) the resources needed to innovate.

Composition of RIS and the Upgrading Strategy of the Clustered SMEs

In the previous sections, we have dealt with the elements of the RIS one by one. We have claimed that human capital, social capital, financial capital and physical capital are important infrastructural elements for the development of SMEs. However, these elements are tightly intertwined. For instance, a cluster of SMEs might be based on strong and very well functioning social ties. The most successful producers in the cluster might provide financial support to other producers for the acquisition of technology. Successful producers might even buy machinery that they rent out to other producers in the cluster, thereby facilitating the technology upgrading to a greater number of SMEs. Technological upgrading may attract the attention of international buyers and human capital, thus reinforcing the overall growth of the cluster. Far from being a hypothetical picture, this process can be observed in several clusters of SMEs in Asia, and points to the systemic character of the different elements of the RIS.

There is not one single best case in upgrading clusters of SMEs, rather there seem to be important differences between industries, as shown in Table 19.2 and discussed below. Furthermore, how SMEs use the RIS infrastructure depends on their upgrading strategy. The main motive for local SMEs to innovate is to reach global markets, as the four cases discussed in this chapter point out. But how they use soft and hard infrastructure in the RIS for that purpose varies significantly across cases.

Traditionally SMEs in the Jepara furniture cluster had focused on the domestic market, where quality standards were low and requirements in terms of design often did not meet the tastes of the international customer. The situation changed in the mid-1980s, when the government sponsored the participation of Java furniture producers at an international fair in Bali. As a consequence, international buyers started to show interest in local production. Since then, large international buyers (for example IKEA) have dominated the cluster. These buyers 'translate' the demands of the final international customer to local producers. Indigenous SMEs have followed two types of strategies to gain access to the global market (Loebis and Schmitz, 2005): although the majority of producers have opted to reduce costs (low salaries, illegal raw materials, avoidance of taxes), few furniture makers have opted to compete by upgrading processes and products. The latter strategy has implied the introduction of new managerial and organizational changes, including compliance with international quality and environmental standards.

In the Taiwan flower industry, the strategy has been quite different. Technological upgrading, especially in orchid production, is clearly linked to the investments in biotechnology, and the linkages with the knowledge providers of the RIS (universities and research centres). Until very recently, Taiwanese producers relied only on 'natural' species that could be produced in most Asian countries, hence not a source of long-term competitiveness. Now they are experimenting with non-natural varieties that display particular aesthetic features and longer durability. These are the outcome of an emerging collaboration between producers and biotech institutes. This collaboration has provided opportunities for developing new species (for example the blue orchid). Realizing the full potential of this collaboration is, however, contingent on establishing the right links between producers, researchers and final markets (through appropriate marketing channels). Currently, collective action is frequent, but limited to one activity of the value chain (that is production or marketing), and hence appears fragmented. Orchids are rather easily copied or imitated, but since Taiwan has and is developing specialized knowledge and related support institutions within these fields, it can engage in constant upgrading and, thus, protect itself against imitators and sustain its long-term competitiveness. SMEs are responsible for the production and, to some extent, the marketing of the product. Most of the activities are based on indigenous Taiwanese firms and TNCs have only a limited role.

However TNCs play a crucial role in the Thai automotive industry, as they control and define the scope of innovation in the cluster. Until recently, the Thai SMEs played a significant role as first or second tier subcontractors for TNCs. Formal policies from the Thai central government stipulated that TNCs locating in Thailand had to guarantee a certain local content in production. TNCs were obliged to link up with local manufacturers. However, over the last few years, Thai SMEs have either been reduced to third or fourth tier subcontractors, or been bought up or gone bankrupt.[11] This can be attributed to the general deregulation enforced by the WTO/GATT. The Thai government interpreted the WTO/GATT agreement as entailing the dismantling of the local content requirement, and a general opening of the economy to FDI. As a result, TNC subsidiaries have established production in the Thai clusters and outcompeted Thai SMEs.

Moreover, new strategies among major assemblers in product innovations impose a new demand on local subcontractors. In this context, it is possible to distinguish between two types of SMEs and upgrading opportunities: foreign and joint venture firms seem to have preferential access to the required technology and resources through their parent companies. Unfortunately this is only a minority in the cluster. For the vast majority of SMEs in the sector, technological improvement is only the result of in-house efforts and the improved experience of employees (Techakanont and Terdudomtham, 2004). Human and organizational capital are the main determinants of the upgrading of these SMEs. Most SMEs do not comply with the international quality standards required by TNC assemblers to be first-tier suppliers.

The provision of human capital does not seem to be a problem anymore in the Bangalore case. Innovation is the result of the interaction with large foreign clients. As in the Thai Automotive cluster, the dynamics of the IT cluster in Bangalore are influenced by the large TNCs located there. It is possible to find two types of SMEs: those tied to a TNC through a subcontracting agreement, and a limited number of independent SMEs. Frequently Thai SMEs undertake a task-specific job, such as moulding specific parts of the car, for the large client firm which settles the parameters of the production and the final outcome, and tightly controls the performance of the SME. For a majority of these SMEs, large firms define innovation, whereas SMEs are only responsible for maintaining quality standards at minimum cost (Nadvi, 1995; Vang and Overby, 2006). Occasionally, SMEs suggest marginal modifications to large firms, in view of their expertise. Beside this large group of SMEs and networks, it is possible to find some independent SMEs, usually driven by highly qualified people that decide to run their own firms. These firms retain their own design and production capacity, and try to position their products in the local market and, to a lesser extent, abroad. The limited cooperation between SMEs and the lack of financial resources are clearly hampering this process.

In sum, the general principle that different (upgrading) strategies demand different combinations of resources can be applied also to the analysis of RIS. Each strategy requires a different combination of soft or hard infrastructure. For example, human capital seems to be more critical for the Jepara furniture and the Thai automotive clusters now than it is for the Bangalore software cluster and the Taiwanese flower industry. And the construction of social capital is more crucial now for the software cluster in Bangalore than for the Jepara furniture cluster. Acknowledging these differences has important implications for innovation policy.

INNOVATION POLICY FOR SMES: LEARNING FROM THE CASES

This section aims at drawing some lessons for the design and implementation of innovation policies to support Asian SMEs from an RIS perspective. The lessons are based on the cases, hence we do not suggest they can be automatically applied to other clusters and RIS. Instead, it serves the purpose of illustrating the need for a diversity of innovation policies to support SMEs. We use the RIS framework critically to discuss how the hard and soft infrastructure of the RIS and their systemic propensities might influence the innovative performance of the Asian SMEs and how the government can invest selectively in the weak and critical nodes of the infrastructure to support SMEs' innovative capabilities and upgrading in general.

Innovation policies usually follow best practice models based on high-tech clusters located in high-performing regions, and only a small number of SMEs benefit from these policy measures. In this chapter, we argue that, when designing innovation policy for SMEs, policy makers need to take into account the different dynamics of regions and clusters of SMEs. We have so far discussed innovation patterns in four clusters of SMEs in Asia, in relation to the hard and soft infrastructure of the RIS in which each cluster is operating. The four clusters represent the four most common industries in the region: traditional industry, resource-based industry, complex product systems industry and specialized software. The cases illustrate how traditional industries or resource-based industries, which tend to be ignored by innovation (technology) policies in Asia, have significant potential in terms of innovation. Hence these cases illustrate that traditional industries remain potential platforms for upgrading in developing countries (Mylteka and Farinelli, 2000) and that policy makers need to adopt a broader perspective on the innovation processes in these industries.

One of the first conclusions to draw from these cases is that there is a need for innovation policies concentrating on the particular needs of SMEs operating in different industries. Unless such measures are taken, SMEs are not likely to engage in noteworthy innovations or upgrading in general. Subsequently, the SMEs will at best maintain their role as low-cost subcontractors to TNCs and will not exploit their economic potential. In the worst scenario, they could even lose their position as subcontractors, by being outcompeted by world players. The cases also suggest that designing and implementing innovative policies for Asian SMEs requires an approach that pays attention to the territorial decision structure, and the specific combination of hard and soft infrastructure that constitutes the appropriate support for Asian innovative SMEs.

Decentralized Decision-making Structure

Applying the RIS approach has proved useful as the point of departure for the design of innovation policies to support SMEs in Asian countries. In contrast to other more atomistic approaches working with the same variables, but in isolation, the systemic approach considers the links and dependencies of the different institutions and organizations that constitute the entire innovation system. Thinking 'systemic' allows selective interventions in the weakest nodes in the system and/or on the most critical nodes. Selectivity is crucial for Asian countries where financial resources are extremely scarce. The systemic approach facilitates the identification of dependencies and complementarities between variables. This in turn can help policy makers to avoid policy interventions focusing on just one variable of the system, which might lead to decreasing returns in the absence of complementary investments. As an example, additional investment in human capital in the Bangalore region will not pay off unless it is combined with demand-side investments.

The cases tend to support the general claim in the RIS and cluster literature, arguing in favour of decentralized decision-making structures. This is supported by the behavioural pattern of the Asian SMEs, whose interactions tend to be embedded locally. Highly centralized government bodies tend to lack relevant local knowledge, and base their interventions on aggregated data that often fail to capture both local and industry specificities. Thus the particular needs of local SMEs, the morphology of local networks, and so forth, are often ignored. For these reasons, centralized governments might even intervene in counterproductive ways. As mentioned earlier, this calls for a decentralized decision-making structure. However, there is a need to highlight the still relevant role of the centralized government agencies and a need to argue against a 'one-size-fits-all' territorial decision-making structure.

Across the industries, centralized government bodies continue to play a crucial role in generating general policies of relevance to the innovative performance of SMEs. The importance of replacing the import substitution industrialization strategy with an export-oriented strategy in the Indian case is almost paradigmatic for illustrating this. Equally important is that centralized governmental bodies need to define the general formal rules of the game, such as formal law and working standards, to avoid a situation in which regions use national policies to engage in a cost-based competition against each other. Decentralization of such policies is likely to hamper the innovation performance of SMEs.

The morphology of the decentralized decision-making structure is also contingent on the industry and institutional setting, as the cases illustrate. It can take two forms: (1) all major decision rights can or should be allocated to the regional governments, or (2) central government bodies have or should have located local government branches, with a high degree of autonomy, in the relevant regions and clusters. In the latter case, there is an additional need to pay attention to the parts of the policy process that have to be decentralized (for example design and/or implementation).

While it is still too early to come up with a rule of thumb on when the first or second type of decentralized decision-making structure should be applied, the cases seem to suggest the following. First, industries relying on highly localized idiosyncratic knowledge tend to benefit most from a decision-making structure based on regional government bodies. The Jepara furniture cluster can illustrate this. The case points to the way the regional government has been effective in identifying some of the weakest and most crucial nodes in the RIS, with respect to the internationalization of the clustered SMEs. Second, industries relying on global standards and/or high capital entry barriers tend to be best facilitated by the central government's premises located in the region. This comes out most clearly in the Bangalore IT software case, where the central government's ISS policies have been important in the development of the cluster, and educational institutions function well, despite being under central rule. The Thai automobile case also suggests the need for a strategy based on the decentralization of central government bodies, as scale economies benefit from a centrally coordinated strategy.

Soft and Hard Infrastructure

The appropriate territorial decision-making structure assures the provision of information on weak nodes and complementarities in the RIS, and thus on where and how to intervene with respect to soft and hard infrastructure. The industry-specific RIS policies can draw on a palette of different supply and/or demand-side policies. Focus can be on providing timely and qualified human resources, supporting the creation of social capital and effective networks between SMEs and TNCs, supplying physical infrastructure, business support services and financial capital, and supporting access to markets. Industry and institutional contingencies dictate the areas (hard and soft infrastructure) in which a governmental intervention is most needed in the RIS, for example investments in human capital or scientific infrastructure, and so on.

Before presenting the case specificities it should be noted that, across all the cases, the innovative performance by Asian SMEs tends to be constrained by a lack of managerial skills in the broadest sense, especially of the manager or the owner of the firm. Intervention in this area seems to be critical for all Asian industries considered in the study. In traditional industries, as illustrated by the Jepara furniture cluster in Indonesia, the major weakness in the SMEs in the cluster is in upgrading the local craftsmanship to meet international demands. This can be solved partly if local manufacturers can link up to international buyers and international markets directly. This is possible when they are price-competitive, provide the right design, comply with required international standards (environmental mainly) and are known actors on the international market. For SMEs not possessing the skills needed for harvesting the benefits from collaborating directly or indirectly with international buyers, the government needs to provide information on international demands, standards and international markets, and to facilitate access to international markets (for example supporting the presence of local SMEs in international trade fairs).

However, providing information is only one variable in the equation. SMEs also need to change their productive competences, according to the demands of the global markets. The government can contribute to the development of SMEs by providing or supporting the development of business development services, such as training, testing, supply chain management and certification. Training aimed at soft elements of the innovation processes, usually marketing or managerial skills or organizational change, is clearly needed. The strength of the local networks can facilitate the dissemination of successful managerial practices.

In resource-based industries, collaboration between knowledge providers (for example universities and research institutions) and producers, as well as the provision of hard scientific infrastructure and qualified human capital, are central cornerstones in the policy agenda. This type of collaboration can facilitate, for example, the invention of new species, more resistant ones, or similar. Local producers can then enter the international market with a knowledge-intensive new product, creating a new niche market. This is clearly the strategy of producers in Taiwan that attempt to become world leaders in orchid production. The Taiwanese government has focused largely on the provision of hard infrastructure for the sector, and not much on the soft infrastructure. Although most producers seem to have the required technical skills, they lack managerial and marketing skills. Their market information is very limited, and their access to new techniques is contingent on formal linkages with biotechnology firms.

The policies in CoPS, like the Thai automotive clusters, are highly dependent on the TNCs' willingness to provide assistance on technological upgrading and building of design competencies, as this is beyond the scope of indigenous SMEs. When TNCs provide this type of information/assistance, it is mainly to first tier suppliers. SMEs do not play a significant role as first tier suppliers, as most indigenous SMEs do not comply with the international quality standards required by TNCs. The cases illustrate that at least two strategies are possible. One is to regulate the relationship between the TNC and the SME, for example, forcing TNCs to subcontract with indigenous SMEs. This regulatory policy may face potential conflicts with the WTO. While this might seem a viable solution in the short term, it does not provide the right incentives for SMEs to acquire new competences, as the Thai case shows.

The second strategy is for the government to focus directly on improving the competences of indigenous SMEs. Centralized government bodies, including technical colleges and universities, need to build organizations physically present in the RIS, as this is where the SMEs are located. This will allow central government bodies to develop the needed local knowledge. Moreover, these government bodies need to be equipped with a sufficiently high degree of autonomy that allows them to act on the basis of local knowledge. The combination of centralization and decentralization will allow for harvesting some economies of scale in the development of indigenous technologies. In a slightly longer time perspective, the decentralized structure might provide a foundation that will allow for more social capital-based horizontal collaboration, which may become relevant when the investments in human and organizational capital are 'in place' and indigenous technologies developed. Increasing the absorptive capacity of firms will set the foundations for the introduction of quality standards in the SMEs that, in turn, will improve the possibilities of recuperating their position in the first tier.

Finally, policies aimed at specialized suppliers, as illustrated by the Bangalore case, initially consist of building the required human capital level to engage in cost-based collaboration with TNCs. Once this level is attained, the biggest problem that the SMEs in these types of industries in Asia are currently facing is getting the high-value assignments that would allow them to position themselves in higher-value parts of the value chain. While several SMEs might have the formally needed competencies for undertaking these activities, TNCs do not know or do not yet trust the ability of indigenous SMEs to undertake these activities. This prevents them from transforming their formal competencies into 'real' competencies; this transformation requires user–producer interaction. This problem is central, as SMEs cannot rely on localized lead users. In parallel, knowledge tends not to be distributed within the clusters of co-located firms. Thus, after initial phases with investments in human capital, public interventions should focus on public procurements, where public government bodies function as lead users demanding local interaction.

CONCLUSION

We started the chapter with the general claim that innovation policies in Asia have tended to support high-tech sectors dominated by large firms. It is estimated that only 3 per cent of the SMEs benefit from these policies, as they are high-tech SMEs. The cases have illustrated that SMEs across industries do have an unrealized potential. They can compete in international markets, even in mature or traditional industries, if there is the right support locally. Unfolding this potential is a matter of understanding the specific needs of local SMEs, and identifying the weakest nodes in the regional innovation system. In order to reach the largest number of SMEs, policy makers need to focus on clusters of SMEs, that is, the policy target should be groups of SMEs, not isolated SMEs.

This chapter has contributed to the current discussion of innovation policies in Asia in many ways. First, we provide an analytical framework (the RIS) to unfold the system propensities in which the activity of the SMEs is embedded, the hard and soft infrastructure, and how they relate to the SMEs needs, and the use of the innovation system approach in practice. Second, we particularize the analysis in relation to four of the most common clusters of SMEs in Asia, identifying some general patterns within the clusters and the main differences across these clusters. And, finally, we provide some guidance to policy makers on how to intervene and support these clusters, with the provision of hard and soft infrastructure.

NOTES

1. It is not the purpose of this chapter to discuss the adequacy of these high-tech oriented policies in the developing world as such, and we do acknowledge that some of the countries have obtained very successful results (for example India, South Korea, Singapore).
2. SMEs are constituted by a variety of types of firms, in terms of size of their financial assets and/or number of employees. No single coherent definition exists (OECD, 2002). The SMEs range from formally established firms engaged in traditional manufacturing to semi-formal sweatshops and informal – and occasionally criminal – activities involving only the household or the family. Moreover, some SMEs are producing intermediaries to firms in global value chains, while others produce end-products to their regional markets only. The definitions used in national statistics are also different for each country in Asia, and the rest of the world for that matter. Currently, the SME department of the World Bank considers the following definitions: micro-enterprises (up to ten employees, total assets of up to US$10 000 and total annual sales of up to US$100 000); small enterprises (up to 50 employees, total assets and total sales of up to US$3 million; medium enterprises (up to 300 employees, total assets and total sales up to US$15 million). We focus on the formal sectors of SMEs in this chapter.
3. Currently, the specific programmes aimed at SMEs in Asia found in almost all countries are high-tech oriented. Most of them, if not all, are aimed at specific groups of firms (start-ups), or specific sectors (ICT, software), where there is a high probability of finding high-tech SMEs. This group, however, only represents about 3 per cent of the SME population. This means that the majority of SMEs are ignored almost completely in all innovation policies. Of the remaining 97 per cent, approximately 65 per cent are considered to be technology users or potential innovators (Clarysse and Uytterhaegen, 1999).
4. Malmberg and Maskell (2002) have recently reduced interaction in clusters to be based on observability only; this might be relevant in some industrial clusters, but mainly for a minor segment based on physical production.
5. For example, the Chilean salmon cluster, the orchid cluster in Taiwan, the apple cluster in Brazil, and so on.
6. Physical capital as infrastructure is crucial for economic development, but this is not the core area of RIS. We therefore refer to UNDP (2004) for detailed elaborations on this topic.
7. South Korea, Singapore and Taiwan are the exception, with net enrolment rates in primary schools close to 100 per cent.
8. Until very recently, formal policies by the Thai central government stipulated that TNCs locating in Thailand had to guarantee a certain local content in the production. TNCs were obliged to link up with local manufacturers. This in turn reduced the incentives of SMEs to increase their qualifications.
9. The World Bank (2002: 3) further notes that, 'Although these two forms of social capital are mutually reinforcing, one can exist without the other. Government-mandated organizations represent structural social capital in which the cognitive element is not necessarily present. Similarly, many relations of mutual trust persist without being formalized in organizations. This description of social capital according to its forms has proven quite useful as a basis for empirical analysis.'
10. For example, one of the consequences of Japanese leadership was the creation of several automobile industry cooperative clubs for assemblers and first-tier suppliers.
11. While bankruptcy was accelerated by the economic crisis in Asia in the late 1990s, this cannot hide the fundamental structural problems faced by the Thai automotive industry.

REFERENCES

Albu, M. (1997), 'Technological learning and innovation in industrial clusters in the south', SPRU electronic working papers, SPRU, University of Sussex.

Amin A. (2004), 'Regulating economic globalization', *Transactions of the Institute of British Geographers*, **29**(2), 217–233.

Asheim, B. and L. Coenen (2005), 'Knowledge bases and regional innovation systems: comparing Nordic clusters', *Research Policy*, **34**(8), 1173–90.

Asheim, B. and M. Gertler (2004), 'Regional innovation systems and the geographical foundations of innovation', in J. Fagerberg, D. Mowery and R. Nelson (eds), *The Oxford Handbook of Innovation*, Oxford: Oxford University Press, pp. 291–317.

Asheim, B. and A. Isaksen (2002), 'Regional innovation system: the integration of local "Sticky" and global "Ubiquitous" Knowledge', *Journal of Technology Transfer*, **27**: 77–86.

Asheim, B., L. Coenen and M. Svensson-Henning (2003), *Nordic SMEs and Regional Innovation Systems*, Oslo: Nordik Industrifond.

Asheim, B., A. Isaksen, C. Nauwelaers and F. Tödtling (2003), *Regional Innovation Policy for Small-Medium Enterprises*, Cheltenham,UK and Northampton, MA,USA: Edward Elgar.

Avnimelech, G. and M. Teubal (2002), 'Venture capital in Israel. A comparative analysis and lessons for other countries', Hebrew University Israel. (http://economics.huji.ac.il/facultye/teubal/VCPolicyBrusselsDraft2.pdf)

Becker, Gary (1998), 'Human capital and poverty', *Religion and Liberty*, **8**(1), pages not numbered, (accessed on http://www.acton.org/publicat/randl/article.php?id=258).

Berry, A., E. Rodriguez and H. Sandee (2002), 'Firm and group dynamics in the small and medium enterprise sector in Indonesia', *Small Business Economics*, **18**, 141–61.

Bitran, E. (2004), 'Sistema de Innovación, Consorcios Tecnológicos y Clusters Dinámicos En Chile', *En Foco*, Santiago de Chile: Expansiva.

Clarysse, B. and M. Uytterhaegen (1999), 'Inside the black box of innovation: strategic differences between SMEs', University of Ghent.

Cohen, W. and D. Levinthal (1990), 'Absorptive capacity: a new perspective on learning and innovation', *Administrative Science Quarterly*, **35**, 128–52.

Cooke, P. and K. Morgan (1998), *The Associational Economy: Firms, Regions and Innovation*, Oxford: OUP.

Cooke, P. and D. Will (1999), 'Small firms, social capital and the enhancement of business performance through innovation programmes', *Small Business Economics*, **13**, 219–34.

Das, T. (2003), 'Promoting resource-based export oriented SMEs in Asia and the Pacific', *Investment Promotion and Enterprise Development Bulletin for Asia and the Pacific*, **1**, 33–76.

Dhungana, B. (2003), 'Strengthening the competitiveness of small and medium enterprises in the globalisation process: prospects and challenges', *Investment Promotion and Enterprise Development Bulletin for Asia and the Pacific*, **1**, 1–32.

Fröbel, F., J. Heinrichs and O. Kreye (1980), *The New International Division of Labor*, Cambridge: Cambridge University Press.

Giuliani, E. (2004), 'Laggard clusters as slow learners, emerging clusters as locus of knowledge cohesion (and exclusion): a comparative study in the wine industry', LEM working paper, Laboratory of Economics and Management -Sant'Anna School of Advanced Studies, Pisa.

Giuliani, E. and M. Bell (2005), 'When micro shapes the meso: learning networks in a Chilean wine cluster', *Research Policy*, **34**(1), 47–68.

Granovetter, M. (1985), 'Economic action and social structure: the problem of embeddedness', *American Journal of Sociology*, **91**, 481–510.

Hsieh, S.-C. (2001), 'Taiwan assisted flower production and marketing in Paraguay', ICDF report.

Kaufmann, A. and F. Tödtling (2002), 'How effective is innovation support for SMEs? An analysis of the region of Upper Austria', *Technovation*, **22**, 147–59.

Lecler, Y. (2002), 'The cluster role in the development of the Thai car industry: some evidence from empirical studies', *International Journal of Urban and Regional Research*, **26**(4), 799–814.

Liu, S.-J. (1998), 'Industrial development and industrial adaptation in Taiwan: some issues of learned entrepreneurship', *IEEE Transactions on Engineering Management*, **45**(4), 338–47.

Loebis, L. and H. Schmitz (2005), 'Java furniture makers: globalization winners or losers?', *Development and Practice*, **5**(3–4), 514–21.

Lundvall, B.Å. (ed.) (1992), *National Systems of Innovation. Towards a Theory of Innovation and Interactive Learning*, London: Pinter.

Lundvall, B.-Å. and S. Borrás (2004), 'Science, technology and innovation policy', in J. Fagerberg,

D. Mowery and R. Nelson (eds), *The Oxford Handbook of Innovation*, Oxford: Oxford University Press, pp. 599–631.

Lundvall B.-Å., I.P. Intarakumnerd and J. Vang-Laurdsen (eds) (2006), *Asia's Innovation Systems in Transition*, Cheltenham, UK and Northampton, MA, USA: Edward Elgar.

Malmberg, A. and P. Maskell (2002), 'The elusive concept of localization economies: towards a knowledge-based theory of spatial clustering', *Environment and Planning*, **34**(3): 429–449.

Martin, R. and P. Sunley (2003), 'Deconstructing clusters: chaotic concept or policy panacea?', *Journal of Economic Geography*, **3**, 5–35.

Mylteka, L. and F. Farinelli (2000), 'Local clusters, innovation systems and sustained competitive-ness', INTECH Discussion Paper Series, Maastricht.

Nadvi, K. (1995), *Industrial Clusters and Networks: Case Studies of SME Growth and Innovation*, Vienna: UNIDO.

NASSCOM (2005) (www.nasscom.org), accessed 20 September 2005.

OECD (2002), *Enhancing Competitiveness of SMEs through Innovation*, Paris: OECD.

Oyelaran-Oyeyinka, B. and K. Lal (2004), *Learning New Technologies by SMEs in Developing Countries*, INTECH Discussion Paper Series (2004-9), **38**.

Paldam, M. (2000), 'Social capital: one or many? Definition and measurement', *Journal of Economic Surveys*, **14**(5), 629–53.

Parthasarathy, B. (2004), 'India's Silicon Valley or Silicon Valley's India? Socially embedding the computer software industry in Bangalore', *International Journal of Urban and Regional Research*, **28**(3), 664–85.

Pavitt, K. (1984), 'Sectoral patterns of technical change: towards a taxonomy and a theory', *Research Policy*, **13**(6), 343–73.

Pietrobelli, C. and R. Rabellotti (2004), 'Upgrading in clusters and value chains in Latin America: the role of policies', Sustainable Department Best Practices Series, Inter-American Development Bank, New York, 97.

Porter, R. (1998), 'Clusters and the New Economics of Competition', *Harvard Business Review*, **76**(6), 77–90.

Ramachandran, V. (1993), 'Technology transfer, firm ownership and investment in human capital', *Review of Economics and Statistics*, **75**, 664–670.

Romer, P. (1990), 'Endogenous technological change', *Journal of Political Economy*, **98**(5), 71–102.

Samart, C. (2004), 'Production networks, trade and investment policies, and regional cooperation in Asia: a case study of the automotive industry in Thailand', paper presented at the 6th ADRF General Meeting, Bangkok, Thailand (http://adrf.trf.or.th/ADRF6update/Full_Papers/Trade&Investment/Samart_Chiasakul/Fullpaper_Samart.pdf).

Sandee, H. (1998), 'Promoting small-scale and cottage industry clusters in Indonesia', *Small Enterprise Development*, **9**, 52–8.

Sandee, H. and P. Rietveld (2001), 'Upgrading traditional technologies in small-scale industry clus-ters: collaboration and innovation adoption in Indonesia', *Journal of Development Studies*, **37**(4), 150–172.

Schmitz, H. (1992), 'On the clustering of small firms', *IDS Bulletin – Institute of Development Studies*, **23**, 64–9.

Sevilla, R.C. and K. Soonthornthada (2000), *SME Policy in Thailand: Vision and Challenges*, Nakhon Pathom: Institute for Population and Social Research, Mahidol University.

Supratikno, H. (2002), 'The development of SME clusters in Indonesia', paper presented at the ASEAN Roundtable on 'Entrepreneurship and Small and Medium-Sized Enterprises (SMEs) in Southeast Asia's Economic Development', ISEAS, Singapore, 7–8 November.

Taiwan Council of Agriculture (2003), *COA Annual Report 2003* (http:// www.coa.gov.tw/coa/end/publications/).

Taiwan Ministry of Economic Affairs (2004), 'White paper on small and medium size enterprises in Taiwan'.

Tambunan, T. (2005), 'Promoting small and medium enterprises with a clustering approach: a policy experience from Indonesia', *Journal of Small Business Management*, **43**(2), 138–54.

Techakanont, K. (2003), 'An analysis of the determinant of inter-firm technology transfer: a case of the Thai automobile industry', *Thammasat Economic Journal*, **21**(3), 145–73.

Techakanont, K. and T. Terdudomtham (2004), 'Evolution of inter-firm technology transfer and technological capability formation of local parts firms in the Thai automobile industry', *Journal of Technology Innovation*, **12**(2), 151–83.

Tsai, J. (2001), 'The comparative advantage of Taiwan's major cut flowers', *Agricultural Economics*, **47**(6), 265–70.

Tsai, K.-H. and J.-C. Wang (2002), 'An examination of Taiwan's innovation policies and R&D performance', Chung-Hua Institution for Economic Research, Division of Taiwan Economy, Taiwan.

Tunzelmann, N.V. and V. Acha (2004), 'Innovation in "Low-Tech" Industries', in J. Fagerberg (ed.), *The Oxford Handbook of Innovation*, Oxford: Oxford University Press, pp. 407–32.

UNDP (2004), 'Unleashing entrepreneurship: making business work for the poor', UNDP report.

UNIDO (United Nations Industrial Development Organization) (1997), 'Progress and prospects for industrial development in least developed countries (LDCs) – towards the 21st century', presented at Fourth LDC Ministerial Symposium: Industrial Capacity Building and Entrepreneurship Development in LDCs with particular emphasis on agro-related industries, United Nations, Vienna.

UNIDO (United Nations Industrial Development Organization) and UUND Program (2004), *Partnerships for Small Enterprise Development*, New York: United Nations.

Vang, J. and B. Asheim (2006), 'Regions, absorptive capacity and strategic coupling with high tech TNCs: lessons from India and China', *Society, Science and Technology*, **11**(1), 39–66.

Vang, J. and M. Overby (2006), 'Transnational communities, TNCs and development: the case of the Indian IT-services industry', in B.-Å. Lundvall, I. Patarapong and J. Vang (eds), *Asia's Innovation Systems in Transition*, Cheltenham, UK and Northampton, MA, USA: Edward Elgar.

Von Hippel, E. (1988), *Sources of Innovation*, Oxford: Oxford University Press.

World Bank (1998), *Social Capital in Africa*, downloaded (http://www.worldbank.org).

World Bank (2002), *Understanding and Measuring Social Capital. A Multidisciplinary Tool for Practitioners*, New York: World Bank.

World Bank (2003), *World Development Indicators 2003*, New York: World Bank.

Zahra, S.A., and G. George (2002), 'Absorptive capacity: a review, reconceptualization, and extension', *Academy of Management Review*, **27**(2), 185–203.

20. Explaining multinational companies from the developing economies of East and Southeast Asia

Paz Estrella Tolentino

Data for 2003 show that developing countries accounted for US$858.7 billion or around 10 per cent of worldwide stock of outward foreign direct investment (FDI), with South, East and Southeast Asia responsible for almost 71 per cent of the stock of outward FDI from developing countries, and around 7 per cent of the worldwide stock of outward FDI (UNCTAD, 2004). The most important home countries of FDI in South, East and Southeast Asia, based on size of outward FDI stock, were, in declining order, Hong Kong (China), Singapore, Taiwan, China, South Korea and Malaysia.[1] Despite the low significance of developing countries in general, and South, East and Southeast Asia in particular, in the worldwide stock of outward FDI, there are at least several striking features that draw attention to the high degree of multinationality of some multinational companies (MNCs) based in the region.

First, there are currently at least 9614 parent companies of MNCs based in the region, which accounts for more than two-thirds of the parent companies based in all developing countries, and 16 per cent of the parent companies based in the whole world. Second, Hong Kong (China), Singapore and Malaysia ranked first, third and fifteenth, respectively, in the list of the world's top 20 countries, in terms of the outward FDI performance index in 2001–3, measured in terms of the size of outward FDI stock.[2] Third, the four leading East Asian newly industrialized economies (NIEs) – Hong Kong (China), South Korea, Singapore and Taiwan – have been the most dynamic foreign investors in Southeast Asia, and constitute the largest or second largest sources of foreign capital in every developing host country in the region (see Hill, 1990, as cited in Lall, 1991).

Indeed, although 'Japan remains the biggest actor for intraregional investment, the East Asian newly industrialized countries have emerged as important investors in the 1980s and 1990s and are, relative to their size, more active foreign investors than Japan. ASEAN and China are also active as outward investors, but on a rather smaller scale compared to the former countries' (Blomqvist, 1995: 280). Riedel (1991) examined the theory of international trade and investment, as it pertains to the intraregional dimension of intra-Asian trade and FDI. The high levels of intraregional trade and investment led in part by MNCs based in developing countries of the region have been a driving force in regional economic integration (Blomqvist, 1995) and the increasing complexity in the regional division of labour (Machado, 1999).

Fourth, some companies based in the region include Hutchison Whampoa, based in Hong Kong (China), Singtel, based in Singapore, and Samsung Electronics, based in South

Korea, are ranked respectively sixteenth, seventieth and ninety-third in the world's top 100 non-financial MNCs, based on the size of their foreign assets, or twenty-ninth, forty-seventh and eighty-eighth, respectively in terms of their transnationality index.[3] Companies based in Hong Kong (China), Malaysia, Singapore and South Korea also count as among the world's largest MNCs in such service industries as electricity, telecommunications, construction, hotels, logistics, restaurants and tourism (see UNCTAD, 2004).[4]

The emergence and evolution of MNCs based in developing countries in general, and those based in South, East and Southeast Asia in particular, are one of the driving forces behind the ongoing changes in the competitive environment of the region, with implications for the competitiveness of MNCs based in the US, Western Europe and Japan operating in the region (see Haley and Haley, 1998; Williamson, 2005). It has also inspired a fairly substantial academic literature in international business, and across the social science disciplines. An indication of the broad scope of the extant literature is evident in the two-volume book edited by Yeung (1999), who organized in seven main themes the subject matter of sixty-five of the most influential research articles on MNCs based in developing countries, published between 1973 and 1998, namely, their origins and characteristics, theoretical perspectives, social and institutional contexts, corporate strategies, business organizations, impact and sectoral studies. A common thread binding the broad research themes is the distinctive nature of MNCs based in developing countries.

The aim of this chapter is to provide a broad critical overview of some of the main empirical and theoretical trends in the academic literature that seek to highlight or explain various aspects of the distinctive features of the emergence and evolution of MNCs based in South, East and Southeast Asia. The review begins in the next section, with the contributions probing the distinctive features of the business or economic organizations, business networks and strategy of firms and MNCs based in Asian developing countries, within the theoretical context of the comparative institutions and strategic management approaches. This is followed by those exploring the distinctive features of MNCs based in developing countries at various levels of economic analysis, in the context of the economic theories of the MNC and international production. The final section reflects on the critical review of the two key strands of the academic literature. It identifies some of the possible future research agenda and hints at some of the key implications for business and government policy.

COMPARATIVE INSTITUTIONS AND STRATEGIC MANAGEMENT APPROACHES

The emergence and evolution of MNCs based in Asian developing countries have inspired in part the analysis of the broad diversity of business systems or societal systems of capitalism that exist in the region, to include those of Japan, South Korea, China, India and the Association of South East Asian Nations (ASEAN). Gordon Redding and Richard Whitley provided pioneering contributions in the examination of the business systems of ethnic Chinese societies (see Redding, 1990, 1995, 2000) and the newly industrialized economies of East Asia (see Whitley, 1990, 1991, 1992). Brown (1995), Carney (1998), Gomez (1999), Mitchell (1995), Ong-Giger (1999), Lim (2000) and Yeung and Olds (2000), amongst others, made further contributions in elaborating the distinctive features of ethnic Chinese business systems. Lim (1996a, 1996b) and Redding (2001) employed a broader approach in explaining the evolution of various Southeast Asian business systems, while the focus of Haley and Haley (1998) and Khanna (2005) had been the comparison of ethnic Chinese and Indian business systems. Indeed the emergence and evolution of MNCs based in Asian developing countries constitute one of the varied aspects of the systems of international business that interlock and interact to make up the evolving world of global trade and investment (see Flowers *et al.*, 1999).

The foremost contribution of Richard Whitley is to advance the societal construction of business organizations from the theoretical perspective of comparative institutionalism, thus providing another angle to the dichotomous debates on the status of business organizations and their relations to the environment as the foci of investigation in organization theory (see also chapters in Part I of this volume).[5] Comparative institutional analysis provides a framework to view variations in the trajectories, patterns and consequences of a business system. A 'business system', as an integral concept in this approach, is the institutionalization, in particular societal contexts, of the configurations of market–hierarchy relations. In Whitley's view, significant institutional legacies and social practices from pre-industrial times, combined with crucial societal institutions developed either during or after industrialization, determine the distinctive nature and success of the modern business systems in the different countries of East Asia, as epitomized in the Japanese *kaisha*, the Korean *chaebol* and the ethnic Chinese family business in Hong Kong (China) and Taiwan. These business organizations and economic rationalities 'display varying degrees of firm interdependence, commitment to particular exchange partners (and expectations of reciprocity), scope of exchange relations, reliance on personal knowledge, vertical integration by quasi-contractual links, and horizontal coordination between sectors through long-term commitments' (Ross, 1993: 118). 'The identification of distinctive and effective forms of economic organization in East Asia has emphasized the close connections between dominant social institutions and ways of co-ordinating economic activities as well as the interrelations between firm and market characteristics in separate business systems' (Whitley, 1994: 153).

Owing to Whitley's contribution, it has become possible in contemporary organization theory to envisage a much broader conception of the societal contexts of modernity to challenge the dominant Anglo-Saxon or, at best, Western conception of modernity (Tsoukas, 1993). This idea puts paid to intellectual endeavours in search of universal features of effective organizations and managerial strategies that apply equally across historical and cultural contexts. On the other hand, it brings into question whether the concepts and theories derived from an analysis of Western societies are useful and appropriate to analyse the institutional and organizational arrangements of East Asia (see Vroom, 1995).

Gordon Redding similarly adopted the societal basis of business organization in examining the business systems of ethnic Chinese societies (Redding, 1990, 1995, 2000) and various countries of Southeast Asia (Redding, 2001). In sharing the views of Whitley, Redding (2001: 762) argues:

> The business system is an evolving and constantly changing pattern of features and owes its shape to its heritage in the way a society chooses to deal with modernization. The features of the system are aspects of the way economic behaviour is held together in stable patterns. . . . These stable

patterns affect three features of the total structure: the way in which ownership holds organizations together, with different forms of ownership producing different forms of company, such that variations are seen in the use of professional management, nepotism, firm size, decision-making, and so on; second, the way in which an economy may be tied together horizontally and vertically in ways which affect the workings of competition, such alliances and understandings being often invisible; and third, the way organizations in a particular society typically go about the job of holding people together in conditions of cooperation within the organization.

It is clear in Redding's view that the above elements of the business system are embedded in the way a society chooses to deal with modernization, through the creation of financial capital, human capital, social capital and trust, which is in turn determined by a society's culture, and, in particular, the vertical and horizontal order that govern relationships. He stresses such social and cultural values, and contexts associated with capitalism and entrepreneurship of ethnic Chinese abroad, analysing the strengths and weaknesses of the family business as a distinctive form of business organization. He associates 'the spirit of Chinese capitalism with the legacy of Chinese social history (defined as paternalism, personalism and insecurity) among owner-managers at the analytical levels of self, kinship and business relations, business organization and role in society' (Cheek, 1992: 209). Similarly, Haley and Haley (1998) advanced the view that there are cultural differences in the social networks composed of family members, friends and trusted colleagues established by ethnic Chinese and Indians. Since such culturally based social networks influence business operations and environments in the region, social networks are, in essence, business networks (see also Khanna, 2005).

In her discussion of the key role of extended family ties, business trust, flexible credit and the 'gift' exchange of information in contemporary decision making in elite Hong Kong Chinese business society, Mitchell (1995) also stressed the social embeddedness of economic practice in explaining business behaviour. In analysing MNCs based in Hong Kong, Yeung (1998: 135) presented the compelling argument that 'the Chinese tend to cultivate personal relationships or guanxi so much so that they tend to personalise their economic relations through business networks'. 'In numerous studies, the family – or clan – based guanxiwang (human relations network) of the "Chinese multinationals" has been singled out as their dominant organizational and behavioural characteristic – so much so that the overseas Chinese business connection is often dubbed the "Bamboo Network"' (Wong, 1999: 18; original reference). However, Ong-Giger (1999) took a cautious view of *guanxi* as an integral element of ethnic Chinese business systems, by highlighting collusion, cronyism and nepotism as its dark aspects (see also Chapter 4 in this volume). Carney (1998) also identified several actual or potential problems with the management style of ethnic Chinese family businesses based in Hong Kong that hinder their competitiveness in technology and capital-intensive industries on a global scale.

This leads on to the academic literature that deals with business networks and a network as a distinct organizational form. On the basis of an investigation into the network form, as it is circumscribed within the institutional and cultural context of ethnic Chinese firms, Li (1998a: 833) advanced the view of a network form as a unique organizational form, consistent with 'a firm with a narrow scope of internal relationships and a broad scope of external relationships . . . who is flexibly connected to a stable web of versatile alliances'. In his view, the Chinese traditional network form, which resembles the emerging network form in the US and parts of Europe, contains the elements of an ideal–typical network form. He described, explained, and prescribed the contours of an ideal–typical network form, in a geocentric framework that synthesized Chinese traditional epistemology with Western methodology. Buckley (2004) examined the nature of Asian network firms, and advanced an analytical framework of three archetypical types cast in a dynamic life-cycle context: Japanese *keiretsu*, South Korean *chaebol* and ethnic Chinese family companies. He showed that the strengths and weaknesses of Asian network firms can be explained, using conventional analysis without the need for situation-specific cultural concepts.

Ghauri and Prasad (1995) lent emphasis to the role of inter-firm networks, such as *keiretsu* and *keiretsu*-type business structures, in the competitive positions and performance of firms in Japan, South Korea, India and other Asian nations. Business groups are generally defined as 'more or less stable networks of legally independent firms that are tied together through some form of shared ownership and common economic strategy' (Hamilton, 1996: 23). They appear in varying degrees of strength in both developed and developing countries (Granovetter, 1994). Lim (1996b) attributed the emergence of business groups and the development of private institutional mechanisms, such as networks and relationships in Southeast Asian business systems (geared to access information, capital and specific business opportunities and to reduce risks and transaction costs) to the fragmented markets for inputs and production associated with the early stages of economic development (see also Chapters 2 and 3 in this volume).

In examining internal (intra-firm) and external (inter-firm) network linkages as determinants of location choice, Chen and Chen (1998) concluded that external linkages are far more important relative to internal linkages for Taiwanese MNCs. Using Taiwanese electronics firms as an example, Chen (2003) illustrated in his network approach that international production entails the management of important domestic and overseas network relations. He argued that the richness and diversity of the linkages to external resources, which enable the assimilation and consolidation of resources in a global context, are often more valuable determinants of the internationalization process than the resources or assets directly owned by the firm. It enables even seemingly small and weak firms that can leverage external network resources to internationalize, and thus the existence of, or close proximity to, abundant network resources determines the choice of location of international production. Li (2003) also argued that the lack of ownership advantages in latecomer MNCs results in a more intensive use of strategic alliance for linkage, leverage and learning at the network level, to enhance dynamic capabilities with an accelerated pattern of evolution to catch up with the MNCs as early movers – a view echoed by Mathews (2002a, 2002b).

On the other hand, in the view of Yeung (1998), the causal mechanisms of transnational business based in East Asian NIEs are simultaneously embedded in complex relational networks at three distinct levels: intra-firm networks, and inter-firm networks and extra-firm networks. Hong Kong MNCs 'are embedded in a perpetual tendency to cultivate complex networks of personal and business relationships' (Yeung, 1998: 229). This networking capability, driven by a socially and culturally determined propensity to establish *guanxi* within and between firms, as well as outside firms, is a more significant component of the competitive advantage of Hong Kong MNCs than more conventional forms of ownership-specific advantages. Through business networking, MNCs based in developing countries, particularly those based in the Asian NIEs, 'are an increasingly potent force in the regional and global economy' (Cho, 2000: 207).

Yeung (1998) did not advocate a 'culturalist' explanation of institutional development, with fundamental economic factors also important, but in a historically and geographically contingent way (Cho, 2000). Gomez (1999) similarly rejected 'culturalist' explanations, based on ideas of the family or networked business, in explaining the growth of the largest Chinese publicly listed business concerns in Malaysia, including Chinese-controlled enterprises that have evolved to become significant MNCs. Given the diminishing clan and dialect group solidarity and cooperation that formed the basis for much of the old-style networking among struggling Chinese immigrants to Southeast Asia a century or more ago, Gomez questioned the significant role of ethnically based business 'networks' as one of the uniquely dynamic qualities of ethnic Chinese capitalism, when explaining large Chinese businesses in Malaysia (see also Chapter 18 in this volume).

The 'business system' concept explains the emergence of the MNC through the interdependent development over time of different varieties of capitalist economic organization in Europe, Asia and the Americas with dominant societal institutions. Indeed the concept suggests that the various ways in which organizations from different business systems internationalize mirrors their varied natures and strategies, which do not change significantly in the absence of a transformation in the fundamental societal institutions. Should the dominant forms of capitalist organization in market economies change as a result of the process of internationalization, the extent and pattern of such change will be path-dependent and reflect their historical legacies and current institutional linkages (Whitley, 1998). In addressing the current controversy over globalization, Guillén (2001) presented a similar argument in explaining that divergence, rather than convergence, of socioeconomic systems is much more likely to be the norm.

In a related light, Li (1993) provided strong evidence to demonstrate the critical influence of national context over the choices of corporate strategy content, through its role in creating (1) the immediate task environment, (2) the basic pool of resources, and (3) the primary cognitive/value system for the indigenous firms. Owing to the heterogeneity in their nation-specific contexts, as measured by the physical and societal profiles, he showed that the indigenous computer firms from South Korea and Taiwan tended to follow contrasting strategies, as measured by strategic intent, posture, mode and thrust. The high degree of sustainability of heterogeneous national advantages, particularly those deriving from nation-specific historical and cultural heritages, ensures continuity in the distinctive nature of corporate strategies of indigenous firms from different countries. Zutshi and Gibbons (1998) provided further evidence to demonstrate the importance of a contextual approach, within which corporate strategies are formed in analysing the internationalization process of government-linked companies in Singapore.

Whitley (2000) advanced the view that the major forms of economic organization or business systems (of which there are six types: fragmented, coordinated industrial district, compartmentalized, collaborative, highly coordinated and state-organized) that are developed and reproduced in particular institutional contexts are associated with distinctive innovation strategies (of which there are five types: dependent, craft-based responsive, generic, complex and risky, and transformative). In this view, institutional differences between market economies explain variations in innovation strategies and patterns of innovative performance (see also Chapter 3 in this volume). Guillén (2001) also recognized that both the dominant form of business organization and organizational strategies are cultivated in the broader political–economic and sociocultural context of established national development regimes, which in turn are determined by country-specific attitudes toward the state, markets and FDI, among other factors. The decisions of the firm, with respect to its size or composition, will determine the mode of its integration with the global economy. He provided quasi-functionalist emphasis on the adaptive capacity of organizations in treading the multiple paths to successful global economic integration, a view challenged by Davis (2003: 241), who proposed that 'there may be more serious limits to firm adaptability and to the relationship between business organizational structure and national developmental gains than Guillén prefers to acknowledge'. Indeed, the various studies linking nation-specific contexts to the dominant form of business organization and corporate strategy may have overlooked or played down the role of organizations themselves in configuring nation-specific contexts, as well as current patterns of globalization.

ECONOMIC THEORIES OF THE MULTINATIONAL CORPORATION AND INTERNATIONAL PRODUCTION

With the emergence and growth of MNCs based in developing countries in general, and those based in the developing countries of East, South and Southeast Asia in particular, the debate in the literature among scholars had always been whether or not economic theories of the MNC and international production, established to explain American and European MNCs, are adequate in explicating the distinctive features of such empirical phenomena. The distinctive features of MNCs based in developing countries lie mainly in the lack or absence of oligopolistic or monopolistic forms of ownership-specific advantages that are usually assumed necessary to enable MNCs from the West and Japan to compete successfully abroad, and in the smaller size of firms engaged in marginally efficient operations, rather than large innovative corporations.[6] The pattern of their outward FDI is different from that of Western and Japanese MNCs, producing typically low technology and undifferentiated goods that take account of lower production costs in foreign locations, using joint ventures as a common international business mode. The relatively smaller size of some firms and home countries means that there is a much higher affinity for cultural, linguistic and geographical proximity in explaining the location advantage of their host countries (Giddy and Young, 1982).[7]

Mirza (2000) contrasted MNCs based in East Asian developing countries with those based in the West and Japan, in terms of their relative technological level, experience and expertise, and the nature of their firm-specific advantages, in the enhanced role of government policies as a determinant of outward FDI, and in the role of ethnic ties as a major factor in the location of a proportion of their outward FDI (see also Yeung, 1994a; Sim and Pandian, 2003). However, the intra-group diversity of MNCs based in developing countries may be more significant than the inter-group distinctions between MNCs based in developed and developing countries (Yeung, 1994b; Mathews 2002b).

Nevertheless various scholars lend support to either the convergence or the divergence hypothesis, depending on whether they believe that the distinctive differences between MNCs based in developed and developing countries will lessen in importance or disappear entirely over time, in a way that will enable the extant theories of the MNC and international production to explain eventually all MNCs. Those that support the convergence hypothesis propose that, notwithstanding the distinctive features of the ownership and internalization-incentive advantages of MNCs based in developing countries in general, and those based in Asian developing countries in particular, and the unique location advantages of production in foreign countries that these MNCs seek, existing economic theories of the MNC and international production can adequately explicate these 'unconventional' MNCs, although it may require that the theories be sufficiently expanded and broadened in scope.

Such were the views of Lecraw (1980, 1981) and Wells (1984) who described the motivations and unique competitive assets of Asian developing countries within the framework of an adapted product cycle model. Dunning (1981a) explained the emergence of developing country MNCs with respect to the eclectic theory of the MNC and international production. He explored 'the proposition that the propensity of a developing country to engage in foreign direct investment is partly a function of its stage of economic development and partly a function of its particular characteristics or those of its firms which make for a unique combination of ownership, location, and internalization advantages whatever its stage of development' (Dunning, 1981a: 6). He explained the rising levels of net outward investment in Brazil and South Korea, in terms of the rising ownership advantages of their indigenous firms rather than falling location advantages of these countries, and these in turn are related to the structure of industry and the strategy of their firms. Shapiro *et al.* (2003) examined the strategic behaviour of ethnic Chinese family firms from the economic perspective of the eclectic theory of the MNE, concluding that, although these firms differ significantly from Western MNCs, their strategic behaviour can be couched within the analytical constructs of ownership, internalization and location advantages.

On the other hand, Li (2003) showed, on the basis of the evidence of one longitudinal embedded case study (the Taiwanese MNC, Acer), that the eclectic theory/paradigm advanced by Dunning and the internationalization theory advanced by Johanson and Vahlne (1977) need modifications (so as to apply to the MNEs from the developing countries as latecomers) and enhancements (so as to better explain all MNEs). Using the eclectic paradigm as a straw man for his alternative OLI approach, Mathews (2002a, 2002b) argued similarly on the basis of the longitudinal embedded case study of the same Taiwanese MNC that firms from developing countries develop an outward association that benefits from a variety of linkages previously offered by globalized firms, and use a 'cellular' structure to integrate their operations.

The emergence and growth of MNCs based in developing countries, along with other new sources of MNCs in developed countries, have profound implications for the advancement of the concept of the investment development cycle/path in international production. Although subsequently extended by Narula (1996) and Dunning and Narula (1997), the concept of an investment development cycle, as it was originally formulated by Dunning (1981a, 1981b), stated that there is a relationship between net outward investment (NOI) and a country's relative stage of development, as measured by gross national product (GNP) per capita. Dunning suggested that the plotted data of the NOI and GNP of different countries, both variables normalized by the size of the population, show the presence of a J-shaped investment development curve, with countries classified as belonging to four main groups corresponding to four stages of development. However, a fifth group corresponding to the fifth stage of development was later added (Dunning, 1988).

Countries at the lowest or first stage of development have little or no inward or outward FDI, and consequently a level of NOI that is close to zero. Countries at somewhat higher levels of development attract increasingly significant amounts of inward FDI, but as the outward FDI is still limited, NOI is negative. The argument then is that, past some threshold stage of development, outward FDI takes off and increases for countries at yet higher levels of development. The continued growth of their outward FDI at a fourth stage results in positive NOI, followed by the growth of cross-investments and intra-industry production that results in the return of their NOI to zero at the fifth stage of development.

In the view of Giddy and Young (1982: 71), 'notionally unconventional multinational business operations may be explained adequately within the broad framework of received theory'. These MNCs base their survival in domestic and foreign markets on the possession of ownership advantages, although those ownership advantages accrue less from large size and heavy R&D intensity. The possession of such unique ownership-specific advantages, whose use is internalized within the firm in combination with favourable location-specific factors of international production in foreign countries, explains their emergence and growth as MNCs. They showed that the ownership-specific advantages of these MNCs determine the location-specific factors sought in foreign countries. With the greater affinity for cultural, linguistic and geographical proximity in explaining the location of their investments, the distinctive pattern of these location-specific factors may be driven more by the dictates of internationalization theory than by economic factors.

This point is later expounded by Erramilli *et al.* (1999), who tested the application of internationalization theory to explain the international expansion patterns of MNCs based in Asian developing countries. By employing South Korean FDI data in manufacturing from 1973 to 1990, they found that (1) physical distance plays a critical role in market selection during the early waves of investment, but economic factors become more important in subsequent waves of investment; and (2) the use of majority ownership modes increases over time, but firms appear to 'leapfrog', when the market potential is good. South Korean MNCs in manufacturing are more likely to seek majority than minority ownership, as the physical distance between the home and the host country increases.

Ferrantino (1992) provided an alternative explanation to the observed pattern of South–South direct investments by firms based in developing countries, in terms of the high entry barriers in high-income markets that include, but may not be limited to, geographical and cultural barriers. Such barriers to investing in developed countries require greater investments in firm-specific competitive advantages such as technological effort to overcome the costs of foreignness. However, Dunning *et al.* (1998) explained that increased investment in developed countries by MNCs based in developing countries may reflect either existing asset-exploiting FDI, where their enhanced ownership-specific advantages help to decrease the costs of foreignness, or new asset-seeking FDI as a means to increase their competitiveness in relation to conventional MNCs on their home turf.

In line with the view of Freeman (1974), the theory of localized technological change advanced by Lall (1981, 1982, 1983a, 1983b) as a dynamic theory of technological competence considers the role of innovation in the multinationality of MNCs based in developing countries. His theory accounted for the capacity of firms from the more advanced developing countries to generate genuinely unique innovation, which is dependent upon, or localized around, the existing conditions of production and which may be based on some occasions on licensed foreign technology. In this theory, the distinctive nature of ownership advantages of MNCs based in developing countries draws on the ability of their firms to innovate on essentially different lines from those of the more advanced countries, that is innovations that are based on lower levels of research, size, technological experience and skills, and to achieve improvements by modernizing an older technique, including foreign outdated technology. Although the different type of innovation pursued by MNCs based in developing countries requires an empirical investigation that recognizes technology creation broader than the sphere of research and patenting activity, Cantwell and Tolentino (1990) demonstrated that the theory of technological accumulation is still a useful means of analysing the international growth of manufacturing firms from quite different environments, and at different stages of development and capacity. Pananond and Zeithaml (1998) demonstrated the relevance of the product cycle model, and the concepts of investment development path, localized technological change and technological accumulation as analytical frameworks, in which to examine the international business expansion of Thailand's Charoen Pokphand (CP) Group (see also Chapter 21 in this volume).

The stages-of-development concept advanced by Cantwell and Tolentino (1990) and Tolentino (1993) further explains the developmental or evolutionary course over time, in the character and composition of foreign activities financed by the outward FDI of countries. The concept, in line with the developmental process described by Vernon and Hirsch in the product cycle model, and by Kojima and Ozawa in the Japanese MNC model, provided another framework in which to elucidate specifically the developmental course of MNCs from developing countries. Although these MNCs are of a more recent vintage, they had been evolving rapidly, and have a distinctive technological tradition, compared to the more mature MNCs from Europe, the US and Japan. The further development of macroeconomic theories of international production enabled a better understanding of the way patterns in the emergence and evolution of MNCs relate to distinctive patterns of national development in different home countries, as determined by their endowment of natural resources, the size of their domestic market and the type of development path pursued in achieving their industrial development (Tolentino, 2000). In relating stages of national development to the form of technological competence of leading indigenous firms, the type of outward FDI and its industrial course over time, MNCs based in the developing countries remain at a much earlier stage of development, compared to the more advanced MNCs from the developed countries, despite the rapid pace in the emergence and in the evolutionary path of their outward FDI.

By contrast, Li (1998b) examined the evolutionary pattern of MNCs based in developing countries on the basis of a longitudinal study of Taiwan's Acer Group as a case study. Combining extant MNC theories (comprising the eclectic paradigm, the internationalization theory and the concept of an investment development cycle/path), strategy analysis and the evolutionary perspective, he developed a model capable of describing both the spatial (that is the antecedent, activity and consequences of MNC evolution) and temporal patterns (that is the simultaneity, directionality and rhythm) of MNC evolution. He derived important implications for MNCs from developing countries from the application of his model to the case study, namely: the sources of initial comparative advantages, the strategies to develop new competitive advantages, the fit between strategy and culture as keys to success and the evolutionary pattern of MNCs.

On the other side of the camp are those scholars who doubt the relevance of the extant theories of the MNC and international production, which were designed to explain the emergence and growth of MNCs based in the developed market economies, in explicating the entirely distinctive nature of MNCs based in developing countries. Those who support this school of thought advocate the view that, although the distinctive differences between MNCs based in developed and developing countries will possibly lessen in importance over time, substantial differences will remain and never disappear entirely, so that the extant theories of the MNC and international production will never adequately explain all MNCs. The alternative paradigm of the Japanese MNC model advanced by Kojima (1973, 1978) – where a distinction was made between anti-trade oriented American MNCs and trade-oriented Japanese MNCs in the manufacturing sector – is firmly rooted in the divergent school of thought. Though Kojima's model of Japanese MNC has become outdated, with the rapid industrial transformation and geographical diversification of Japanese MNCs over time, the model provides a cogent framework in which to view the persistent substantial differences in the nature of MNCs based in developed and developing countries.

In addition, the study of Tolentino (1993) showed how the general trend towards internationalization of business, associated with the rapid emergence and growth in the levels of outward FDI from newer home countries, including developing countries, had profound implications for Dunning's concept of an investment development cycle/path in international production. She showed a structural change in the relationship between NOI and GNP per capita that has occurred since the mid-1970s, as a result of the general rise of newer MNCs based in countries at intermediate stages of development, including the richer developing countries, that have acquired the capacity and incentive to engage in outward FDI at a much earlier stage in their development, when compared to the conventional MNCs based in Europe and the US. As a consequence of the increased significance of outward FDI from the newer home countries, resulting from the general trend towards internationalization of business, a country's overall NOI can no longer be determined or predicted solely by its relative stage of development.[8]

By promoting the view that the phenomenon of MNCs based in developing countries is an exception to established theories of MNCs and international production, Pangarkar (1998) also supported the divergence hypothesis. In addition to the absence of monopolistic or oligopolistic ownership advantages in developing country MNCs due to superior technology, brand name capital or some kind of management expertise associated with conventional MNCs, he argued that the presence of ownership advantage did not always precede their international business expansion. Although the importance of asset-augmenting FDI has more recently been incorporated in the eclectic paradigm, the presence of ownership advantages, or more generally the necessity of ownership advantages, in explaining the emergence and evolution of MNCs remains an ongoing contestable issue in the academic literature. Using a network perspective to explicate the international expansion in the ASEAN region of firms based in Hong Kong, Yeung (1998: 230) similarly challenged 'essentially economistic and Western-centric models of international production by shifting the focus of explanation from transaction cost economising to the on-going socio-spatial embeddedness of transnational corporations'.

Finally, Mathews (2002a, 2002b), on the basis of evidence gathered from the longitudinal case study of the Taiwanese MNC, Acer, advanced the view, that, although the basic tenet of learning and growth inherent in the Uppsala model of internationalization continues to be an influential analytical tool for understanding the growth of MNCs in general, the approach is institutionally inappropriate in explaining the growth of the latecomer MNC in a global marketplace, via leapfrogging that, in contrast to the slower process of learning associated with careful expansion, facilitates rapid learning to build the dynamic capabilities necessary for competition in global markets (see Roehl, 2003, and Chapter 16 in this volume). This supports the earlier findings of the study of Oh *et al.* (1998) based on the Daewoo Motor Company. They provided compelling evidence to show that developing country MNCs, as latecomers, must undertake simultaneous technological accumulation and internationalization. This involves, inter alia, learning to stretch and leverage their resources, and to be open to access technology through various cooperative arrangements, providing emphasis on process rather than product innovation, being prepared to take risks by the takeover of ailing companies, and a focus on geographic markets ignored by developed country MNCs.

CONCLUSION

This section reflects on the critical review of the two key strands of the theoretical and empirical literature, as a foundation in which to identify some of the agenda for future research and hint at some implications for business and government policy. It has become abundantly clear, when reflecting on the contributions of those scholars who support the convergence hypothesis, that at least some of the extant theories of the MNC and international production at a macroeconomic level (that is the product cycle model, the concepts of the investment–development cycle/path and stages of development, and the internationalization theory) and at a mesoeconomic level (that is the concept of localized technological change and the theory of technological accumulation) hold up reasonably well in explaining the emergence and evolution of MNCs based in developing countries in general.

Similarly, the expansion and broadening of the concepts of ownership, location and internalization advantages in the evolution of the eclectic paradigm of international business (a theory that applies at all levels of economic analysis) has enabled it to become a broad framework to explain all MNCs in all types of international business activity. And so indeed does the internalization theory of the MNC, based on a theory of a firm as well as the strand of organizational theory and new institutional economics, that argue commonly on the view of the firm, or the organization as a creature of market failure, as a result of significant transaction costs in market trading. Additionally, given the key role of inter-firm networks (such as *keiretsu* and *keiretsu*-type business structures or business groups) in the competitive positions and performance of firms and MNCs based in Japan, South Korea, India and other Asian nations, one could speculate on the relevance of Hymer's [1960] (1976) theory of the MNC, in the presence of oligopolistic interdependence to explain this empirical phenomena.

However, the broad framework of received theory seems to explain MNCs based in developing countries only in part, for a closer scrutiny reveals the underlying distinctive nature of MNCs in different market economies, a view strongly advocated by the alternative paradigm of the Japanese MNC model advanced by Kojima at the macroeconomic level, and by those advocating the different varieties of societal systems of capitalism school of thought in comparative institutional analysis. As mentioned previously, although Kojima's model of Japanese MNCs has become outdated with the rapid industrial transformation and geographical diversification of Japanese MNCs over time, the idea behind the model is pertinent to the examination of the substantial differences in the nature of MNCs based in developed and developing countries; and such differences are highly likely to persist. The exceptionally brisk pace in which Japanese firms developed their innovative capabilities, which formed the basis of the rapid transformation of the Japanese economy and the evolution of Japanese MNCs, is unlikely to be replicated by developing countries or their firms.

Some lay the blame on the failure of the concept of structural diversification described by the FDI-led flying geese theory of economy development of Kojima (2003), particularly in advanced technologies. Others attribute it to more fundamental factors such as the steeper learning curves, increased costs of R&D and the rapid pace of technological advancement, combined with the absence of suitable institutional and policy mechanisms to absorb and adapt foreign technologies during the learning process. All of these factors have been considered to exacerbate the problems faced by developing economies in their quest to reduce their technological dependence on developed countries (Bernard and Ravenhill, 1995; Ray *et al.*, 2004).

Yet, before we jump hastily to prescribe that government policy provide appropriate and adequate institutional and policy mechanisms to support the technological advancement and competitiveness of local firms, we need to draw renewed enlightenment from Dunning (1992), who had long reminded us of the necessity to design and adopt a systemic, integrated and holistic macro-organizational strategy, or horizontal policy, to encompass policies on education and training, science and technology, competition, protection of property rights, regional development, trade and inward and outward FDI, all of which exert an important impact on the productivity and competitiveness of firms and resources within the jurisdictions of national governments. The desired outcome of a successful macro-organizational strategy (the greater enhancement of the international competitiveness of domestic firms, with a structure of output and innovation patterns consistent with high productivity levels) requires integrated loci of governance at the local, national, regional and international levels (see also chapters in Part III of this volume).

Those advocating the different varieties of capitalism approach argue in a similar fashion, but on the basis of adopting a different theoretical approach. Their proponents would be opposed to the contingency theoretic tradition in organization theory that argues, on the basis of the ontological distinction and separation of organizations and their environment, that all firms vary hypothetically on a continuum of set dimensions. 'Businesses, however, are never isolated economic actors; they always operate in complex social settings and always reflect the social and organizational dynamics of those settings' (Hamilton, 1996: 40). The salient ideas derived from comparative institutionalism that there are various types of effective organizations and managerial strategies that emerge and evolve distinctively across historical and cultural contexts, and that there are divergent pathways to modernity in different national contexts, carry important business policy implications for strategic planning and implementation in 'unconventional' MNCs, including those based in developing countries. The process of catching up of MNCs based in developing countries in general, and those based in Asian developing countries in particular, with those of more established MNCs based in developed countries is a path-dependent one, which will reflect the inimitable historical legacies and institutional linkages in different national contexts.

Nevertheless, current studies in this school of thought may have placed more emphasis on linking nation-specific contexts to the dominant form of business organization and corporate strategy, at the expense of analysing the active role of organizations themselves in configuring their strategies and structures, nation-specific contexts, and mode of integration into the world economy, as mentioned previously. This constitutes a vital research agenda for the future, along with the comprehensive analysis of the limits of the adaptive capacity of capitalist economic organizations to tread the multiple paths to successful global economic integration. To do full justice to this research agenda would require an expansion of the time period and a broadening of the circle of factors taken into account when examining business organizations, including a more critical examination of their social and political power (Davis, 2003). The interdependent development over time of different varieties of capitalist economic organization in different market economies with dominant societal institutions is worthy of further scholarly attention, as is the nature and extent to which the dominant forms of capitalist organization in different market economies may change or be influenced over the course of their evolution by a range of economic, political and social forces at the local, national, regional, international and global levels.

NOTES

1. Hong Kong (China) registered the highest levels of outward FDI stock, even after taking into account round tripping FDI to China and the channelling of funds to non-operating companies in tax havens (see UNCTAD, 2004). Some of the outward FDI from Singapore and Malaysia represent the outward FDI of foreign affiliates operating in those economies.
2. The outward FDI performance index, as calculated by UNCTAD (2004), is the world share of a country's outward FDI, as a ratio of its share in world GDP. The index can be derived on the basis of outward FDI flows or stocks: flows reflect current FDI activity, while stocks reflect accumulated activity.
3. The transnationality index, as calculated by UNCTAD (2004), is based on the average of the following three ratios: foreign assets to total assets, foreign sales to total sales and foreign employment to total employment.
4. Korea Electric Power, CLP Holdings (Hong Kong, China) and Hong Kong Electric Holdings belong to the world's 25 largest electricity MNCs, ranked by size of foreign assets. Singapore Telecommunications and Telekom Malaysia belong to the world's 30 largest telecom MNCs, ranked by the number of host countries. Keppel Corporation (Singapore) belongs to the world's ten largest MNCs in construction, based on size of foreign assets. Shangri-La Asia (Hong Kong, China), City Developments Limited (Singapore), Hong Kong & Shanghai Hotel (Hong Kong, China) and Raffles Holdings (Singapore) belong to the world's 15 largest MNCs in hotels, based on size of foreign assets. Neptune Orient Lines (Singapore) and Orient Overseas International (Hong Kong, China) belong to the world's ten largest MNCs in logistics, based on size of foreign assets. Inno-Pacific Holdings (Singapore) belongs to the world's 15 largest MNCs in restaurants, based on size of foreign assets. China Travel International (Hong Kong, China) belongs to the world's ten largest MNCs in tourism, based on size of foreign assets.
5. Thus organizations could be analysed in one of three ways in organization theory. In the contingency theoretic tradition, organizations and their environments are ontologically distinct and separate, and therefore not mutually constituted. In regarding organizations as creatures of market failure with markets and hierarchies considered mutually exclusive, economic rationalists accord a derivative status to organizations. To those that examine the societal construction of business organizations, business organizations are intrinsically related to their environments, and markets and hierarchies are mutually constituted (see Tsoukas, 1993).
6. Evidence gathered from an analysis of conventional MNCs based in the US and the UK suggest that it may be misleading to link multinationality exclusively with large, technologically advanced firms (see, for example, Newbould, Buckley and Thurwell, 1978; Stopford, 1976). Freeman (1974) highlighted other

characteristics or strategies that can influence multinationality, including investments that do not necessarily require large size to achieve the required scale economies. In outlining a typology of strategies that firms could adopt under technological change – to include offensive strategy, defensive strategy, imitative strategy, dependent strategy, traditional strategy and opportunist or niche-dependent strategy – he proved that innovative competition and multinationality need not be synonymous with heavy R&D expenditures. Guillén (2001), amongst others, similarly doubted the proposition that only large consolidated business groups can achieve international competitiveness in an increasingly global context, a finding that brings his ideas in sync with the flexible specialization theories (Davis, 2003).

7. Not all studies of MNCs based in developing countries are in agreement with the stylized facts of the typical 'unconventional MNC'. See, for example, Lall (1981, 1982, 1983a, 1983b), Tolentino (1993) and the various studies on MNCs based on the Asian newly industrialized economies by Li (1994), Ulgado *et al.* (1994), Hobday (1997), Oh *et al.* (1998), van Hoesel (1999), Ernst (2000) and Mathews (2002b), amongst perhaps others, which provide a contrasting view (see also Chapters 21 and 22 in this volume).

8. For related findings on the investment–development cycle, see Hobday (1995).

REFERENCES

Bernard, Mitchell and J. Ravenhill (1995), 'Beyond product cycles and flying geese: regionalization, hierarchy, and the industrialization of East Asia', *World Politics*, **47**(2), 171–209.

Blomqvist, Hans C. (1995), 'Intraregional foreign investment in East Asia', *ASEAN Economic Bulletin*, **11**(3), 280–97.

Brown, Rajeswary Ampalavanar (ed.) (1995), *Chinese Business Enterprise in Asia*, London and New York: Routledge.

Buckley, Peter J. (2004), 'Asian network firms: an analytical framework', *Asia Pacific Business Review*, **10**(3/4), 254–71.

Cantwell, John and Paz Estrella E.Tolentino (1990), 'Technological accumulation and third world multinationals', University of Reading discussion paper in international investment and business studies, no. 139, Department of Economics, University of Reading, Reading.

Carney, Michael (1998), 'A management capacity constraint? Obstacles to the development of the overseas Chinese family business', *Asia Pacific Journal of Management*, **15**(2), 137–62.

Cheek, Timothy (1992), 'Review of S. Gordon Redding, The Spirit of Chinese Capitalism', *Social Science Quarterly*, **73**(1), 208–9.

Chen, Homin and Tain-Jy Chen (1998), 'Foreign direct investment as a strategic linkage', *Thunderbird International Business Review*, **40**(1), 13–30.

Chen, Tain-Jy (2003), 'Network resources for internationalization: the case of Taiwan's electronics firms', *Journal of Management Studies*, **40**(5), 1107–30.

Cho, Myung-Rae (2000), 'Review of Henry Wai-chung Yeung, Transnational Corporations and Business Networks: Hong Kong Firms in the ASEAN Region', *Regional Studies*, **34**(2), 207.

Davis, Diane E. (2003), 'Review of Mauro F. Guillén, The Limits of Convergence: Globalization and Organizational Change in Argentina, South Korea, and Spain', *Economic Development & Cultural Change*, **52**(1), 239–42.

Dunning, John H. (1981a), 'Explaining outward direct investment of developing countries: in support of the eclectic theory of international production', in K. Kumar and M.G. McLeod (eds), *Multinationals from Developing Countries*, Lexington, MA: Lexington Books, pp. 1–22.

Dunning, John H. (1981b), *International Production and the Multinational Enterprise*, London: Allen & Unwin.

Dunning, John H. (1988), 'The eclectic paradigm of international production: a restatement and some possible extensions', *Journal of International Business Studies*, **19**(1), 1–31.

Dunning, John H. (1992), 'The global economy, domestic governance, strategies and transnational corporations: interactions and policy implications', *Transnational Corporations*, **1**(3), 7–45.

Dunning, John H. and Rajneesh Narula (1997), 'The investment development path revisited: some emerging issues', in J.H. Dunning and R. Narula (eds), *Foreign Direct Investment and Governments: Catalysts for Economic Restructuring*, London: Routledge, pp. 1–41.

Dunning, John H., R. van Hoesel and R. Narula (1998), 'Third world multinationals revisited: new developments and theoretical implications', in J.H. Dunning (ed.), *Globalization, Trade and Foreign Direct Investment*, Amsterdam: Elsevier, pp. 255–86.

Ernst, Dieter (2000), 'Inter-organizational knowledge outsourcing: what permits small Taiwanese firms to compete in the computer industry?', *Asia Pacific Journal of Management*, **17**(2), 223–56.

Erramilli, M. Krishna, R. Srivastava and S. Kim (1999), 'Internationalization theory and Korean multinationals', *Asia Pacific Journal of Management*, **16**(1), 29–45.

Ferrantino, Michael J. (1992), 'Transaction costs and the expansion of third-world multinationals', *Economics Letters*, **38**(4), 451–6.

Flowers, Edward B., T.P. Chen and J. Shyu (eds) (1999), *Interlocking Global Business Systems: The Restructuring of Industries, Economies and Capital Markets*, Westport, CT and London: Greenwood, Quorum Books.

Freeman, Christopher (1974), *The Economics of Industrial Innovation*, Harmondsworth: Penguin.

Ghauri, Pervez N. and S. Benjamin Prasad (1995), 'A network approach to probing Asia's interfirm linkages', in S. Benjamin Prasad (ed.), *Advances in International Comparative Management*, vol. 10, Greenwich, CT and London: JAI Press, pp. 63–77.

Giddy, I.H. and S. Young (1982), 'Conventional theory and unconventional multinationals: do new forms of multinational enterprise require new theories?', in A.M. Rugman (ed.), *New Theories of the Multinational Enterprise*, London: Croom Helm, pp. 55–78.

Gomez, E.T. (1999), *Chinese Business in Malaysia: Accumulation, Accommodation and Ascendance*, Richmond: Curzon Press.

Granovetter, Mark (1994), 'Business groups', in N. Smelser and R. Swedberg (eds), *The Handbook of Economic Sociology*, Princeton, NJ: Princeton University Press, pp. 453–75.

Guillén, Mauro F. (2001), *The Limits of Convergence: Globalization and Organizational Change in Argentina, South Korea, and Spain*, Princeton, NJ: Princeton University Press.

Haley, G.T. and U.C.V. Haley (1998), 'Boxing with shadows: competing effectively with the Overseas Chinese and Overseas Indian business networks in the Asian arena', *Journal of Organizational Change Management*, **11**(4), 301–20.

Hamilton, Gary G. (1996), 'The organization of capital in South Korea and Taiwan', in A.E. Safarian and W. Dobson (eds), *East Asian Capitalism: Diversity and Dynamism*, Hongkong Bank of Canada Papers on Asia, vol. 2, Toronto: University of Toronto Press, pp. 19–44.

Hobday, Michael (1995), *Innovation in East Asia: The Challenge to Japan*, Aldershot, UK and Brookfield, US: Edward Elgar.

Hobday, Michael (1997), 'Latecomer catch-up strategies in electronics: Samsung of Korea and Acer of Taiwan', *Asia Pacific Business Review*, **4**(2/3), 48–83.

Hymer, Stephen H. [1960] (1976), *The International Operations of National Firms: A study of Foreign Direct Investment*, Cambridge, MA: MIT Press.

Johanson, J. and J.E. Vahlne (1977), 'The internationalization process of the firm – a model of knowledge commitment', *Journal of International Business Studies*, **8**, 23–32.

Khanna, Tarun (2005), 'Asia's new business giants', *Global Agenda*, **3**, 166–8.

Kojima, Kiyoshi (1973), 'A macroeconomic approach to foreign direct investment', *Hitotsubashi Journal of Economics*, **14**(1), 1–21.

Kojima, Kiyoshi (1978), *Direct Foreign Investment: A Japanese Model of Multinational Business Operations*, London: Croom Helm.

Kojima, Kiyoshi (2003), *The Flying-Geese Theory of Economic Development*, Tokyo: Bunshindo.

Lall, Sanjaya (1981), *Developing Countries in the International Economy: Selected Papers*, London and Basingstoke: Macmillan.

Lall, Sanjaya (1982), *Developing Countries as Exporters of Technology*, London and Basingstoke: Macmillan.

Lall, Sanjaya (1983a), 'The rise of multinationals from the third world', *Third World Quarterly*, **5**(3), 618–26.

Lall, Sanjaya (1983b), 'The theoretical background', in S. Lall (ed.), *The New Multinationals*, Chichester: John Wiley.

Lall, Sanjaya (1991), 'Direct investment in South-East Asia by the NIEs: trends and prospects', *Banca Nazionale del Lavoro Quarterly Review*, **179**, 463–80.

Lecraw, Donald J. (1980), 'Intra-Asian direct investment: theory and evidence from the ASEAN region', *UMBC Economic Review*, **16**(2), 20–25.

Lecraw, Donald J. (1981), 'Internationalization of firms from LDCs: evidence from the ASEAN region', in K. Kumar and M.G. McLeod (eds), *Multinationals from Developing Countries*, Lexington, MA: Lexington Books, pp. 37–51.

Li, Peter Ping (1993), 'How national context influences corporate strategy: a comparison of South Korea and Taiwan', in S. Benjamin Prasad and R.B. Peterson (eds), *Advances in International Comparative Management*, vol. 8, Greenwich, Connecticut and London: JAI Press, pp. 55–78.

Li, Peter Ping (1994), 'Strategy profiles of indigenous MNEs from the NIEs: the case of South Korea and Taiwan', *International Executive*, **36**(2), 147–70.

Li, Peter Ping (1998a), 'Towards a geocentric framework of organizational form: a holistic, dynamic and paradoxical approach', *Organization Studies*, **19**(5), 829–61.

Li, Peter Ping (1998b), 'The evolution of multinational firms from Asia', *Journal of Organizational Change Management*, **11**(4), 321–37.

Li, Peter Ping (2003), 'Toward a geocentric theory of multinational evolution: the implications from the Asian MNEs as latecomers', *Asia Pacific Journal of Management*, **20**(2), 217–42.

Lim, Linda Y.C. (1996a), 'The evolution of Southeast Asian business systems', *Journal of Asian Business*, **12**(1), 51–74.

Lim, Linda Y.C. (1996b), 'Southeast Asian business systems: the dynamics of diversity', in A.E. Safarian and W. Dobson (eds), *East Asian Capitalism: Diversity and Dynamism*, Hongkong Bank of Canada Papers on Asia, vol. 2, Toronto: University of Toronto Press, pp. 91–117.

Lim, Linda Y.C. (2000), 'Southeast Asian Chinese business: past success, recent crisis and future evolution', *Journal of Asian Business*, **16**(1), 1–14.

Machado, Kit G. (1999), 'Complexity and hierarchy in the East Asian division of labour: Japanese technological superiority and ASEAN industrial development', in K.S. Jomo and G. Felker (eds), *Technology, Competitiveness and the State: Malaysia's Industrial Technology Policies, Studies in the Growth Economies of Asia*, vol. 23, London and New York: Routledge, pp. 65–97.

Mathews, John A. (2002a), 'Competitive advantages of the latecomer firm: a resource-based account of industrial catch-up strategies', *Asia Pacific Journal of Management*, **19**(4), 467–88.

Mathews, John A. (2002b), *Dragon Multinational: A New Model for Global Growth*, Oxford: Oxford University Press.

Mirza, Hafiz (2000), 'The globalization of business and East Asian developing-country multi-nationals', in N. Hood and S. Young (eds), *The Globalization of Multinational Enterprise Activity and Economic Development*, London: Macmillan.

Mitchell, Katharyne (1995), 'Flexible circulation in the Pacific Rim: capitalisms in cultural context', *Economic Geography*, **71**(4), 364–82.

Narula, R. (1996), *Multinational Investment and Economic Structure: Globalisation and Competitiveness*, London: Routledge.

Newbould, G.D., P.J. Buckley and J.C. Thurwell (1978), *Going International: The Experience of Smaller Companies Overseas*, New York: John Wiley.

Oh, Donghoon, Chong Ju Choi and Eugene Choi (1998), 'The globalization strategy of Daewoo Motor Company', *Asia Pacific Journal of Management*, **15**(2), 185–203.

Ong-Giger, Kim (1999), 'Review of Henry Wai-chung Yeung, Transnational Corporations and Business Networks: Hong Kong firms in the ASEAN region', *ASEAN Economic Bulletin*, **16**(1), 127–9.

Pananond, Pavida and C.P. Zeithaml (1998), 'The international expansion process of MNEs from developing countries: a case study of Thailand's CP Group', *Asia Pacific Journal of Management*, **15**(2), 163–84.

Pangarkar, Nitin (1998), 'The Asian multinational corporation: strategies, performance and key challenges', *Asia Pacific Journal of Management*, **15**(2), 109–18.

Ray, Pradeep Kanta, M. Ida, Chung-Sok Suh and Shams-Ur Rahman (2004), 'Dynamic capabilities of Japanese and Korean Enterprises and the "flying geese" of international competitiveness', *Asia Pacific Business Review*, **10**(3/4), 463–84.

Redding, S. Gordon (1990), *The Spirit of Chinese Capitalism*, Berlin and New York: Walter de Gruyter.

Redding, S. Gordon (1995), 'Overseas Chinese networks: understanding the enigma', *Long Range Planning*, **28**(1), 61–9.

Redding, S. Gordon (2000), 'What is Chinese about Chinese family business? And how much is family and how much is business?', in Henry Wai-Chung and Kris Olds (eds), *Globalization of Chinese Business Firms*, New York: St. Martin's Press and London: Macmillan Press, pp. 31–54.

Redding, S. Gordon (2001), 'The smaller economies of Pacific Asia and their business systems', in A.M. Rugman and Thomas L. Brewer (eds), *The Oxford Handbook of International Business*, Oxford: Oxford University Press, pp. 760–81.

Riedel, James (1991), 'Intra-Asian trade and foreign direct investment', *Asian Development Review*, **9**(1), 111–46.

Roehl, Tom (2003), 'Review of John A. Mathews, Dragon Multinational', *Asia Pacific Journal of Management*, **20**(3), 411–13.

Ross, Douglas N. (1993), 'Review of Richard Whitley, Business Systems in East Asia: Firms, Markets and Societies', *International Journal of Organizational Analysis*, **1**(1), 117–19.

Shapiro, Daniel M., E. Gedajlovic and C. Erdener (2003), 'The Chinese family firm as a multi-national enterprise', *The International Journal of Organizational Analysis*, **11**(2), 105–22.

Sim, A.B. and J.R. Pandian (2003), 'Emerging Asian MNEs and their internationalization strategies – case study evidence on Taiwanese and Singaporean firms', *Asia Pacific Journal of Management*, **20**(1), 27–50.

Stopford, John M. (1976), 'Changing perspectives on investment by British manufacturing multi-nationals', *Journal of International Business Studies*, **7**(2), 15–27.

Tolentino, Paz Estrella E. (1993), *Technological Innovation and Third World Multinationals*, London: Routledge.

Tolentino, Paz Estrella E. (2000), *Multinational Corporations, Emergence and Evolution*, London: Routledge.

Tsoukas, H. (1993), 'Review of Richard Whitley, Business Systems in East Asia: Firms, Markets and Societies', *Journal of Management Studies*, **30**(4), 681–4.

Ulgado, Francis M., Chwo-Ming J. Yu and A.R. Negandhi (1994), 'Multinational enterprises from Asian development countries: management and organizational characteristics', *International Business Review*, **3**(2), 123–33.

UNCTAD (2004), *World Investment Report 2004: The Shift Towards Services*, New York and Geneva: United Nations.

Van Hoesel, Roger (1999), *New Multinational Enterprises from Korea and Taiwan*, London: Routledge.

Vroom, C.W. (1995), 'Review of Richard Whitley, Business Systems in East Asia: Firms, Markets and Societies', *Organization Studies*, **16**(1), 159–61.

Wells, Louis T. Jr. (1984), 'Multinationals from Asian developing countries', in R.W. Moxon, T.W. Roehl and J.F. Truitt (eds), *International Business Strategies in the Asia-Pacific Region: Environmental Changes and Corporate Response, Research in International Business and Finance*, Vol. 4(A), Greenwich, CT: JAI Press, pp. 127–43.

Whitley, Richard D. (1990), 'Eastern Asian enterprise structures and the comparative analysis of forms of business organization', *Organization Studies*, **11**(1), 47–74.

Whitley, Richard D. (1991), 'The social construction of business systems in East Asia', *Organization Studies*, **12**(1), 1–28.

Whitley, Richard D. (1992), *Business Systems in East Asia: Firms, Markets and Societies*, Newbury Park, CA, London and New Delhi: Sage.

Whitley, Richard D. (1994), 'Dominant forms of economic organization in market economies', *Organization Studies*, **15**(2), 153–82.

Whitley, Richard D. (1998), 'Internationalization and varieties of capitalism: the limited effects of cross-national coordination of economic activities on the nature of business systems', *Review of International Political Economy*, **5**(3), 445–81.

Whitley, Richard D. (2000), 'The institutional structuring of innovation strategies: Business systems, firm types and patterns of technical change in different market economies', *Organization Studies*, **21**(5), 855–86.

Williamson, Peter J. (2005), 'Strategies for Asia's new competitive game', *Journal of Business Strategy*, **26**(2), 37–43.

Wong, John (1999), 'Southeast Asian ethnic Chinese investing in China', *Global Economic Review*, **28**(1), 3–27.

Yeung, Henry Wai-chung (1994a), 'Transnational corporations from Asian developing countries: their characteristics and competitive edge', *Journal of Asian Business*, **10**(4), 17–58.

Yeung, Henry Wai-chung (1994b), 'Third World multinationals revisited: a research critique and future agenda', *Third World Quarterly*, **15**(2), 297–317.

Yeung, Henry Wai-chung (1998), *Transnational Corporations and Business Networks: Hong Kong Firms in the ASEAN Region*, London: Routledge.

Yeung, Henry Wai-chung (ed.) (1999), *The Globalization of Business Firms from Emerging Economies*, Cheltenham, UK and Lyme, USA: Edward Elgar.

Yeung, Henry Wai-chung and Kris Olds (eds) (2000), *Globalization of Chinese Business Firms*, New York: St. Martin's Press and London: Macmillan Press.

Zutshi, Ravinder K. and Patrick T. Gibbons (1998), 'The internationalization process of Singapore government-linked companies: a contextual view', *Asia Pacific Journal of Management*, **15**(2), 219–46.

21. Explaining the emergence of Thai multinationals

Pavida Pananond[1]

The increasing participation of Asian firms in the global economy has been one of the key indications of the development of Asian business over the past few decades. Starting with the Japanese firms that emerged after the 1970s, but sharply increased their foreign direct investment (FDI) as a reaction to the rapid and steep appreciation of the yen in 1985 (see Itami, 1994), new players from the four Asian newly industrialized economies (NIEs) – Hong Kong, Singapore, South Korea and Taiwan – joined their Japanese predecessors in rapidly increasing their outward FDI during the 1980s (see Yeung, 1998). Household names, such as the Acer group of Taiwan and Samsung of South Korea, became renowned across the globe, not just in Asia. Later in the 1990s, a new generation of firms from smaller Southeast Asian economies began to venture beyond their borders, contributing favourably to the rise of outward FDI from Asian developing economies (see also Chapters 9 and 20 in this volume). Among the *World Investment Report* 2004's top 50 non-financial multinational enterprises (MNEs) from developing economies, [2] 14 hailed from Southeast Asia, including the CP group of Thailand (UNCTAD, 2004: Table I.3.1).[3] Although the CP group was dropped from the list in 2005 (UNCTAD, 2005: Annex table A.1.10), partly owing to the rise of many MNEs from China (see Chapter 22 in this volume), its prominence remained high. The group's president, Dhanin Chearavanont, was included as one of Asia's top 25 most powerful business leaders in *Fortune*'s October 2005 ranking (Demos, 2005).

Although outward investment of Thai firms is a recent phenomenon that became discernable only in the 1990s, its significance has rapidly increased over the years, until the 1997 economic crisis put a halt to this trend. From a negligible amount of US\$13 million in 1980, outward FDI stock from Thailand rose more than 200 times to exceed US\$3 billion in 1996 (UNCTAD, 1999: 498). Although the 1997 crisis led to a sharp downturn of Thai outward FDI in the years following the crisis, Thai FDI outflows resurged in 2001, and reached a level that surpassed the pre-crisis years for the first time in 2003 (UNCTAD, 2004: Annex table B.2). The continuing growth of outward FDI from Thailand represents undeniable evidence of the growing emergence of Thai multinationals in the international business arena.

While attempts to explain Thailand's outward FDI were available (see Vatchratith, 1992; Intarak and Thanaekcharoen, 1995), studies that addressed the institutions conducting the outward investment – the Thai multinationals – have been scarce. The majority of information was popular press reports, celebrating the 'borderless' stage of Thai firms. Much less emphasis was placed on explaining why and how these firms expanded abroad. The lack of academic studies on the emergence of Thai multinationals was in stark contrast to the revived interest in multinationals from other East and Southeast Asian countries (see, for example, Lecraw, 1993; Tolentino, 1993; Hoesel, 1997; Yeung, 1998; Chapter 20 in this volume). Peng *et al.* (2001) clearly indicated that Thai firms had been historically underresearched and deserved more empirical attention.

Despite the limited interest in Thai firms and their international expansion, two strands of literature that addressed the emergence of Thai multinationals can be identified. The first line of work considers Thai firms as representatives of the 'overseas Chinese'[4] capitalism that has been dominant across Asia (cf. Chapter 18 in this volume). Proponents of this view suggest that the emergence of Thai multinationals is part of the overall internationalization process of the 'overseas Chinese' businesses in Asia. The key concepts underpinning this line of argument are usually drawn from the social, cultural and institutional theories.

The second line of research on the emergence of Thai multinationals is based on the economic theories of the multinational enterprises (MNEs), especially those that focused on the 'Third World MNEs',[5] sometimes referred to as developing country MNEs. Drawing on the theoretical concepts that have been used to explain the emergence of multinationals from other developing countries, this line of work attempted to explain the dynamics behind the emergence of Thai multinationals, with particular emphasis on their ownership advantage. This chapter is divided into four sections. The first two sections trace the arguments forwarded by the aforementioned two strands of research. The third section looks at the changing dynamics of the Thai multinationals, while the last section suggests directions for future research to broaden the understanding of the issue.

THAI MULTINATIONALS AS PART OF THE 'OVERSEAS CHINESE' DIASPORA

Like their competitors elsewhere, Thai multinationals are usually firms that have already enjoyed a successful presence in the domestic market. These leading firms often share two main characteristics. First, they are generally large firms owned by either a single family or a group of families. Typically, these firms are organized as conglomerates or business groups, involved in a variety of related and unrelated business activities (Suehiro, 1992; see also Chapters 2 and 3 in this volume). Second, the majority of families that own these firms are founders or descendants of ethnic Chinese families who had migrated to Thailand (Phipatseritham, 1982; Phipatseritham and Yoshihara, 1983; Suehiro, 1989, 1992). Estimated to comprise only about 10 per cent of the total population, ethnic Chinese in Thailand controlled approximately 81 per cent of listed companies in the Stock Exchange of Thailand in the pre-crisis years (East Asia Analytical Unit, EAAU, 1995: 74). In a recent study of the post-crisis ownership structure of firms in Thailand, Suehiro (2004: 183) confirmed that the dominant role of ethnic Chinese in the Thai business community still continued, despite the transfer of ownership of some ethnic Chinese families to foreign multinationals following the 1997 economic crisis.

In his first extensive research on the capital accumulation of Thailand, Suehiro (1989: 275–77) concluded that the development of domestic capitalist groups was a product of the historical development of the 'tripod' relationships among these business groups, state and public enterprises, including military-related firms, and foreign multinationals. He stressed that the understanding of Thai capitalist groups be achieved through the analysis of these relationships. Various chapters in McVey (1992) similarly pointed out that the evolution of ethnic Chinese entrepreneurs in Thailand and other Southeast Asian countries was a product of political, economic, social and cultural forces that involved these entrepreneurs and other key actors in the society, particularly the state (see also Mackie, 1992; Doner, 1992). Yoshihara (1988) took a harsher view of these relationships, and concluded that the Southeast Asian entrepreneurs' relationships with foreign multinationals and the state were considered a dependence that prevented them from proper technological accumulation, and led to an ersatz capitalist development process, where rent-seeking activities were rampant.

In addition to relationships with the state and foreign multinationals, ethnic networks among the other 'overseas Chinese' and the mainland Chinese were also considered significant in these firms' domestic development and international expansion. Since China opened its doors to foreign investment in 1979, ethnic Chinese have been the largest source of foreign investment in China, with Hong Kong ranking as the number one investor (East Asia Analytical Unit (EAAU), 1995). Southeast Asian firms became an additional important source of investment during the 1990s (Brown, 1998: 612). Close ties between Southeast Asia, Hong Kong, Taiwan, and China attracted much attention from scholars, and exotic terms, such as the 'bamboo network' (Weidenbaum and Hughes, 1996) or the 'worldwide web of Chinese business' (Kao, 1993) were coined to describe these links. Many scholars have suggested that these 'overseas Chinese' networks provide entrepreneurs with necessary business intelligence, alternative sources of capital and necessary political linkages (see, for example, Hamilton and Biggart, 1988; Biggart and Hamilton, 1990; Redding, 1990, 1995; Ch'ng, 1993; EAAU, 1995; Brown, 1998). These resources served as competitive advantages for ethnic Chinese entrepreneurs in their domestic development (Haley *et al.*, 1998).

Moreover, advocates argued that networks among these 'overseas Chinese' were extended across borders to benefit business dealings in East and Southeast Asia, as their common cultural background promoted trust and reduced transaction costs. Some scholars suggested further that a common ethnic and cultural background was an important source of ownership advantage for these firms, vis-à-vis Western competitors, when investing in the Asian region, especially in China (see Limlingan, 1986; Redding, 1990, 1995; EAAU, 1995). Most scholars agreed that doing business in China required much use of *guanxi* or personal relationships and connections (see also Chapters 4 and 6 in this volume). Luo and Chen (1997) suggested that these personal connections contributed significantly and positively to the performance of firms operating in China. They stated that, compared with their Western counterparts, ethnic Chinese investors were more at ease using these *guanxi*, and that in turn had benefited their ventures in China. With the increasingly significant role played by these ethnic Chinese firms in the regional economy, many scholars have therefore linked the international expansion of Thai firms to the overall internationalization process of the ethnic Chinese businesses in Southeast Asia (see, for example, Yeung, 1999, 2000; Sikorski and Menkhoff, 2000).

While the 'overseas Chinese' business framework may help to explain the behaviour of some business groups in Thailand, lumping all Thai firms that have expanded abroad as part of the 'overseas Chinese' diaspora may be misleading. Not all Thai multinationals identify themselves as ethnic Chinese. For example, four key case studies on Thai multinationals (Pananond, 2001a) pointed out that only the CP group had shown particular interest in China, and had benefited from the shared cultural background. The notion that ethnic Chinese business firms are similar within the same home economies and across different countries has already met with strong criticism for oversimplification (see, for example, Jomo, 2003; Yeung, 2004; Gomez and Hsiao, 2004). To imply that the international expansions of all Thai and other Southeast Asian firms are part of an overall internationalization process of the 'overseas Chinese' capitalism could lead to more inaccurate representations in the field that has already been criticized as 'fraught with misconceptions' (see Gomez and Hsiao, 2004: 3). In a study of Singaporean multinationals, Dahles (2002) concluded that ethnic Chinese ties were not exclusively applicable to Singaporean Chinese business expansion beyond the region. Nor were these ties significant for the younger generation of businesses that had been established since the 1990s.

In addition, the predominance of the cultural and institutional view on the development of these ethnic Chinese firms has led to the limited analysis of the issue from the economic and business perspective. Shapiro *et al.* (2003) stressed that, despite the considerable amount of research on ethnic Chinese family firms, few had examined the strategic behaviour of these firms from an economic viewpoint, hence resulting in the cultural heritage and institutional context taking the primary role in explaining their strategic behaviour. This leads us to the next strand of literature that explains the emergence of Thai multinationals from the economic theories of multinational enterprises.

THAI MULTINATIONALS AS 'THIRD WORLD' MULTINATIONALS: TECHNOLOGICAL AND NETWORKING CAPABILITIES

Studies that focused on the international expansions of Thai firms as a phenomenon in itself, not as part of the globalization of the 'overseas Chinese' business, only emerged in the late 1990s (see Osotsapa and Chirathiwat, 1997; Pananond and Zeithaml, 1998). This line of research is part of the continuing interest in the emergence and activities of 'Third World multinationals'. The literature on 'Third World multinationals' dated back to the early 1980s, and could be broadly categorized under two different waves, based on the timing of their emergence and their views on the nature of the competitive advantages of these firms (see also Chapter 20 in this volume). Despite their differences, the two groups shared a strong emphasis that, without their own proprietary technology, the competitive advantages of multinationals from developing countries lay in their ability to gradually adapt and accumulate technological skills from the technology originally imported from the more advanced economies.

The first wave, or those that emerged in the late 1970s and early 1980s, argued that the competitive advantages of developing country multinationals were derived from their ability to reduce costs of imported technology through descaling techniques, such as reducing operation scale, replacing machinery with human labour, and replacing imported inputs with cheaper local ones. These cost advantages forced these firms to concentrate their operations in the low-cost market of other developing countries with a similar or poorer economic status. The sustainability of these firms was thought to be untenable, as their cost advantages would erode over time once local firms caught up.

Proponents of this view included Wells (1977, 1981, 1983), O'Brien (1980), Aggarwal (1984), Lecraw (1977, 1981) and Kumar (1982). This perspective was not shared across all its contemporaries, however. Lall (1983a, 1983b) argued that the ownership advantages of multinationals from developing countries were derived from the *knowledge* of operation in less developed markets, rather than the cost advantages from descaled operations. These knowledge-based advantages could therefore be sustained in the long term, through sufficient R&D efforts and continued learning. Lall's conclusions formed the basis of what was to become the second wave of literature on 'Third World multinationals'.

Though attention to the subject faded in the late 1980s, there has been a renewed surge of interest since the early 1990s. The second-wave literature on 'Third World multinationals' focused particularly on the capability of these firms to catch up with their developed-country counterparts, through the learning-by-doing technological accumulation process. It was suggested that developing country multinationals built their competitive advantages from the incremental learning process that started with lower value-added activities, and worked their way up the value chain. Proponents of this view included Vernon-Wortzel and Wortzel (1988), Cantwell and Tolentino (1990), Tolentino (1993), Lecraw (1993), Ulgado *et al.* (1994), Dunning *et al.* (1997), and Hoesel (1997). In sum, the more recent works on multinationals from developing countries suggested that the competitive advantages of these firms were derived from their technological capabilities accumulated through the incremental learning process.

Notwithstanding its valuable insights, the literature on 'Third World multinationals' is not without limitations. In his study of 'dragon multinationals', latecomer firms that internationalized from the periphery, Mathews (2002) criticized the mainstream literature for its implication that multinational firms expanded abroad to exploit their existing advantages. He aptly pointed out that latecomer firms suffered from an initial lack of resource endowment, and therefore had to turn their disadvantages into potential sources of advantage through clever and innovative strategies and organizational forms. Beausang (2003) also confirmed that the precondition of ownership advantage at the outset of internationalization was not applicable to Brazilian and Chilean multinationals. The notion that multinationals from developing countries had had to construct their competitive advantage throughout their internationalization process was a major deviation from the conventional wisdom.

In addition, Pananond (2001a, 2001b, 2002) contended that the existing literature offered a rather limited and deterministic interpretation of what constituted the competitive advantages of developing country MNEs and of their development. She argued that the conventional approach of comparing multinationals from developing countries with their counterparts from developed economies led to deterministic implications that the former could catch up with the latter only through becoming like them. With proprietary technology being the most important competitive advantage of MNEs from developed economies, the only way for developing country multinationals to emerge was therefore to accumulate their technological skills and to work their way up from the lower value-added activities of the value chain. The key implication of this view was that the emergence of multinationals from developing countries would be an incremental process, reflecting the learning-by-doing nature of the dynamics behind these firms' emergence. Given this strong hypothesis, other explanations of alternative routes to the development of multinationals from developing countries were often unobserved, despite the diverse and complex reality of these MNEs' emergence.

The strongest critique Pananond (2001a) put forth, however, was that the 'under-socialized' nature of the existing literature on 'Third World multinationals' led, not only to a narrow interpretation of what constituted a firm's competitive advantages, but also to a disregard of the way the firm's development in the domestic market influenced its inter-national expansion behaviour. The classical and neoclassical view of economic institutions as atomized and rational actors independent of all social relations had been previously criticized by economic sociologists (see Granovetter, 1985, 1992, 1995). Theories on MNEs and 'Third World multinationals' were no exception to this view. As a consequence, most insights on the development of MNEs were dominated by economic explanations, without much consideration for their social *embeddedness* (Yeung, 1994, 1998).

As a consequence, theories on the MNEs implied that ownership advantages of the firm reside only within the boundary of the firm, in the form of efficiency-enhancing assets, such as technological and managerial skills, financial prowess or proprietary innovations. Although attempts have been made to address the growing significance of cooperative alliances of firms across borders (see, for example, Dunning, 1995), these networks were perceived mainly as a form of governance structure that could contribute to the develop-ment of their R&D and innovation development (see Dunning, 2001). This undersocial-ized approach reinforced the implication that efficiency-enhancing activities, such as the technological accumulation process, were the most crucial factors in the emergence of multinationals from developing countries.

In addition, economic theories on 'Third World multinationals' paid little attention to the domestic development of these firms, and how that pattern might influence their inter-national expansion. Kogut (1988, 1991, 1993) asserted that firms remained imprinted by their domestic growth strategy, even as they internationalized. Similarly, Li (2003) stressed that the process of international expansion was an integral part of an overall MNE evo-lution, and, therefore, the context of the firm's evolution had to be taken into consider-ation, when explaining the MNEs' internationalization process.

To complement the undersocialized economic perspective of the theories on multina-tionals from developing countries, an interdisciplinary approach that would integrate issues, such as networks and the firm's domestic development, is highly desirable. The combination of these two perspectives could explain Thai multinationals, not simply as a product of their historical development, but also as emerging MNEs that are faced with growing competition in the global economy. Although the literature on the 'overseas Chinese' business pointed out that the development of domestic firms in East and Southeast Asian countries was a product of its cultural, historical and social environ-ment, little was mentioned about how these institutional factors affected the development of business organizations within those economies.

One line of research that attempted to unveil how institutional context affected the development of domestic firms in Asia placed emphasis on the timing of a country's entry into industrialization. According to this view, the timing of industrialization served as one of the most important contingencies that influenced domestic firms' strategy and structure. Unlike leading enterprises of countries that went through indus-trialization early, firms from countries that only entered the industrialization process after the Second World War were driven by a different mechanism. Without a core set of proprietary technology, firms from late industrialized countries were obliged to develop an additional set of generic skills that were not specific to any particular industry, and could be transferred across industries. While the early proponents of this view stressed the knowledge-based generic skills that were mainly found in the production function (see Amsden, 1989, 1995, 2001; Amsden and Hikino, 1993, 1994; Hikino and Amsden, 1994; Hoesel, 1997),[6] some recent works identified some broader generic organizational skills, such as contact capabilities (the ability to combine foreign and domestic resources to enter other industries quickly and cost-effectively), as key resources in the development of business groups from late industrializing countries (see Kock and Guillén, 1998; Guillén, 2000).

Combining this with the view that Asian firms benefited tremendously from the extensive network of relationships, it can be interpreted that networking has been an important organizational skill of firms from late industrializing countries. While network ties are considered as assets, networking can also be regarded as an important organizational skill. Ebers (1997) defined networking capabilities as organizational skills through which firms could gain competitive advantages, by getting access to the desired resources and capabilities that were complementary to their own. Mathews (2002) similarly concluded that the ability to leverage resources through global partnerships and linkages was a crucial element in the international expansion of newcomer firms from developing economies.

Following this view, Pananond (2001a) argued that networking capabilities, or the firm's ability to draw on complementary resources of partners and to turn them to the firm's benefit, formed an equally critical part of the Thai multinationals' competitive advantages by serving as generic skills that could be transferred across industries. In other words, the emergence of Thai multinationals depended on not only their industry-specific technological skills, but also their generic networking capabilities. Based on the in-depth studies of four Thai multinationals, namely the Charoen Pokphand (CP) group, the Siam Cement group, the Dusit Thani group and the Jasmine group, Pananond (2001a) concluded that the internationalization process of these firms was guided not only by their accumulated technological skills, but also by their networking capabilities, or the ability to draw on complementary resources of different partners, and to turn them to the firm's benefit. While industry-specific technological skills, such as scale and scope in the domestic market, were fundamental in creating these Thai multinationals' competitive advantages, networking capabilities served as an additional source of advantage that could be exploited across industries during these firms' domestic growth as well as international expansion.

Four types of network relationships vital to the emergence of these Thai multinationals were close ties with domestic and international financial institutions, relationships with both home- and host-country governments, alliances with foreign technology partners, and social relationships based on ethnic ties. First, close ties with financial institutions were among the most important networks that facilitated the rapid international expansion of Thai multinationals. Not only did these networks endow the four Thai multinationals with financing ability and valuable information on international expansion opportunities, they also provided indirect links to international financial sources that helped contribute to the financing of many international projects.

Second, network relationships with the home-country government, including bureaucrats, technocrats and the military, brought several benefits to these Thai multinationals. Examples of these advantages included valuable information, government contracts, favourable policies and, sometimes, privileged access to expansion opportunities granted through concessionary rights. While close relationships with the home-country government contributed favourably toward these firms' domestic growth, the applicability of these networks in other countries remained limited. To enhance the business-to-government networks in host countries, the four Thai multinationals under study relied on forming ties with the carefully selected local partners, who were well connected in the selected host countries.

The third type of network relationships, business-to-foreign partners, could be further subdivided into ties with foreign technology partners, and with host-country business partners. While the technological expertise of foreign multinationals remained significant throughout the domestic and international expansion of the Thai multinationals studied, the role of local business partners was limited to providing necessary business and political connections for activities in each of the host markets. It should be noted that, while these Thai multinationals selected the most advanced technology partner in their respective industry, their local partners were chosen, not so much for their technological excellence, but for their strong local knowledge and connections.

The fourth type of network that contributed to the emergence of the Thai multinationals under study was social networks. Although much emphasis had been given to ethnic Chinese networks in Asia and how these deep ethnic ties contributed to the development of ethnic Chinese firms in Southeast Asia (see, for example, EAAU, 1995; Limlingan, 1986; Weidenbaum and Hughes, 1996; Brown, 1998), Pananond (2001a) found that this emphasis might be exaggerated. Although common cultural background was indeed helpful in the early development of some firms by facilitating business dealings, later development was led more by business objectives than by sentimental ethnic ties. Among the four cases, Pananond contended that only one, the Charoen Pokphand (CP) group, identified themselves as ethnic Chinese, whereas the others considered themselves as Thai groups, with no particular ties to other ethnic Chinese businesses. Even for CP, whose common language and cultural background facilitated its investment in China to a certain extent, the group's expansion in China resulted from many other factors that were beyond ethnic ties or ancestral loyalty (see also Pananond and Zeithaml, 1998; Pananond, 2005). Among these four types of networks, relationships with financial institutions and with foreign technology partners played the most crucial role throughout the emergence of the four Thai multinationals under study (see also Chapters 8 and 18 in this volume).

These networks relationships endowed the firms with resources they previously lacked. More importantly, the ability to combine a variety of resources from these different partners and to package them together served as an important organizational skill that helped these firms to emerge in a way that they could not have done on their own. Links with foreign technology partners allowed these Thai multinationals to skip the incremental technological accumulation process, and yet provided them with sufficient technological skills needed for regional investments. Similarly, the easy access to funding sources prompted them to invest in projects they might not have been able to afford on their own. In other words, these networking capabilities, or the ability to combine resources from different partners and to turn them to the firm's benefit, were significant generic organizational skills that served to enhance their competitive advantages, in addition to their industry-specific technological skills.

The finding that Thai multinationals benefited from the resources of others was congruent with Peng *et al.* (2001). In a study that looked at the top 200 listed firms in the Stock Exchange of Thailand (SET), the authors found that firms that they classified as multinationals[7] drew resources from others through the appointment of board directors. While previous research on business networks placed emphasis on ethnic ties or global partnerships in R&D and other value-chain networks, studies on Thai multinationals mentioned above have brought attention to other types of network relationships. In particular, the focus was placed on these Thai firms' ability to manage different types of networks, and to benefit from their partners' resources.

The mutually advantageous interaction of technological, as well as networking, capabilities allowed the four selected Thai multinationals to bypass the incremental technological process, and to undertake a rapid internationalization process prior to 1997. This pattern contradicted the existing literature on 'Third World multinationals' that suggested their emergence follows an incremental process driven by the improved and accumulated technological capabilities. By integrating the institutional perspective into her framework, Pananond (2001a) explained how the symbiotic interaction of industry-specific technological skills and generic networking capabilities was pivotal to the rapid international expansion of Thai multinationals in the early 1990s. The next part discusses how the balance between these two types of capabilities changed in the years following the crisis (see also Chapter 8 in this volume).

THE CHANGING CONTEXT AND CHANGING DYNAMICS OF THAI MULTINATIONALS: POST-CRISIS ADJUSTMENTS

Over a brief period, Thai multinationals, whose ownership advantages were largely based on networking capabilities, were able to expand and seize opportunities in nearby markets. Investing in other Asian developing countries, where market institutions were still weak, enabled these firms to exploit their networking capabilities, sometimes at the expense of accumulating necessary technological expertise. It has become evident that rapid international expansions, based largely on network relationships, led to Thai multinationals' imprudent and ill-advised decisions. The close ties with domestic and international financial institutions, along with a more relaxed regulatory requirement, prompted these Thai multinationals to borrow extensively to finance their domestic and international expansions. Such leveraging and the accompanying high debt–equity ratios became disastrous after the Baht was floated in July 1997, almost doubling their foreign currency debts. The difficult period that ensued both at home and in the region forced many firms to give up their overseas objectives, and they focused instead on domestic survival.

Although it is still too early to determine conclusively how Thai multinationals have changed after the crisis, some trends are discernable. Pananond (2004) classified the emerging patterns of the post-crisis reactions of Thai multinationals into four groups: decline, replication of pre-crisis behaviour, reform and refocus, and new emergence. While the first group of multinationals succumbed to their financial and managerial burdens, the second one acted in a similarly opportunistic manner that characterized its hasty pre-1997 international expansion. Quite to the contrary, the third pattern observed among Thai multinationals showed that this group of firms took the crisis as a wake-up call to refocus their strategy and restructure their operations. The last trend introduced a new set of Thai multinationals that enjoyed its growth and international expansion in the years following the crisis, thanks partly to government support and favourable business conditions.

To put these trends in a theoretical perspective, Pananond (2004) proposed that the decline in international activities of the first group of multinationals reflected their weaknesses in both technological and networking capabilities. When competition and the financial burden heightened, these shortcomings became much more pronounced, and forced this group of Thai multinationals to reduce considerably their international activities. The second pattern – replication of pre-crisis behaviour – indicated the tendency of Thai multinationals to continue their dependence, primarily on their networking capabilities, without paying much attention to developing their technological expertise. With increased competition and less favourable market conditions, Thai multinationals in this group were likely to find it more difficult to rely principally on the resources of others, thus resulting in the potential loss of competitive advantages in the long run.

The third trend, reform and refocus, could be viewed as attempts to sharpen their core technological capabilities without relying too much on networking capabilities. For the last trend, it can be hypothesized that these newly emerging multinationals were the latecomers in the Thai economic development. The competitive environment surrounding their activities was much more intense, leading to these firms' emphasis on developing their core technological capabilities. The intense competition and their young age may discourage these firms from diversifying away from their core industries. Consequently these firms are primarily concerned with developing their core technological capabilities.

A greater commitment to the development of industry-specific technological capabilities signified a changing dynamic of the Thai multinationals. From relying more on their networking capabilities during the pre-crisis international expansion, it appeared that Thai multinationals placed more emphasis on creating their competitive advantages from their own efforts. Strategies that had been widely adopted after the crisis included selection of core industries and reduction of non-related activities, increased emphasis on profitability over growth, and introduction of value-adding activities, such as brand creation and service provision. Some Thai multinationals started to integrate their international activities into their overall value chain in a much more coordinated manner. Rather than leaving activities in each host market as a stand-alone unit, these Thai multinationals became more selective in using their overseas investments in different locations for different purposes (see, for example, Burch and Goss, 2005; Pananond, 2005).

In sum, there appeared to be a shift in the dynamics of Thai multinationals. From a heavy reliance on networking over technological capabilities in the pre-crisis years, the re-emergence of Thai multinationals in the years following the crisis appeared to be based more on their technological capabilities. Although these trends are far from being conclusive, they can serve as a basis for future studies of the emergence of Thai multinationals. The next section discusses some directions for future research.

CONCLUSION AND FUTURE RESEARCH AGENDA

As there is still limited academic interest in Thai multinationals, or even Thai firms in general, numerous avenues for future research can be explored. This broad review has raised a number of theoretical issues that can be further explored. First, one of the most important theoretical issues addressed in this review is that networking capabilities can be considered generic organizational skills that enhanced Thai firms' competitive advantages. This conclusion is consistent with the resource-based perspective in the strategic management literature (Wernerfelt, 1984; Barney, 1991; Peteraf, 1993). Based on this framework, several research questions can be developed further. For example, whether networking capabilities are common among other Thai multinationals may be one direction that could increase the generalizability of the concept and the empirical representation of Thai multinationals. In addition to database studies on listed firms in the SET, like Peng *et al.* (2001), in-depth case studies of individual firms are much in demand.

To link the resource-based view with the firm's institutional context, attempts to explore whether networking capabilities are generic skills, which lead to the preference of business group and conglomerate structure among firms from late industrializing countries, can contribute to the understanding of the most prevalent organizational structure in those countries. The business group literature (see, for example, Khanna and Palepu, 1997; Ghemawat and Khanna, 1998; Khanna, 2000) had long argued that the business group structure was a product of market imperfections, political economy and cultural heritage. The resource-based concept of networking capabilities can be extended to explore whether these generic skills contributed to the ease in expanding into the diversified activities of business groups (see also Chapters 2 and 3 in this volume).

The relationship between a country's institutional context and the nature of firm development is another aspect that could benefit from the resource-based perspective. The late industrialization literature discussed earlier already suggested that the timing of a country's entry into the industrialization process had a strong impact on the development of the indigenous firms. Having integrated the resource-based view in this line of thought, Van de Ven (2004) arrived at a similar conclusion: that much of the knowledge that provided distinctive competence for sustained competitive advantage was context-specific. He suggested that this implication could be significant for firms from developing countries, whose context-specific competence could lead to more successful outcomes in other developing countries with similar institutional contexts. Firms from developed countries that had not acquired this type of tacit knowledge may find it more difficult to operate in these developing countries.

The notion that a firm's competence was context-specific could lead to inquiries as to whether the change in institutional context would affect the sustainability of resources that had been developed as a response to a different institutional context. Pananond (2001a) indicated that networking capabilities might have worked well in some specific environments, particularly in booming developing economies where multiple opportunities reward early movers. However, markets do not permanently remain under such conditions, as witnessed in the aftermath of the 1997 crisis. A legitimate question that calls for some rigorous research is whether networking capabilities can still be counted on in a more demanding environment of increasing market liberalization and global competition (see also Chapter 3 in this volume).

The second theoretical concept that can be examined further concerns the nature of the 'Third World multinationals'. As discussed earlier, this strand of literature has principally explained the emergence of MNEs from developing countries as an incremental learning process that started in the lower value-added activities of production, and later moved up the value chain. However, the rapid globalization of technology has made it more difficult for firms to rely on an extended, learning-by-doing technological accumulation process. Various authors (see, for example, Mathews, 2002; Dahles, 2002; Beausang, 2003) have already indicated that the internationalization process of firms from developing countries is about not only exploiting their existing ownership advantages, but also attempts to find more opportunities and strategic advantages that could benefit these firms' growth. This concept has been empirically supported, particularly in East Asia.[8]

Another new trend, whereby firms from developing economies are enhancing their competitive advantage, is the international expansion of their R&D activities to developed, as well as developing, countries (UNCTAD, 2005). Moreover, many firms from developing countries have taken the shorter route of merger and acquisition to obtain their desired technology. The acquisition of the IBM personal computer business by the Chinese multinational Lenovo demonstrated that multinationals from developing countries could bypass the incremental process of technology accumulation through acquisition (see also Chapter 22 in this volume). Future research on 'Third World multinationals' may therefore explore whether the production-based technological capabilities are being shifted toward the acquisition and management of technology, the service activities of technology products and the application rather than the innovation of technological know-how. The significance of these questions has recently increased, as multinationals from developing countries are becoming more and more engaged in technology-related activities.

Given all these diverse forms and strategies of multinationals from developing countries, it is appropriate to question the implicit suggestion in the 'Third World multinationals' literature that these firms remain the non-traditional MNEs that would eventually have to become like their predecessors from developed economies. As Pananond (2001a) argued, the comparative undertone intrinsic in this strand of literature inevitably led to the conclusion that MNEs from developing countries could emerge only when they became like the 'conventional' multinationals from developed economies. Future studies that could examine whether the complex and diverse reality of multinationals from developing countries generates different patterns of emergence would be a much needed addition to this stream of literature.

Finally, future research can be done to examine further the literature on 'overseas Chinese' multinationals. This chapter suggested earlier that this stream of literature could benefit from integrating the economic and business perspectives with the cultural explanations. More importantly, the question whether emerging multinationals from Asia, whose commonality happened to be their ethnicity, could all be lumped together as part of the globalization of 'overseas Chinese' capitalism remains to be debated much further. Despite its recent emergence, the international expansion of Thai firms has become one of the most salient strategic issues facing multinationals in the era of globalization. Having presented a short review of the existing literature dealing with the issue, this chapter is intended to point out further avenues into the study of Thai multinationals.

NOTES

1. I would like to thank Dr Pasuk Phongpaichit, Dr Somboon Siriprachai and Dr Henry Wai-chung Yeung for suggestions and comments on earlier drafts. The excellent research assistance provided by Veerayooth Kanchoochat is also highly appreciated.

2. The United Nations Centre on Transnational Corporation defined 'multinational enterprises' (MNEs) in 1978 as 'all enterprises which control assets – factories, mines, sales offices and the like – in two or more countries' (UNCTC, 1978: 158). Although many changes and additions have been made to define the term to encompass the changing nature of the MNE since then, attempts to restrict the definition inevitably led to more difficulties than when a more general definition was used (Jones, 1996: 4). This chapter therefore adopts the 1978 UN definition of the term and uses it interchangeably with 'multinationals'.
3. It should be noted, however, that, if multinational enterprises from the more developed Singapore are excluded, only five MNEs in the top 50 list originated from Southeast Asia.
4. Strictly speaking, the term 'overseas Chinese' is misleading, as it is a direct translation from the term *huaqiao* (sojourner). This term implies that the 'overseas Chinese' are temporarily residents outside of, and intend to return to, China. Recently, scholars have cautioned against the use of the term 'overseas Chinese', and proposed that 'ethnic Chinese' be used instead (Jomo and Folk, 2003, Gomez and Hsiao, 2004; Yeung, 2004). In Thailand, Chinese descendants are often referred to as Sino-Thais or Chinese Thais.
5. Yeung (1994: 302–3) strongly criticized the term 'Third World multinationals' as 'imperialistic' and 'not a theoretically fruitful way to conceptualise the nature of international business and production'. He suggested that a more unbiased and less derisory term, 'developing-country multinationals' be used instead. However, the term 'Third World multinationals' has been associated with the established stream of literature that dated back to the 1970s. This chapter uses this term specifically as a reference to this existing literature.
6. Amsden (2001) identified three types of generic technological capabilities: *production capabilities* (the skills necessary to transform inputs into outputs), *project execution capabilities* (the skills necessary to expand capacity), and *innovation capabilities* (the skills necessary to design entirely new products and processes).
7. The authors classified the 200 firms as either MNEs or non-MNEs in a two-step procedure. First, a threshold of having operations in at least three countries during 1994–6 must be met. Second, an MNE must have at least 5 per cent of its sales derived internationally during 1994–6, or 5 per cent more of its assets must have been invested overseas at the end of 1996 (Peng *et al.* 2001). Under this classification, 102 firms were classified as MNEs and 98 as non-MNEs. Although this is a rather innovative way to identify who the Thai MNEs are, the number of MNEs might be exaggerated as the practice of many Thai business groups is to list several of its subsidiaries in the stock market. For example, the CP group had four listed firms in agribusiness in the SET before the crisis, namely Charoen Pokphand Feedmill (CPF), Charoen Pokphand Northeastern (CPNE), Bangkok Agro-Industrial Products (BAP) and Bangkok Produce Merchandising (BKP). Only after the crisis did the group consolidate its operation in agribusiness under Charoen Pokphand Food (CPF), while the rest were delisted (CPF Notification to SET, 8 June 1998). Meanwhile, the CP group still maintains its listed subsidiaries in other sectors, such as Telecom Asia in telecommunications, 7-Eleven (Thailand) in retailing and Vinylthai in petrochemicals.
8. See, for example, Hoesel (1997) for studies of multinationals from South Korea and Taiwan, Yeung (1998) for Hong Kong firms, and Mathews (2002) for the Acer group of Taiwan.

REFERENCES

Aggarwal, R. (1984), 'The strategic challenge of third world multinationals: a new stage of the product life cycle of multinationals?', in R.N. Farmer (ed.), *Advances in International Comparative Management: A Research Annual, Vol. 1*, Greenwich, CT and London: JAI Press.
Amsden, A. (1989), *Asia's Next Giant: South Korea and Late Industrialisation*, Oxford and New York: Oxford University Press.
Amsden, A. (1995), 'Like the rest: South-East Asia's "Late" Industrialization', *Journal of International Development*, 7(5), 791–9.
Amsden, A.H. (2001), *The Rise of 'the Rest': Challenges to the West from Late-industrialising Economies*, Oxford: Oxford University Press.
Amsden, A.H. and T. Hikino (1993), 'Borrowing technology or innovating: an exploration of the two paths to industrial development', in R. Thompson (ed.), *Learning and Technological Change*, New York: St Martin's Press, pp. 243–66.
Amsden, A.H. and T. Hikino (1994), 'Project execution capability, organisational know-how and conglomerate corporate growth in late industrialisation', *Industrial and Corporate Change*, 3(1), 111–47.
Barney, J. (1991), 'Firm resources and sustained competitive advantage', *Journal of Management*, 17(1), 99–120.

Beausang, F. (2003), *Third World Multinationals: Engine of Competitiveness or New Form of Dependency?*, New York: Palgrave Macmillan.

Biggart, N.W. and G.G. Hamilton (1990), 'Explaining Asian business success: theory no.4', *Business and Economic Review*, **5**, 13–15.

Brown, R.A. (1998), 'Overseas Chinese investment in China – Patterns of growth, diversification and finance: the case of Charoen Pokphand', *The China Quarterly* (September), 610–36.

Burch, D. and J. Goss (2005), 'Regionalisation, globalisation and multinational agribusiness: a comparative perspective from Southeast Asia', in R. Rama (ed.), *Multinational Agribusiness*, New York: Haworth Press.

Cantwell, J. and P.E.E. Tolentino (1990), 'Technological accumulation and third world multinationals', Discussion Papers in International Investment and Business, no. 139, University of Reading.

Ch'ng, D. (1993), 'The overseas Chinese entrepreneurs in East Asia: background, business practices and international networks', CEDA Monograph M 100.

Dahles, H. (2002), 'Transborder business: the "capital" input in Singapore enterprises venturing into ASEAN and beyond', *SOJOURN*, **17**(2), 249–73.

Demos, T. (2005), 'Asia's 25 Most Powerful', *Fortune*, October.

Doner, R. (1992), 'Politics and the growth of local capital in Southeast Asia: auto industries in the Philippines and Thailand', in R. McVey (ed.), *Southeast Asian Capitalists*, Southeast Asia Program, Ithaca, NY: Cornell University.

Dunning, J.H. (1995), 'Reappraising the eclectic paradigm in the age of alliance capitalism', *Journal of International Business Studies*, **26**(3), 461–91.

Dunning, J.H. (2001), 'The key literature on IB activities: 1960–2000', in A.M. Rugman and T.L. Brewer (eds), *The Oxford Handbook of International Business*, Oxford: Oxford University Press.

Dunning, John H., R. Van Hoesel and R. Narula (1997), 'Third world multinationals revisited: new developments and theoretical implications', Discussion Papers in International Investment and Management, Series B, no. 227, University of Reading.

East Asia Analytical Unit (1995), *Overseas Chinese Business Networks in Asia*, Canberra: Department of Foreign Affairs and Trade.

Ebers, M. (1997), 'Explaining inter-organisational network formation', in M. Ebers (ed.), *The Formation of Inter-Organisational Networks*, Oxford: Oxford University Press.

Ghemawat, P. and T. Khanna (1998), 'The nature of diversified business groups: a research design and two case studies', *Journal of Industrial Economics*, **96**(1), 35–61.

Gomez, E.T. and H.-H.M. Hsiao (2004), 'Chinese business research in southeast Asia', in E.T. Gomez, and H.-H.M. Hsiao (eds), *Chinese Business in Southeast Asia: Contesting Cultural Explanations, Researching Entrepreneurship*, London: RoutledgeCurzon.

Granovetter, M. (1985), 'Economic action and social structure: the problem of embeddedness', *American Journal of Sociology*, **91**(3), 481–510.

Granovetter, M. (1992), 'Problems of explanation in economic sociology', in N. Nohria and R.G. Eccles (eds), *Networks and Organisations*, Boston, MA: Harvard Business School Press.

Granovetter, M. (1995), 'Coase revisited: business groups in the modern economy', *Industrial and Corporate Change*, **4**(1), 93–130.

Guillén, M.F. (2000), 'Business groups in emerging economies: a resource-based view', *Academy of Management Journal*, **43**(3), 362–80.

Haley, G.T., C.T. Tan and U. Haley (1998), *New Asian Emperors: The Overseas Chinese, their Strategies, and Competitive Advantages*, Oxford: Butterworth Heinemann.

Hamilton, G.G. and N.W. Biggart (1988), 'Market, culture, and authority: a comparative analysis of management and organisation in the Far East', *American Journal of Sociology*, **94**(Supplement), S52–S94.

Hikino, T. and A.H. Amsden (1994), 'Staying behind, stumbling back, sneaking up, soaring ahead: late industrialization in historical perspectives', in W.J. Baumol, R.R. Nelson and E.N. Wolff (eds), *Convergence of Productivity: Cross-national Studies and Historical Evidence*, Oxford: Oxford University Press.

Hoesel, R.V. (1997), *Beyond Export-Led Growth: The Emergence of New Multinational Enterprises from Korea and Taiwan*, Rotterdam: Erasmus University.

Intarak, C. and A. Thanaekcharoen (1995), Karn Longtun nai Tangpratet duoy Khon Thai: Tittang Mai tee na Jabta (Outward investment by Thais: a new direction to watch), *Bank of Thailand Monthly Report*, **35**(3), 11–24.

Itami, H. (1994), 'The globalisation of Japanese firms', in N. Campbell and F. Burton (eds), *Japanese Multinationals*, London and New York: Routledge.

Jomo, K.S. (2003), 'Chinese capitalism in Southeast Asia', in K.S. Jomo and B.C. Folk (eds), *Ethnic Business: Chinese Capitalism in Southeast Asia*, London: RoutledgeCurzon.

Jomo, K.S. and B.C. Folk (eds) (2003), *Ethnic Business: Chinese Capitalism in Southeast Asia*, London: RoutledgeCurzon.

Jones, G.G. (1996), *The Evolution of International Business: An Introduction*, London: Routledge.

Kao, J. (1993), 'The worldwide web of Chinese business', *Harvard Business Review*, (March–April), 24–36.

Khanna, T. (2000), 'Business groups and social welfare in emerging markets: existing evidence and unanswered questions', *European Economic Review*, **44**, 748–761.

Khanna, T. and K. Palepu (1997), 'Why focused strategies may be wrong for emerging markets', *Harvard Business Review*, (July–August), 41–51.

Kock, C. and F. Guillén (1998), 'Strategy and structure in developing countries: business groups as an evolutionary response to opportunities for unrelated diversification', Paper presented at the Annual Academy of International Business Conference, Vienna.

Kogut, B. (1988), 'Country patterns in international competition: appropriability and oligopolistic agreement', in N. Hood and J.-E. Vahlne (eds), *Strategies in Global Competition*, London, New York, Sydney: Croom Helm, pp. 315–40.

Kogut, B. (1991), 'Country capabilities and the permeability of borders', *Strategic Management Journal*, **12** (Special Issue on Global Strategy), 33–48.

Kogut, B. (1993), 'Learning, or the importance of being inert: country imprinting and international competition', in S. Ghoshal and D.E. Westney (eds), *Organization Theory and the Multinational Corporation*, New York: St Martin's Press, pp. 136–54.

Kumar, K. (1982), 'Third world multinationals: a growing force in international relations', *International Studies Quarterly*, **26**, 397–424.

Lall, S. (1983a), 'The rise of multinationals from the Third World', *Third World Quarterly*, **5**(3), 618–26.

Lall, S. (1983b), *The New Multinationals: The Spread of Third World Enterprises*, New York: John Wiley & Sons.

Lecraw, D. (1977), 'Direct investment by firms from less developed countries', *Oxford Economic Papers*, **29**(3), 442–57.

Lecraw, D. (1981), 'Internationalization of firms from LDCs: evidence from the ASEAN region', in K. Kumar and M.G. McLeod (eds), *Multinationals from Developing Countries*, Lexington, MA: D.C. Heath, pp. 37–51.

Lecraw, D. (1993), 'Outward direct investment by Indonesian firms: motivations and effects', *Journal of International Business Studies* (Third Quarter), 589–600.

Li, P.P. (2003), 'Toward a geocentric theory of multinational evolution: the implications from the Asian MNEs as latecomers', *Asia Pacific Journal of Management*, **20**(2), 217–42.

Limlingan, V.S. (1986), *The Overseas Chinese in ASEAN: Business Strategies and Management Practices*, Manila: Vita Development Corporation.

Luo, Y. and M. Chen (1997), 'Does quanxi influence firm performance?', *Asia Pacific Journal of Management*, **14**(1), 1–16.

Mackie, J. (1992), 'Changing patterns of Chinese big business in Southeast Asia', in R. McVey (ed.), *Southeast Asian Capitalists*, Southeast Asia Programme, Ithaca, NY: Cornell University.

Mathews, J.A. (2002), *Dragon Multinational: A New Model for Global Growth*, Oxford: Oxford University Press.

McVey, R. (ed.) (1992), *Southeast Asian Capitalists*, Southeast Asia Program, Ithaca, NY: Cornell University.

O'Brien, P. (1980), 'The new multinationals: developing-country firms in international markets', *Futures*, 303–16.

Osotsapa, S. and S. Chirathiwat (1997), 'Business strategies of transnational corporations from

Thailand', *Competitive Business Strategies of Asian Transnational Corporations*, New York: United Nations, pp. 71–82.

Pananond, P. (2001a), 'The making of Thai multinationals: the internationalisation process of Thai firms', unpublished PhD Thesis, University of Reading.

Pananond, P. (2001b), 'The making of Thai multinationals: a comparative study of Thailand's CP and Siam cement groups', *Journal of Asian Business*, **17**(3), 41–70.

Pananond, P. (2002), 'The international expansion of Thailand's Jasmine Group: built on shaky ground?', in M. Bhopal and M. Hitchcock (eds), *Asean Business in Crisis*, London: Frank Cass.

Pananond, P. (2004), 'Thai multinationals after the crisis: trends and prospects', *ASEAN Economic Bulletin*, **21**(1), 106–26.

Pananond, P. (2005), 'A great leap forward? The changing dynamics of the CP Group's international expansion', paper presented at the Workshop on Ethnic Chinese Economy and Business in Southeast Asia in the Era of Globalisation, Institute of Southeast Asian Studies, Singapore, 21–22 April.

Pananond, P. and C.P. Zeithaml (1998), 'The international expansion process of MNEs from developing countries: a case study of Thailand's CP Group', *Asia Pacific Journal of Management*, **15**(2), 163–84.

Peng, M.W., K.Y. Au and D.Y.L. Wang (2001), 'Interlocking directorates as corporate governance in third world multinationals: theory and evidence from Thailand', *Asia Pacific Journal of Management*, **18**(2), 161–81.

Peteraf, M.A. (1993), 'The cornerstones of competitive advantages: a resource-based view', *Strategic Management Journal*, **14**, 179–88.

Phipatseritham, K. (1982), *Wikroh Laksana Karn Pen Chao Khong Turakij Khanat Yai* (The Distribution of Ownership in the Thai Big Business), 1st edn, Bangkok: Thai Studies Center, Thammasat University.

Phipatseritham, K. and K. Yoshihara (1983), *Business Groups in Thailand*, research note and discussion paper no. 41, Institute of Southeast Asian Studies, Singapore.

Redding, S.G. (1990), *The Spirit of Chinese Capitalism*, New York: Walter de Gruyter.

Redding, G. (1995), 'Overseas Chinese networks: understanding the enigma', *Long Range Planning*, **28**(1), 61–9.

Shapiro, D.M., E. Gedajlovic and C. Erdener (2003), 'The Chinese family firm as a multinational enterprise', *International Journal of Organisational Analysis*, **11**(2), 105–22.

Sikorski, D. and T. Menkhoff (2000), 'Internationalisation of Asian business', *Singapore Management Review*, **22**(1).

Suehiro, A. (1989), *Capital Accumulation in Thailand 1855–1985*, Chiang Mai: Silkworm Books.

Suehiro, A. (1992), 'Capitalist development in postwar Thailand: commercial bankers, industrial elite, and agribusiness groups', in R. McVey (ed.), *Southeast Asian Capitalists*, Ithaca, NY: Cornell University, pp. 35–63.

Suehiro, A. (2004), 'Misunderstood power structure in Thailand: politics, business leaders, and the Chinese community', paper presented at the Core University Program Workshop on 'Middle Classes in East Asia', Center for Southeast Asian Studies, Kyoto University, 6–8 October.

Tolentino, P.E.E. (1993), *Technological Innovation and Third World Multinationals*, London and New York: Routledge.

Ulgado, F.M., C.-M.J. Yu and A.R. Negandhi (1994), 'Multinational enterprises from Asian developing countries: management and organisational characteristics', *International Business Review*, **3**(2), 123–33.

United Nations Centre on Transnational Corporation (1978), *Transnational Corporations in World Development: A Re-examination*, New York: United Nations.

United Nations Conference on Trade and Development (1999), *World Investment Report 1999: Foreign Direct Investment and the Challenge of Development*, New York and Geneva: United Nations.

United Nations Conference on Trade and Development (2004), *World Investment Report 2004: The Shift Toward Services*, New York and Geneva: United Nations.

United Nations Conference on Trade and Development (2005), *World Investment Report 2005: Transnational Corporations and the Internationalization of R&D*, New York and Geneva: United Nations.

Van de Ven, A.H. (2004), 'The context-specific nature of competence and corporate development', *Asia Pacific Journal of Management*, **21**, 123–47.

Vernon-Wortzel, H. and L.H. Wortzel (1988), 'Globalizing strategies for multinationals from developing countries', *Columbia Journal of World Business* (Spring), 27–35.

Vatchratith, V. (1992), 'Thai investment abroad', *Bangkok Bank Monthly Review*, **33**(April), 10–21.

Weidenbaum, M. and S. Hughes (1996), *The Bamboo Network: How Expatriate Chinese Entrepreneurs are Creating a New Economic Superpower in Asia*, New York: The Free Press.

Wells, L.T. (1977), 'The internationalisation of firms from developing countries', in T. Agmon and C.P. Kindleberger (eds), *Multinationals from Small Countries*, Cambridge, MA and London: MIT Press.

Wells, L.T. (1981), 'Foreign investors from the third world', in K. Kumar and M.G. McLeod (eds), *Multinationals from Developing Countries*, Lexington, MA: D.C. Heath, pp. 23–36.

Wells, L.T. (1983), *Third World Multinationals: The Rise of Foreign Investment from Developing Countries*, Cambridge, MA: MIT Press.

Wernerfelt, B. (1984), 'A resource-based view of the firm', *Strategic Management Journal*, **5**, 171–80, reprinted in N.J. Foss (ed.) (1997), *Resources, Firms and Strategies: A Reader in the Resource-based Perspective*, Oxford: Oxford University Press.

Yeung, H.W.-C. (1994), 'Third World multinationals revisited: a research critique and future agenda', *Third World Quarterly*, **15**(2), 297–317.

Yeung, H.W.-C. (1998), *Transnational Corporations and Business Networks*, London and New York: Routledge.

Yeung, H.W.-C. (1999), 'The internationalisation of ethnic Chinese business firms from Southeast Asia: strategies, processes and competitive advantage', *International Journal of Urban and Regional Research*, **23**(1), 103–27.

Yeung, H.W.-C. (2000), 'The dynamics of Asian business systems in a globalising era', *Review of International Political Economy*, **7**(3), 399–433.

Yeung, H.W.-C. (2004), *Chinese Capitalism in a Global Era*, London: Routledge.

Yoshihara, K. (1988), *The Rise of Ersatz Capitalism in South-East Asia*, Singapore: Oxford University Press.

22. Corporate China goes global

Friedrich Wu

Recent high-profile international acquisitions and takeover bids by mainland Chinese companies have dramatically shifted media attention from spotlighting China as a 'giant sucking vacuum cleaner' for global inward foreign direct investment (FDI) to characterizing the country as a cash-rich 'predator' embarking on a global buying binge. Despite the latest public frenzy stirred up by Chinese companies' accelerated cross-border merger-and-acquisition (M&A) forays, a large number of these enterprises have actually been discreetly internationalizing their operations for some years, without attracting a lot of media limelight (Wu, 1993, 1994). Nonetheless, the phenomenon of China's rising outward FDI has provoked some intense interest lately. Among academic studies, even the most recently published delineation at the macro level (Wong and Chan, 2003; see also Wang, 2002) was rather dated, as it was based on 2000–2001 data. The purpose of this chapter is therefore two-fold: to update the macro picture with the latest available data and to offer a more micro-analysis from the firm-level perspective.

THE MACRO PICTURE

Accelerated Outward FDI in the 2000s

While cross-border acquisitions and takeover bids by mainland Chinese companies have only recently captured international news headlines, the Beijing government has been formulating and executing the 'Go-Out' policy since the early 1990s. The latter was conceived as a critical component of the 'Open-Door' policy promulgated in late 1978. As President Jiang Zemin declared during the 14th Chinese Communist Party (CCP) Congress in 1992, 'to open wider to the outside world . . . we should encourage enterprises to expand their investments abroad and their transnational operations'. Between 1991 and 1997, the State Council had assembled a 'national team' of 120 state-owned industry groups – from 'strategic sectors', such as power generation, mining, automobiles, electronics, iron and steel, machinery, chemicals, construction, transport, aerospace, pharmaceuticals – that could spearhead the internationalization of Chinese enterprises (Nolan, 2001). To build the 'national team', these enterprise groups were given high levels of protection and generous state financial support, as well as special rights in management autonomy, profit retention and investment decisions. By 1997, in a reference to the government's drive to nurture globally competitive firms, President Jiang asserted during the 15th CCP Congress that 'the state-owned sector must be in a dominant position in major industries . . . we shall effectuate a strategic reorganization of state-owned enterprises by managing large enterprises well . . . China will establish highly competitive large enter-prise-groups with . . . transnational operations'.

With official encouragement, Chinese outward FDI flows surged to an average of nearly US$3.0 billion per annum during 2001–4, compared to an average annual of US$2.3 billion during 1991–2000 (see Table 22.1). By the end of 2004, accumulated outward FDI stock by Chinese companies reached US$38.8 billion – almost on a par with South Korea's US$39.3 billion, a country whose *chaebol* had a longer track record of internationalization (see Table 22.2). To help Chinese firms to invest abroad, the Beijing government had signed bilateral investment treaties with 103 countries, and double taxation treaties with 68 countries by early 2003. Accelerated outward FDI during 2000–2004 was likewise fuelled by Chinese companies' increasingly aggressive cross-border M&A purchases. Averaging US$948.2 million a year, they nearly doubled

Table 22.1 China's outward FDI flows in comparative perspective (in US$ billion)

Outward FDI flows (average annual)	1980–1990	1991–2000	2001–2004
China	0.4	2.3	2.8
South Korea	0.5	3.3	3.3
Taiwan	1.6	3.6	5.8
Singapore	0.4	4.9	10.3
Malaysia	0.2	1.7	1.4
Thailand	0	0.4	0.3
Indonesia	0	0.7	0.1
India	0	0.1	1.4

Source: UNCTAD, 2005.

Table 22.2 China's outward FDI stock in comparative perspective (in US$ billion)

Outward FDI stock	1985	1995	2004
China	0.1	15.8	38.8
South Korea	0.5	10.2	39.3
Taiwan	0.2	25.1	91.2
Singapore	4.4	35	100.9
Indonesia	0.1	1.3	*
Malaysia	1.4	11	13.8
Philippines	0.2	1.2	1.6
Thailand	0	2.3	3.4
India	0	0.3	6.6
Japan	44	238.5	370.5
United States	238.4	699	2 018.2
United Kingdom	100.3	304.9	1 378.1

Note: *Negative stock value.

Source: UNCTAD, 2005.

the figure of US$575.2 million per annum during 1995–9, according to the United Nations Conference on Trade and Development (UNCTAD, 2005). In contrast to UNCTAD that adopts the more inclusive data, based on balance of payments statistics from the People's Bank of China, China's Ministry of Commerce (MoC) has consistently reported significantly lower outward FDI value figures. However, MoC's data do not include reinvested earnings, intra-company loans and non-financial and private-sector transactions. Consequently MoC has grossly underestimated the total value of China's outward FDI, as it fails to capture the amounts invested abroad by firms using, for example, earnings from exports or loans raised in international capital markets (Wu and Yeo, 2002; Wu and Tang, 1999).

Geographical Spread of Global Reach

By the early 2000s, Chinese enterprises were present in almost every corner of the earth. According to MoC, there were 7470 Chinese foreign affiliates spreading across 168 countries/economies at the end of 2003 (see Table 22.3). While understandably a disproportionately large number of them could be found in Hong Kong (2336), reflecting the latter's special role as an offshore platform for Chinese firms to raise funds and spearhead their regional business activities, the US, surprisingly, was the next biggest host country for Chinese foreign affiliates (786). As regions, Southeast Asia (857), as well as Central and Eastern Europe (865), were also important hosts to Chinese enterprises. Other regional hosts with significant presence of Chinese foreign affiliates were the Middle East and Africa (769), EU-15 (432) and Latin America (384). Like MoC's reported outward FDI value figures, the enterprise numbers could also turn out to be significant underestimates. For example, while, according to MoC, there were only 188 Chinese enterprises doing business in Singapore in 2003, the latter's officials asserted that the number was about 1500.

Table 22.3   Geographical distribution of Chinese enterprises abroad

	Number of Chinese enterprises abroad, by country/region	
	End 1995	End 2003
Total	1 882	7 470
Hong Kong/Macau	182	2 336
Central and Eastern Europe	280	865
ASEAN	289	857
United States	229	786
Middle East and Africa	241	769
EU-15	102	432
Latin America	130	384
Japan	80	250
Australia	88	225
Canada	76	155
Rest of the World	185	411

Source: Ministry of Commerce, China.

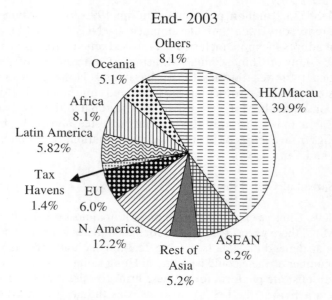

End- 2003

Source: Ministry of Commerce, China.

Figure 22.1   Regional distribution of Chinese outward FDI in value terms

In value terms, the geographical distribution of China's outward FDI stock seems to mirror the regional/country spread of enterprises (see Figure 22.1). Apart from Hong Kong, that claimed a significant 40 per cent share at the end of 2003, Chinese outward-bound capital seemed to favour developed economies, like North America, the European Union and Australia/New Zealand, which together accounted for 23 per cent of China's outward FDI stock. According to MoC's rankings, Australia, Canada, Denmark and the US were also among the top ten country destinations for Chinese outward FDI. Among developing economies, Southeast Asia managed to attract more (8.2 per cent) Chinese outward FDI vis-à-vis Africa (8.1 per cent) and Latin America (5.8 per cent) at the end of 2003. Of the five largest member countries in the Association of South East Asian Nations (ASEAN), Indonesia and Thailand also made it to the top ten country destinations for China's outward FDI. Reflecting a continuous thaw in bilateral relations, resource-rich Russia had emerged as the third most important country destination for China's outward FDI at the end of 2003 with a 4.8 per cent share. Overall, the geographical distribution largely coincides with the various motivating factors that have prompted Chinese companies to make offshore forays.

'Pull' and 'Push' Motivating Factors

A closer examination of the geographical distribution of China's outward FDI, as well as the recent history and patterns of overseas acquisitions/takeover bids, suggests that Chinese firms are motivated by a handful of 'push' and 'pull' factors to internationalize their operations. Essentially, they boil down to four factors.

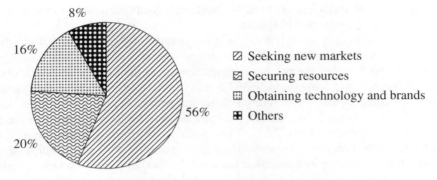

Source: Von Keller and Wei (2003).

Figure 22.2 Motivations of outward FDI from survey of China's 'Top 50 industry leading firms'

1. To establish local sales and distribution networks in host countries, especially in industries with excess production capacity and diminishing domestic demand at home (for example, kitchen-appliance maker Haier's manufacturing plant and distribution centre in the US, and TCL's acquisition of Schneider Electronics AG in Germany).
2. To support exports and open up new markets (for example, worldwide trading offices of Sinochem, COFCO and China Minmetals to purchase and sell raw materials, intermediate and finished goods).
3. To acquire advanced technology, cutting-edge manufacturing know-how, and/or global brands (for example, TCL's majority joint venture with French TV maker Thomson, Lenovo's purchase of IBM's personal computer business, and Haier's aborted takeover of American home-appliances maker Maytag).
4. To secure access to raw materials and natural resources (for example, CNOOC's failed takeover of Unocal, and CNPC's proposed purchase of PetroKazakhstan in Canada).

A 2003 survey of China's 50 largest, 'industry-leading' firms by the Shanghai office of the Germany-based Roland Berger Strategy Consultants (Von Keller and Wei, 2003) corroborated the above observations. Some 56 per cent of the participating firms, many of them large trading houses and manufacturers, named 'seeking new markets' as the overriding imperative for globalizing their business activities (see Figure 22.2). Among this group of firms, manufacturers in particular cited growing competitive pressure from MNCs in the home market, excess capacity and sliding profit margins as key reasons to search for new markets abroad. According to McKinsey & Co., in China's home-appliances market for example, overcapacity is estimated at over 30 per cent in washing machines, 40 per cent in refrigerators, 45 per cent in microwave ovens and 87 per cent in televisions (Woetzel, 2003). Small wonder that Chinese home-appliances and consumer-electronics manufacturers, like Haier, TCL and Huawei Technologies, have made repeated forays into more affluent developed economies, such as the US and the EU, in the hope of gaining market share; together, these two host regions had garnered a more than 18 per cent share of China's outward FDI stock.

Apart from 'seeking new markets', the most compelling reason for China's top 50 'industry-leading' firms to look offshore was to 'secure resources'. This factor was identified by 20 per cent of the participating enterprises in the Roland Berger survey. This was not altogether surprising, in view of China's rapid ascent in recent years to become the world's biggest consumer of many key natural resources and commodities, such as iron ore, aluminium, steel, copper, cement, and the world's second largest consumer of crude oil (see Appendix, Table 22.7). This explains why resource-rich countries, like Australia, Canada, Indonesia, Peru and Russia, were among the top ten country destinations for China's offshore investment, circa 2003. In fact, estimates show that resource-rich countries roughly account for 25–30 per cent of Chinese outward FDI stock, and this share will certainly rise in the future, as China's consumption needs increase in tandem. Occasional setbacks, such as CNOOC's failed bid for Unocal in 2005 and China Minmetals' aborted takeover of Noranda, a Canadian mining giant, in 2004, are unlikely to deter Chinese commodity companies from scouring the world for resource assets.

Last but not least, 16 per cent of China's top 50 'industry-leading' firms from the Roland Berger survey specified 'obtaining technology and brands' as the critical reason for making international acquisitions. It is a truism that Chinese consumer-product manufacturers suffer from the 'twin deficits' of global branding power and advanced technology, including critical design knowledge. As the Japanese and South Korean experiences have demonstrated, building these capabilities through in-house, organic growth would take two to three decades and billions of dollars (see also Chapter 16 in this volume). In these days of rapid technological changes and shorter product cycles, Chinese companies simply do not have the luxury of time to pursue this protracted option. Hence outright acquisitions and strategic joint ventures in developed economies, such as the US and the EU – like the Lenovo–IBM, TCL–Thomson, and the aborted Haier–Maytag deals – become the shortcut route to address these 'twin deficits'. Acquiring advanced technology also means establishing R&D facilities in developed economies to tap the cutting-edge knowledge of foreign engineers, designers and scientists. Haier, for example, has founded R&D and design centres in both Germany and the US, while Huawei Technologies and ZTE Corp have each established R&D centres in Sweden. Witnessing the growing global ambitions of Chinese consumer-goods manufacturers, brand and technology acquisitions as rationales for internationalization will gain increasing weight in the corporate boardrooms of Chinese companies.

FIRM-LEVEL PERSPECTIVE

The World Begins to Take Notice

After more than a decade of taking the incremental, one-step-at-a-time approach to globalization during much of the 1990s, some Chinese companies are beginning to attract international attention with the dawn of the new century. By way of recognition, UNCTAD published in 2002 a list of what it considered the 'top 12 Chinese TNCs [transnational corporations]' that collectively controlled over US$30 billion in overseas

Table 22.4   15 Chinese enterprises on the Fortune Global 500

	Revenues (US$ millions)	Profits (US$ millions)
SINOPEC	75 076.70	1 268.90
State Grid	71 290.20	694
China National Petroleum	67 723.80	8 757.10
China Life Insurance	24 980.60	74.3
China Mobile Communications	23 957.60	4 077.90
Industrial & Commercial Bank of China	23 444.60	279.2
China Telecommunications	21 561.80	2 422.00
SINOCHEM	20 380.70	229.7
Shanghai Baosteel Group	19 543.30	1 537.30
China Construction Bank ·	19 047.90	5 846.20
China Southern Power Grid	18 928.80	231.4
Bank of China	17 960.40	2 529.00
Agricultural Bank of China	15 284.60	242
COFCO	14 189.40	121.4
China First Automotive Works	13 825.40	293.4

Source: Fortune, 25 July 2005.

assets, with over 20 000 foreign employees and US$33 billion in offshore sales (see Appendix, Table 22.8). Of the 'top 12 Chinese TNCs', at least six had amassed foreign assets worth between US$2.8 billion and US$9.4 billion, seven had recorded offshore sales of between US$1.2 billion and US$9.1 billion, and four employed between 2000 and 6800 overseas workers. Many of these on the UNCTAD list – such as the COSCO Group, CNOOC, COFOC, CNPC, Sinochem, Shougang Group, China Minmetals, Shanghai Baosteel, Haier and ZTE Corp – would later move on to capture international headlines in their subsequent global M&A forays.

In 2003, the *BusinessWeek* magazine compiled and published a list of 'Top 200 Emerging-Market Companies', ranked by market value (see Appendix, Table 22.9). Among them were 20 (or 10 per cent of the total) Chinese companies. While the ranking yardstick was not a measurement of the extent of a company's global reach, some Chinese companies made it to the list – notably, the CITIC Group, CNOOC, COSCO Group, Lenovo, PetroChina (listed concern of CNPC) and SINOPEC were already making waves on the international business scene. The latest (2005) *Fortune Global 500* roster increases the number of Chinese companies by one to 15 (see Table 22.4). By now, China can boast the largest number of companies on the list among emerging economies (for example surpassing South Korea's 11). It also compares favourably with developed economies, overshadowed only by Britain (35), France (39), Germany (37), Japan (81) and the US (176), and trumping the rest (see Table 22.5).

However, as total revenue, rather than overseas assets and sales, is the ranking criterion for the *Fortune Global 500*, a majority of the 15 Chinese companies can only be considered as state-owned domestic corporate behemoths, rather than internationally-active business concerns. The exceptions are CNPC, COFOC, Sinochem and Shanghai Baosteel (all on

Table 22.5 Number of enterprises on the Fortune Global 500 *from emerging economies and developed economies*

Developed economies	No of companies on the *Fortune Global 500*	Emerging economies	No of companies on the *Fortune Global 500*
Australia	9	Brazil	3
Belgium	3	*China*	*15*
Britain	35	India	5
Canada	13	Malaysia	1
Denmark	2	Mexico	2
Finland	3	Russia	3
France	39	Singapore	1
Germany	37	S Korea	11
Italy	8	Taiwan	2
Japan	81	Thailand	1
Netherlands	14		
Norway	2		
Spain	8		
Sweden	7		
Switzerland	11		
United States	176		

Source: *Fortune*, 25 July 2005.

the 2002 UNCTAD list of 'top 12 Chinese TNCs'), plus Bank of China and SINOPEC. However, the financial performances of these six firms are very uneven. According to 2004 figures published by the *Fortune* magazine, while Bank of China, CNPC and Shanghai Baosteel recorded a respectable average profit-to-revenue ratio of 11.6 per cent, the average ratio for COFCO, Sinochem and SINOPEC was a dismal 1.2 per cent. This suggests that, for Chinese firms with high global ambitions but low profitability, they would have to turn to government coffers to sustain their international expansion, with the attendant risks of provoking political opposition from the host countries.

Different Modes of Globalization: Three Case Studies

While evidence from the earlier-cited Roland Berger's 2003 survey of China's top 50 'industry-leading' firms indicates that organic growth was the preferred mode of cross-border expansion (48 per cent of participating firms) over strategic alliance/joint venture (39 per cent) and outright acquisition (13 per cent), more recent trends suggest that the latter two routes are increasingly gaining ascendancy inside China's corporate board-rooms, particularly for commodity companies and consumer-goods manufacturers (see Table 22.6). As McKinsey management consultants have trenchantly pointed out, 'it took years, and a great deal of money, before the giant Japanese and S. Korean consumer-goods companies established themselves abroad'. 'Chinese companies don't have that much choice but to acquire overseas companies. Very few companies can build organically any more. If they wait 10 to 15 years, they could be dead' (Gao, Woetzel and Wu, 2003;

Table 22.6   Recent actual and proposed overseas acquisitions by Chinese firms

Selected overseas acquisitions by Chinese companies (actual & proposed)		
Buyer	Target	US$ million
Nanjing Automotive	MG Rover Group (UK)	Not yet disclosed
CNPC	PetroKazakhstan	4 180
Lenovo Group	IBM PC Division (US)	1 250
China Netcom	PCCW (HK, 20%)	1 000
Shanghai Auto Industry	Ssangyong Motor (Korea, 49%)	500
BOE Technology	Hynix Semicon Flat-Panel Display Division (Korea)	380
Petro China	Devon Energy (Indonesia)	262
China National Chemical Import/Export Corp	Atlantis Holding AS (Norway)	215
SINOPEC	Northern Lights Project (40%, Canada)	124
TCL International	Schneider Electronics AG (Germany)	8

Source: Various press reports.

also *New York Times*, 30 June 2005). The three cases below illustrate a trend shift in the globalization strategy of Chinese corporations.

Haier: Limits to Organic Growth

The Qingdao-based home appliances maker has come a long way since its humble beginning in 1984 as a near-bankrupt OEM (original equipment manufacturer) refrigerator producer for MNCs. By the mid-1990s, under new and more disciplined management, Haier had built a reputation in the domestic market for price, quality, innovation and customer service and, with that, gained a dominant position in China's home appliances market. It also started to expand abroad during this period through a typical organic growth route. Beginning with exports whose products now reach 160 countries, Haier has subsequently built and operated more than 20 production plants outside China. By the early 2000s, Haier had risen to become the world's fifth largest home appliances producer, with the declared ambition eventually to reach the number three position. Worldwide sales (80 per cent in China) hit US$12.2 billion in 2004, compared to US$4.9 billion in 2000.

Haier first entered the US market in 1994. While it has managed to persuade large retail chains, like Best Buy, Home Depot, Sears and Wal-Mart, to carry a variety of its products, such as air-conditioners, microwave ovens, washing machines, dishwashers, and so on, it is in the niche segments of mini refrigerators and wine coolers that Haier has been able to grab market shares. This is because US market leaders, like Whirlpool, General Electric and Maytag, have already abandoned these segments for reasons of low profit margins and/or volume. By 2002–3, Haier had cornered 50–60 per cent of the US market share for these two products. Having achieved some modest success on the US turf and facing rising competitive pressure from MNCs at home (especially after China's WTO accession in January 2002), it is natural that Haier harbours bigger commercial ambitions in the US. As Haier's Chairman and CEO Zhang Ruimin sombrely pointed out, 'every multinational sets up in China. Margins are low here. If we don't go outside, we cannot survive' (*The Economist*, 20 March 2004).

As an indication of increasing competition in the home market where it commands 80 per cent of Haier's worldwide sales, the company experienced zero profit growth in 2004 for a third consecutive year, while gross margins from sales of air-conditioners and refrigerators (in combination constituting 80 per cent of core revenue and operating profits in 2003) fell to 11.2 per cent and 16.5 per cent, respectively, in 2004, from 2003's 12.4 per cent and 19.2 per cent, respectively (*Asian Wall Street Journal*, 8 April 2005). During the first six months of 2005, Haier's net profit fell sharply by 22 per cent (*Asian Wall Street Journal*, 8 April; 19 August 2005). In the US, beyond niche segments, the biggest challenge for Haier is to expand its market shares in mainstream home appliances and compete head-on with the top three or four American manufacturers. To this end, CEO Zhang has set an ambitious target of winning 10 per cent of US market share for full-size refrigerators by 2005, from 2.0 per cent in 2002 (Wu, 2003). The target would exceed the production capacity of Haier's US$40 million manufacturing plant in South Carolina, with the balance being made up by imports from China.

Despite having a design centre in Los Angeles and a rising R&D budget of up to 4.0 per cent of revenue in 2004 (close to the international benchmark of 5.0 per cent or more), Haier is still handicapped in a number of ways in the US. As *The Economist* (20 March 2004) bluntly observed, compared to Whirlpool and General Electric, 'Haier lacks such firms' R&D, their design skills, their distribution or their service networks . . . Haier does not have their established brands.' In other words, as the competition shifts from niche to mainstream product lines, Haier is confronting some hard-to-surmount barriers that its hitherto organic growth globalization strategy cannot help the ambitious firm to overcome. Hence Haier executives have turned to acquisition to enable it to leapfrog to the next stage of development.

In June 2005, when loss-making Maytag (America's third largest home-appliances manufacturer with a 15 per cent market share versus Whirlpool's over 30 per cent and General Electric's 20 per cent) became a target for takeover, Haier, in partnership with Bain Capital and the Black Stone Group, immediately jumped into the fray, offering US$1.28 billion to Maytag shareholders against the US$1.1 billion bid by Ripplewood. As one Haier senior executive had put it, 'Haier's target is Maytag's prestigious brand name as well as its mature sales channels' (*Asian Wall Street Journal*, 23 June 2005). The merged entity, had it been successful, would have catapulted Haier overnight to become the third, or even second, largest home appliances producer in the US. Haier could be an immediate threat to Whirlpool and General Electric, despite doubt about whether Haier would have the management skills to integrate successfully the two concerns.

Alas, Haier's aspiration was thwarted by Whirlpool, which foresaw the threat to its market-dominant position from this merger, with a higher counter-bid of US$1.35 billion, prompting Haier to abort its takeover attempt a month later. Though temporarily foiled, the Maytag setback is unlikely to deter CEO Zhang's ambition 'to make

Americans feel that Haier is a localized US brand instead of an imported Chinese brand' (Wu, 2003). Corporate America will undoubtedly see Haier returning to the M&A scene when the next takeover opportunity arises.

TCL-Thomson: a not-yet Profitable Strategic Alliance

Like Haier's humble inception, the Huizhou-based TCL started as a small-time producer of cassette tapes in 1981. It diversified into telephone production in 1985, and television manufacturing in 1992. By the late 1990s, TCL had emerged as the largest television producer in China. Aside from selling its own brand of televisions in China and exporting them to developing countries, its manufacturing prowess and quality control were recognized by OEM contracts from international brands like Philips and Toshiba, and even the luxurious Bang & Olufsen of Denmark. However, it had no market presence in Europe and North America, because of protectionist barriers such as import quotas and high tariffs (for example 21.25 per cent from the US). Nonetheless, these obstacles were not formidable enough to deter TCL management's ambition 'to become a global brand' (*Asian Wall Street Journal*, 4 November 2003). As Chairman and CEO Li Dongsheng had declared, 'our goal is to become a Chinese Sony or Samsung' (*The Economist*, 8 January 2005).

To circumvent Europe's import quotas, TCL established a beachhead in Germany in 2002, by purchasing an insolvent television maker, Schneider Electronics, for US$8.0 million. However, Schneider's production capacity, distribution network and brand profile proved to be too small and insignificant to help the ambitious and impatient TCL executives realize their aspiration for global reach. So when the loss-making French television manufacturer Thomson Electronics, which also owns the venerable RCA brand in the US, looked for a cash-rich partner to help resuscitate its moribund business, TCL saw the opportunity of using a joint-venture vehicle to leapfrog entry barriers and penetrate both the European and US markets simultaneously. Like Haier, TCL executives recognized that the organic growth globalization strategy would be time consuming and tortuous for latecomers. As TCL's Chief Financial Officer, Vincent Yan, admitted, 'it would take 5 or 10 years [for TCL] to reach the level of recognition that Thomson and RCA have in their markets' (*Asian Wall Street Journal*, 26 November 2004).

In fact, Yan's time-frame for TCL to conquer the European and US markets by going it alone must be considered highly optimistic, compared to the globalization experiences of Japanese and South Korean MNCs during the 1980s and the 1990s. Hence, when TCL and Thomson announced in November 2003 the US$520 million strategic alliance – TTE (TCL-Thomson Electronics) – to create the world's largest television manufacturer, with the Chinese partner owning a majority stake of 67 per cent, industry leaders and the media marvelled at the bold move and received it with aesthetic approval (*Asian Wall Street Journal*, 4 November 2003; *BusinessWeek*, 17 November 2004). Representing corporate America's endorsement of the deal, TCL Chairman Li was named 2003 'Asian Businessman of the Year' by the *Fortune* magazine. By combining the two partners' 29 000 employees and a dozen production facilities worldwide (in China, France, Indonesia, Mexico, Philippines, Poland, Thailand and Vietnam), and using common designs for chassis and chipsets, executives from both sides touted the enhanced efficiencies, cost savings and (it was hoped) improved profits that the joint venture's size would eventually yield.

Unfortunately, instead of focusing sharply on turning the unprofitable Thomson around (185 million euro loss in 2003), TCL soon jumped into another, what would turn out to be an ill-fated, joint venture with the mobile phone arm of Alcatel, the world's biggest supplier of broadband Internet equipment, in 2004. In August, TCL paid US$60.5 million for a 55 per cent stake in a US$110 million joint venture with Alcatel to manufacture and sell mobile phones in Europe. However, the marriage proved to be short-lived. Citing losses (US$45.7 million in first quarter 2005) and management discord, Alcatel backed out of the joint venture after nine months, and sold its entire stake to TCL in May 2005. As one Alcatel senior executive lamented, 'the cultural differences between the two companies were huge . . . there was no synergy at all' (*International Herald Tribune*, 29 July 2005).

Meanwhile, TCL's insufficient attention to turning around Thomson's unprofitability resulted in unabated financial haemorrhage for the latter, and dragged down TCL's own profitability. As TCL's CFO Yan admitted on the one-year anniversary of the strategic alliance, 'in the past [few] months of operations, we found out the challenges and difficulties are deeper than we thought' (*Asian Wall Street Journal*, 26 November 2004). As a reflection of this belated realization, TCL's net profits fell by half in 2004 to US$41.0 million. In the first half of 2005, TCL's Hong Kong-listed concern, through which it controls the 67 per cent-owned joint venture, announced a surprising loss of US$12.4 million, caused mainly by operation losses of US$42.0 million from its joint-venture partner. Accordingly, the originally optimistic plan to make TTE profitable by 2005 had to be pushed back by two years to 2007, according to CFO Yan (*BusinessWeek Online*, 22 August 2005). While TCL's executives might eventually be able to swing Thomson back into profitability, near-term prospects are not rosy. As the *Financial Times* (24 May 2005) observed, 'TCL's buying spree has become a cautionary tale about the limits of Chinese companies' management capabilities.' In other words, there is still a steep, and financially costly, learning curve to climb for Chinese companies that opt for the strategic-alliance mode of globalization.

Lenovo: Jury still out on the Acquisition of IBM's PC Business

When Lenovo announced its US$1.75 billion purchase of IBM's PC business in December 2004, the *Financial Times* (9 December 2004) hailed the deal as 'the dawn of a new era in China's M&A market', while the *Asian Wall Street Journal* (9 December 2004) praised it as a 'milestone in China's integration in world business'. But for Lenovo's founders, led by its former Chairman Liu Chuanzhi, it was a 20-year haul to the global stage, begun at the Chinese Academy of Sciences in 1984 by several entrepreneurial scientists. They succeeded in developing a circuit board that would allow IBM PCs to process Chinese characters. As their breakthrough research product, the Chinese language system enabled them to sell imported PCs, which in turn helped them gain distribution experience and an understanding of customer needs. Legend, as the corporate label was then, before it was rebranded as Lenovo in 2003, started to assemble PCs under its own brand name in 1990, and went on to attain a listing in Hong Kong four years later. By tailoring reliable products to local customers and keeping inventories and costs down, Legend soon emerged to become China's biggest PC supplier, with a domestic market share of 30 per cent.

By the early 2000s, however, the PC market in China began to suffer from falling margins and overcrowding, with the entry of more domestic and foreign players. 'Price wars are raging at the high-end of the Chinese PC market,' as the *Far Eastern Economic Review* (19 June 2003) reported, 'and foreign competitors like Hewlett-Packard and Dell are nipping at Legend's heels'. Confronted by rising competitive pressure at home, like Haier, Legend began to look overseas for growth opportunities. As Legend's Chief Financial Officer, Mary Ma, pointed out retrospectively, 'if we just focus on China, we cannot generate returns for our shareholders' (*The Economist*, 30 June 2005). In 2003, President Yang Yuanqing, who was later promoted to Chairman after the IBM purchase, while admitting that Lenovo was 'a brand name no one knows' outside China, was more forthright in articulating Lenovo's global ambitions: 'We want to take ourselves to an international scale, to the scale of a world first-class enterprise,' he told the *Far Eastern Economic Review* (19 June 2003).

So when IBM put its unprofitable PC business up for sale, Lenovo saw the acquisition as a vehicle to help the firm leapfrog from local to global league overnight. The US$1.75 billion purchase, announced in December 2004 and sealed in May 2005, would quadruple Lenovo's annual revenue to US$13 billion and catapult the company to become the world's third largest PC supplier, after Dell and Hewlett-Packard, with a 9–10 per cent global market share. Over 72 per cent of its revenue would come from overseas sales, compared to almost zero before the acquisition. Not only would Lenovo be allowed to use the IBM brand under licence for five years, most significantly it would also own IBM's premium *Think* trademark that covers the prestigious *ThinkPad* notebook brand and the *ThinkCenter* desktop line. Equally important would be Lenovo's gaining access to IBM's international expertise, especially in areas such as the management of manufacturing and distribution channels in the 160 countries where IBM had already established its presence.

To secure IBM's continuous technical support and unflagging customer loyalty to the new acquirer, IBM would be given an 18.9 per cent stake in the post-acquisition Lenovo. The takeover was not free from political controversy in Washington, however. After three Republican congressmen raised their concerns on national security grounds, because of IBM's status as a major US government contractor and Lenovo's majority ownership by the Chinese government, the deal was subjected to a long review by the Committee on Foreign Investment in the US (CFIUS). Even though PC manufacturing had already become a low-margin, commoditized production, it took three months of investigation before CFIUS granted security clearance for the sale, and only on condition that Lenovo agreed to move the acquired PC division out of IBM's headquarters at Raleigh, North Carolina. In April 2005, as a vote of confidence in the acquisition, three US private-equity firms (Texas Pacific, General Atlantis and Newbridge Capital) paid US$350 million to buy a 10.8 per cent stake in Lenovo. Since May 2005, Lenovo has had in its possession an iconic global brand: IBM was ranked as the world's third most-valuable brand, after Coca-Cola and Microsoft, in 2005 by *BusinessWeek*/Interbrand in their joint annual scoreboard of 'The 100 Top Brands' (*BusinessWeek*, 1 August 2005).

But the multiple challenges facing Lenovo have just begun. First is financial. IBM's PC business has been unprofitable for several years (first half 2004 loss was US$139 million, after being in the red to the tune of US$258 million in 2003). To turn the business around would be a critical test for Lenovo's management expertise. Should it fail to do so within one to two years, the acquired entity would be a drag on Lenovo's balance sheet in the medium term. Next is integration. The *Asian Wall Street Journal* (8 December 2004) rightly asked 'how a Chinese company with a proud history and no experience running extensive overseas operations will integrate a flagship US company with its own strong identity'. Lenovo has inherited IBM's 9000 worldwide employees, who had been operating within a corporate culture very different from that of the acquirer. Lenovo's initial responses to this challenge are to relocate its corporate headquarters to New York and share management with ex-IBMers.

Steve Ward, ex-head of IBM's PC division and a 26-year veteran of the company, has been appointed CEO of Lenovo, and ex-IBMers have filled half of the top 30 executive positions in Lenovo. By themselves, however, these moves would not guarantee a seamless integration of the two merged corporate entities. CFO Mary Ma has candidly admitted the divide between the two management styles. In an interview with *Business Week Online* (22 August 2005), she observed: 'Lenovo China would normally approach something top down. But the IBM PC division has a very strong executive culture. It's a very different approach.' It remains to be seen whether Lenovo could successfully meld the two distinctively different corporate cultures/management styles into a unified whole to help advance Lenovo's global ambitions.

Finally, and most crucially, Lenovo has to tackle the challenge of sustaining the IBM brand and retaining customer loyalty in the next five years, as well as executing a credible and effective brand-transition strategy before the licence to use the IBM brand expires in five years' time. Buying an internationally recognized brand seems to be a breeze, when compared to the arduous task of sustaining and managing the acquired brand. Existing and potential customers would need to be convinced that Lenovo would possess the capability to deliver to them the same high-quality products and after-sales service as IBM did, especially after the latter's brand name exits the scene in 2010. In this respect, a hitherto China-centric Lenovo has no track record. Hence only time will tell whether this bold acquisition turns out to be a boom or bust to Lenovo's ambitious global agenda.

CONCLUSION AND IMPLICATIONS

From the foregoing macro- and micro-analyses, several conclusions can be drawn. As late entrants (compared to their Asian and Western counterparts) to transnational commerce with less than two decades of globalization experience, mainland Chinese firms are likely to be disadvantaged in a number of ways. Majority government ownership of many of these enterprises can present additional roadblocks on their international acquisition trails, particularly in foreign assets that may be deemed strategic resources by host countries. For example, economic nationalism had not only foiled CNOOC's high-profile takeover attempt of Unocal in July 2005, but had also derailed China Minmetals' proposed purchase of Noranda, a Canadian mining giant, in early 2005 (*Asian Wall Street Journal*, 15 July 2005), and SINOPEC's bid for Slavnet, Russia's ninth biggest oil company, in December 2002 (*South China Morning Post*, 12 July 2005). However, one hesitates to single out Chinese firms as especially vulnerable to such political risk. Denying a foreign investor's taking control over a host country's strategic resources has happened even between friendly allies. For instance, in 2001, the Canberra government blocked a bid by Shell to acquire Woodside Petroleum, an Australian oil and gas company, on the grounds that 'it wasn't in the national interest [of Australia]' (*Asian Wall Street Journal*, 15 August 2005). Consequently, Chinese firms, like other MNCs, would just have to accept the fact that certain politically sensitive cross-border targets are beyond their reach, even if their government ownership is reduced to minority status.

Besides political risk, Chinese enterprises have not yet, largely because of their limited M&A experience, demonstrated the requisite skills to turn around, integrate and/or sustain the brands that they have acquired. Delay or failure to address these tasks swiftly and urgently in the post-acquisition phase can prove costly, not only financially but also for the fate of the merged entity. As the case studies in this chapter show, tardiness in repairing Thomson's bottom line has come at the expense of TCL's own profitability, while successfully integrating and sustaining the IBM brand will be a litmus test of Lenovo's management savvy in the coming critical months. Aspiring Chinese MNCs, investment analysts and business-school professors will follow these two cases with ardent interest to see what valuable insights and lessons they may eventually yield.

Notwithstanding the obstacles described above, they would not be formidable enough to deter Chinese firms with global ambitions from internationalizing their operations. On the home turf, accelerating competitive pressure from foreign MNCs will remain a relentless 'push' factor for Chinese enterprises to 'go out'. Intense pressure will be especially felt by services companies in the next two years, as Beijing completes its liberalization schedule by 2007 on the services sector under WTO accession requirements, and allows majority foreign ownership in many service industries. This liberalization will inevitably squeeze the profit margins of local service firms and push them to look for off-shore growth opportunities. Furthermore, with a predicted medium-term average trend growth rate of 7.0 per cent–9.0 per cent per annum, there will be no abatement in China's ferocious appetite for key commodities. Rapid urbanization, rising car ownership, and accelerated infrastructure construction, especially in the western region, will spur China's resource companies to scour the world for energy, building materials and key minerals.

Foreign acquisitions will be backed by massive financial resources from the government, which had amassed US$769 billion in official foreign exchange reserves as of September 2005. On just the 21 months between the end of 2003 and September 2005, such reserves had risen at an astonishing pace, averaging US$17.4 billion per month (that is allowing China to bid for more than 20 Unocals over this period). Moreover, with the RMB's (Chinese currency) recent modest revaluation and switching to peg against a basket of currencies, instead of the US dollar, market consensus (*Bloomberg Financial News*, July 2005) expects the RMB to move onto a trend appreciation trajectory, hitting RMB 6.8/US$1.0 by 2010, from RMB 8.3 before the change in the exchange-rate regime in July 2005. Hence, with a stronger RMB going forward (like Japan's surging Yen after the 1985 Plaza Accord), Chinese companies are anticipated to speed up on the international acquisition trail.

Finally, the Beijing government is not expected to relent in its support for the 'Go-Out' policy in the medium term. If anything, it has recently enacted policies that will make outward FDI by Chinese companies easier. In October 2004, for instance, MoC announced that it would not only start to accept outward FDI applications and issue approvals online, but also cease to scrutinize the feasibility of each proposal (*Asian Wall Street Journal*, 13 October 2004). This was followed by the announcement nine months later that the Export-Import Bank of China (Chexim) would receive a substantial capital injection, in order to enable it to support the cross-border expansion of Chinese companies (*Asian Wall Street Journal*, 12 July 2005). As Chinese Vice Premier Wu Yi forcefully articulated, 'We will actively foster our own multinational companies [and] we will create all kinds of favorable conditions to help our multinational companies further explore overseas markets and engage more strongly in global economic competition and operation' (*China Daily*, 7 November 2003).

Consequently, recent high-profile international acquisitions and takeover bids by Chinese companies can be seen as only the tip of the iceberg. The world community is merely witnessing the first step in Corporate China's ascent to the international business stage. Its outsized global ambitions have been fittingly illustrated by a recent issue of the *China Entrepreneur* magazine. On its cover, it puts the brash question: 'Should China Buy Wal-Mart?' (*New York Times*, 30 June 2005). Despite getting a bloody nose from the foiled takeover bid of Unocal, there is no reason to doubt that ambitious and tenacious Corporate China would not one day set its sights on the top company on the *Fortune Global 500* scoreboard. That day may come sooner than anybody can expect.

Overall, the emergence of China as a significant capital exporter, through a continuous recycling of its huge domestic savings and external surpluses, should be beneficial to the global economy, resulting in a win–win situation for all. In developed markets, Chinese acquisitions of distressed assets – should they manage to turn the latter around – could help resuscitate failed or near-failed companies and prevent job losses. Such successful turnarounds would in turn generate political good will, instead of hostility and suspicion, as in the case of CNOOC's takeover bid for Unocal, in the host countries. Moreover, the relocation of labour-intensive light manufacturing facilities to emerging economies by Chinese producers would translate into a deepening of capital investment, as well as employment creation, skills transfer and wage improvement for the poor and unskilled workers in these capital-scarce economies. This would in turn raise China's stature among developing economies, which it had already successfully cultivated during the 1960s and the 1970s through its generous technical assistance programmes.

Investing in commodity-rich countries by China's resource companies would help revitalize some once-moribund industrial sectors, enhance commodity prices and raise export earnings for these countries. While some of these recipient countries of Chinese investment (for example Australia, Canada, South America) are Washington's long-standing political allies, over time they might refrain from leaning toward the US, when bilateral disputes between Beijing and Washington arise. Some more neutral countries, such as Indonesia and Russia, could even side with China.

Last but not least, Chinese companies operating in developed markets would benefit from the need to conform to higher standards of corporate governance, accountability, transparency and social responsibility, for failing which they would be disciplined by foreign market regulators, as in the case of the 2005 China Aviation Oil débâcle in Singapore. Thus, over time, many Chinese transnational corporations would come to accept, and implement, international best business practices, if they wanted to be regarded as respectable global corporate citizens. Parent companies domiciled in China would also feel the transnational pressure that would spur them to accelerate enterprise reforms at home (see also Chapter 6 in this volume).

REFERENCES

Asian Wall Street Journal (2003), 'China's TCL emerges on world screen', 4 November.
Asian Wall Street Journal (2004), 'China cuts red tape on investing abroad', 13 October.
Asian Wall Street Journal (2004), 'Returning to a clear picture', 26 November.
Asian Wall Street Journal (2004), 'Lenovo near deal to take control of IBM's PC unit', 8 December.
Asian Wall Street Journal (2004), 'Lenovo agrees to purchase IBM unit amid doubts', 9 December.
Asian Wall Street Journal (2005), 'Haier's net profit is flat despite revenue surge', 8 April, 3.
Asian Wall Street Journal (2005), 'Haier's Maytag bid taps brand loyalty', 23 June.
Asian Wall Street Journal (2005), 'China increases reserves for "Go Out" plan', 12 July.
Asian Wall Street Journal (2005), 'Canada welcomes China's cash', 15 July.
Asian Wall Street Journal (2005), 'CNOOC shares arcs to new high', 15 August.
Asian Wall Street Journal (2005), 'Qingdao Haier's net profit falls 22% in competitive Chinese market', 19 August.
Bloomberg Financial News (2005), 'Survey of foreign exchange traders', 22–5 July.
BusinessWeek (2003a), 'Emerging might', 14 July, pp. 66–9.
BusinessWeek (2003b), 'Top 200 emerging-market companies', 14 July.
BusinessWeek (2004), 'Bursting out of China', 17 November, pp. 20–22.
BusinessWeek (2005), 'Global brands', 1 August, pp. 86–94.
BusinessWeek Online (2005), 'TCL's multimedia's global agenda', 22 August.
BusinessWeek Online (2005), 'Lenovo's long march', 22 August.
China Daily (2003), World Economic Development Declaration Conference, Express, Supplement.
Economist (2004), 'Haier's purpose', 20 March, p. 67.
Economist (2005), 'The struggle of the champions', 8 January, pp. 57–9.
Economist (2005), 'Chinese companies abroad: the dragon tucks in', 30 June.
Far Eastern Economic Review (2003), 'Legend goes for the big league', 19 June.
Financial Times (2004), 'Deal divides opinion over further M&A trends', 9 December.
Financial Times (2005), 'Win–win turns into "well . . . may be" ', 24 May.
Fortune (2005), 'World's 500 largest corporations', 25 July, F1–10.
Gao, Paul, J.R. Woetzel and Yibing Wu (2003), 'Can Chinese brands make it abroad?', *McKinsey Quarterly* (Special Edition), 55–65.
International Energy Agency (2005), 'China eats the world: sustainability of the dragon's appetite for commodities' (Hong Kong: CLSA Asia-Pacific Markets, Spring) (www.iea.org <http://www.ea.org>).
International Herald Tribune (2005), 'China's push abroad gathers pace', 29 July.
Ministry of Commerce, China (www.mofcom.gov.cn <http://www.mofcom.gov.cn>).
New York Times (2005), 'China seeks known brands to go global', 30 June.
Nolan, Peter (2001), *China and the Global Economy: National Champions, Industrial Policy and the Big Business Revolution*, New York: Palgrave.
South China Morning Post (2005), 'Win or lose, CNOOC remains key play in "Go Out" policy', 12 July.
UNCTAD (2002), *World Investment Report 2002*, Geneva: United Nations.
UNCTAD (2005), *World Investment Report 2005*, Geneva: United Nations.
Von Keller, Eugen and Zhou Wei (2003), 'From middle kingdom to global market: expansion strategies and success factors for China's emerging multinationals', Roland Berger Strategy Consultants, Shanghai.
Wang, Mark Y.L. (2002), 'The motivations behind China's government-initiated industrial investment abroad', *Pacific Affairs*, **75**(2), 187–206.

Woetzel, Jonathan R. (2003), *Capitalist China: Strategies for a Revolutionized Economy*, Singapore: John Wiley & Sons.

Wong, John and Sarah Chan (2003), 'China's outward direct investment: expanding worldwide', *China: An International Journal*, **1**(2), 273–301.

Wu, Friedrich (1993), 'Stepping out the door: Chinese companies are becoming major investors overseas', *China Business Review*, **20**(6), 14–19.

Wu, Friedrich (1994), 'China's rising speculative capital outflows', *Asian Wall Street Journal*, 7 March, p. 6.

Wu, Friedrich and Leslie Tang (1999), 'Tracking China's mysterious money flows', *Asian Wall Street Journal*, 24 February, p. 8.

Wu, Friedrich and Han Sia Yeo (2002), 'China's rising investment in Southeast Asia: trends and outlook', *Journal of Asian Business*, **18**(2), 41–61.

Wu, Yibing (2003), 'China's refrigerator magnate', *McKinsey Quarterly*, **3**, 106–15.

APPENDIX

Table 22.7   China's consumption of world commodities as shares of world total

	1995	2003
Iron ore	30	35
Aluminium	9	19
Steel	12	27
Copper (refined)	10	20
Zinc (refined)	12	20
Cement	33	37
Oil	5	8 (2004)

Source: UBS Investment Research; International Energy Agency (2005).

Table 22.8   UNCTAD's list of the twelve largest transnational corporations from China, 2002

Rank	Corporation	Assets (US$ million)		Sales (US$ million)		Employment (no.)	
		Foreign	Total	Foreign	Total	Foreign	Total
1	China Ocean Shipping (Group) Company (COSCO)	9 382	16 926	2 149	6 757	4 124	74 669
2	China National Offshore Oil Corporation (CNOOC)	4 814	8 635	976	3 669	13	24 406
3	China State Construction Engineering Corporation	3 739	8 099	1 818	5 790	6 833	236 464
4	China National Cereal, Oils and Foodstuff Import & Export Corporation (COFOC)	3 707	5 014	6 446	13 004	359	25 000
5	China National Petroleum Corporation (CNPC)	3 350	83 254	1 600	41 089	4 400	1 167 129
6	China National Chemicals Import & Export Corporation (Sinochem)	2 788	4 928	9 148	16 011	350	7 950
7	Shougang Group	969	6 678	467	4 401	2 086	179 997
8	China National Metals and Minerals Import & Export Corporation (China Minmetals)	729	2 797	998	4 277	570	7 145
9	China Harbour Engineering Company (Group)	520	3 271	6 579	17 826	812	70 160
10	Shanghai Baosteel Group Corporation	383	19 389	1 211	8 643	50	113 896
11	Haier Group Corporation	328	3 188	976	7 260	803	31 281
12	Zhongxing Telecommunications (ZTE Corporation)	17	1 205	260	1 685	120	12 961

Source: UNCTAD (2002).

Table 22.9   20 Chinese enterprises on BusinessWeek*'s 'Top 200 Emerging-Market Companies', 2003*

Name of Chinese company	Market value (US$ million)	Profits (US$ million)
China Mobile (Hong Kong)	44 899	3 956
Petrochina	43 512	5 668
China Petroleum & Chemical (SINOPEC)	35 696	1 943
China Telecom	16 386	2 038
CNOOC	11 481	1 116
Huaneng Power International	10 252	474
China Unicom	7 444	552
Jiangsu Expressway	6 049	103
CITIC Pacific	4 015	500
Guangdong Electric Power Development	3 240	127
Sinopec Shanghai Petrochemical	3 066	14
Shanghai Lujiazui Finance & Trade Zone Development	2 800	13
Yanzhou Coal Mining	2 587	148
Maanshan Iron & Steel (MA Steel)	2 459	18
Lenovo Group	2 333	134
Beijing Datang Power Generation	2 251	170
Aluminium Corp of China (Chalco)	2 248	169
Cosco Pacific	2 147	155
China Eastern Airlines	2 061	10
China Shipping Development	1 896	71

Source: BusinessWeek (14 July 2003).

Index

Index